INDIAN JUDICIARY AND POLITICS

The Changing Landscape

Indian Judiciary and Politics

The Changing Landscape

Edited by

B.D. DUA • M.P. SINGH • REKHA SAXENA

MANOHAR
2008

First published 2007
Reprinted 2008

ISBN 81-7304-723-5

Published by
Ajay Kumar Jain *for*
Manohar Publishers & Distributors
4753/23, Ansari Road. Daryaganj
New Delhi 110 002

Typeset by
Kohli Print
Delhi 110 051

Printed at
Lordson Publishers Pvt. Ltd.
Delhi 110 007

Contents

Acknowledgements

The idea for this volume matured when the three of us—M.P. Singh, Rekha Saxena, and B.D. Dua, then vice-president of the Shastri Indo-Canadian Institute, New Delhi—met informally to discuss Rekha Saxena's Ph.D. thesis on a comparative study of inter-governmental agencies in India and Canada in August 2001. The discussion, interspersed with reminiscences of graduate days when the two of us—M.P. Singh and B.D. Dua—were students at the University of Alberta (Canada) in the early 1970s, turned to some reflections on the current itinerary of the Indian political system. Our academic interests converged into a commitment to do two volumes, one on Indian federalism and the other on Indian judiciary. The federalism volume was published—B.D. Dua and M.P. Singh (eds.), *Indian Federalism in the New Millennium* (Manohar: 2003). We now deliver on our second commitment with the publication of this volume in collaboration with Rekha Saxena.

As in the case of the first volume on federalism, we are greateful to Rekha Saxena for not only prompting us to do this volume, but also for her untiring efforts in coordinating with our contributing authors and the publishers. It was not an easy job for her to do, given her other scholarly commitments, but she did it with exceptional grace and dignity. And we are pleased that she has joined us as one of the editors for this volume.

We are proud of the scholarship of our authors. We are grateful that they agreed to contribute to this volume and trusted our editorship of their scholarly works. We would like to acknowledge our gratitude to Mr. V.K. Ohri, Advocate, Supreme Court of India who was helpful in getting contributions from some eminent jurists. We appreciate the exceptional patience and understanding of our publishers, M/s Manohar Publishers & Distributors, in particular of Ramesh Jain, for accommodating our undue delay in the submission of our completed and revised manuscript.

Finally, B.D. Dua would like to thank the University of Lethbridge for research grant and research facilities given to him in editing and preparing this volume.

B.D. DUA, M.P. SINGH, REKHA SAXENA

Contributors

DOUGLAS V. VERNEY is Professor Emeritus of Political Science, York University, Toronto, Canada, and Professor of South Asian Regional Studies, University of Pennsylvania, USA. He has published several books and numerous articles on comparative parliamentary and federal systems in American, British, Canadian, and Indian journals, and is widely recognized for his excellent scholarship.

RAJEEV DHAVAN was educated at Allahabad, Cambridge, and London universities. A former academic, he taught at Queen's University (Belfast, Ireland) and at the University of West London, with visiting and other assignments at the Universities in London, Austin, Madison and Delhi. He is an honorary professor of the Indian Law Institute and Director of Public Interest Legal Support and Research Centre. He has authored several books and articles on constitutional law, policy and public affairs and was called to the Bar in India and England, he is now a Senior Counsel practising in the Supreme Court of India.

SOLI J. SORABJEE, former Attorney General of India; President, United Lawyers' Association; Member, UN Sub-Commission on Prevention of Discrimination and Protection of Minorities; Member, Permanent Court of Arbitration at The Hague. He has held assignments on behalf of the United Nations Human Rights Commission and has appeared and argued for the Government of India before the International Court of Justice. He was conferred the Padma Vibhushan by the President of India in March 2002. He is a prolific writer and an ardent champion of human rights.

MAHENDRA PAL SINGH, Professor and former Dean of Law, University of Delhi. He has published several articles in a variety of scholarly journals. His lecture at the Waseda University, Tokyo, in June 2002, was published in the 5 *Waseda Proceedings of Comparative Law* 72.

JUSTICE RAJINDER SACHAR, former Chief Justice, High Court of Delhi, Delhi. He was UN Special Rapporteur on Housing; Member, UN Sub-Commission on Prevention of Discrimination and Protection of Minorities; and President, Peoples' Union for Civil Liberties (PUCL), India.

PRASHANT BHUSHAN, Senior Advocate, Supreme Court of India, has written a well-researched book on the Bofors controversy. He is well-known for his focus on accountability in public life and has made sterling contributions in the area of public-interest petitions and changing contours of judicial activism.

R.K. BARIK, Reader in Public Administration, Indian Institute of Public Administration, New Delhi.

DHARMENDRA S. SENGAR, Professor of Law and Chairman, Legal Management Group, Indian Institute of Management, Lucknow, India. He has held a Fulbright Fellowship (GWU, Washington DC), the Shastri Indo-Canadian Institute Fellowship (University of Calgary Law School, Canada), and has made several scholarly contributions in his specialized area of environmental law and business.

SUBHENDU RANJAN RAJ, Reader, Postgraduate DAV College, University of Delhi, Delhi.

JOHN R. WOOD, Professor of Political Science, University of British Columbia, Vancouver, Canada. He is widely published and highly regarded for his scholarly contributions to India Studies. Currently, he is the Vice-President of the Shastri Indo-Canadian Institute, New Delhi.

C.P. BHAMBHRI, Distinguished Scholar, Centre for Political Studies, Jawaharlal Nehru University, New Delhi. He has authored several books and numerous scholarly and popular articles.

SANGHAMITRA PADHY, a former student of Jawaharlal Nehru University, is a doctoral student (thesis: Indian Supreme Court's Environmental Defence) at the University of Southern California, Los Angeles.

MAHENDRA PRASAD SINGH, Professor, University of Delhi. He was Head of the Department of Political Science and the Dean of the Faculty of Social Science at the University, and a Director of the Indian Council of Social Science Research. He has authored, edited, and co-edited several books on Indian politics and contributed scholarly papers in professional journals in India and North America.

GEORGE MATHEW, Director, Institute of Social Sciences, New Delhi. He is a scholar-administrator, well-published in his area of specialization of Local Governments in professional scholarly journals. As a Shastri Indo-Canadian Fellow (2005), he was associated with Trent University in Canada and was invited to a seminar at the World Bank in Washington, DC.

K.G. KANNABIRAN, Senior Advocate, Andhra Pradesh High Court, Hyderabad. He is the President of the Peoples' Union for Civil Liberties (PUCL) who has championed the cause of human rights for the past fifty years, and campaigned for democratizing the Indian court system.

B.D. DUA, Dean (Emeritus), Faculty of Arts and Sciences, and Professor (Emeritus), Department of Political Science, University of Lethbridge, Alberta, Canada. He was the Vice-President of the Shastri Indo-Canadian Institute, New Delhi for the year 2001–2. He has several publications to his credit and is well-published in prestigious journals. Currently, he holds Adjunct Professorship at the University of Lethbridge.

REKHA SAXENA, Reader, Centre for Federal Studies, Hamdard University, New Delhi. She was twice awarded the Shastri Indo-Canadian Fellowship (1999, 2002) and was affiliated with the Department of Political Studies at the Queen's University, Canada. Besides contributing articles to professional journals, newspapers, and news magazines, she has published and edited a number of books. Her latest book is *Situating Federalism: Mechanisms of Intergovernmental Relations in Canada and India.*

S.K. VERMA, Director, Indian Law Institute, New Delhi. She was formerly Head of Department and Dean, Law Faculty, University of Delhi. She has written widely on international law and intellectual property laws in various national and international journals and has authored a book on public international law, in addition to co-editing *Fifty Years of the Supreme Court of India: Its Grasp and Reach.*

DOLLY ARORA, Reader in Political Science, Indian Institute of Public Administration, New Delhi. She is well-published; one of her latest works is: *Democracy and Competing Claims: Should Privileges be Privilege over Rights?* New Delhi: Indian Institute of Public Administration, 2003.

V.K. OHRI, Advocate, Supreme Court of India and Human Rights activist.

Introduction

DEMOCRACY AND CONSTITUTIONALISM

As democracy initially came to be largely equated with majority rule, the relationship between law and politics increasingly acquired critical importance. This was so both in terms of institutionalization of procedures and values as well as in terms of individual and minorities' rights. In the trajectory of growth of democratic thought and institutions, law and politics developed as two indispensable pillars of democracy. Maravall and Przeworski perceptively observe: 'The conflict between rule of majority and rule of law is just a conflict between actors who use votes and laws as their instruments. Whether legislatures or courts prevail in particular situations is a matter of politics.'[1] Majoritarianism or rule of law are both at heart, political outcomes, by political choice. Majoritarianism is the antecedent and the rule of law the consequent. The rule of law is the natural outcome in a divided society and a divided government which must govern by consensus. Democracy is constitutive of law and law is constitutive of democracy. One can't survive without the other.

In political thought sources of law have variously been discovered in customs and conventions (Edmund Burke), popular sovereignty (civic republicanism drawing on Plato, Aristotle, and Jean-Jacques Rousseau), and legitimate government premised on the guarantee of individual liberties and human rights (classical liberalism tracing its origins and elaboration to John Locke and others). In the former two approaches, social control, and in the latter, individual autonomy, are the basis of legitimacy. In Jurgen Habermas' discourse theory of law and democracy, all the three foregoing strands are, in a way, pulled together into theorizing a constitutional state in which legal as well as democratic legitimacy are internally related to a series of concentric circles of deliberative democracy. To quote Habermas:

> The establishment of the legal code, which is undertaken with the help of the universal right to equal individual liberties, must be completed through communicative and participatory rights that guarantee equal opportunities for the public use of communicative liberties. In this way, the discourse principle acquires the legal shape of a democratic principle.[2]

In the course of evolution of comparative constitutional theory and practice in democratic societies, at least three models of constitution have crystallized in modern times: (a) the Westminster parliamentary system whose two organizing principles—parliamentary sovereignty and rule of law—were delineated by A.V. Dicey in his 1885 classic, *An Introduction to the Study of the Law of the Constitution*;[3] (b) the U.S. American model of presidential federalism established in 1787 in the wake of the war of independence (and the failure of the Articles of Confederation) and premised on the separation of powers on the horizontal plane, and federal division of powers between the federal and state governments on the vertical plane; and (c) the nineteenth and first-half-twentieth century Commonwealth parliamentary federations in Canada (1867), Australia (1901) and India (1950).

In British constitutional history, tendencies towards royal absolutism were gradually checkmated by assertion of power and legality by Parliament and law courts by the early eighteenth century. This trend to deinstitutionalize royal absolutism was more or less firmly established in the nineteenth century. The two key principles of the English constitution—parliamentary sovereignty and rule of law—were thus magisterially stated by Dicey:

> All that [is] necessary to insist upon is [that] the essential property of representative government is to produce coincidence between the wishes of the sovereign and the wishes of the subjects; to make, in short, the two limitations on the exercise of sovereignty absolutely coincident. This, which is true in its measure of all real representative government, applies with special truth to the English House of Commons.[4]
>
> In England the idea of legal equality, or of the universal subjection of all classes to one law administered by the ordinary courts, has been pushed to its utmost limit. With us every official, from the Prime Minister down to a constable

or a collector of taxes, is under the same responsibility for every act done without legal justification as any other citizen.[5]

The challenge to royal absolutism was born in politics, legitimized by law soon thereafter. Having questioned the power of the Crown in the name of representativeness of the Parliament and legality of the courts, constitutionalism in the United Kingdom inevitably culminated in parliamentary sovereignty tempered by rule of law. Subject to willing acceptance of international law and European constitution and law, these twin tenets of British constitutionalism, delineated by Dicey in the last quarter of the nineteenth century are still largely valid. However, it must be noted that since the early 1990s, the Executive and Parliament have found the judiciary more and more self-righteous and assertive. One observer goes to the extent of saying that it is 'virtually certain that the current level of tension between the judiciary and the executive will continue; it will [rather] intensify. So it looks as though the British judiciary will have to hold the line against the Executive until the House of Commons starts scrutinizing legislation properly.'[6]

In contrast to more or less gradual evolution of British constitutionalism and the survival of feudal relics from the past due to this reason, the United States was founded after the trial of a war of independence, and a rupture with the past. The Americans therefore tried to codify their constitutional principles on a *tabula rasa* in 1787. They had suffered at the hands of the arbitrary British colonial executive. Hence they devised a constitution which created a democratic version of Tudor monarchy in the two orders of government set up at federal and regional levels, countervailed by separate and more or less co-equal legislative and judicial authorities. The hallmark of this branch of constitutionalism—judicial review of congressional enactments and executive orders was only dimly realized initially, but came to be firmly established by early nineteenth century (*Marbury* v. *Madison*, US Supreme Court, 1803). As Cox observed:[7]

The doctrine of judicial supremacy and the people's attachment to this form of constitutionalism drew their principal sustenance from the rich soil of necessity. Without a supreme expositor for constitutional distribution of power and popular acceptance of its decisions, the enterprise upon which the American people launched themselves in the constitution could hardly have survived. With the court as expositor the system worked so well that history legitimated the power, and then habit took over to guide men's actions so long as the system worked well enough.

More recently, the American constitutional device of separation and division of powers has also caught the imagination of theorists of deliberative democracy. This constitutional device 'is a way to insure that competing perspectives, competing arrays of reasons and considerations, are brought to bear on major issues of public policy'.[8]

In interpreting Indian constitutionalism, its historical context of origin would suggest that the independence of India from British colonial rule was partly evolutionary and partly 'revolutionary' in as much as the transfer of power was through legal means rather than by any violent overthrow of the established political authority. Yet it came at the culmination of a freedom struggle in which extra-legal methods of political agitation were used in a mass movement of long duration and depth. The making of the Indian Constitution represented continuity as well as transformation. These paradoxes are amply reflected in the Independence of India Act 1947, an enactment of the British Parliament, and the opening lines of the Preamble to the Constitution which begins with 'We the People of India . . .', a ringing declaration of popular sovereignty as the source of the basic law. The constitution also instituted electoral democracy as the basis for the five-yearly renewal of popular mandate for the Parliament and state legislatures. As members of the Constituent Assembly were particularly obsessed with democratic representation and citizen's fundamental rights and welfare securities, the Indian nationalists had to compromise with limited franchise and indirect elections for the Constituent Assembly, under constraints of the time and the process of transfer of powers by the British colonial rulers.[9]

The Constituent Assembly was indirectly elected in 1946 by members of the provincial legislatures who were themselves elected in 1936 under the Government of India Act 1935, by a franchise extended to about 25 per cent of Indians on the basis of education and property ownership. Representatives of princely states were nominated by their rulers.

In stable and institutionalized democracies, it is difficult to differentiate between majoritarianism, consensualism, and the rule of law. As a matter of fact, constitutionalism believes in a government by law. In Indian constitutional law, the constitutional mandate overrides a transient electoral mandate. For the former epitomizes a fundamental consensus at a historical and defining moment in the history of the nation (*B.R. Kapur* v. *State of Tamil Nadu*, Supreme Court, 2001).

DEMOCRACY AND INSTITUTIONAL FRAMEWORK

Democratic regimes, irrespective of the form of government they choose, work best when the three organs of government function in harmony with each other. The constitution, written or unwritten, defines the functional parameters of the legislative, executive, and judicial branches of the government so that they do not run afoul of each other, but work in tandem for the smooth and stable governance of the country. The form of government—parliamentary (based on the fusion of executive and legislative powers) or presidential (based on the separation of powers), unitary or federal or some other hybrid type—does impact the degree of friction that may mark the relationship between and among the three branches of government, but the organic unity of the political regime is sustained through a delicate system of 'checks and balances' built either into the constitutional framework of the country or institutionalized through customs, traditions, and conventions (particularly in the case of an unwritten constitution). The distribution of state power (and its further vertical division in the case of a federal system) to the three organs of government makes for the de-monopolization of political power, and the system of 'checks and balances' ensures that no organ of the government becomes a law unto itself nor thrives at the cost of the other organs of the government to the detriment of constitutional law and public good. While public participation and political contestation constitute the essence of democratic regimes, the dispersion of power and the dynamic operation of the system of 'checks and balances' nourishes the growth of constitutionalism and the rule of law.

To the extent that all political systems are embedded in their historical past, even somewhat similar constitutional arrangements (as in Canada and India) work differently in different political and social settings. Human ingenuity of which institutions are made of, innovates new operational modes to cope with new challenges without necessarily modifying the formal constitutional structures. This is as much true of the American system which has a more than two centuries-old written and relatively rigid constitution, with a few dozen constitutional amendments to it as it is of the British system which has no written but a flexible constitution. In this evolutionary process, the functional parameters of each branch of the government—the legislative, executive, and judiciary—change over time, with one or two branches gaining more ground or glitter than the others at different times. The overall decline of legislatures (more so in the parliamentary system of the British variety than in the US presidential system), for example, has strengthened the executive branch of government in the same way as the contemporary thrust all the world over for human rights has made the courts expand their reach to vindicate human freedoms. Such a dynamic or organic response to evolving ground realities establishes a new *modus operandi* among the three branches of government, but the basic ground rules of constitutionalism, of 'checks and balances' among government branches and the rule of law stand unaffected in stable democratic systems, unless the constitutional order is altered or amended by appropriate constituent authorities according to procedures laid down in the constitution or established by traditions and conventions.

Unlike the other two branches of government (more closely related because policy-making and policy-implementation are not mutually exclusive functions) which draw their strength from their representative character based on popular mandate, the judiciary is placed on a different pedestal. In most democratic systems, the higher judiciary in particular is neither elected nor does it have the power of purse or sword. It draws its strength from its professionalism and jurisprudential competence. To ensure that it performs its adjudicatory functions without fear or favour, it is fairly independent of the other two branches of government—the men in the black robes enjoy long-term tenure and their impeachment is rare, if ever. Its power to interpret the constitution and to see that all legislative and executive actions are in conformity with the constitutional law of the land (though the scope of judicial review may vary from country to country) allows it wide interpretative discretion (reading into, or reading down, articles of the constitution) in decision-making. It is the guardian of fundamental rights, customary or written in a charter, and the repository of justice. It is not accountable in the same sense as the other two branches are, but it must exercise its powers with restraint—ruling according to the constitution and not over the constitution—to sustain the legitimacy of its decisions. It is expected to guard the constitution against its violations, and not be the custodian of the constitution (the doctrine of 'sovereignty of the parliament' is still alive and well in most parliamentary systems though it is increasingly being questioned) though the distinction disappears when one is reminded of what one US Chief Justice once said: 'The Constitution is what the Supreme Court says it is.'

INDIAN CONSTITUTION AND THE HIGHER JUDICIARY

Besides approximately one hundred amendments, some not very consequential, the Constitution of India, commenced at the dawn of the Republic in 1950, has undergone some radical changes through judicial interpretations. While the Supreme Court in particular has earned public applause for its innovative jurisprudence, it has exercised, some constitutional pundits would argue, extravagant jurisdiction, transgressing the executive and legislative domains, contrary to the original 'checks and balances' design of the Constitution. This judicial transformation of the original scheme of the Constitution, it is further argued, has been facilitated because of the dysfunctionality and ineffectiveness of the other two branches of government both at the Centre and in the States, and on account of the widespread criminalization of politics. In the process of correcting this abnormality, the Court has, critics say, over-reached its adjudicating role to become the governing institution of the country.

Of the many concerns that have been articulated, the Supreme Court's invention of the doctrine of 'basic structure of the Constitution' as the litmus test for the validity of constitutional amendments has been the most significant and controversial one. The doctrine evolved as a reaction to the assertion of unfettered constituent powers by the Parliament but the 'argument of fear' lest the Parliament should damage or undermine the essential democratic features of the Constitution prompted the Supreme Court (as if it was anticipating the 1975–7 Emergency which practically unnerved where it mattered the most) to restrain the amending power of the Parliament.

Article 368 read with Articles 2, 3, and 4 outline three processes for amending different parts of the Constitution. First, Articles 2, 3, and 4 give the Parliament the power to admit or form new states by simple majority in each House of the Parliament and with the assent of the President. In fact, laws made under Articles 2 and 3 amending the First and the Fourth schedules of the Constitution (containing a list of the States and of the Union Territories and allotting seats to each of these federating units in the Rajya Sabha respectively) are not to 'be deemed to be an amendment this Constitution for the purposes of Article 368' (Article 4, clause 2). The only precondition laid down for this category of amendment by simple majority, is that if it related to the formation of new states or alteration of areas, boundaries, or names of existing states, no such bill can be introduced in either House of the

Parliament without the prior consent of the President and prior consultation with the affected states and their legislatures (Article 3).

Second, other parts of the Constitution, excepting federal features, can be amended by a bill initiated in either House of Parliament and with a majority of the total membership of the House plus not less than two-thirds of the members present and voting.

Third, federal features of the Constitution (relating to the President of India and other members of the Union Executive and Executives of State Governments and Union Territories, Supreme Court and High Courts, legislative relations between the Union and States—Union/States/Concurrent Lists, representation of States in Parliament, and provisions of Article 368) may be amended by special majority (two-thirds) in each House of the Parliament plus (as a check on parliamentary majoritarianism) ratification by the legislatures of at least 50 per cent of States (Article 368, clauses 1 and 2). There is no provision for a joint session of the two Houses of the Parliament to resolve a deadlock between the two, nor is there any provision for President's request for reconsideration (on only once basis) of amendment bills. Thus the Rajya Sabha has veto power on amendment of the above federal provisions of the Constitution. However, the President has no delaying power.

The late 1960s and 1970s were a period that transformed the pattern of judicial behaviour in India in a significant way. After initial acquiescence (*Sankari Prasad* v. *Union of India*, 1951; *Sajjan Singh* v. *State of Rajasthan*, 1965), the Supreme Court asserted its judicial power in *Golak Nath* v. *State of Punjab* (1967). Faced with continuous circumvention of its rulings (primarily with respect to property rights) by governments amending the Constitution itself to disempower the judiciary, the Supreme Court offered the first major resistance in the Golak Nath case by setting its foot down in curbing the amending power of the Parliament, at least in relation to Part III of the Constitution on Fundamental Rights, and entrenching the judicial review. In the Court's view, Fundamental Rights appeared to have a certain permanence in the intents and purposes of the constitutional scheme. Parliament replied by a series of constitutional amendments, asserting full power to amend any and all parts of the Constitution, and declaring the judiciary out of bounds in case of laws and amendments brought about to implement the Directive Principles of State Policy. This, however, did not settle the issue of parliamentary sovereignty *versus* judicial review.

In a landmark judgement in *Keshavananda* v. *State of Kerala* (1973), the Court conceded Parliament's power to amend the entire Constitution, but then boomeranged, by adding that in doing so, the Parliament/aggregate legislature could not 'damage', 'abrogate', 'emasculate', 'destroy', or 'change or alter' the 'basic features/elements', 'fundamental features', or 'framework' of the Constitution.[10] This was a masterstroke by the Court—it overruled Golak Nath much to satisfaction of the government, returned to its earlier position in the Shankari Prasad case by conceding the Parliament's power to amend the Constitution and, at the same time, strengthened and enhanced its own power of judicial review of constitutional amendments. It was a 13-judge bench ruling by a sharply divided Court (7 to 6). The illustrative enumeration of the features of the basic structure varied from judge to judge with overlaps in some, but not in all cases. The features common to all or most were the democratic nature of the Constitution, Fundamental Rights, Indian secularism, separation of powers, and federal division of powers, etc. One judge ominously mentioned the Preamble and its elaboration in the rest of the Constitution. The judgement was criticized by some as vague and divided. The government's reaction was swift and strong. In the upcoming judicial promotions that were soon due, the executive appointed a Chief Justice of India, superceding four senior judges on the bench who had delivered the Keshavananda judgement.

Since Keshavananda, the doctrine of 'basic structure' has been used so often to test the validity of constitutional amendments and even ordinary legislation[11] that it has become, as Upendra Baxi anticipated, 'in some sense, the Indian Constitution of the future'.[12] However, criticism of the doctrine still abounds. Even if it be admitted, some argue, that the doctrine has been used, throughout the 1980s and 1990s, to enhance constitutionalism and the rule of law, it is still a text beyond the text of the Constitution. Leaving aside the fact that the doctrine is indeterminate, and is continuously in the making at the hands of a few judges,[13] it is unsafe at best, because it gives too much power to a few unelected judges to determine the style of future governance of the country (even the most desirable amendments may not be made for fear lest the judiciary should veto them). As Raju Ramachandran has argued: 'The basic structure doctrine proceeds upon a distrust of the democratic process, which itself must be part of the basic structure. In limiting the amending power, the basic structure doctrine in fact stifles democracy, a basic feature.' And he advises: 'The basic structure doctrine has served a certain purpose: it has warned a fledgeling democracy of the perils of brute majoritarianism [reference to 1975–77 Emergency]. . . . The doctrine must now be buried.'[14]

Besides the 'basic structure' doctrine, the Supreme Court has invented yet another test to determine the constitutionality of any legislation and executive action. In *Maneka Gandhi* (1978), the Court declared that all Fundamental Rights were inter-related; that any law for taking away the life and personal liberty of an individual under Article 21 (procedure established by law) to be valid, must also satisfy the requirements of Article 19 (equality before law); and that the 'procedure established by law' must be 'reasonable, fair, and just'. Thus, in one stroke the Court (shifting from its earlier position in *A.K. Gopalan* v. *State of Madras*, 1950) did what was purposely rejected by the Constituent Assembly: it imported the American doctrine of 'due process of law' in place of the 'procedure established by law'. The Maneka decision was well received by people disenchanted with government administration. (Article 21 has since been used creatively and expansively to improve criminal justice, ecology, and the quality of life in the country[15]), but some experts still express reservation if the Court acted properly in reconstructing the text of the Constitution to its own power advantage, relative to the other two branches of the government.

The Supreme Court did this again in 1993, when it wrested control of higher judicial appointments from the executive. Articles 124 and 217 speak of 'consultation' that the President of India shall have with the Chief Justice of India, other judges and constitutional functionaries before he makes appointments to the Supreme Court and various High Courts. The expression is not 'concurrence'—an expression that was not agreed to by the Constituent Assembly[16]—yet the Court's juridical reasoning boiled down to this expression in the *Supreme Court Advocates on Record Association* v. *Union of India* (SCAORA 1993) decision (re-affirmed in 1998), which passed the appointment powers to the higher judiciary (in a collegium), while reducing the role of the executive to a mere formality. Since the SCAORA decision, the higher judiciary has virtually become self-appointing, contrary to the original design of the Constitution. While the decision has been justified to protect the independence of the judiciary from executive interference (that began in the 1970s and increased during the 1975–7 Emergency and thereafter), some critics have foamed at the mouth. 'Save the Constitution from the Supreme Court.'

Juristocracy prospers when the elected representatives fail to provide good governance in a democratic polity. Notwithstanding the fact that the Supreme Court carries the burden of some serious concerns about its interpretation of the Constitution, it has acquired enormous public acclaim for expanding the ambit of human rights, and protecting individual and collective freedoms in the midst of growing political corruption and criminality in public life. The Court (and the higher judiciary) has relaxed the strict legal rules of locus standi (allowing a 'third party' to petition in public interest litigation), to reach the poor and disadvantaged sections of society and to enable individuals or groups to raise common concerns arising from inefficient or dishonest governance.[17] Public Interest Litigation (PIL) has further enhanced the popularity of the higher judiciary much to the embarrassment (for the exposure of many political scandals in high places) of government(s) which would like to see some parameters set for admitting PIL petitions. 'Let the government govern' has been the outcry of many political leaders against the growth of unprecedented activism of the courts, which have not hesitated to intervene in executive administration to ensure implementation of their decisions (in a variety of areas—environmental pollution, prison reforms, bonded labour, etc.). Even the National Commission to Review the Working of the Constitution (NCRWC) advised judicial restraint and offered some loaded comments:[18]

> Judicial activism has not gone too well with groups of democratic theorists who object to the kind of judicial activism which has tended to turn social and political processes to legal processes and obliterating the then line of demarcation between interpretation and adjudication and exhibiting an ever-eager tendency to intervene in the governing process. Constitution adjudications do have an inevitable legislative element. Judges need great wisdom and restrain in wielding this great judicial power lest they should erect their own predilections into principles.

The judicial response to this criticism is well summed up by the former Chief Justice, Dr. A.S. Anand:[19]

> The expanded role of the judiciary has been given the title of 'Judicial Activism' by those who are critical of this expanded role. The main thrust of the criticism is that the judiciary by its directives to the administration is usurping the functions of the legislatures and of the executive and is running the country, and according to some, even ruining it. What these critics of the judiciary overlook is that it is the tardiness of legislatures and the indifference of the executive to address itself to the complaints of the citizens about violations of their human rights and unfair treatment which provides the necessity for judicial intervention. . . . When

the court is apprised of and is satisfied about gross violations of basic human rights, it cannot fold its hands in despair and look the other way.

Although the number of public interest petitions has increased over time, Dr. Anand sensitized the courts to the need for judicial restraint, when he added: 'Care has to be taken to see that PIL essentially remains *Public* Interest Litigation and does not become either *Political* Interest Litigation or *Personal* Interest Litigation or *Publicity* Interest Litigation or used for *Persecution*. If that happens, it would be unfortunate.'[20]

There is no doubt that the 'victim-abuse' jurisprudence of the higher judiciary has been loudly cheered by the public, but how long the applause will last is anybody's guess. Public disappointment is likely to set in, given that the judiciary alone can neither quick-fix all problems of justice nor enforce probity in public life. In respect to the Constitution, the power shift from the elected representatives to the unelected judiciary may not be of immediate concern to the masses struggling for justice, but a serious concern it must remain for 'We the People of India'. As a former Attorney-General, Santosh Hegde, once cautioned: 'Things are so bad today that any and every approach adopted by the courts is applauded. But the damage suffered by the checks and balances of our Constitution makes me apprehensive about tomorrow.'[21]

The papers in this volume are written by well-known scholars, lawyers, and academics. They reflect on the itinerary of the higher judiciary and its contributions to constitutional law and public good, in the context of the developmental path of the political system since the commencement of the Republic in 1950. The papers cover a variety of topics—the struggle for judicial review and governance by the judiciary, judiciary and bill of rights, ecology, secularism, parliamentary institutions, executive relations, market economy, and judicial reforms—and focus primarily, though not exclusively, on the ramifications of judicial activism.

We recognize the diversity of topics, the gaps and the overlaps, but this was bound to happen in a venture of this nature. For the convenience of the readers however, we have organized the volume into six parts—Part I: Judiciary and Judicial Activism; Part II: Judiciary and Ecology; Part III: Judiciary and Secularism; Part IV: Judiciary and Parliamentary-Local Institutions; Part V: Judiciary and Central Executive; Part VI: Judiciary and Reforms. The abstracts of the papers presented in the volume are as follows:

Douglas A. Verney, in his comparative historical discussion of Judicial Review in the Anglo-American and the Commonwealth traditions, delineates five types of precursive or contemporary varieties of judicial review. These five variants are: Britain in the seventeenth century, when Chief Justice Coke abortively tried to review royal prerogatives on the basis of conventional common law, the classical American constitutional doctrine of judicial review discovered by Chief Justice Marshall, the review of laws of British colonial legislatures by the Judicial Committee of the Privy Council in London, a rather limited judicial review of parliamentary and provincial laws by the Supreme Court of Canada, and the vigorous judicial review of parliamentary and state laws by the Supreme Court of India. In all these instances, Verney demonstrates that although judicial review first 'emerged out of a crisis or crises of governance', it has acquired relevance and salience over a period of time. 'In none of the political systems', concludes Verney, 'is judicial review widely considered to be opposed to the principles of liberal democracy. There has been a balance between the various branches of government, a balance which shifts from time to time, but which has left the legislative and judicial branches largely intact.'

Rajeev Dhavan, in his incisive analysis of the judicial process in India, discusses the trajectory of the Supreme Court from the 1950s to the beginning of the next millennium, through what he calls the 'three Rebellions': 1950–5, 1960–71, and 1972–5, and a qualitative shift into a fourth phase, from the immediate post-Emergency years to the onset of the 2000s. The first rebellion took the form of declaring land reforms laws unconstitutional, which provoked the Nehru regime, the Shastri interregnum, mainly in the early years of Indira Gandhi's premiership. In this period, the Court raised issues of the philosophy of the Constitution and empowerment of the people. Unlike the first, the second rebellion confronted the executive with greater determination. The third rebellion flared up into sharper confrontation when the Court invented the theory of 'basic structure' of the Constitution and its unamendability. But during the Emergency, the executive mounted serious reprisals and practically coerced the Court to cave in. However, after the electoral defeat of the Emergency regime in 1977, the Court reactivated itself with a vengeance. It not only re-established judicial review, which it had never formally surrendered, but entered into a phase of activism on an unprecedented scale, more than any other judiciary in the world. Dhavan observes: 'The judiciary ceased to be an institution of State, and became an institution of governance in its own right'—a position (or 'usurpation') it cannot legitimize 'unless it responds to some sense of the peoples' voice'.

Soli J. Sorabjee, in his scholarly and comparative analysis, starts with the premise that 'individuals possess basic human rights independently of any Constitution by reason of the basic fact that they are members of the human race', and that 'a purposive, rather than a strictly literal' judicial interpretation keeps a constitutionally-entrenched Bill of Rights alive and flexible to changing conditions and emerging challenges. 'A most generous Bill of Rights,' says Sorabjee, 'can be reduced to a parchment of promises by narrow and insensitive judicial interpretation.' Recognizing that 'judicial review is a very delicate exercise and can also cause problems', Sorabjee reviews many cases to compliment the Supreme Court for an expansive interpretation of Article 21 (right to life and personal liberty) of the Constitution to include, among others, 'reasonable, fair and just' procedures established by law, reasonably expeditious trials, the right to live with human dignity and all that goes along with it, the right to travel abroad, and (in conjunction with Article 14) protection against inhuman and degrading punishment or treatment. The Court has deduced fundamental rights (freedom of the press; freedom of information) not specifically mentioned in the chapter on Fundamental Rights, scrutinized whether the restrictions imposed on fundamental rights in the 'public interest' are reasonable and not excessive or disproportionate, awarded compensation for infringement of a person's fundamental right, reviewed bona fide, the pre-requisites for the declaration of emergencies, and exercised enough care in 'reading into' or 'reading down' the language of statutes to prevent any unnecessary challenge to their constitutionality. But the most notable achievement in the protection and promotion of fundamental rights, says Sorabjee, has been by the development of Public Interest Litigation (PIL) where the Court has 'departed from the traditional requirement of locus standi . . . and forged new tools, devised new methods and adopted new strategies' to deliver justice to the weaker and marginalized sections of society.

Mahendra Pal Singh discusses judicial activism in India against the background of comparative development of this trend (that emerged with the conception and development of constitution or limited government) in other countries, particularly in the United States. He takes a more balanced and constitutionalist view on this matter than the generally pro-judiciary view of the recent phase of judicial review in the literature. It is apparent from his discussion, that judicial activism developed in fundamental rights and constitutional amendment review cases, and only recently has it extended its reach to the federal dysfunctionality of government, including the protection of the human rights of the poor and the unorganized. He divides the history of judicial behaviour in India into the pre-Emergency period which was marked by economic liberalism, and the post-Emergency period which is more in line with the underlying principles of constitutionalism, egalitarianism, and social justice. He concludes that the judiciary 'must accelerate the pace' of accomplishing the goals—'Justice: social, economic, and political'—as enshrined in the Preamble of the Constitution 'through its activism'.

Rajinder Sachar maps the journey of the Indian judiciary, particularly of the Supreme Court, since the Emergency (1975–7), reviews the apex Court's judgements in some very critical cases such as the *habeas corpus* case, the civil liberties issues under the Prevention of Terrorism Act 2002, the right of privacy in the *Peoples' Union for Civil Liberties* case, the misfeasance in public office in the *Satish Sharma* case, the denial of right to vote to under-trials under the Representation of People Act 1951, the Vajpayee government's privatization decision in the *HPCL–BPCL* case, and reflects on the Court's view in respect of capital punishment and the government employees' right to collective bargaining. Sachar speaks with the voice of an insider; he concludes with a brief narrative of his own personal experience as the Chief Justice of the Delhi High Court, to reaffirm his central theme: the courts should be bold enough to challenge unworthy laws and active enough to humanize justice in the interest of the poor and the marginalized people, notwithstanding the erroneous impression that the judiciary is intervening in the political domain and over-stepping its jurisdiction. The Supreme Court has done reasonably well to retrieve its reputation since its surrender during the Emergency; overall however, 'the judiciary is still a mixed bag—it does seem to be on right track but the journey is still long and hazardous'.

Prashant Bhushan recognizes the contribution of the Supreme Court in expanding the scope and breadth of public interest litigation from its initial concerns for environment, to social issues such as bonded labour, child labour, the rights of detenus and inmates of various asylums, the rights of the poor to education, shelter and other amenities. The Court took a holistic view of fundamental rights, relaxed the rules of locus standi to provide for easy access to justice to the socially and financially weaker sections of society, and expansively interpreted

Article 21 of the Constitution, much to the rumbling discontent of political and bureaucratic elites. This approach which started in the 1970s and continued through the 1980s and the major part of the 1990s, the author argues, seems to have come to a halt in recent years. The Court has tried to put unreasonable conditions into the PIL to discourage it, and has very rarely invalidated measures of the governments and the industries in pursuit of what has come to be known as 'economic reforms'. The recent case laws leave the author with the inescapable conclusion that the Court has unduly endorsed economic reforms even when they have been pursued at the cost of the rights of the poor and the helpless public, and in ways that show infirmities of corruption. The Court has diluted its earlier expansive interpretation of rights to life and liberty in its more recent judgements.

R.K. Barik analyses the reasons for the present crisis in our judicial system in the context of fragmentation in the political process, assumption of policy-making function by the judiciary, absence of a system of review of decisions taken by the apex court, playing of politics by courts and the huge dependency of court cases, impact of globalization, and the persistence of anti-poor biases even in PIL cases. The judiciary, writes Barik, has many challenges but the most significant, is for it to respond to the needs of the common people for quick justice in line with the constitutional mandate of promoting social democracy. The Preamble of the Constitution, says Barik, should be central to all judicial interpretations of national laws and international contractual obligations. The conservatism of the judicial elite must be tempered with the virtues of social justice as outlined in our Constitution.

Dharmendra S. Sengar examines the importance of Public Interest Litigation (PIL) as a legal instrument for public access to environmental justice through an in-depth study of notable judicial pronouncements and the norms and principles that flow from them. He reviews constitutional and legal provisions relating to environmental matters, and critically examines the role of Indian courts in the evolution and development of environmental jurisprudence. He focuses both on the reported and unreported judicial decisions and discusses significant developmental and environmental issues that have been brought before the Supreme Court through PILs. In diluting the concept of locus standi, the Indian activist judiciary, he argues, has undertaken the task of protecting the environment in a big way and its efforts have been successful to a certain extent. 'But it is unfortunate', writes Sengar, 'that in spite of constitutional, legal and administrative measures, the problem of pollution of environment and exploitation of natural resources is increasing at an alarmingly high rate.' Keeping in view the lack of people's awareness of environmental hazards, the limited number of bona fide social action groups, and the limitations of the judiciary to implement its own pronouncements, Sengar recommends the search for innovative measures to make the existing system of environmental compliance and enforcement more effective and proactive.

Subhendu Ranjan Raj discusses the general principles relating to environmental jurisprudence as evolved and laid down by the Supreme Court, but more specifically the process that culminated in the introduction of CNG buses in Delhi in 2002, much to the relief of Delhi residents, who were virtually getting suffocated by the ever-increasing air pollution in the city. But for the valiant efforts of M.C. Mehta who was the first to file the PIL petition in 1986 on this issue, and the perseverance and persistence of the Supreme Court to the extent of virtually monitoring the progress of its directives at the two levels of government (Delhi Administration and the Union of India), relating to pollution reduction (despite some criticism that the Court was transgressing its legitimate boundaries), Delhi would have continued to suffer from the hazardous effect of polluted air mostly caused by the increasing number of diesel-driven vehicles. Despite rich scientific data supporting positive correlation between air pollution and diseases and deaths, many stops were pulled, the author says, by vested interests, including the government at the two levels, to switch from diesel fuel to the cleaner CNG fuel.

John R. Wood, in his insightful and comprehensive analysis of the politics of Narmada River dam's controversy and its final resolution by the Supreme Court, draws attention to aspects of Indian development and politics that have not as yet received much attention from political scientists. As it emerges from his detailed narrative, the protagonists in this dispute were the governments of riparian States, the Narmada Bachao Andolan (NBA), the Supreme Court, and the World Bank. After a long and protracted mobilization of a movement by the NBA, the net gain to the movement was that the governments had to respond to the public grievances. The World Bank withdrew from its funding, but finally the construction of the dam was not stopped. The Supreme Court balked from its activist PIL activism and allowed the dam to be built with a judgement that met the public demand by making some concessions. The judges validated the existing procedures for water dispute settlement, but laid down certain conditions for the completion of the dam which the politicians and the administ-rators had to attend to. Although criticized for its judgement (as pro-development, anti-people), the Court made it clear that it could not intervene in government policy matters, nor could it allow PIL to become Publicity Interest Litigation or Private Inquisitiveness Litigation.

C.P. Bhambhri focuses on the difficult odyssey of a secular state in India in a hyper-religious society. Drawing on case law, he explicates the nature of Indian secularism under the Constitution and applauds the judiciary for taking a 'balanced' approach in settling inter-communal religious conflicts without compromising the role of the state in reforming unsustainable religious practices. In recent years, the rise of 'militant and aggressive anti-minority ideology of Hindutva' did pose a severe challenge (the demolition of the Babri Masjid, the Best Bakery riots), to the tenets of secularism and to the overall democratic governance of the country, but the judiciary came alive as the most reliable defender of constitutional values. Bhambhri concludes: 'The Indian judiciary, on the basis of its continuous involvement in dealing with contentious issues concerning "religion", "religious practices", and threats to "religious practices", and "religious freedoms", has done a commendable job in a very difficult social situation.'

Sanghamitra Padhy examines the Supreme Court's decisions on issues of secularism, religion, and a uniform civil code over the last two decades and argues that the 'judgements defy the logic of the positivist determination of outcomes. Judicial deliberations on issues of secularism reveal rather, that context takes centre-stage in decision-making.' Consequently, judicial pronouncements have been inconsistent and contradictory. While in some cases, the Court has 'promoted majority interests, eroding the rights of minority groups, in others, it has privileged minority groups'. All in all, 'the vision of secularism endorsed by the judiciary', Padhy concludes, 'favours the majority, as the emphasis is on uniformity based on oneness rather than respect for difference'.

Mahendra Prasad Singh observes that the law relating to privileges and immunities of Parliament/State legislatures in India continues to rely on ill-understood conventions and to be largely lacking in positive constitutional law emanating from the constitution, legislation, and/or case law. He traces the slow growth of these immunities in British India and reviews the uncritical, and contradictory import of British monarchical democratic conventions and laws in republican and federal India. The 44th Amendment (1978), he argues, provides a deceptive 'solution', a remedy worse than the disease, by dropping reference to the British House of Commons [as originally provided in Article 105(3) of the Indian Constitution in 1950], and adding that the privileges and immunities of parliamentary bodies in India would be those that had evolved and been adopted by the year of the said amendment. For Singh shows that but for (a) a case-specific judicial opinion offered by the Supreme Court in a Presidential reference case under the Court's advisory jurisdiction, and (b) unsuccessful, often bizarre, assertions by State legislatures of their 'neo-feudal' privileges vis-à-vis individual and press freedoms that are easily shot down by courts and weighty, juristic, academic, and media experts, there has been no attempt on the part of legislative bodies until today, to codify their privileges that the constitution mandates them to do, nor has there been a clinching case-law laid down by the Supreme Court under its original jurisdiction. Singh makes a solid and cogent argument for the codification of legislative privileges subject to judicial review.

George Mathew describes the significance of the 73rd and 74th amendments to the Constitution of India (1992), which accorded constitutional status to 'institutions of local self government' and regrets that several state governments, which passed their own acts in conformity with the amended constitutional provisions, have been hesitant in 'giving the panchayats and the municipalities their due share of powers'. According to Mathew, there are vested interests—contractors, bureaucrats and politicians—who feel threatened and humiliated by the new local governments. He examines several cases of judicial interventions where the higher judiciary, on the initiative of social and community groups or on the basis of public interest litigation, acted as the 'saviour' of local governments, directing regular and timely elections (in Karnataka, Andhra Pradesh and Bihar), and safeguarding the legitimate functions and powers of local government institutions against the onslaughts of senior bureaucrats (Punjab and Tamil Nadu), and anti-local government forces. There have been exceptions to this otherwise very positive judicial support to local governments as in the on-going case of *Perumatty Panchayat* v. *Coca Cola Factory in Kerala*, and in the case where the Supreme Court validated the undemocratic 'two child norm'—imposed by some states—on candidates for contesting panchayat elections. But Mathew appreciates the overall 'progressive and pro-active role of the judiciary in overseeing the sustained progress of local institutions in the interests of grass-roots democracy; he expects the judiciary to clarify many grey areas in Article 243 of the Constitution (dealing with a local government institution) and to act promptly in disposing of cases relating to them.

K.G. Kannabiran argues that the process of appointments to the High Courts and the Supreme Court lacks transparency, despite the fact that the higher judiciary has virtually become 'self-appointing' in its struggle to be independent of the executive. The Constitution provides a general framework and eligibility requirements for appointments, but the Constituent Assembly laid down no merit criteria or guidelines to assure that only persons, who have the 'intellectual capabilities to understand the constitutional scheme, its goals, an enthusiasm to mould the law, and interpret it in a manner that would secure the objectives set out in the Preamble to the Constitution' would get selected as judges. Being a lawyer even with a large clientele does not, says Kannabiran, 'fit the bill'. The selection process should assess candidates for their philosophical understanding of the Constitution and orientation to judicial values and norms. Further, although judges enjoy tenure during good behaviour, the Ramaswamy case exposes the politics of impeachment to remove judges for misbehaviour. The author welcomes the recommendation of the National Commission to Review the Working of the Constitution (NCRWC: 2000) for a National Judicial Commission to streamline judicial recruitment and disciplinary procedures, though he would like to see the larger community of lawyers included in the composition of the Commission. Wider representation and consultation, Kannabiran believes, will democratize the appointment process which 'need not be shrouded in opacity'.

B.D. Dua, in a comprehensive and detailed paper, describes the ebb and flow in executive-judicial relations through the changing leadership at the Centre (Nehru to Manmohan Singh), to argue that the higher judiciary has become so powerful relative to the other two dysfunctional branches of the government, that matters of judicial appointments to higher judiciary and transfer of High Court judges should be decided by a Judicial Commission wider in composition, to include more stakeholders than the one recommended by the National Commission to Review the Working of the Constitution (2002). Few will deny, he writes, that the Supreme Court in particular has come a long way to earn public applause for its creative jurisprudence to enlarge the scope of human rights, but it has, in the process, titled the balance of power in its favour with its juridical reasoning and crusading activism to check the vagaries of a malfunctioning political system and its self-aggrandizing leadership. Its judgement in *Supreme Court Advocates-on-Record Association* v. *Union of India* (re-affirmed in 1998) which makes the judiciary virtually 'self selecting' (in collegium) may be an appropriate reactionary response to the long-drawn out executive interference in judiciary, but it is neither in consonance with the design of the Constitution, nor does it lend transparency to the process of judicial appointments and transfers—a matter too important to be left to the enclosed community of judges alone.

Rekha Saxena argues that the Union government should develop mechanisms of consultation with State governments before signing international treaties and conventions which affect state jurisdictions, notwithstanding the fact that the Centre has been given exclusive jurisdiction in foreign affairs under the Constitution of India. The Indian polity, needless to emphasize, is more federated today than it was during the dominance of the one-party system. Not only have some of the state governments protested against the Union Executive unilateralism (aside from entertaining foreign investors in their competitive bids to attract foreign investment and multinational corporations), in signing some trade treaties, but have also approached the Supreme Court (Tamil Nadu, Rajasthan, Orissa) to adjudicate in such matters. Although the cases have been withdrawn, the pressure from the State governments to be partners in treaty making is not likely to disappear in the growing context of federalization within and globalization without. Before the docket of the Supreme Court gets flooded with such petitions, the politics of current federalism demands that the interests of the State governments should be accommodated within an institutionalized Centre-State consultation framework.

S.K. Verma examines the current state of the judiciary and argues for its modernization to meet the challenges of new economic regime in India in the wake of globalization. 'The judiciary', Verma writes, 'has not only to play its role more effectively to ensure that the new dispensation works in the national interest towards the goal of development, but it has also to ensure security, predictability and transparency in the working of the legal regime with a well-entrenched legal mechanism for quick disposal of cases, under which the foreign entrepreneurs, the multinational corporations, and investors work towards the national goals' enshrined in our Constitution. Our country has a 'vibrant legal system with progressive laws, well established institution' and an 'independent judiciary', but the system, according to the author, faces 'a few insurmountable challenges, namely, the huge backlog of court cases and delay in dispensing justice, lack of accountability and transparency, high cost of litigation, and large-scale acquittals in the criminal cases'. Drawing on several studies, Verma makes valuable suggestions which will not only improve the delivery of justice in the country, but also create 'an atmosphere of trust in the judicial system for the foreign entrepreneurs and investors' to do business with India.

Dolly Arora, in her paper, discusses the agenda of judicial reforms embedded in the market ideology of international financial institutions and aid agencies, and analyses whether the diagnosis as well as the solution reflect the interest and priorities of those providing assistance for reforms (i.e. to create a reliable environment for foreign investment, enforcement of individual rights, and the establishment of accessible and efficient judicial mechanism to settle complex market disputes). The blueprint for these reforms, often thrust upon loan conditions, accomplishes neither the goals of the donor agencies, nor helps the recipient countries because the suggested reforms are not contextualized in the local economic, social, and cultural conditions of the Third World countries. While the Third World countries do need aid, they should be careful not to accept a gift horse without looking into its mouth.

V.K. Ohri's paper is a practitioner's attempt to review the debate on critical reforms in criminal justice system in the context of criminalization of political process and subsequently to take a comprehensive view of the law and administration of criminal justice from the perspective of civil society. It begins with an indepth treatment of the N.N. Vohra Committee Report (July 1993), which made a very perceptive comment that our criminal law was originally devised with the individual criminal within its frame of reference, but now it must deal with criminal activities by syndicates of mafia. The article also gives account of various efforts made by the Government of India to make criminal justice more effective with a special focus on Malimath Committee Report. It also highlights various inadequacies and deficiencies in these efforts and makes various recommendations based on the author's first hand experiences.

We hope that the volume will be of interest and value to readers from all scholarly disciplines.

EDITORS

NOTES

1. Jose Maria Maravall and Adam Przeworski (eds.), *Democracy and the Rule of Law*, Cambridge, 2003, p. 15.
2. Jurgen Habermas, *Between Facts and Norms: Contributions to a Discourse Theory of Law and Democracy* translated by William Rehg, Oxford, 1996, p. 458.
3. A.V. Dicey, *An Introduction to the Study of the Law of the Constitution* with introduction by E.C.S. Wade, Delhi, 1994, first published in 1885.
4. Ibid., p. 84.
5. Ibid., p. 193.
6. *The Hindu* (New Delhi), 17 December 2005, p. 10.
7. Archibald Cox, *The Role of the Supreme Court in American Government*, Delhi, 1976, pp. 29–30.
8. Jeffery K. Tulis, 'Deliberation Between Institutions', in James S. Fishkin and Peter Lasett (eds.), *Debating Deliberative Democracy*, Philosophy, Politics and Society Series 7, Oxford, 2003.
9. Shefali Jha, 'Representation and its Epiphanies: A Reading of the Constituent Assembly Debates', *Economic and Political Weekly* (*EPW*), vol. XXXIX, no. 39, 25 September–1 October 2004, p. 4357.
10. See Granville Austin, *Working A Democratic Constitution: The Indian Experience*, Oxford, 2000, p. 265.
11. It is difficult to list all the cases, but a few noteworthy cases are: *Indira Gandhi* v. *Raj Narain* (1975) where the Supreme Court declared 'free and fair' elections as part of the basic structure of the Constitution; *Minerva Mills Ltd.* v. *Union of India* (1980) where sections 4 and 55 of the Emergency regime's authoritarian 42nd Amendment (1976) was declared as beyond the amending power of the Parliament and hence unconstitutional; *Waman Rao* v. *Union of India* (1981) validated all amendments till *Keshavananda* Judgement (24 April 1973) but amendments relating to Ninth Schedule after that dateline were declared as transgressing the basic structure of the Constitution; *S.P. Sampath Kumar* v. *Union of India* (1987) where the rule of law was declared as a basic feature; *Prakash Singh Badal* v. *Union of India* (1987) and *Kiholta Hollohan* v. *Zachilhu* (1993) where speakers' ruling in dispute concerning defection and disqualification from membership of legislators in relevant legislative bodies, were considered open to judicial review; *Indira Sawhney* v. *Union of India* (1992) where the powers of the Supreme Court under Articles 32, 136, 141, and 142 of the Constitution, judicial review, and rule of law were adjudicated as basic features of the Constitution; *S.R. Bommai and others* v. *Union of India* (1994) where federalism and secularism were declared as parts of the basic framework of the Constitution.
12. Quoted in Austin, ibid., p. 275.

13. Durga Das Basu, in his *Introduction to the Constitution of India*, Agra, 2001 observes: 'The Supreme Court has refused to foreclose the basic features'. He proceeds to draw up a long list gleaned from a variety of judgements: Supremacy of the Constitution; Rule of Law; Separation of Powers; Preamble objectives; Judicial review and Articles 32 and 226; Federalism; Secularism; The Sovereign, Democratic, Republican structure; Freedom and Dignity of the individual; Unity and Integrity of the Nation; Equality, not every feature of equality, but the quintessence of equal justice; Fundamental Rights; Social and Economic Justice; Balance between Fundamental Rights and Directive Principles; Parliamentary System of Government; Free and fair elections; Limitations upon amending power conferred by article 368; Independence of the Judiciary; Effective access to justice; Powers of Supreme Court under articles 32, 136, 141, 142; Legislation seeking to mollify the awards made in exercise of judicial power of the state, by arbitration tribunals constituted under an Act.
14. Raju Ramachandran, 'The Supreme Court and the Basic Structure Doctrine', in B.N. Kirpal et al. (eds.), *Supreme But Not Infalliable*, Oxford, 2000. Also see, M.P. Singh in Shukla's *Constitution of India*, Lucknow, 2001, p. 896. Singh opines that 'the existence of the doctrine of basic structure is no more a matter of dispute. The only dispute remains about its basic contents.'
15. See M.P. Jain, 'The Supreme Court and Fundamental Rights', in S.K. Verma and Kusum (eds.), *Fifty Years of the Supreme Court of India: Its Grasp and Reach*, Oxford, 2000, pp. 22–37.
16. B. Shiva Rao, *The Framing of India's Constitution*, vol. 4, p. 193.
17. S.P. Sathe, *Judicial Activism in India: Transgressing Borders and Enforcing Limits*, Oxford, 2002, p. 202.
18. *Report of the National Commission to Review the Working of the Constitution*, Delhi, 2002, p. 136.
19. A.S. Anand, 'Indian Judiciary and Challenges of 21st Century', in *Indian Judicial System: Need and Directions of Reforms*, Delhi, 2004.
20. Ibid., p. 15.
21. Quoted in *India Today*, 31 October 1996, p. 54.

PART I

Judiciary and Judicial Activism

1

The Struggle over Judicial Review: Supreme Court and Limited Government

DOUGLAS V. VERNEY

INTRODUCTION: FIVE TYPES OF JUDICIAL REVIEW

It has long been accepted that there are two basic models explaining the political role of the judiciary. As the Dutch jurist, Tim Koopmans, has observed:

> . . . in the first, laws passed by the legislative bodies can never be challenged before the courts, because these laws are the very foundation of the constitutional system in question; in the second, the constitutional system is founded on a written constitution which defines or limits the powers of the legislature and allows the courts to check whether legislation tallies with constitutional provisions.

Koopmans goes on to say: 'The first model is very close to the British doctrine of the "sovereignty of Parliament"; the second embodies systems characterized by judicial review of legislation, such as the American or the German.'[1]

There have, therefore, been two concepts of the role of the courts: judicial interpretation (in Britain) and judicial review (in the United States). Judicial review is assumed to date from the 1803 case of *Marbury* v. *Madison*, in which the American Supreme Court assumed the power to invalidate legislation as unconstitutional.

The Supreme Courts of India and Canada retained the British tradition of judicial interpretation until the mid-twentieth century, after which they are presumed to have gradually shifted to judicial review. At the same time, their parliamentary federal political systems have come to be viewed less as parliamentary on the British (or Westminster) model, and more as federations, like the United States.[2]

This may not be entirely correct. The two courts still take for granted a number of features of the Westminster tradition. One of these is the convention that the government is responsible to the lower house of parliament. The upper chamber, which represents the federation and not simply the national popular majority, has less power. Moreover, to some extent the courts still accept the principle of parliamentary (or legislative) supremacy. The courts have often deferred to Parliament.

Unlike the American constitution, the constitutions of Canada and India permit the government to refer matters of public importance to the Supreme Court for an advisory opinion. These 'Reference' cases have played a large part in expanding the jurisdiction of the two Courts.

India is also interesting because there has developed a form of judicial review called 'judicial activism'. In the 1970s, the Court appears to have concluded that Parliament was unable to act in the public interest. Perceiving a vacuum in governance, it began to hand down important judgements dealing with the constitution (in the 1970s), the weaker sections of society (in the 1980s), and the environment (in 1990s).

In both Canada and India, therefore, the Supreme Courts have carved out niches of their own. With the experience of India and Canada in mind, the presumption of a dichotomy between British judicial interpretation and American judicial review needs further examination. There are several types of judicial review.

Nor is this all. If notice is taken of events in England before 1701, and in the British Empire after 1833, there appear to have been even in England two forms of judicial review.[3] The struggle for judicial review in the common law world can therefore be examined from at least five perspectives: those of England, the United States, the British Empire, Canada and India.[4]

Something approximating judicial review was first attempted in England. It involved outspoken judges in the common law courts. In the early seventeenth century, when America was first being settled, the English Court of Common Pleas attempted to curb the prerogative powers of the monarch. Indeed, under Chief Justice Sir Edward Coke, the court is sometimes alleged to have even asserted the primacy of the common law over parliamentary statutes, notably in Dr. Bonham's case (1610). For a few scholars, this case has been 'widely regarded as foreshadowing . . . the power which American courts today exercise in the disallowance of statutes. . .'.[5] In sum, the Court attempted to introduce what may be described as an early type of judicial review, albeit one that may only be called *tentative.*

The second form of judicial review, the American, is one that is often called *classical.* The American constitution assumed the separation of the executive and legislative powers of government, not their fusion in Parliament. It also assumed that the American people wanted to limit the powers of government. What remained unclear was how the Supreme Court could limit the powers of either the President or Congress. In 1803, after the victory of the Democratic–Republicans over the Federalists, a direct confrontation of the Court with the Administration of President Jefferson seemed for a while unavoidable. Chief Justice Marshall avoided a conflict by focusing on Congress, which, he argued, had erred in passing Section 13 of the Judiciary Act of 1789. This section had purported to give the Supreme Court original jurisdiction, but in a matter not provided for in the constitution. The justices declared that the Court had original jurisdiction only in those matters stipulated in the constitution. In his judgement, Chief Justice Marshall declared that the powers of the other branches of government were limited by the Constitution, a document to be interpreted by the Supreme Court. In establishing judicial review, the Court also put an end to the popular assumption in the United States that there was still legislative supremacy.[6]

The third type of judicial review became prominent a generation later. It was one that applied to the British colonies, and can best be described as an *imperial* judicial review. It was exercised by the Judicial Committee of the Privy Council, a peculiar body that legally was part of the executive branch of the British government. The Judicial Committee remained the highest court of appeal for India and Canada until 1949. (It still accepts appeals from a number of Commonwealth countries.[7])

Canada and India each developed their own form of judicial review. This may be called a *parliamentary* judicial review. They retained their British-inspired parliamentary system in which the executive and legislative branches of government were fused into what Canadians called 'responsible government'. Because of the tradition of parliamentary supremacy, judicial review, when it came, had to take a different form from the American, with its suspicion of government. Instead there was the presumption that parliaments acted constitutionally. 'The courts in India started with the ingrained traditions of the British administration of justice according to which judges do not get involved in political or social controversies.'[8] And the Supreme Courts of both nations had to come to terms with a parliamentary tradition, where powerful politicians were unsympathetic to any claim to exercise judicial review. The provincial premiers made this explicit in Canada in 1981 when the Government of Canada needed the support of the provinces for a constitutional amendment procedure. It had to agree to allow both Parliament and the provincial Legislative Assemblies the constitutional right to override parts of the Charter of Rights in what became the 1982 Constitution Act. This meant that in certain circumstances legislative supremacy could still trump judicial review.

In India, where the Supreme Court from the beginning emphasized its right to review legislation, Parliament insisted that it had the last word. Laws were placed in a new Schedule (the Ninth), which protected them against judicial review. There was a long struggle between the Supreme Court and Parliament, with Parliament insisting on its supremacy and the Supreme Court declaring that the basic structure of the constitution could not be amended.

In other words, there has been no common pattern of judicial review. In the common law world there have been at least five types. These we have called tentative, classical, imperial, parliamentary/Canadian and parliamentary/Indian.

Because of their parliamentary political systems, the Supreme Courts of Canada and India have not played the same role as has the American Supreme Court. In both countries the evolution from judicial interpretation to judicial review has taken place gradually.[9]

There were good reasons for this evolutionary approach. Unlike the Americans, neither the Canadians nor the Indians made a revolutionary break with Great Britain. As a result they experienced nothing comparable to *Marbury* v. *Madison*. They did not abandon the Westminster tradition of parliamentary government, adopted by the provinces of British North America in the 1840s, by the Dominion of Canada in 1867, and by the Indian Constituent Assembly in 1949.

1. ENGLAND: FROM TENTATIVE JUDICIAL REVIEW TO PARLIAMENTARY SUPREMACY TO JUDICIAL REVIEW

It was in the nineteenth century that the British fully evolved the doctrine of parliamentary sovereignty, putting an end to the traditional belief in the separation of powers between the executive and legislative branches of government. When A.V. Dicey published his magisterial *Law of the*

Constitution in 1885 he stated that there were three principles of British government: the rule of law; conventions of the constitution; and parliamentary sovereignty. With Parliament supreme, he concluded, the role of the British courts was limited to that of judicial interpretation.[10] As a result, it was long argued that there was no judicial review in the United Kingdom.

Dicey did not produce his doctrine of parliamentary supremacy in a vacuum. In the 1880s the United Kingdom was bitterly divided over the question of Home Rule for Ireland. The Liberal Prime Minister, William Ewart Gladstone, believed that some sort of federal solution, similar to the Canadian, might be worth considering. Dicey was one of those who disagreed, favouring what was called 'Union' instead. The doctrine of parliamentary supremacy preserved England's dominance in the United Kingdom and at the same time prevented court cases from being used to further the cause of Home Rule.

However, to assume that in the United Kingdom, Parliament is supreme, is to ignore not only the recent past but also the long history of the courts in England. As early as 1610, Chief Justice Coke attempted to exercise judicial review over the monarch by declaring, 'the King hath no prerogative, but that which the [common] law of the land allows him'.[11]

In due course the English managed to curb royal power, but in the end they did so not by judicial review but by the evolution of what came to be called 'parliamentary government'. However, in the course of that evolution, in which arbitrary royal power was replaced by the rule of law, the English courts played a not unimportant role, harking back to ancient laws and customs.

They asserted that the rule of law dated from King John's agreement to sign Magna Carta (the Great Charter) in 1215.[12] The notion that on the island of Runnymede the king had assented to a limit to his prerogative may have been a myth, but it was a powerful myth in the centuries of monarchical rule that followed, centuries during which the rule of law did not always prevail.[13]

Matters reached a head after James I of Scotland came to the throne of England in 1603 to succeed the popular Queen Elizabeth. It was then that the limits of the monarch's power became an issue. With his belief in the Divine Right of kings, James was determined to extend the royal prerogative, and to make greater use of the prerogative courts, unpopular institutions created by monarchs over the years.[14] One of these courts was the notorious Star Chamber.

In the struggle between the executive, legislative and judicial branches of government that ensued, it was at first the common law judges, particularly Chief Justice Coke, who fought against the use of the prerogative as arbitrary power. In the 1610 *Case of Proclamations*, Coke declared that the King could not use the prerogative to issue Proclamations whenever he wished.[15] However, Coke's success was short-lived. In 1616 he was dismissed for refusing to defer to James I in giving judgement. Ten years later James's son, Charles I, dismissed another judge, Chief Justice Sir Ranulph Crew, for refusing to admit the legality of a forced loan.

Because judges sat at the pleasure of the king, the attempt to curb the prerogative power through judicial review was clearly doomed. It was only after judges were granted tenure by Parliament in 1701 that the rule of law became something that monarchs had to learn to live with.

By then the battle with the king had been waged, and won, by the third branch of government, the legislature. Known in England as Parliament, it was a body in which (following his dismissal), Coke played a leading role in the 1620s. Until the Civil War, Parliaments were also subject to the monarch, being summoned and dismissed at his or her pleasure. In the 1630s, when the king governed (and taxed) without summoning Parliament, popular resentment increased. Ultimately another Parliament had to be called in 1640. When the king resisted the demands of the so-called Long Parliament, civil war broke out. Parliament then abolished a number of prerogative courts, including the Star Chamber.

Victory by the parliamentary forces in the civil war, which ended with the execution of Charles I in 1649, did not lead to the supremacy of the legislature over the executive. Instead it was the army that took over governance. (After 1640 no parliamentary elections were held until the restoration of the monarchy in 1660; hence the name 'Long Parliament'.) With the declaration of a republic (or Commonwealth), a successor to the king, supported by the army, was appointed to govern the country. The army's leading general, Oliver Cromwell, was chosen as Protector, and ruled until his death in 1658. Although a former Member of Parliament, Cromwell too governed without a Parliament for much of the time.[16]

The civil war therefore did not resolve the fundamental problem of governance: the conflict between the legislative, executive and judicial branches of government. In 1654, Parliament tried to establish its sovereignty when it 'proceeded to draft a new constitution in which its own supremacy over executive, Army, taxation and the Church should be clearly established'.[17] However, this annoyed Cromwell, who then dissolved Parliament. Thomas Hobbes appeared to have argued correctly that government could be in the hands of either one man or an assembly of men, but not both.

The search for a solution to the tensions between the various branches of government continued after the demise of the Commonwealth and the return of the Stuart monarchy in 1660. England failed to establish parliamentary supremacy in the seventeenth century. However, it was fortunate to escape the experience of most Continental countries. There, and especially in the France of Louis XIV, absolutism triumphed. In due course, England, and later Great Britain, proved to be lucky in its political development, not least as a consequence of substituting the dour Hanoverian dynasty for the mercurial Stuarts (1603–1714). Power gradually passed from the monarch, but it did so informally and to ministers. It did not pass to them formally, and it did not pass to Parliament as legislature.

Instead, by convention, ministers came to play a dual role. They remained 'ministers of the Crown'. On taking office they were sworn in as members of His Majesty's Privy Council. However, a clever distinction came to be made between the Crown as an abstract symbol and the monarch as a person. The government was legally responsible to the Crown, not to the monarch. By the nineteenth century monarchs became reconciled to the fact that although they reigned (as monarchs) with traditional pomp and circumstance they did not rule (as the Crown). Most of the Crown's prerogatives (especially in appointments and finance), were taken over by the ministry. They took decisions as a 'cabinet' under a Prime Minister who lived modestly in 10 Downing Street. The ministers then went to the Palace, meeting the king as his Privy Council. Here they had their decisions formally ratified by the monarch in council.

At the same time the ministers were also members of Parliament, with seats in either the Commons or the Lords. The House of Commons gradually established itself as the superior house. Here, the MPs took it upon themselves to decide whether they approved of the actions of the ministry. They proved their supremacy when they voted to replace a government. In due course the notion evolved of ministries (or cabinets) being politically responsible to Parliament, which in practice meant responsibility to the House of Commons, where the MPs had the power to dismiss them from office.

This did not mean the triumph of the legislature as such over the executive. Instead the two branches were fused in what became known as 'parliamentary government', but in which the Prime Minister and cabinet played a leading role. It was also a fusion accompanied by a new form of the separation of powers. First, there was separation of the Crown as an institution from the person of the monarch as Head of State. Secondly, there was the separation of the Head of Government, the Prime Minister, from the Head of State. The Prime Minister and his cabinet were politically responsible only to the House of Commons, not to the House of Lords or the monarch. Although, until 1832, the House of Commons was hardly a democratic body, it was elected and could claim to be more representative of the people than either the monarch or the hereditary House of Lords.

The triumph of Dicey's doctrine of parliamentary sovereignty in the 1880s did not mean that a shift of power had taken place from the executive branch to the legislature. British government was not comparable to government in the radical Third Republic of France after 1875, in which the National Assembly exercised its power to dismiss ministries at will. In conservative Britain the term 'parliamentary supremacy' meant in law, the supremacy of the Queen-in-Parliament, that is to say of the executive branch and both houses of the legislature. Through the fusion of the two branches of government, the cabinet retained the power of the Crown. British subjects [*sic*] received notices from the government by the Royal Mail in envelopes headed by 'On Her Majesty's Service'.

As Dicey noted, much of the operation of the British government depended not on law but on conventions. There was the convention of a powerful cabinet acting in secrecy; the assumption that government oscillated between two increasingly disciplined political parties; the acceptance of the supremacy of Parliament; and the belief that a government should resign when it lost the confidence of the house. It was this Westminster form of parliamentary government that the Dominion of Canada inherited in 1867 and the Republic of India in 1947, and which they had to codify into law. And somehow they had to modify it to suit their vast federations.

In Britain, parliamentary government came into being not through a written constitution but by convention—though changes in conventions did in effect, change the British constitution. For a while there might not be a single document called the constitution, yet, there *was* a constitution. It consisted of a combination of statutes, royal prerogatives, conventions and case-laws that had developed over the centuries. While some enactments were more important than others, legally none had a superior position. All acts of parliament could be changed by a majority vote. There was no process of formal constitutional amendment.[18]

Parliament was a very different body from the American Congress, whose members could not at the same time serve in the President's cabinet. Moreover, the term 'parliamentary supremacy' remained ambiguous. Legally it continued to mean 'the King-in-Parliament', the entity (King, Lords and Commons) that formally governed the country. But by the middle of the twentieth century the principle of 'parliamentary supremacy' meant in practice, the supremacy of the House of Commons alone. The Parliament Acts of 1911 and 1949 had stripped the House of Lords of its power. There was now a debate over whether power lay with the House of Commons or the prime minister and cabinet.[19]

By the year 2000, the very notion of parliamentary supremacy appeared to be outmoded, in practice if not in theory. The United Kingdom was now a member of the European Union. Acts of Parliament were subject to judicial review by a European Court that could on occasion override the doctrine of parliamentary supremacy.[20] (In 2004 the British government proposed to replace the law lords of the House of Lords by a Supreme Court.)

In retrospect, then, it would seem that the doctrine of judicial interpretation was one that succeeded tentative attempts at judicial review in the seventeenth century, reaching its zenith around 1900, after Dicey popularized the principle of parliamentary sovereignty. However, by the year 2000 there was in place a new form of judicial review, introduced after the United Kingdom joined the European Union and became subject to European courts.

2. CLASSICAL JUDICIAL REVIEW: THE AMERICAN SUPREME COURT'S DEFUSING OF PARTISAN TENSIONS AFTER THE 1800 ELECTIONS

It is easy to forget on what an uncharted course the Americans set out after independence. The nearest counterpart to the new republic was the English Commonwealth of 1649–60. It was during the Commonwealth that Parliament made its only attempt to have a written constitution, the Instrument of Government. But in those days what remained of Parliament was struggling to find a role in a political system dominated by the army. After the army's leader, Oliver Cromwell, became head of the executive branch of government as Protector, he rejected Parliament's proposal. Like the Stuart monarchs, Cromwell was unable to resolve the tensions between the executive and legislative branches of government, and in 1660, two years after his death, England reverted to the monarchy.[21]

Unlike the English, the Americans had the advantage of a popularly ratified written constitution, an elected legislature, and an army leader (George Washington) who was not only the first President, but was a leader prepared to abide by the constitution. After two terms he stepped down from office in 1797 to be succeeded by another Federalist President, John Adams.[22] By the end of the 1790s there were deep social and political tensions, which increased when the Federalist Party was defeated in the elections of 1800 by the Democratic-Republicans, led by Thomas Jefferson. A group of politicians called the 'High Federalists' refused to accept the fact that they had lost the presidency, the Senate and the House of Representatives.[23]

The unwillingness of these Federalists to admit their defeat was to create a crisis of governance. The situation in the United States was complicated by the fact that there was now a federal judicial system headed by a Supreme Court established by Congress in accordance with the constitution. Unless both the (Federalist) Chief Justice and the (Democratic-Republican) President behaved with circumspection, there was the possibility of the Supreme Court confronting the President and possibly the Congress. Tensions were increased by the decision of the last Federalist President, John Adams, to make a number of 'midnight' appointments of Federalist sympathizers to the judiciary. Among them was William Marbury, whose commission had not been delivered by the time the new administration took office. He appealed to the courts, where the High Federalists were trying to use appointments to the courts to preserve what little power their party retained. Because of the Federalists' hold on power since 1789, when Thomas Jefferson became President, there was not a single judge from his own Democratic-Republican Party on the bench.[24]

In 1801 the new Congress passed a second Judicature Act, but with a slim majority in the Senate. It aroused the ire of the High Federalists, who looked to the courts for redress. Adams had appointed as Chief Justice, John Marshall, his Secretary of State. Marshall and his fellow justices had to find a way to defuse a very ugly situation in which partisan passions were aroused and the future of the constitution itself was in doubt. The flashpoint proved to be the case of *Marbury* v. *Madison.* The issue was whether the Supreme Court could strike down a federal statute that Congress had enacted believing it was consonant with the constitution, but which the Court thought to be in conflict with it. Madison was the new Secretary of State, and he declined to intervene to ensure that Marbury received his commission.[25] There seemed no way out for the Supreme Court. Either (through Madison), it challenged the new president, who would undoubtedly win the contest, or it admitted its incompetence to handle the issue, which would harm the reputation of the court.

Marshall resolved the issue by an astute judgement. He declared that Marbury was entitled to his commission; he stated that under American law he was entitled to redress; and he agreed that a writ of mandamus was the proper instrument. However, he argued, the Supreme Court was not the proper tribunal. The constitution had not given Congress the power to authorize the Supreme Court to use its power of original jurisdiction to compel the Secretary of State to deliver Marbury his commission. He concluded that in the Judicature Act of 1789, Congress had exceeded its authority, for the constitution explicitly limited the matters over which the Supreme Court exercised original jurisdiction. The Court had no original jurisdiction over appointments, to the bench. In sum, Congress's authority to demand action by the Court over judicial appointments, had no constitutional sanction.

The significance of Marshall's judgement was not only that it provided the Supreme Court with the rationale for what became known as the judicial review of the constitution. In delivering his judgement he was also able to show that the court was able to rise above the emotions of party politics. Marshall (who remained Chief Justice until his death in 1835) established a respect for the court, whatever its decisions, that has continued to the present. (This has not prevented appointments to the court from continuing to lead to passionate debates in the Senate.)

Marbury v. *Madison* would probably not have become so important had it not been for the crisis of governance after the 1800 election. And Marshall's judgement would not have been accepted in a system in which Parliament claimed to be supreme. It required a separation of powers in which both branches of government were responsible to the constitution. Its significance lay in the recognition that there was a third branch of government, the judiciary, which was also independent and could act as an umpire in disputes between the executive and legislative branches.

How did Marshall manage to produce such an impressive and momentous decision? One explanation is, that he was fortunate enough in his youth to have studied under one of the most eminent American scholar-statesmen of his day, George Wythe, at the College of William and Mary in Virginia. Each day, Wythe taught constitutional law in the morning and political philosophy in the afternoon. Under Wythe, Marshall therefore studied not only Sir William Blackstone's *Commentaries on the Laws of England* (1765–9) but also *The Spirit of the Laws* (1748) written by Charles Louis de Secondat, known to posterity as Baron de Montesquieu. Montesquieu advocated the separation and balance of powers within government as a means of guaranteeing the freedom of the individual. His exposition of the British constitution as one in which there was such a separation of powers (as against of the absolutism of the Bourbon monarchs), had a profound impact on Captain Marshall, then on leave from the revolutionary army.[26]

As Chief Justice, Marshall provided a solution that had eluded both Hobbes and Cromwell. There were now two ways of resolving the problem of executive-legislative relations. One was the parliamentary form of government, with its fusion of the executive and legislative powers, then evolving in Great Britain. The other was the presidential-congressional government of the United States Constitution with its formal separation of the legislature (Article I), the executive (Article II), and the judiciary (Article III), in which the Supreme Court was the guardian of the constitution.[27]

The two countries had faced very different crises. In Britain executive power, including the prerogative, had traditionally lain with the monarch. After the early seventeenth century, courts had unsuccessfully attempted to limit this power, Parliament tried to make Thomas Hobbes' 'an assembly of men' supreme. But this also failed. Instead, Parliaments in the eighteenth and nineteenth centuries resolved the issue of the royal prerogative differently. They left the form of royal power intact (with the monarch), but transferred the substance of power to a ministry responsible to Parliament. In the nineteenth century, Britain's much vaunted 'cabinet government' retained all the powers of the Crown. The government added to these powers by insisting that Parliament (which it often controlled) was sovereign. The cabinet, under a determined Prime Minister like Winston Churchill in wartime, was a very powerful body indeed.

In the United States, proponents of presidential-congressional government had a very different goal: limited government. They succeeded in separating the three powers of government in the constitution, a document that divided the national legislature into two powerful chambers. The constitution also distributed power between the Federal authorities and the States. Judicial review came to be accepted because it contributed to the goal of limiting government through checks and balances.

3. IMPERIAL JUDICIAL REVIEW: THE JUDICIAL COMMITTEE OF THE PRIVY COUNCIL AND ITS LIMITS ON PARLIAMENTARY SUPREMACY IN THE COLONIES

When the English Parliament abolished the prerogative courts in 1641 it left intact the Privy Council's role as highest court of appeal for the colonies. This was because England was just beginning to embark on colonization, and the parliamentarians were unsure what authority Parliament itself had over the colonies. It therefore left the empire to be handled by the Privy Council. At the time of the Revolution, the American colonists were therefore familiar with having colonial legislation rejected by the Privy Council as *ultra vires.* Despite the loss of the thirteen colonies, the British Empire continued to grow. Following the Napoleonic wars, the Privy Council had to deal not only with English common law but also with European civil law cases from Quebec and Malta. There were also cases from India involving Muslim and Hindu law.

Clearly, in due course the composition of the ancient Privy Council, like that of the unreformed House of Commons would have to be reviewed. And so in 1833, thirty years after *Marbury* v. *Madison,* and one year after the bill reforming the British Parliament, the Council was transformed, with a Judicial Committee created to handle all legal appeals from the colonies to the Privy Council. Parliament provided statutory authority for its composition. This Judicial Committee of the Privy Council (JCPC) became the final court of appeal throughout the empire. It was entitled to declare colonial legislation void if it were to be repugnant to an imperial statute.[28] In other words, it exercised the power of judicial review.

The Judicial Committee was composed of a variety of eminent judges, most of them Law Lords who were members of the House of Lords. Judges familiar with civil, Muslim and Hindu law were added. In due course, Commonwealth judges such as the Chief Justice of Canada were sometimes appointed. In law, the JCPC remained an integral part of the Crown, and part of the executive branch of government. It was an imperial body associated with Whitehall, not Westminster. But by convention its decisions were regarded as final.

As an indication of their formal status as advisers to the Crown, members of the Judicial Committee met in private, as a committee not as a court, and did not wear robes. As an advisory body to the Sovereign, the Judicial Committee published no dissenting opinions (until 1966). Its report on each case was published as an Order-in-Council. The Judicial Committee played a different role from the American Supreme Court. Legally, it still depended in part on the royal prerogative. By contrast, the US Supreme Court was governed by a written constitution emanating from the sovereign people.

The Judicial Committee served as the final court of appeal for Canada and India until well into the twentieth century. Its function was not judicial review in the American sense, but a careful interpretation of dominion and colonial legislation in conformity with the doctrine of parliamentary supremacy—that is to say, the supremacy of the Imperial Parliament. The documents that were considered constitutional by the Dominions, such as the British North America Act (BNA Act) of 1867 (known since 1982 as the Constitution Act, 1867) were in fact 'imperial statutes' of the British Parliament. This meant that the British Parliament treated them as ordinary statutes, thus maintaining the doctrine of parliamentary supremacy.[29] It also meant that the amendment of the Canadian 'constitution' required no special treatment.

As a result of imperial judicial review, ultimate authority over the colonies and dominions remained with London. But it was only one of the ties that bound the British Empire to the mother country. From the colonial perspective, Britain exercised control through three distinct branches of government. First there was the Executive (the Crown), which exercised control through Viceroys, Governors-General and Provincial Governors. Second there was the legislature, Parliament at Westminster, which exercised its authority through the enactment of such important statutes as the BNA Act of 1867 and the Government of India Act of 1935. While the British treated these statutes as part of their ordinary legislation, for the Canadians and Indians, they were important constitutional documents.

Consequently, imperial authority rested not only with the Judicial Committee but also with the Crown and Parliament. Although, as we have seen, the JCPC was formally a part of the executive branch, in practice it was the Empire's Supreme Court, exercising the power of imperial judicial review over such documents as the BNA Act. In other words, although by 1900, tentative judicial review had long given way to judicial interpretation in England, throughout the empire (including Ireland) the imperial judicial review still played an important role.

For Canada the role of the JCPC proved significant primarily because it became involved in dominion-provincial relations, thereby in preserving Canada's federal structure. In particular it ensured that the provinces (especially Quebec) retained their autonomy. The JCPC was therefore an important element in Canada's evolution as a federation. By contrast, *Marbury* v. *Madison* had nothing to do with federalism. The significance of the American decision lay in making it clear once and for all that the tradition of legislative (or parliamentary) supremacy had no place in the American constitution, that the constitution was supreme, and that the Supreme Court was its guardian.

In India and Canadá, where the doctrine of parliamentary supremacy has been modified but not rejected, there have been no cases equivalent to *Marbury* v. *Madison.* To understand the changes in the form that judicial review has taken in Canada and India, then, it is not enough to consider it either in the context of the Westminster form of parliamentary government or of the American alternative of judicial review. Another influence was the form of judicial review practised by the JCPC. In both Canada and India, the Supreme Court took over from the JCPC the role of final court of appeal.[30]

Neither court thought of itself, initially, as playing the role of the American Supreme Court. It was only when, in the course of time, the courts became involved in constitutional crises, that they too embarked on a form of judicial review. This took different forms in India and Canada. In India, the Supreme Court became involved in a struggle with the Government, as in seventeenth century England. In Canada there was less conflict. Instead, the Supreme Court was asked by the Government and Parliament to help resolve a number of constitutional issues.

The emergence of these two unique forms of judicial review has to be understood in the context of their own experience of constitutional crises. It is to these crises that we now turn.

4. PARLIAMENTARY JUDICIAL REVIEW IN CANADA: ITS RECONCILIATION WITH LEGISLATIVE SUPREMACY

The Supreme Court became Canada's highest court of appeal when the British Parliament passed a new BNA Act in 1949. In the years that followed, the court continued to pay respect to the tradition of parliamentary supremacy. No federal law was struck down between 1950 and 1972.[31] However, for the people of Quebec, they were exchanging an impartial external umpire in London for a largely English-Canadian Supreme Court and Parliament, something which often went unnoticed by English-speaking observers, who welcomed a strong national government.[32]

Preparation for the passage of the Constitution Act of 1982, together with a number of constitutional crises, impelled Parliament to ask the Supreme Court to undertake a judicial review. Resentful of its role in Canada in the 1970s, the Parti Quebecois Government of Quebec had proposed the separation of the province from Canada and the formation of a Quebec nation state. Referenda on secession were held in Quebec in 1980 and 1995.

Three of the crises that involved the Supreme Court are worth noting. The first occurred over the federal government's proposal for a new amendment procedure to the Canadian constitution. Because the BNA Act of 1867 was in law an Act of the British parliament, it had contained no amendment provision, and in principle, could be amended whenever the British parliament chose to do so. After the Statute of Westminster of 1931 recognized the virtual independence of the dominions, the responsibility for deciding on an appropriate amendment procedure lay with the Canadians. But the provinces could never agree with the federal government on the proper procedure.

In 1981, an exasperated Prime Minister, Pierre Trudeau, persuaded the Canadian Parliament to go it alone and to ask the British to agree to what was termed 'the patriation of the constitution'. However, there was such an outcry from the provinces, and then such concern in Britain, that he relented and agreed to ask the Supreme Court for an opinion as to whether the provinces needed to be involved. Such a 'reference' was something the American court was not permitted to do, and was one of many indications of the different role that the Supreme Court played in Canada. The reference invited the Court to move beyond its traditional practice of judicial interpretation and concern itself with judicial review. In its judgement the Court agreed that legally Parliament could act alone in approaching the British Parliament. But it added that by convention, on an issue affecting all the provinces the federal government should consult them before doing so. The Court declared that a 'substantial number' of provinces should agree to patriation.

The Supreme Court did not specify the number required. It was willing in this crisis to enter the murky waters of parliamentary conventions, but it wisely decided to let the politicians decide how many provinces should agree to an amendment. In the end it was a decision with which all the provinces except Quebec agreed. Trudeau's government gave way and permitted a debate over the patriation of the constitution, to take place at conferences of First Ministers.

Trudeau's fears of the consequences of consulting the provinces proved well founded. The price he paid was the insertion of an 'override' clause (sometimes called the 'notwithstanding' clause) in the Constitution Act of 1982. This clause (Section 33) permitted both Parliament and the provincial legislatures to override provisions of the Charter of Rights in the Act for up to five years.[33] The Quebec National Assembly took advantage of the provision to reject Court decisions that it felt unduly protected linguistic minorities, and hindered the policy of making Quebec, francophone. Other provinces also used the clause, sometimes without the publicity that accompanied its use by Quebec.[34]

Adoption of the 'override' clause indicated that the Supreme Court's power of judicial review was to be nothing like as sweeping as in the United States. *Marbury* v. *Madison* had put an end to the possibility of legislative supremacy in the United States. By contrast, the immediate effect of the override clause in Canada was to sustain the doctrine of parliamentary supremacy at both the federal and provincial levels. In the long run, however, the override clause proved relatively benign. It enabled Quebec to pursue its promotion of the French language, but in due course, all children who graduated from Quebec schools were able to speak French, so that the provision was no longer necessary.

Debate over the 1982 Constitution Act had followed an unsuccessful referendum on secession in Quebec. Passage of the Act did not, however, satisfy those in Quebec who wished to secede from what they called 'the Rest of Canada' (or ROC). In 1995, another Parti Quebecois government of Quebec ordered a second referendum. This nearly succeeded. However, the question put to the voters was ambiguous, suggesting to some respondents that a 'yes' vote might result in more autonomy for the province, but would not necessarily lead to outright separation.

Moreover, the margin of victory was very slim (50.6 per cent against secession and 49.4 per cent in favour). The Government of Canada decided that secession was too important an issue to leave in the hands of a separatist, and possibly manipulative, Quebec government, that asked ambiguous questions and that would take the slimmest of majorities as authorizing secession. Fearful of the result of a third referendum, the Government of Canada asked the Supreme Court to rule on several issues. One was the nature of the question posed and another was on the sort of majority needed for separation to be allowed by the rest of Canada. Here the Court was given another opportunity to exercise judicial review.

Not surprisingly, in the *Quebec Secession Reference* case (1998), the court ruled unanimously that any question on secession should be 'clear'. Subsequently Parliament passed a Clarity Act in 2000 to prevent ambiguous referendum questions. The Court also declared that the vote on secession should provide a clear majority, though this too was not specified.[35] In the years since this ruling, the demand for outright secession has diminished, though of course if an English-speaking Prime Minister from outside Quebec were to win a federal election the mood might change again.[36]

While a foreign observer might think that a ruling demanding a qualified majority in support of secession was only fair, this did not reflect the views of staunch Quebec nationalists. They regarded the 80 per cent of the people of Quebec who were of French extraction as having a special role in provincial affairs. The views of the 20 per cent who were Anglophone or 'allophone' were less important. Those Quebec residents who were not of French extraction tended to look more kindly on Canada and to oppose separation. This meant that for the nationalists to win even a 51 per cent vote for separation over 63 per cent of the francophone vote had to be in favour.

Much has happened in Quebec since the Quiet Revolution of the 1960s led to the creation of the Parti Quebecois in 1968, and the first PQ government in 1976. The population is now nearly 80 per cent urban. By 1996 the number of declared francophones had declined to 56 per cent. There were now only 5 per cent who were anglophone. No fewer than 38 per cent declared themselves bilingual.[37]

Even so, a number of problems remain. While the Court's ruling established the principle of judicial review, it also made it legitimate for Quebec to propose secession. Moreover, the ruling required the Government of Canada to negotiate with Quebec should a qualified majority be in favour of separation.[38]

Nor must it be forgotten that the 1982 Constitution Act remains one of a series of documents to which Quebec has never formally consented. Quebec was opposed to the reference of the 1995 referendum issue to the Supreme Court.[39] The province's commitment to Canada therefore has remained in doubt. At the very least, as one wag has put it, whereas the other nine provinces can be described as treating the Government of Canada as a mother, for the *Quebecois* it remains a mother-in-law. This is hardly surprising. The English-Canadian preference for monarchy over a republic, for conventions over law, and for a general fuzziness on issues that are disputed, are all indications that English-speaking Canada has a different political culture. Canadians celebrate Canada Day on 1 July. But Quebec has its own national day of celebration, Saint-Jean Baptiste Day, on 24 June. Federal buildings in Quebec fly Canada's maple leaf flag, but other buildings fly the traditional French *fleur-de-lys*. Yet, awkward though the relationship between Ottawa and Quebec City may be at times, the frictions are far less than they were forty years back. It seems a long time since the chairman of the Canadian National Railways, a public corporation based in Montreal, explained why none of his seventeen directors was a francophone: there was, he insisted, no French Canadian who was qualified!

In sum, the Supreme Court has contributed to a lowering of the temperature by exercising judicial review on a number of constitutional issues, notably on amendments, parliamentary supremacy and the conduct of referenda. It has been required in times of crisis to offer advice to the Government of Canada through references, and has been willing on occasion to offer opinions that have not been confined to points of law. But judicial review in Canada remains more limited than in the United States. The Supreme Court must take into account the tradition of parliamentary supremacy, the important role played by conventions, and the override provision of the 1982 Constitution Act.[40]

5. PARLIAMENTARY JUDICIAL REVIEW IN INDIA: THE CHALLENGE TO PARLIAMENTARY SUPREMACY

In India, as in Canada, there has been a shift from judicial interpretation to judicial review. Indeed, the practice of declaring acts of Parliament *ultra vires* was a power exercised by the Supreme Court almost from the beginning. However, in the early days, if the Court opposed legislation, Parliament simply amended the constitution under Article 368 or placed the law in a special schedule (the Ninth) where it was not justiciable. In India, as in other federations, it was taken for granted that the legislative branch had the last word. As we shall see below, the Supreme Court challenged this assumption in 1967 in the *Golak Nath* case. On this occasion the Court drew a line: the Government and Parliament could not tamper with fundamental rights. From now onwards there was confrontation. The struggle was not between the federal and regional (state or provincial) governments as in Canada, but between the Indian Parliament and the Supreme Court over which was supreme. The judges now claimed a 'discharge of a duty plainly laid upon them by the Constitution'.[41] In some ways the Court's role was similar to that of Coke's Court of Common Pleas in seventeenth century England: opposition to arbitrary power.

Even then, the Court was unwilling to challenge the government on one very important issue: the government's use of emergency powers to dismiss state governments. 'To begin with, Indian courts were reluctant to submit any proclamations under Article 356 to judicial review.'[42] It was not until 1977 that the Court took its first tentative step towards judicial review of emergency powers in the case of the *State of Rajasthan* v. *Union of India.* It then examined a presidential order under Article 356, the Article used to proclaim President's Rule in a state. But the Court still hesitated to challenge the government's use of its powers. It stated that there was no need for the President to give reasons for introducing President's Rule. The Court merely wanted the President to satisfy himself that the order was justified.

The second and major step taken was in the *Bommai* case of 1994. On this occasion, the Court unanimously agreed that when conditions in a state were proclaimed to require emergency powers it could approach the Court and ask for judicial review of the Proclamation. The Court declared that this could be undertaken even if Parliament had approved of the Proclamation. Now the Court was insisting on disclosure of the full facts on which the Proclamation was based. For, it now asserted, federalism was part of the basic structure and the states were sovereign within their own sphere.

On a number of other issues in the Bommai case, including the decision that the union government had the power to remove a state government because it was not upholding the principles of secularism, the court was split 5–4. On this issue the court indicated that it had not moved away completely from its previous deference to the Government and the Parliament of India. But as one commentator noted, it was unlikely that the court would retreat from the defence of secularism taken by the majority.[43] Ajit Mozoomdar went on to conclude that the decision of the court provided a safeguard against the misuse of Article 356 by the Union government. He did not foresee the violence in Gujarat in 2002 when neither the union nor the state governments (both in the hands of the BJP) appeared to be committed to upholding the secular state.[44]

What caused the early confrontation of Parliament by the Supreme Court, confrontation that caused Parliament to pass constitutional amendments that in effect overrode the court's rulings?[45] The main disagreement was between socialism and conservatism. In the 1950s the Congress party, and especially Jawaharlal Nehru's government, wanted to bring about land reform. The Supreme Court stood in the way, upholding the rights of property owners under Part III of the Constitution: Fundamental Rights. Just as there had been ideological differences in the fledgling United States between the Adams Federalists and Jeffersonian Republicans, also over land, so in India there was popular feeling against large landowners. In each instance the courts proved conservative in their handling of private property.

Matters did not reach a crisis point in India until after the deaths of both Jawahailal Nehru and his successor, Lal Bahadur Shastri. With the appointment of the inexperienced Indira Gandhi as Prime Minister in 1966, conservatives feared that Fundamental Rights, particularly the right to property, would come under attack. To protect the Constitution, the Supreme Court ruled in *Golak Nath*, that the fundamental rights in the Constitution could not be abridged or abrogated by Parliament—even through constitutional amendment.

This dispute raised a number of important issues. For conservatives and some liberals, the constitution had to be defended at all costs against subversion by radicals (often communists), who did not appreciate the importance of the rule of law. One of the problems, as they saw it, was the ease with which the Constitution could be amended.

They argued that while it was one thing to amend the document to keep up with the times, it was another thing to use that power to in effect destroy the protections of the constitution. In the opposing camp were communists, socialists and some liberals, for whom defence of the constitution was a ploy to thwart necessary social change. They believed that reactionary forces, whose deep pockets enabled them to challenge legislation in the courts, should not be allowed to use the courts to overturn the will of Parliament.

After 1967 Mrs. Gandhi responded to popular pressure by passing constitutional amendments that challenged private property and the practice of judicial review. She persuaded Parliament to nationalize the banks and abolish the pensions (called 'privy purses') of the former princes, and after further amendments to the constitution, she was re-elected to power in 1971. In another important case, *Keshavananda* in 1973, the Supreme Court overruled *Golak Nath* and agreed that her Twenty-fourth Amendment was constitutional. At the same time it insisted that no change to 'the basic structure' of the constitution was permissible.[46]

Nevertheless, in 1976, Mrs. Gandhi's government did indeed transform 'the basic structure' of the constitution by a wholesale reform euphemistically called the Forty-second Amendment. One clause in this amendment overrode judicial review and reaffirmed the supremacy of Parliament. Following her defeat in the 1977 elections, the period 1977–9 saw the repeal of much of her government's Forty-second Amendment by the Janata government's Forty-fourth Amendment. The Supreme Court then ruled once again (in *Minerva Mills*, 1980), that Parliament could not change the basic structure. This decision was not challenged, and suggested that on this issue the Supreme Court has had the last word. (However, if a government came into power dependent on the support of organizations that rejected the Constitution per se, there could be another battle royal.)[47]

There were many different forces at work throughout this period. There were able, dedicated (and often conservative) constitutional lawyers who wanted to promote the principles of judicial review as one of the checks and balances that had served the US so well. There were devoted (and sometimes liberal) parliamentarians who believed that parliamentary supremacy was necessary if economic and social reforms (and the democratic process) were to prevail. And there were socialists who admired the achievements of the USSR and China, and felt that India was falling behind.[48] In the end, India chose the middle way, accepting parliamentary supremacy as a general principle and adopting judicial review to preserve the principles of the constitution. When the fiftieth anniversary of the constitution was being celebrated in 2000, the Government of India set up a National Commission to Review the Working of the Constitution. Its terms of reference accepted parliamentary supremacy, but also specified that there should be no change to the constitution's basic structure.

The period between the Emergency and the year 2000, saw yet another development. A divided Parliament often seemed incapable of responding to public needs, for example in helping the poor, in curbing pollution and protecting the environment. Now an activist court became the champion of reformers and the disadvantaged. It responded to what is called Public Interest Litigation. In other words, the Supreme Court and Parliament exchanged the roles before 1977. Now it was the Supreme Court that favoured reforms, and Parliament that was reluctant to respond to popular pressures.[49]

More recently in India, there has been concern over the activity of Muslim extremists on the one hand and Hindu nationalists on the other. This has affected centre–state relations and raised questions regarding the proper role of the Supreme Court. In particular there has been the fear that a state government might be unable (and even unwilling) to defend law and order (as happened in 1992 in Uttar Pradesh when Hindu activists tore down a mosque).[50] In addition there has been concern that the Government of India might not use its powers to introduce President's Rule to dismiss an elected state government. For in the *Bommai* case the Court had carefully restricted the grounds on which the centre could interfere in state affairs.

Events in Gujarat in 2002 suggested that *Bommai* might have to be reconsidered. In 1994 the Court had not considered the possibility of an outbreak of violence following which the national government was unwilling to confront a state government in the hands of the same party. To seek redress, some of the victims turned to the courts. In 2004, cases dealing with the 2002 Gujarat riots were still pending.

CONCLUSION

In each of the five instances, judicial review emerged out of a crisis or crises of governance. In seventeenth century England, there was fear that the Stuart dynasty would extend the royal prerogative too far. It was an age when monarchs had their own prerogative courts and governed for much of the time without summoning Parliament. The common law courts were not able to prevent James I or Charles I from governing as they chose. Tentative judicial review, which saw the judiciary confronting the executive, therefore, enjoyed only a brief popularity before successive monarchs dismissed Chief Justices Coke and Crew. The task of confronting the king fell to Parliament, and to a civil war, which the king lost. With the emergence of parliamentary government over the next two centuries, power passed from both the executive and judiciary to Parliament. The courts accepted a limited role, later called judicial interpretation. Acts of Parliament could not be declared *ultra vires.*

But this too represented only a stage in the constitutional development of Great Britain, a stage particularly associated with A.V. Dicey's late-nineteenth century doctrine of parliamentary supremacy. By the 1930s, British constitutional lawyers were rejecting much of what Dicey had asserted fifty years earlier.[51] At the end of the twentieth century, the European Courts were exercising a judicial review of acts of the British Parliament, which in practice was no longer sovereign.

The second and most important example, the classical judicial review of the United States, was the brainchild of Chief Justice Marshall. He established the principle that the judiciary, not the legislature or the executive, was the guardian of the Constitution. Commentators have drawn attention to the importance of *Marbury* v. *Madison* not only for the United States, but also for Supreme Courts elsewhere. Yet the case became important mainly because of a crisis of governance. It is easy to forget how turbulent were American politics in the years leading up to the 1803 decision and how concerned were the Chief Justice and the President that matters should not get out of hand. Though modern political parties had yet to emerge, partisan passions ran high and there were fears that the constitution itself was in danger.[52] The Supreme Court handled itself admirably. Charles Warren commented on *Stuart* v. *Laird,* the case that followed *Marbury* v. *Madison*: 'No more striking example of the non-partisanship of the American judiciary can be found than this decision by a Court composed wholly of Federalists, upholding, contrary to personal and political views, a detested Republican measure.'[53]

The third type of judicial review, exercised by the imperial Judicial Committee of the Privy Council (JCPC), developed as a result of a somewhat different crisis. This was the inability of the ancient Privy

Council (with a majority of laymen), to handle appeals from an expanding empire in which some knowledge of civil, Muslim and Hindu law (by at least one privy councillor), became necessary. Unlike the other courts, the JCPC was not part of the judicial branch of government. In law, as its name indicated, it was a prerogative court and a part of the executive (i.e. the Crown).

Even so, the imperial government treated it as a court, beyond which there was no appeal. The Judicial Committee became important because it set legal standards for the whole of the British Empire. In addition, it introduced countries like Canada and India to the idea of judicial review. Even so, when their Supreme Courts became independent it was some time before they too, fully exercised this power, perhaps because the JCPC itself accepted the doctrine of parliamentary supremacy—the supremacy of the British Parliament. In initially accepting the supremacy of their own parliaments, the courts in India and Canada demonstrated that they were willing to change course, only if they felt impelled to do so by constitutional crises.

Canada offers a fourth type of judicial review, one that involves gradual change and may be classified as an evolutionary hybrid. From being primarily concerned with Federal-Provincial relations, it has evolved into a court concerned with citizens' rights. For a while after 1949, the Supreme Court was careful not to encroach on the doctrine of parliamentary supremacy, in this case the supremacy of the Canadian Parliament. A crisis of governance led to a change in the court's behavior. After the Quebec government proposed secession in 1980, and Parliament with nine of the ten provinces, agreed on an amendment formula and a Charter of Rights, it became clear that the Supreme Court was expected to exercise judicial review. The court then showed little hesitation in going beyond the law proper and exploring the role that convention played in Canada's affairs. Canada avoided India's conflict between the Supreme Court and Parliament over the issue of parliamentary supremacy, by inserting the override clause in the 1982 Constitution Act. The result was a hybrid system in which Parliament and provincial legislatures could on occasion override the constitution. This provided a means for avoiding confrontation between two schools of thought: English-Canadian stress on individual rights, and the Quebec government's defiant defence of the collective rights of the province's francophones.

Inevitably, some fundamental differences remain between Quebec and the rest of Canada. To the Quebec government, the Federal government looms large and has to be constantly watched lest it should encroach on the province's powers. To the rest of Canada, it is the United States that looms large, making a strong national government that includes both Parliament and the Supreme Court necessary to protect Canada's interests. So long as there is a lack of consensus on the constitution, it is difficult to pronounce judgement on the success of the Court.[54]

The fifth type of judicial review is the Indian. For various reasons, the Supreme Court has been less hesitant from the start to declare acts of parliament *ultra vires.* Over the years, judicial review has taken various forms. When it was first adopted, soon after the constitution was enacted, Parliament was able to exclude legislation from judicial review by amending the constitution. It was therefore able to override the Court's defence of property rights, at a time when the Government wanted land reform. During the Nehru years of the 1950s and early 1960s, parliamentary supremacy was successfully defended on the grounds that it alone would ensure the modernization of the country's economy and society.

In 1967, after Mrs. Gandhi came to power, the case of *Golak Nath* took judicial review a step further. Some of the justices began to see themselves as protecting the constitution against what they considered to be arbitrary executive power. Their concerns were reminiscent of the judges in early seventeenth century England. But whereas the English courts failed to prevent the monarch from exercising the prerogative, the Supreme Court of India appears to have proved successful, in Keshavananda (1973) and *Minerva Mills* (1980), in convincing both the public and Parliament that it was defending the basic structure of the constitution.[55]

Even so, after 1967, the Indian Supreme Court long remained reluctant to review actions of the government, especially in emergencies. It was only after Hindu-Muslim tensions led to the destruction of the mosque at Ayodhya in 1992 that the court decided to intervene on the issue of President's Rule, in the *Bommai* case of 1994. This case was notable for upholding the autonomy of the states, long threatened by the Centre's misuse of judicial review. In the decade since then, both the Centre and the States have respected that judgement: Delhi no longer misuses Article 356 by interventions that are unwarranted. However, as we have noted, the *Bommai* case can be used by the national government to defend an unjustified policy of non-interference only when human rights issues are at stake.

Although Canada and India may be said to have gradually shifted from judicial interpretation to judicial review of the Constitution, they may have paid a considerable price in doing so. Because of Canada's new amendment procedure requiring federal-provincial unanimity, it will be difficult for Canadians to alter the basic structure of their constitution. This means that Canada may be destined to retain the British monarch as Head of State. India too may have difficulty in altering the basic structure of its Constitution, even if federalism proves incompatible with certain features of the Westminster parliamentary tradition.

In all four countries, the greatest battles have been fought over the Constitution. On the one hand there have been those who have seen themselves as partisans of needed reforms. To liberal reformers, the Supreme Court has sometimes been criticized as an unelected and conservative body. To their opponents, the reformers have seemed to be radicals willing to subvert the Constitution to achieve their ends.

Conservatives have thought they were defending the Constitution and the political system. Their opponents have been convinced that the conservatives are committed at best to the status quo, and at worst to preserving their own privileges.

Fortunately, in all four countries, the courts, though often conservative, have in the end managed to move with the times, responding to changes in public opinion. In all of them the courts have the respect of the people. In none is judicial review widely considered to be opposed to the principles of liberal democracy. There has been a balance between the various branches of government, a balance which shifts from time to time, but which has left the various branches largely intact.

An issue that has emerged in both Canada and India in recent years, and has yet to be resolved, is the position of a permanent minority. In Canada, Quebec has not signed on to the 1982 Constitution, and no one seems to know how to persuade the province to do so. In India, the role of the Muslims in a changing society is unclear. What seems certain is that the courts and judicial review will continue to play an important role in resolving these and other social conflicts.

NOTES

1. Tim Koopmans, *Courts and Political Institutions,* Cambridge, UK: Cambridge University Press, 2003, p. 12.
2. In Canada instead of a comparison between judicial interpretation and judicial review, a distinction is drawn between ordinary judicial review and constitutional judicial review. See Patrick Monahan, *Constitutional Law,* Toronto: Irwin Law, 2nd edn., 2002, p. 23.
3. Since judicial interpretation, and early attempts to apply judicial review, originated in England before the union with Scotland in 1707, it is more precise to refer to 'England'.
4. The five types have been selected because of their relevance for India. There are other examples, notably in the civil law of countries in Europe, where there are constitutional courts. See Vernon Bogdanor (ed.), 'Judicial review', *The Blackwell Encyclopaedia of Political Institutions,* Oxford: Blackwell, 1987, pp. 305–6.
5. S.E. Thorne, 'Dr. Bonham's Case', in his *Essays in English Legal History,* London: The Hambledon Press, 1985, p. 269. However, Thorne went on to argue that Coke's famous remark on the superiority of the common law over statutes has been taken out of context, and 'proves to be not a *dictum*', p. 274. He concluded: '. . . Coke's ambitious political theory is found to be not his, but the work of a later generation of judges, commentators, and lawyers', p. 278.
6. 'The Supreme Court of the United States was a court of law, not a constitutional court. It was established to hear law cases, not to expound the Constitution. Its jurisdiction was expressly limited, and its appellate role was determined by statute. Congress and the President enjoyed far more extensive constitutional authority. . . . *'The authority of the legislature derived from the concept of legislative supremacy, which the Continental Congress had inherited from the British Parliament*' (my italics). Jean Smith, *John Marshall,* p. 283.
7. Koopmans, p. 26, n. 25.
8. H.M. Seervai, *Constitutional Law of India,* Bombay: Tripathi, 1991, vol. I, p. 264.
9. In Canada it has been suggested that the *Drybones* case of 1970 was something of an aberration and that the transition to judicial review came dramatically after the 1982 Constitution Act. Monahan, *Constitutional Law,* p. 16.
10. 'English judges do not claim or exercise any power to repeal a Statute, while Acts of Parliament may override and constantly do override the law of the judges. Judicial legislation is, in short, subordinate legislation, carried on with the assent and subject to the supervision of Parliament.' A.V. Dicey, *Introduction to the Study of the Law of the Constitution,* with an introduction by E.C.S. Wade, London: Macmillan, 9th edn., 1945, pp. 60–1.

11. *Case of Proclamations* (1610). Quoted by Peter W. Hogg, *Constitutional Law of Canada*, Toronto: Carswell, 2nd edn., 1985, p. 10.
12. Chief Justice Coke is reported to have said: 'Magna Carta is such a fellow that he will have no sovereign.' Christopher Hill, *The Century of Revolution 1603–1714*, Edinburgh: Nelson, 1961, p. 63.
13. 'The historical origin of due process may be traced to chapter 39 of Magna Carta (1215). . . .', A.W. Bradley, 'due process of law', in Vernon Bogdanor, *The Blackwell Encyclopaedia of Political Institutions*, p. 182. In the 1970s, J.P. Narayan attacked authoritarian government in India by referring to Magna Carta.
14. 'King James defined his prerogative as absolute. He believed that all institutions of government and law existed solely by his grace.' Louis A. Knafla, *Law and Politics in Jacobean England*, Cambridge, UK: Cambridge University Press, 1977, p. 65.
15. Several American scholars have claimed that Coke anticipated American ideas of judicial review. See Raoul Berger, 'Doctor Bonham's Case: Statutory Interpretation or Constitutional Theory?' *University of Pennsylvania Law Review*, 117 (1969), pp. 521–45; and Charles M. Gray, 'Bonham's Case Revisited', *Proceedings of the American Philosophical Society*, 116 (1972), pp. 35–58.
16. Cromwell himself had served as a Member of Parliament from 1628 until the civil war.
17. Hill, *Century of Revolution*, p. 137.
18. This was something that later bedevilled the Canadians, who discovered that they had a written constitution.
19. The Introduction by R.H.S. Crossman to a new edition of Walter Bagehot's, *The English Constitution*, 1st pub. in 1867, London: Watts, 1964.
20. After quoting A.V. Dicey on parliamentary supremacy, Patrick Monahan noted 'that with the enactment of the, *Human Rights Act, 1998*, Britain has taken an important step in the American direction, by granting courts the power to declare statutes to be "incompatible" with guarantees in the European Convention on Human Rights. *Constitutional Law*, p. 20, fn. 31.
21. For two years, England was governed by his son, Richard, who then retired.
22. He was also childless.
23. It took over thirty ballots before Jefferson was declared to have been elected as President.
24. Jean Smith, *John Marshall*, 303.
25. The Federalist administration, which included John Marshall, had failed to deliver the commission before it left office.
26. Marshall's father had been a charter subscriber to the first American edition of Blackstone, published in 1772.
27. Curiously enough, many intellectuals failed to appreciate the significance of these developments, preferring to admire the French Revolution of

1789. Yet it was to take France nearly a century before it overcame its revolutionary heritage by settling on parliamentary government in 1875. It was to take nearly another century before it produced its own interesting (and successful) hybrid of presidential-parliamentary government under Charles DeGaulle in 1959.

28. According to the Colonial Laws Validity Act of 1865.
29. The three paragraphs above draw on Douglas V. Verney, 'The "Reconciliation" of Parliamentary Supremacy and Federalism in Canada', *The Journal of Commonwealth and Comparative Politics,* XXI, 1, 1983, especially p. 36.
30. 'Before India adopted the Constitution, the highest judicial body in the land was the Federal Court, although prior to independence appeals could be made from this Court to the Privy Council in London. After January 1950 the Federal Court became the Supreme Court.' Granville Austin, *The Indian Constitution: Cornerstone of a Nation,* Bombay: Oxford University Press, 1966, p. xvi.
31. It has also been argued that until the 1980s, Canadian judges were less well educated in matters of constitutional law. See Ian Greene, 'The Charter, Democracy and National Unity', mimeo, p. 4, to be published in a volume edited by Ray Bazowski.
32. 'Generally, the notion of a strong central government was emasculated by interpretations of the Judicial Committee of the Privy Council in the 1920s and 1930s. However, stronger federal legislative authority has been restored by the Supreme Court of Canada since it became the final court of appeal for all criminal and civil matters in 1949.' Gerald L. Gall, *The Canadian Legal System,* Toronto: Carswell, 3rd edition 1990, p. 103.
33. Section 33 (1) stated: 'Parliament or the legislature of a province may expressly declare in an Act of Parliament or of the legislature, as the case may be, that the Act or a provision thereof shall operate notwithstanding a provision included in Section 2 or Sections 7 to 15 of this Charter.' (Section 2 dealt with fundamental freedoms, sections 7–14 with legal rights, and section 15 with equality rights.)
34. The override clause was used at least sixteen times in the first twenty years.
35. *Reference Re Secession of Quebec,* [1998] 2 S.C.R. 217.
36. For 77 of the first 101 years, from 1867 to 1968, Canadian Prime Ministers were English Canadian. The exceptions were Wilfrid Laurier (1896–1911) and Louis St. Laurent (1948–57). In the 36 years since the appointment of Pierre Trudeau in 1968, the Prime Ministers, apart from three minor exceptions who governed for a few months each (in 1979, 1984 and 1993), have all been from Quebec.
37. *The 1999 Canadian Global Almanac,* Toronto: Macmillan, 1998, p. 28.
38. Patrick Monahan, *Constitutional Law,* Toronto: Irwin Law, 2002, 2nd edn., pp. 486–7.
39. The Quebec members of the Supreme Court voted with their colleagues in the ruling on the 1995 Quebec secession referendum. Separatists could

argue that these justices were appointed by the Government of Canada and were inevitably biased against their point of view on constitutional issues.

40. For some authorities the doctrine of parliamentary supremacy has been challenged by the notion of the separation of powers. In 1996, Chief Justice Lamer stated: 'One of the defining features of the Canadian Constitution, in my opinion, is the separation of powers.' Quoted in Michael Bryant and Lorne Sossin, *Public Law*, Toronto: Carswell, 2002, p. 101.
41. Austin, *Working a Democratic Constitution*, p. 39.
42. Ian Greene, 'The Judicial Dimension of Federalism in India and Canada: A Comparative Analysis', in Rekha Saxena (ed.), *Mapping Canadian Federalism for India*, New Delhi: Konark, 2002, p. 263.
43. Ajit Mozoomdar, 'The Supreme Court and President's Rule: A Comment', in Balveer Arora and Douglas V. Verney (eds.), *Multiple Identities in a Single State: Indian Federalism in Comparative Perspective*, New Delhi: Konark, 1995, p. 168.
44. Some years after Mozoomdar, Ian Greene also concluded optimistically: 'the *Bommai* decision is a major contribution . . . to furthering the principles of democracy in India . . .', in Saxena (ed.), *Mapping Canadian Federalism*, p. 266.
45. In the first thirty years or so after 1950, the Supreme Court held over 100 Centre and State Acts to be invalid, mostly through unanimous decisions.
46. See Granville Austin, *Working a Democratic Constitution: The Indian Experience*, New Delhi: Oxford University Press, 1999, Part II: The Great Constitutional Confrontation: Judicial Review *versus* Parliamentary Supremacy, pp. 167–73.
47. In the 1990s, the Vishva Hindu Parishad floated the idea of a body of holy men, a *dharma sansad*, superior to Parliament. Manjari Katju, *Vishva Hindu Parishad*, New Delhi: Orient Longman, 2003, pp. 71ff.
48. See Douglas V. Verney, 'Understanding India as a Federation: Conservative Tradition, Liberal Principles, Conservative Tradition and Socialist Ideology', in B.D. Dua and M.P. Singh, eds., *Indian Federalism in the New Millennium*, New Delhi: Manohar, 2003, pp. 27–47.
49. Some observers have attributed the Court's tendency towards judicial activism after 1977 to guilt over its failure to oppose the Emergency of 1975–7.
50. See the articles in the, *Journal of the National Human Rights Commission*, vol. 1, 2002.
51. E.C.S. Wade, in his Introduction to Dicey's *Law of the Constitution*, p. xliv.
52. Together with *Stuart* v. *Laird*, *Marbury* v. *Madison* 'threatened to produce a constitutional crisis, which Marshall recognized the Court could not win. Even more seriously, each threatened to end the nonpartisan stance the justices had adopted and, with it, the Supreme Court's legitimacy as the nation's highest tribunal.' Smith, *John Marshall*, p. 315.

53. Quoted by Jean Smith, *John Marshall*, p. 324n.
54. 'It is unclear whether Canadians are capable of agreeing on a single organizing vision of what the country is about or what it should aspire to become', Patrick Monahan, *Constitutional Law*, pp. 482–3.
55. In the cases of *Keshavananda* (1973) and *Minerva Mills* (1980).

2

Governance by Judiciary: Into the Next Millenium

RAJEEV DHAVAN

In the inevitable chemistry of social change,
judges are certainly not anti-catalysts!

JUSTICE KRISHNA IYER (1969)[1]

Written in 1969, Justice Krishna Iyer's remonstrance that judges were certainly not anti-catalysts in the path of India's progress, captured both the politics of the present and prophesied a promise for the future. As an institution of government, India's judiciary was born in 1950, by and through the new Constitution. Its creation was a distinct break from the past. The 'imperial' judiciary of the British had served its masters well. It had brought a sprawling empire under the suzerainty of an occidental 'rule of law', empowered it to support the 'law and order' needs of the Raj, subordinated the personal and customary laws of diverse peoples into a governable coherence, and left behind an aura of law, justice and courts for the natives to whom governance was to be transferred—in Nehru's inimitable words—on the stroke of midnight of 14 August 1947, whilst the rest of the world slept.

India's constitution makers did not know what to do with the judiciary. British courts were to remain—partly out of reverence and partly because they were convenient and familiar. That part was easy. But, the retention of 'British' courts did not engage the more serious questions of constitutional politics over the political role of the judicial power to protect people from their democratic masters. In an imperial state, the judiciary was simply an adjunct to imperial governance—an autonomous bureaucracy which was 'fair', but not entirely independent in its aims and perspectives. That the British had designed a slightly more enlightened judicial model for its own people is irrelevant. The question before Independent India was: would India's future Constitution create a new post-imperial judiciary which would reinforce its democracy, interrogate majoritarianism, protect governance, from the innumerable vices of governance, and empower people to pursue their version of the good life within the framework of a commonweal? If such a creature was to be institutionally embedded in the constitutional structure, it would have a far more significant role than any imperial judiciary could have ever possessed.[2]

There were too many djinns and demons in the cupboards. Warnings came from everywhere. Nehru's 'fabian' instincts, learnt from Laski and others, warned that judges were anti-labour and fuelled by biases in favour of the propertied classes. There was a long line of instances from the turn of the century confirming his worst fears. America's record had been no better. The American Supreme Court's turn of the century record was buttressed by the liberal voice of a Holmes or Brandeis. America's New Deal crisis, with President Roosevelt's threat to pack the judiciary, coupled with advice given to B.N. Rau, the Constituent Assembly's constitutional advisor, that judiciaries can stand in the way of 'regulatory', 'welfare state' progress, sealed the fate of the future judiciary.[3] Judges were all right; but, not entirely to be trusted. The djinns and demons remained. Committed to a Bill of Rights, the judiciary became the custodian of the enshrined Fundamental Rights. Confronted with a federal design, it had to be left to the judiciary to interpret the federal allocation of powers and, perforce, determine federal disputes. This latter task had already been entrusted to the Federal Court (1937–50) with relatively unobstrusive results.[4] But, in fact, the custodianship of fundamental rights and arbitration of disputes within the federal system itself, instituted a dramatic transformation of the Indian judiciary in the emerging constitutional system. It meant that the higher judiciary had a power which no British or common law judiciary (outside America) had even claimed since the seventeenth century. It was an enormous power empowering India's new judiciary to strike down government decisions and parliamentary statutes because the judges thought they were unconstitutional. This was an American style judiciary with American style powers. The djinns and demons returned. All kinds of changes were made in the constitutional text. The 'due process' clause was converted into an 'any procedure' clause. This meant that it was not for judges to lay down a due process of their own choosing, but simply to follow the one laid down by the legislature. Each Article of the 'Bill of Rights' was written and re-written so that the power of the government and legislature triumphed, to leave as little room for ambiguity as possible. The biggest debates were overdue process, property rights and the social welfare provisions. Protests were absorbed. As far as the managers of the Constituent Assembly were concerned, the future judiciary had been neutralized—nipped in the bud.[5] 'Modern' in its design, India's judiciary was to play a secondary role—an adjunct to the new State, but never quite to be its master.[6]

But, one more step had to be taken before the djinns and demons could be confined to the lumber room. This concerned the power to appoint judges. This was critical. Who was to make these appointments? The range of choices was limited. The English model was a political appointment model in which the will of the Prime Minister and his cabinet prevailed. Informally, the judiciary had its say—even a decisive say in many instances. The American approach built 'senate' confirmations around appointments. This was thought to be cumbersome. India retained the political model, with the judiciary to be consulted. So, what was created was a potentially powerful judiciary, partly neutered by the constitutional text and partly controlled by the executive in whose hands lay the appointment of future judges to replace existing incumbents. Perhaps, this is why Nehru held the view that the main qualification for a future Supreme Court judge was that he must have served in the High Court somewhere.[7]

II

Whether brought together in a single document or not, constitutions are expressed through innumerable texts. Designed to bring governance together, constitutions potentially conceal the seeds of discord and divisiveness. The various 'texts' create 'institutions' 'empowerments' and 'processes'. Each institution or process attracts a power politics of its own. Into the working of the Constitutions are inducted 'custodians' of various ranks, and empowerments of differing shapes and sizes—each one vying for their own turf , though not generally unmindful of the whole. To the 'maha' or 'grand' custodians of the executive and legislative power who claim to be the rulers of India, were added many others. Institutional rebellions and processual hang-ups take place in any constitutional system—not necessarily dramatically but often quietly. A million mutinies seem to take place all the time. They are not really mutinies—but consist of claims, demands, protests, refusals, inhibitions, restraints, delays. Sometimes by minor functionaries. Sometimes these are ironed out, sometimes overruled, sometimes crushed, and sometimes simply left in the air to be resolved some other day. Constitutions are veritable hotbeds of controversy inviting contention and divisiveness amidst pleas of harmony. Each custodian and each player in any institution or of any process, may play his own games subject to his own rules while accepting the discipline imposed on him from some but not all quarters. Of course, Constitutions are not always tested to the extremities of their impossible limits. But it is these tensions that make constitutions interesting, exciting, conflict driven, tested for their tensile strengthen, ingenuity and, sometimes, unworkable. But the ones that endure, develop practices to keep them together. These practices (or conventions) change over time. But without these institutional practices and the morality they portray, constitutions can fail—partially or even fully. Independent India has had its fair share of constitutional rebellions. Presidents have tried to curb their Prime Ministers who, in turn, have had to confront their parties, colleagues and legislatures. Speakers of legislatures have not only threatened but created crises. Legislatures have claimed unlimited privileges. Judges have constantly written over and rewritten the constitutional text, to successfully claim powers never intended for them. Election Commissions have flexed their muscles. The federal system is constantly re-negotiated—with State democracy being undermined by the imposition of the Union's President's Rule. Indeed, India went through a draconian Emergency (1975–7) through an abuse of the constitutional provision—when every check and balance seemed to fail except the power of the people, which threw Mrs. Gandhi's regime out of power in 1977 to return her back to power in 1980. Generally, constitutional skirmishes and rebellions are not necessarily destructive of the constitutional fabric, but they can be. The Indian Constitution has been put at risk as a result of a policy of 'maximization' with the consequence, that each constitutional player sometimes has 'maximized' its understanding of the use and abuse its own empowerments at the cost of developing working ground rules, institutional practices and conventions.[8] As I remarked when closing a now dated study of President's Rule:

> The ground rules of Indian political system, as they are constituted today, work on the theoretical assumption that every sectional interest in India can be politically effective if it uses the political and constitutional structure expediently, ruthlessly and without obeisance to the operational morality that the

parliamentary system envisages. This theoretical assumption rests on the premise that various interests seek a quick translation of their ambitions and frustrations into political reality, even if this means breaking existing conventional norms of political behaviour. This idea of a 'quick translation' of aspirations into reality induces a certain speed into system. The political system begins to reflect every twist and turn of political behaviour instead of stabilizing itself. In time, the system itself, having compromised all its ground rules, begins to weaken unless some alternative rules are found to replace the previous ground rules. . . . India today (has) compromised to existing ground rules without providing an alternative.[9]

Yet, the Indian Constitution has creatively muddled through amidst tensions. It is still not secure from both constitutional lawlessness and the collapse of the rule of law which threatens India's governance as a whole.

The struggle for judicial supremacy is concerned with the tension between the 'political' and 'justice' texts of the Constitution. The 'political' texts constitute how political power is institutionalized, distributed and exercised. They set up the parliamentary and federal system to create 'political rulers'. The 'justice' texts create 'judicial custodians' who ensure that constitutional empowerments stay within their designated bounds, interpret and defend the Bill of Rights, resolve federal disputes and generally bind all rulers, great and small, within the rule of law. Judicial custodians were generally expected to behave conservatively with due deference to the exercise of power by the political rulers; and, if needs be, interpret constitutional texts and doctrines harmoniously rather than use their awesome power to strike down governmental action or legislation as unconstitutional.

When the Constitution began its journey in 1950, Nehru was convinced that the voice of the people and democracy, history and justice spoke through him and his government—both for now and the future. Given the Congress's antecedents, he could not be grudged this winning admiration and support. But, he was a vacillating ruler seeking to evolve a working 'consensus' which paid due deference to the political, and, therefore, democratic power vested in himself.[10] The judiciary was simply there to get on with its job without creating a fuss to defy the unravelling of India's history. Nehru had a clear concept of 'law and development'—borrowed from a mixture of Soviet planning, American New Deal bureaucratic regulation, and English Fabian socialism—by which law was to instrument social change albeit through tough controls and sanctions. In retrospect such 'instrumentalism' appears crude, but it was the fashion of the day and still not entirely irrelevant to India, even if not too complete a faith cannot be reposed on it.[11] By contrast, the judges of the Supreme Court of the 1950s had no constitutional philosophy as such, no distinct approach, no real disquiet with the 'law and development' approach, but a sense of the enormous power that they possessed in ways, and to an extent, not possessed by any other constitutional functionary. There were some libertarians (Fazl Ali, Bose, Mahajan later, Subba Rao and, possibly, Hidayatullah), some conservatives (Sastri, N. Chandrasekhar Aiyer, possibly Mukerjea) and some pragmatists (like S.R. Das and later Gajendragadkar) who wanted to quell confrontation. But these positions were often fluid. This resulted in an inconsistent and untidy approach as the judges cautiously and in different ways tested the temperature of the water.

THREE REBELLIONS: THE FIRST REBELLION 1950–1955

Till the Emergency, the Supreme Court broadly speaking posed three rebellions. The first rebellion (1950–5), would generally have gone unnoticed if it had confined itself to claiming the power of judicial review and issues related to personal liberties. The Court had agreed to a narrow due process, accepted administrative preventive detention with limited judicial intervention, upheld the regulatory state, permitted vast delegated legislations and generally allowed differential criminal procedures for speedy trials. They struck down certain public order statutes which infringed on press freedom (necessitating a constitutional amendment); but generally relented on all fronts.[12] If so, what went wrong? The fly in the ointment was the Courts' striking down 'land reform' legislation aimed at directly wiping out the old zamindars and created at least new kulaks with some benefits to the peasantry. This was Nehru's dream from his earlier days in UP and part of the Congress's political statement since, at least, the Karachi Resolution of 1931. Several High Courts had rebelled. That was enough for Nehru to react. In the Supreme Court, emerged the figure of M.C. Mahajan (puisne judge from the Federal Court and later to become Chief Justice of India). Had the judges succeeded in their endeavours, India's exchequer would have been bankrupted. No less its radical image of abolishing vestiges of feudalism would have been tarnished. Along with others, the Supreme Court fought for higher market value compensation for the landlords. The middle class background of the judges began to reveal itself as they drew support from Anglo-American theories of eminent domain requiring full compensation for all acquired property.[13] The more the Supreme Court fought, the stronger the response of Nehru's parliament which kept amending the Constitution to reverse court decisions. Mahajan and his colleagues were at the receiving end. This was a real crisis. Nehru even contemplated ignoring the 'seniority' principle to seek (perhaps, Roosevelt-like) to by-pass and supercede the claims of Mahajan and others to become Chief Justices of India. But, the informal story is that all the judges of the Supreme Court threatened to resign if such a supercession took place.[14] Constitutional amendments, supercession threats, public obliquy—all this and more. Such a battle had not taken place in common law judiciaries since the seventeenth century. Nehru's onslaught was not simply that the judges had—as he put it—'purloined the constitution' but stood in the way of the nation's progress.[15] Eventually, the judges simply backed off—but gracefully, without wholly surrendering their power of judicial review. The onslaught had been too great. Mahajan was sent off to hear some Privy Council appeals in Hyderabad. Chief Justice Sastri gave a speech on his retirement that the judges had been misunderstood.[16] Many decisions were re-worked. Some of the libertarians simply retired. By the mid-1950s, the first judicial rebellion died down.

The first judicial rebellion of the 1950s had a very disquieting effect on the judges—forcing introspection. After all, who were the judges? Were they playing Anglo-American hopscotch with the Indian Constitution, unmindful of the tasks that lay ahead? What was wrong with Nehru's 'law and development' approach? Did Indian judges not have an Indian response to an Indian situation? Apart from the strategic retreat of backing off whilst retaining their power of judicial review, judges began to look for Indian answers for the Indian situation(s). Two significant responses emerged. The first was the role of the Supreme Court as 'problem solver'. Controversies abounded. These included the Kerala Education Bill crisis (1958), the cowslaughter cases (1958–61), issues relating to the Press (1958 and 1962), the UP High Court legislature crisis (1964), controversies over religious endowments (1954–64), and on the power within faiths of ex-communication (1959). This problem solving function continues.[17] Without abandoning issues of principle, the Supreme Court struck balances which both diffused the issues and sought pragmatic answers.[18] The second response of some of the judges, was to broadly embrace Nehru's law and development approach. These judges saw themselves as part of the task of 'social engineering'. To begin with, they had to move away from the image that judges stood in the way of progress. Hence, Justice Krishna Iyer's protest that judges were not to be seen as anti-catalysts. Many High Court judges took a similar view. But, the towering exponent of 'social engineering' (borrowed from the no less towering American jurist, Roscoe Pound) was Justice Gajendragadkar (Chief Justice 1964–6), who brought the Court together on many issues concerning labour and workers rights, the welfare state and secularism. In a sense, the second response was akin to the first 'problem solving' response. But, it added ideological purpose to juristic exercise. It also created a new concept of 'committed judges' seeking to separate those committed to the constitutional' (or was it 'regime'?) goals from those who did not.[19]

THE SECOND REBELLION: 1960–1971

By this time, the second rebellion was under way. It is very easy to regard these rebellions as intra-governmental palace rebellions led by individual persons and judges. In a sense, they are. But, judges are part of the politics of the day. India's mixed economy yielded mixed responses. Within the Congress itself, there were powerful voices protecting landed and corporate interests. The judiciary is a natural location for 'establishment' wars. Even if judges falter, lawyers and the interests they represent, keep chipping away. Even if the first rebellion had eventually yielded a sort of Nehruvian judiciary, not everyone was happy with it. The legal establishment was divided. Lawyers like Palkhivala and judges like Subba Rao tried to re-work the juristic losses of the 1950s. The first thrust was to generally try and enlarge the meaning of 'due process' and the broad sweep of the life and liberty and property provisions. To this was added the fight over compensation for acquired property. All of a sudden, a debate that had been closed by constitutional amendment in 1954 was revived.[20] This was done by clever arguments and twists of meaning. Parliament's threats to rewrite the Constitution were struck down by a slim 6:5 majority in 1967, to succeed more fully in the third rebellion that was to follow.[21] But these were rendered 'prospective' so that the constitutional amendments of the past hurt only the government's political plans for the future. Meanwhile, in 1969, the Congress split into two 'socialist' and 'capitalist' halves with Mrs. Gandhi's Congress bringing in Bank Nationalization and the abolition of Privy Purses on her agenda. The *Bank Nationalization* case (and, to a lesser extent, the *Privy Purses* case) culminated the second rebellion. The foundation for a more integrated due process was laid. The 'compensation' debate ended partly against the government. Along with the *Times of India* newsprint case (1972),[22] the Supreme Court overcame its earlier inhibitions to take an oppositional stand against the government.

The second rebellion of the Supreme Court had distinct features of its own. Unlike the first rebellion, it had been taken to its logical conclusion. Some of the judges of the Supreme Court had not only taken the government on, but also threatened to do so in future. No doubt, the Court was divided. But, the posture of the Supreme Court went beyond threat into opposition. If the present pattern of judicial appointments were to be continued, the opposition of the Supreme Court would increase. Just as Mahajan was a key factor in the first rebellion to unite the 'libertarians', Justice Subba Rao and Shah, possibly Hidayatullah, and no less significantly, later Hegde were seen as the incoming tide of opposition. The second rebellion was over many things—no less the philosophy of the Constitution, and the role of the judiciary. At the root lay the old issue of 'empowerment'. Nehru, and now his successors, claimed the 'power' to effect social change without being distrusted by the reactionary eyes of judges. If the prime minister was the democratic leader in charge of a socialist constitution, who were the judges to disabuse that position and challenge his authority? The second rebellion was unrelenting. Like Nehru, Mrs. Gandhi could have let it go and let things work themselves out. But, she had decided not to do so. Like Nehru, she was going to use the power of constitutional amendment to undermine existing and future judicial decisions. Unlike Nehru, she had decided to take on the judiciary fully and put it in its place.

THE THIRD REBELLION: 1972–1975

It was Mrs. Gandhi's actions that prompted the third rebellion to climax. The power to make judicial appointments continued to lie with the Prime Minister—with inputs from the judges. The final say lay with Mrs. Gandhi. On advice, she eyed several people who would be in the Court for a long time for appointment. In this list were prominent names like Justice Chandrachud, Dwivedi, Bhagwati and Krishna Iyer and others such as Ray and Beg. Krishna Iyer had been part of the first Communist government of Kerala (1957–9) which Mrs. Gandhi had personally pressured Nehru to dethrone by the use of President's Rule.[23] Her 'left' advisors wanted Krishna Iyer but were apprehensive about him. He was appointed first to the Law Commission on some spurious reason invented by Mohan Kumaramangalam—one of Mrs. Gandhi's advisors. Later he joined the Supreme Court in 1973. By this time, the remaining judges had already been appointed—with politics playing its inevitable role in the timing of their respective appointments.[24] In this way, she secured ballast for the future. From 1977 to 1986 onwards, the Chief Justice of India would be chosen from her list. To all intents, she had a 'socialist' court which would, at least, do her ideological bidding. The Law Minister could act as a go-between. But, in between, lay a shadow. There were a series of Chief Justices in between: Hidayatullah (1968–70) who had struck down constitutional amendments prospectively in 1967, Shah (1970) who wrote the majority *Bank Nationalization* judgement, Sikri (1970–3) who was a part of the rebellion, but otherwise described as a forbearing gentleman, Shelat, Hegde and Grover (to be Chief Justices from 1973 in quick succession) who would control the court after they were appointed. The future had been taken care of. But, what about the present ?

In 1972, Mrs. Gandhi's constitutional amendments sought to reverse the 'compensation' jurisprudence of the *Bank Nationalization* case (1970), push many statutes beyond judicial review, and make it clear that if Parliament amended the Constitution, the Courts could not strike these amendments down. Meanwhile, Mrs. Gandhi got a jolt in the *Times of India* case (1972), when judges she could rely on struck down her attempt to control newspapers by rationing the 'newsprint' on which papers are printed and subjecting them to direct governmental regulation. Even if this was seen as a hiccup, in 1973, an emboldened Supreme Court made its famous ruling in the Fundamental Rights case, that the basic structure of the Constitution was inviolate even from constitutional amendments. The judgement itself makes dull reading. However, few can deny that it is one of the momentous constitutional rulings of all time.[25] The judges had blocked Parliament's sovereign power; and claimed to share the constituent power to remould the Constitution. No change could alter the 'basic structure' of the Constitution. The judges would decide what the basic structure was. They now controlled the Constitution, and any change to it.

After the third rebellion recorded its more than partial victories, Mrs. Gandhi—the recent victor of the Bangladesh war and the landslide victory that followed—struck back. Her chosen appointees (especially Chandrachud, Ray, Beg and Dwivedi) had been loyal to her even in the *Fundamental Rights* case (1973). She wanted socialists judges who agreed with her. In 1973, the three immediate future Chief Justices (Shelat, Hegde and Grover) were superceded and Ray appointed Chief Justice of India. The supercession was punitive. The three superceded judges resigned. Later in 1976, during the Emergency, Beg superceded Khanna who had halfheartedly supported the Fundamental Rights majority decision in 1973; but, more significantly, gave a lone dissent in the infamous *Prevention Detection* case (1976), to make him a kind of folk hero amongst libertarians and the political opposition.[26] Nehru may have threatened supercession to confront rebellion, but never got round to doing so. Mrs. Gandhi had ventured beyond a threat to indicate the possible shape of things to come. The third rebellion was over; but ostensibly nipped in the bud *ex post facto*; but not really.

Although Mrs. Gandhi tried to give an ideological explanation for her actions by claiming that capitalist judges were not 'committed' to the socialist goals of the Constitution, nobody quite bought this explanation.[27] In Mrs. Gandhi's conception, a 'committed judge' had to be committed not just to a goal, but also to the regime. That is, to her regime. Deep down, Mrs. Gandhi had a distrust of any kind of oppositional politics. She tolerated this because parliamentary democracy obliged her to do so. But, she was not used to disquiet—wherever it came from. The Supreme Court represented a kind of oppositional politics to which she had no answer. The Court out-trumped her over constitutional amendments in 1967, tried to kill her taking over the Privy Purses, aborted part of her Bank Nationalization ventures and set aside her plans to control the media. To top it all, after 1973, the Court claimed suzerainty over the constitutional empire in ways that placed amending the constitution beyond her reach. She could not control judges. No doubt, friendly and unfriendly words may have been passed on. But, judges were a law unto themselves. She needed judges around her whom she could trust. Most judges could not be so trusted. When a single judge of the Allahabad High Court set aside her election in 1975 with the possibility that she might—even if momentarily—cease to be prime minister, her worst fears were confirmed. Her conclave of advisors showed the way. After Krishna Iyer granted her an injunctive stay of the Allahabad decision but reminded her that she was subject to the rule of law, she declared an Emergency the next day on 27 June 1975. From 1975–7, vast constitutional changes were made by the infamous 42nd Amendment. Judicial interference with her electoral verdict was contained. The general purpose of the amendments was to consolidate her power and render the judiciary relatively powerless.[28] A huge number of detentions without trial were unleashed. Some High Court judges protested they had the power of judicial review. But, many were ignominiously transferred to other High Courts by way of punishment. When the Supreme Court refused to interfere even in malafide detentions, the Emergency was at its peak; and, the judicial power reached its nadir. Since the judiciary had faltered during the Emergency, it lost what it had gained. In 1977, Mrs. Gandhi herself was voted out of power.

The second and third judicial rebellions (1960–75) had been crushed by supercessions, judicial appointments and, eventually the Emergency. But, some of the juristic seeds sown by that rebellion remained. These seeds were not over the right of the privileged to property or the compensation they would receive. They concerned the basic power of the higher judiciary to impose due process norms on the government and legislature; and asserted that it was the judiciary, in its role as the custodian of not just the 'justice texts', but the Constitution itself, that was supreme. But, the story was not over. There was more to come.

III

The story of the Indian judiciary after the Emergency is as remarkable as it is instructive. A judiciary tainted with the charge of cowardice cannot easily resurrect itself by its own bootstraps. But, after the Emergency a new kind of judiciary was created in India which, in my view, altered the basis of constitutional governance in India. A new kind of judiciary had been created which was not just a break from the past, but no less a unique experiment for the future. The judiciary ceased to be an institution of state; and, became an institution of governance in its own right.

In 1977, the Emergency came to an end. Mrs. Gandhi lost the Election and was voted out of power. The Supreme Court had reached its lowest ebb. In peoples' minds it had failed the nation during the Emergency. Many of the Emergency judges were still on the Bench—especially three of those had decided the *Prevention Detention* case, namely Justices Beg, Chandrachud and Bhagwati, who, in that order would become Chief Justices of India from 1977–86. The bad taste of the Emergency was not over. Justice Chandrachud simply apologized. Justice Bhagwati wrote a judgement in the *President's Rule* case (1977) which not only undermined Indian federalism by permitting emergency take overs in nine constituent States, but which also contained approbatory comments for the phenomenon which brought the post-Emergency Janata government into power, specifically using fulsome words in praise. He was later to evoke even greater praise in favour of Mrs. Gandhi when she returned to power in 1980.[29] Meanwhile, the press opened up against the 'Emergency' judges. Chief Justice Beg issued contempt notices to silence the press to protect his reputation and those of his emergency colleague. For the Court to have taken the 'press' (and the lawyers and other people behind it) on would have been disastrous. With some behind the scenes activity, Justice Krishna Iyer persuaded Chief Justice Beg to drop the contempt charge. It was quite clear that if the Supreme Court wanted to revive its reputation, Beg's way was not the right way to go about it.[30]

The answers lay in the genius of Krishna Iyer. He was a former politician, minister in the first Communist government of Kerala, original thinker and with a flair for both words and strategy. What, then, was the Supreme Court? In Krishna Iyer's understanding, it was not a bunch of judges appointed by the executive on the basis of seniority of service and their ideological commitment to Congress (or anti-Congress? as the case may be). To him a judge was not a mason or a plumber but an architect. This architectural design flowed from the Constitution whose custodianship had been vested in the judiciary.[31] The judiciary was not a satellite to the government. It had an independent existence with independent duties not just to the State but to the people directly. This was a distinct shift from the earlier approach of the 'socialist' judges. Amidst the turbulent calm of the second rebellion, Gajendragadkar's approach (from which Krishna Iyer's approach did not earlier entirely distance itself) was to assure the government that judges would strive for social justice by playing a supportive role in empowering the government to achieve its goals, solving problems as they emerged and retain the power to play a 'rule of law' conscience keeper in dealing with what was capricious. Indeed, this is what Krishna Iyer meant when he said that in 'the inevitable chemistry of social change, judges were certainly not anti-catalysts'. Perhaps, he meant a little more than that; certainly so, after the Emergency. Now, Krishna Iyer wanted to appeal to the people themselves to bring their problems to the Court directly for the Court to forge reliefs, including schematic solutions if the occasion demanded it. This was designed to alter the very basis of the operation of the judiciary as an institution of governance.

It may well be said that to attribute this change entirely to the fecundity of Krishna Iyer's genius may not be entirely fair to the other judges who had, in fact, moulded the new Court and its work. After all, Krishna Iyer retired in 1980—having delivered just a view of the public interest judgements which did no more than point a direction. No less, there was a gang of 'four' that structured this response, including Justices Bhagwati and Chandrachud (from before the Emergency), and Desai and Chinappa Reddy (appointed after the Emergency). History cannot rob these and other judges of their inevitable contribution to the creation of the new judiciary. Yet somewhere in embryo of this design, Krishna Iyer emerges as possibly the most significant designer. Once within the domain of possibility, each of the 'four'—and, indeed, the many others to follow—crafted the jurisprudence of the new dispensation.[32]

There were several new and strengthened strands to the judicial metamorphosis—none entirely divorced from the past, and, yet part of something new that was emerging. To begin with the scope of judicial review itself was enlarged to suggest that there were no 'no go' areas other than those dictated by judicial restraint. Thus, it did not matter if the exercise of power imposed the union's Emergency rule on the constituent states, exercised the power of pardon or concerned itself with exercises of any other kind of prerogative power.[33] Judicial review was enlarged. With this, the American dilemma that judges would not entertain 'political questions' or enter the 'political thicket' seemed resolved in favour of the judges—even if some Indian judges several years later, seemed to favour the 'English' doctrines that judges should not entertain what was not judicially manageable.[34] English fashions appeared to have their sway on post-colonial minds. But, these were just formulas which did not seriously upset the broad enlarged claim of judicial power while holding a promise of discipline on the part of the judges—if they were so advised. Connected to the claim of judicial review was securing the new due process—the foundation for which was laid in the second rebellion.[35] The new 'due process' greatly enlarged the meaning of the 'life' and 'liberty' provisions to include various aspects of livelihood, health, social welfare concerns, the environment, the right to governance and potentially virtually every aspect of the social and public interest. Linked to this expansionist approach was a new emphasis on due process procedures, public participation in decision making, anti-arbitrariness principles, and enlarged versions of governance and the public interest.[36] But, beyond this lay another important transition. If hitherto, the approach of judicial review was to tell the executive or legislature where they had gone wrong but leave it to them to structure the right decision, the new approach in many cases was to tell the government what the right decision was, structure the decision making process and, in fact, ensure the implementation of the new decisions ordained by the court. Despite the Court's protestation that it was not taking over governance but simply fulfilling the mandate of the Constitution, the Supreme Court was doing precisely what it protested it was not doing. It was a monumental usurpation. Every usurpation demands a justification. The justification of the judges that they were merely fulfilling the Constitution had a divine right ring to it. In this, it was not the 'will of God' but the 'will of the Constitution' which the Court had already endowed with a soul included its inviolate core which it called its 'basic structure'. The Court claimed to be fighting for the Constitution's soul, whilst, amidst many dissensions, also claiming an independent role and empowerment for itself. It started expanding schemes on bonded labour, health, mining and the environment.[37] What else is the assumption of governance, if the Court, against political opposition, shifted industries out of Delhi, imposed a cleaner CNG fuel on Delhi for public transport, to the exclusion of petrol and diesel and better fuel standards for the huge automobile industry, and brought forests and coastlines within the control of the Supreme Court? Governments were coerced into doing what they did not want to do. This was more than the usual 'rule of law' oversight.[38] It was taking over governance, substituting the Court's decision on what needed to be done; and in what proportion and in what way. This process was no secret, was often brazen in its approach and, more often than not, in its style—even if the judges protested their innocence many times over.[39] They claimed they were simply keeping a watch to ensure that the government did its job; and, this, alas, was the will of the Constitution.

Beyond the consequentialist analysis of the Supreme Court's direct inroad into governance, the Court secured its intrusive strategy, by and through, developing new juristic techniques. The Court appealed to the Preamble of the Constitution, and the mandate of the Directive Principles to argue that the Constitution was a social document proclaiming socio-economic goals for all—especially the underprivileged, dalits and tribals [designated by the Constitution as Scheduled Castes (ST) and Scheduled Tribes (ST)]. The Court claimed to champion the cause of the 'poor' and 'downtrodden' who had no other champion (other than the elusive promises of politics).[40] This sought to relegate the Court's record of the Emergency behind it, and to launch new concerns which the Court was not just prepared to declare, but also fulfil. To strengthen its tentative initiative, the Court began by concentrating on two distinct areas: (i) human atrocities—many of which were unspeakable, such as the blindings of accused by the police in Bihar, conditions in prisons, and excesses of the police and other custodians of the law including deaths, torture and rape—to create an interventionist 'anti-atrocity' jurisprudence; and (ii) the socio-economic conditions of bonded and other labour to elaborate an active socio-economic justice—whilst tentatively expanding to other areas. In addition to the first technique of claiming to fulfil a constitutional duty to actively prevent and deal with atrocities and no less actively help the poor, powerless and disadvantaged, three other techniques were elaborated. The second change was to open up the Court's procedures for direct access by and to the people. People could normally only approach the Court if they had a 'cause'; and, that too by complicated legal procedures. Now, the Court opened up its doors. As long as they acted in a bona fide manner, any one with a worthy cause (especially on behalf of the disadvantaged) could approach the Court simply by writing a letter, indicate their social, economic or other disaffection and leave it to the Court to devise answers and solutions.[41] The third technique was to enlarge the powers of the Court to investigate a problem by appointing commissions and committees if needs be.[42] This was linked to the fourth technique of devising schematic solutions with oversight and management often vesting in the Court and its agents and by introducing new laws and procedures, otherwise unimaginable for a judiciary to create.[43] These powers were not to be exercised in each and every case—certainly not where the PIL was itself bonafide or privately motivated; and also not necessarily in other cases. Which issues were to be selected, and to what extent the Court would go, depended on the judicial intuition, the fashion of the day, the vulnerability of the government and the individual judges and lawyers involved.[44]

The effect of all this was to enable the judiciary to become an institution of governance in its own right. Even though judges disagreed themselves and many stayed away from the new jurisdiction, the Court had claimed a new role in constitutional governance. This was not always well received. Those at the receiving end of PIL (which often included industries, mining corporates, timber and other merchants), were happy neither with this increased jurisdiction nor the procedures adopted. Often, draconian orders were passed. Equally, the vulnerable on whose behalf the court claimed to speak got few direct benefits;

and, in many instances were pawns to enlarge the Court's power. *Amicus Curiae* were appointed to assist the Court. Many *amicus* silenced those who protested—acting both arbitrarily and as hit men for the court. No out-of-Court meetings took place to resolve matters. Things were invariably done in a hurry in many cases. For those attending court hearings, it seemed that if the Court had taken a view it would persist in its plan. Some of the committees appointed by the Court were entrusted with wide powers; and, sometimes behaved as if they were the court themselves. There are many aspects of PIL which expand the horizons of governance. There are also many things which make it suspect.[45]

At one stage, academics who helped mould the PIL of the Court preferred to describe this litigation as 'social action litigations' (SAL).[46] This description sought to create exaggerated illusions. The invocation of the term SAL was to try and show that avenues of a new kind of people-based 'social democracy' had been created which not only democratised the court processes but democracy itself. Thus, unlike PIL, SAL suggested that behind the Supreme Court's endeavours was the full support of many social movements whose spirit the Court imbibed. An analysis of the Court's PIL record showed that this was far from the truth. In environment matters, one individual filed many of the cases which the Court transformed to suit itself. Many of the groups that came to the Court were self-styled groups—some seeking publicity (to invite the derogatory description that PIL was 'publicity interest litigation) and, some genuinely involved in some causes to varying depths of social involvement. The so-called NGO (non-governmental organizations) groups were varied in their description. The stronger—better funded—individuals and groups flocked to PIL to use and abuse it. But, PIL remains a temperamental jurisdiction, even if artful, creative and with much to its credit. For those actually involved in social action movements, it could be a trap. The solutions of PIL remain imperfect to create institution traps to imprison the scope of social action. From the point of view of those who struggle, the critical decision is whether 'law' courts and their newly invented populist fora could genuinely be the *site* of struggle. It is not an open-ended choice. People are oppressively drawn into the tentacles of the law whether they like it or not. PIL opens up a possible arena of struggle—more for the advantaged NGOs than others.[47] The 'social democracy' of NGO's, collectivities and people are as complex in their range and as biased in their diverse purposes as society itself. To even suggest that the new PIL (or SAL—by whatsoever name called) created a peoples' Court, is based on too many mal-understandings about how these processes work and at whose behest. Yet some avenues for some were opened up, which had not existed before.

Side by side with the quest to share the power of governance lay the old concern of the judges that if they provoked the government too much, the latter would pack the Court. In the original design, the judges were to be consulted, but the ultimate selection lay with the executive. Nehru had not abused this partnership; but Mrs. Gandhi had—both by seeking to appointing judges of her choice (even if not the less distinguished for being so), transferring High Court judges from one State to another, as well as superceding those she did not want and, thus, forcing them into retirement. In this area, the Court was vulnerable. At first, the post-Emergency Court in 1982 was inclined to allow the transfer power and the power to make judicial appointments to remain with the executive, but mandating consultation with the judges as a safeguard. But, the Congress governments of the 1980s seemed to exercise a seemingly pervasive influence whilst consulting the judges. In two further important decisions of 1993 and 1998, the Supreme Court virtually wrested these appointment and transfer powers, from the exclusive domain of the executive.[48] The judges placed themselves in the primary role even though the tradition of compromise with the executive may have continued. Judicial cabals were invented which made the judges a law unto themselves in the matter of appointments. The guiding formula was that judges to the Supreme Court would be appointed on the basis of seniority in the High Court subject to an integrity and efficacy test but leaving open the possibility for exceptional appointments. The cabal has not necessarily behaved rationally. Friendships and caste and other associations have played a role to triumph over choices based on ability, the experience of seniority and constitutional ideology. Successive governments have not been entirely happy with this further usurpation—even though some Law Ministers have played their cards well in both High Court and Supreme Court appointments. What has strengthened the government's hand is public concern that there is corruption and indiscipline in the judiciary. One Chief Justice of India estimated that 1 in 5 judges may be corrupt.[49] In India's single solitary impeachment case of a Supreme Court judge, the tribunal found against the judge, but the Congress party abstained in the vote, to ensure that the requisite majority did not exist in Parliament to complete the impeachment. The various in-house mechanisms to deal with judicial corruption have not succeeded in allaying well-grounded fears and suspicions. This has triggered renewed demands for a National Judicial Commission which will be responsible for both appointments to the judiciary as well as matters of discipline. The real tussle here, is over who will have the upper hand; and, whether the new proposed commission and its procedures will consist of cozy arrangements amongst the judiciary and government or also other watchful and participatory persons without compromising the independence of judges.[50]

Over the post—Emergency years, the Supreme Court has consolidated its power and influence. Even though there are many governments, politicians, interests and persons who are wary of the new-found power of India's higher judiciary, the foundations on which this power has been built are not as shaky as they might be made out to be. Through its new jurisdiction and jurisprudence, the Courts have been able to expose aspects of Indian governance to be rotten, corrupt, vicious and cruel. By addressing issues that need attention and exposure, the Court has gathered support for itself even if it is criticized for its methods, decisions and undemocratic status. With this support, it has altered its place in the nature and style of Indian governance, by winning enough public support to sustain its initiatives so that, at any given point in time, supporters and detractors balance out.

IV

The latter part of the twentieth century has seen vast changes in the nature of governance. The advent of electoral democracy has empowered people to vote governments in and out of office. As this power has increased in its significance, other aspects of democratic involvement have also intervened to create new processes for interrogating power. But, the power of government while mindful of the pressures of electoral democracy is not its prisoner. The sheer complexity of governance has created much participations and many expectations. The scale of governance and the enlarged scope and rapidity of technological change and development has created enormous temptations. Real power evades the people to vest in many interlocking interests—some more powerful than others. In different measures, a democracy theoretically founded on accountability, and responsibility to the people, has also unleashed corruption, greed, venality and atrocity. Many areas of governance have failed to find the balance between governance and its antithesis.

Frightening reports of the collapses of governance would haunt India's constitutional imagination.[51]

It is in this volatile world that the judiciary of the second part of the twentieth century has been pushed to seek its baptism by fire. In its original design, the judiciary was an institution of state—an adjunct to the political institutions who through their legislatures and executive exercised constitutional power. As an adjunct, the judiciary had a role to play so that the exercise of power was disciplined and, at least, mindful of the liberties of the people. This role was accepted by some but not all constitutional jurisdictions. But, somewhere in the 1950s, a dramatic change seem to have occurred when the American Supreme Court in *Brown* v. *Board of Education*, picked up a long standing issue of racial justice which lay at the root of American governance and tried to resolve it directly. The Supreme Court, thus, placed itself in a position of direct custodianship of this issue to relate directly to the people. This may, in fact, be something of an exaggeration; but this is how the judgement was welcomed and remonstrated against. This paved the way for a creative the Warren Court to consider many more interventions to alter the constitutional landscape. This brought the American Court system into a new lime light, even if it was criticized for non-neutral decisions and government by judiciary.[52] What was hitherto an institution of government had become an institution of governance in its own right with its own charismatic relationship with the people.

The American example was not exactly followed by the common law and other judiciaries of the world. There may have been some reluctant admiration; but these new developments and changes were seen as distinctly for and by Americans. The first three Indian judicial rebellions may have derived some juristic support from American examples; but, in many cases went much further to respond to, and take advantage of, the problems of Indian governance. India's post-Emergency Court set alight a pattern which was innovatively distinct and relevant for future constitutional developments in India and elsewhere. The Indian judiciary too, is no longer an institution of state but an institution of governance in its right. We need to ponder a little over these developments rather than simply dismiss them as exaggerated claims of temporary significance. Governance changes over time not just to alter the balance of power between institutions, but to alter the nature of governance available from the array of institutions and processes available for use and abuse.

The rise of the new judiciary forces us to re-think democratic governance. As an institution of State, the judiciary wrapped itself in many myths including the well known defences that judges did not make laws but simply interpreted them to retain a watch-dog function over governance. No one watching the sweep of judicial governance can apply any of these erstwhile understandings to the Indian judiciary with any integrity. But, if indeed, a new institution of governance has, willy nilly, been created, many other challenges exist both for the theory and practice of this kind of judiciary as a part of democratic governance. The Indian judiciary is not a democratic institution. Appointments to the judiciary are enmeshed in innumerable conspiracies. The system of internal and external discipline over the judiciary itself creates dilemmas, about how these disciplines can be maintained without undermining the independence of the judges. Even if the judges sit in public and give reasons for their decisions, that may not, by itself, make the judiciary a democratic institution. These are vexed issues. But, many such issues will arise as part of post-modern governance which throws up new fora of activity around which new pressures create new institutions, procedures and interactions which compete with each other for recognition. The end result is not just that 'more-is-more' but to qualitatively change governance itself.

It is tolerably clear that democracy is not a self-fulfilling prophecy. Its gifts are replete with much that is imperfect, wrong, questionable and undemocratic. Perhaps, if constitutional and other processes are strengthened, democracy may generate its own self cleansing. But, electoral democratic governance is not by itself enough. In the late twentieth century, many institutions and procedures have been created which render the classical description of government as a separation of powers between the executive, legislature and judiciary over-simplistic. We now have a plethora of institutions at various levels of governance with independent access to the various interests that compose the people. Amidst these institutions is the new judiciary—but no longer as an adjunct to the executive or legislature but as a self-standing exercise opening up far greater possibilities than any other judiciary that may have preceded it.[53]

The prospects of the Indian judiciary as an institution of governance, draw from an untidy past, but project some new ideas into the future of democratic constitutional governance.

But, where does all this take us? For some Indian judges, all this leads to the 'promised land' in which the disadvantaged will find 'social justice' and—to use their phrase—to wipe the tear from every unfortunate poor person's eye. Would such things be possible by a wave of the judicial wand? Nor, indeed, is it vouchsafed that all judges at all times would be prompted by such social heroism—if, indeed they were, in all cases. Even though the judges claimed to speak to the people directly and invite if not solicit their partnership in their quest for judicial power, the 'people' were pawns in the game. The 'people' were only those whom the Court sought to recognize as worthy. 'Peoples concerns' were those which the court agreed to recognize within the time and place constraints which the judiciary was placed. No legal system—no less its supreme judicial power as any other—can by itself fundamentally alter the power structure of a society. It cannot bring an end to exploitation, injustice, race, caste or gender discrimination, or basically alter power structures, property relations and the range of opportunities available to others. But, it can assist in these struggles and make a dent where it was inconceivable before. It will be a long time before India's Constitution speaks for its peoples. But, it has played some role in bringing the 'idea of India' together, and open up some possibilities for some people for some causes. Democracy visits a Constitution when more and more people visit more and more of its processes to yield even-handed and equitable dividends for all. This is no less true of the new judiciary which, too, cannot legitimize its usurpation unless it responds to some sense of the peoples' voice. Will it make a difference? Depending on how it goes about it, perhaps. If it turns its back on the people, they will turn their backs on the judges. But, if it carries the people, it will secure its place in Indian governance more firmly to set an example for others—which, to some extent, it has already done.

NOTES

1. Justice Krishna Iyer in *Kunhu Mohammed* v. *T.K. Ummayithi* (1969), *Kerala Law Reports* 629. The full text of the passage reads 'Courts, which within strict limits have to essay social engineering, are not the sanctuary of age-old but unwholesome customs even if they are not the refuge of social reformers working to emancipate women in the spirit of the Constitution. In the inevitable chemistry of social change courts certainly are not anti-catalysts.'
2. During the long years of British rule British courts did not have the right to strike down governmental action as such. Only the Presidency High Courts of Calcutta, Bombay and Madras were given the prerogative writ jurisdictions, to review and discipline the exercise of the government's power; and,

that, too *within the limits of these towns.* Later, as we shall see, the Federal Court (1937–50), could strike down legislation on limited grounds. Thus, the 'Western' model which built a working polarity between the executive and judicial power was singularly absent: see further R. Dhavan, 'On the future of "Western" law and justice in India: Reflections on the predicament of the post-Emergency Court' (1981) 8, *Journal of the Bar Council of India*, pp. 61–86.

3. Even during the Independence movement, the demand for a Bill of Rights was somewhat weak. This is self-evident from the text of the Home Rule Scheme 1889, the Constitution of India Bill 1895, The Nehru Report 1928 and other documents (see B. Shiva Rao, *The Framing of India's Constitution*, Delhi: Indian Institute of Public Administration, 1968—hereafter cited as *Study Volume* or by volume number, I, pp. 3–4, 5–14, 48–75 *et.seq.* On this see R. Dhavan, 'Tidy Intuitions, Untidy Discourse: Conversations and Exchanges in the Constituent Assembly' (1995, mimeo and Working Paper No. 20 for the Public Interest and Legal Support And Research Centre [PILSARC]). For general accounts of discussion on Fundamental Rights, see B. Shiva Rao, *Study Volume* (1968), pp. 170–318; and for a more optimistic account, G. Austin, *The Indian Constitution: Cornerstone of a Nation*, Delhi: Oxford University Press, 1966, pp. 50–115.
4. See George H. Gadbois Jr, 'Evolution of the Federal Court of India' (1963) 5 *Journal of the Indian Law Institute* 19 (hereafter *JILI*); George H. Gadbois Jr, 'The Federal Court of India 1937–50' (1964), 6, *JILI*, 253. For a less incisive but readable account see M.V. Pylee, *The Federal Court of India*, Bombay: Manaktalas, 1966.
5. While the real discussion on the judiciary's powers were on the 'fundamental rights' provisions, there was a less meaningful discussion on the judiciary on which see R. Dhavan, *Justice on Trial: The Supreme Court Today*, Allahabad: A.H. Wheeler, 1980, pp. 27–64 and B. Shiva Rao, *Study Volume* (1968) (supra n. 3), pp. 480–510.
6. After a vigorous involvement in 'Independence' movement, lawyers and judges were in two minds about their continuing relevance. A resolution of UP lawyers in 1947 blew their own trumpet about their own importance while judges talked of the great role ahead and, guardedly, saw courts as the Constitutional Assembly in continous session ! Few knew what was ahead. One thing was clear, the profession was not about to give up anything even if it did not quite know what it wanted. For a collection of the responses of the lawyers and judges, see R. Dhavan, *The Supreme Court of India: A Socio-legal Critique of its Juristic Techniques*, Bombay: N.M. Tripathi, 1977, pp. 2–19.
7. Nehru, Speech in the Constituent Assembly (1948), VIII, *Constituent Assembly Debates* (hereafter *CAD*), 247 (24 May 1949).

8. Although Indian judges have given due recognition to certain 'conventions' to treat them as part of the Constitution [such as the rules of parliamentary governance in *Samsher Singh* v. *State of Punjab* (1974) 2 SCC 831, pr. 105–33, pp. 861–76], they have also invented conventions in their own favour whilst usurping the controlling power to make higher judicial appointments (see cases cited infra n. 48); but note specially Justice Kuldip Singh in *Supreme Court Advocates-On-Record Association* v. *Union of India* (1993) 4 *SCC* 441, pr. 357–76, pp. 657–64 specifically at pr. 375, p. 363). No doubt institutional practices are themselves a conspiracy amongst elites to regulate the sharing and exercise of power. But the absence of such practices could create problems that defy resolution.
9. R. Dhavan, *President's Rule in the States*, Bombay: N.M. Tripathi, 1979, 181.
10. R. Segal, *The Crisis of India*, London, 1963, has an insightful description comparing Nehru with Hamlet—a remark that drew stinging criticism when it was published.
11. There is no 'Nehru text' on law and development, but a powerful developmental approach is self-evident from the policies and laws of his regime. For a construction of his views see R. Dhavan, 'If I contradict myself, well, then, I contradict myself . . . Nehru, Law and Social Change' in R. Dhavan (ed.), *Nehru and the Constitution*, New Delhi: Indian Law Institute, 1992, pp. 45–62; and more generally R. Dhavan's long 'introduction' in the same volume, pp. (i)-(xcii).
12. In the very first year the Supreme Court agreed to a narrow due process clause (*Gopalan* v. *State of Madras*, AIR 1950 SC 27 over the dissent of Fazl Ali J.), struck down pre-publication censorships (*Brij Bhusan* v. *State of Delhi*, AIR 1950 SC 129; *Ramesh Thappar* v. *State of Madras*, AIR 1950 SC 124) and made a stray remark on educational opportunities for the backward classes (*State of Madras* v. *Champakam Doraijan*, AIR 1951 SC 226 and *Venkataramana* v. *State of Madras*, AIR 1951 SC 229). These along with various High Court decisions on zamindari (feudal landlord) abolition [which were later decided in appeal by the Supreme Court (see *State of Bihar* v. *Kameshwar Singh*, AIR 1952 SC 252)] led to the Constitution (First Amendment) Act 1951. Perhaps, as some judges suggested later, these amendments were not entirely necessary. But, it appears that the Supreme Court had bared a steely smile to which parliament responded with an overwhelming show of strength.
13. The right to property disputes led to significant decisions on zamindari abolition (*Kameshwar* v. *State of Bihar*, AIR 1952 SC 252), public purpose and compensation (*State of West Bengal* v. *Subodh Gopal*, AIR 1954 SC 92; *Dwarkadas* v. *Sholapur Spinnning and Weaving Mills*, AIR 1954 SC 119; and *State of West Bengal* v. *Bella Banerjee*, AIR 1954 SC 170). In fact, in the 1950s, after *Kameshwar's case* (supra), the Supreme Court did not strike down agrarian reform legislation (perhaps, because of parliament's

reaction), generally upheld regulatory state control measures and denied itself the power to strike down constitutional amendments (*Shankari Prasad* v. *Union of India*, AIR 1951 SC 458). For the best account of these controversies see H.C.L. Merrillat, 'Compensation for taking property—A historical footnote to Bella Banerjee's case' (1959) 1, *JILI*, 375 and more comprehensively H.C.L. Merrillat, *Land and the Constitution*, Bombay: N.M. Tripathi, 1970.

14. This story is set out in G. Austin, *Working a Democratic Constitution: The Indian Experience*, New Delhi: Oxford, 1999, at p. 134 on the threatened supercession and more generally on the Nehru government's record of interference with judicial appointments at pp. 123–42.
15. Nehru: Speech in the debate on the Constitution (First Amendment) Bill 1951 [see (1951)] *XII–XIII Parliamentary Debates* 8819-21 (16 May); see generally Alice Jacob: 'Nehru and the Judiciary', in R. Dhavan, *Nehru and the Constitution*, New Delhi: Indian Law Institute, 1992, pp. 63–76.
16. Chief Justice Patanjali Shastri in a speech after his retirement from the Supreme Court reported in AIR 1955, *Journal* 25.
17. The Supreme Court has diffused many a crisis, both in its advisory jurisdiction and otherwise, including the Kerala Education crisis of 1958 (Bill In Re *Kerala Education, 1957*, AIR 1958 SC 956); UP Judiciary-Legislature crisis in 1964 (Singh In Re *Keshav, Special Reference No. 1 of* 1964, AIR 1965 SC 745), Presidential Election crisis of 1974 (In Re *Presidential Poll* (1974) 2 *SCC* 33); Pakistan Border Dispute Crisis of 1960 (In Re *Berubari Union*, AIR 1960 SC 845), the uproar over 'reservations' by implementing the controversial Mandal Commission in 1992 (*Indra Sawhney* v. *Union of India*, 1992 Supp (3) SCC 212); Babri Masjid controversies (*Dr Ismail Faruqui* v. *Union of India* (1994) 6 SCC 360), Judicial appointments controversy in 1998 (In Re *Special Reference No. 1 of 1998* (1998) *7 SCC* 739), and the Gujarat Post Godhra Election Controversy (In Re *Special Reference No.1 of 2002* (2002) 8 SCC 237). All this is in addition to the many other controversies over ex-communication by religious leaders (*Syedna Tahir Saifuddin Saheb* v. *State of Bombay*, AIR 1962 SC 853; *Most Rev. P.M.A. Metropolitan* v. *Moran Marthoma*, 1995 Supp (4) SCC 286), or over cow slaughter (*Mohd. Hanif Qureshi v. State of Bihar*, AIR 1958 SC 731; *Abdul Hakim Qureshi* v. *State of Bihar*, AIR 1961 SC 448). No doubt, the Court has also been a source of controversy as, for example, in its controversial statements on the right to strike even if it diffused a major showdown between the Tamil Nadu Government and its civil servants in that state in 2003 (*T.K. Rangarajan* v. *Govt. of Tamil Nadu* 2003 (6) SCALE 84).
18. The role of courts as problem solvers is eclipsed by controversies over the courts as problem creators. This is an area that needs further elucidation to understand the Supreme Court's role as an institution of state and governance.

19. Earlier, there was simply a distinction between judges who supported the 'socialism' of the Constitution and those who resisted it. Thus the archetypical 'socialist' judge was Chief Justice Gajendragadkar and his alleged 'right-wing' antithesis Justice Subba Rao. The later 'right-wing' judges took care to wear their 'social justice' on their sleeve, emphatically by declaring adherence to the 'Directive Principles'. This was a smart move to obviate assertions that they were against the poor—see in this context K.S. Hegde's B.N. Rau Lectures on 'Directive Principles of State Policy' reprinted in (1971) 1 *Supreme Court Journal* 50 and his judgement with Justice Mukherjea in *Kesavananda* (infra n. 25) at prs. 712–6, pp. 502–3.
20. Despite the fact that the Constitution has neutralized the controversy over the 'compensation' to be paid for the acquisition of property, Justice Subba Rao revived this controversy in *Special Deputy Collector* v. *Vajravelu* AIR 1965 SC 1017). Later, Justice Hidayatullah who was a party to this decision explained that he had got confused over it, and another pre-amendment decision, in *State of Gujarat* v. *Shanti Lal*, AIR 1969 SC 634.
21. *Golak Nath* v. *State of Punjab*, AIR 1967 SC 1643, totally broke the complacency of the Indira Gandhi government with a 6:5 majority taking the view that constitutional amendments could be reviewed and declared unconstitutional by the Supreme Court. Apart from anything else, this raised the general question of who was supreme: a duly elected legislature or an elite judiciary? For some of the problems see R. Dhavan, *The Supreme Court and Parliamentary Sovereignty*, New Delhi: Sterling, 1976. Earlier Chief Justice Gajendragadkar presiding in *Sajjan Singh* v. *State of Rajasthan*, AIR 1966 SC 845 led a majority to thwart a judicial attempt to invalidate a constitutional amendment; on which see A.R. Blackshield: 'Fundamental Rights and the Institutional Viability of the Indian Supreme Court' (1966) 8, *JILI*, 139.
22. Broadly note the Bank Nationalization Case [*Rustom Cavasjee Cooper* v. *Union of India* (1970), 1 SCC 248]; the Privy Purses Case [*Madhav Rao Scindia* v. *Union of India* (1971) 1 SCC 85]; and the Newsprint case [*Bennett Coleman and Co.* v. *Union of India* (1972), 2 SCC 78].
23. There is a photograph in Justice Krishna Iyer's study showing Iyer with Nehru in a large tent with the latter wearing a sad and pensive expression. Krishna Iyer says that this was because Iyer had agreed to all the terms to avoid President's Rule; but Nehru had told him that he was helpless and that the decision lay with the then President of the Congress, Indira Gandhi. This was 1959, Mrs. Gandhi was not one to forget.
24. Too much concentration on the 'supercession' of judges in 1973 overlooks the fact that Mrs. Gandhi—on the advice of P.N. Haksar, Kumaramangalam and Gokhale (her Principal Secretary, the Minister of Petroleum and Chemicals and Law Minister respectively in her government)—was already 'packing' the court on which see further Granville Austin, *Working a Democratic Constitution* (supra n. 14), pp. 269–77.

25. *Keshavananda Bharati* v. *State of Kerala* (1973), 4 SCC 225. For critical reactions see S. Malik (ed.), *Fundamental Rights Case: The Critics Speak*, Lucknow: Eastern Book Co., 1975, anthologizing the lead articles; and contrast R. Dhavan, *The Supreme* Court *and Parliamentary Sovereignty* (supra n. 21), for a different view. For an account from the judges see P. Jagmohan Reddy, *The Judiciary I Served* (Hyderabad, Orient Longman, 1999), pp. 225–54; and more comprehensively G. Austin, *Working a Democratic Constitution* (supra n. 14), 258–77.
26. Justice Khanna was somewhat ambivalent in *Kesavananda* (supra n. 25) even though he signed the summary conclusions of nine judges in that case. But, his place in history comes from his dissent in the Preventive detention case in the Emergency (*ADM Jabalpur* v. *Shivkanta Shukla*, AIR 1976 SC 1207), in gratitude for which his portrait was installed by the Bar in Court 2 of the Supreme Court. Later Khanna accepted the post of Law Minister and Chairman of the Law Commission of India—somewhat to the peoples' dismay.
27. The 'committed' judges metaphor was circulated by Mohan Kumaramangalam whose speech in parliament was reproduced as a book entitled *Judicial Appointments*, Delhi: Oxford, IBH, 1973. See also the *Lok Sabha Debates* (*LSD*) in the Vth Series, Part 27, No. 46 col. 311–402 (2 May 1973), No. 45 col. 136–46 (26 April 1973); No. 43 col. 228–32 (27 April 1973). For a response see K. Nayar (ed.), *Supercession of Judges*, New Delhi: Indian Book Company 1973; N. Palkhivala (ed.), *A Judiciary Made to Measure* (Bombay, 1973), and K.S. Hegde, *Crisis in the Judiciary* (Delhi, 1973).
28. For the background and passage of the Constitution (42nd Amendment), Act 1976, see especially the summary of the debates in R. Dhavan: *Amendment or Conspiracy*, Allahabad, A.H. Wheeler, 1978, pp. 86–111. Taken to its logical conclusion, the Amendment would have enfeebled the judiciary necessitating correction by the Constitution (43rd Amendment), Act 1977 and Constitution (44th Amendment), Act 1979. Some of the effects of the amendments in respect of the judicial power lingered on. It was years later in 1997 that the Supreme Court restored the power of the High Courts over service cases [*L. Chandrakumar* v. *Union of India* (1997) 3 SCC 261].
29. Note Justice Bhagwati's comments on the return of the Janata government in the *Dissolution* case (*State of Rajasthan* v. *Union of India*, AIR 1977 SC 1361 at pr. 146, pp. 1416–17). This seems of the same genre as his letter to Prime Minister Indira Gandhi on 15 January 1980, following her return to power. At the time, I had written an article on this (see R. Dhavan: 'On the Future of Western Law in India: Reflections on Justice Bhagwati's Letter to the Prime Minister', 1980, mimeo) which I did not publish after due deference to Justice Bhagwati's wishes, that if published at that time would only add fuel to the fire.

30. The contempt notices were discharged (see In Re *Sham Lal* (1978), 2 SCC 479; In Re *S. Mulgaonkar* (1978), 3 SCC 399). I personally know from interviews with Justices Krishna Iyer, Bhagwati and Beg that there was a considerable behind-the-scenes activity to persuade Chief Justice Beg to withdraw the contempt notices which he did with some reluctance. For a legal analysis, see R. Dhavan and B.Singh: 'Publish and be damned: The Contempt Power and the Press at the Bar of the Supreme Court' (1979), 21 *JILI,* 1–30.
31. Thus Krishna Iyer quotes freely in *Fuzlunbi* v. *K. Khader Vali* (1980), 4 SCC 125, pr. 5 from Lord Denning's 'Introduction' to R. Dhavan: *Supreme Court of India* (supra n. 6), vii to claim the role of an architect not a plumber. On Krishna Iyer's contribution, see Hari Swaroop, *For Whom the Law is Made,* New Delhi: Veena, 1981; and for an analysis of his juristic contribution see K.M. Sharma: 'The judicial universe of Mr. Justice Krishna Iyer' in R. Dhavan et al. (ed.), *Judges and the Judicial Power: Essays in Honour of Justice V. Krishna Iyer,* London, Sweet and Maxwell, 1985, pp. 316–36.
32. There is a vast literature on public interest law. The first spontaneous reaction came from U. Baxi, 'Taking Suffering Seriously: Social Action Litigation in the Supreme Court', in R. Dhavan et al. (supra n. 31), pp. 289–315. The next phase is commented on in R. Dhavan: 'Law as Struggle: Public Interest Law in India' (1994), 36 *JILI,* 302. A decade later, public interest litigation cases were critically reviewed by Ashok Desai and S. Murlidhar: 'Public Interest Litigation: Potential and Problems' in B.N. Kripal et al. (ed.), *Supreme But Not Infallible: Essays in Honour of the Supreme Court of India,* New Delhi: Oxford University Press, 2000, pp. 159–92. For a collection of the Supreme Court and High Court decisions see the now dated S. Ahuja, *People, Law and Justice,* New Delhi, Orient Longman, 1997, in two volumes.
33. The power to review prerogative powers is now firmly established in respect of the imposition of President's Rule [see *S.R. Bommai* v. *Union of India,* (1994) 3 SCC 1, at prs. 364–83, pp. 261–73 specifically at prs. 373–5, pp. 266–9] Now even the Presidential power of pardon is subject to review [see *Kehar Singh* v. *Union of India* (1989), 1 SCC 204], *Swaran Singh* v. *State of UP* (1998), 4 SCC 75; *Satpal* v. *State of Haryana* (2000), 5 SCC 170.
34. The 'political question' doctrine was seen as a big hurdle to judicial intervention, but it was eclipsed in a serious of cases including [*Golak Nath* v. *State of Punjab* (supra n. 21), at prs. 154–7, pp. 1702–3]; the Dissolution case [*State of Rajasthan* v. *Union of India* (1977) 3 *SCC* at pr. 39, p. 616, pr. 131, pp. 644–5, pr. 149, pp. 660–2, pr. 150, pp. 662–3, pr. 183, p. 672 and pr. 208, p. 289.] and the Second Dissolution case [*S.R. Bommai* v. *Union of India* (1994)] 3 SCC 1 at prs. 97, pp. 112–115 (Kuldip Singh and Sawant JJ), pr. 202, pp. 178–9, pr. 204, p. 180, pr. 211, pp. 183–4, (Ramaswami J), pr. 258, p. 208, pr. 329, pp. 245–6 (*Jeevan*

Redy and Agrawal JJ). However, in the latter case some judges in varying degrees accepted the new concept of 'judicial manageability (see Justice Ahmadi at pr. 35, pp. 81–2, Justices Verma and Dayal, at prs. 40–5, p. 85, Justices Kuldip Singh and Sawant, prs. 98–100, pp. 115–16, Justices Jeevan Reddy and Agrawal, pr. 330, pp. 246–7 but cf. Justice Ramaswami, prs. 215–16, pp. 187–8) which they have borrowed from English law [*Puhlofer* v. *Hillingdon London Borough Council* (1986), 1 All ER 467] This begs the question: why is it not judicially manageable? Clearly, because it is a political question best left to politics than to judges.

35. The new due process was laid down in Maneka Gandhi's Passport case (*Maneka Gandhi* v. *Union of India* AIR 1978 SC 597) which drew from the Bank Nationalization case (supra n. 22). Gradually, due process was extended to criminal law and justice (On the new jurisprudence on the rights of prisoners see *D.B.M. Patnaik* v. *State of Andhra Pradesh* (1975) 3 SCC 135; *Sunil Batra* v. *Delhi Administration* (1980), 3 SCC 488; *Mohd. Ghiasuddin* v. *State of A.P.* (1977), 3 SCC 287; *Rama Murthy* v. *State of Karnataka* (1997), 2 SCC 642, including investigations by the police [*D.K. Basu* v. *State of West Bengal* (1997), 1 SCC 416; *Joginder Kumar Singh* v. *UP* (1994), 4 SCC 260]. In administrative cases, the new due process can be seen in various cases [*E.P. Royappa* v. *State of Tamil Nadu*, (1974), 4 SCC 3; *R.D. Shetty* v. *International Airports Authority of India* (1979), 3 SCC 489 and *Ajay Hasia* v. *Khalid Mujib* (1981), 1 SCC 722], even though these decisions of the court have been criticized (see T.R. Andhyrujina, *Judicial Activism and Constitutional Democracy*, Bombay, N.M. Tripathi 1992).

36. Although the judges generally take the view that public policy is an unruly horse [(*Gherulal Parekh* v. *Mahadeodas Maiyya*, AIR 1959 SC 781; *P. Rathinam v. Union of India* (1994), 3 SCC 394) and they are generally forbearing in their review of public policy (In Re *Delhi Laws Act*, 1912, AIR 1952 SC 332; *Alembic Chemicals Work* v. *Their Workmen*, AIR 1961 SC 647; *State of M.P.* v. *Nandlal Jaiswal* (1986), 4 *SCC* 566, pr. 34, p. 605; *Tata Cellular* v. *Union of India* (1994), 6 *SCC* 651; *Delhi Science Forum* v. *Union of India* (1996), 2 SCC 405, pr. 5, p. 412; *Association of Industrial Electricity Users* v. *State of A.P.* (2002), 3 SCC 711); *Kanishka Trading* v. *Union of India* (1995), 1 SCC 274; *Shriji Sales* v. *Union of India* (1997), 3 SCC 398; *G.B. Mahajan* v. *Jalgaon Municipal Council* (1991), 3 SCC 91, pr. 22, p. 104; *Pearless General Finance & Investment Co.* v. *R.B.I.* (1992), 2 SCC 243, pr. 31, p. 375; *Premium Granite* v. *State of Tamil Nadu* (1994), 2 SCC 691, pr. 54, p. 715; *Narmada Bachao Andolan* v. *Union of India* (2000), 10 SCC 664, pr. 229, p. 762).] Judicial policy is invariably inconsistent. Judges clearly support policies when they want to—under the guise of not interfering with them (*Balco Employees Union* v. *Union of India* (2002), 2 SCC 333).

37. See on bonded labour, health and environment, *Bandhua Mukti Morcha* v.

Union of India (infra n. 40); *Paschim Banga Khet Mazdor Samity* v. *State of West Bengal* (1996), 4 SCC 37; *Tarun Bharat Sangh* v. *Union of India*, 1992 Supp (2), SCC 448; *Tarun Bharat Sangh* v. *Union of India*, 1993 Supp (1), *SCC* 4; *Tarun Bharat Sangh* v. *Union of India*, 1992 Supp (2), SCC 750; *Tarun Bharat Sangh* v. *Union of India* (1995), 1 *SCC* 150; *Rural Litigation and Entitlement Kendra* v. *Union of India*, 1986 Supp SCC 517.

38. The imposition of Compressed Natural Gas (CNG), as a compulsory fuel for public transport was clearly a policy decision [See the various orders of the Supreme Court in the CNG Case—*M.C. Mehta* v. *Union of India*, (1999) 6 SCC 14; (2000) 9 SCC 519; (2001) 3 SCC 756; (2001) 3 SCC 763; (2002) 10 SCC 191; (2002) 4 SCC 356]. Much of the impetus for this came from the Centre for Science and Environment (CSE), which officially was not even allowed to intervene in the case.

39. Despite their massive interventions, judges constantly claim that they are merely following a law and correcting an imbalance [Justice A.M. Ahmadi 'Speech Delivered on the Occasion of Law Day' (1997), 2 SCC Journal 3; Justice A.S. Anand 'Public interest litigation as aid to protection of Human rights' (2001), 7 SCC Journal 1; Justice A.S. Anand 'Protection of Human rights—judicial obligation or judicial activism' (1997), 7 SCC Journal 11; Justice Dharamadhikari 'Nature of judicial process' (2002), 6 SCC Journal 1; Justice B.N. Kripal 'Environmental justice in India' (2002), 7 SCC Journal 1]. If this is so, public interest litigation will cease after the imbalance is corrected. But, perhaps, it will never be corrected. Such feigned innocence on the part of the judges does a disservice to what they have done and are doing, even if they prefer to take the stance that since they cannot tell a lie, they did not do it!

40. Thus, the original strategy was to concentrate on public interest litigation for the downtrodden [*Bandhua Mukti Morcha* v. *Union of India* (1984), 3 SCC 161; *Forward Construction Company* v. *Prabhat Mandal* (1986), 1 SCC 100; *M.C. Mehta* v. *Union of India* (*Oleum Gas Case*), (1987), 1 SCC 395; *People's Union for Democratic Rights* v. *Union of India* (1982), 3 SCC 235; Note also the Court for these origins of public interest litigation in *Janata Dal* v. *H.S. Chowdhary* (1992), 4 SCC 305], and atrocities by State functionaries (*Charles Sobhraj* v. *Supdt. Tihar Jail*, AIR 1978 SC 1514 (conditions of imprisonment of undertrials); *Hussainara Khatoon* v. *State of Bihar*, AIR 1979 SC 1360 (undertrials); *Kadra Pahadiya* v. *State of M.P.*, WP No. 8322 of 1981 (torture of young prisoners); *Munna* v. *State of U.P.*, AIR 1982 SC 806 (sexual exploitation of young children in jails); *Sheela Barse* v. *State of Maharashtra*, AIR 1983 SC 378 (custodial violence towards women prisoners); see also Justice P.N. Bhagwati, 'Judicial Activism and Public Interest Litigation' (1985), 23 *Columbia Journal of Transnational Law* 561.

41. Thus, the rules of locus standi were enlarged to allow any one with a

worthy cause to approach the court as long as they were bona fide in their pursuit [*Krishnaswami v. Union of India* (1992), 4 SCC 605; *S.P. Gupta* v. *Union of India* (infra n. 48); *Janata Dal* v. *H.S. Chowdhary* (supra n. 40); *Dr. Meera Massey* v. *Dr. Mehrotra* (1998), 3 SCC 98; *Bandhua Mukti Morch* v. *Union of India* (supra n. 40)].

42. The letter petition was a popular way to attract judicial attention [*R.K. Mishra* v. *State of Bihar*, AIR 1984 SC 547; *Sheela Barse* v. *Union of India* (1988), 4 SCC 226; *Sunil Batra* v. *Delhi Administration* (1980) 3 SCC 488; *Tushar Gandhi* v. *State of Orissa* (1997), 1 SCC 1; *Chhetriya Pradushan Mukti Sangharsh Samiti* v. *State of U.P.* (1990), 4 SCC 449; *State of H.P.* v. *Parent of a Student of Medical College* (1985), 3 SCC 169]. Even though the Supreme Court has now a procedure to deal with such petitions, it sometimes issues notice as in the CSE petition on bottled water and pesticides.

43. The power to appoint committees and commission is borrowed from the Civil Procedure Code, but enlarged for public interest cases [e.g. *Bandhua* (supra n. 40)]. To add to such committees and commissions comes the court's concept of a continuing mandamus through which it continues to monitor a case [e.g. *Vineet Narain* v. *Union of India* (1998), 1 SCC 226]. Some of the court's committees have become standing committees to advise the court [See the Bhurelal Committee in the CNG Case (supra n. 38) and even taking over the court's work (see the Central Empowered Committee in the Forest Case *T.N. Godavarman Thirumulkpad* v. *Union of India* (1998), 2 SCC 59 and (2002), 10 SCC 606].

44. The degree of inconsistency amongst judges is generally high; see generally R. Dhavan: *The Supreme Court of India* . . . (supra n. 6). In public interest litigation, these inconsistencies have increased.

45. For sharp criticism of the Supreme Court note see especially the views of Arun Shourie: *Courts and Their Judgements*, Delhi, Rupa and Co., 2001. Ironically, Shourie was a staunch supporter of public interest law (see A. Shourie: 'On why the Hon'ble Court Must Hear Us' (1981), 4 SCC (Journal), 1-30. Other criticisms from within the legal academy include S.K. Agarwala, *Public Interest Litigation: A Critique* (New Delhi 1981), and D.C. Jain, 'The Phantom of Public Interest' (1986), 3 SCC Journal, 30–7. But, a great deal of this criticism has died down, as lawyers, academics and judges try to come to grips with this new phenomenon—sometimes comprehensively but not always with perceptive subtlety (e.g. S.P. Sathe: *Judicial Activism in India*, New Delhi: Oxford University Press, 2002, to lose the wood for the trees.

46. The term social action litigation comes from U. Baxi: 'Taking Suffering Seriously . . .' (supra n. 32) and was adopted by Justice Bhagwati (supra n. 40). In some senses Bhagwati saw himself as leading a 'social movement'. While a judge, he had to have a 'village' and 'meeting halls' named after him!

47. Non-Governmental Organizations (NGOs), have taken over the initiatives of democracy in civil society to the point of excluding the voices of others. This is no less true of the 'take over of public interest law'. Following reports from Marc Galanter to the Ford Foundation in 1980–1, foreign funding agencies have poured huge funds into new and old NGOs to mobilize 'law' and social action. Despite some efforts (see the bibliography to M. Sidel's introductory essay: 'Recent Research Philanthropy and the non-profit sector in India and South Asia' (2001), 12 *Voluntas International Journal of Voluntary and Non Profit Organizations* 171; this area eludes systematic research. Some grassroot NGOs see courts as an institution trap which will imprison their dispute within its entrails, rather than liberate their cause into a renewed efficacy.
48. Through the three Judges cases of 1981, 1993 and 1998 [*S.P. Gupta* v. *Union of India*, 1981, SCC Supp 87; *Supreme Court Advocates-On-Record Association* v. *Union of India* (supra n. 8); *In Re Special Reference No. 1 of 1998* (supra n. 17)], the Supreme Court has totally hi-jacked control over judicial appointments to the higher judiciary, even though the text of the Constitution [Articles 124(2) and 217(1)], gave them only a consultative role. The High Courts already have control over appointments to the lower judiciary and its working (on which see Article 217 of the Constitution; and note in particular the various orders in the, *All India Judges Association* v. *Union of India* (1999), 5 SCC 185; *All India Judges Association* v. *Union of India* (2002), 4 SCC 247; *All India Judges Association* v. *Union of India* (1997), 8 SCC 520; *All India Judges Association* v. *Union of India* (1998), 3 SCC 34.
49. A comment made by Chief Justice Bharucha that one out of five judges in the lower judiciary were corrupt; see for comments on the Chief Justice's statement, P.P. Rao, 'The Judiciary', *The Hindu*, 15 May 2003; R. Dhavan, 'Transferred Justice', *The Hindu*, 28 November 2003.
50. Several in-house mechanisms have been tried, including appointing informal committee of Supreme Court judges (as was done in the case of Justice V. Ramaswamy whilst he was being impeached), leaving it to the good offices of the Chief Justice of India as was done in the case of the Bombay judges in 1994–5 (which proved to be successful), and the appointment of outside High Court judges to probe allegations as was done in 2001–2 in the case of allegations against the judges of Punjab and Karnataka (which failed to be effective). Clearly, the Supreme Court favoured some kind of informal response [see *C. Ravichandran Iyer* v. *A.M. Bhattacharjee* (1995), 5 SCC 457]. Eventually, some kind of machinery is required to both sustain judicial appointments through a 'national commission', as well as examine complaints against High Court and Supreme Court judges [on which see R. Dhavan, 'Removing Judges: The quest for fair solutions' (1991), 17 *Indian Bar Review* 42–57]. At last a National

Commission Bill 2003 has been tabled which gives the edge to politicians in the matter of appointments and seems to repose disciplinary powers in the same Commission which includes politicians.

51. The *Vohra Committee Report*, New Delhi, Government of India, mimeo 1993—made public in 1995, created a stir in parliament and shook public confidence in governance since it revealed the nexus of political power and money and muscle at all levels of governance. The Supreme Court case on the Vohra Committee (*Dinesh Trivedi* v. *Union of India* (1997), 4 SCC 306), led to an inconclusive judgement which reposed the problem back in the hands of the problem makers.
52. *Brown* v. *Board of Education* (1954), 347 US 483. For reactionary comments see H.H. Weschler: Neutral Principle of Constitutional Law (1959), 73 *Harvard L. Review* 1; ibid., *Principles, Law and Politics*, Cambridge: Cambridge University Press, 1961, and *R. Berger*: *Congress* v. *The Supreme Court*, Cambridge, Harvard University Press, 1969; ibid.: *Government by Judicary*: *The Transformation of the Fourteenth Amendment*, Cambridge: Harvard University Press, 1977, as illustrative comments. More generally see J. Agresto: *The Supreme Court and Constitutional Democracy* (New Delhi, Prentice Hall 1984, which examines the literature; cf. J. Ely: *Democray and Distrust: A Theory of Judicial Review* (Boston Harvard University Press, 1980, which sees judges as reinforcing the democratic process but not acting in substitute of it. American governance has become more used to the idea of the judiciary as an 'institution of governance' even though controversy abounds. Thus, there is clear acceptance—howsoever reluctant—of the transformation of the judiciary into a new constitutional incarnation.
53. I explore the idea of the India judiciary as an 'institution of governance' rather than a mere institution of state in R. Dhavan: 'Judges and Indian Democracy: The Lesser Evil' in Francine Frankel et al. (ed.) *Transforming India: Social and Political Dynamics of Democracy*, New Delhi: Oxford University Press, 2000, pp. 314–52.

3

Bill of Rights: Judicial Approach, Principles of Interpretation and Remedies—The Indian Experience

SOLI J. SORABJEE

INTRODUCTION

The Constitution of a State essentially reflects the aims and aspirations of the people who gave unto themselves the Constitution. A Bill of Rights is the conscience of the Constitution. An independent judiciary is its conscience keeper.

Neither the Constitution nor the Bill of Rights is a self-executing instrument. It is what the judges say it is. And whether the judiciary is the safeguard of our rights under the Constitution will depend upon its interpretation of the Constitution and, in particular, of the Bill of Rights. A most generous Bill of Rights can be reduced to a parchment of promises by narrow and insensitive judicial interpretation.

It is well to remember that the Constitution is not an ephemeral, legal document embodying a set of legal rules for the passing hour. It sets out 'principles for an expanding future'[1] and is 'intended to endure for ages to come and consequently to be adapted to the various crises of human affairs'.[2]

Therefore a purposive, rather than a strictly literal approach to the interpretation, should be adopted. 'A constitutional provision must be constructed, not in a narrow and constricted sense, but in a wide and liberal manner so as to anticipate and take account of changing conditions

*Published with author's permission from Soli J. Sorabjee (ed.), *Law and Justice: Anthology*, Delhi: Universal Law Publishing Co., 2003.

and purposes so that the constitutional provision does not get atrophied or fossilized but remains flexible enough to meet the newly emerging problems and challenges.'[3]

This principle of interpretation is particularly apposite to the interpretation of a Bill of Rights. It is a fallacy to regard a Bill of Rights as a gift from the State to its citizens. Individuals possess basic human rights independently of any Constitution, by reason of the basic fact that they are members of the human race. A Bill of Rights does not 'confer' fundamental human rights. It confirms their existence and accords them protection. Its very purpose is 'to withdraw certain subjects from the vicissitudes of political controversy, to place them beyond the reach of majorities and officials and to establish them as legal principles to be applied by the courts'.[4]

Consequently, 'a constitution, and in particular that part of it which protects and entrenches fundamental rights and freedoms to which all persons in the state are to be entitled, is to be given a generous and purposive construction'.[5] Courts should place 'a generous interpretation avoiding what has been called 'the austerity of tabulated legalism',[6] remembering that 'the letter killeth, but the spirit gives the life'.[7]

In construing the Hong Kong Bill of Rights, the Privy Council in *Lee Kwongkut's*[8] case has struck a note of warning. Lord Woolf speaking for the Judicial Committee whilst reaffirming the principles of construction of Bill of Rights enunciated in *Fisher*[9] and *Momodou Jobe*[10] observed that 'while the Hong Kong judiciary should be zealous in upholding an individual's rights under the Hong Kong Bill, it is also necessary to ensure that disputes as to the effect of the Bill are not allowed to get out of hand. The issues involving the Hong Kong Bill should be approached with realism and good sense, and kept in proportion.'[11] No one can quarrel with the prescription of realism and good sense so long as these observations made in the context of the Hong Kong legislature's effort to combat serious crime, are not regarded as a general prescription for undue judicial deference to the judgement of the executive.

INTERPRETATION OF FUNDAMENTAL RIGHTS

The Supreme Court of India has held that while considering the nature and content of fundamental rights the Court must not be too astute to interpret the language in so literal a sense as to whittle them down. The Court must interpret the Constitution in a manner which would enable the citizen to enjoy the rights guaranteed by it in the fullest measure.[12]

An instance of literal and narrow interpretation of a vital fundamental right in the Indian Constitution is the early decision of the Indian Supreme Court in the case of *A.K. Gopalan.*[13] Article 21 of the Constitution of India provides that 'no person shall be deprived of his life and personal liberty except according to procedure established by law.' The Supreme Court by a majority, held that 'procedure established by law' means any procedure established by law made by the Union Parliament or the legislatures of the States. It refused to infuse the procedure with principles of natural justice and concentrated solely upon the existence of enacted law.

It was after three decades that the Supreme Court overturned its previous decision in *Gopalan* and held in its landmark judgement in *Maneka Gandhi*[14] that the procedure contemplated by Article 21 must answer the test of reasonableness. It must be 'right, just and fair', and not arbitrary, fanciful or oppressive; otherwise, it would be no procedure at all and the requirements of Article 21 would not be satisfied. The Court further held that the procedure should also be in conformity with the principles of natural justice.

Based on this broad interpretation, Article 21 has been invoked in the case of numerous under-trials languishing in Indian jails, in which the Supreme Court ruled that 'speedy trial, and by speedy trial we mean reasonably expeditious trial, is an integral and essential part of the fundamental right to life and liberty enshrined in Article 21 and a procedure whereby under-trials remained in jail for periods longer than the maximum term for which they could have been sentenced if convicted, was not a fair, just and reasonable procedure'.[15] It was held that Article 21 was violated and these under-trials were ordered to be released.

There is no central legislation in India providing for legal aid. Perhaps by way of atonement for its previous niggardly treatment of Article 21 the Court construed it very liberally in the case of *Madhav Hoskot* v. *State of Maharashtra.*[16] It held that free legal services to the poor and needy is an essential element of any 'reasonable, fair and just' procedure and rules: '(1) Where the prisoner is disabled from engaging a lawyer, on reasonable grounds such as indigence or incommunicado situation, the court shall, if the circumstances of the case, the gravity of the sentence, and the ends of justice so require, assign competent counsel for the prisoner's defence, provided the party does not object to that lawyer; (2) The State which prosecuted the prisoner and set in motion the process which deprived him of his liberty shall pay to assigned counsel such sum as the court may equitably fix.'[17]

The most significant instance of expansive interpretation of a fundamental right is the decision in *Francis Coralie* v. *Union Territory of Delhi.*[18] The Court held that the expression 'life' in Article 21 does not connote merely physical or animal existence but embraces something more. 'We think that the right to life includes the right to live with human dignity and all that goes along with it, namely, the bare necessaries of life such as adequate nutrition, clothing and shelter over the head.' On the basis of this interpretation the Court ruled that a prisoner 'as part of the right to live with human dignity and therefore as a necessary component of the right to life, would be entitled to have interviews with the members of his family and friends, and no prison regulation or procedure laid down by prison regulation regulating the right to have interviews with the members of the family and friends can be upheld as constitutionally valid unless it is reasonable, fair and just'.[19]

A highly controversial issue is whether a Court can, in construing a Bill of Rights, deduce fundamental rights which are not expressly set out in the Constitution. In the United States of America, rights of privacy and parenthood have been deduced on the basis that the specific guarantees in the Bill of Rights 'have penumbras formed by emanations from those guarantees that help give them life and substance'.[20] A similar approach has been adopted by Irish Courts in the Republic which have held that 'the Constitution guarantees various other rights which are not expressly referred to or are obviously a part of the expressly referred to rights'. These additional rights have been termed 'unspecified' or 'unenumerated' rights.[21]

The Indian judiciary has deduced fundamental rights which are not specifically mentioned in the Chapter on Fundamental Rights, on the principle that certain unarticulated rights are implicit in the enumerated guarantees. For example, in several decisions of the Supreme Court, freedom of the press has been held to be implicit in the guarantee of freedom of speech and expression.[22] In India there is no legislation securing freedom of information. The Supreme Court by a liberal interpretation deduced the right to know and the right to access to information, on the reasoning that 'the concept of an open government is the direct emanation from the right to know which seems to be implicit in the right of the free speech and expression guaranteed under Article 19(1)(a)'.[23]

The right to travel abroad has been spelt out from the expression 'personal liberty' in Article 21 of the Constitution.[24] Although there is no specific provision in the Constitution prohibiting cruel, inhuman and degrading punishment or treatment, the Court has evolved this right, by its expansive interpretation of Article 21, which protects the right to life, in conjunction with Article 14 which prohibits discrimination and arbitrary action.[25] In a recent landmark judgement, the Court has ruled that the right to education until the age of fourteen, is a fundamental right the emanating from the all-pervasive Article 21.[26]

No fundamental right can be absolute. Every Constitution provides for regulation and restriction of fundamental rights in the general interest and welfare of society. The crux of the problem is that the restriction imposed should not be unnecessary or excessive and disproportionate. In determining this issue judicial subjectivity is bound to play a part. But that surely is no ground for declining or unduly restricting judicial review. The Indian Supreme Court in the celebrated case of *State of Madras* v. *V. C. Rao*[27] acknowledged that 'it is inevitable that the social philosophy and the scale of values of the judges participating in the decision should play an important part, and the limit to their interference with legislative judgement in such cases can only be dictated by their sense of responsibility and self-restraint and the sobering reflection that the Constitution is meant not only for people of their way of thinking but for all, and that the majority of the elected representatives of the people have, in authorizing the imposition of the restrictions, considered them to be reasonable.'

The Court at the same time emphasized that if the legislation in question violated a fundamental right it would have to be struck down 'in discharge of a duty plainly laid upon them by the Constitution. This is especially true as regards the "fundamental rights", as to which this Court has been assigned the role of a sentinel on the *qui vive*.'[28]

A well settled principle of constitutional adjudication is to construe the statute in a manner as will save it from constitutional challenge. Courts in the USA have in a long series of decisions acted on this principle. In the words of Mr. Chief Justice Taft, 'it is our duty in the interpretation of federal statutes to reach a conclusion which will avoid serious doubt of their constitutionality'.[29]

The Supreme Court of India has also adopted the same principle when considering the constitutionality of a statute. In some cases the Court has *read into* a statutory provision qualifying words and expressions in order to sustain its validity. A glaring instance is its decision in

R.M.D.C. v. *Union of India.*[30] The definition of 'prize competition' in the statute was wide and unqualified, and there was nothing in the wording of it which limited it to competitions in which success depended on exercise of skill as distinct from those which depended on chance. The provision was challenged on the ground that it unreasonably restricted the fundamental right of trade and business. It was conceded by the counsel for the State that the restrictions contained in the Act could not be upheld in respect of competitions which were not in the nature of gambling and involved substantial skill. The Court in order to sustain the constitutionality of the statute read into the definition the words 'only those competitions in which success does not depend on any substantial degree on skill'.[31]

In *Tinsukhia Electric Supply* v. *State of Assam*[32] the Supreme Court read into the provisions of the Act several requirements and thereby repelled the challenge of constitutionality. In a recent decision in *Kartar Singh* v. *State of Punjab*[33] where the Court had to deal with the constitutional challenge to a draconian piece of legislation, Terrorist and Disruptive Activities (Prevention) Act 1987 (TADA), the Court read into the definition of the expression 'abet' the words: 'with the actual knowledge or reason to believe'.[34]

In more than one case the Supreme Court of India has also *read down* the wide and unqualified language of a statute, limiting it to certain categories of persons or activities on the principle that 'it is well settled that if certain provisions of law construed in one way would make them consistent with the Constitution, and another interpretation would render them unconstitutional, the Court would lean in favour of the former construction'.[35]

The judicial technique of reading down, or reading into a constitutional or statutory provision is not permissible where the intention of the legislature is clear and manifest and the language is unambiguous and intractable. In such cases it would not be permissible to either read into, or read down, the statutory provision in question.[36]

It is a sound principle that restrictions on fundamental rights should be narrowly construed and should not be enlarged inferentially or by implication beyond the heads of restriction specified in the Constitution. Article 19(2) of the Indian Constitution set out specific heads of restrictions which may be imposed on the exercise of freedom of expression. The head of 'interests of the general public' which is specified in regard to other fundamental rights is not mentioned in Article 19(2). The Supreme Court rejected the plea that press freedom in that case could be restricted on the ground that the restriction imposed in that case was in the interests of the general public because, 'the only restriction which may be imposed on the rights of an individual under Article 19(1)(a) are those which clause (2) of Article 19 permits and no other'.[37]

The Court also emphasized that in considering the nature of the restrictions in construing the Constitution it is the substance and the practical result of the act of the State that should be considered rather than its purely legal aspect. The correct approach in such cases should be to enquire as to what in substance is the loss or injury caused to the citizen, and not merely what manner and method has been adopted by the State in placing the restrictions.[38]

If the restrictions imposed are unreasonable, a reasonable manner of administering the statute is immaterial. The constitutional validity of the statute would have to be determined on the basis of its provisions and on the ambit of its operation, properly construed.[39]

On whom does the burden lie, of proving that the restriction imposed on the exercise of fundamental rights is unreasonable and therefore the statute is unconstitutional?

On first principles the initial burden would lie on the party assailing the constitutionality of the statute in whose favour there is a presumption of constitutionality. After a prima facie case is made out by placing credible, factual and legal materials, the burden shifts to the State which must place materials before the Court to bring the legislation within the prescribed permissible limits.[40] The European Court on Human Rights at Strasbourg has ruled that the necessity for any restrictions on fundamental rights 'must be convincingly established'.[41]

Utmost judicial vigilance is necessary with regard to restraints on freedom of expression and personal liberty. Experience has shown that these basic human rights are the frequent and favourite targets of attack by authoritarian regimes and their suppression enables the regime to proscribe debate and discussion, eliminate the dissenter, jettison accountability, and ensure the government's continuance in office.

As pointed out by the Privy Council in *Hector*'s case[42] 'in a free democratic society it is almost too obvious to need stating that those who hold office in government and who are responsible for public administration must always be open to criticism. Any attempt to stifle or fetter such criticism amounts to political censorship of the most insidious and objectionable kind.' Therefore, any statutory provision which criminalizes statements likely to undermine public confidence in the conduct of public affairs must be viewed with the utmost suspicion.[43] The Indian Supreme Court has emphasized that the voicing of a contrary opinion is a powerful and wholesome weapon in the democratic reportoire.[44]

Preventive detention is anathema to the Rule of Law. A person is deprived of his liberty not by way of punishment for his acts, but on suspicion of the likelihood of his committing acts in the future which are detrimental to public peace and order. This can be tolerated only as a necessary evil in times of war or other grave national emergencies.

Consequently detention orders should receive strict judicial scrutiny. There must be meticulous compliance with all the procedural requirements for the passing of a detention order. Courts in India have quashed detention orders which are not in strict conformity with constitutional and statutory procedural requirements and released the detainees, uninfluenced by the gravity and magnitude of their alleged illegal activities.[45]

Again there should not be undue deference to the subjective satisfaction of the detaining authority. The satisfaction must be grounded on materials which are of rationally probative value. The grounds on which the satisfaction is based, must be such as a rational human being can consider, connected with the fact in respect of which the satisfaction is to be reached. They must be relevant to the subject matter of the inquiry and must not be extraneous to the scope and purpose of the statute. No relevant factor should be omitted from consideration and there should be full application of mind to the factors enjoined by the statute.[46]

The most serious violations of human rights occur during emergencies. The usual explanation offered is that fundamental rights are required to be suspended temporarily in order that the nation may survive. Theoretically this is unexceptionable. But actual experience establishes that those to whom supreme authority has been confided are reluctant to give it up. Temporary dictatorship often becomes a permanent tyranny because when the safeguards of the Constitution are surrendered to the rulers, the means of getting them back have been also surrendered.

Judicial protection is most needed during emergencies. Judicial review can be legitimately exercised to determine whether the constitutional pre-requisites for declaration of emergency were satisfied, and also whether continuance of emergency after the disappearance of conditions which occasioned its promulgation is mala fide and a fraud on the Constitution. The erstwhile doctrine that these issues are totally non-justiciable is outdated and cannot hold good. The general judicial trend is in favour of reviewability of declarations of emergency, albeit on limited grounds. The human rights jurisprudence developed by the European Commission and the European Court of Human Rights functioning under the European Convention on Human Rights (ECHR) at Strasbourg has established that the existence of a 'public emergency threatening the life of the nation' is a justiciable issue.[47] The Inter-American Commission at San Jose functioning under the American Convention on Human Rights, 1969, has asserted its authority to consider the validity of declaration of emergency by analysing whether the circumstances warranted such a declaration.[48]

In the *Minerva Mills* case, Justice Bhagwati in his minority judgement has clearly held that 'a proclamation of emergency is undoubtedly amenable to judicial review though on the limited ground that no satisfaction as required by Article 352 was arrived at by the President in law or that the satisfaction was absurd or perverse or mala fide or based on an extraneous or irrelevant ground.'[49] The majority judgement has not dissented from this view nor expressed any reservations about it.

Rights without remedies are useless. A mere declaration of invalidity of a detention order, or seizure of the press or revocation of a licence to carry on a business, would not provide a meaningful remedy to a person where fundamental rights have been violated. To drive such a person to adopt separate proceedings for recovery of damages would be onerous. The Court which has found violation of a fundamental right would be the most appropriate forum for giving compensatory relief. In some Constitutions there is a provision for award of compensation to victims of unlawful arrest or detention. What is the position when there is no such provision? Although the Indian Constitution contains no provision for awarding compensation for infringement of a person's fundamental right, the Supreme Court has, in some cases, ordered compensation by the State.[50] In a recent case of custodial death, the Court emphasized that the compensation awarded by it was not to be equated with damages in a civil action, but was grant of relief under public law 'for the wrong done due to breach of public duty of not protecting the fundamental rights of the citizen'.[51] It was clarified that the sum awarded would be adjusted, if other proceedings are taken for recovery of compensation on the same ground so as to prevent payment twice over.[52]

In principle, there is no reason why compensation should not be awarded in cases of violations of fundamental rights other than life or personal liberty. A person whose restaurant licence has been unconstitutionally cancelled or whose freedom of expression has been infringed by a patently illegal ban on his book or play should also be entitled to compensation for the injury caused.

The Sri Lankan judiciary has awarded monetary compensation in cases where fundamental rights of freedom of expression and association, in addition to personal liberty have been violated. In one case, instead of making the State pay—which in reality means the tax payer—personal liability for payment was fixed on the offending official.[53]

The most notable achievement in the protection and promotion of fundamental rights has been by development of Public Interest Litigation (PIL) in India. PIL is a form of legal proceedings in which redress is sought in respect of injury to the public in general, and for the enforcement of the rights of a determinate class or group of people directly injured by the act or omission complained of, but who are unable to approach the court on account of indigence, illiteracy or social or economic disabilities. For example, prisoners or inmates of care centres or mental homes or landless labourers. In view of these harsh realities, the Supreme Court has departed from the traditional requirement of locus standi and, in its landmark judgement in *Gupta*'s case,[54] declared that where judicial redress is sought for legal injury to disadvantaged persons, any member of the public acting bona fide and not for oblique considerations, can maintain an action on their behalf. The Court has forged new tools, devised new methods and adopted new strategies. For example, it has appointed commissions for the purpose of gathering facts and data in regard to a complaint of breach of fundamental rights. It has sometimes appointed a district magistrate, or a district judge, sometimes a professor of law, and at times, a practising advocate for the purpose of carrying out an inquiry and making a report to the court.[55] The Supreme Court also adopted the practice of treating letters and telegrams addressed to it as writ petitions and acting upon them. This has been described as the Court's 'epistolary jurisdiction'.

Thanks to PIL, enjoyment of fundamental rights has become a living reality, to some extent, for at least some illiterate, indigent and exploited Indians. Numerous prisoners languishing in prisons awaiting trial have been released;[56] persons treated like 'serfs' and held in bondage have secured freedom and have been rehabilitated;[57] conditions of inmates in care homes and in asylums for the insane,[58] and of workers in stone quarries and brick kilns,[59] have been ameliorated. Juristic activism in the arena of environmental and ecological issues,[60] and accountability in the use of the hazardous technology, has been made possible and has yielded salutary results.[61]

No doubt there can be problems with PIL. It can be abused, it can add to the burden of arrears, and in some cases lead to confrontation with the executive. An activist court will need to move in the area of PIL with tact and circumspection to secure public acceptability and official acceptance and cooperative implementation of the orders and directives passed by the court. However, in a society where freedoms suffer from atrophy and activism is essential, some risks have to be taken.

CONCLUSION

Judicial review is a very delicate exercise and can also cause problems. Besides, in countries where fundamental rights are being widely violated every day, whether in flouting of labour laws, illegal detentions, discriminatory actions, and other violations, a cynic may well question its utility. The answer is that it empowers citizens and groups fighting for justice to approach the court and provides opportunities for vindicating the Rule of Law. It also establishes norms and standards which can be used to educate people to know, demand, and enforce their basic rights. It has a salutary effect on administration which knows that it has to conform to the discipline of fundamental rights. Above all, a Bill of Rights is a constant reminder that the powers of the State are not unlimited and that human personality is priceless.

NOTES

1. Cardozo, *Nature of the Judicial Process.*
2. *M'Culloch* v. *Maryland,* 4 L.Ed. 579, 603.
3. *Francis Coralie* v. *Union Territory of Delhi,* AIR 1981 SC 746, 752.
4. *West Virginia State Board of Education* v. *Barnette,* 87 L.Ed. 1628, 1638.
5. *Atorney General of the Gambia* v. *Momodou Jobe* [1984] A.C. 689, 700; *Attorney General of Hong Kong* v. *Lee Kwong-kut (P.C)*, [1993] 3 W. L. R., 329, 338.
6. *Minister of Home Affairs* v. *Fisher* [1980], A.C., 319, 328.
7. *People* (D.P.P.) v. *O'Shea* [1982], I.R.384, 426 Henchy J dissenting.
8. See *Hong Kong* case, supra n. 5.

9. Supra n. 6.
10. Supra n. 5.
11. Ibid., at 346.
12. *Sakal Papers* v. *Union of India*, AIR 1962 SC 305, 311.
13. AIR 1950 SC 27.
14. AIR 1978 SC 597.
15. *Hussainara Khatoon* v. *Home Secretary, Bihar*, AIR 1979 SC 1360; 1369.
16. AIR 1978 SC 1548.
17. Ibid., at 1557.
18. Supra n. 3.
19. Ibid., at 753.
20. *Griswold* v. *Connecticut*, 381 US 479.
21. Michael Forde, *Constitutional Law of Ireland* 264 (1987); generally *Kelly, The Irish Constitution*, pp. 756–8 (3rd edn. 1994).
22. *Brij Bhusan* v. *State of Delhi*, AIR 1950 SC 129; *Bennett Coleman & Co.* v. *UOI*, AIR 1973 SC 106; *Indian Express Newspapers* v. *UOI*, AIR 1986 SC 515.
23. *S.P. Gupta* v. *Union of India*, AIR 1982 SC 149, 232–3.
24. *Satwant Singh* v. *Union of India*, AIR 1967 SC 1836.
25. *Sunil Batra* v. *Delhi Administration* (1978), 4 SCC 494.
26. *Unni Krishnan* v. *State of Andhra Pradesh*, 1993 1 SCC 645.
27. AIR 1952 SC 196, 200.
28. Ibid., at 199.
29. *Richmond* v. *U.S.*, 72 L.Ed.303; *U.S.* v. *Rumby*, 97 L.Ed. 770, 775.
30. 1957 SCR 930.
31. Ibid., at 939.
32. (1989) 3 SCC 709, 755.
33. (1994) 3 SCG 569.
34. Ibid., at 649, 712.
35. *Kedar Nath* v. *State of Bihar* (1962) Supp 2 SCR 769; *Shah & Co.* v. *Maharashtra* (1967) 3 SCR 466; *Jagdish Pandey* v. *Chancellor, University of Bihar*, AIR 1968 SC 353, 357; *N.C. Dalwadi* v. *State of Gujarat*, AIR 1989 SC 1933; *Charan Lal Sahu* v. *Union of India*, AIR 1990 SC 1480.
36. *Minerva Mills* v. *Union of India*, AIR 1980 SC 1789, 1809 para 68; *Delhi Transport Corporation* v. *DTC Mazdoor Congress*, AIR 1991 SC 101, 180, 203 para 274.
37. Supra n. 12 at 315.
38. Ibid., at 311.
39. *Collector of Customs* v. *N.S. Chetty*, AIR 1962 SC 316, 331–2; *Kantilal Babulal* v. *H.C. Patel*, AIR 1968 SC 445.
40. *Saghir Ahmed* v. *State of Uttar Pradesh*, AIR 1954 SC 728; *Kheyerbari Tea* v. *State of Assam*, AIR 1994 SC 925; *Wrajlal Manilal & Co.* v. *State of Madhya Pradesh*, AIR 1970 SC 129.

41. *Observer and Guardian* v. *United Kingdom* (1992), 14 EHRR 153 at para 59; *Thorgeirson* v. *Iceland* (1992), 14 EHRR 843 at para 63.
42. [1990] 2 All ER 103.
43. Ibid., at 106.
44. *Ram Bahadur Rai* v. *State of Bihar*, AIR 1975 SC 223.
45. *Prabhu Dayal* v. *D.M. Kamrup*, AIR 1974 SC 183; *Icchu Devi* v. *Union of India*, AIR 1980 SC 1983; *Vijay Narain Singh* v. *State of Bihar* (1984), 3 SCC 14; *Hem Lal Bhandari* v. *State of Sikkim* (1987), 2 SCC 9; *Mohinuddin* v. *D.M.* (1987), 4 SCC 58, 63.
46. *Khudiram* v. *State of West Bengal*, AIR 1975 SC 550, 557.
47. *Lawless* case, 1 EHRR; *Greek* case, 1969 Year Book ECHR 1; *Ireland* v. *UK*, 1978 (2), EHRR 25.
48. Report on the Situation of Human Rights in the Republic of Columbia, OEA/Ser.LV/11.53, doc. 22, 3 June 1981; Report on the Situation of Human Rights in the Republic of Bolivia, OEA/Ser. L/V/11.53, doc. 6, 1 July 1981; Report on the Situation of Human Rights of a Segment of the Nicaraguan Population of Miskito Origin, OEA/Ser. L/V/II 1.62, doc. 10 rev. 3, 29 November 1983.
49. (1980) 3 SCC 625, 693–4.
50. *Rudal Sah* v. *State of Bihar* (1983), 4 SCC 141; *Sebastian M. Hongray* v. *Union of India* (1984), 1 SCC 339; *Sebastian M. Hongray* v. *Union of India* (1984), 3 SCC 82; *Bhim Singh* v. *State of J & K* (1984), Supp SCC 504; *Bhim Singh* v. *State of J & K* (1985), 4 SCC 677; *Saheli: A Women's Resources Centre* v. *Commissioner of Police, Delhi Police Headquarters* (1990), 1 SCC 422, *State of Maharashtra* v. *Ravi Kant S. Patil* (1991), 2 SCC 373.
51. *Nilabati Behera*, AIR 1993 SC 1960, 1969 per Verma J.
52. Ibid., at 1970.
53. *Ratanasara Thero* v. *Udugampola* (1983), 1 Sri Lanka Law Reports 461; *V. Amaratunga* v. *Sirimal*, SC. App. No. 468/92, decided on 6 March 1993, 5–6, quoting *De Jonge* v. *State of Oregon*, 299 US 353 (1937).
54. Supra n. 23.
55. *Bandhua Mukti Morcha* v. *Union of India* (1984), 3 SCC 161, 189, 190–1.
56. Supra n. 15.
57. Supra n. 55.
58. *Veena Sethi* v. *State of Bihar* (1982), 2 SCC 583; *Vikram Dev Singh Tomar* v. *State of Bihar* (1988), Supp SCC 734, 736.
59. Supra n. 55.
60. *M.C. Mehta* v. *Union of India* (1987), 4 SCC 463.
61. *M.C. Mehta* v. *Union of India* AIR 1987 SC 1086.

4

Inconclusive Overview of Judicial Activism in India

MAHENDRA PAL SINGH

JUDICIAL ACTIVISM

There may be different versions of judicial activism in legal literature but, to me it comes into play, when courts do not confine themselves to adjudication of legal conflicts, but venture out to make social policies, affecting many more people and interests than the ones that would have been affected, had they confined themselves to the resolution of narrow disputes before them. The judges who believe that it is legitimate for them to formulate social policy are called judicial activists; the others who would confine the judiciary to the task of applying to specific case laws and regulations made by the other or political branches of the government are known as advocates of judicial restraint. The heart of the issue between the two is the proper relationship between the courts on the one hand, and the legislature and administration on the other. The activism of a court may, thus, be measured by the degree of power that it exercises over citizens, the legislature, and the administration.[1]

Judges all around the world must have always been exercising that power in some measure ever since they undertook the responsibility of judging. But such an exercise of power was not noticed for a long time.

*This paper is a revised and updated version of a lecture delivered at Waseda University, Tokyo in June 2002, and published in 5 *Waseda Proceedings of Comparative Law 72*. I thank Swati and Surya Deva in helping me in the revision of the paper.

It was not noticed because the judges themselves disclaimed any power of making the law and if they ever did, as Chief Justice Coke is alleged to have attempted, they were restrained or snubbed on the ground that their job was to apply and not to make the law.[2] Before the establishment of democracy, lawmaking was within the domain of the ruler or his agents while in democracy it came within the domain of a representative body such as parliament. Logically, if the people were to be ruled by a government freely elected by them, the task of law making could not be assigned to the non-elected judges. The establishment of constitutional democracies, starting with the Constitution of the United States, however, changed this logic. The constitution laid down certain limitations within which alone, the elected government must act. In case of a dispute somebody had to decide whether those limits were exceeded. That task was assigned to the courts. Any doubts in this regard were removed by that legendary judge, Chief Justice Marshall, in *Marbury* v. *Madison*[3] as far back as 1803. Time has settled all doubts about *Marbury* v. *Madison* in its favour. Now in all democracies, including to some extent the United Kingdom, the courts perform the function of determining whether the other branches of the government have crossed the limits set for them.

Such limits may be set in several ways such as by the separation of powers between different branches of government, division of powers between the general and the regional governments, and denial of power to the government about certain matters, prominently the basic rights of the individual. The courts in the United States and other countries have been performing the job of keeping different branches of the government within these limits. In some countries like the United States, Canada and Australia, they have played an important role in determining the limits of respective powers of the general and the regional governments. Quite often they have been credited or discredited for certain developments in the relations between the two governments. Equally but less often, they have also resolved the disputes between the executive and the legislature about the extent of their powers. Sometimes they have also declined to intervene in such disputes for the same reason for which they are brought before them, i.e. the separation of powers.

But the limitation of basic rights has become the most important subject since World War II. Even in the United States the basic rights remained almost dormant until the beginning of the twentieth century, coming into full bloom only after 1950s. Even though, as already observed, the Supreme Court of the United States was exercising the power of judicial review since 1803, perhaps excepting *Dred Scott* v. *Sandford*[4] in 1857 and *Plessy* v. *Ferguson*[5] in 1896, it also started exercising this power in relation to the basic rights after the advent of the twentieth century, though not so intensely until 1945 or thereafter. Some of these cases like *Lochner* v. *New York*[6] exclusively under the due process clause of the bill of rights, and some others in association with other limitations like the separation of powers stirred the American society, compelling it to propose drastic changes in the composition of the Supreme Court. This exercise of power by the Court was termed as judicial activism. But apparently the term judicial activism was coined only after World War II, particularly after Warren Court's decisions starting with, *Brown* v. *Board* of Education.[7] While in Lochner and other cases until the end of 1930s, the Court was propagating a conservative ideology of freedom of contract for the employer and the industry, the Brown and post-Brown Court was propagating a welfare social policy of equal rights for all. That is, in both cases the judges conceived a particular model of society under the Constitution. Any legislative or executive action that was not consistent with that model was seen unconstitutional. In this exercise the Court has almost as many supporters as critics. But supporters have an upper hand because it is now universally recognized that the judges not only apply, but also make law and, secondly, the democratic model is subject to certain values enshrined in the Constitution. Therefore, the debate about judicial activism is not so much about its existence or non-existence as about its modalities and parameters. In the early part of the nineteenth century, judges were influenced by the positivist approach to law propounded by Bentham and Austin. But in the later half of the nineteenth century, already the sociological and realist schools of jurisprudence which taught that judges not only interpret but also make law had started emerging. The constantly shifting law crafted by judges, they said, reflected society's ever-changing needs. By definition, say the realists, there can be no conflict between social utility and law. Consequently by 1890, the judges were heavily influenced by the sociological school and rendered a pattern of decisions, best exemplified by *Lochner*, in which it invalidated scores of state and federal laws regulating business, such as the minimum wage, maximum working hours and child labour laws, on the ground that they would be harmful for the country and its economy and values. The first activist justices were political conservatives, attempting to preserve economic freedom. This was the period up to the end of the 1930s. The period from the end of the 1930s onwards has, however, been a period of left activism. The conventional wisdom that John Marshall was the first activist Supreme Court Justice is not necessarily true. Judicial activism is clearly the product of the doctrines of legal positivism, historicism, and sociological jurisprudence, each of which seized intellectuals in the United States long after Marshall's death (and whose seeds cannot be found in the opinions of the Marshall Court). Activism emerges when judges no longer feel restrained by the law, and it has captured the imagination of judges on both the right and the left of the political spectrum over time.

SOME FINDINGS ABOUT JUDICIAL ACTIVISM

From a comparative study of judicial activism in eleven countries, namely, the United States, England, Canada, Australia, Israel, Italy, France, Germany, Sweden, Japan and the Soviet Union conducted in 1989, Kenneth Holland has drawn the following seven points:[8]

Firstly, judicial activism is a phenomenon distinct from judicial review. Judicial review is expressly provided for in the Japanese Constitution, but the Japanese Supreme Court has rarely invalidated a law of the Diet. Secondly, judicial activism, generally speaking, serves the ends of liberalism. Among others, the Japanese Court has invalidated laws based on Confucianism, such as a patricide law that made murder of a parent a more serious crime than homicide involving a sibling, child, or non-relative.[9] Thirdly, civic education is a prominent non-adjudicative function often performed by courts. Fourthly, the most activist courts display a penchant for a higher law, eschewing legal positivism—that law is the will of the sovereign backed by force. Fifthly, the judicial activism tends to erode both the parliamentary system and majoritarian democracy. Sixthly, the courts are playing an active role not only in constitutional cases, but in review of administrative decisions as well. And seventh, the activism of the U.S. Supreme Court has been both an inspiration and an admonition for the leaders and the jurists of other countries. Courts in countries as disparate as Italy and Japan still frequently cite *Marbury* v. *Madison*.

On the basis of the same study, Holland has also drawn a list of conditions conducive to judicial activism. Certain structural and intellectual conditions seem to make more likely the emergence of an activist judiciary. Among the structural features associated with judicial activism are federalism, a written constitution, judicial independence, absence of separate administrative courts, a competitive political party system, and generous rules of access to the courts. Certain traditions, doctrines and ideas can also galvanize the courts: the common law tradition, the concept of limited government, high esteem for judges, and a social consensus on fundamental regime questions. I proceed to examine the judicial activism in India in the light of some of the above conditions.

CONDITIONS CONDUCIVE TO JUDICIAL ACTIVISM IN INDIA

1. *Written Constitution*

It need hardly be said that not only is the Constitution of India written, it is also the lengthiest constitution in the world. It provides for a federal structure with division of powers between the Union and the States. It includes a detailed bill of rights along with directive principles of state policy and fundamental duties. The basic values of the Constitution are expressed in its preamble, the fundamental rights, directive principles of state policy and some other provisions for the protection of the interests of the weaker sections of society and minorities.[10] All organs of the state including the judiciary are expected to act towards the realization of constitutional goals and values.

2. *Judicial Review*

The Constitution of India does not expressly provide for judicial review except to the extent that in matters of fundamental rights the Supreme Court of India and the High Courts can be approached for their enforcement, and that any law abridging them shall be unconstitutional.[11] But it has always been assumed and accepted without any doubt that any law or executive action contrary to the Constitution is null and void and can be so declared by the courts. The Courts have been exercising the power of judicial review since the very first constitutional dispute brought before them. The other branches of the government, however, did not always approve the exercise of judicial review. Therefore, they often amended the Constitution to curtail, at times drastically, the scope of judicial review and to nullify the effect of Court decisions. In *Golak Nath* v. *State of Punjab*,[12] the Supreme Court stemmed this process in 1967 by holding that any amendment of the Constitution abridging the fundamental rights was impermissible and unconstitutional. Later, in 1973, in *Keshavananda Bharati* v. *State of Kerala*,[13] the Court overruled *Golak Nath* but laid down a broader limitation on the power of amendment of the Constitution, by holding that the basic structure of the Constitution or its essential features could not be amended in the exercise of that power. It also invalidated a provision of an amendment, which denied the power of judicial review in a specific matter. Later, the Court expressly held that judicial review is one of the essential features of the Constitution, which could not be taken away or curtailed by an amendment of the Constitution.[14] It also invalidated an amendment of the Constitution, which provided for the establishment of administrative tribunals exempted from the power of judicial review of the High Courts, though these tribunals were subject to judicial review by the Supreme Court.[15] Thus no action of the state including the power to amend the Constitution is free from judicial review in India.

As the Constitution does not expressly grant the power of judicial review it also does not lay down any limitations on it. Unlike the Constitution of the United States, it does not even require that a matter must be brought before the courts in the form of a case or controversy Therefore, the courts themselves must evolve any limitations on their power of judicial review. Of course, they have evolved certain norms in this regard, but they are flexible and can be relaxed in appropriate cases. Thus, for example, the courts have held that they will not refuse to entertain a matter simply because it involves political questions.[16] Nor would they insist upon a strict requirement of locus standi. As the requirement of locus standi is important for access to courts, it shall be discussed under that head.

3. *Access to Courts*

Access directly to the highest court of the land, i.e. the Supreme Court, is the most fertile area of judicial activism, namely, the 'fundamental rights' is itself a fundamental right.[17] Access to the High courts is not a fundamental right, but it is available as a matter of course, if not of right, not only to enforce the fundamental rights but also for other purposes.[18] Traditionally only an aggrieved person, i.e. the person whose rights or interests were adversely affected could seek access to the courts. But the emergence of pro bono publico litigation has considerably relaxed this requirement. In a non-fundamental rights case of *S.P. Gupta* v. *Union of India*,[19] the Supreme Court held:

Any member of the public having sufficient interest can maintain an action for judicial redress for public injury arising from breach of public duty or from violation of some provision of the Constitution or the law and seek enforcement of such public duty and observance of such constitutional or legal provision.

One of the several propositions laid down in support of this extended approach was repeated in a fundamental rights case, Bandhua Mukti *Morcha* v. *Union of India*,[20] in the following words:

[W]here a person or class of persons to whom legal injury caused by reason of violation of a fundamental right is unable to approach the court for judicial redress on account of poverty or disability or socially or economically disadvantaged position, any member of the public acting bona fide can move the court for relief under Article 32 . . . so that the fundamental right may become meaningful not only for the rich and the well-to-do who have the means to approach the court but also for the large masses of people who are living a life of want and destitution and who are by reason of lack of awareness, assertiveness and resources unable to seek redress.

Following this liberalized approach to locus standi or standing, the Court has allowed various public spirited persons and social organizations to bring petitions before it of persons like under-trials, bonded labourers, tribal people, children and women in protected homes, hutment and pavement dwellers, victims of gas leak or mass disasters. Not only that, the Court has also acted on its own on the basis of newspaper reports and letters or post cards written to the judges about the violation of fundamental rights. To facilitate the epistolary proceedings, the Supreme Court has opened a Public Interest Litigation Cell to which all letters addressed to the Court or individual judges, are forwarded and are placed before the Chief Justice after scrutiny by the staff attached to the cell.

Further, as regards the enforcement of fundamental rights, the Supreme Court can be approached by 'appropriate proceedings'. The Court has held that there is no limitation in regard to the kind of proceedings except that they must be appropriate. The requirement of 'appropriate' must be judged in the light of the purpose for which the proceedings are to be taken, namely, enforcement of a fundamental right. The word 'appropriate' does not refer to any form but to the purpose of the proceeding and, therefore, so long as the purpose of the proceeding is enforcement of a fundamental right, it is appropriate and when it relates to the enforcement of the fundamental rights of the poor, disabled or ignorant by a public spirited person, even a letter addressed by him to the court can legitimately be regarded as an appropriate proceeding. Moreover, the appropriate proceedings need not be adversary proceedings; they can be inquisitorial also. The Court has emphasized that the Court and the State must act in collaboration and co-operation in enforcing the fundamental rights.[21] The fundamental right to approach the Court cannot, of course, be taken away or curtailed by any legislation or executive act. The Court has held that a law, which has the effect of retarding the assertion or vindication of the fundamental right of the petitioner, would be unconstitutional. For this reason the Court struck down its own rule which required the petitioner to furnish security as a condition precedent to the hearing of the petition, because it imposed financial obligation on the petitioner (which if he failed to discharge, his petition would fail).[22]

Not only have the courts opened wide the gates of access, they have also simplified the procedures and innovated remedies to meet the ends of justice in each case. They have held that procedures are the handmaids of justice and should not become an obstacle to it. Similarly, whatever relief—preventive, restitutive or compensatory—is suitable in any case for the enforcement and protection of the rights of an individual, it must be given. Therefore, in cases of violation of fundamental rights, the courts have awarded compensation to the victims of rape, police excesses, and medical negligence. The Supreme Court has also liberally used its power of passing such decree or order as is necessary for doing complete justice in any matter pending before it.[23]

JUDICIAL ACTIVISM AND THE FUNDAMENTAL RIGHTS

As we have already noted, fundamental rights have in general become the most fertile ground for judicial activism everywhere. This is natural because they are expressed in terms of concepts and values such as life, liberty, equality, dignity, etc. These concepts are dynamic and require constant exploration and exposition. The constitutional grant of these rights withdraws the final say in such exposition and exploration, from the hands of the legislature and the executive, and transfers it to the courts. The courts thus become natural expositors and explorers of these concepts. We may agree or disagree with their exposition, but we cannot deny their power and responsibility in this regard. The fundamental rights have thus been the most prominent subject matter for judicial activism. In view of the composition and working of the Supreme Court of India (which is equally true about the High

Courts)—that the Court does not sit *en banc* but sits in small benches, that the judges are not for life, but retire at the age of sixty-five, that they are for a short duration in the Court and that the senior most judge of the Supreme Court becomes the Chief Justice of India on the retirement of his predecessor, which sometimes gives him as short a tenure as a few months or weeks—it is not possible to examine judicial activism in India on the same lines as in the United States or some other countries. Therefore, I have decided to examine it by dividing the period since the commencement of the Constitution, substantially into two periods, i.e. from 1950 to 1975 and from 1977 to the present. In between these two periods, the period from June 1975 to March 1977 was the period of internal emergency during which fundamental rights were partly suspended. In my opinion there is a difference between the activism of the Court before and after the emergency. Let me briefly examine that difference. I may also examine the extent to which the emergency induced this difference.

1. *From January 1950 to June 1975*

This in my view is the period of the Court's reliance on economic liberalism. At the cost of ignoring the egalitarianism of the Constitution, the Court defended property and capital interests. It failed to appreciate the revolutionary spirit of social and economic transformation enshrined in the Preamble, the fundamental rights, the Directive Principles of State Policy and other provisions of the Constitution. On the contrary it defended and supported the social and economic status quo. This is evident from the first to the last decision during this period. *A.K. Gopalan* v. *State of Madras*[24] was its first decision on life and liberty where, declining to rely upon the due process clause in the US Constitution, it justified State action in terms of fundamental rights. But when it came to property rights it imported and employed some elements of the due process clause to the property right provision which excluded due process clause as much, if not more, as did the life/liberty provision.[25] It even invalidated land reforms laws, which had been at the national reforms agenda even before independence and were specifically protected under the property right clause.[26] Similarly, it invalidated a Madras State measure for the promotion of educational interests of the weaker and deprived sections of the society, a measure that the State sought to defend under a directive principle of state policy.[27] To reject the State's defence it took an argument which was patently wrong and which the Court itself had to abandon later.[28]

As the decisions on property as well as on the promotion of the educational interests of the weaker and deprived sections of the society were not in harmony with the letter and spirit of the Constitution, the Constitution makers, who had just got converted into the provisional parliament, decided to overrule them by amendments to the Constitution. As these decisions, especially on property rights, were capable of further mischief, the Constitution was so drastically amended that it gave almost unlimited power to Parliament to save any laws not only from challenge on ground of property rights but even on ground of any fundamental right.[29] Another amendment in the right to property also excluded from it some of the aspects of due process clause.[30]

But these amendments also could not have the desired results. Firstly, the validity of the amendments themselves was challenged on ground of their inconsistency with the fundamental rights.[31] Secondly, the Court continued to read the right to property in a manner not intended by the Constitution-makers.[32] As such a reading was not consistent with the egalitarianism of the Constitution specifically expressed, inter alia, in Article 39 (b) and (c), the right to property had to be amended again and again. While in the first instance of challenge to such amendments, the Court unanimously held that the fundamental rights were not immune from amendments, in the second instance after about one and a half decades later, it stood divided.[33] Though the majority still upheld the previous position, it opened the way for future challenges. Consequently, after about two years the majority of the Court moved to the other side, and in *Golak Nath*,[34] it held that the fundamental rights could not be abridged or taken away even by an amendment of the Constitution. Of course, the decision was revolutionary but in the context of India and its Constitution, it was also reactionary. It supported status quo and decried urgently needed and overdue change. After disabling the parliament from amending the Constitution, the Court became even bolder in its defence of property rights. Among others, it invalidated a major initiative on the part of the Union government to nationalize fourteen major banks.[35] It also invalidated abolition of the privy purses paid to the former princes, which were a drain on the state treasury.[36] Before these decisions in 1967, there was also a split in the ruling political party, i.e. the Indian National Congress, at the regional or state level and in 1969 at the national level. Roughly speaking, those who sympathized with the status quo got separated from those who campaigned for change. The government, however, at the Union and in many states, remained in the hands of the supporters of change.

Finding itself so helpless in bringing about social and economic changes desired by the Constitution (and on account of the politics of defection), the government had to call for premature elections to Parliament. Court's limitation on the amendment of the Constitution and its interpretation and application of the right to property were one of the major items in the election manifesto of the party in power. In the ensuing elections in 1971, the party in power returned with a thumping majority, and proceeded to remove the obstacles created by the Court. It amended the Constitution, among others, overruling *Golak Nath* and giving precedence to the Directive Principles in Article 39(b) and (c), which provided for socialization of the means of production and redistribution of resources, over the fundamental rights to property, equality and business.[37] The later amendment also prohibited the courts from examining whether a law implemented Article 39(b) or (c) or not (if the law so declared). These and some other amendments also became a matter of dispute before the Supreme Court in the *Keshavananda Bharati* case. The Court upheld all of them except the provision excluding the judicial review of legislation. In the same case, as we have already noted, the Court by a 7: 6 majority also held that though fundamental rights could be amended, no amendment could change or destroy the basic structure of the Constitution. Thus, though the Court upheld major amendments to the Constitution, it sustained its power of judicial review and also expanded it to the review of constitutional amendments. But by this time realization dawned upon the Court, that the right to property was at the centre of all controversies and posed a threat to other fundamental rights too. One of the judges, J. Khanna who tilted the balance in *Keshavananda*, expressly said that the right to property was not part of the basic structure of the Constitution.

Before I move to the next stage of judicial activism, let me also examine its operation in one more area of fundamental rights. It also concerns distribution of social resources. Much before the commencement of the Constitution, some of the States were executing affirmative programs for the benefit of the socially and economically backward classes of society.[38] One of such programmes, introduced by the State of Madras well before the commencement of the Constitution providing opportunities for such classes for admission to the medical and engineering schools by assigning quotas for different classes, was challenged in the courts immediately after the commencement of the Constitution on the ground that it violated Article 15(1) of the Constitution, which prohibited discrimination on the basis of race, religion, caste, sex, etc. The State defended the programme under the directive principle in Article 46 which requires the State to take special care of the educational and economic interests of such classes. The Supreme Court rejected the State's defence on the plea that the directive principles were subsidiary to fundamental rights and invalidated its programme.[39] As the decision was contrary to the understanding of the Constitution by its makers, who had thought of the directive principles as important as the fundamental rights, the first amendment to the Constitution had to take care of this issue also. Accordingly, Article 15(4) was introduced, which secures special provisions for the socially and educationally backward classes irrespective of Articles 15(1) or 29(2), which, among others, prohibit discrimination in matters of admission to educational institutions on grounds of race, religion, language, caste, etc. After the amendment it was expected that the government was free to make any special provisions for these classes to improve their educational, social and economic conditions. But the Supreme Court did not let it happen when the matter came before it after about a decade. In *M.R. Balaji* v. *State of Mysore*[40] it held that the determination of backwardness was subject to judicial review; the caste of a person could not be the sole or dominant criterion for determining his backwardness, and that national or public interest required that the special provisions should be kept below the fifty per cent limit. Soon after, the fifty per cent limit was also extended to a programme of the Union Government, which provided for twenty-two and a half per cent reservation in jobs to the lowest amongst the backward classes, namely the Scheduled Castes and the Scheduled Tribes under Article 16(4) that expressly provides for such reservation. The special provision said that in case the jobs reserved for the Scheduled Castes and the Scheduled Tribes were not filled in a particular year, the unfilled vacancies could be carried forward to the next two years. In invalidating the carry forward scheme the Court accepted the abstract mathematical argument that twenty-two and a half multiplied by three would become more than fifty per cent of the total. It did not even examine whether in any particular case it had actually exceeded the fifty per cent limit.[41] As both Articles 15(4) and 16(4) are part of the constitutional scheme that envisages social and economic transformation of Indian society, and redistribution of its resources, the Court's approach in the above cases appears status quoits. Denial of caste as the basis of backwardness in India is similar to denial of race as the basis of affirmative action in the United States. Similarly in justifying the less than fifty per cent limit on the ground of public interest, the Court reverses its role of defending fundamental rights against the state action sought to be taken in the public interest. The Court defends the fundamental rights against their encroachment by the state on the plea of public interest. In Balaji, without going into the question whether the fifty per cent or any other limit violates anybody's fundamental right, the Court simply invented that limit in support of public interest, which apparently is not the domain of the courts. A re-thinking on these issues emerged only during and since the emergency, to which I return a little later.

Soon after *Keshavananda*, the government also moved to change the composition of the Supreme Court. Disregarding the practice of appointing the senior-most judge of the Court as the Chief Justice of India, on the superannuation of the then Chief Justice, it appointed the judge at number four in seniority, superseding three others senior to him. Remarkably, the three superceded judges constituted the majority in *Keshavananda*, which limited the power of amendment, while the fourth supported no limits on such power. This was perceived as a direct interference in the independence of the judiciary and became a matter of debate as much, if not more, as the *Keshavananda* case.

Before any major decisions could come from the newly-constituted Court, the government imposed an Emergency in June 1975 on grounds of internal disturbance, while already an Emergency on ground of external aggression was in force. The Emergency lasted until March 1977. During this period a few developments notable from the point of view of judicial activism took place. As regards the right to life and liberty the Court went to the extreme in conceding unlimited power to the government to deprive people of their life and liberty and expressed its inability to provide any relief to the victims. It went to the extent of holding that even the common law principle that no one could be deprived of his life or liberty without the authority of law did not apply during the emergency.[42] But as regards equality, it took a progressive view of affirmative programmes. It said that the right to equality included not merely formal but also substantive equality and the provision for reservation in jobs in Article 16(4) was an example of substantive equality, and not an exception to the right to equality. Article 16(4) not only provided for reservation in jobs but also included any other concessions such as relaxation in qualifying marks or exemption from clearing a test. The Court rejected the argument that the Scheduled Castes were castes, and, casting its doubts on the legitimacy of the 50 per cent limit, upheld the special provision which exceeded that limit.[43]

During the Emergency, the Constitution was drastically amended, curtailing among others, the courts' power of judicial review of legislation and constitutional amendments[44] The independence of the judiciary was also threatened by transferring to inconvenient locations those High Court judges, who gave judgments causing embarrassment to the government. The courts were unable to give any relief against these actions of the government, except that they invalidated an amendment which had the effect of deciding a pending election appeal about the then Prime Minister. But ultimately it decided the appeal in favour of the Prime Minister.[45]

2. *From 1977 to the Present*

The emergency proved a catalyst for judicial activism in India. The first and the most important change in 1978 came in the Court's approach to the right to life and liberty. By giving an expansive and unifying approach to the application of the fundamental rights, it discovered the due process clause in the right to life and liberty. It held that the right to life and liberty could not be read in isolation; it had to be read with other fundamental rights such as the right to equality in article 14, which prohibited arbitrariness and unreasonableness in all state actions. No state action, either legislative or executive, could survive article 14 if it failed the test of reasonableness. Therefore, any law that deprived a person of his life or liberty must satisfy the requirement of reasonableness.[46] Following this line of arguments the Court has invalidated some of the provisions of substantive and procedural laws and administrative actions.[47] Expanding the right to life in *Francis Coralie* v. *Delhi*,[48] it held:

> We think that the right to life includes the right to live with human dignity and all that goes along with it, namely, the bare necessaries of life such as adequate nutrition, clothing and shelter over the head and facilities for reading, writing and expressing oneself in diverse forms, freely moving about and mixing and co-mingling with fellow human beings.

And thus followed a long line of cases recognizing such rights as the right to clean environment,[49] drinking water,[50] livelihood,[51] medical care,[52] preservation of culture and heritage,[53] self-preservation,[54] protection against sexual molestation and harassment[55] and education.[56] Special rights of accused and convicts such as legal aid,[57] speedy trial,[58] prohibition on hand cuffing,[59] human conditions inside the prisons,[60] availability of the fundamental rights during detention,[61] prohibition on cruel and unusual punishments[62] and compensation for violation of the right to life[63] were also recognized.

What was remarkable about all the cases establishing these rights is that, as I have already noted, almost all of them involved the interest of the vulnerable sections of society such as contract workers, bonded labourers, under-trials, prisoners, women, children, tribals, pavement-dwellers, hawkers, riksha-pullers and prostitutes. They did not concern big property holders, smugglers, political figures or industrialists. Judicial activism in the field of fundamental rights has not been as vigorous in the 1990s as it was in the 1980s.

In the arena of affirmative action, after taking a somewhat progressive approach in upholding the reservation for backward classes in the central government jobs in the *Mandal* case[64] in 1992 (where it rejected most of the propositions laid down in *Balaji* and *Devdasan*), the Court has fallen back on its policy of finding fault with these programmes since the late 1990s.[65] Such policy has again led to several amendments of the Constitution, some of which have been challenged in the Court and are pending decision.[66]

JUDICIAL ACTIVISM AND POLITICAL CORRUPTION

Since 1996, the Court appears to be getting more active in matters of political and economic corruption in high places. It ordered the investigation and prosecution of crimes involving political figures, including a former Prime Minister and some Chief Ministers.[67] It has called for the independence of the investigating and prosecuting agencies from political influence.[68] It has also invalidated the appointment of a chief Minister on the ground that she was disqualified to be so appointed because of her conviction for corruption.[69]

JUDICIAL ACTIVISM IN SUPPORT OF JUDICIARY

I have already noted the strengthening of the power of judicial review and its extension to constitutional amendments by the Court. Besides that, after holding in 1982 that the independence of the judiciary was a basic feature of the Constitution,[70] it established its primacy in the appointment of judges of the Supreme Court and the High Courts, and in the transfer of High Court judges in 1993, fortified in 1998.[71] Since 1993 it has given several decisions directing the union government to ensure the independence and efficiency of the subordinate judiciary by improving the working conditions and financial position of its members.[72]

JUDICIAL ACTIVISM AND FEDERALISM

The judiciary has hardly shown any activism in the arena of federalism except that soon after the revocation of emergency in *State of Rajasthan* v. *Union of India*,[73] and later in 1993 in *S.R. Bommai* v. *Union of India*,[74] it held that the imposition of central rule in a state requires satisfaction of certain conditions in the absence of which the Court could invalidate the action of the union government and restore the *status quo ante*. The latter decision has considerably reduced the frequency of the President's Rule in the states.

JUDICIAL ACTIVISM AND ADMINISTRATIVE ACTION

Courts have contributed immensely through their activism in the arena of administrative action. They have held that no administrative action including the decision of the head of the state to pardon people for their crimes, or to impose President's rule in a State, is beyond judicial scrutiny, because administrative discretion is never unlimited.[75] They have extended the application of the principles of natural justice to all actions of the administration having adverse civil consequences and to government contracts.[76] These principles are not confined to bias and hearing but also include the requirement of reasoned decisions and fairness.[77] Among the principles of judicial review of administrative action, the principle of reasonableness has been given a constitutional status through Article 14, the right to equality.[78] The principles of proportionality and legitimate expectations have also been introduced in several decisions.[79] There is hardly any area of administrative action in which the courts have not shown their willingness to intervene, including, as I noted above, investigation and prosecution of crimes.

CONCLUSION

The foregoing inconclusive detour through the Courts' activism shows that our judiciary has been quite active since the commencement of the Constitution in 1950. It has never been assumed that the exposition and implementation of the Constitution is exclusively the job of the political branches. Vigilant citizens from different walks of life have been approaching the courts, for their determination as to whether the actions of the political branches are consistent with the Constitution. And though the courts have always been invoking the well-known presumption of constitutionality of actions of those branches, they have never shirked the responsibility of invalidating them if found in conflict with the Constitution. Not only that, in appropriate cases they have also invoked the political branches to perform their constitutional obligations because omission could be as pernicious as commission.

But it must be remembered that judicial activism as such is not an end or a virtue as such. The Constitution envisages a judiciary capable of protecting and defending the individual against the unconstitutional exercise of power by the state. It also envisages that all social, economic, and other policies and decisions shall be taken by our elected representatives and not by the Courts. If the Courts start sitting in judgement over all these policies and decisions, they exceed their constitutional limits. Determination of those limits is, however, a delicate task, which nobody has yet been able to fix with accuracy. Accuracy may also not be possible or even desirable in all matters. Efforts must, however, continue towards obtaining as much accuracy and drawing as fine a balance as possible between different constitutional goals and values.

The Constitution and its goals and values themselves are not static and definite. They continue to change and grow. Some of them decay and die. The judges must be as conscious of their growth and decay as the members of the other two branches of the state. They must also acknowledge that the members of the other two branches have somewhat better means and opportunities of perceiving growth and the decay, and that they are immediately answerable to the people if they fail in their perception. They must also remember that there are matters which the Constitution excludes from the domain of all branches of the state. They must, therefore, carefully draw the difference between what is and what is not assigned to the state.

After a long and hard struggle, for example, the US Supreme Court could realize that economic matters are not excluded from the domain of the state in the same way as the freedom of speech or religion.[80] The Indian courts also took too long to realize that the right to property does not stand on the same footing as the right to life and liberty. They are still having difficulty in realizing that affirmative action, particularly in the domain of distribution of social and economic resources, is as much part of equality as non-discrimination, and the Constitution expressly sanctions it, and that 'Justice, social, economic and political' is boldly enshrined in the Preamble to the Constitution and repeated in the directive principles demands social and economic restructuring of the society as expeditiously as possible. The judiciary must accelerate the pace of accomplishment of that task through its activism.

NOTES

1. Compare, S.P. Sathe, *Judicial Activism in India,* 4ff., New Delhi: Oxford University Press, 2002, who seems to be drawing no difference between judicial review and judicial activism. He seems to be suggesting that a court is activist if it frequently invalidates the actions of the legislature and the executive. Sathe's work is the most recent and intensive on the subject. Among the earlier works, see U. Baxi, *The Indian Supreme Court and Politics,* Lucknow: Eastern Book Co., 1980.
2. See Bonham's case (1610) Co. Rep. 107a and subsequent developments in J.M. Kelly, *A Short History of Western Legal Theory,* 222ff., Oxford: Clarendon Press, 1992.
3. 1 Cranch 137 (US 1803).
4. 19 How. 393 (1857).
5. 163 US 537 (1896).
6. 198 US 45 (1905).
7. 347 US 483 (1954).
8. Kenneth M. Holland, *Judicial Activism in Comparative Perspective,* New York: St. Martin Press, 1991.
9. See, Yosiyuki Noda, *Introduction to Japanese Law, 120–1,* University of Tokyo Press, 1976.
10. See, Parts III, IV, V, & XVI, Constitution of India.
11. See Articles 13, 32 & 226. Under Article 226, High Courts can also be approached for any other purpose. Judicial review of laws is also traced to Article 245, but it is doubtful whether that is a sound proposition. See, M.P. Singh, 'Legislative Powers in India: Some Clarifications', 4 & 5, *Delhi Law Review* 73 (1975–6); also, V.S. Deshpande, *Judicial Review of Legislation,* 55 (1975) and D.D. Basu, *Limited Government and Judicial Review,* 291 (1972).
12. AIR 1967 SC 1643.
13. AIR 1973 SC 1461.
14. *L. Chandra Kumar* v. *Union of India,* AIR 1997 SC 1125.

15. Ibid.
16. *State of Rajasthan* v. *Union of India*, AIR 1997 SC 1361.
17. Article 31, Constitution of India.
18. Article 226.
19. AIR 1982 SC 149, 216.
20. AIR 1984 SC 802.
21. See, among others, *M.C. Mehta* v. *Union of India*, AIR 1987 SC 1086.
22. *Prem Chand Garg* v. *Excise Commissioner, U.P.*, AIR 1963 SC 996.
23. For details, see M.P. Singh, *Shukla's Constitution of India*, 277ff., Lucknow: Eastern Book Co., 10th ed., 2001; U. Baxi, 'Taking Suffering Seriously: Social Litigation in the Supreme Court of India', 8 & 9 *Delhi Law Review* 91 (1979-80); Parmanand Singh in the *Annual Survey of Indian Law*, Indian Law Institute, New Delhi, and his several other writings on the subject including, 'Access to Justice: Public Interest Litigation and the Indian Supreme Court', 10 & 11, *Delhi Law Review* 156 (1981–2).
24. AIR 1950 SC 27.
25. See, *State of West Bengal* v. *Bela Banerjee*, AIR 1954 SC 170.
26. See, among others, *Kameshwar Singh* v. *State of Bihar*, AIR 1951 Pat. 91; and *State of Bihar* v. *Kameshwar Singh*, AIR 1952 SC 252.
27. *State of Madras* v. *Champakam Dorairajan*, AIR 1951 SC 226.
28. See, *Mohd. Hanif Qureshi* v. *State of Bihar*, AIR 1958 SC 731; Kerala Education Bill, 1957, AIR 1958 SC 956, and P.K. Tripathi, 'Directive Principles of State Policy', 17 *Supreme Court Journal* 7 (1954). Also, *Minerva Mills Ltd.* v. *Union of India*, AIR 1980 SC 1789.
29. See Article 31B.
30. See the first and the fourth amendment to the Constitution.
31. *Sankari Prasad Singh Deo* v. *Union of India*, AIR 1951 SC 458.
32. *Vajravelu* v. *S.P. Dy. Collector*, AIR 1965 SC 1017; *R.C. Cooper v. Union of India*, AIR 1970 SC 1318.
33. *Sajjan Singh* v. *State of Rajasthan*, AIR 1965 SC 845.
34. AIR 1967 SC 1643.
35. *R.C. Cooper* v. *Union of India*, AIR 1970 SC 1318.
36. *Madhav Rao Scindia* v. *Union of India*, AIR 1971 SC 530.
37. 24th and 25th amendments to the Constitution.
38. See, Marc Galanter, *Competing Equalities*, New Delhi: Oxford University Press, 1984.
39. *State of Madras* v. *Champakam Dorairajan*, AIR 1951 SC 226.
40. AIR 1963 SC 649.
41. *Devadasan* v. *Union of India*, AIR 1964 SC 179.
42. *A.D.M. Jabalpur* v. *Shivakant Shukla*, AIR 1976 SC 1207.
43. *State of Kerala* v. *N.M. Thomas*, AIR 1976 SC 490.
44. See, among others, 42nd Amendment to the Constitution, 1976.
45. *Indira Nehru Gandhi* v. *Raj Narain*, AIR 1975 SC 2299.

46. *Maneka Gandhi* v. *Union of India*, AIR 1978 SC 597.
47. See, for example, *Mithu* v. *State of Punjab*, AIR 1983 SC 473; Karnataka *S.T.D.C.* v. *Karnataka S.T.A.T.* (1986), 4 SCC 421; *Sudhir Chandra Sarkar* v. *Tata Iron & Steel Co. Ltd.* (1984), 3 SCC 369.
48. AIR 1981 SC 746, 753.
49. *R.L.E.K.* v. *State of U.P.*, AIR 1987 SC 2426, and a series of cases since then.
50. *N.B.A.* v. *Union of India* (2000), 2 SCC 465.
51. *Olga Tellis* v. *Bombay Municipal Corporation*, AIR 1986 SC 180.
52. *Vincent* v. *Union of India*, AIR 1987 SC 990; *Murli S. Deora* v. *Union of India* (2001), 8 SCC 765.
53. *Ramsharan* v. *Union of India*, AIR 1989 SC 549.
54. *Surjit Singh* v. *State of Punjab* (1996), 2 SCC 336.
55. *Chairman Railway Board* v. *Chandrima Das*, AIR 2000 SC 988.
56. *Unni Krishnan* v. *State of U.P.* (1993), 1 SCC 645.
57. *Khatri* v. *State of Bihar*, AIR 1981 SC 928.
58. Hussainara cases, AIR 1979 SC 1360, and later including *P. Ramachandra Rao* v. *State of Karnataka* (2002), 4 SCC 578.
59. *Prem Shankar* v. *Delhi Administration*, AIR 1980 SC 1535.
60. *Upendra Baxi* v. *State of U.P.* (1983), 2 SCC 308.
61. *Sunil Batra* v. *Delhi Administration*, AIR 1978 SC 1675.
62. *Deena* v. *Union of India*, AIR 1983 SC 1155; *Daya Singh* v. *Union of India*, AIR 1991 SC 1548.
63. *Rudul Shah* v. *State of Bihar* (1983), 4 SCC 141.
64. *Indira Sawhney* v. *Union of India*, AIR 1993 SC 477.
65. See, for example, *Ajit Singh* (II) v. *State of Punjab* (1999), 7 SCC 209; also, *Ajit Singh* (III) v. *State of Punjab* (2000), 1 SCC 430.
66. See, for example, the Constitution (81st Amendment) Act, 2000 (82nd Amendment) Act, 2000, and (85th Amendment) Act, 2001.
67. For example, the trial of former Prime Minister Narasimha Rao, former Chief Minister A.R. Rahman, and Chief Minister Jayalalithaa.
68. *Vineet Narain* v. *Union of India*, AIR 1998 SC 889
69. *B.R. Kapur* v. *State of Tamil Nadu* (2001), 7 SCC 231.
70. *S.P. Gupta* v. *Union of India*, AIR 1982 SC 149.
71. *S.C. Advocates on Record Assn.* v. *Union of India*, AIR 1994 SC 268, and in re, Presidential Reference, AIR 1999 SC 1.
72. See, for example, *All India Judges' Assn.* v. *Union of India*, AIR 1992 SC 165, and AIR 1993 SC 2493.
73. AIR 19977 SC 1361.
74. AIR 1994 SC 1918.
75. See, the cases cited in the preceding two notes and *Maru Ram* v. *Union of India*, AIR 1980 SC 2147; *Kehar Singh* v. *Union of India*, AIR 1989 SC 653; *Swaran Singh* v. *States of U.P.* (1998), 4 SCC 75.

76. See, for example, *Eurasian Equipment & Chemicals Ltd.* v. *State of West Bengal.*, AIR 1975 SC 266, and *R.D. Shetty* v. *International Airport Authority*, AIR 1979 SC 1682.
77. See, M.P. Singh, 'Duty to Give Reasons for Quasi-Judicial and Administrative Decisions', 21 *Journal of Indian Law Institute*, 45 (1979).
78. *Ajay Hasia* v. *Khalid Mujib*, AIR 1981 SC 487. Also see M.P. Singh, 'The Constitutional Principle of Reasonableness' (1987), 3 SCC (Journal), 31.
79. *Chintamanrao* v. *State of Madhya Pradesh*, AIR 1951 SC 118; *Union of India* v. *Rajesh P.U.* (2003), 7 SCC 285; *Chanchal Goyal* v. *State of Rajasthan* (2003), 3 SCC 485; *Union of India* v. *International Trading Co.* (2003), 5 SCC 437.
80. See the developments since Justice Stone's footnote 4 in *United States* v. *Carolene Products Co.*, 304 US 144 (1938).

5

Judicialization of Politics

RAJINDER SACHAR

There seems to be an impression, though not fully accurate, that the judiciary is intervening in matters which are in the political domain, and thus over-stepping its jurisdiction. This impression is broadly incorrect and reflects inadequate understanding of the role of the judiciary in our constitutional set-up.

It will be readily conceded that interpretation of laws is the proper and exclusive province of the courts. Yet, judges are many a time faulted on the ground of either giving decisions which, according to the critics, stretch the law or trespass on fields reserved for other instrumentalities. This paper suggests that such a censure is only partially correct. It is of course a truism to say that judges must give objective, impartial, and impersonal judgements. Such judgements must be arrived at in a spirit of humility, and in full consciousness of the limitations which are inherent in every decision given by any mortal person. But being mandated to give a decision, the judge cannot shirk the responsibility of giving what might turn out to be an unpopular decision—of course, he must be stoic enough to accept criticism, both informed and uninformed.

Judges are not vain enough to hold that courts have answers to every problem that concerns society. They lay no claim to such infallibility. No doubt, the interpretation and emphasis by each judge will depend upon his or her socio-economic, philosophical, and political background. Decisions will also be affected by the judge's conception of such policies which respond to the social, economic, and political environment. Acceptance of all these variables influencing the judge's decisions may weaken the mystique of the so-called judicial process, but to put it under wraps will give a wrong idea of the way the judiciary functions.

The force of Justice Cardozo's statement is as applicable to judges as to anyone else: '. . . the great tides and currents which engulf the rest of the men do not turn aside in their course and pass the Judges idly by'. Judges' decisions are influenced by what writers like Pound and Frankfurter called 'the sociological jurisprudence', and what Justice Holmes called 'the major inarticulate premise':

> One of the usual misunderstanding in the exercise of judicial review of action of legislature and executive seems to arise as if the courts consider themselves superior to Executive and Legislature. This controversy being generated over the supremacy of the three wings of democracy—judiciary, legislature and executive—was a futile exercise. Neither the legislature nor the executive nor even the judiciary was superior. It were the people who (were) supreme.

The criticism of judicial activism as such is untenable. Courts have since long been judicially active in giving relief in social action litigation to labour, to the victims of custodial violence, and to the excesses committed by the executive. But for too long, the judicial targets were comparatively junior officials and not the politicians. Hence, the issue of judicial activism was not raised by the executive. The charge of alleged interference by the courts has only now been made into an 'issue' because the fire of judicial activism has come too close to the vicinity of high officials and politicians, who had falsely hypnotized themselves into believing that they were above the law. They seemed oblivious of what Chief Justice Coke (England) had said as far back as over 300 years ago: 'Be you ever so high, the law is above you.'

It is in this context that one recapitulates with nostalgia the response given by an anguished but determined Chief Justice Patanjali Sastri to the highest of political leaders like Jawaharlal Nehru, who were visibly upset at some of the earlier judgements of the Supreme Court for striking down legislation because it violated fundamental rights of the citizens:

> . . . that we think it right to point out, what is sometimes overlooked, that our Constitution contains express provision for judicial review of legislation as to its conformity with the Constitution. If then, the Courts in this country face up to such an important and none too easy task, it is not out of any desire to tilt at legislative authority in a crusader's spirit, but in discharge of a duty plainly laid upon them by the Constitution. This is especially true as regards the fundamental rights, as to which this Court has been assigned the role of a sentinel on the 'qui vive',—and that while the Court naturally attaches great weight to the legislative judgement, it cannot desert its own duty to determine finally the constitutionality of an impugned statute.

These are wise and strong words which still continue to act as a beacon to the legal fraternity.

It may well be true, as some critics have said, that the courts' interference in the normal functioning of administration (like the directions as to which particular authority is to take a decision), may, and does cause administrative anomalies and loss of morale. Besides, I am not sure that judges can properly monitor the daily disposal of garbage by the civic administration, or the actual steps taken to meet the problem of malaria, or the shortage of electric supply, etc. In this regard, I would rather agree with critics that such matters are too technical for the courts to monitor.

NEED TO PRIORITIZE HUMAN RIGHTS OVER ENVIRONMENTAL CONCERNS

While environmental concerns are important, the courts, I believe, should be more concerned with human rights. Many environmental groups, using the cloak of fear of pollution and over-indulgent consideration for the welfare of wild animals, seek the aid of courts for direction, to evict the poor slum dwellers from the sites they have lived on for generations, resulting in great suffering for the poor evictees. I do not mind confessing but I do feel bitter that the courts let themselves be persuaded to invoke the language of the first world and seek to apply the same tests in developing countries, even though such tests are most inappropriate in different situations. After all, the greatest violation of human right is poverty, homelessness, and lack of ordinary shelter. I may sound reactionary but if ever a choice was to be made between preserving the human right to shelter for a slum dweller, or the so-called environmental standards laid down by the first world, I would unhesitatingly opt for the former, because to me no one takes precedence over human brotherhood.

In the past few years, the alleged judicial activism of the Supreme Court has been projected as a repudiation of the charge of a conservative face of the Court. But that was due more to the concern shown to the alleged environmental pollutions—an obsession of the affluent section of society—than to the misery of hundreds of thousands of slum dwellers and the oustees of projects like Narmada who have not received a similar response. Lest it should be assumed that that the Court has always been on the side of the politically weak or socially neglected, it would be proper to review the Court's judgements for its flattering and not so flattering decisions.

THE EMERGENCY (1975–7) AND THE COURT

The Supreme Court struck a completely dominant role in *Golak Nath* case when it held that fundamental rights, including the right to property, were sacrosanct. A near revolt erupted in the executive and the legislature. The judiciary took note of it and adopted a larger perspective which combined the command of the Preamble of the Constitution to build a nation on justice—social and economic. So we had *Keshavananda Bharti* case evolving the 'doctrine of basic structure'. I know there are a number of entities especially in the executive branch of the government which are uncomfortable with this doctrine, and challenge its legitimacy. I, however, believe that this judgement has been able to secure the country at its most delicate period and is a guarantee that (sans absolute surrender of judicial independence) the basic principles of our Republic—democracy, social justice, secularism—will be preserved by the judiciary. But it has not been an easy journey, because the Court had to wrestle a lot to establish this base. Thus, notwithstanding *Keshavananda Bharti* case, the Court in the wake of 1975–7 Emergency (except for the rare courage of Justice Khanna) wilted in the ADM Jabalpur case and delivered the most damaging blow to the liberty of citizens. How it fell into this error, or possibly into a state of 'judicial surrender', will continue to haunt us! At times, I wonder if the Emergency could have survived had the Supreme Court shown the necessary courage to follow the well-established law, which the Indian Courts had been following since the very beginning: that in cases of habeas corpus, every imprisonment is prima facie unlawful and that it is for a person directing imprisonment to justify his act—a principle which is one of the pillars of liberty in English law.

It will be recalled that many eminent politicians, journalists, and social activists were arrested by Prime Minister Indira Gandhi's Emergency regime under the Maintenance of Internal Security Act (MISA), on non-existent or frivolous grounds. The detentions were challenged but the petitioners were met with the government's plea that Article 21—the sole repository of liberty—had been suspended by the Presidential Order of 27 June 1975, as a consequence of which the petitions were liable to be dismissed at the threshold. This objection having been over-ruled by nine High Courts, the appeal was heard by a

5-Judge Bench of the Supreme Court. Here, it was only Justice Khanna who showed rare courage in negating this totalitarian claim. Justice Chandrachud and Justice Bhagwati (who were widely expected to side with the liberties of citizens), however, wilted and joined Chief Justice Ray and Justice Beg (who, in any case, was expected not to go against the government) in dismissing the habeas corpus petitions. Sadly, it was to take another twenty-one months and the peoples' simmering anger to get rid of the emergency.

There are still many unexplained reasons as to why the two Justices (Chandrachud and Bhagwati J.J.), decided as they did. For their conclusion, they relied on one single most important case of *Liversidge* v. *Anderson,* wherein the House of Lords in England, by majority (the sole dissenter being Lord Acton), had held that the Home Secretary's opinion to the effect that a person should be detained was final, and not reviewable by the Court. Justice Khanna, in his powerful dissent, held that Article 21 could not be considered to be the sole repository of the right to life and personal liberty, and that this right could not be taken away under any circumstances without the authority of law in a society governed by the rule of law. On the contrary, Chandrachud and Bhagwati J.J. allowed themselves to be persuaded by the majority decision in Liversidge, to the effect that the opinion of a detaining authority was not challengeable, even to the extent that if a policeman was to shoot down a citizen maliciously and capriciously, there was no remedy in a court of law.

It is, indeed, surprising that both Chandrachud and Bhagwati J.J. ignored the dissent of Lord Acton who was caustic about judges who 'show themselves more executive-minded than the executive', and who commented that the 'unchallengeability', argument in Liversidge 'might have been addressed acceptably to the Court of King's Bench in the times of Charles I'. Soon after the Liversidge decision was given, Lord Acton received vociferous support from parliamentarians and jurists, who viewed the majority judgement as antithetical to the liberties of citizens. In fact, Justice Stable, a Judge in High Court London, was so upset with the majority judgement as to observe that the status of the judiciary had been reduced 'to mice squeaking under a chair in the Home office'. Lord Radcliffe (1951: HL), said that 'it would be a very unfortunate thing if Liversidge's case was regarded as laying down any general rule', and Lord Reid (1963: HL), referred dismissively to 'the very peculiar case in *Liversidge* v. *Anderson*' and said: 'It should be confined apparently to a wartime context and that it is already clear that the decision was regarded as an aberration.'

All this trenchant criticism of the Liversidge judgement was available in various law quarterly reviews since the start of the case. A review available in the *Law Quarterly Review* (1970), clearly spelled out how embarrassing the decision in Liversidge was for the English judiciary. And yet our Supreme Court surprisingly chose to follow the discredited majority view in Liversidge which was becoming increasingly embarrassing for the men in the robes in England as time went on. That is why Lord Tiplock (HL) in 1979 was constrained to rule: 'For my part I think the time has come to acknowledge openly that the majority of this House in *Liversidge* v. *Anderson* were expediently and, at that time, perhaps, excusably wrong and the dissenting speech of Lord Acton was right.' And Lord Scarman hammered the final nail when he said that 'the ghost of that decision need no longer haunt the law'.

Some commentators have ironically described the majority in the Liversidge case as the court's contribution to the war efforts of England. Similarly, some in this country are inclined to describe the majority in the *ADM Jabalpur* case as the Supreme Court's contribution to the continuance of the 1975 Emergency. I am inclined to agree. Had the Supreme Court taken the same view as the nine High Courts in the states, the Emergency would have collapsed immediately, because no court would have upheld the detention of stalwarts and patriots like Jayaprakash Narayan, Morarji Desai, Madhu Limaye, and thousands of others, on the ground that they were a danger to the security of the country. The inevitable result would have been the immediate release of these leaders leading to an overwhelming opposition movement, which would have swept away Mrs. Gandhi's regime by the end of 1975. But, alas, all this is in the realm of speculation. The Supreme Court did not show courage. This case will continue to haunt the Court and the judicial fraternity, and the Supreme Court will never be able to live it down. How the fate of nations can be influenced by the pusillanimity of a few individuals is amazing, but then such is life.

However, we may fortunately not have to pass through that darkness again because the 44th Amendment to the Constitution (1978), has taken away the power of the President to suspend Article 21, though we must still continue to remember that eternal vigilance is the price a nation must pay for safeguarding the liberties of its citizens.

Possibly, the Court itself felt uncomfortable with the *ADM Jabalpur* case; that alone may explain its reticence and restraint in upholding the action of the Janata Centre (Janata Party replaced the Indira regime in

1977), in dismissing the state government of Rajasthan by the wrongful invocation of Article 356 of the Constitution. It was, however, to take a decade and half before the Supreme Court would take cudgels in the *Bommai* case to uphold the dismissal of state governments for violation of secularism—a basic feature of the Constitution.

THE POTA 2002 AND THE COURT[1]

By rejecting the challenge to the Prevention of Terrorism Act 2002, the Supreme Court does not appear 'liberal' in the matter of civil liberties of individuals when faced with the government's plea (excuse) of national security. Somehow, the Court seems inclined to accept the 'national security', plea rather too easily.

The two-Judge decision in December 2003, upholding the validity of POTA, must understandably cause disappointment. The judgement negated the submission that legislative competence to pass POTA rested in State (Public Order Entry), jurisdiction, and not in the Union. It read down the State Entry, notwithstanding earlier constitutional Bench judgements holding that the security of a state (the alleged justification for POTA), was also a facet of the public order. Even in as critical a situation as in Kashmir, in the aftermath of the Pakistan tribal invasion in 1947, the State Assembly of Jammu and Kashmir was held competent to legislate under Public Order. The Court, however, put terrorism under a residuary category which is not defined in the Constitution.

The challenge to Section 14 of POTA, in that it gives unbridled powers to the investigating officer to force even lawyers and journalists to disclose their confidential information on pain of being proceeded under POTA was rejected. It is a settled principle, the Court observed, that the lawyers and journalist have no privilege even with regard to the confidentiality of information, notwithstanding that a substantial opinion (though there is some conflict of opinion), in the United States is in favour of journalists' privileges. With regard to lawyers' privilege, the House of Lords has held (1995) that the legal professional privilege is a fundamental condition on which the administration of justice rests and there can be no exception to the absolute nature of legal professional privilege.

The challenge to Section 18 of POTA which gives government the power of including a terrorist organization on its own belief, without giving a prior hearing to the organization, was negated. The Court held that as organizations so included could apply subsequently to the Government to get de-listed, this was a sufficient safeguard, and a post-decisional hearing satisfied the rule of natural justice. This was in direct conflict with an earlier case (1994), dealing with the Unlawful Activities Act (1967), which empowered the Government to declare any association as 'unlawful' if its activities tended to disrupt the integrity of India, but with a safeguard that such an order could not become effective until it was upheld in appeal by a High Court.

Under POTA, there is no regular appeal against the Government's order. The remedy before a Review Committee is illusory because the jurisdiction of the Committee is limited to considering the matter in the light of principles applicable to judicial review. This means that the Committee will not be competent to examine the case either on merits, or law. Thus, there is no full right of appeal on facts and law; and it is a settled law that in such a case, post-decisional hearings are illusory and a violation of natural justice and, consequently, the order could be void.

The other illegality is that the Review Committee may be headed by a retired Judge, which earlier decisions of the Court have struck down in the case of election tribunals; even worse is that the Judge would be in a minority in the Committee, because the majority would consist of non-judicial members. This goes counter to the earlier judgement where the Court held that unless an Administrative Tribunal was headed by a High Court judge and the majority of the members were judicial, the provision would be unconstitutional. It is ironic that while in the case of government servants, the Administrative Tribunal must have judicial pre-dominance, the Tribunal under the POTA (dealing with the most serious matter of fundamental right of a citizen under Articles 14, 19, and 21), consisting of majority of non-judicial members should be held to be valid.

Another serious infirmity under the POTA of keeping back the identity of a witness (thus denying the fundamental right of cross-examination of the accused), was upheld, though the Court softened the blow by holding that the identity would be withheld only in exceptional cases, and for weighty reasons, to be recorded in writing. The Court accepted that keeping secret the identity of a witness was a deviation from the usual mode of trial. It also approvingly referred to the decision of Inter-American Court of Human Rights and the recommendation of the Law Commission of New Zealand, affirming that keeping the identity of a witness would seriously prejudice the accused and deny his right to a fair trial. Yet the Court yielded to the panicky view of the Executive that in the fight against terrorism, even the fundamental right of cross-examination could be circumscribed.

Although the constitutionality of POTA has been upheld, it is to the credit of the Court that it has read down many of its provisions which should make it difficult for the government to misuse it. Thus Sections 21 and 22 (under which the Tamil Nadu government detained Vaiko, its political opponent), have been liberally interpreted by holding that the support *per se*, or a mere expression of sympathy for a terrorist organization, or arrangement of a meeting which is not intended and does not have the effect of furthering activities of any terrorist organization, are not within the purview of POTA. The provision on bail which in its language prohibited asking for bail in the first year was saved, but modified so that the provision, in the language of the Court, would not 'lead to an absurdity or become meaningless'. Thus interpreted, the accused can be granted bail even in the first year of detention subject to certain strict provisions, and thereafter under the ordinary law, thereby keeping somewhat of a check on the partisan use of POTA.

The central government seems to have gone on a victory dance. Its spokesperson described this decision as a slap in the face of the opposition, tending to suggest as if the Court had upheld the *need* for POTA. Nothing is farther from the truth. On the contrary, the Court specifically noticed the argument of misuse of law but restrained itself by saying that it 'cannot go into and examine the *need* of POTA'. It is a matter of 'policy' for the government.

The central government, however, needs to be reminded that the need or the legality of POTA was doubted by successive National Human Rights Commissions which are headed by retired Chief Justices of India, and include the retired Judges of the Supreme Court and High Courts. Though strictly in terms of the binding effect, the view of the 2-Judge Bench of the Supreme Court will naturally prevail, but the fact that eight or ten Supreme Court Judges, though retired, adversely commented on the need or the legality of the POTA, should not be lightly brushed aside. One would have thought that the central government would, in view of the reservations expressed and in the context of increasingly relaxed Indo-Pakistan relations, withdraw POTA which, by any standard, is a draconian law unworthy of a civilized nation. Let the government heed the warning words of the judgement: 'if human rights are violated in the process of combating terrorism, it will be self-defeating'.

INTERNATIONAL CONFERENCES AND THE COURT

The rejection summarily by the Supreme Court, without giving any reasons, the writ petition challenging the circulars of the central government, by which prior approval is to be obtained from the Ministry of Home Affairs, in regard to international conferences to be organized by Indian Non-Governmental Organizations (NGO), Associations, Universities (even on subjects of human rights), and worse, and also from the Ministry of External Affairs, if the participants are from friendly neighbours like Bangladesh, Sri Lanka, and Pakistan, may be considered by government apologists as a shot in its arm. But it has also revived the vitriolic debate about the effectiveness of the judiciary in safeguarding the fundamental right of freedom of speech guaranteed to citizens and has occasioned the caustic comment that while the legislatures are one generation behind public opinion, even the judiciary is one generation behind the legislatures.

Why does this suspicion exist about public bodies? The danger of foreign invitees being in fact saboteurs does injustice to responsible individuals, NGOs, and the Universities. Such an approach shows greater confidence in the ability and patriotism of small minions of officials, than in top academics, intellectuals, and public men. It is comical, if not a tragic paradox, that while seeking to improve relations with our neighbouring countries specially Pakistan, by opening sensitive lines of control and borders, the circular should insult their citizens. If participants from these countries are attending a conference on as innocent a subject as International Arbitration Law, clearance has to be taken from both the Ministry of Home Affairs and also from the Ministry of External Affairs which would not be the case, if the participants were from other countries of Asia and Europe.

RIGHT OF PRIVACY AND THE COURT

Although there is no specific provision in our Constitution guaranteeing the right of privacy, the judgement in the *Peoples' Union for Civil Liberties* (PUCL) case has taken a view somewhat favourable to the citizens, that the 'right to privacy' is part of the right to life and personal liberty, and that telephone tapping, unless it comes within the grounds of restrictions provided under Article 19(1), 19(1)(a) of the Constitution, is improper.

But the judgement has not provided any firm and satisfactory safeguards against the continued misuse of telephone tapping. PUCL's plea that no telephone tapping be permitted without obtaining prior *ex parte* judicial authorization, has not been accepted. Instead, interception has been permitted if authorized by Home Secretaries, whose order is subject to review by a committee consisting of Cabinet Secretary at the centre, Chief Secretary in states, along with some other secretaries. This is unfortunate because reports of interception were sent regularly to the Cabinet and Home Secretaries even prior to this judgement, and yet the Central Bureau of Investigation (CBI) report was frank enough to admit that its enquiries had revealed unjustified interceptions of telephones of a larger number of journalists, members of Parliament, Chief Ministers, and even some central ministers.

Provision in the judgement for a review committee is equally toothless as it would be an appeal from Caesar to Caesar, all within the intimate obliging circle of the elite bureaucracy. This touching, but misplaced, faith in bureaucracy is a serious flaw in the judgement, especially in view of the Court's own finding that several lapses had occurred in the execution of the orders passed under the Act.

SATISH SHARMA AND THE COURT

A pall of gloom must spread over all the Public Interest Litigation (PIL) activists with the Review judgement in the case of Satish Sharma, setting aside an earlier Bench decision imposing exemplary damages of Rs. 50 lakhs on him, for his illegal action of wrongfully allotting 15 petrol pumps. The earlier Bench had held that all allotments made by Satish Sharma, in his discretion as the then Minister of State for Petroleum and Natural Gas in the central government, were wholly arbitrary, nepotistic, and motivated by extraneous considerations. The Review Court also recorded its own findings in more devastating form as follows:

> The conduct of the petitioner in making allotment of petrol outlets was atrocious, specially those made in favour of the Members of Oil Selection Board or their sons, etc., . . . and reflects a wanton exercise of power by the petitioner. This court has already used judicial vituperative in respect of such allotments and we need not strain our vocabulary any further in this regard.

Notwithstanding these strong observations, the Court has surprisingly gone ahead to review the earlier judgement. It is a little difficult to appreciate how, having held that the conduct of Sharma was wholly unjustified, the Court could go on nevertheless to say, that it fell short of misfeasance in public office. It is a settled law that misfeasance in public office is the name given to the tort which includes malicious power and deliberate mal-administration. In such cases, the courts have the power to impose damages because no public servant can say 'you may set aside an order but you cannot hold me personally liable for it'.

The Court accepted the principle that in action for tort, exemplary damages can be awarded when the conduct of a government or its officers is found to be arbitrary. However, it accepted the review by laying down a principle, which if allowed to prevail, would damage the whole fabric of representative democracy, namely, its findings that Sharma 'did not, on becoming a minister, assume the role of a trustee in the real sense, nor does a "trust" come into existence in respect of government properties'. Directors of public oil companies are trustees of their company finances and are liable for breach of trust. But inexplicably, the Court holds that Mr. Sharma who, as Minister of Petroleum and Natural Gas, appointed directors is blameless, even when the finding is that he has betrayed his position as a minister. Can anything be more cynical?

The principle of ministerial responsibility for any maladministration is well established and was expressed by a British Foreign Secretary (1968) thus: 'we will breach very serious constitutional position if we start holding officials responsible for things that are done wrong—if things are wrongly done, then they are wrongly done by the ministers'. In *Roncarelli* v. *Duplessis*, the Supreme Court of Canada (1959), awarded damages against Quebec's premier personally, for cancellation of a liquor licence of a restaurant owner on the ground that the cancellation was an abuse of discretion.

Another reason given in the review is that unless there is an identifiable plaintiff, there cannot be any order for compensation or damages to redress the loss. But this proposition ignores the distinction between private and public law remedy, namely, that the purpose of public law is not only to civilize public power but also to assure the citizens that they live under a legal system which aims to protect their interests and preserve their rights.

Another worrisome finding of the Court, is the proposition that as Common Cause (an NGO as litigant), had not applied for a petrol pump, it could not have obtained damages for itself, and therefore no tort of misfeasance had been committed by Sharma. This finding ignores the warning given decades ago that if because of a technical plea of locus standi people are denied the right to judicial remedy, they may turn to the streets and in the process, rule of law will be seriously impaired.

THE REPRESENTATION OF PEOPLE ACT 1951 AND THE COURT

PYUCL had challenged Section 62(5) of the Representation of People Act 1951 which denies the right to vote to under-trials who are in prison or police custody, but gives this right to persons accused of heinous offences if they are out on bail. The plea that this provision favours the rich smugglers and black marketeers who can afford bail bonds against the poor under-trials, failed to persuade the Court to hold this provision as unconstitutional. We can now perhaps understand what provoked George Chapman (1559–1634) to say: 'I am ashamed the law is such an ass'.

The Court has upheld this restriction on under-trials by seeking support from the well-accepted proposition that criminalization of politics is the negation of democracy, and thus subversive of free and fair election which is a basic feature of the Constitution. A lay man, however, would find absurdity in a law which at one and the same time permits a convicted person sentenced to two years, to contest elections (even from jail), and vote at an election (if on bail), even though sentenced for 10 years. One wonders as to how this discrimination advances the cause of fair and free elections!

The Court has also justified permitting a person in preventive detention to vote by postal ballot while denying the same right to undertrials in detention. Preventive detention, the Court has held, is to prevent the breach of law while imprisonment on conviction or during investigation is subsequent to the commission of crime, and, therefore, this classification is reasonable. Persons under preventive detention are those who are alleged to be involved in smuggling and narcotic offences, and who can only be kept in detention, if justified on a review by three High Court judges. If a detenue, after such a review process, is permitted to vote at the election, one may ask as to what the logic is for denying this right to a poor under-trial in jail against whom there is only an allegation of guilt? In the United Kingdom, the right to vote is denied only if a person is convicted and during the time he is detained in a penal institution. In Israel, even a convicted person in jail is allowed to vote.

Another justification mentioned for upholding the law, is that it would require deploying a larger police force for conducting elections if under-trials are permitted to vote. But it was never pleaded that under-trials would be taken personally to the polling booths to cast their votes; all that was claimed was the right to vote by postal ballot, as was the case with detenues under the preventive detention law. This did not require any extra police force to accomplish.

But what is of distorting consequence, is the reasoning that as the right to vote is subject to the limitations imposed by the statute, the challenge to any provision of the election law cannot be made with reference to a fundamental right. This is contrary to Article 13(2) of the Constitution, which mandates that a law which contravenes any of the fundamental rights shall be void. Thus, the election law is no holy cow to claim immunity from the sweep and protection of Article 14. The guarantee of equal protection under Article 14, according to earlier Supreme Court decisions, embraces the entire realm of state action, even in the matter of granting privileges and contracts. How then can it be said that the statute on election law is immune from scrutiny under this Article?

CAPITAL PUNISHMENT AND THE COURT

The Court has been rather cautious in matters in which legislation and public opinion have strong views, say about capital punishment. In this regard, the role of the judiciary has been too conservative, notwithstanding the fresh thinking in favour of abolition of death penalty throughout the world. The rationale for the abolition of death penalty was wisely expressed by President Eduardo Frei of Chile: 'I cannot believe that to defend life and punish the person that kills, the State should in its turn kill. The death penalty is as inhuman as the crime which motivates it.'

The support for the death penalty has remained strong in India. In 1946, the then Home Minister stated that the government did not think it wise to abolish capital punishment. Ten years later, when the centre asked the states for their opinion, most expressed support for the death penalty. In its 35th report (1967), the Law Commission took the view that capital punishment acts as a deterrent to crime, though it conceded lack of statistical data to prove or disprove its view.

The Supreme Court traditionally has not questioned capital punishment, though some liberal judges have tried to develop the alternative by holding that if more than two years have passed since the imposition of a death sentence, the accused could invoke Article 21 and demand that the death sentence be quashed. However, in Triveniben (1989), the Supreme Court unanimously upheld the death penalty to be constitutional, and held that the 'delay' could only be counted from the day the Supreme Court's judgement was pronounced (in other words when the judicial process comes to an end). The Court added a caveat that the time consumed by repeated petitions at the instance of the convicted person should not be considered 'delay' to benefit the accused. In April 1991, however, the Supreme Court reduced the death sentence that it had confirmed in 1988 on Daya Singh, who had murdered Punjab Chief Minister Pratap Singh Kairon, to life imprisonment because of 'delay'. Strangely, this was done without any examination of the causes of the delay, apparently in contravention of its 1989 decision.

The cacophony of differing judicial views is bound to continue so long as the death penalty remains on the statute book. Each judge, it seems, reaches for his own interpretation of the retributive or reformative aspect of criminal punishment. So we have confusing signals on the death penalty. Ironically, after the rarest of the rare doctrine of 'delay' was propounded in the 1980s, the Supreme Court confirmed death penalty in 40 per cent of the cases in 1980–90 as against 37.7 per cent of the cases in 1970–80—an increase of 3.3 per cent. For the High Courts, the figures confirming death sentence rose from 59 per cent in 1970–80 to 65 per cent in 1980–90.

The vociferous opposition to the abolition of death penalty comes from the myth that it will lead to higher rate of murders. As many as 118 countries have abolished death penalty either in law or in practice, and the mountain of statistical data collected in most of these countries suggests no positive correlation between the abolition of capital punishment and the rate of murders or homicides. In 1988, a United Nations survey concluded that research has failed to provide any evidence that executions have a greater deterrent effect over life imprisonment. And a survey by the *New York Times*, in 2000 found that the homicide rate in states with death penalty was 48 to 101 per cent higher than in states without death penalty during the last twenty years. On top of this, the irreversibility of the death sentence and the danger of executing the 'innocents'—one exoneration for every seven executions since the US Supreme Court reinstated the death penalty in 1976—demands our serious consideration to abolish the death penalty.

The Baldus report prepared in the United States, found that if a homicide victim was white, his or her killer was four times more likely to get the death sentence than if the victim was black. The same disadvantage would occur in India in case of a Dalit or a poor person. It cannot be disputed that the outcome of any trial depends to a fairly large extent on the quality of legal advice that the accused receives. This loads the scales in favour of the rich who find it easier to avoid the death penalty rather than the poor. The arbitrariness, sometimes approaching freakishness, of the sentencing mechanism in India persuades one to strongly urge (and the Court can allow itself to take some bold initiative), that retaining capital punishment is less just and is a violation of human rights.

CRIMINALIZATION OF POLITICS AND THE COURT

The peoples' anger at the criminalization of politics found a sympathetic ear with the judiciary, when it held that the 'right to know', mandates all candidates to disclose their involvement in criminal cases, and to list all their assets in their nomination papers for elections. Although the Court only gave restricted directions, it invited total unanimous criticism from all political parties close to the 2004 parliamentary elections. Surely, this correct stand of the Court could not be said to be interfering in the political field; rather, it was a step in the preservation of the citizens' democratic right to know—an aspect of the right of full speech guaranteed by Article 19 of the Constitution. And yet, political parties let loose a flood of calumny against the judiciary, and charged it for dabbling in politics and transgressing its judicial boundaries. This was a ploy of the political parties to prevent the glare of publicity on the hidden skeletons in their closets. Notwithstanding, the Court stood by the fundamental right of the citizens to know and rightly went ahead in giving the necessary direction.

The ghastly murder of Graham Staines and his sons (Orissa), on the night of 22 January 1999, shocked the nation. It was a communal demon let loose with no restraint. Investigation by the police did not seem to work. A small time criminal (Dara) was given the mantle of a Hindu militant showing that he was out to save Hinduism from the

Christians. The burning of the Staines' family—a law abiding and compassionate family which had been in the country for a long time—was a disgusting and loathsome act. An inquiry by a sitting judge of the Supreme Court failed to find a communal angle in the murder; his findings invited serious adverse comments. A criminal trial began, but years rolled by and the public became cynical and despondent. Here again, the judiciary demonstrated its resilience. A Sessions Judge, unfazed by the earlier inquiry report given by a Supreme Court judge, convicted the culprits, notwithstanding the blatantly communal twist given to this case in the highly-charged Hindutva-Sangh Parivar environment. The Session, Judge, for sure, deserves our compliments for his courage and impartiality.[2]

PRIVATIZING HPCL-BPCL AND THE COURT

In 2000, all the opposition parties were unanimous in their view that the Vajpayee Centre should seek the approval of Parliament before privatizing two oil public sector undertakings: HPCL-BPCL. The stubbornness of the government in resisting such a sensible demand was hard to explain. The will of the people is reflected in the Parliament—the Executive is a temporary incumbent—and it is the Parliament which speaks the voice of the nation. There was abundant public demand that the oil industry, which in modern days is the kernel for development of any society , should remain in the public sector, and not be parcelled out to private oil buccaneers including foreign operators. Mass protest by political parties and trade unions created no ripples for the Government. All seemed lost for a while until a public interest litigation in the Supreme Court restored the democratic right of the people and asked the government to seek the approval of Parliament.[3] It is indeed ironic that an ultra-nationalist government which should have been supportive of public undertakings particularly in the oil sector so critically needed for economic development, required the intervention of the Supreme Court to safeguard the national interest and recognize the supremacy of Parliament.

GENERAL REVIEW

But as in life, so in judiciary; not all is rosy. Thus, we have the unfortunate and demonstrably erroneous decision by the Supreme Court, denying government employees the right of collective bargaining and strikes and, more important, purporting to give gratuitous advice on the morality and ethics of this most prized right of workers—a view that has pitted the working class against the Court.[4]

We also have instances of superior courts showing, at times, undue over-sensitivity and self-projection by using their power of contempt by ignoring the warning given by Chief Justice Gajendragadkar: 'We ought never to forget that the power to punish for contempt, large as it is, must always be exercised cautiously, wisely and with circumspection.' Frequent or indiscriminate use of this power in anger or irritation would not help to sustain the dignity or status of the courts; it may rather affect the courts adversely. Wise Judges never forget that the best way to sustain the dignity and status of their office is to earn the respect of the public at large by the quality of their judgements, based on fearlessness, fairness, and objectivity—a view reinforced by Justice Krishna Iyer: 'If Judges decay, the contempt power will not save them.'

It often happens that a Judge is faced with an iniquitous provision while the legislature, for reasons of political sensitivity or even sheer lethargy, is unable to bring in a fresh, desired legislation.[5] So a situation arises where literal interpretation of the law seems grossly unjust to a Judge. The traditional view would be to leave the matter to the legislature. I would beg to differ; when faced with such a situation a Judge cannot hide behind the legislative skirt. I myself was faced with such a situation when dealing with the case of a young man who was being prosecuted for attempting to commit suicide, under Section 309 of the Indian Penal Code (IPC), because the parents had refused him to marry a girl of his choice.

My state of mind can be understood from the observations I made in my judgement: 'The continuance of Section 309 is an anachronism unworthy of a humane society like ours . . . there was no justification for a provision like Section 309 IPC to be on the statute book. It seems paradoxical that a person who (if the prosecution is to be believed), is so unhappy that he makes an attempt to commit suicide. But if he fails in his attempt, he should be arrested and roughed through by the police and face the criminal courts . . . which will coarsen him further . . . instead of being attended to by medical doctors and psychiatrists.'

I, therefore, called to my file 120 cases filed under Section 309 of the IPC that were pending in Delhi Courts. My justification for adopting this unusual course of action was expressed in my judgement: 'It is true that Section 309 IPC still continues to be on the statute book and, technically speaking, the offence continues to be there . . . if the police send up a charge sheet under Section 309 IPC, the Courts cannot *per se* hold that a case has been sent up for an offence which is not a part of the statute. But I see no reason why (there is) the delay in repealing this provision, which no longer finds place in almost all the civilized nations of the world. . . . As it is, there is enough of criminality in society which would keep the police, the prosecution, and the courts busy for all the time; and there is no reason to put more stress on these institutions than is absolutely necessary. I can only hope that this provision is removed from the statute book at the earliest. Personally speaking, I see no justification for the police to send up a case under Section 309 IPC.'

As a consequence, the proceedings in all 120 cases were quashed. The dilemma of a Judge who believes that the prosecution under Section 309 IPC is unjust and cruel, clearly had to find some place in determining his choice of the sentence, though he may be somewhat rightly criticized as having taken on the role of the legislature. But it is difficult for the courts to observe restraint when dealing with an obviously uncivilized provision of law; the courts would rather take a risk, than be a party to such a monstrosity of law. It is a different matter that my satisfaction was short-lived; later, a full Bench of the Supreme Court took a contrary view. But these are the normal hazards of the administrative hierarchy of the court system. On its part, the judiciary roots for justice in the hope that legislatures would be persuaded into giving a genuine consideration to such and other substantial matters of public concern.

Overall, the judiciary is still a mixed bag—it does seem to be on the right track but the journey is still long and hazardous.

NOTES

1. The Vajpayee Government lost the 2004 parliamentary elections. The new government under the leadership of Prime Minister Manmohan Singh (UPA) at the centre repealed the Act in 2004. For arguments against POTO, see, *The Hindu International Edition*, editorial, 4 October 2005.
2. Ibid.
3. See, *India Today*, 29 September and 20 October 2003.
4. Ibid. Also see, *Frontline*, 29 August and 12 September 2003. 'The Supreme Court's observations', writes Venkatesan, '"on government em-

ployees" right to strike are in sync with a series of recent verdicts on democratic rights and labour issues in the era of liberalization'.

5. The Supreme Court in the *Islamic Academy* case (2005), declared that unaided professional institutions were entitled to autonomy in their administration and that the state governments could not impose a seat-sharing quota or reservation policy in admissions in such institutions. The Parliament criticized the decision but the Court reminded the government that it had failed to bring in a piece of legislation to enforce the reservation policy as advised in the T.M.A. Pai case years ago. For controversies, see *Frontline*, 9 September 2005; *The Statesman Weekly*, 27 August 2005.

6

Public Interest Litigation: Supreme Court in the Era of Liberalization

PRASHANT BHUSHAN

The foundations of public interest litigation were laid in the late 1970s with cases like the Ratlam Municipalities case. The scope and breadth of public interest litigation were expanded in the eighties from the initial environmental concerns, to concerns like bonded labour, child labour, the rights of detenues, inmates of various asylums, the rights of the poor to education, to shelter and other essential amenities which would enable them to lead a life of dignity. Article 21 was expansively interpreted to include all these rights, and the rule of locus standi was relaxed to enable any public spirited citizen to move the courts on behalf of a person or persons, who may not have the social or financial capacity to move the courts themselves. Subsequently, in the early nineties the courts also took up cases, as public interest litigation, involving corruption in high places and the accountability of public servants.

This new activism on the part of the courts naturally created serious rumblings of discontent in the political and bureaucratic establishments which charged that the courts were going beyond their normal role and were assuming extra-constitutional powers. The political establishment also threatened from time to time to curb the powers of the courts with regard to public interest litigation by legislation. However, since this activist role of the courts gained increasing public support, the political establishment desisted from such legislative misadventures. However, the charges of usurpation of extra-constitutional powers by the activist courts continued to be made by all sections of the ruling establishment. Unfortunately however, these charges appear to have struck a sympathetic chord among a significant section of the court, as it appears from some of their pronouncements recently. There is now a large body of cases decided in the last decade, where the court has not only betrayed a lack of sensitivity towards the rights of the poor and disadvantaged sections of society, but has also made gratuitous and unmerited remarks regarding the abuse of public interest litigation.

This decade has also been the decade of 'economic reforms' as they are called. Several public interest cases were filed during this period challenging alleged perversions, corruption, and other illegalities involved in the implementation of the new economic policies. Almost all of these cases were dismissed. In several of them, the court hinted at and made remarks suggesting an abuse of public interest litigation. Since I had, myself, been involved in many of these cases as a lawyer, I thought that it would be interesting to investigate, whether one could see a change in the philosophy of the Supreme Court with regard to public interest litigation during the era of economic reforms. This is what I have set out to do briefly in this presentation. The results are quite illuminating and, indeed distressing.

In *BALCO Employees' Union* v. *Union of India*,[1] where the employees' union of the government company had challenged its disinvestment on various grounds, including the arbitrary and non-transparent fixation of its reserve price, the Supreme Court, while dismissing the petition, went on to make the following observations:

> There is, in recent years, a feeling which is not without any foundation that public interest litigation is now tending to become publicity interest litigation or private interest litigation and has a tendency to be counter-productive. . . . PIL is not a pill or a panacea for all wrongs. It was essentially meant to protect basic human rights of the weak and the disadvantaged, and was a procedure which was evolved where a public-spirited person filed a petition in effect on behalf of such persons who on account of poverty, helplessness or economic and social disabilities could not approach the court for relief. There have been, in recent times, increasing instances of abuse of PIL. Therefore, there is a need to re-emphasize the parameters within which PIL can be resorted to, by a petitioner and entertained by the court.

The court in this case refused to consider the petition of B.L. Wadhera, a lawyer known for having taken up many serious public interest cases, on the ground that he was not directly affected by the disinvestment of Balco. It went on to observe:

(I)t will be seen that whenever the court has interfered and given directions while entertaining PIL, it has mainly been where there has been an element of violation of Article 21, or of human rights, or where the litigation has been initiated for the benefit of the poor and the underprivileged who are unable to come to court due to some disadvantage. In those cases also, it is the legal rights which were secured by the courts. We may, however, add that public interest litigation was not meant to be a weapon to challenge the financial or economic decisions which had been taken by the government in exercise of their administrative power. No doubt a person, personally aggrieved by such decisions which he regards as illegal, can impugn the same in the court of law, but, a public interest litigation at the behest of a stranger could not to be entertained. Such a litigation cannot *per se* be on behalf of the poor and the downtrodden, unless the court is satisfied that there has been violation of Article 21, and the persons adversely affected are unable to approach the court. The decision to disinvest and the implementation thereof is purely an administrative decision relating to the economic policy of the State and challenge to the same, at the instance of a busybody, cannot fall within the parameters of public interest litigation. On this ground alone, we decline to entertain the writ petition filed by Shri B.L. Wadhera.

This effectively meant that a citizen could not challenge the loot of the public exchequer by way of PIL unless he was personally affected. It is significant that these observations were made in a case involving a challenge to an element of the so-called 'economic reforms' of the government. It will be seen that the Supreme Court has almost without exception, negated all challenges to any element of the economic reforms package of the government, even when such challenges were based on specific violation of law or evidence of corruption.

In Balco itself, the challenge to the sell-off of the public sector undertaking was based, inter alia, on a completely non-transparent and arbitrary valuation of the company conducted in less than a week by an evaluator of immovable property, having no experience in the valuation of companies. It had been pointed out that the valuation of the captive power plants of the company alone were worth more than the price at which it was being sold. The Court, however, refused to examine this challenge by saying that the valuation was done by one of the known methods of valuation.

In *Citu* v. *Union of India*,[2] where the validity of the Enron power project had been challenged on the ground that it was being set up in violation of Section 29 of the Electricity Supply Act, that the project would be ruinous to the finances of the State Electricity Board, and that there was adequate circumstantial evidence of corruption in the sanction of the project, the court restricted the challenge, only to examine the accountability of the public servants involved in the sanction of the project. It refused to examine the challenge to the project itself on the ground that it would not be in the public interest to go into the validity of a project which had been substantially set up and against which several previous challenges had been rejected by the courts. This was said despite the fact that the construction of Phase 2 of the project (which was more than twice the size of Phase 1), had not even commenced at the time, and that none of the previous challenges to the project were based on the grounds and material on which the CITU challenge was based. One of the grounds on which CITU had challenged the project was that under Section 29 of the Electricity Supply Act, it was only the Central Electricity Authority (CEA) which had the power to examine and grant technical and economic approval to the project. In this case, when the CEA was protesting the cost of power from this project as too high, the Finance Ministry told the CEA not to examine the financial aspects of this project and proceed to grant only the technical approval. This is how the project came to be approved, which went on to supply power to the State Electricity Board at too high a cost of up to Rs. 27 per unit, as a result of which the supply from the project had to be stopped, leading to claims of thousands of crores of rupees by Enron in an arbitral tribunal in London.

In *State of Karnataka* v. *Arun Kumar Agarwal*,[3] the Karnataka High Court had ordered a CBI investigation into the circumstances in which a 1,000 MW power project had been approved in Karnataka. Among others, the series of highly suspicious circumstances found by the High Court which warranted such investigation were:

a. That the financial capacity of the company, Cogentrix, which had been approved to set up this project was such that no reasonable person could think that it was capable of executing such a project. Its paid-up capital was only US $130,000, as against a project cost of over $1 billion. Its debt equity ratio was 19.2 to 1 as against the norm of 2:1.
b. That Cogentrix had falsely claimed in its techno-economic feasibility report, that General Electric Co. would be its technical partner for it to piggyback on the technical experience of GE.
c. That China Light and Power, which was subsequently brought in as a partner by Cogentrix, had shown an amount of 191 million Hong Kong dollars as development costs in India (through its Hong Kong

subsidiary, CLP international), though they did not have any ongoing project in India, and had not shown how and on what projects these costs had been incurred. This Hong Kong subsidiary was subsequently shut down and another subsidiary by the same name was opened in the British Virgin Islands, a known tax haven for money-laundering.

d. That though the requirement for power in Karnataka would mainly be in the Bangalore area, and that is why originally the application of Cogentrix was for setting up a 500 MW plant in Bangalore, and another 500 MW plant in Mangalore, later however, they were allowed to set up the entire 1,000 MW plant in Mangalore, necessitating expensive transmission of power by the state authorities from Mangalore to Bangalore.
e. That though the original permission for setting up the plant was given on the basis, that Cogentrix would sell this power privately to whoever was willing to purchase it from them at mutually negotiated rates, thereafter, the State Electricity Board entered into the power purchase agreement with Cogentrix to purchase the entire power at very high rates.

The Supreme Court, however, made short shrift of the elaborate High Court judgement, holding that . . . 'none of the 13 circumstances noticed by the High Court can be characterized as giving rise to any suspicion, much less the basis for investigation by a criminal investigating agency'.

In the *Centre for Public Interest Litigation* v. *Union of India*,[4] the Supreme Court dismissed the plea for an independent investigation into the government's decision to sell off developed offshore gas and oilfields, from the Oil and Natural Gas Commission (ONGC) to a private joint venture. The challenge was based on a large number of facts and circumstances suggesting corruption in the deal such as:

a. The government's own estimates of the oil and gas deposits kept arbitrarily varying at different points of time and the deal was evaluated at the lowest of such estimates.
b. A Superintendent of Police (SP) of the anticorruption unit of the Central Bureau of Intelligence (CBI) had filed a source information report to the effect that the deal involved a loss of thousands of crores of rupees to the public exchequer, and recommending that an FIR (First Information Report), be registered so that a regular investigation could be commenced, and searches and seizures made.

However, instead of registering an FIR, the SP was transferred out of the CBI soon after he made this report, and the file on which he made the report was made to disappear. The CBI went on to file a false affidavit in the High Court, denying the existence of the file on which the SP's note had been made.

c. The CBI, in another case being investigated by it, had recorded the statement of the private secretary of the Minister of Petroleum (who had signed the deal) that the Minister had received Rs. 4 crores from Reliance Industries, one of the joint venture partners to whom the oilfields had been sold.
d. Various high officials of the Ministry of Petroleum and ONGC who were involved in the evaluation of this deal, gave up their jobs, joining Reliance immediately thereafter.
e. The Comptroller & Auditor General (CAG) of India had submitted a report on this deal pointing out that:

   i. the government had not studied the comparative economics of running the gas fields and oilfields through the ONGC versus giving them to a private joint venture;
   ii. the estimates of gas and oil deposits kept arbitrarily varying at different points of time;
   iii. though the deal was evaluated on certain claimed levels of operating expenses by the joint venture, the operating expenses were not capped in the contract, leading to a situation, whereby the operating expenses actually claimed by the joint venture in the first few years of operation were higher than those of the ONGC; and
   iv. the royalties and cess payable to the Government of India by the joint venture on the extraction of oil and gas were frozen for the duration of the contract, though the joint venture was allowed to sell the oil and gas at international market prices prevailing at any point of time.

However, despite the above-mentioned host of highly suspicious circumstances surrounding the deal, the report of the CAG, and the report of the SP of the CBI, the Court did not think it fit to even order an investigation in the matter, though it castigated and passed strictures against the CBI, for the loss of the file containing the SP's report and their false affidavits filed in the High Court.

In *Delhi Science Forum* v. *Union of India,*[5] the petitioners had challenged the award of telecom licences to private companies on various grounds, including one of the companies, HFCL, which had made by far the highest bids in nine circles had a very small net worth which made it ineligible. It, however, sought to make up its net worth by entering into a joint-venture with a foreign company which had a minor equity in the joint-venture, but 90 per cent of its net worth. The petitioners also challenged the decision of the government to place a cap of three circles for any single company, which effectively allowed HFCL to vacate its other six circles, where it was by far the highest bidder, without the penalty of Rs. 50 crores per circle which it would have otherwise had to pay, since it could not have possibly paid the licence fees of all 9 circles. Again, the court dismissed the challenge by saying that the matter had been cleared by the tender Evaluation Committee and there were no allegations of malafides against it. All other challenges were repelled on the ground that they amounted to challenges to the economic policies of the government.

In *Union of India* v. *Azaadi Bachao Andolan*,[6] the High Court had struck down a government circular which compelled the Income Tax (IT) authorities to exempt post box companies registered in Mauritius as 'offshore companies' from taxation in India on the ground that such a direction violated the IT Act, and prevented the IT authorities from lifting the corporate veil of these post box companies in order to examine their real place of residence. The Supreme Court, however, reversed the High Court decision, holding that the government could, in terms of its economic policies, grant a tax holiday to foreign companies in order to attract foreign investment. It gave short shrift to the argument that this would violate the Income Tax Act under which non-resident companies are taxable on their domestic income, and that any change in the tax regime would have to be done by means of a Finance Act passed by Parliament and could not be made by the executive alone.

The Oil companies case (*HPCL-BPCL* v. *Union of India*[7]), is the only case to my knowledge, in which the Supreme Court has allowed a challenge to any purported implementation of the new economic policy. It held here that the government oil companies nationalized by Acts of Parliament which specifically mandated the companies to remain government companies could not be privatized without amending the Acts and thus taking the approval of Parliament.

So we see that barring the exception of the oil companies case, the court dismissed all other petitions challenging any executive act taken under the cover of economic reforms. While it may be possible to take the view that all these decisions are technically correct, it is difficult not to get the feeling that the court's decisions were influenced by its own approval of the new policies of liberalization, privatization and globalization.

> Indeed, the court in Balco went on to say that . . . lastly, no ex parte relief by way of injunction especially with respect to public projects and schemes or economic policies or schemes should be granted. It is only when the court is satisfied for good and valid reasons that there will be irreplaceable and irretrievable damage that an injunction be issued after hearing all the parties. Even then the petitioner should be put on appropriate terms such as providing an indemnity or an adequate undertaking to make good the loss or damage in the event the PIL filed is dismissed.

A similar proposition, virtually restraining the court from granting any interim orders in PILs challenging any 'development projects', was also laid down by the court in Raunaq International.[8] Obviously, if a public interest petitioner is asked to give a bank guarantee or even an undertaking that he will make good the loss that may occur to the government or any other person, because of an interim order obtained in his petition (in the event of his petition eventually being dismissed), no interim order can ever be granted in a PIL. No petitioner, especially the one who moves the court in the public interest, can be held responsible for the vagaries of the court. Different judges have completely different views, even on matters of law. The Narmada matter, for example, came to be heard and decided, by a bench different from the one which had originally stayed the construction of the dam. Even the bench which eventually dismissed the petition and allowed the construction to proceed had continued the stay order in various hearings. Could or should the Narmada Bachao Andolan (NBA) be saddled with any loss occasioned to the government, or the project authorities, or the contractors, on account of the stay order which stopped the construction for four years? It would completely stultify PILs if such a pernicious view is allowed to prevail.

The activism of the Supreme Court in the last decade is most evident in environmental cases, particularly cases involving the urban environment or deforestation. Thus, the court has taken sweeping and bold steps to move polluting industries out of Delhi, to improve the air quality of Delhi by forcing commercial vehicles to convert to CNG, and to stop deforestation across the country. But it must be noted that in a number of cases where the cause of the environment was pitted against 'development projects', such as large dams, or even hotels and housing colonies, the cause of the environment gave way to the interest of such development. It is important to note that in many of these cases, the legal soundness of the case was also evident from the fact that some of the judges gave dissenting judgements, or that the court went against the advice of its own expert committees.

In *Narmada Bachao Andolan* v. *Union of India*,[9] despite the strong dissenting judgement of Justice Bharucha (pointing out that the Sardar Sarovar project was proceeding without a comprehensive environmental appraisal and without even the necessary environmental impact studies having been done, as was evident from the documents of the government itself), the majority judges still went on to approve the project and allowed it to go ahead, without any comprehensive environmental impact assessment which was necessary, even according to the government's own rules and notifications. The underlying reasons and ideology behind the subordination of the cause of the environment to the cause of 'development' is evident from the majority judgement. There are several passages in the majority judgement, extolling the virtues of the kind of development brought in by large dams. The judgement even goes on to gratuitously emphasize the myth that the Bhakra dam was responsible for the green revolution in the country. This, despite the fact that the court had specifically restrained the Narmada Bachao Andolan from making any submissions on the pros and cons of large dams. The court also goes on to make disparaging remarks against the NBA as being an anti-development organization.

The same subordination of environmental interests to the cause of 'development' is evident in the Supreme Court's judgement in the Tehri dam case (*N.D. Jayal* v. *Union of India*[10]), where the government's own expert committee known as the Hanumantha Rao Committee had given an elaborate report, pointing out a series of violations of the conditions on which environmental clearance to the project, had been given by the Ministry of Environment. The Committee had pointed out that a number of studies which were necessary to evaluate the environmental impact of the project, had not been conducted and had recommended that these studies be conducted forthwith. However, despite this, though Justice Dharmadhikari held, that in order to ensure compliance with the conditions of environmental clearance, it was necessary to constitute an independent expert committee which would monitor the compliance and that further construction of the dam could only proceed on the green signal of this expert committee, the majority judgement did not even bother to ensure compliance with the conditions of environmental clearance of the project. Again, the judgement makes remarks extolling the virtues of development projects such as Tehri and other large dams.

This attitude showing the Court favouring 'development' over the rights of oustees or the environment is most clearly evident in the manner in which the court has sought to push the Mega project called 'Interlinking of rivers'. Consider the circumstances. On Independence Day in 2003, a paragraph was added in the President's speech to the effect that the problems of floods and drought could perhaps be solved by interlinking the rivers. This paragraph was enough for a lawyer, appointed by the Supreme Court as amicus curiae (to assist the Court) in the Yamuna pollution case, to file a short application praying that the court should direct the government to take up this project. As if on cue, the bench headed by the then Chief Justice B.N. Kripal issued notices to all the states and the centre. On the next day of hearing, which was the day before the retirement of the then Chief Justice, an order was passed which is now effectively being treated by the government as a direction by the court to undertake this project and complete it within the shortest possible time. The order noted that only the Union of India and the State of Tamil Nadu had filed responses to the notice issued by the court. The Union of India pointed out that the project would cost Rs. 5,60,000 crores, would take forty-three years, and would need the consent of the states. The State of Tamil Nadu had filed an innocuous affidavit, virtually saying nothing. The Court noted that no other state had filed any affidavit and therefore it could be assumed that none had any objection to the implementation of this project! After orally noting that funds cannot be any constraint for the government for a project in the national interest, the Court observed in its order that the project should be completed within 10 years! It also went on to advise the union government that in case the consent was not forthcoming from the states, it should consider passing a legislation to obviate consent of the states for this project.

All this for a project which would require funds equal to the total irrigation budget of the country for the next forty-four years, if the Ninth Plan expenditure is any guide. And all this without hearing any interested party, not even the states, without any discussion or debate whatsoever, without completing even feasibility studies, leave aside the question of social, environmental, economic or optimality assessments! Such is the casual nonchalance with which this country is being pushed to a course, which would have unparalleled and unprecedented, financial, social, and environmental consequences.

In *TATA Housing Development Company* v. *Goa Foundation*,[11] the Court went against the report of its own expert committee in allowing the construction of a housing colony on land which had been held by the committee to be forest land. The Court held that the committee had wrongly classified this land as forest land, by holding that the committee had deviated from its own norms. The court also relied on the reports of some other private experts filed by the Tata Housing Development Company. Without entering into an elaborate discussion of the merits of this judgement, it may only be noted, that such microscopic examination of a report of the courts own expert committee has never been made at the instance of a poor or weak petitioner. For example, the court did not critically examine or interfere with the report and recommendations of the centrally-empowered committee (appointed by the Court), regarding fishing by poor local fishermen in the Jambudvip islands. The court's orders based on the committee's report had effectively deprived hundreds of poor fishermen, who were using the Jambudvip islands for fishing for their livelihood.

The period of economic reforms also appears to have coincided with an apparently decreased sensitivity of the Courts to the rights of the poor. This is evident from the attitude that the Court has displayed towards slum dwellers, oustees, and workmen. In *Almitra Patel* v. *Union of India*,[12] the court, while adversely commenting upon the government's policy to rehabilitate slum dwellers, remarked that 'the promise of free land, at the taxpayers' cost, in place of a *jhuggi*, is a proposal which attracts more land grabbers. Rewarding an encroacher on public land with the free alternative sites is like giving a reward to a pickpocket.' This, despite that the court was aware of the fact that most of the dwellers live in sub-human conditions and do not have access to other houses, and contrary to the court's earlier repeated pronouncements, that the right to shelter and housing was a fundamental right of every citizen of the country.

In *Ekta* v. *Union of India*, the Supreme Court refused to stop the eviction of slum dwellers in Calcutta, who had been living in those slums for the last more than thirty years, despite the fact that they had no other access to housing nor were they being offered any alternative place to go to, by the government. This was a case where the High Court had ordered the eviction on the ground that the slums were a public nuisance. In *Azaadi Bachao Andolan* v. *Union of India* (2003), the Supreme Court even refused to examine the question whether the Land Acquisition Act in so far as it allowed compulsory acquisition of land from persons who are dependent upon that land for their livelihood, is violative of their fundamental rights, since the Act does not obligate the government to provide them with alternative land or an alternative means of livelihood. The challenge to the validity of the Act was made in the circumstances that the monetary compensation given under the Act does not enable the oustees to recover what they lose by their displacement as a result of compulsory acquisition of the land, and that they are in effect deprived of their livelihood by such compulsory acquisition.

The recent decision of the Supreme Court (*T.N. Rangarajan* v. *State of Tamil Nadu*[13]), holding that there is neither any fundamental nor legal nor any moral right to strike on the part of workmen (which not only goes against the Statute where this right has been recognized, but also against several earlier judgements), has further strengthened the perception among a significant class of poor and disadvantaged sections of society that, despite its expansive pronouncements on the ambit of fundamental rights under Article 21 of the Constitution, the ideology of the Supreme Court has, during this phase of 'reforms', shifted decisively in favour of the rich and powerful sections of society.

The above cases provide more than anecdotal evidence for the propositions that: (a) the Supreme Court as an institution has frowned upon challenges to any action of the executive taken in the purported furtherance of 'economic reforms', even when such challenges were based on violations of statute and evidence of corruption; and (b) the Court appears to have diluted its interpretation of Article 21, in the recent past. At the very least, it has often not acted to enforce the rights that it had declared earlier in favour of the poor and the weak.

In these circumstances, it is indeed tempting to argue that the recent drawing back of the Court in PIL, and the fears expressed by it of the possible abuse of PIL, is because the Court has in fact bought into the ideology underlying the economic reforms—an ideology which venerates the virtues of free market, and minimizes the role of the state in providing education, jobs, and the basic amenities of life to its citizens. Such an ideology runs counter to the Court's earlier expansive interpretation of Article 21. This hypothesis does seem to offer the simplest, though not the most exhaustive, explanation for the above decisions of the Court.

NOTES

1. (2000) 2 *Supreme Court Cases* 343
2. (1997) 4 SCALE(SP-16)
3. (2000) 1 *Supreme Court Cases* 210
4. (2000) 8 *Supreme Court Cases* 606
5. AIR 1996 *Supreme Court Cases* 1356
6. (2003) 8 SCALE 287
7. (2000) 7 *Supreme Court Cases* 532
8. (1999) 1 *Supreme Court Cases* 492
9. (2000) 10 *Supreme Court Cases* 664
10. 2003(7) SCALE 54
11. (2003) 11 *Supreme Court Cases* 714
12. (2000) 3 *Supreme Court Cases* 575
13. (2003) 6 *Supreme Court Cases* 581

7

Politics of Judicial Administration

R.K. BARIK

INTRODUCTION

Judiciary is an important pillar of a democratic State. It has a long history but in the present capitalist world it plays a critical role. This is so because market economy is based on contractual obligations which, in turn, require (a) predictable laws governing marketplace; and (b) a legal regime that protects capital formation and ensure property rights. Judiciary adjudicates conflicts to ensure that contractual obligations are discharged according to the rules of the game. This enhances investors' trust in the economy and in the marketplace. Neither the national nor the global economies can work without a fair and impartial adjudication process. For that matter, even a civil society is 'civil' to the extent that it conducts itself according to the rules of the game. The essence of a constitutional democracy is that it respects the rules of the game and accords universality to the rule of law which limits the concept of absolute sovereignty or absolute state. Whether such rules are written (in a constitution), or unwritten (based on traditions and conventions), they are considered sacrosanct in constitutional democracies. The United States articulates the philosophy of a limited state through its constitutional separation of powers and checks and balances. Article 1 of the American Constitution vests legislative powers in the Congress; Article 2 vests executive powers in the President; and Article 3 vests powers in the Judiciary, to settle disputes arising out the legislature and the executive. This recognizes the supremacy of judiciary, which has the power of judicial review to ensure that the laws passed by the Congress and the executive actions taken by the President are constitutionally valid.

India is a constitutional democracy. The Constitution of India provides for a parliamentary-federal structure of government, recognizes the supremacy of a long list of fundamental rights guaranteed to citizens, and commits itself to the promotion of liberty, equality, and justice. Indian democracy affirms its faith in the promotion of a social welfare state (acknowledged through the 'directive principles of state policy'), with the positive provisions made for the protection of minority rights, as well as for the promotion of the weaker sections of society (scheduled castes and scheduled tribes, among others). As the Indian society has been hierarchical in its social structures for centuries, measures taken by the government to promote social welfare and egalitarianism often create conflicts in the process of modernization of traditions. Additionally, the special provisions for affirmative action to enhance the welfare of the marginalized sections of society create their own political dynamics versus the rule of law. Notwithstanding the recent thrust towards privatization and globalization, the promise of the Indian state to promote the distribution of wealth, for the benefit of the hitherto excluded sectors of society generate a variety of policy and constitutional challenges, which require complex and sober mediation. Although the Indian Constitution, unlike the American Constitution, does not subscribe to the theory of separation of powers—the executive and legislative organs of the government are fused in the parliamentary system, it does recognize the independence of the judiciary and assigns to the higher judiciary, the role of the guardian of the Constitution. In fact, what is said of the US Supreme Court is more than true for our Supreme Court: the Constitution is what the Supreme Court says it is. Our apex Court has not only acquired the power of judicial review of legislation but has also the power to review constitutional amendments. In the context of the moorings of the Indian state in welfare and egalitarianism democracy, the judiciary has a very difficult and complex umpiring role to play. In the vibrant political democracy that India is, the judiciary has to do a tight rope walk, in balancing several social and economic demands with due regard for the rule of law and the basic principles of the Constitution, and without compromising the constitutional role of the other two branches of government.

THE CRISIS OF THE JUDICIAL SYSTEM

It is believed by many, that the failures of executive and legislature are glaring. The judiciary is over-active and performs functions which should have been performed by the other two organs of the government. I shall examine this presumption of our intelligentsia. Both legislature and executive are experiencing decay and unable to perform up to expectations. Rajni Kothari argues that both these institutions were manipulated by a powerful personality. During Nehru's time, these institutions started flowering, but decayed under the authoritarian leadership of Indira Gandhi. She wanted committed bureaucracy and servile politicians. The Congress party had a democratic tradition which got throttled by her.[1] Atul Kohli has agreed to a point that the institutions of the Indian State are in a state of decay, but the reasons are not necessarily those given by Kothari. Kohli argues that these institutions have limited capability to accommodate the demand of surging political participation in the wake of socio-economic mobilization of the country.[2]

Kohli stresses that a large section of society, hitherto excluded, is entering into the political process making more demands on the system which does not have the capacity to handle these demands. The system functions at a low level of performance, which results in the alienation of the people. In the case of the judiciary, one can say that a larger section of our society has not visited the judicial process because of poverty and ignorance. But this section, already in the middle of political battle to capture political power, is poised to enter the judicial process. As the judicial system is already under stress even without its participation, one wonders what will happen when this section storms into the system. Kohli, however, is optimistic. He recognizes the strength of Indian democracy and believes that the Indian system is set for more inclusiveness based on the principle of justice and equality. He appreciates the West Bengal model which has combined economic development with greater mass participation, at various levels of the State. It brings, he argues, economic growth with social justice.

I shall analyse the underlying reasons for the crisis in the judicial system. In our constitutional scheme, the Supreme Court of India has been given so many powers, that Rajeev Dhavan characterizes the Court as the most powerful federal court in the world.[3] In the Constituent Assembly, the lawyers were the most vocal group who demanded all sorts of powers for the Supreme Court. In comparison with the American and British courts, our Supreme Court is the most powerful

Court. In a parliamentary system of government however, it is clear that sovereignty lies with the legislature. They are the elected members. They are supposed to play a definite role in making laws. However, the judiciary has become progressively active in the law-making process. It has usurped new powers. Recently, in a judgement over the Jharkhand Assembly (2005), the apex Court has made a clear breach in the balance of powers. It has trespassed into the legislative boundary by directing the Speaker of the Assembly how to conduct the proceedings of the Assembly.[4]

FRAGMENTATION OF THE POLITICAL PROCESS

The political process is getting fragmented. Non-ideological politics has given rise to politics of identities, caste, and ethnic community. Identities have taken the central place. Issues affecting common masses do not get articulated. Political groups have emerged around these identities. These groups do not articulate the demands of masses. Lack of ideology and lack of proper perspective have brought a class of politicians into the political landscape, who are basically very short-sighted in nature. The Indian National Congress, once a dominant political party, has declined as a monolithic political party. Coalitional politics have not succeeded in creating a coalitional political culture based on shared values. The political leadership is weak and indecisive and has been so for more than a decade. It has been unable to play a decisive role in the law-making process. Policy-making demands better legislations, but the leadership fiddles in the midst of disorderly legislature(s). Lack of policy consensus also accounts for years of delay in passing many urgent pieces of legislation.

ASSUMPTION OF POLICY-MAKING ROLE

The judiciary is exploiting the situation and is getting involved in the policy-making process. Judges give judgements that have wider policy implications. Policy-making is a serious political and administrative business. The policy-makers are supposed to evaluate a variety of alternatives and accept one in the end. It is, however, ironic that the judges, who are neither elected nor accountable to the people, are trespassing into an area for which they are not professionally qualified. No doubt, most of the democratic countries in the world are experiencing this over-domination of the judiciary. Handberg observes: 'A number of scholars in recent years have noted the increasing judicialisation occurring across diverse societies and legal cultures'.[5] Judicialization has been defined by Neal in terms of two inter-related processes: (1) the process by which courts and judges come to dominate increasingly the making of public policies that had previously been made specially by legislatures and executives; and (2) the process by which non-judicial negotiating and decision-making fora come to be dominated by quasi-judicial (legalistic) rules and procedures. The increasing judicialization, it has been argued, has had a damaging effect on the social capital of civil societies. In a comparative study of American and South Asian societies, Fukuyama states that when a lot of money has gone into the litigation process, it signifies the decline of social trust among people and the diversion of productive capital into the non-productive sector of the economy.[6] Unlike as in the United States, social capital is active in Korea, China, and Japan with the consequence that these societies do not spend so much money in litigation. This helps in the economic development of Asian societies.

In the classical sense, the judiciary has never played such a decisive role in the policy-making process as it does now. The courts have played a role but a limited one in democratic systems. Judges are not the elected members. They cannot represent the general will of the people. They belong to a professional class of people who are, generally speaking, socially conservative relative to the non-conservative and 'popularity driven' values of the political elite(s). No wonder, the global companies and even international organizations such as the World Bank and the International Monetry Fund find it more congenial to deal with the judicial and bureaucratic elite, rather than with the political elite. Wherever the political elite is active in separating the chaff from the grain in the national interest, the process of globalization has been slower than otherwise.

NO PROVISION FOR THE REVIEW OF THE SUPREME COURT DECISIONS

American democracy is based on the principle of separation of powers where judicial review was constitutionally permitted. During the nineteenth century, America was experiencing a limited democracy where blacks, minorities, and women did not have basic political rights. Lazare states that 'the result was . . . deliberately ambiguous power arrangement in which it was impossible to determine where ultimate authority lay whether with the Congress, the Presidency or the Supreme Court, or with the people at large in their capacity either as a State or Federal Citizen'.[6] As a consequence of this ambiguous situation, the Supreme Court emerged as the dominant force in political change.

No Western parliamentary democracy accepts the American concept of judicial supremacy. Nor is there a provision in our Constitution for judicial review. The makers of our Constitution were clear that sovereignty lay with the Parliament and not with the judiciary. The judges have expanded the power of judicial review by re-interpreting the Constitution in *Golak Nath* case where they stated that the Parliament had the right to change the Constitution through amendments but did not have the power to change its basic structure. But the very interpretation as to what part of the Constitution is 'basic' depends on the personal whim of the judges. As Rajeev Dhavan has correctly observed: 'Through the Golak Nath case, the Court thrives.'[7] There is no other supreme body or council to review the decision of the Supreme Court except the Supreme Court itself.

THE POLITICS OF COURTS

The trajectory of judicial history tells us that the courts have played politics. The lawyers' lobby in the Constituent Assembly framed the right to property in such a confused manner, that it gave a handle to the courts to interpret the constitutional provision of property in favour of the landlords. The first amendment to the Constitution was made because land legislations were struck down by the courts. Baxi is right in observing that the combination of judges, lawyers, and scholars, conspired to propagate what he calls the 'truth of lies'.[8]

The crisis in judiciary can be located in the number of cases piling up in courts and justice getting delayed. While judges have acquired more and more powers, they have not handled their job well. Needless to say, that when institutions fail to provide justice to common people, the country runs into a deep moral crisis.[9] Notwithstanding the fact that the higher judiciary has opened its doors to the marginalized sections of our society through the public interest litigation process, there is a widespread perception that the judiciary has ignored the Dalits, the Scheduled Tribes and other Backward Classes. The Supreme Court judgement against quotas in private colleges has proved the point once more. As Gallanter puts it, these neglected classes question the legitimacy of the judiciary. From this perspective, Trubeek and Gallanter correctly say that the legal system reaches small sections of the population in most developing countries.[10]

IMPACT OF GLOBALIZATION

Globalization is affecting the judiciary. The judges undersand very well the underlying philosophy of globalization. They reinterpret laws to satisfy the interests of the global order. The World Bank and other international agencies are interested in structural reforms that require that the legal framework should be market-friendly and conducive to balanced development.[11] The judges of the Supreme Court have already observed that 'sovereignty' of the preamble is not applicable in the present day situation. The judges interpret the laws according to the philosophical ideals of globalization. Justice Fernandez is right in observing: 'The widespread process of economic and political liberalization currently taking place in developing countries . . . has brought about a renewed interest in the role of law and legal institutions.'[12]

David Held raises a critical point in his latest book on globalization and democracy. His argument is that globalization would affect democracy negatively.[13] Democracy is nurtured in an environment where there is a low level of inequality between the rich and the poor. Globalization has increased inequality, which threatens the basic fabric of democracy. India is already a land of inequalities. Ambedkar underlined this point in the Constituent Assembly:

> We must begin by acknowledging the fact that there is a complete absence of two things in Indian society. One of these is equality on the social plane. We have in India a society based on the principle of graded inequality which means elevation for some and degradation for others. On the economic plane, we have a society in which there are some who have immense wealth as against many who live in abject poverty. On January 26, we are going to enter into a life of one man, one vote, one value. In our social and economic life we shall by reason of our social and economic structure continue to defy the principle of one man, one vote, one value. How long shall we continue to live this life of contradiction? How long shall we continue to deny equality in our social and economic life? If we continue to deny it for long we shall do so by putting our political democracy in peril.[14]

Gramsci, in his *Prison Notebooks*, raises a similar point that political rationality would come into conflict with economic and social irrationality. That would militate the poor against the rich. The politicians, not the judges, can understand these contradictions. The judges belong to a conservative elite which is more concerned with the procedural rather than the substantive dimensions of such problems. The conservative outlook of the judges is reflected in many of their judgements which have struck down important pieces of social legislation on the ground of due process, an American constitutional provision. The conservatism of the Indian judges will have to be tempered with the social welfare and egalitarian goals of the Constitution, to undo some of the negative impact of globalization and liberalization. In other words, the preamble to our Constitution should be central to judicial interpretation of both national laws and international contractual obligations in order to keep ourselves anchored in social democracy.

PERSISTENCE OF ANTI-POOR BIAS EVEN IN PIL CASES

Some Supreme Court judges had the vision to see the inbuilt bias of the judicial system against the poor. They tried their best in the name of social justice to change the public perception of courts. As Sharma notes: '. . . Justice Bhagwati used his professed philosophy of constitutional interpretation and his kind of activism to serve the constitutional good of securing justice to millions of downtrodden, exploited and mistreated masses of Indian society'.[15] Situations have changed. Many of the judgements in Public Interest Litigation (PIL) are against the poor—for instance, closing down industries in Delhi where lakhs of people lost their livelihood, or providing inadequate relief and rehabilitation to the people displaced in the construction of Sardar Sarovar dam. Articles 38 and 39 of the Indian Constitution are not taken seriously by judges all over India, although there are popular movements on the question of livelihood. Justice Chandrachud observed in the *Dissolution* case in 1977: 'In the last analysis, people for whom the constitution is meant, should not turn their faces away from it in disillusionment for fear that justice is a will-of-the-wisp.'

Several explanations can be looked for if the PILs have not necessarily worked in favour of the poor. Leaving aside the macro-environmental explanations, focus can be turned towards the socio-economic background of judges that populate our benches. Recently, for example, the President of India talked about inadequate representation of Scheduled Castes, Scheduled Tribes, and women in the higher judiciary. The assumption here being that the socio-economic background of judges gets reflected in their judgements. The experience of American courts where judges belonging to the black community and minorities have rendered judgements that are different in nature supports this assumption. To some extent, the crisis of our judicial system can be attributed to the unchanging pattern of judicial recruitment: most of the judges of the Supreme Court have been drawn from four courts—Madras, Bombay, Ahmedabad, and Calcutta; and most of the judges in the higher judiciary have a high socio-economic background.

CONCLUSION

The political system which is engulfing all major institutions, especially the judiciary is in crisis. The majority of the people do not feel that they can get justice from the courts. Surveys conducted by both the print media and visual media have come to the same conclusion. At the same time, the judges have been trying to organize the judiciary, independent of the other two branches of government without bringing basic changes in constitutional positions. This may create problems for democracy in our developing country. If the people are denied justice, they may as well be pushed into a corner and may realize that the struggle for human rights and justice lies beyond law.[16] The way the judiciary is working, it is bringing distortions into the philosophical unity of the State. One organ of the State is waving against the other organs. It is like one part of the body being in disharmony with the other parts of the body.

NOTES

1. Rajni Kothari, 'The Congress System Revisited: A Decennial Review', *Asian Survey*, 14/12, December 1974.
2. Atul Kohli, *Democracy and Discontent: India's Growing Crisis of Governability*, Cambridge, 1994.
3. Rajeev Dhavan, *Justice on Trial: The Supreme Court Today*, Allahabad, 1980.
4. *Frontline*, 8 April 2005.
5. R. Handberg, 'Judicialisation Across Societies: The Spread of Judicial Power and Societal Change', *International Journal of Public Administration*, vol. 22, no. 8, 1999.
   Tate C. Neal, 'Why the expansion of judicial power', in Neal and V. Torbjorn, eds., *The Global Expansion of Judicial Power*, New York, 1995, pp. 27–35.

6. Fukuyama, F., Trusts: the social virtues and the creation of prosperity, London, 1995. Daniel Lazare, 'America the Undemocratic', *New Left Review*, no. 232, 1998, and John Zresper, 'The Separation of Powers in American Politics', *Government and Opposition*, vol. 34, no. 1, Winter 1999.
7. Rajeev Dhavan, *The Supreme Court of India: A Socio-Legal Critique of its Justice Techniques*, Bombay, 1997.
8. Upendra Baxi, *The Indian Supreme Court and Politics*, Lucknow, 1980.
9. John Rawls, *A Theory of Justice*, Cambridge, 1971.
10. David M. Trubeek and Marc Gallanter, 'Scholars in Self-Estrangement: Some Reflections on the Crisis in Law and Development Studies in the US', *Wiscosin Law Review*, 1974, p. 1079.
11. Leila Frischtak, *Governance Capacity and Economic Reforms in Developing Countries*, Washington, 1994, p. 301.
12. Julio Fernandez (ed.), *Good Government and Law, Legal and Institutional Reform in Developing Countries*, The British Council, 1977, p. 1
13. David Held, *Democracy and the Global Order*, Cambridge, 1995.
14. B.R. Ambedkar, *Constituent Assembly Debates*, pp. 667–922, 938–95.
15. M.C. Sharma, *Justice P.N. Bhagwati, Court, Constitution and Human Rights*, Delhi, 1995; R.K. Barik, 'Conflict between Politicians and Judges', *Deccan Herald*, 16 February 1997.
16. Mass All Derecho, 'Beyond Law: Stories of Law and Social Change from Latin America and Around the World', *Issues* 1, 2 & 3, 1991–2, quoted in R. Dhavan, 'Ambedkar's Prophecy: Poverty of Human Rights in India', *Journal of the Indian Law Institute*, January–March 1994.

PART II

Judiciary and Ecology

8

Environmental Justice through Public Interest Litigation

D.S. SENGAR

INTRODUCTION

A very high priority has been accorded to industrial development in India for speedy economic growth. Such progress, however, brings along with it a lot of ecological problems. Environmental pollution caused by hazardous industries is a present and potential challenge to life and to the harmony between man and nature. It is true that industrial development should not proceed at the cost of environmental health but, simultaneously, environmental protection measures should not deprive a country of the opportunities for economic development. As there is always a conflict between industrial development and conservation of the environment, there is an obvious need to balance the values of development and environmental health.

The natural environment provides the most hygienic and healthy conditions for the survival of mankind. However, these conditions have been modified by mankind for productive ends, and hazardous materials such as concrete, charcoal, plastics, smoke, toxic chemicals, wastes, etc., have been added to the environment. Industrialization, urbanization, over-exploitation of natural resources, depletion of traditional sources of energy and the search for new ones, as well as the disruption of ecological balances for economic development, are the major factors responsible for environmental pollution and consequent health hazards to human beings and other biota.

Industries predominantly chemical in nature, pose potential as well as real health hazards. Besides regular pollution, industrial accidents causing air pollution and human health hazards have been reported from many parts of the country. These accidents have virtually created a killer environment in their wake, by destroying overnight what nature has taken thousands of years to create, as shown tragically in the Bhopal disaster. In this accident, at least 5,000 people were killed and some 50,000 people were seriously injured.[1] About one-fifth of the resident population of the gas-affected areas of Bhopal are the children, born in the post-tragedy period to gas-exposed women, with gas-related ailments.[2]

As every industrial activity causes some kind of environmental pollution, we cannot aspire to achieve the state of purity of the environment as existed in pre-industrial societies. However, at present, we are facing the problem of rapid deterioration in environmental quality due to the huge amount of pollutants released from hazardous industries which, in turn, expose humans to greater health hazards. As industrial growth has become inevitable to fulfil human needs, reverting back to the life style of a pre-industrial society is inconceivable. The consequential ill effects of industrialization, therefore, are great challenges for us and call for adopting effective measures to regulate hazardous activities in public interest. This also calls for providing an instrument to the public for accessing justice in matters relating to environment.

NATIONAL RESPONSE TO INTERNATIONAL URGE

While in the environmentally conscious countries, the environmental problems are being handled through legislative action, in India, unlike as in other Commonwealth countries including Canada,[3] these problems have been given a constitutional status for the State to deal with.[4]

The Indian Constitution, as adopted in 1950, did not deal with environmental protection as such. The environmental movement in India has its genesis in the United Nations Conference on Human Environment held at Stockholm in June 1972, in which India actively participated. The participating countries resolved to take appropriate steps for the protection and improvement of human environment. In line with the recommendations of the conference, the Government of India took the necessary steps and, for the first time, specific provisions relating to environmental matters were inserted in the Indian Constitution by way of an amendment in 1976.

One of the Directive Principles added through amendment provides for the protection and improvement of public health as one of the primary duties of the State. Article 48A of the Indian Constitution thus enables the State not only to adopt protective measures but also take all suitable steps to improve an already polluted environment. It is now within the powers of the State to impose restrictions on the use of those resources which adversely affect life and its development.[5] The State is also obliged to direct its policy towards the control of material resources of the community to subserve the common good.[6]

The responsibility for abatement of pollution and protection of environment is also the obligation of every citizen, so that an individual may not overlook his duties to the community and commit wanton destruction of the natural environment. The duty which a citizen owes is specified in Article 51A(g) of the Constitution of India. It states that every citizen should care for the protection and improvement of the natural environment. Since the citizens' fundamental duties are not addressed to the State, a citizen cannot claim that he must be properly equipped by the State for the performance of such duties, though the Supreme Court has issued many directions to the State in this matter, in various environmental cases.[7]

Regarding the importance of constitutional provisions to protect the environment and the roles of the courts to deal with the problem of ecology, the Supreme Court in *Sachidanand Pandey* case[8] held that, 'Whenever a problem of ecology is brought before the Court, the Court is bound to bear in mind Art. 48A of the Constitution, the Directive Principle which enjoins that the State shall endeavour to protect and improve the environment and to safeguard the forests and wild life of the country, and Art. 51A(g), which proclaims it to be the fundamental duty of every citizen of India to protect and improve the natural environment including forests, lakes, rivers and wild life, and to have compassion for living creatures.' The Supreme Court further held: 'when the Court is called upon to give effect to the Directive Principle and the Fundamental duty, the Court is not to shrug its shoulders and say that priorities are a matter of policy and so it is a matter for the policy-making authority'.[9]

The need to conserve natural resources and to improve environmental quality, particularly to prevent damage to fragile and irreplaceable ecosystems, has been increasingly reflected in the national policy of India. The policy elements seek the actual implementation of environmental objectives with the increased use of legislation and regulations in addition to other instruments.[10] Thus, in responding to the international call, the Indian Constitution became the first constitution in the world to attempt to secure the protection of fragile environment at the national level. It laid down the basic foundation for environmental legislation under the directive principles of state policy, in addition to making provision for the citizens' duty towards environmental protection in India.

LEGISLATIVE MEASURES AND INNOVATIONS

Although, the conservation of environment need not be construed as non-intervention, the industrial production process cannot be permitted to go unhindered to pollute the environment. In the words of Paton, 'We cannot have an absolute right to an unspoiled environment, for modern industry must at least in some areas destroy rural beauty. The best that law can do is to curb the worst excesses of industrialization by town planning. Noise and pollution are two of the greatest offenders—the later affects air, water, natural growth and health of humanity.'[11]

India has a large body of environmental laws and regulations. These include laws executed by the central and state governments as well as judicial decisions affecting hazardous activities causing pollution. There are more than 200 statutes that have a direct and indirect bearing on environmental matters. In the pre-independence era, the protection and improvement of the environment was regulated mainly by general laws, i.e. the Indian Penal Code 1860,[12] the Code of Criminal Procedure 1898,[13] and the Police Act 1861.[14] The specific Acts to deal with the problem of water pollution were the North Canal and Drainage Act 1873, the Obstruction of Fairway Act 1881 and the Indian Fisheries Act 1897. The air pollution was regulated by the Oriental Gas Company Act 1857, the Explosives Act 1908, the Indian Boilers Act 1923 and the Motor Vehicle Act 1938.[15] The pesticides were regulated by the Poison Act 1919, and the wild life and conservation of the forests were governed by the Indian Forest Act 1927. Besides these Acts, some provinces had also made their own laws and regulations to protect the environment.

In free India, the Damodar Valley Corporation (Prevention of Pollution of Water) Regulation Act 1948, the River Board Act 1956, and the Merchant Shipping (Amendment) Act 1970 were enacted to curb water pollution. Similarly, the Atomic Energy Act 1962 and the Radiation Protection Rules 1971 attempted to curb atomic radiation.

It is, however, worthy of note, that hardly any case law on pollution has occurred under the Indian Penal Code, which exposes its infirmity in dealing with the problems of pollution. Although the director and managers of the Gwalior Mills were prosecuted under Sections 268, 269, 277, 288 and 290 of the Indian Penal Code for polluting the Chambal River by putting certain industrial wastes into it, the Madhya Pradesh High Court in *Babu Lal* v. *Ghanshyamdas Birla*[16] held that the directors and other officials could not be prosecuted, unless a specific act or omission was attributed to them or there was *mens rea* or an overt act done by them. This is a glaring example of the penal provision under the Indian Penal Code being without teeth to remedy the wrong.

A comprehensive environmental legislation, the Water (Prevention and Control of Pollution) Act 1974, exclusively dealing with the control of water pollution, was enacted only after the Stockholm conference. It not only provides for the prevention and control of water pollution, but also for maintaining and restoring the water quality. Thereafter, the Indian Parliament also enacted other statutes for the purpose of protecting the environment and compensating the pollution victims.[17] The statutes include: The Water (Prevention and Control of Pollution) Cess Act 1977; the Air (Prevention and Control of Pollution) Act 1981; and the Environment (Protection) Act 1986. Besides, the Government of India also enacted the Public Liability Insurance Act 1991 to deal with issues relating to liability arising out of Industrial disasters, and the National Environment Tribunal Act 1995,[18] for effective and expeditious disposal of cases arising out of any accident (occurring while handling any hazardous substance), with a view to giving relief and compensation for damages to persons, property, and the environment. In addition, the National Environment Appellate Authority Act 1997 has been enacted to establish an appellate authority to hear appeals with respect to restriction of areas in which industries, operations or processes shall be carried out, subject to certain safeguards under the Environment (Protection) Act 1986.

However, in spite of an industrial policy,[19] environmental policy,[20] environmental planning,[21] and constitutional and legal protections given to environment in India, the pollution caused by hazardous processes and substances has continued to increase. This situation has been largely caused by the continuing and worsening failure of the legislature and the executive to frame and implement proper laws. In the absence of suitable enforcement, regulatory and monitoring mechanisms, environmental degradation has affected the public interest which has attracted the attention of the judiciary.[22]

EMERGENCE OF PUBLIC INTEREST LITIGATION

Like other socio-economic problems, the equal access to courts is a world-wide problem. The indigent and disabled persons have difficulties in obtaining adequate legal advice and representation in the courts. There are also difficulties in asserting diffuse, collective, and meta-individual rights. Access to the courts is an essential aspect of providing justice which presupposes the existence of an accessible legal system that makes sure that a person can achieve a just solution by approaching a court.[23]

The preamble of the Constitution of India and the directive principles of state policy play a very pivotal role in the development of Indian legal system. The preamble secures to all citizens social, economic and political justice, and also equality of status and opportunity. A new and recent feature fulfilling the objectives laid in the preamble and the directive principles is the rapid growth and development of Public Interest Litigation, which has opened a new chapter in the Indian judicial system.

PIL is the strategic arm of a legal movement to bring justice within the reach of disabled and poor people. These people constitute the low visibility area of the humanity.[24] The legal movement shaping PIL in India has been influenced strongly by the movement in the USA.[25] It was meant to fulfil the need of a large number of people, who individually lacked the resources or operational capacity to vindicate social values and their own specific interest through the courts. The PIL litigants are now able to participate actively and ensure that institutions behave lawfully.[26]

Though the various movements and programmes that contributed to the shaping of the underlying ideology of public interest law in the USA reach back to 1876, when the first legal aid office was established in New York city, the famous Gideon case[27] has really formed the basis for the concept of PIL in the United States.

In India, the concept of PIL was initiated by Justice Krishna Iyer in the year 1976, in the *Mumbai Kamgar Sabha* case.[28] He observed that test litigation, representative actions, *pro bono publico*, and broadened forms of legal proceedings, are in keeping with the current imperative on justice to the common man, and a necessary disincentive to those who wish to bypass the real issues on merit, by suspect reliance on peripheral, procedural shortcomings. . . . Public interest is promoted by a spacious construction of locus standi in our socio-economic circumstances, while conceptual latitudinarianism permits taking liberties with individuali-zation of the right to invoke the higher courts where the remedy is shared by a considerable number, particularly when they are weaker. Less litigation, consistent with fair process, is the aim of adjective law.[29] In the Fertilizer Corporation case,[30] this concept was further developed both by C.J. Chandrachud, and J. Krishna Iyer. On the issue of locus standi, J. Krishna Iyer stated that the Law, as 'I conceive it, is a social auditor and this audit function can be put into action only when someone with real public interest ignites the jurisdiction of the court'. However, the full scope of Public Interest Litigation was analysed by C.J. P.N. Bhagwati, in *S.P. Gupta.*[31] Speaking for the Court, he quoted with approval, Lord Diplock's judgement and opined that it would be a grave lacuna in our system of Public law if a pressure group, like the federation or even a single public-spirited taxpayer, was prevented by outdated technical rules of locus standi from bringing the matter to the clarification of the Court to indicate this rule of law and get such unlawful conduct stopped. It is not a sufficient answer to say that judicial review of the action of the officers of departments of central government is unnecessary, because they are accountable to Parliament for the way in which they carry out their functions. They are accountable to Parliament for what they do, so for as regards efficiency and policy, of Parliament is the sole judge, they are responsible to a court of Justice for the lawfulness of what they do, and of that the Court is the only judge.[32]

C.J. Bhagwati, further held in this case that 'We would, therefore, hold that any member of public having sufficient interest can maintain an action for judgement, redress for public injury arising from breach of public duty or from violation of some provision of the Constitution, or the law, and seek enforcement of such public duty and observance of such constitutional or legal provision. This is also absolutely essential for maintaining the rule of law furthering the cause of justice and accelerating the pace of realization of the constitutional objective of law.'[33]

The USA and Canada (I believe) draw no distinction between 'public interest' cases and ordinary law suits. It only means a provision of lawyers for individuals, groups and for specific types of cases that otherwise go unrepresented.[34] Comparatively speaking, public interest judges in India are doing much more work than the work done by public interest judges in the United States and Canada. However, as the public interest cases increase the burden on the Indian courts and judges (and in the light of heavy backlog of cases which are already pending in the courts), there may be an incentive for public interest and public spirited lawyers[35] to bring public interest cases before the court for mass justice. In Thorson[36] and Nova Scotia Board of Censors[37] cases the Supreme Court of Canada relaxed the 'standing' requirements for obtaining injunctions in a constitutional litigation, diverting attention from the interest of applicant to the interest of lawful administration. Thus, in Canada attempts have been made to broaden the scope of access to socio-economic and environmental justice through PIL.

Public Interest Litigation is a procedural innovation,[38] and a cooperative or collaborative effort to secure observance of legal and constitutional rights,[39] benefits or privileges conferred upon the vulnerable section of the community.[40] It is important to note that procedural rigidities [41] should not be permitted to frustrate the efforts of overcoming the magnitude of hazards, caused by multifarious developments that are taking place in the society as well as in the polity. The extended use of this procedure has facilitated poor and illiterate people, non-governmental organizations, social action groups, and public-spirited persons to bring cases before the appellate judiciary and, thereby, get an easy access to socio-economic[42] and environmental justice.[43]

PUBLIC INTEREST LITIGATION AND ACCESS TO ENVIRONMENTAL JUSTICE

Generally, in environmental litigation, the parties affected by pollution are a large, diffuse and unidentified mass of people. Therefore, the question arises as to who ought to bring such cases to the courts' notice where no personal injury in particular has been noticed. As the human environment belongs to nobody but is *res communis,* any degradation of environmental conditions should be actionable by the community at large, or by any public spirited member of the community. However, procedural norms do not exactly support this proposition. Therefore, in cases of pollution nuisance, where an injury to health is too indirect for any individual to start a legal proceeding for collective wrong, a representative as well as collective action is needed.

The Indian judiciary has been very active and dynamic in transforming fundamental rights into living realities for the poor, the oppressed, and the downtrodden people through PIL. The state is charged with the duty to bring socio-economic and environmental justice to everyone.[44] PIL provides an opportunity to the courts to examine the socio-economic and environmental conditions of the oppressed. It has proved to be a vehicle for fixing the judicial lenses on environmental matters, affecting the public health and safety. In PIL cases brought before the courts by individuals, social action groups, legal aid societies and non-governmental protective organizations, the locus is not a vital question. This is true particularly in those cases where the public authorities have failed to carry out their obligations, resulting in injury to general public.

The biggest hurdle in the way of litigation for environmental justice has been the traditional concept of locus standi.[45] Earlier, when environmentalists approached the courts on behalf of others for seeking relief against the injury, the actions were not maintainable as courts focused their attention on the identity of the petitioner rather than on the subject of petition. However, now the courts' attitudes have changed drastically, and any member of the society having sufficient interest may be allowed to initiate the legal process to assert diffused and meta-individual rights. This sort of standing is meant to defend the rights which are so diffused among the public generally, that no individual right per se can be enforced. The environmental cases falling in this category include those where a citizen is able to enforce his/her right as a member of the society to whom a public duty is owed.[46]

The PIL movement got statutory recognition in 1970 in the United States with the passing of the National Environment Protection Act, 1970. Further, the US Clean Water Act 1970, the Federal Water Pollution Act 1970, the Clean Air Act 1972, and now the Clean Water Act 1977, all provide that, 'any person' or 'any citizen' may bring an action even though the breach of law has not directly affected him.[47] The PIL provided an opportunity for judicial reconsideration of the requirement of locus standi and as a result, attempts were made to broaden the scope of access to environmental justice. However, it is surprising to note that PIL in the United States, which once stood as an example for India, is now losing its importance and the United States Supreme Court has repeatedly insisted on locus standi to reject public interest petitions without consideration of the merits of the case.[48]

On the other hand, the Indian judiciary has developed a totally new environment-oriented jurisprudence which, although still young, is in the process of rapid development. In recent years, the idea of extending legal protection to cases of public environmental interest has resulted in making environmental laws more effective. This has partly been accomplished by the expansion of the principle of locus standi by the Indian courts to challenge administrative decisions.[49] Any individual or association who claims a right to conserve and improve the environment in the social interest, may approach the courts (through the PIL process) for environmental justice even though he/she may not be directly affected by the case.[50]

In India, one of the oldest cases in environmental pollution where PIL found its way was in the case of Society For Protection of Silent Valley.[51] Here the case was filed by a voluntary organization seeking a writ to make the State of Kerala refrain from proceeding to construct a hydroelectric project at Silent Valley. The organization asserted that the project would disturb the ecological balance of the area. But the High Court dismissed this petition without giving sufficient reasons. However, this case created public awareness about the importance of ecological balance. In another PIL case of Joseph John,[52] the Kerala High Court decided that the petitioner, the president of a voluntary organization, was a mere *pro bono publico*, having no locus standi to challenge the action of State to clear the tropical forest of the Silent Valley.

The judicial attitude towards a clean environment gained popularity throughout the country when the higher judiciary diluted the concept of *locus standi* and entertained public interest petitions pertaining to environmental matters. Under Article 32 of the Constitution,[53] the Supreme Court has directed the government to implement the fundamental right to life and liberty, and (as part thereof) execute environmental protection measures in the public interest.The High Courts have not lagged behind the Supreme Court and have invoked jurisdiction to this effect under Article 226 of the Constitution.[54] The practice of encouraging public interest litigation by the High Courts was approved by the Supreme Court in the *Chaitanya* case,[55] wherein it was held that if the public interest faced a threat of being undetermined by arbitrary and vicious executive action, it was the duty of the High Court to issue a writ. In bonafide cases, the High Courts were required to act promptly by giving appropriate directions, and without insisting on locus standi, if the matter involved was of great public importance for its impact on the social system and values.[56]

PUBLIC INTEREST ENVIRONMENTAL PETITIONS BEFORE THE SUPREME COURT

A very high priority has been accorded to industrial development in India for speedy economic growth. Such progress, however, brings along with it a lot of ecological problems. Environmental pollution caused by hazardous industries is a present and potential challenge to life and the harmony between man and nature.

Citizens have invoked the jurisdiction of the superior courts on becoming aware of the fact that environmental pollution and ecological-imbalances have the potential to affect fundamental rights under the Constitution of India. Under their writ jurisdiction, the courts have given wide-ranging relief to citizens, which were not even contemplated under the existing environmental laws of India. In its power to review a state action under Article 32 of the Constitution, the Supreme Court has expanded the ambit of fundamental rights to include pollution-free environment.

Since the Supreme Court included the right to a wholesome environment under Article 21 of the Constitution of India[57] in the Rural Litigation case,[58] litigants have asserted their right to a pollution-free environment against the State. The Court interpreted the right to life, as the right to have a living atmosphere congenial to human existence. As environmental pollution causes disabilities leading to the non-functioning of vital organs of the body, the Court treated it as amounting to a violation of the right to life. In this case, a group approached the Supreme Court under Article 32 and demanded the closure of a limestone quarry on the ground that mining operations were causing ecological-imbalances and hazards to human health and environment.[59] The Court ordered the closure of the mining operations and responded to those who protested: '. . . (B)ut it is a price that has to be paid for protecting and safeguarding the right of the people to live in healthy environment with minimal disturbance of ecological balance'.[60] The Supreme Court, however, did not pass an order and treated the matter as a policy matter which the government was directed to look into for a decision.[61] Similarly, in Tarun Bharat Sangh,[62] the Supreme Court recognized the public interest petition brought by a social action group complaining against the permission of the Rajasthan government given for large-scale mining operations causing environmental harm in the protected area. Here, what is significant to note, is that the Supreme Court has come to consider petitions involving environmental matters as suitable PIL cases.

The ambient air in the mining area gets highly polluted by the dust generated by the blasting operations, vehicular movement, and the exhaust gases from equipment and machinery used in the mining operations. The mining may disturb the rain water drains which may badly affect the water level and water quality of water bodies. Therefore, in order to preserve environment and control pollution within the vicinity of the tourist resorts, it is necessary to stop mining in the area. In M.C. Mehta,[63] the Supreme Court directed that there should be no mining activity within 2 km radius of the tourist resorts of Bhatkal and Surajkund in Haryana. All the mines which fall within this radius shall not be reopened and no construction of any type shall be permitted now onwards within 5 km radius of the tourist resorts. All open areas shall be converted into green belts. The mining leases within the area from 2 to 5 km radius shall not be renewed without obtaining prior 'no objection' certificate from the Haryana Pollution Control Board as well as from the Central Pollution Control Board, New Delhi.[64] In another petition by M.C. Mehta,[65] the Supreme Court issued directions for the closure of stone-crushing operations in Delhi and Haryana as the process was causing air pollution. Similarly, in ARC Cement Ltd., and Others, the Supreme Court stopped the manufacturing process and ordered the cement factories to shift elsewhere beyond the jurisdiction of Mussoorie and Dehradun, keeping in view the environmental protection of the Doon Valley. The Court also advised the petitioner and the State of UP to find alternative use for the factory area to avoid waste of land.[66] These are important cases where the Court recognized that mining activities cause severe impact on local ecology, bring extensive alterations into the natural land profile, and pollute tourist resorts.[67]

In the *Shriram Chemicals* case,[68] the judiciary gave constitutional status to the right to pollution-free environment. The Supreme Court adopted a liberal attitude and recognized the petitioner's role as a representative in a public interest action which raised questions concerning the scope and ambit of Articles 12, 21 and 32 of the Constitution. These provisions relate to the principles and norms applicable in determining the liability of a hazardous industry causing environmental and health hazards. The issue before the Court was to identify the basis upon which damages could be quantified, and whether such large enterprises should be allowed to continue to function in the thickly-populated areas.

The issues involved in the Shriram Chemicals were complex. Though the Court had reminded the government and the citizens of their social responsibility to preserve and maintain the ecological balance in the *Sachidanand Pandey* case,[69] it took the view that ecological balance could be maintained by the courts, in spite of the fact that such obligations were merely part of the directive principles of state policy under the Constitution of India—an approach that is also reflected in the judicial pronouncements of various High Courts.[70]

After balancing various considerations such as the welfare of the people, the possibility of management's negligence, and the effects of unemployment in the event of closure of the plant, the Supreme Court, in *Shriram Chemicals*,[71] permitted conditional continuation of its operation. While acknowledging the important public and signal service of the petitioner, M.C. Mehta, for fighting a valiant battle against a giant enterprise like Shriram Chemicals with substantial success,[72] the Court drew a balance between the value of trade and industrial development vis-à-vis value of environmental protection and human health.

In the *Ganga Pollution* (by tanneries) case,[73] the Supreme Court observed that the closure of polluting units could be justified as life, health and ecology had greater roles to play in the life of people than lack of employment opportunities and loss of revenue. The Court exercised its writ jurisdiction on the ground that the statutory agencies had failed to prevent pollution of the river Ganga, and rejected the plea of financial constraint in setting up the effluent treatment plants. The Court stated that, just like an industry which cannot pay minimum wages to its workers cannot be allowed to exist, a tannery without setting up a primary treatment plant can not be permitted to continue at the cost of social interest.[74]

Thus, for the existence of any industry, the setting up of an effluent treatment plant is as essential as the payment of wages to the workers. The Court also justified its intervention on the ground that the statutory authorities, local people and the state pollution control board were ineffective in implementing environmental laws and regulations. The strong judicial prejudice against the polluting industries is reflected in the judgement which ordered the denial of licenses to new hazardous industries who did not have effluent treatment plants.[75] Although, in some cases the developmental activities have been favoured, at the same time the courts have also laid down detailed guidelines so that the development process should not result in adverse effects on environment and human health.

In the *Bhopal Gas disaster* case, about one hundred cases were filed in the US and more than three hundred civil and criminal cases were filed in Bhopal, on behalf of the victims in order to obtain compensation from Union Carbide and to establish liability for the escape of toxic gas.[76] The Supreme Court by upholding the validity of the Bhopal settlement,[77] nullified its own ruling of absolute liability as pronounced in the Shriram case for inflicting damage on citizens through the use of hazardous substances. As the Supreme Court order did not attribute liability to Union Carbide, it was thought that it might have long-term implications for the development of environmental jurisprudence by Indian courts[78] but later on, the Supreme Court reaffirmed the principle of absolute liability in the cases of Indian Council for Enviro-legal Action[79] and the Vellore Citizens Welfare Forum.[80]

Restoration of the damaged environment is a part of the process of sustainable development and as such, the polluter is liable to pay the cost to the individual sufferer as well for reversing the damaged ecology. The Supreme Court in the Vellore Citizens Welfare Forum defined 'the Precautionary principle' and the 'Polluter Pays principles' and viewed the 'the Precautionary Principle' and 'The Polluter Pays principle' as being essential features of 'Sustainable Development'. The 'Precautionary Principle' in the context of the municipal law means: (i) environmental measures—by the State Government and the statutory authorities—which must anticipate, prevent and attack the causes of environmental degrada-tion; (ii) where there are threats of serious and irreversible damage, lack of scientific certainty should not be used as a reason for postponing measures to prevent environmental degradation; and (iii) the 'onus of proof' is on the actor or the developer/industrialist to show that his action is environmentally benign.[81]

'The Polluter Pays Principle' was already held to be a sound principle in the Indian Council for Enviro-Legal Action.[82] The Supreme Court observed, 'We are of the opinion that any principle evolved in this behalf should be simple, practical and suited to the conditions obtaining in this country.' The Court ruled that 'once the activity carried on is hazardous or inherently dangerous, the person carrying on such activity is liable to make good the loss caused to any other person by his activity irrespective of the fact whether he took reasonable care while carrying on his activity. The rule is premised upon the very nature of the activity carried on'. Thus, the polluting industries are 'absolutely liable' to compensate for the harm caused to human health, soil and underground water. The industries are bound to take measures to remove sludge and other pollutants lying in the affected areas. Here, the 'Polluter Pays principle' means the absolute liability for harm to the environment, and extends not only to compensate the victims of pollution but also the cost of restoring the degraded environment.

The Supreme Court, in Delhi polluting industries case,[83] ordered the Delhi Administration to hold an inquiry and fix the responsibility on the officers who had been negligent in the performance of statutory duties entrusted to them. The Court held that it was the sole responsibility of the Delhi Pollution Control Committee to check pollution, conduct a survey, and submit a complete list of hazardous industries in the town. The master plan for Delhi provides the shifting of hazardous industries but this could not be done within a reasonable time period. Therefore, keeping in mind the increased level of pollution, the Court directed the Member Secretary, Central Pollution Control Board, New Delhi, to issue notices for relocation of the polluting industries with reasonable time given to the industries for filing objections.[84] Thus, PIL acted as an instrument to enforce the environmental provisions under the Master Plan.

While directing the closing down of hazardous industries in Delhi,[85] the Court observed that law alone can not help in controlling pollution. There is a need to adopt result-oriented strategic action[86] and make people aware of the hazards of pollution.[87] Thus, the Supreme Court's attitude reflects not only an appreciation of the people's right to a clean environment, but also the government's responsibility to make the people aware of the hazards of environmental pollution. This may result in increased people's participation in pollution prevention programmes of the country.

The Supreme Court was not satisfied with the efforts of concerned authorities in addressing the issue of acute vehicular pollution in Delhi. It was distressed to find that the periodic instructions of the Court evoked no response from them. The Court stressed that the state was obliged to follow instructions under Article 144 of the Constitution, and directed the time-bound implementation of the recommendations of the Environment Pollution (Prevention and Control) Authority for the National Capital Region, with the caveat that failure to do so would invite contempt proceedings. One of the main directions was the phasing out of commercial vehicles more than 15 years old and the use of catalytic converters on new and existing vehicles. This led to Delhi being declared 'unleaded' from 1 September 1998.[88]

The Supreme Court of India in the M.C. Mehta petition[89] observed that Articles 39(e), 47 and 48-A of the Constitution collectively cast a duty on the State to secure the health of the people, improve public health and protect and improve the environment. Notwithstanding adequate laws being in place, the quality of air in Delhi was steadily deteriorating due to lack of effort on the part of the enforcement agencies. Therefore, in order to protect the health of the present and future generations, the Court for the first time in 1986, directed the Delhi Administration to take appropriate steps to control pollution, emission of smoke, noise, etc., from vehicles plying in Delhi. It is as a result of the intervention by this Court that measures were taken in controlling pollution to some extent. It included: (a) lowering of sulphur content in diesel, first to 0.50 per cent and then to 0.05 per cent; (b) ensuring supply of only lead-free petrol; (c) requiring the fitting of catalytic converters; (d) directing the supply of pre-mix 2T oil for lubrication of engines of two-wheelers and three-wheelers; (e) directing the phasing out of grossly-polluting old vehicles; (f) directing the lowering of the benzene content in petrol; and (g) ensuring that new vehicles, petrol and diesel, meet Euro II standards by September 2000.[90]

The Environment Pollution (Prevention and Control) Authority was also established under Section 3 of the Environment (Protection) Act 1986 which directed the phasing out of non-CNG buses. As owners of diesel buses continued to ply diesel buses beyond 31 January 2002, contrary to the Court's orders, it directed that the Director of Transport, Delhi would collect from them costs at the rate of Rs. 500 per bus, per day, increasing to Rs. 1,000 per day, after 30 days of operation of the diesel buses with effect from the next day (5 April 2002), and the amount so collected shall be deposited in this Court by the Director of Transport by the tenth day of every month.[91] This speaks volumes for the concern of the Court since 1986, to protect the health of the people of Delhi.

In a PIL based on community need of conservation of environment,[92] the Supreme Court held that the most vital 'community need' was the conservation and the reversal of environmental degradation. The quality of ambient air was so hazardous in Delhi, that lung and respiratory diseases were on the increase. Therefore, the Court in case of shifting of hazardous industries out of Delhi viewed that the land surrendered by the owners and occupiers of the shifted hazardous industries should be used for the development of green belts and open spaces for clean and green environment,[93] and to meet other community-needs. It would, therefore, be in conformity with the broader concept of 'community need' under the Master Plan to permit the owner to develop part of the land for his own benefit and surrender the remaining land for the use of the community at large.[94] This reflects the Court's concern about individual ownership right to land, and the community interest of conservation of environment.

A writ petition was allowed in the Supreme Court to proceed under Article 32 of the Constitution to enforce the right to life of the people but without any reference to Article 21. In the *Ganga Pollution* case, [95] the Court did not discuss the crucial question of whether the tanneries and other private industries could be held liable for violation of the fundamental rights guaranteed under the Constitution.[96] It may be inferred from this case, that in an environmental litigation, it is not necessary for the Court to conclude that a particular fundamental right is likely to be violated by the polluter. It is also not necessary that the polluter be a public enterprise or an agency of the State.[97] Article 32 enables the Court to issue directions to prevent public nuisance caused by environmental pollution, provided the statutory authorities are not taking any initiative to rectify the grievances. Regarding the maintainability of a petition the Court, in the *Ganga Pollution* case,[98] concluded that the annoyance caused by the polluted river water was a public nuisance. As it was widespread in range and indiscriminate in its effect, it would be reasonable to accept the petition initiating the proceedings to stop the nuisance to the public.

Actions against the indiscriminate exploitation of natural resources have been the subject matter of PILs before the higher judiciary. In the *F.K. Hussain* case,[99] the Supreme Court held that the right to fresh drinking water was a part of right to life. Since it was in short supply in Lakshdweep, the large scale withdrawal of ground water could upset the fresh water equilibrium. In the *Bangalore Medical Trust* case,[100] the Court entertained a PIL against the decision of the Karnataka government to convert an open space reserved for a park into a private nursing home, holding that the government order was null and void, and without jurisdiction. Thus, the Court appreciated the people's right to fresh water for drinking and an open space for recreation. However, the Court also dismissed the petitions where the state authority was found to have adequately considered the potential environmental impacts of a development project. In Dahanu taluka,[101] the Court agreed with the Bombay High Court's dismissal order as the government was found to have considered the environmental issues before setting up the public project. But in *Sachidanand Pandey* case,[102] the Court held that it could intervene where irrelevant considerations had influenced the government decisions.[103]

A PIL was filed in the Supreme Court to protect the Taj Mahal,[104] a monument of international repute, from atmospheric pollution. The petition was filed for appropriate directions to the authorities concerned, for taking immediate steps to prevent air pollution in the Taj Trapezium (TTZ). The foundries, chemical industries and the refinery at Mathura, were the major sources of air pollution. The sulphur dioxide emitted by the Mathura Refinery and other industries when combined with Oxygen—with the aid of moisture—forms a sulphuric acid known as 'Acid rain' which has a corroding effect on the gleaming white marble of the Taj.[105] The Supreme Court, based on the expert reports, found that the industrial emissions had a damaging effect on the Taj and on the health of people living in the TTZ. The Court viewed that the precautionary principle requires that environmental measures must anticipate, prevent and attack the causes of pollution and environmental degradation. The 'onus of proof' would be on an industry to show that its operation was environmentally benign. As it was proved beyond doubt that the emissions generated by the use of coke/coal by industries were the main polluters of the ambient air, the Court held that the polluting industries should change over to the natural gas as an industrial fuel.[106] The industries unable to obtain gas connections should stop or relocate in new industrial estates. The Uttar Pradesh government was also directed to assist the industries in the process of relocation and provide incentives for relocation in the new industrial estates. The workmen employed in relocating industries were allowed certain rights and benefits.

In another PIL filed by M.C. Mehta,[107] the Supreme Court pronounced three judgements. In the first case (decided in 1997), the Court applied the doctrine of 'Public Trust', which means resources like water, air, sea and forests have such a great importance to the people as a whole, that it is not justifiable to put them under private ownership. In the second judgement (decided in 2000), the Court held that any disturbance to air, water and soil would be hazardous to life within the meaning of Article 21 which guarantee the right to clean environment. The Court also referred to the 'polluter pays principle', and held that in addition to damages for the restoration of environment, a person guilty of causing pollution can also be held liable to pay exemplary damages so that it may act as a deterrent for others. The Court, in the third judgement (decided in 2002), awarded special damages of Rs. 10 lakhs in addition to damages on the basis of the 'Polluter Pays Principle'. The Court observed that the special damages of Rs. 10 lakhs would be used for flood protection in the area of Beas River affected by the action of Span Motels Pvt. Ltd.

In the *Narmada Bachao*[108] case, the Supreme Court held that the Sardar Sarovar Dam project was not inconsistent with the mandate of sustainable development as it would result in the up-gradation of ecology. The precautionary principle would not apply here, as it is generally applied in case of pollution or other project or industry, where the extent of damage likely to be inflicted, is unknown. The Court agreed that the construction of the dam would result in some change in the environment and there is every reason to presume that the Sardar Sarovar would also result in ecological disaster but when steps are taken to preserve and improve the ecology and environment, it would not amount to violation of Article 21 of the Constitution. Here, the PIL was filed on the ground that the construction of the dam would violate the fundamental rights of the tribals, as well as the right to a pollution-free environment under Article 21 of the Constitution.

The Supreme Court in the *Church of God* case,[109] also clarified that noise pollution amounts to violation of Article 21 of the Constitution which gives the right to live in a healthy environment. Noise pollution violates this right. In order to protect forests for maintaining ecological balance needed to preserve bio-diversity, the Court in the case of the Godavarman case,[110] held that the Forest Conservation Act 1980, must be applied to all forests irrespective of the nature of ownership or classification thereof. The Court further held that any non-forest activity was prima facie in violation of the provisions of the Act, if it did not have the prior approval of the central government. The Court directed the state governments of Arunachal Pradesh and Assam to ensure that the mining of minerals for non-forest purposes was stopped, and that a complete ban was imposed on the felling of trees. It further directed these governments, to close saw mills, veneer mills and ply-wood mills in Tirap and Changlang and within a distance of 100 km from its border in Assam. In addition, the Court directed that workers employed in all closed units would continue to be paid their emoluments and should not be removed from service for this reason.

Although the Supreme Court deserves well-earned credit for developing a healthy environmental jurisprudence—it has extended Article 21 of the Constitution to include pollution-free environment for citizens—its decisions have not been without some social costs. Industries have been moved (Delhi, Agra, and other places), much to the lament of the industrialists, and labourers have been displaced, creating unemployment in this process of dislocation and relocation without due respect for the directions of the Court that they be paid their salaries and benefits.[111] The Court has faced difficult and complex issues, though one wishes that the poor and the downtrodden were not to pay such a heavy price for environmental protection.

In addition to the Supreme Court's jurisdiction under Article 32, the High Courts in India have also used Article 226 of the Constitution to entertain PILs. They have awarded a wide range of remedies in matters litigated in the public interest, despite the lack of formalities which would normally be required in an ordinary law suit. Under its epistolary jurisdiction, simple letters and telegrams have been sufficient to attract judicial attention.[112] PIL claimed the higher peak and further diluted the concept of locus standi when a news item published in a daily was treated by the Rajasthan High Court as a writ of petition.[113] From time to time, both the Supreme Court and the High Courts have acted in an inquisitorial manner to enforce their directives relating to pollution-free environment, under the rubric of fundamental rights, and instead of relying on the petitioner to produce evidence to support a claim, the courts have adopted an 'investigative role' by appointing commissions of enquiry to collect evidence and produce the facts before them.[114]

BASIS FOR ENTERTAINING PIL

There are no set admissibility parameters for the PILs. The Supreme Court has restricted PIL cases to the substantive violations of fundamental rights. In the *M.C. Mehta* (Shriram Chemical) case, the Court observed that ordinarily a petition under Article 32 of the Constitution could not be used as a substitute for the enforcement of the right to claim compensation for the infringement of fundamental rights, through an ordinary processes of a civil court.[115] The Court advised the Delhi Legal Aid Board to file compensation claims on behalf of the victims in an appropriate lower court.[116] It further observed that in the past, monetary damages have been ordered by the Supreme Court, but only in those cases where the violations shocked the judicial conscience.[117] Thus, the nature of the relief granted was futuristic and corrective, rather than compensatory. Similarly, in the *Sachidanand Pandey* case,[118] Justice Khalid held that the Supreme Court should put aside procedural shackles and hear only such petitions which involved gross violations of fundamental rights, or basic human rights, or such cases which shocked the judicial conscience. In the light of the above observation of the Court it seems that the High Courts may also restrict the public interest cases either to those cases that violate fundamental rights or which involve a blatant violation of other legal rights.

As the Indian High Courts under Article 226 of the Constitution have jurisdiction to issue writs to enforce any legal right and not just fundamental rights, the Kerala High Court in the *Mampilly* case,[119] has correctly proposed that whenever there was a public injury or substantial public health hazard, any member of the public could approach the High Court to issue a writ under the Article 226. Similarly, the Rajasthan High Court in the *Koolwal* case,[120] held that citizens were entitled to utilize the court's jurisdiction to ensure that the state performs its legal duties. However, the Allahabad High Court in the *Umesh Chandra* case,[121] had gone a step further by deciding that it would accept public interest writ petitions, even though neither fundamental rights nor conscience shocking facts were involved. Thus, the rules and standards regarding the nature of the rights violated and the extent to which these violations are accepted for admission of public interest claims are in a state of flux, uncertainty, and variation.[122]

RESTRAINING THE ABUSE OF PROCESS: *PUBLIC* V. *PRIVATE INTEREST LITIGATION*

Regarding the alleged fears that the Public Interest Litigation would lead to the opening of floodgates of the Court with litigation, P.N. Bhagwati (CJ), referred with approval, to the following observations of the Australian Law Commission:

> The idle and whimsical plaintiff, or dilettante who litigates for a lark, is a spectre which haunts the legal literature, not the court room . . . A major expressed reason for limiting standing rights is fear of a spate of actions brought by busybodies which will unduly extend the resources of the court. No argument is easier put, one more difficult to rebut. Even if fear be justified, it does not follow that present restrictions should remain. If proper claims exist it may be necessary to provide resources for their determination. . . . Professsor Scot (has) commented on the liberalized standing accorded by the US Supreme Court by observing 'when the floodgates of litigation are opened to some new class of controversy by a decision, it is noticeable how rarely one can discern the flood that dissenters feared'. Professor Scot went on to point out that the liberalized

standing rules had caused no significant increase in the number of actions brought, arguing that parties will not litigate at considerable personal cost unless they have a real interest in the matter.[123]

The Indian courts have always taken care to see that the public interest petitioners are not misusing the process. The Supreme Court has warned the High Courts to ensure that they were acting bonafide, and were not out to abuse the process for personal gains or private profit or political motivation, or other oblique considerations. The Court should not allow its process to be abused for political gains or to delay legitimate administrative action. The distinction between locus standi and justiciability should be kept in mind, because every default on the part of the State or public authority may not be justiciable. The Court should take care to see that it does not overstep the limits of its judicial function and trespass into the areas reserved for the executive or legislature under the Constitution. Public Interest Litigation being a new jurisprudence evolved by the Indian courts, demands judicial statesmanship and high creative ability.

The Supreme Court has been discriminating in the admissibility of public interest petitions. In the *Sangharsh Samiti* case,[124] the Court dismissed the petition as being devoid of any public interest as it reflected a long history of personal enmity. The Court held that prima facie, the provisions of Water Act and Air Act were complied with, and there was no conduct which could be attributed to the respondent, herein leading to pollution of air or ecological imbalance calling for interference by this Court. Again, the Court in the *Dahanu taluka* case,[125] dismissed the public interest petition as the State of Maharashtra was found to have adequately considered the potential environmental problems. Similarly in the *Subhash Kumar* case,[126] the Court held that the petition was not in the public interest; rather it reflected petitioner's personal interest and was therefore dismissed.

Like the Supreme Court, the High Courts have been equally careful and discriminating in entertaining PILs. In the *Goa Foundation* case,[127] the Bombay High Court declined to interfere with the continuation of a project of large magnitude and observed that PIL could not be used to serve the private interest of some local people to the detriment of the public at large. Again in the *K.K. Vasant* case,[128] the Karnataka High Court refused to grant relief under public interest petition as this would amount to unnecessary judicial interference in the sphere reserved for the state executive. Similarly, in the case of Shastrinagar[129] the Punjab and Haryana High Court held that no interference under Article 226 of the Indian Constitution was called for, provided an enforcement machinery of the state had already initiated proceedings under the relevant statutes.[130]

In a recent case, a project got delayed and consequently the cost escalated due to the High Court's interim order in a PIL case.[131] Therefore, in order to compensate the public, the Supreme Court gave a major ruling which may have the impact of checking the abuse of PIL in the future. The public may also claim compensation, if a project meant to benefit them becomes costlier or gets delayed, due to the Courts' interim order on a fake PIL. The apex Court cautioned the High Courts against entertaining PILs, the consequences of which could be detrimental to the public good. The Supreme Court further held that the party at whose instance interim orders were obtained, must be made accountable for the consequences, otherwise public detriment might overweigh public benefit in granting such interim orders.[132]

CONCLUSION

India has given the environmental matters a constitutional status and created an ambitious and highly developed system of environmental laws. But it is unfortunate to note that in spite of constitutional, legal and administrative measures, the problem of pollution of environment and exploitation of natural resources is increasing at an alarmingly high rate. In a developing country like India where people are not aware of the hazards of environmental pollution, nor are they aware of their constitutional and legal rights to fight against it, mere enactment and amendments of environmental laws are not enough. What has been more crucial is the judicial interpretation of environmental laws in favour of the people-oriented sustainable development. The judicial innovation and interpretation should promote effective implementation of pollution prevention laws through the existing enforcement machinery. India's activist judiciary has undertaken the task of protecting environment in a big way (for reasons of failure on the part of the executive to do so), and to a certain extent its efforts have also been successful.

PIL in India has revolutionized the concept and procedure for access to environmental justice. Indian courts have diluted the concept of locus standi to entertain public interest environmental petitions. It is a welcome step, as it provides opportunities to the courts to focus its lenses on environmental matters affecting public health and sustainable development. The judiciary has passed orders against bureaucrats, enforcement officers, and the industrialists, in the cause of protecting environment. The judiciary has also done a commendable work in arousing social awareness about the importance of environmental protection. However, environmental education, legal awareness and legal aid, assistance in understanding the procedure of filing environmental complaints in courts, as well as better advocacy may help the public interest litigants in achieving speedy and better results.

Needless to say, the problems of environmental justice cannot be solved unless and until the judicial pronouncements are enforced effectively. Given the limitations of the judiciary, the limited number of bonafide social action groups or the public-spirited lawyers eager to file PILs in environmental matters, and the continuing and increasing instances of environmental degradation, the search for new and innovative measures to make the system of environmental law enforcement more effective and pro-active must continue.

NOTES

1. See, Timmy Katyal and M. Satake, *Evironmental Pollution*, 16 (1989).
2. *Indian Express*, New Delhi, 21 February 1992. For details, also see, D.S. Sengar, 'Mitigating the Miseries of Pollution Victims—A Statutory System in India', *Indian Bar Review*, 107 XIX (1 & 2), 1992.
3. See, *Friends of the Oldman River Society* v. *Canada (Minister of Transport)* [1992] 1 SCR 3, 88 DLR (4th) 1. The Oldman decision is the most recent Supreme Court of Canada pronouncement on environmental jurisdiction under the Constitution Act 1867. In reviewing the consti-tutional basis for a federal environmental assessment (EA) of the Oldman River Dam, La Forest J. acknowledges the difficulty of addressing environmental issues within the framework of the Canadian Constitution: It may be realized that the environment is not an independent matter of legislation under the Constitution Act 1867. It is a constitutionally obtruse matter which does not comfortably fit within the existing division of powers without considerable overlap and uncertainty. Also see for case comments, Steven A. Kennet, 'Federal Environmental Jurisdiction After Oldman', 38 (1) *McGill Law Journal*, 180 (1993). For general studies in Environmental Law and

Policy in Canada, see Elaine L. Hughes, et al. (eds.), *Environmental Law and Policy* (1993).

4. C.M. Jariwala, 'The Constitutional 42nd Amendment Act and the Environment', in S.L. Agarwal (ed.), *Legal Control of Water Pollution* (1980).
5. See, Constitution of India 1950 as amended for Article 48A. Also see, O.P. Dwivedi and B. Kishore, 'India's Environmental Policies: A Review', in Shekhar Singh (ed.), *Environmental Policy in India* (New Delhi: IIPA, 1984), p. 49.
6. Article 39(b), Constitution of India. Also see, Delhi Master Plan Case, infra n. 107.
7. See, Rural Litigation Case, infra nn. 58 and 61.
8. *Sachidanand Pandey* v. *State of West Bengal,* AIR 1987 SC 1109. In this case, the Supreme Court did not agree with the opposition to construct a five-star hotel on the land near a Zoological Garden as it will disturb ecological balance.
9. Ibid.
10. Government of India (1992), *Policy Statement for Abatement of Pollution,* Ministry of Environment and Forest, New Delhi.
11. G.W. Paton, *A Textbook of Jurisprudence,* pp. 160–1 (1972).
12. Sections 268, 270, 290, 291, 426, 430, 431, 432; and Section 277 for controlling water pollution; and Section 278 IPC 1860 for controlling atmospheric pollution.
13. Section 133 of Cr.P.C., 1973 for controlling public nuisance.
14. Sections 89, 119, 120 of the Central Motor Vehicle Rules, 1989 for noise level and prevention of noise.
15. Section 110 of the Motor Vehicle Act 1988; Sections 112–16 of the Central Motor Vehicle Rules, 1989 for controlling vehicular pollution.
16. The case was decided on 19 May 1976.
17. For comments on the Public Liability Insurance At 1991, see, D.S. Sengar, supra n. 2.
18. The creation of National Environment Tribunal in 1995 may effect the frequency of PIL. See Michael Anderson, 'Individual Rights to Environmental Protection in India', in Alan E. Boyle and Michael R. Anderson (eds.), *Human Rights Approaches to Environmental Protection,* 1996.
19. *National Industrial Policy(2) 1989,* Government of India.
20. Supra n. 10.
21. It was the Fourth Five Year Plan (1969-74) which observed that the planning for harmonious development was possible only if the environmental aspects were introduced in the planning and development process.
22. For comments on enforcement issues of pollution laws in India, see D.S. Sengar, 'Enforcement Issues of Pollution Laws in India: With special emphasis

on hazardous industries and water pollution', 2 *Lucknow University Law Journal*, 77 (1995).

23. See, Herihert A. Hirte, 'Access to the Courts for Indigent Person: A Comparative Analysis of the Legal Framework in the United Kingdom, United States and Germany', 40, *International and Comparative Law Quarterly* 91 (1991).
24. See, *People's Union for Democratic Rights* v. *Union of India*, AIR 1982 SC 1473 at 1476.
25. The Council for Public Interest Law set up by the Ford Foundation in USA defined the PIL as follows: 'Public Interest Law is the name that has recently been given to efforts to provide legal representation to previously unrepresented groups and interests. Such efforts have been undertaken in the recognition that the ordinary market place for legal services fails to provide such services to significant segments of the population and to significant interests. Such groups and interests include the poor, environmentalists, consumers, racial and ethnic minorities, and others.' A Report by the Council for Public Interest Law, U.S.A. 1976—quoted in V.G. Ramachandran's *Law of Writs*, 4th edn., p. 301. Also see, Carl Tobias, 'Public Law Litigation and Federal Rules of Civil Procedure', 74, *Cornell Law Review* 270, 282 (1989).
26. Ibid.
27. *Gideon* v. *Wainwright*, 372 NS 335 (1876). In this case, one Clarence Earl Gideon had sent to the US Supreme Court one handwritten scrawl informing the apex Court that he was a pauper and prayed the Court to listen and act upon his plea. He pleaded that the Florida Trial Court had refused to appoint counsel for his defence and that it was contrary to the Constitution. This letter was treated as a petition and allowed by the Supreme Court by a majority of 9.0. The SC by relaxing its procedural law has created history and it has become a judicial precedent.
28. *Mumbai Kamgar Sabha* v. *Abdullabhai*, AIR 1976 SC 1455.
29. Justice Iyer expressed similar view in many cases including *Sunil Batra* v. *Delhi Administration*, AIR 1980 SC 1579; *Municipal Council of Ratlam* v. *Vardhichand*, AIR 1980 SC 1622; (3) *Akhil Bharatiya Soshit Karmchari Sangh (Railways)* v. *Union of India*, AIR 1981 SC 298; *Azad Rickshaw Pullers Union, Amritsar* v. *State of Punjab*, AIR 1981 SC 14.
30. *Fertilizer Corporation Kamgar Union* v. *Union of India*, AIR 1981 SC 344.
31. *S.P. Gupta* v. *Union of India*, AIR 1982 SC 149.
32. Ibid., p. 190.
33. Ibid.
34. See, Lance Liebman, 'Public Interest Law in India and in the United States', 21, *Law Quarterly* (West Bengal) 1,3 (1984).
35. Ibid., p. 4.
36. Case referred in R.S. Gupta, 'Widening the Rules of Locus Standi', 26 *Journal of India Law Institute* (*JILI*), 427 (1984).

37. Ibid.
38. Public Interest Litigation (PIL) is a comparatively recent concept of litigation but it occupies an important status in the new regime of public law. It seeks to relax the rule of locus standi. A few writers like Upendra Baxi and judges like Justice P.N. Bhagwati have preferred to call Indian PIL cases as Social Action Litigation (SAL), as it is a representative action for access to justice for the poor. But PIL terminology is frequently used by the courts and the academicians in their legal expressions. See Upendra Baxi, 'Taking suffering seriously: Social Action Litigation in the Supreme Court of India', 8 and 9, *Delhi Law Review* 91, 94 (1979–80), and Rajeev Dhavan, 'Law As Struggle: Public Interest Law in India', 36 (*JILI*) 302 (1994).
39. The Indian Constitution guarantees a number of fundamental rights and the violation of a fundamental right is the *sine-qua-non* of the exercise of the right to constitutional remedies under Article 32. See *Fertilizer Corporation case* (1981) 1 SCC 568; AIR 1981 SC 344.
40. The relaxed procedural; rules under PIL can be invoked in cases where the plaintiff is seeking enforcement of the constitutional or legal rights of those persons or group of persons who by reason of poverty, disability or due to socially or economically disadvantageous position find it difficult to approach the courts for redress. See *S.P. Gupta* v. *Union of India*, AIR 1982 SC 149; *State of Himachal Pradesh* v. *A Parent of a Student of Medical College, Shimla*, AIR 1985 SC910. Also, *P. V. Kapoor* v. *Union of India* 1992 *Cri. L.J.* 128.
41. The rigid rule of standing evolved by Anglo-Saxon jurisprudence that only a person wronged can sue for judicial redress, may not hold good in the present socio-economic settings of the country, and if public spirited citizens having faith in the rule of law are rendering great social and legal service, they cannot be ignored on technical grounds, nor measured by the conservative yardstick of the rule of locus standi. See, *Ishwar Singh* v. *State of Haryana*, AIR 1996 P & H 30, pp. 40–1. The Court held that the question of locus standi would not be material if litigation involves a public interest issue.
42. The appellate courts have entertained socio-economic petitions under PIL for claiming right to work and means of livelihood, as well as the right to education and right to reside in the working women's hostel as part of Article 21 of the Constitution of India, which speaks about the protection of life and personal liberty. The petitioners were seeking a direction to the government to eliminate the system of bondage, to improve the conditions of female prisoners, regarding custodial restraint on children, for compensating the death due to falling of a person into an uncovered sewage tank and for the victims of communal riots. See, *Olga Tellis* v. *Bombay Municipal Corporation*, AIR 1986 SC 180; *Sheela Barse* v. *Union of India*, AIR 1988 SC 2211; *Munna* v. *State of Uttar Pradesh*, AIR 1982 SC 806 (sexual exploitation of under trial juveniles); *Veena Sethi* v. *State of Bihar*, AIR 1983 SC 339 (illegal detention for three decades); *Kadra Pahadiya* v.

State of Bihar, AIR 1982 SC 1167 (under trials in prison for eight years without trial); *Lakshmi Kant Pandey* v. *Union of India*, AIR 1984 SC 469 (trafficking in children by foreigners); *Shivajirao Patil* v. *Mahesh Madhav Gosavi*, AIR 1987 SC 294 (tampering with the mark sheet of the Chief Minister's daughter); *Sheela Barse* v. *Union of India*, AIR 1986 SC 1773 (release of children below 16 years detained in jails); *Municipal Corporation of Greater Bombay* v. *Prabhat Mandal* (the hut dwellers' case), AIR 1986 SC 391; *Kishan Patnayak* v. *State of Orissa*, AIR 1989 SC 1783 (sexual exploitaton of blind girls in a blind school).

43. The appellate courts have entertained environmental petitions under PIL against the conversion of a park into a private nursing home, against polluted butter, against the setting up of a project involving environmental pollution, against the establishment of a super thermal power industry in a forest area, and also for prohibiting a contractor from cutting bamboo trees in forests. See, *Bangalore Medical Trust* v. *B.S. Mudeappa*, AIR 1991 SC 1902 at 1915; *Shivarao Shantaram Wagle* v. *Union of India*, AIR 1988 SC 1952; *Dahanu Taluka Environment Protection Group* v. *Bombay Suburbal Electric Supply Company Ltd.* (1991), 2SCC 539; *F.K. Hussain* v. *Union of India* 1990 Ker. 321; *M.C. Mehta* v. *Union of India*, AIR 1991 SC 113; *Banwasi Seva Ashram* v. *State of U.P.*, AIR 19987 SC 374; *Executive Engineer, Attapaddy Valley Irrigation Project* v. *Environmental and Ecological Protection Samiti, Agali*, AIR 1993 Ker. 320.
44. Supra nn. 42, 43.
45. Differences over questions of standing, reflects diverging opinions about the role of public law, about the distinction between public and private interest and about whether individuals have a legitimate role in asserting the public interest. See, David Feldman, 'Public Interest Litigation and Constitutional Theory in Comparative Perspective', 55, *Modern Law Review* 53 (1992). For various discussions on locus standi, N.N. Chaturvedi, 'Liberalizing the Requirement of Standing in Public Interest Litigation', 26 *JILI* 42–54 (1984); K.S. Mohan, 'Public Interest Litigation and Locus Standi', 8 *Cochin Uni. L.R.* 425–6 (1984).
46. Clarke D. Cunningham, 'Public Interest Litigation', in the Indian Supreme Court: A Study in the light of American Experience', 29 *JILI* 501 (1987); see, supra n. 41 and the accompanying text.
47. See, Satish K. Shastri, *Pollution and Environmental Law* 18–19 (1990).
48. *Warth* v. *Seldin* 422 US (1975); *Simon* v. *Eastern Kuntuchy Welfare Rights Organisation*, 426 US 26 (1976); *Valley Forge Christian College* v. *Americans United for Separation of Church and State* 454 US 464 (1982); also, Sonia Hurra, *Public Interest Litigation in Quest of Justice*, 253 (1993).
49. A number of environmental protection and pollution control laws have encouraged the suits by the individuals or groups or intended beneficiaries. These measures have liberally granted the locus standi and authorized citizens' suits. See, section 19(b) of Environment Protection Act 1986.

50. See, *S.N. Rao* v. *State of Maharashtra*, AIR 1988 SC 712 at 716. In this case, the petitioners, members of Ecological Action Group, were interested in seeing that sufficient area is kept reserved for a park for the benefit of the members of the public.
51. See, *Society for Protection of Silent Valley* v. *Union of India*, unreported judgement, O.P. No. 3025 of 1979 of the Kerala High Court.
52. See, *Joseph John* v. *State of Kerala*, Unreported judgement, O.P. No. 2949 of 1979 of the Kerala High Court. Also see, M.K. Prashad, 'The Silent Valley Case: An Ecological Assessment', in P. Leelakrishnan (ed.), *Law and Environment* 116, 123 (1992).
53. Article 32 of the Constitution of India provides remedies for the enforcement of fundamental rights.
54. High Courts in India can entertain PIL under Article 226 of the Constitution.
55. *Chaitanya* v. *State of Karnataka*, AIR 1986 SC 825.
56. Ibid.
57. Article 21 of the Indian Constitution provides that no person shall be deprived of his life or personal liberty except according to the procedure established by law.
58. *Rural Litigation and Entitlement Kendra, Dehradun* v. *State of Uttar Pradesh*, AIR 1985 SC 652. It was the first reported case of its kind in the country invoking the issue relating to 'Right to Pollution Free Environment and Ecological Imbalance'.
59. Ibid.
60. Ibid., at 656.
61. *Rural Litigation and Entitlement Kendra, Dehradun* v. *State of Uttar Pradesh*, AIR 1987 SC 359.
62. *Tarun Bharat Sangh* v. *Union of India*, AIR 1993 SC 293.
63. *M.C. Mehta* v. *Union of India*, AIR 1996 SC 1977 at 1979–80. M.C. Mehta sought a direction to the Haryana Pollution Control Board to control the pollution caused by the stone crushers and mine operators in Faridabad.
64. Ibid.
65. *M.C. Mehta* v. *Union of India*, AIR 1992 SC 382.
66. *ARC Cement Ltd. and Others* v. *State of UP*, 1993 Supp.(1) SSC 57, 426.
67. Supra n. 63.
68. *M.C. Mehta* v. *Union of India*, AIR 1987 SC 965 at 982. Here, leakage of Oleum gas resulted in injury to a large number of persons. One public spirited lawyer, M.C. Mehta, approached the Supreme Court on behalf of the victims.
69. Supra n. 8.
70. See *Goa Foundation and Other* v. *Konkan Railway Corporation and Others*, AIR 1992 Bombay 471.
71. *M.C. Mehta* v. *Union of India* (Shriram Chemical case), AIR 1987 SC 1086.

72. Supra nn. 68, 71, 98.
73. *M.C. Mehta* v. *Union of India* (Ganga Pollution by Tanneries case), AIR 1988 SC 1037; (1987) 4 SCC 463.
74. Ibid.
75. *M.C. Mehta* v. *Union of India* (Ganga Pollution by Municipality case), AIR 1988 SC 1115 at 1126–27. In this follow-up case, the Supreme Court directed the Mahapalika to arrange for the removal of accumulated dairies' wastes and take action against existing industries responsible for pollution.
76. See, *Charan Lal Shahu* v. *Union of India*, AIR 1990 SC 273.
77. *Union Carbide Corporation* v. *Union of India*, AIR 1990 SC 273.
78. Upendra Baxi, 'Supreme Court Judgement on Bhopal Settlement', *Times of India* (New Delhi), 6 October 1991. Also, Michael Anderson, 'Litigation and Activism: The Bhopal Case', *Third World Legal Studies*, 1993: 177 (1993).
79. For details see, *Indian Council for Enviro-Legal Action* v. *Union of India* (1996) 2 JT (SC) 196: (1996) AIR SCW 1069.
80. *Vellore Citizens Welfare Forum* v. *Union of India* (1996) 7 JT (SC) 375: (1996) AIR SCW 3399. Also see, *M.A.P. Pollution Control Board* v. *Professor. V. Nayudu* (*Retd.*) 1999 SOL case No. 53 (available on http://www.scjudgements.com/visited on 15 March 2004).
81. Ibid.
82. Supra n. 79.
83. *M.C. Mehta* v. *Union of India*, AIR 1996 SC 2231.
84. Ibid., Also see, *Fertilizers and Chemicals Travancore Ltd. Employees Association and Ors.* v. *Law Society of India and Ors.* SC judgement: 2 February 2004. The issue before the Supreme Court was whether the risk factors associated with setting up of sensitive plants like electricity generators can be a sole ground for their closure or relocation. Keeping in mind their utility to the public, the Court held that sabotage, attack by terrorists, earthquake, etc., are the events which can not be foreseen. Therefore, there is need to strike a balance between existing utilities which exist in public interest on the one hand, and human safety conditions on the other.
85. *M.C. Mehta* v. *Union of India* (closure of hazardous industries in Delhi case), 1991 2 SCC 253.
86. Ibid.
87. *M.C. Mehta* v. *Union of India*, AIR 1992 SC 382.
88. *M.C. Mehta* v. *Union of India* (1998) 6 SCC 63. Also, 13, *From The Lawyers Collective*, November–December 1998, p. 32.
89. *M.C. Mehta* v. *Union of India*, AIR 2002 SC 1696; 2002 Indlaw SC 1929 decided on 5 April 2002. Available at http.//www.scjudgements.com
90. Ibid.
91. Ibid.

92. *M.C. Mehta* v. *Union of India* (Delhi Master Plan case), AIR 1996 SC 3311.
93. Idid., at 3316.
94. Idid., at 3317.
95. Supra n. 73.
96. Ibid. Also see, Parmanand Singh, 'Public Interest Litigation', *Annual Survey of Indian Law* (ASIL) 145 (1987).
97. Idid., at 145–6.
98. Supra n. 73.
99. See, *F. K. Hussain*, supra n. 43. Also, *Mukti Sangharsh* v. *State of Maharastra* 1990 Supp. SCC 37. This was a PIL against commercial exploitation of sand from the river bed.
100. See, *Bangalore Medical Trust*, supra n. 41.
101. *Dahanu Taluka*, supra n. 43. Also, Parmanand Singh, op. cit.
102. *Sachidanand Pandey*, supra n. 8.
103. Idid., at 114.
104. *M.C. Mehta* v. *Union of India* (The Taj case), AIR 1997 SC 734.
105. Ibid. Also see, *Samata* v. *State of Andhra Pradesh*, 1997(8) SCC 191 and in *Madhu Kishore* v. *State of Bihar*, 1996(65) SCC 125; and *State of Himachal Pradesh* v. *Ganesh Wood Products*, 1995(6) SCC 363.
106. *M.C. Mehta* v. *Union of India* (The Taj case), AIR 1997 SC 762, 763.
107. *M.C. Mehta* v. *Kamal Nath*, 1997(1) SCC 388, and *Vellore Citizens* case (put cita); *M.C. Mehta* v. *Kamal Nath and others*, AIR 2000 SC 1997; 2002 (2) SCALE 564.
108. *Narmada Bachao Andolan* v. *Union of India*, AIR 2000 SC 3751.
109. *Church of God (Full Gospel) in India* v. *KKR Majestic Colony Welfare Assocation*, AIR 2000 SC 2773.
110. *T.N. Godavarman Thirumulkpad* v. *Union of India*, AIR 1997 SC 1223 at 1230.
111. Over 60,000 artisans and craftsmen of the Shaharanpur wooden handicraft industry have been rendered jobless after the closure of sawmills following the recent SC judgement in respect of illegal felling of trees. *Hindustan Times*, New Delhi, 3 May 1997. Also see supra n. 98.
112. The Supreme Court entertained a petition on the basis of a letter in *Sheela* v. *State of Maharashtra*, AIR 1983 SC 378, *Veera* v. *State of Bihar*, AIR 1983 SC 339.
113. *Ram Pyri* v. *Union of India*, AI 1988 Raj 124.
114. See, *Bandhua Mukti Morcha* v. *Union of India* (1984) 3 SCC 161; *Rural Litigation and Entitlement Kendra* v. *State of UP* (1986) Supp. SCC 517; and *Shivarao Shantaram Wagle* v. *Union of India*, AIR 1988 SC 1952.
115. Supra n. 71 at 1091.
116. Ibid. Also see, Richard K. Gordon, Jr., Jonathan M. Lindsay, 'Law and the

Poor in Rural India: The Prospects for Legal Aid', 5 *The American University Journal of International Law and Policy*, pp. 756–62 (1990).

117. See, *Shriram Chemical*, supra n. 71.
118. See, supra n. 8.
119. *Mampilly* v. *State of Kerala*, AIR 1985 Ker. 24.
120. *K.L. Koolwal* v. *State of Rajasthan* AIR 1988 Raj. 2.
121. *Umesh Chandra* v. *Samiti*, AIR 1984 All. 46
122. Also see, Richard K. Gordon, supra n. 115.
123. Supra n. 31 at 194.
124. *Chhetriya Pradushan Mukti Sangharsh Samiti* v. *State of UP*, AIR 1990 SC 2060; J.T. 1990(3) SC 685 (1990) 4 SCC 440.
125. Supra n. at 43.
126. *Subhash Kumar* v. *State of Bihar* 1991 (1) SCALE 8. Also, *Dattaraj Nathuji Thaware* v. *State of Maharashtra*, AIR SC 2005.
127. *Goa Foundation* v. *Konkan Railway*, AIR 1992 Bom. 471; also , *Citizen Consumer and Civic Action Group* v. *Union of India*, AIR 2002 Madras 298.
128. *K.K. Vasant* v. *State of Karnataka*, AIR 1992 Kant. 256.
129. *Shastri Nagar–Kanchghar Sudhar Sabha* v. *State of Haryana*, AIR 1997 Punjab and Haryana 172.
130. Ibid.
131. SC rules against abuse of PILs, the *Times of India* (New Delhi), 12 December 1998.
132. Ibid. In this case, Sujata V. Manohar (J) and B.N. Kripal (J) set aside a Bombay High Court verdict through which the execution of Khaparkheda Thermal Power Station Project was delayed. The apex Court judgement was the fall-out of an appeal by a private company which had been given the contract for supply, manufacture, design, erection and commissioning of the project.

9

Supreme Court Environmental Crusade: Enforcing CNG Alternative for World's Third Most Polluted City

SUBHENDU RAJAN RAJ

Evolution has so ordained that of all creatures, *homosapiens* should be the most responsible for the maintenance, preservation, and survival of the benign environment that can support and nurture all living creatures, including humankind. The genetic composition of all species is such that it cannot adjust beyond a certain threshold in environmental changes. The maintenance of this harmonic mean is too great a responsibility, and the state, in all societies, is therefore required to undertake a very pro-active role in this regard. It is the state's bounden responsibility to endeavour and help create an environment that aids and nourishes the life and health of all of its citizens.

The Indian state has been found woefully wanting in this regard. There is a need to visualize the significance of environmental concern in a larger perspective because environment is not just protection of tigers or forests. The political debate in post-independent India has been broadly focused on two major issues: economic growth and the equitable distribution of wealth. Environmental concerns and sustainable alternatives to development have been left out in the process. The biggest challenge contemporaneously is to search and implement a development process that can allow greater growth, equity, and sustainability which demands respect for the environment.

Development can take place at the cost of the environment only until a point. Beyond that point it will be like the foolish man who was trying to cut the very branch on which he was sitting. Development without concern for the environment can only be short-term development. In the long term, it can only be anti-development and can go on only at the cost of enormous human suffering, increased poverty and oppression.[1]

But for the pioneering role of the Supreme Court in matters concerning the environment (and its persistence that its writ is respected to the extent of even performing functions that legitimately belong to the executive), the citizens would have continued to be exposed to unmitigated sufferings. The Court has intervened, over the years, but more noticeably since the seventies, to enforce and implement measures in the wake of complaints of the citizens (as also suo motu), against environmental degradation and administrative negligence. For sure, there is no dearth of laws in the country regarding the protection of the environment—if the sheer number of such enactments was to be considered, India would perhaps be the least polluted country in the world. We have more than 200 central and state statutes which have at least some concern, directly or indirectly, with environmental protection such as the Water (Prevention and Control of Pollution) Act 1974, Air (Prevention and Control of Pollution) Act 1981, Environment Protection Act 1986, Environment (Protection) Rules 1986, and others. Besides, the Indian constitution is amongst the few in the world that contain specific provisions on environmental protection—the directive principles of state policy and the fundamental duties chapters explicitly enunciate the national commitment to protect and improve environment. Unfortunately, the multitude of such enactments has not resulted in preventing environmental degradation which, on the contrary, has increased over the years.

This paper looks closely at where the State has reneged its responsibility of providing a clean environment (despite its constitutional responsibility), in the capital city of the country: Delhi. If it were not for the tireless efforts of the Supreme Court, Delhi would still be suffering from the ignominy of being the third most polluted city in the world. The CNG case, as it became known, is an apt example of how the cleaning of Delhi had to be enforced by the highest judiciary of the land, which in reality should have been done by the state. In fact, the case speaks volumes for the abysmal failure of the state in India in discharging its basic obligation of providing a healthy environment for its citizens, an environment which is considered as the basic minimum requirement for a healthy living in civilized societies all across the world.

PRIORITY TO ENVIRONMENT

India's regulatory instruments, in terms of laws to preserve and safeguard its natural resources, have proliferated over the years. These laws, however, work badly, if they work at all. Legislatures, both at the central and state levels, have enacted environmental laws as and when necessary, to regulate most aspects of industrial and development activity, but feeble enforcement budgets and political and administrative sloth have hampered their implementation. Throughout the country, governmental agencies wield vast powers to regulate industry, mines, and other polluters, but are reluctant to use their powers to discipline the violators. This has forced the judiciary to step in. The High Courts and the Supreme Court have, time and again, cast upon themselves the responsibility of protecting the environment for the collective well-being of citizens, notwithstanding the fact that it is an onerous duty of the state, under Articles 39(e), 47 and 48A, 51A(g), 253 of the Constitution of India, to secure the health of the people, improve public health, and protect and improve the environment. This responsibility of the state is further reinforced by the fact that constitutional sanctity has been given to the eco-system, to comply with the principles of the Stockholm Conference, 1972 (to which India is a signatory). The amended Constitution has given every citizen the fundamental right to live in an unpolluted environment, and has cast a fundamental duty on the state and every individual to maintain the purity of environment. This has been accompanied by a spate of specific environment laws and the establishment of a Ministry of Environment and Forests.

The Supreme Court, in particular, adorning the mantle of an ombudsman as it were, has filled the lacunae in the laws (as some of the earlier laws on environment were badly made) and enforced their implementation by its landmark and innovative decisions. The Court, right from the *Ratlam* case (1980), has evolved and re-affirmed the right to a clean environment in India. The *Ratlam* case was the first important decision of the Supreme Court where a statutory obligation of a civic body towards protection of the environment was categorically acknowledged. Treating environmental degradation as a violation of the fundamental right under Article 21 (right to life), it was proclaimed that 'environment protection is a constitutional mandate and the judiciary cannot be a mute spectator'. The Environment Protection Act (EPA) of 1986 brought more effective environmental regulations. The Act established a Ministry of Environment and Forests to administer and enforce environmental laws and policies. The Environmental Action Plan of the government integrated environmental considerations with development strategies, with an emphasis on the reduction of industrial pollution and the adoption of cleaner technologies. And yet, it must be admitted that air and water pollution remains the most severe environmental problem due to industrialization, rapid urbanization, and inconsistent regulation enforcement.

Until 1986, the environmental statues had a system of licensing for the use of natural resources, and criminal sanctions against those who violated the conditions of licensing. This system was aimed at recovering civil compensation from private citizens. The agencies which implemented these statues, issued permits and prosecuted violators in ordinary criminal courts. Invariably, these agencies ignored imposition of pollution charges, penalties, or other economic sanctions to discourage pollution. Since 1986, the enforcement techniques have been strengthened. The law now does not permit private prosecution, and empowers state agencies to shut polluting industries. The EPA was the first comprehensive statue to give the Central Government authority to issue direct written orders, including orders to close, prohibit, or regulate any industry, operation or process, or to stop or regulate the supply of public utilities such as electricity, water or any other service to ensure compliance with the Act. Among other powers granted to the Central government include the power of entry for examination, testing of equipment, taking of samples of air, water, soil or any other substance, from any place for analysis. The Act explicitly prohibits discharge of environmental pollutants in excess of prescribed regulatory standards.

Notwithstanding that the Environment Protection Act 1986 strengthened the regulatory regime, the pollution control boards set up under the Act did not perform as well as could be expected. As a consequence, the Supreme Court continued to entertain many public interest litigation cases having to do with the prevention of hazardous environment, through an expansive definition of the fundamental right to life and liberty. In the *Sariska* case the Court stated: 'this litigation concerns environment. A great American judge emphasizing the imperative issue of environment said that he placed government above big business, individual liberty above Government and environment above all. . . . *The issues of environment must and shall receive the highest attention from this court.*'[2] Such an approach has led the Supreme Court to derive, adopt, and apply a wide range of principles in environmental jurisprudence. Some of the notable fundamental principles recognized by the Court are:

1. Enforcement agencies of the state are under bounden obligation to strictly enforce environmental laws in India.[3]
2. Every citizen has the right to a wholesome environment, which is a facet of the right to life guaranteed under Article 21 of the Indian constitution.[4]
3. Government agencies may not plead non-availability of funds, inadequacy of staff or other insufficiencies, to justify the non-performance of their obligations under environmental laws.[5]
4. The 'polluter pays' principle, which is a part of the basic environmental law of the land, requires that a polluter bears the 'remedial or clean up' costs as well as the amounts payable to compensate the victims of pollution.[6]
5. The 'precautionary principle' requires government authorities to anticipate, prevent, and attack the causes of environmental pollution. This principle imposes the burden of proof on the industrialist or developer to show that his or her action is environmentally benign.[7]
6. In matters of environment, the burden of proof shall lie on the party that wants to change the status quo.[8]
7. Government development agencies charged with decision making are under a solemn commitment to give due regard to ecological factors including the environment policy of the central and state governments and the need for sustainable development in the utilization of natural resources; they are under the obligation of the present generation to preserve natural resources and to pass on to future generations an environment which would be liveable as we inherited from our predecessors.[9]
8. The state is considered a trustee of all natural resources which are by nature meant for public use and enjoyment. The citizens are the beneficiaries of the sea shore, running waters, air, forests and ecologically fragile lands. These resources cannot be converted into private ownership.[10]

The above principles were enunciated by the Supreme Court in many of the cases of environmental pollution it dealt with. Generally, the Court was much more critical of the central and state governments and the pollution control boards (set up under the EPA) for failing to prevent environmental hazards than of the private industrial units that caused the environmental pollution. Many of the public interest litigation (PIL) cases involved the Court in balancing the competing claims of economic development and the need to sustain healthy environment, and/or taking care of the weaker sections of society adversely affected by such developments. As S.P. Sathe, in his scholarly work (*Judicial Activitism in India*), has summarized:

> Objections that a development scheme was approved by the government without taking into consideration the environmental hazards,[11] or without providing for the rehabilitation and relief to the people displaced by such a scheme,[12] or without considering its probable adverse effects on the rights of tribals or adivasis[13] were considered in PILs. Where lands were acquired for the construction of a dam and tribals were evicted from the land, it was held that no possession could be taken until the tribals were given alternate land and compensation.[14]

However, in the recent judgement delivered on 18 October 2000, in the case of the Sardar Sarovar Dam, it appears that the need for development overwhelmed the Court against the principle of 'alternative land and compensation' principle. In this case, the Court allowed the raising of the height of the Dam though the Narmada Bachao Andolan had vociferously stated any increase in the height beyond 90m would submerge homesteads and displace thousands of tribals. In a 2 to 1 majority judgement, the Court allowed immediate construction on the dam up to a height of 90 m. Further, the judgement authorized construction up to the originally planned height of 138 m in 5-m increments subject to receiving approval from the Relief and Rehabilitation Subgroup of the Narmada Control Authority. *This essentially unfettered clearance has come from the Court despite major unresolved issues on resettlement, the environment, and the project's costs and benefits analysis.*[15] In Sathe's analysis, the concerns for development have often over-ridden concerns for the weaker sections of society and the degradation of the environment. 'The judicial relief,' writes Sathe, 'has, however, been limited to providing protection against decision-making by government without taking into consideration all the relevant aspects'. He adds:

The courts have ensured that all relevant aspects of environment are considered and the persons likely to be adversely affected are heard. The Court has, however, said that the scope of judicial review in such cases is limited. . . . A court cannot go into whether a policy is right or wrong [a preserve of the legislature]. It only goes into whether the decision has been taken after considering all the relevant factors or without considering any irrelevant factors and whether the persons likely to be affected were heard and provided against the loss, if any.[16]

Notwithstanding its decision in the case of the Sardar Sarovar Dam, the Court deserves compliments for its persistence and perseverance in enforcing the use of Compressed Natural Gas (CNG) as alternative clean fuel for public transportation to reduce pollution in Delhi. In fact, as the case pertaining to Delhi's CNG project shows, the Supreme Court has gone a great step forward, or it may be said many steps ahead of its strictly adjudicatory role. The *M.C. Mehta* v. *Union of India* [WRIT PETITION (CIVIL) NO. 13029 OF 1985] is notable in the annals of environment-related matters in India. In this case, the Supreme Court showed itself as a crusader, as it were, in the last seventeen years (decision given in 2002), and assumed the role of a legislature, a perspicacious and trenchant critic, and an administrator overseeing the progress of its directives being implemented. Even though some observers warned that this was not the legitimate territory of the Court, it turned itself into a registry while tracking the day-to-day progress of the conversion of diesel buses into CNG in its forthright zeal to ensure improvement in the quality of ambient air of the capital city. This role was brought upon itself by the Court when it encountered first hand, the deep embedded inertia, lackadaisical intent, almost criminal neglect and vested complicity, not to shift to an alternative clean fuel (CNG) in place of diesel which, all scientific studies showed, was patently lethal and carcinogenic to the health of the public. The Court noted that both the sets of governments (at the centre as well as in Delhi) were party to a great extent, if not in equal measure, to resisting the conversion to compressed natural gas. In no small measure, behind the success of this pioneering crusade were the efforts of the titan of environmental initiatives—M.C. Mehta, who indefatigably brought to the Court many instances of neglect of the environment and the sensitivity of eminent legal cognoscenti, such as J.J. B.N. Kirpal, V.N. Khare and Ashok Bhan.

DELHI—THE CAULDRON OF POLLUTION

Delhi, due to a variety of reasons of which the ever-burgeoning population is a major one, the peculiar topography, the spread of the urban conurbation which lives in a spread that grows, extending in a periphery all around some 40–50 kms from the centre, aggravated by the typical winter fog and summer humidity, was not only considered one of the country's worst polluted cities but also the world's third-most polluted city until the Supreme Court stepped in. It had airborne particulate levels of pollution which were twice the standards set by WHO. Industrial vehicles—their number ever-growing—were heavily contributing to the air pollution load. In January 1999, Delhi had 2.6 million vehicles and the number was increasing by 500 vehicles per day, raising the Suspended Particulate Matter (SPM) load to 5 times the load according to WHO norms. Poor quality fuels provided by filling stations had further aggravated the problem. SPM produced by diesel fumes, which remains in the atmosphere and can be easily inhaled, had become a major health hazard due to its carcinogenic effect. Although the lead content at traffic intersections was reduced by approximately 60 per cent after the introduction of unleaded petrol, high levels of benzene and polyaromatic hydrocarbons were a great cause for concern. Although somewhat dated, the statistics of annual emissions for the year 1996 give evidence of the pathogenic air quality in Delhi: SPM: 116,000 tons (Kolkata: 200,000); Sulphur Dioxide: 46,000 tons (Mumbai: 157,000). The emission of Carbon Monoxide in Delhi on a daily basis for the year 1996 was 810 tons (Mumbai: 470; Kolkata: 180).

Besides vehicles, thermal power plants, industries and domestic emissions contributed 16, 12 and 7 per cent of the total air pollution load in Delhi. Deforestation had led to loss of green cover, open desiccation, moisture loss, and soil textural adversities. And as we know, the depletion of tree cover is responsible for high levels of dust in the air leading to diseases like bronchitis, asthma, and acute respiratory infections. Pesticides in the air also affect the liver and cause neuropathy. Intestinal pneumonitis, chronic kidney disorder, diabetes, hypertension and atheroma in blood vessels are some of the ailments due to the oxidant effect of nitrogen dioxide, and on account of the presence in air of aldehydes and hydrocarbons.

Delhi was certainly making some efforts to control air pollution through improved traffic management (by the introduction of computerised traffic signalling to avoid congestion and delays at traffic intersections), construction of flyovers on major highways, and bypasses at major peripheral colonies, and through the process of rigorous vehicle inspection and certification. Although these measures were becoming effective, something more was needed to be done. The Delhi government had to take the hard decision in the matter of promoting livelihood for a small group of taxi operators vis-à-vis the health of a large section of the urban population and phased out outdated vehicles most grudgingly. Efforts to increase tree cover to reduce dust and smog in the air was another step. In Delhi, although green cover had increased from 26 sq kms to 60 sq kms in the last few years, much was needed to be done. Improving public transport system was another step—currently, Delhi is in the process of introducing an alternative transport system, such as the underground or elevated high-speed rail transit facility under the ambitious Delhi Metro project. Delhi is one of the few capitals in the world where no alternative mass transit system has been available so far. Hopefully, the rail link under the Delhi Metro project would cover the entire area with feeder or subsidiary links to enable a commuter to reach his destination without having to transfer to road transport and vice-versa.

Notwithstanding the above measures, there was a need to tackle the mother of all problems of air pollution: how to provide a safer and cleaner fuel concomitant to minimize the content of benzene and sulphur, especially for diesel vehicles, for the millions of vehicles that the city possessed which, at the last count, were more than the sum total of all vehicles in the metros of Kolkata, Mumbai and Chennai with obvious harmful effects. There is no dearth of data which co-relates increased air pollution with an increase in cardiovascular and respiratory diseases, giving rise to increase in terminal diseases among the residents of Delhi.

That the health of the Delhi resident was at risk on account of air pollution is borne out by many scientific studies which indicate that air pollution leads to considerable levels of mortality and morbidity. Fine particulate matter, or respirable particulate matter (RSPM) PM10, is particularly dangerous. The *Journal of American Medical Association* (*JAMA*) has published in 2002 the findings of a study, conducted over 16 years, involving over 500,000 people in different cities of the US. It has found that fine particle-related pollution leads to lung cancer and cardiopulmonary mortality. The *JAMA* research further indicates that with an increase of every 10 microgramme per cum (mg/cum) of fine particles, the risk of lung cancer increases by 8 per cent. The US

Environmental Agency has mandated that the annual average levels of PM 2.5 particles in air should not exceed 15 mg/cum. The Indian annual national average standard for PM10 is 60 mg/cum, but most cities, including Delhi, register PM10 levels above 150–200 mg/cum on an annual basis. A study conducted with regard to children in Bangalore shows that the incidents of asthma of children rose from 9 per cent in 1979 to 29.5 per cent in 1999 with the increase of vehicles from 1.46 lakhs in 1979 to 12.23 lakhs in 1999 in that city. Similarly, a study by the Chittaranjan Cancer Institute and Environmental Biology Laboratory of the Department of Zoology of Kolkata University, carried out between November 1997 and May 1999, found that about 43 per cent of the children in Kolkata were suffering from respiratory disorders compared with 14 per cent of the children in rural areas. Alarmingly, 94–96 per cent of the children were found producing sputum which would usually be reflective of habitual smokers, though only 5.5 per cent of the children were found to be occasional smokers. According to the study reflected in the *Indian Journal of Medical Research* (July 2000), the culprit for this situation was pollution in the ambient air. According to an estimate by the World Bank study using 1992 data, the annual health cost to India was up to about Rs. 5,550 crores due to ambient air pollution. Out of this, the health cost of air pollution in Delhi alone was found to be about Rs. 1,000 crores.[17]

SUPREME COURT INITIATIVES

When the State was found wanting, in action to control pollution, the Supreme court stepped in. By reason of the fact that neither the Delhi administration nor the central government (since both have parallel control over Delhi), seemed willing to discharge their constitutional obligation to protect the health of the present and future generations, the Supreme Court, for the first time on 23 September 1986, directed the Delhi Administration to file an affidavit, specifying steps taken by it for controlling pollution emission of smoke, noise, etc., from vehicles plying in Delhi. The concern of the Court in passing various orders since 1986 has only been one, namely, to protect the health of the people of Delhi. It was with this objective in mind that directions were issued by the Court to persuade the governmental authorities to take such steps as would reduce the air pollution. Consequent upon the Court's direction, the following measures were taken in reducing pollution to some extent:

a. lowering of sulphur content in diesel, first to 0.50 per cent and then to 0.05 per cent;
b. ensuring supply of only lead-free petrol;
c. requiring the fitting of catalytic converters;
d. directing the supply of pre-mix 2T oil for lubrication of engines of two-wheelers and three-wheelers;
e. directing the phasing out of grossly-polluting old vehicles;
f. directing the lowering of the benzene content in petrol; and
g. ensuring that new vehicles, petrol and diesel, meet Euro-II standards by September 2000.

Additionally, the issue of substituting the use of diesel for the CNG was on the anvil of the Environment Pollution (Prevention and Control) Authority, which is a statutory authority constituted under section 3 of the Environment (Protection) Act 1986, and whose directions are final and binding on all persons and organizations concerned.[18] The Authority, first on its own, and later endorsing the recommendations of the Bhure Lal Committee, had directed the conversion to CNG mode and the phasing out of the non-CNG buses. It may be mentioned here that the need for finding an alternative fuel to diesel had been drawing the attention of the Supreme Court as well for quite some time. This is evident from its order dated 21 October 1994, in which the Court had observed:

> On an earlier occasion when these matters came up before this Court it was suggested that to begin with, Government vehicles and public undertaking vehicles including public transport vehicles could be equipped with CNG cylinders with necessary modification in the vehicles to avoid pollution which is hazardous to the health of the people living in highly polluted cities like Delhi and the other metros in the country.[19]

Although references to conversion of government vehicles to CNG, as well as to the installation of CNG stations and kits, were made in the Court's orders dated 28 March 1995, and 9 February 1996, it was after the report of the Bhure Lal Committee (which was set up, under section 3 of the EPA, during the course of the proceedings of the Supreme Court in various writ petitions filed before it), that the Court passed orders, dated 28 July 1998, fixing the time-limit within which the switch-over to CNG was to take place. It is, however, unfortunate that the efforts of the governmental authorities did not keep pace with the orders passed by the Supreme Court. For more than a year, under one pretext or the other, first the National Capital Authority (NCT) of Delhi and then the Union of India sought extension of time for conversion of commercial vehicles to CNG. With a view to seeing that the disruption in bus services did not take place and unnecessary hardship was not caused, the Court extended the time-limit again with regard to the conversion of commercial vehicles (first extended to 30th September 2001, and then to 31 January 2002). Despite these two extensions, the governments at the two levels were slow to act. At long last, 'it (was) during the period January 2001 to February 2002, that action was taken by the Union of India, which leaves us with no doubt that its intention, clearly (was), to frustrate the orders passed by this Court with regard to conversion of commercial vehicles to CNG. The manner in which it has sought to achieve this object is to try and discredit CNG as the proper fuel, and, secondly, to represent to this Court that CNG is in short supply and, thirdly, delay the setting up of adequate dispensing stations.'[20]

The Supreme Court served a serious indictment and held the State responsible for the abysmal state of affairs when it stated:

> The increase in respiratory diseases specially amongst the children should normally be a cause of concern for any responsible government. The precautionary principle enshrined in the concept of sustainable development would have expected the government and the health authorities to take appropriate action and arrest the air pollution. However, children do not agitate or hold rallies and, therefore, their sound is not heard and the only concern of the Government now appears to be is to protect the financial health of the polluters, including the oil companies who by present international desirable standards produce low quality petrol and diesel at the cost of public health. Statistics show that the continuing air pollution is having a more devastating effect on the people, than what was caused by the Bhopal gas tragedy. In that case, the nation, including the Union of India, was rightly agitated and sought action and compensation from the multinational company, who was held to be responsible for the same. Here, in the case of CNG, the shoe is on the other foot because the government is not facilitating measures for clean air and water including the supply of CNG or an other clean unadulterated fuel. It is due to the lack of proper concern on the part of the governmental authorities that people are suffering from respiratory and other diseases. The Bhopal gas tragedy was a one-time event which, hopefully, will not be repeated, but here, with not enough concern for action being undertaken by the Union of India, far greater tragedies in the form of degradation of public health are taking place every day. Under these circumstances, it becomes the duty of this Court to direct such steps be taken as are necessary for cleaning the air so that the future generations do not suffer from ill-health.[21]

As usual, the Government of India tried to buy time once again. In 2001, the government hurriedly set up a Committee headed by R.A. Mashelkar to give a report with regard to vehicular pollution. It was surprising that since 1986 (when the pollution issue became the subject of PIL), the Union of India had not thought of establishing such a Committee until after 31 January 2001, when an order was passed by the Court in which the apathy on the part of the government in carrying out the Court's orders was taken note of, and the authorities were required to comply with the orders so passed. The composition of the Mashelkar Committee was such that none of its members was either a doctor, or an expert in public health. The said Committee submitted its report, which did not show any serious concern in protecting the health of the people. The Committee recommended that emission norms should be laid down, and that the choice of the fuel should be left to the users.

The Court was fully convinced that vehicular pollution, though one among the many sources of air pollution, was the *major* source of pollution in metropolitan towns such as Delhi. Even the journal (*Parivesh*) published by the Central Pollution Control Board in September 2001 had acknowledged, based on scientific analysis, that diesel emissions, relative to gasoline emissions, were much more harmful to health and quoted approvingly, the findings of a study on the subject done by a Swedish Consultancy, *Eco Traffic* (Peter Ahlvik and Ake Branberg: 1999), which showed that 'the cancer potency of diesel vehicles (was) more than two times than that of petrol vehicles in India. But if only the most harmful of the exhaust emissions, that is particulate emission, is considered, the carcinogenic effect of one new diesel car (was) equivalent to 24 petrol cars and 84 new CNG cars on the road.'[22] While Parivesh listed pollution related diseases in India, the *Down to Earth* publication of the Council for Science and Environment (an independent Non-governmental Organization) warned of the increasing death toll on account of pollution:

The number of people dying in urban India due to deteriorating air quality is rising every year and very little is being done to deal with pollution in Indian cities. A stupendous 51,779 people are estimated to have died prematurely in 36 Indian cities due to air pollution in 1995 as against 40,351 in 1990–1, a rise of 28 per cent over the three-year period. Calcutta, Delhi, Mumbai, Kanpur, and Ahmedabad account for 10,647, 9859, 7023, 3639, 3006 premature deaths respectively. This accounts for 66 per cent of total premature deaths in India. The number of air pollution-related ailments requiring medical treatment and hospital admissions have sky-rocketed to 25 million cases, indicating an increasingly ruined state of health in Indian cities. The estimate was 19 million in 1991–2.[23]

Notwithstanding such overwhelming data about the harmful effect of diesel fuel on public health and despite the recommendations of the Bhure Lal Committee to which all parties, including the Government of India, agreed (herein after referred to as agreement), the Supreme Court had to persevere until 2002 (when it mandated a ban on running of diesel buses in Delhi), to make sure that CNG was used at least in the Delhi public transport system. The Court had passed orders based on this agreement as early as in July 1998, but the Government of India did not live up to its commitment. Interestingly, it was submitted in the Court on behalf of the Union of India at that time, that diesel and CNG were not materially different in the matter of air pollution and that, instead of a 100 per cent switchover to CNG, a mix of CNG and diesel buses in equal proportion would make a difference of only 2 per cent in the pollution levels. The Supreme Court was not convinced. Data from the Automotive Research Association of India (submitted by the petitioner, M.C. Mehta) at Pune showed that the pollution potential of emissions from CNG was far less than even the Euro-IV standards. The Court averred that:

> With the emissions from the CNG vehicles being more than comparable with the EURO-IV standards, the contention of the Union of India that a mix of diesel buses and CNG buses would make a difference of only 2 per cent in the pollution levels is patently untenable. In the case of particulates, current CNG vehicles are 15 times better than Euro-II diesel vehicles (with 500 ppm sulphur), and only Euro IV diesel vehicles are comparable to CNG vehicles. In fact, the certificate issued by the Automotive Research Association of India (ARAI) to the bus manufacturers says that particulate emissions were negligible and could not be measured. The aforesaid analysis emphasizes the need for change to non-liquid fuel like CNG or LPG so as to improve the air quality in this country and not merely of Delhi. Such change-over may perhaps obviate the need to manufacture vehicles meeting Euro III or Euro IV standards.[24]

THE AFTERMATH

It was as a result of the various orders passed by the Court that the air pollution level in Delhi has stabilized. In 2000, the annual average levels of RSPM declined to 186 from 222 mg/cum. This was no small achievement given that the city was adding over 2,00,000 vehicles each year. Despite the improvement, Delhi RSPM pollution remains roughly 3 times above the national standard for annual average concentration of RSPM mandated under the Air Act 1981. Perhaps, the use of Metro and the change-over to CNG for private vehicles would ameliorate the current situation.

It must, however, be put on record, that but for the laudable perseverance of the Supreme Court and the PIL petitioner, M.C. Mehta, this feat would have not been accomplished. The Court faced concerted opposition of the vested interests, apart from the lethargy of the two levels of governments, who were stalling the CNG-fitted transport vehicles. Initially, it was said that nowhere in the world had the CNG buses been introduced on the scale directed by the Court, while the two levels of government urged that the CNG technology was still evolving and experimental, and hence a few years away from implementation. On the contrary, the Court maintained that even though the CNG technology was experimental, it was worth implementing, given that stringent norms on pollution were emanating from the West as well as from the rest of the world that would have to be enforced in the country in the near future. In the United States, the Court pointed out, CNG buses accounted for 18 per cent of the current and 28 per cent of the potential bus orders. Under pressure to clean up the air because of the approaching Olympic Games, the Beijing government has resorted to an alternative fuel strategy—the latest figures from Beijing indicate that the city was planning to have 18,000 buses fuelled by CNG, LPG, and electricity. The Ministry of Environment in South Korea has since inducted more than 20,000 natural gas buses to its current fleet.

Though the final judgement in the writ petition filed by M.C. Mehta was given in 2002, now some years down the line, it can be realized that the Supreme Court looked ahead of time in the future and set a precedent of sorts by forcing the State to convert the entire Delhi metro public transport fleet, to a cleaner fuel. Today as Delhi Transport Corporation buses sport the banner of *World's Largest Eco Friendly Bus Service* and close to 11,000 such buses are plying on the road, Delhi-ites experience cleaner air on account of a fall in the RSPM emission levels in the city. The Court stood its ground against the Government's arguments that there was insufficient CNG as it were and that a breakdown in the Hazira pipeline carrying CNG could paralyse the transportation system. Among the directions it delivered, the Court asked the Government to allocate more gas to Delhi (with increased supply of CNG, the queues at the vending stations have disappeared), the consolidated intake of the city is a mere 4.8 of the current supply of gas by the Hazira pipeline—and assign top priority to the transport sector (private vehicles all over India included), over the industrial sector in the allocation of CNG. This means that CNG will be allocated to Delhi and to other air-polluted cities of India for the transport sector prior to its allocation (if available) to the industries, with preference for the public-sector undertakings and power projects. Although there does not seem to be any effective or systematic plan at this stage to clean up air pollution in other cities, air quality is critical in Agra, Lucknow, Jharia, Kanpur, Varanasi, Faridabad, Patna, Jodhpur, and Pune as per the CPCB data. The situation may improve now that LPG (which is environmentally acceptable), has also been permitted to be used as an alternative fuel to CNG.

CONCLUSION

The Supreme Court crusade in the Delhi context did suffer some criticism. Although the Court accomplished the goal of pollution reduction much to the relief of Delhi residents, its dogged persistence to achieve the goal by enforcing CNG as an alternative fuel was not well received in some quarters. Besides vested interests, the Court noted the apathy, if not utmost resistance, of the State to switch over to the CNG mode for public transportation. Although it was the function of the governments at the two levels to provide healthy environment to the citizens, the Court's minute monitoring of the progress in the field and its final direction to convert the entire Delhi metropolitan public transport system to CNG, invited questions about the limits and legitimacy of its judicial activism. At another level, some unfair critics asked, as to why had the Court not demonstrated as much eagerness and enthusiasm for giving justice to the oustees in the Sardar Sarovar Dam project, as it did in enforcing the CNG as an alternative fuel in the capital. However, it needs no emphasis that such comparisons are not proper as each case is sui generis, and no amount of downplaying the achievement of the Court can undermine the service it has rendered to the people of Delhi.

From a broader perspective, the Delhi case has enhanced the cause of sustainable development. Perhaps, none of this would have been possible without the emergence of PIL as developed by the Supreme Court during the last more than two decades and without the Court's innovative interpretation of the Constitution which has brought many ecological and environmental concerns within the expanding ambit of Article 21 of the Constitution. The environmental jurisprudence in our country is at the developmental stage (the Court has already laid down 'precautionary principle' and 'polluter pays principle'), and we expect further developments in this area as the Court pursues more environment-related issues in the context of domestic sustainable development and 'reduce global warming' according to the international Kyoto accord.

NOTES

1. Anil Aggarwal, *The State of India' Environment 1984-5: The Second Citizen's Report,* New Delhi, Centre for Science and Environment (1986) 362.
2. Tarun Bharat Sangh, *Alwar* v. *Union of India,* Writ Petition (Civil) No. 509 of 1991, SC.
3. *Indian Council for Enviro-Legal Action* v. *Union of India,* 1996 (5) SCC 281.
4. *M.C. Mehta* v. *Union of India* (Delhi Stone Crushing Case), 1992 (3) 256; *Subhash Kumar* v. *Bihar,* AIR 1991 SC 420; *V. Gaur* v. *Haryana* 1995(2) SCC 577.
5. *B.L. Wadhre* v. *Union of India* (Delhi Garbage case), AIR 1996 SC 2969.
6. *Indian Council for Enviro-Legal Action* v. *Union of India,* 1996; Vellore Citizens' *Welfare Forum* v. *Union of India,* AIR 1996 SC 2715; *S. Jagannath* v. *India,* AIR 1997 SC 811.
7. Vellore Citizens' *Welfare Forum* v. *Union of India,* AIR 1996 SC 2715; *S. Jagannath* v. *India,* AIR 1997 SC 811; *AP Pollution Control Board* v. *M.V. Nayudu,* AIR 1999 SC 812.
8. *AP Pollution Control Board* v. *M.V. Nayudu,* AIR 1999 SC 812.
9. *Himachal Pradesh* v. *Ganesh Wood Products,* AIR 1996 SC 149.
10. *M.C. Mehta* v. *Kamal Nath,* 1997 SCC 388; *M.I. Builders* v. *Radhey Shyam Sahu,* AIR 1999 SC 2468.
11. *DLF Universal Ltd.* v. *Prof. A.L. Sagar,* 1998 7 SCC 1.
12. *Narmada Bachao Andolan* v. *India,* 1998 SCC 586; *Banwasi Sewa Ashram* v. *UP,* AIR 1992 SC 920.
13. *Animal and environmental Legal Defence Fund* v. *Union of India* 1997 3 SCC 549.
14. *Karjan Jalasay Yojna Assar grasth Sahkarane Sangarsh Samiti* v. *State of Gujarat and others,* AIR 1987 SC 532.

15. The comments in italics are to emphasize the point.
16. Sathe, S.P. *Judicial Activism in India*, New Delhi: Oxford University Press (2002), p. 225.
17. The scientific findings contained here were presented before the Court during the arguments in the *M.C. Mehta* v. *Union of India*, Writ Petition (Civil) No.13029 of 1985 (decision given in 2002), judgement (mimeo).
18. This position has been reiterated by this Court in Sector 14 Residents' *Welfare Association and Others* v. *State of Delhi and Others* (1999) 1 SCC 161.
19. Cited in *M.C. Mehta* v. *Union of India* Writ Petition (Civil) No.13029 of 1985 (decision given in 2002), judgement (mimeo), p. 4.
20. Ibid., p. 5.
21. Ibid., pp. 18–19.
22. *Parivesh,* September 2001—a Journal published by the Central Pollution Control Board, New Delhi, relating to air pollution and human health, p. 34; quoted in the judgement, op. cit., pp. 21–2.
23. *Down to Earth,* 'Death is in the Air', Council for Science and Environment, Delhi, 15 November 1977, p. 29.
24. *M.C. Mehta* v. *Union of India*, op. cit., p. 24.

Resolving River Water Disputes in India: The Supreme Court and the Narmada River Dams Controversy

JOHN R. WOOD

After what seemed like an inordinate delay, the Supreme Court of India handed down its judgement in the case of *Narmada Bachao Andolan* v. *Union of India and Others* on 18 October 2000.[1] Few anticipated that the verdict would go so clearly against the petitioner, the Narmada Bachao Andolan ('Save the Narmada Movement', NBA), and so in favour of the government. The NBA had been fighting to stop the construction of the Sardar Sarovar dam on the Narmada River since 1989. The immense dam, located in eastern Gujarat near its borders with Maharashtra and Madhya Pradesh, was nearing the halfway mark in its completion when the Supreme Court, in response to the NBA's writ petition of 1994, imposed a stay order on increasing the height of the dam in 1995. This was to protect villages soon to be submerged by Sardar Sarovar's projected 200 km long reservoir and allow time to deal with a host of issues affecting the resettlement and rehabilitation of displaced villagers, in India called 'oustees', as well as the environmental damage caused by dam construction.

The controversy over the development of the Narmada River basin's water resources stretched back over decades.[2] The project to build the terminal dam and irrigation canals had been inaugurated by Prime

*Paper presented at the Annual Meeting of the South Asia Council of the Canadian Asian Studies Association, Dalhousie University, Halifax, 1 June 2003.

Minister Jawaharlal Nehru in 1961 and named in honour of Sardar Vallabhbhai Patel. Eventually, a network of 30 major, 125 medium and 3,000 minor dams was planned to be built on the river and its 41 tributaries. But first, the conflict over how much water and hydroelectric benefits should be allocated to the riparian States had to be resolved through the formation of the Narmada Water Disputes Tribunal (NWDT) in 1969. As in the case of other Indian inter-state river water disputes, the NWDT, created under The Inter-State Water Disputes Act, 1956, consisted of three judges who carried out extensive investigations before handing down their award in 1978. The award, which was to be final and beyond the jurisdiction of the courts, was not to be reviewed until 2025. It not only determined the share of benefits and costs for the states of Gujarat, Madhya Pradesh, Maharashtra and Rajasthan, but also the resettlement and rehabilitation (R&R) process, by which oustees would be compensated for their losses. Still, construction could not begin until 1987 when the Prime Minister, Rajiv Gandhi, under much pressure from drought-stricken Gujaratis, gave the project its environmental clearance.

A number of NGOs emerged to fight for improvement in the R&R and environmental protection provisions, especially when the World Bank made its contribution of a $ 500 million start-up loan. The NBA, under the leadership of the renowned activist Medha Patkar, fought primarily on behalf of the *adivasi* (aboriginal) population of the upstream States of Maharashtra and Madhya Pradesh. After NBA-led clashes with the police and government officials in 1990–1, the World Bank appointed an Independent Review headed by Bradford Morse. The Morse Review argued that the Sardar Sarovar project was flawed and that the World Bank should reconsider its involvement.[3] In 1992, after the Government of India decided to forego the last instalment of World Bank support, the latter withdrew from the project.[4] This led to a further review of the project by Indian experts, known as the Five Member Group, whose investigation was boycotted by the Gujarat government and whose ultimate report was divided and inconclusive. It was then that the NBA began its last round of agitations against the dam, culminating in its petition to the Supreme Court in 1994.

In an effort to explain the outcome of the conflict, I will first outline some important changes that had occurred in the political background to the struggle over Sardar Sarovar, between 1995 and 2000. I will then review the content of the Supreme Court judgement, and its impact on the anti- and pro-dam forces on the Narmada, and the long-range significance for river water dispute resolution and the politics of water in India in general.

LARGE DAMS: THE CHANGING CONTEXT OF A CONTROVERSY

The six years between the filing of the NBA's writ petition and the Supreme Court judgement (1994–2000) were among the most politically chaotic and uncertain in India since independence. In particular, the years following the ending of Congress party rule under Narasimha Rao in the elections of 1996, up to the shaky consolidation of Bharatiya Janata Party (BJP) rule under Atal Behari Vajpayee in the elections of 1999, were fraught with turmoil. Three general elections in four years reflected an uncertain, fragmented electorate, while continual coalition formation, break-up and reformation resulted in weak governance.

One of the consequences of this political disarray was a new assertiveness on the part of India's judiciary, particularly at its highest level, the Supreme Court of India. The SC had begun to expand its role in the late 1970s by encouraging Public Interest Litigation (PIL), that is, class action suits aimed at promoting social and economic justice. This developed further into what Upendra Baxi has called Social Action Litigation (SAL) in the 1980s, when the court itself took the lead on behalf of downtrodden people such as bonded labourers, *adivasis*, women, the homeless, undertrials and others.[5] Supreme Court justices became widely admired for taking up issues that politicians and the political system, for reasons of corruption, indifference or the kind of political impasse just noted, seemed incapable of resolving.

Judicial activism, however, also had its critics and opponents. The judges, they said, had reached too far beyond their normal area of competence, had become overly ambitious in trying to effect social change and, in the process, had stimulated an immense increase in India's already staggering litigation backlog. There was mounting evidence too, that judges, as they moved into territory hitherto regarded as political, were themselves becoming politicized. By 2000, there was increasing worry, not least among responsible judges themselves, that the courts could lose their reputation for impartiality and integrity, without which their effectiveness would be seriously impaired.[6]

Nonetheless, when the NBA filed its writ petition in 1994 it had high hopes, not only that the Supreme Court would find in its favour regarding the injustices it alleged were being inflicted on the Sardar

Sarovar oustees and the environment, but also that the Court would stop the building of the dam altogether. Medha Patkar and the NBA, through their creation of the National Association of People's Movements, had moved their struggle on to a higher and wider plane, demanding that not only dams but any development projects that were top-down and insensitive to the needs of adversely affected people, should be stopped. When the Supreme Court issued its stay order on the Sardar Sarovar construction in January 1995, the NBA appeared to be at the height of its success: it had defied the State and interrupted work on India's most prestigious and expensive dam project. It had won the support of the Morse Independent Review and forced the World Bank to withdraw. The story of its (NBA leaders would say 'the people's') heroic struggle had spread worldwide through print and visual media and, outside of Gujarat, it appeared that the NBA was winning the battle of Indian public opinion regarding large dams and water resource development.

It should be noted, however, that the Supreme Court stay order against construction at Sardar Sarovar, that is, against raising the dam's height above the 80.3 m mark reached in 1994, did not apply to other important aspects of the project, such as the canal network or the hydro-electric powerhouses.[7] From the Gujarat government's point of view, carrying on with their construction had several positive consequences. First, the government would not be seen as sitting idle: it was pressing on with the work. Second, the many kilometres of empty cement-lined canal snaking their way across central and northern Gujarat would be a constant reminder to all passers-by of the water Gujaratis desperately needed, and were being denied. Moreover, there was a widespread belief that the more Gujarat invested in the project, the less likely it would be cancelled.

Towards the end of the 1990s, meanwhile, the context of the NBA's struggle had begun to change, not least thanks to its own and other like-minded organizations' success. Internationally, 'sustainable development' had become the watchword of all aid donor organizations, conferences, seminars and publications dealing with the Third World. Sustainable development, as a concept, had acquired many and diverse meanings and was looked at cynically by some protagonists on both sides of the pro- and anti-development divide.[8] However, it provided an opportunity for discussion by hitherto die-hard enemies, in the process, moderating the views of both. New emphasis was placed on dialogue and finding compromises. A good example of this change could be seen in the World Bank itself. Stung by criticism of the damaging impact of megaprojects it had funded around the world, the Bank began a process of self-examination and reform. In re-thinking its policies regarding large dams, a turning point was reached in April 1997, when the Bank, in conjunction with the World Conservation Union (IUCN), held an International Workshop on Large Dams at Gland, Switzerland. Attended by stakeholders from eighteen countries representing all shades of pro- and anti-dam opinion, the Workshop sought a consensus on 'whether dams have a major role to play in land, water and energy development and how particular dams should be selected, constructed and operated'. The three participants from India included Shripad Dharmadikary of the Narmada Bachao Andolan.[9]

One of the workshop's main accomplishments was to set up the World Commission on Dams (WCD), whose report was eventually published as *Dams and Development: A New Framework for Decision-Making*, widely circulated on the Internet and CD Rom.[10] India was prominently involved in several ways. Medha Patkar of the NBA and L.C. Jain, formerly of the Planning Commission, were two of the twelve Commissioners of the WCD.[11] Although Narmada dams were not featured in the six major case studies of dam projects in different parts of the globe, India and China were asked to prepare country reports that provided comprehensive analyses of their entire dam-building experience. The Indian report, *Large Dams: India's Experience: A Report for the World Commission on Dams*, was a massive (p. 279) compilation of data, review and appraisal of the history of dam-building in India, including analysis of the legal-institutional framework, the economic performance, as well as the environmental and social impacts of India's dams.[12] The report noted that large dams in India have made important contributions to the development of irrigated agriculture, improving production of food as well as contributing hydro-electric power and enhanced domestic and industrial water supply. However, in a tough, exhaustive appraisal of costs, not only economic and financial, but also environmental and social, the report concluded that many dam projects undertaken since the 1980s were, and remain, unviable.

Despite the frank acknowledgement of mistakes and miscalculations, the overall thrust of both the Indian and the WCD reports, was that ways can be found to improve dam-building, so that the injustices and harm they have inflicted can be minimized, if not eliminated altogether. What was most noticeable, however, was that the debate on large dams internationally, as well as in India, had come a long way since the first protests were launched against the Sardar Sarovar in the early 1980s.

As suggested earlier, a lot of the credit for creating the new climate of public concern, was due to the Narmada Bachao Andolan, whose dogged persistence and many sacrifices had kept the relevant issues in the public eye. By the end of the 1990s, however, the NBA's categorical opposition to the Sardar Sarovar seemed to be out of tune with the new search for compromise and, as a result, losing its support. Key journalists (for example, Tavleen Singh in the widely read *India Today*), were beginning to question the obstinacy of Medha Patkar.[13] When Arundhati Roy, the author who had won the Booker Prize for her novel, *The God of Small Things*, became the latest celebrity to join the NBA's cause in 1999, the result was an upsurge in media attention. But Roy's essays on the Sardar Sarovar, long on sympathy for the oustees and short on understanding of the complexities of water resource management, eventually built up resistance, not only among government officials but also middle class opinion in general. In the summer of 2000, Roy was the star of a 'Rally in the Valley' protest at the submerging village of Domkhedi in Maharashtra, that attracted large numbers of NBA supporters and unprecedented amounts of international media attention. During the same summer, Gujarat was entering its second year of severe drought and demands for Narmada water there reached a new high in intensity. Arundhati Roy's book, *The Greater Common Good*, was burned publicly in Ahmedabad. 'The argument against the dam is not anti-Gujarat,' insisted Roy. The argument, she maintained, was about basic fundamental rights: 'Go to the valley and see for yourself how the people are suffering.'[14]

On the political front, the hopes of Gujaratis for an end to the Sardar Sarovar stalemate rose when the BJP, already ruling in Gujarat, was able to form a 13-party coalition government in New Delhi, in March 1998. Although that government fell in April 1999, when one of the coalition partners defected, the BJP and its allies returned strongly in the general election in October of that year, eventually putting together a 23-party coalition government. Altogether 19 Gujarati BJP MPs sat with the government in 1998 and 20 in 1999.[15] The most prominent, Lal Krishna Advàni, who held the Gandhinagar seat in Gujarat, was regarded as the number two man in Vajpayee's government. Throughout the election campaign, he had declared that if the BJP were elected, the Narmada dams would become a 'National Project', meaning that all obstacles would be removed to build SSP to its full height.[16]

Meanwhile, the BJP government in Gujarat was renewing its efforts to deal with the rehabilitation and resettlement of oustees. Here too some moderating change can be seen. The new minister in charge of Narmada Development, Jainarayan Vyas, announced on 16 March 1998, that the Gujarat government would allow 8,000-odd project-affected families in Madhya Pradesh to decide where they would like to relocate when their villages—121 of them, according to one account—were submerged.[17] Hitherto, if the Gujarat government were to pay for R&R, the oustees would have to relocate to Gujarat. The new policy was good news for Madhya Pradesh oustees, many of whom did not want to move away from their *janmabhoomi* (the place of their birth), and into a different linguistic area. It also reduced the problem of finding suitable resettlement land in Gujarat. But primarily, the announcement showed that the Gujarat government was doing its utmost to impress the Supreme Court with its reasonableness in dealing with resettlement and rehabilitation.

The most convincing evidence of this reasonableness came in February 1999 when the Government of Gujarat created the Grievance Redressal Authority for Sardar Sarovar Project Affected Persons (GRA). This body was to provide a means whereby oustees resettled in Gujarat could get redress for their grievances until the entire resettlement process was completed. By a Government resolution of 17 February 1999, Justice P.D. Desai, Retired Chief Justice of the Bombay, Calcutta and Himachal Pradesh High Courts, was appointed the Chairman of the GRA. Desai quickly established a reputation for integrity and fairness. He insisted on two stipulations in his appointment: (1) that the Chief Justice of the Supreme Court concur in the Chairman's appointment and that the Chairman not be removable except with the concurrence of the Chief Justice; and (2) that all decisions and directions of the GRA regarding project-affected families be final and binding on the state of Gujarat. Clearly, Desai wanted to act autonomously, free from any political or bureaucratic pressure, and he wanted everyone to know that he could do so.

The headquarters of the GRA was established in the old buildings of the Gujarat High Court in downtown Ahmedabad, but the effective work was decentralized through the creation of two mechanisms: the Tatkal Fariyad Nivaran Samiti ('Immediate Complaint Resolution Committee), and the Single Window Clearance System. The former was an on-the-spot investigative team that would hear and attempt to resolve oustee grievances at regular intervals at, or near, the resettlement sites. The latter was a mechanism whereby officers from various state government departments—Revenue, Land Records, Agriculture, Health, Electricity Board, etc.,—could be quickly brought together to expedite the disposal of grievances. According to GRA records, between April 1999 and December 2000, the GRA dealt with 14,158 grievances; out of these, 10,725 were decided in favour of the oustee complainants.[18] Remarkably, the work of the GRA was commended not only by Keshubhai Patel, the Chief Minister of Gujarat, but also by the NBA, which submitted an affidavit appreciating the role played by the GRA and the access it provided to project affected families.[19] But perhaps the greatest compliment paid to the GRA came a year later, when the Governments of Maharashtra and Madhya Pradesh, ordered that GRAs be set up in their states as well.

Meanwhile, in Madhya Pradesh further developments complicated the picture for the NBA. The NBA's relations with the Chief Minister, Digvijay Singh, had started off well in 1993, when he proposed that the projected height of the Sardar Sarovar dam be lowered to 436 ft in order to save 67 villages from submergence. However, the Madhya Pradesh government had begun its own construction work on dams upstream of the Sardar Sarovar, at Bargi, Mann and Maheshwar. It was particularly at Maheshwar that the NBA took up cudgels with the builder, a private firm called S. Kumars Ltd., as well as the police and the government. When blasting to lay the foundations of the Maheshwar Dam began in 1997, local residents contacted the NBA and with the help of fasting by NBA activists got the MP government to concede the establishment of a Task Force to investigate the impact of the dam. Before the Task Force could finish its report, however, S. Kumars announced that 'safety-related work', would have to be undertaken to protect the construction already completed. The NBA saw this as a guise under which construction might be continued, and became agitated when the MP government sided with S. Kumars, and moved over a thousand police on to the dam site. By April 1998, a major confrontation was underway, with the MP government imposing prohibitory orders on the dam site under Section 144, which bans the assembly of more than four persons. Hundreds of protestors, including large numbers of women, were jailed. With the help of international NGOs, the NBA succeeded in deterring foreign investors, which according to the NBA would be responsible for 76 per cent of project equity.[20] But the NBA now found itself fighting on several fronts at once and stretching its resources more thinly.

To sum up thus far, during 1995–2000, the struggle over the development of the Narmada Valley had reached such an impasse, that there was ostensibly no work going on at the Sardar Sarovar dam site. The pro- and anti-dam forces, it seemed, had fought each other to a standstill. Both looked to the Supreme Court, hoping to win. While the judges worked on their decision, however, significant changes had taken place in a variety of interrelated 'realms': first, in the realm of ideas about development in general, and large dams in particular; second, in the realm of Indian public opinion; and third, in the realm of politics. In none of these realms was the change a simple movement from position 'A' to position 'B'; rather, there were crosscurrents and complexities.

In the realm of ideas about water resource development, as we have seen, despite all the angry rhetoric, a dialogue was now taking place that brought die-hard opponents to the same table and forced each to take the other's point of view into consideration. The World Commission on Dam Debates were being played out in gatherings all over India, from academic seminars to conversations among villagers. The discussions were aided by a communications revolution that made far more people aware of the issues than ever before. Government officials and engineers could no longer pretend that only they knew all the answers to the questions being asked. Meanwhile, those who opposed dam projects were being forced to study the scientific-technical realities of water management in India, and come up with viable (workable, affordable and sustainable) alternatives.

Change in the realm of Indian public opinion about dams and development, and its effects on decision-makers, is much harder to grasp, let alone explain. There is no adequate quantitative data with which to determine what the opinions were and what difference they made. Moreover, there are obviously many and diverse 'publics' in India, different, for example, in downstream versus upstream states, in urban versus rural settings, or among agriculturalists versus non-agriculturalists. Several things however were new. One was that public opinion mattered: otherwise, governments, on the one hand, and the NBA, on the other, would not have striven so diligently to try to influence it. A related phenomenon was international opinion and the globalization of the Narmada controversy. No other dam in India had attracted so much attention abroad, or been so extensively discussed in the world's media. A second change was that, perhaps for the first time in India, not only elite opinion mattered. The Narmada issues—issues like displacement, environmental impacts, the costs versus the benefits of megaprojects, the rights of aboriginals—were so fundamental to development issues in other parts of India that far more people *had* opinions. And whether they were for or against the Sardar Sarovar project, they were more ready to express them, in letters to the editor, in casual conversations, and in protest demonstrations.

All of the foregoing changes were undoubtedly going to have their effects in the political realm, which, as has been already outlined, was undergoing changes of its own. The uncertainty and deadlock in all-India politics in the last half of the 1990s, related developments in state level politics, the increasing assertiveness of NGOs, the new activism of the judiciary—all of these could be expected to have an effect on the Supreme Court decision. The SC was no doubt an independent body, but it was a Court operating in a democracy. All of the changes so far described were connected in some way to democratization processes in an open, pluralistic and highly mobilized-polity. The three judges called upon to decide the fate of the Sardar Sarovar project were no doubt aware of the swirling waters into which they would cast their judgement.

THE JUDGEMENT

The judgement was a 2-1 split decision. Justice B.N. Kirpal wrote the majority judgement; Chief Justice A.S. Anand agreed with it. Justice S.P. Bharucha wrote the dissenting minority judgement. The 183-page majority judgement will be dealt with first, followed by the 32-page minority judgement. References are given according to the page numbers in the judgement.

Justice Kirpal began with a synopsis of the history of the dispute over Narmada waters, the provisions of the Narmada Water Disputes Tribunal award, the terms of the clearances given by the Government of India and the findings of the Five Member Group. After listing the main points of contention under: (1) general issues; (2) issues regarding the environment, (3) issues regarding relief and rehabilitation, and (4) issues regarding review of the Tribunal's award (p. 30), Kirpal focused on three points of law. The first was that the petitioner, the NBA, was guilty of 'laches' in not approaching the Court earlier (pp. 32–4). Laches is a legal term meaning negligence in the observance of a duty or opportunity, or more specifically, an undue delay in asserting a legal right or privilege. According to Kirpal, although the NBA was formed in 1986 and the Government of India gave the Sardar Sarovar project environmental clearance in 1987, the NBA was guilty of laches in that it did not challenge the decision to construct the dam until 1994, that is, long after construction was undertaken and large amounts of public money were spent.

This led to the second point of law: whether issues such as the height of the dam, the extent of submergence, environmental impact and clearance, hydrology, seismicity and so on, could be permitted to be raised at such a late stage. Justice Kirpal said no: 'it was only the concern of this Court for the protection of the fundamental rights of the oustees under Article 21 of the Constitution of India which led to the entertaining of this petition' (p. 35). The Court would therefore only be really concerned with Relief and Rehabilitation measures, even if it would deal with some of the other issues raised by the NBA. The third point of law cited in the majority judgement was that '[o]nce [a Tribunal] Award is binding on the States, it will not be open to a third party like the petitioners to challenge the correctness thereof'(p. 37). The Court, in other words, would not deal with any contention that would challenge the correctness of an issue decided by the Tribunal.

General Issues

Under general issues, Justice Kirpal rejected the NBA's claim that according to Article 21 of the Constitution of India, read with the International Labour Organization Convention Article 107, the displacement caused by the Sardar Sarovar was not in the national interest and was a violation of the oustees' fundamental rights. Instead, he maintained that in view of 'the need of water for burgeoning population' (p. 45), increased water storage was essential.[21] He went on to extol the benefits of the dam for food security, domestic and industrial water supply, hydro-electric power and flood control. Regarding the rights of *adivasis*, Kirpal said that once they were rehabilitated at new locations they would be 'better off than what they were . . . [T]hey will have more and better amenities than which they enjoyed in their tribal hamlets. The(ir?) gradual assimilation in the mainstream of the society would lead to betterment and progress' (p. 48).

Environmental Issues

With regard to environmental issues, Justice Kirpal first tackled the question of whether proper impact studies had been made before environmental clearance was given for the Sardar Sarovar. According to the NBA, the decision in 1987 to give clearance was political, not a considered decision taking into account the environmental effects of the project, and thus, it constituted a violation of the rights of the affected people under Article 21 of the Constitution (p. 49). Shri Shanti Bhushan, advocate for the NBA, argued this point on the basis of the findings of the Morse Independent Review. Like Morse, Bhushan argued that the studies that had been made were of poor quality, based on improper data. He charged that remedial measures were 'lagging behind *pari passu*', that is, were not keeping sufficiently ahead of dam construction (p. 51).

Justice Kirpal went into fifty pages of extraordinary detail regarding the institutional procedures, the studies undertaken and the reports submitted prior to Sardar Sarovar's environmental clearance based on the *pari passu* condition. In 1986 the Ministry of Water Resources, unable to get the agreement of the Ministry of Environment and Forests, had forwarded a note to Prime Minister Rajiv Gandhi's office, arguing that either the project could be delayed for two to three years while plans and studies were drawn up, or clearance could be given, subject to the stipulation that environmental studies and appropriate monitoring arrangements be taken up 'in a time bound manner' (p. 62). The Ministry of Environment and Forests wanted stricter monitoring by a Narmada Management Authority. When in January 1987, a note was put up to Prime Minister Rajiv Gandhi asking his approval for giving clearance subject to conditions—especially that plans for rehabilitation, catchment area treatment, compensatory afforestation and command area development be prepared, and a Narmada Management Authority be created to ensure that environmental management plans were imple-mented, *pari passu* with engineering and other works—he did not immediately give his approval (p. 67). Ultimately a press note was issued by the Prime Minister's Office on 13 April 1987 announcing agreement by Gujarat, MP and Maharashtra that a high level River Valley Authority would be set up for control and development of the river basin, and also that the Narmada Sagar and Sardar Sarovar projects had been cleared (p. 69). Later, the Prime Minister replied to various requests for confirmation of project clearance with a statement on 4 May 1987, that this had been given conditionally.

The majority judgement concluded from this recitation of events that the environmental clearance was a 'conscious decision'. Aware that a number of impact studies had yet to be completed, the Government of India had imposed the *pari passu* condition and made arrangements to monitor the completion. As for the implementation of the conditions, Justice Kirpal rejected Shanti Bhushan's reference to the Morse Independent Review's findings regarding non-implementation, since the Review's *Report* was accepted neither by the World Bank nor the Government of India (pp. 76–7).[22] Then, he examined issues such as catchment area treatment, compensatory afforestation, downstream impacts, archaeological remains and health concerns. Justice Kirpal found that the collection of impact data was adequate: 'we are satisfied that this has been and is being done' (p. 98). In sum, '[c]are for environment is an on-going process and the system in place would ensure that ameliorative steps are taken to counter the adverse effect, if any, on the environment with the construction of the dam' (ibid.). The 'system in place' referred to the operations of the Environmental Sub-Group of the Narmada Control Agency, a 'watchdog' which can recommend stoppage of work to the NCA. If the NCA is divided, an appeal can be made to the Review Committee, of which the Minister of Environment and Forests is a member. Justice Kirpal quoted the commendation of the Five Member Group, that '[i]t seems doubtful whether any more effective mechanism could have been devised or made to work within the framework of our existing political and administrative structures, particularly in the context of a federal system' (p. 92).

Relief and Rehabilitation Issues

The main contentions of the NBA regarding the oustees were: First, that the number of families affected by dam construction had risen drastically; beyond these, there were many non-recognized oustee categories, people who should additionally be compensated. Second, the R&R policies of the different states differed, with the result that MP and Maharashtra oustees were being forced to resettle in Gujarat. Third, there was no Master Plan for resettlement, no systematic arrangements made for oustees prior to the submergence of their villages. Finally, the existing R&R sub-group of the NCA as a governmental agency did not have the requisite independence with which to monitor and see to the compliance of R&R provisions in the NWDT Award.

In his majority judgement, Justice Kirpal acknowledged that the number of Project Affected Families (PAF) had risen from 7,000, as stated in the NWDT Award, to 40,227 as of 1990 (p. 116). He made the point that much of the project-affected land belonging to these people would only be minimally submerged. The reason for the rise in numbers was principally because of the liberalization of the eligibility rules for R&R benefits. Justice Kirpal rejected the idea that PAF status should be extended further, for example to non-agriculturalists in affected villages or those displaced by the building of the dam construction colony at Kevadia, or to canal-displaced families. He argued that in the two foregoing cases, those affected by construction would be rewarded by new opportunities for employment, while for the latter category, there would be new opportunities in increased land productivity (pp. 123–5).

As regards the differential in the R&R packages offered by Gujarat, Maharashtra and Madhya Pradesh, Justice Kirpal argued that it stemmed from inevitable differences in geography, economic conditions and availability of land. He saw no need to force the three states to offer identical packages; oustees were free to choose the option that worked best for them (p. 122). Justice Kirpal pointed out that the Tribunal Award never called for a Master Plan, but that one had evolved through individual state action plans presented to the NCA, beginning in 1989, and eventually coordinated as an integrated Master Plan in 1993 and 1995 (pp. 114–15). This was designed to take care of R&R policy and procedures, implementation machinery, monitoring and evaluation, empowerment of women and youth, special care for vulnerable groups, financial planning, etc. He cited important inter-state meetings in 1996 and 1999, where commitments had been made to review the implementation of resettlement and rehabilitation measures so that implementation would in fact progress *pari passu* with the raising of the dam's height. Justice Kirpal reviewed and approved all the measures designed to protect the welfare of the oustees, including those to preserve their social and cultural environment, provide civic amenities, improve agricultural production and extend health care facilities (pp. 119–20).

Finally, Justice Kirpal agreed with the Government of India that the R&R sub-group and the Rehabilitation Committee of the NCA constituted 'a well-established mechanism . . . for coordination and monitoring . . . R&R programmes in case of Sardar Sarovar Project'. According to Justice Kirpal, the R&R sub-group of the NCA would closely monitor R&R progress with regard to land acquisition, rehabilitation of PAFs and implementation of R&R *pari passu* with the raising of the height of the dam. The Rehabilitation Committee of the NCA, headed by the Secretary of the Ministry of Justice and Empowerment and including representatives of the three states, would regularly visit submerging villages and R&R sites in order to report to the NCA as well as to monitor compliance. Finally, the Review Committee of the NCA, consisting of the Union Ministers of Water Resources and of Environment and Forests plus the Chief Ministers of Gujarat, Maharashtra and Madhya Pradesh had the authority to review any decision of the NCA.

But Justice Kirpal saved his strongest praise for the Grievances Redressal Authority, which he described as 'an effective monitoring and implementing agency with regard to relief and rehabilitation of the PAFs in Gujarat' (p. 137). After extolling Justice P.D. Desai's 'innovative steps', in setting up cells for improving agricultural productivity, health extension and education facilities, he noted:

> There now seems to be a commitment on the part of the Government of Gujarat to see that there is no laxity in the R & R of the PAFs. It appears that the State of Gujarat has realized that without effective R & R facilities no further construction of the dam would be permitted by the NCA and under the guidance and directions of the GRA meaningful steps are being undertaken in this behalf. (p. 154)

The majority judgement revealed that on 9 May 2000, the Supreme Court had directed the state governments of Gujarat, Maharashtra and Madhya Pradesh to file affidavits, disclosing the latest status of R&R work for both existing and prospective oustees likely to be affected by raising the height of the dam (p. 140). The object was to ascertain whether the states were prepared for the next stage of R&R if the dam was raised to 90 m. After reviewing the affidavits, Justice Kirpal declared that 'this Court is satisfied that more than adequate steps are being taken by the State of Gujarat' (p. 156). In reviewing the Maharashtra affidavit, he concluded that the state would be in a position to make land available to all, the relevant PAFs (p. 162).

He was critical, however, of the effort of the Madhya Pradesh government: 'There seems to be no hurry to effectively rehabilitate the Madhya Pradesh PAFs in their home state' (p. 159). He noted that the main effort of the MP government had been to convince PAFs that they should go to Gujarat. However, if PAFs wanted to remain in MP, the MP government was obliged to resettle them. It could not plead that the cost was too great as Gujarat had agreed to pay for their resettlement. Justice Kirpal was not, however, harsh in his criticism of the MP government. In fact, he provided a rationale for its behaviour: the main benefits of the Sardar Sarovar would go to the other states (p. 160). However, he asserted that:

[I]n a federal setup like India whenever any such Inter-State project is approved and work undertaken the States involved have a responsibility to co-operate with each other. . . . The Award of the Tribunal being binding the States concerned are duty bound to comply with the terms thereof. (pp. 160–1)

Justice Kirpal's final comments on the reviewability of the Tribunal Award and the court's role in decision-making regarding dam projects like Sardar Sarovar have been mentioned earlier. In his conclusion he went out of his way to state the limits of Public Interest Litigation:

With the passage of time the PIL jurisdiction has been ballooning so as to encompass within its ambit subjects such as probity in public life, granting of largese in the form of licenses, protecting environment and the like. But the balloon should not be inflated so much that it bursts. Public Interest Litigation should not be allowed to degenerate to becoming Publicity Interest Litigation or Private Inquisitiveness Litigation. (p. 166)

According to Kirpal, the Court must not 'transgress its jurisdiction' or be called upon to 'undertake governmental duties or functions' (pp. 166–7). 'The Courts cannot run the Government,' he maintained; moreover, 'it has been consistently held by this Court that in matters of policy the Court will not interfere' (pp. 167–8).

When there is a valid law requiring the Government to act in a particular manner the Court ought not to . . . give any direction which is not in accordance with law. In other words the Court itself is not above the law. (p. 168)

Again:

In a democratic set up, it is for the elected Government to decide what project should be undertaken for the benefit of the people. Once such a decision has been taken . . . unless and until it can be proved or shown that there is a blatant illegality in the undertaking of the project or in its execution, the Court ought not to interfere with the execution of the project. (p. 171)

Justice Kirpal affirmed the ability of river valley projects to improve the environment and increase prosperity, including for *adivasis*:

It is not fair that tribals and the people in un-developed villages should continue in the same condition without ever enjoying the fruits of science and technology for better health and have a higher quality of life style. . . . In the present case the R&R packages of the States, especially of Gujarat, are such that the living conditions of the oustees will be much better than what they had in their tribal hamlets. (pp. 172–3)

THE COURT'S DIRECTIONS

As he laid down his directions at the end of the judgement, Justice Kirpal emphasized two principles: first, that the project should be completed at the earliest, and second that the states must comply with the conditions regarding relief and rehabilitation, as well as ameliorative measures for the environment. The directions, which have been slightly abridged, follow:

1. Construction of the dam will continue as per the Award of the Tribunal.
2. As the R&R sub-group has cleared the construction up to 90 m, it can proceed immediately. Raising of the height can only be *pari passu* with R&R implementation and after clearance by the R&R sub-group.
3. The Environment sub-group must give environmental clearance before the stages of construction beyond 90 m.
4. Permission for raising the dam height will be given by the NCA after it obtains clearances from the R&R sub-group and the Environment sub-group.
5. Gujarat, Maharashtra and Madhya Pradesh must comply with any direction given by the NCA or the Review Committee or the GRAs in implementing the Award according to the terms of the packages offered to the oustees.
6. The NCA and the Environmental sub-group will continue to ensure that all steps are taken not only to protect but to restore and improve the environment.
7. In four weeks, the NCA will draw up an Action Plan in relation to further construction and R&R work, fixing a time frame with which the states must comply.
8. The Review Committee will meet whenever required to resolve any dispute which cannot be resolved by the NCA, or at least once every three months, to oversee the construction and implementation of R&R programmes. If any serious differences remain that cannot be resolved by the Review Committee, the Committee may refer the same to the Prime Minister, whose decision shall be final and binding on all concerned.
9. The Grievances Redressal Authorities will be at liberty to issue appropriate directions to the respective States for implementation of the R&R programmes and in case of non-implementation, the GRAs will be at liberty to approach the Review Committee for appropriate orders.
10. Every endeavour shall be made to see that the project is completed as expeditiously as possible.

THE MINORITY UDGEMENT

Justice S.P. Bharucha's judgement did not differ from the majority judgement with regard to the facts. He started off with the assertion that the Project, per se, did not need to be re-examined, for example in regard to its cost-effectiveness, or the seismicity question. He largely agreed with the stipulations laid out by Justice Kirpal regarding resettlement and rehabilitation, emphasizing the importance of the Grievance Redressal Authorities' role in carefully sanctioning increases in the height of the dam only after satisfactory oustee rehabilitation, and the acquisition of land for the oustees to be displaced by further construction (pp. 31–2).

Justice Bharucha's main point of dissent, however, was in his interpretation of whether environmental clearance was properly given in 1987, when, according to notes prepared at the time by the Ministry of Environment, Forests and Wildlife, 'what has been done so far whether by way of action or by way of studies does not amount to much and [that] many matters are yet in the early and preliminary stages' (p. 22). In Justice Bharucha's view: 'An environmental clearance based on next to no data in regard to the environmental impact of the Project was contrary to the terms of the then policy of the Union of India in regard to environmental clearances . . .' (p. 22).

Without the impact data, no assessment could be made as to whether the project could proceed. Moreover, 'What the environmental safeguards measures the Narmada Control Authority was to ensure were, and what their cost would be, was not known when the environmental clearance was given. There was, therefore, no way in which this cost could be included in the cost of the Project, which was a requirement of the Guidelines' (p. 23).

In view of these shortcomings, Justice Bharucha called for the Environmental Impact Agency of the Ministry of Environment and Forests to appoint a Committee of Experts to gather all necessary data on the environmental impact of the Sardar Sarovar project. The Committee would 'take into consideration the fact that the construction of the dam and other work on the Project has already commenced' (p. 31). However, until the Committee gave environmental clearance, 'further construction work on the dam shall cease' (Ibid.).

REACTION

Needless to say, in Gujarat, widespread jubilation greeted the Supreme Court decision. Chief Minister Keshubhai Patel summed up the feelings of relief this way: 'For long we were under pressure. Many asked why we were not launching a counter-agitation on Narmada. But we said that we have full faith in the court. Today we stand vindicated. It is a victory for us.'[23]

Patel's government planned a big celebration for 31 October. It diverted 3,200 Gujarat State Road Transport Corporation buses, roughly one-third of the fleet, to carry some two hundred thousand people to join in the festivities at Kevadia Colony, near the Sardar Sarovar dam site. The ensuing chaotic traffic jam in the small town soon turned ugly. Mobs vented their fury by attacking ministers' cars. Meanwhile, at the Kevadia Colony celebrations, while Gujarati politicians took an exultant pledge to complete the construction of Sardar Sarovar 'at the earliest', representatives from the other riparian states were conspicuous by their absence. Medha Patkar, in a telephone interview, was quoted as saying that the function to relaunch the construction of Sardar Sarovar was a 'manifestation of the arrogance of state power which would be resisted by the people of the Narmada Valley'.[24] Later, in an NBA publication, *People* v. *Verdict*, she issued a call for action: 'Till date our struggles have been against a corrupt system, against a false concept of development and against undemocratic planning. But now the struggle of the Narmada Valley will be a fight to bring the Constitution of India to its reality. If neither politicians, nor bureaucracy and not even the judiciary are able to safeguard the Constitution, then how do the common people of the country do it? That is what the Narmada Andolan has to demonstrate now.'[25]

On 13 December 2000, the NBA held a protest demonstration outside the gates of the Supreme Court in New Delhi. Five lawyers, finding their way blocked, berated the crowd. They later alleged that Medha Patkar exhorted the crowd to kill them, that Prashant Bhushan, the NBA counsel, had pulled one person by the hair and that Arundhati Roy tried to incite the crowd to violence by branding the Supreme Court a 'thief'. The allegations developed into a case of contempt of court that dragged on for over a year. Eventually, Patkar and Roy, arguing that the charges were an attempt to stifle legitimate dissent and inviting the SC to send them to jail, were given one-day sentences. The Court was clearly trying to deny martyrdom to the activists, even as it insisted on respect for the Court and its decisions. Eventually, the litigation seemed to take the wind out of the sails of the NBA. It appeared that the NBA activists, who had struggled relentlessly against politicians for the past fifteen years, had finally found their match in the justices of the Supreme Court.

The critiques of two former administrators who had been members of the Five Member Group, Ramaswamy Iyer and L.C. Jain, met the judges' points more cogently. Iyer argued that it was wrong to trust the NCA and its sub-groups to monitor the fulfilment of R&R or environmental conditions for raising the dam to 90 m or beyond when they had failed to do so up to 85 m.[26] Second, he objected to the judges' advocacy of dams in general, given the case against dams and in favour of other means of water-harvesting in the recent literature. Third, he felt that the justices were unfair to the NBA. It had not come to the Court earlier because it was pursuing its cause by pressuring the World Bank to set up the Independent Review, and later, the Government to set up the Five Member Group. If the Court had suspended construction for several years, was that not prima facie evidence that the NBA had a case? Fourth, Iyer argued that the non-reviewability of the Tribunal award was debatable: changes in the form of liberalization in R&R policy had already been made. Moreover, where a Tribunal has not consulted dam-affected people, questions of human rights should not be overridden by an award on the inter-state sharing of water. Finally, Iyer found it 'unfortunate and disquieting' that all the good work of Public Interest Litigation over the previous two decades could be 'nullified at one stroke by this single judgement'. In sum, the judgement was 'a negative answer to those who sought relief, and a severe blow to people's movements'.

L.C. Jain decried the 'ideology' of the majority judgement, which he saw as unequivocally pro-development and pro-large dams. In particular, he lamented its view that the displacement of *adivasis* was a 'desirable goal by itself'.[27] He then proceeded to review the recent criticism of large dams by numerous experts—their cost-effectiveness, their impact on the environment, the living standards of displaced persons, and so forth. What he found most disturbing in the judgement was the knowledge-base of the judges who had discounted all the negative evidence regarding large dams—'surely our courts are not so completely insulated from glaring living reality'.[28] Jain similarly found it surprising that the majority judgement seemed blind to the controversies raging for over two decades about the specifics of the Sardar Sarovar project, such as the utilizable quantum of water in the river or the height of the dam, which, he argued, had been determined by political expediency. Finally, like Iyer, Jain argued that the NBA had been treated unfairly by the Court: [n]ot once has the Majority Judgement acknowledged that NBA was representing the problems of the affected people, who after years of trying, were forced to turn against the dam itself by the obduracy and excesses of the executive. . . .[29]

CONCLUSION

Whatever controversies surrounded the Supreme Court judgement, its immediate significance was that the Narmada Water Disputes Tribunal Award, however much it had been altered by pressure and protest since 1978, in its essentials stood firm. Work on Sardar Sarovar and other dams on the Narmada River could now, with important conditions, resume. A project that had become bogged down in uncertainty could now proceed with certainty. Even if disputes persisted about the feasibility and process of implementing the Award, the Court had laid down a formula for resolving them, and getting on with completion of the Sardar Sarovar Dam. Pointing to its past record, many observers, like Ramaswamy Iyer, had doubts about the NCA's capacity to live up to the Court's expectations. However, the enhanced authority and credibility of the GRAs, pointed to the fact that a new institution had been validated, one which should probably have been functioning from the very beginning.[30]

The Supreme Court's upholding of the Tribunal's work and its Award reinforced the credibility of similar tribunals whose decision-making regarding other Indian rivers has often been under attack. If the work of the NWDT had been overturned by the SC, it would be very difficult to prevent a domino effect in the challenging and invalidating of other Tribunal awards. What judge would want to serve on a tribunal and what disputants would respect a tribunal's decisions, if the decisions could be so easily discarded? Why spend huge amounts of taxpayers' money and engage judges, lawyers, engineers and other experts in years of deliberation if the award they arrived at carried no weight?

The answer to such questions from those opposed to dam-building in the first place, was that tribunals like the NWDT may resolve interstate disputes over river water, but not the more essential problems that happen to people, some of whom are victimized by dam construction while others benefit. There is much truth in the charge that river water dispute tribunals in India, thus far, have not consulted the people most affected by their decisions. But in October 2000, the Supreme Court was saying that it could not resolve conflicts that arise from tribunal decisions: they belonged in the political, not the judicial sphere. The Court would look into allegations of violation of the rights of oustees as they were defined in the Tribunal Award and subsequent agreements. Anything in the Tribunal Award or the government undertakings that went beyond that—the height of the dam or the extent of submergence, for instance—must be regarded as a political decision.

Was this an evasion of responsibility, a 'cop-out' by the Supreme Court? Certainly most observers who support the NBA position have seen it that way. It was no doubt surprising after nearly two decades of judicial activism in India for the Court to abandon the interventionist role it had recently played in similar cases. But the Court did not evade its responsibility: it came out foursquare for the state's position and emphatically rejected the arguments of the petitioner. We can only speculate as to whether the Court's almost belligerent support of dam-building was its way of seizing the initiative in what would inevitably be a controversial decision, a sort of 'dam-the-torpedoes' approach to all the countervailing arguments, because it knew that anything else would only produce more controversy, more delay, more cost and more suffering. Perhaps in the eyes of the majority judges, the Narmada case was the straw that had broken the back of the PIL camel? Their remark about 'Publicity Interest Litigation' certainly revealed their frustration with the NBA leadership's attempts to use the Court to attract public attention to its cause.

More importantly, Justice Kirpal was arguing that the judiciary could not resolve issues that properly belonged in the political sphere. In the case of the Narmada dispute, elected politicians and state-employed bureaucrats had the responsibility to make and implement decisions about the Sardar Sarovar and other dams. If they failed in this task, they would be accountable to voters at the ballot box. Meanwhile, if judges, not accountable at the ballot box, were to take the responsibility, several consequences would ensue. First, politicians, not having to live up to their responsibility, would become even more unaccountable and negligent. Second, although judges could hand down judgements in the public interest as they understood it, they did not have the means to see through the implementation of their rulings. As Justice Kirpal said, 'The Court cannot run the government'. And third, if the politicians neglected their duty to 'run the government', they would leave inordinate power in the hands of bureaucrats, already accused of insensitivity to the needs of people affected by development policy decisions.

The case of *Narmada Bachao Andolan* v. *Union of India and Others*, seems likely to become a landmark in the history of river-water dispute resolution in India. Although the Supreme Court may not have delivered the kind of justice sought by human rights and environmental protection activists, it did not just reaffirm the status quo. The judges, in effect, said that the existing institutions for water dispute resolution—supplemented by the new Grievance Redressal Authorities—were adequate to deal with conflicts over the development of India's water resources. In laying down conditions for the completion of the Sardar Sarovar project, they were challenging those responsible for India's water governance, both politicians and administrators, to get on with their job.

NOTES

1. Writ Petition (C) No. 319 of 1994, a civil original jurisdiction of the Supreme Court of India.
2. For critiques of the project, see, Claude Alvares and Ramesh Billorey, *Damming the Narmada: India's Greatest Planned Environmental Disaster*, Dehra Dun: Natraj, 1988; Vijay Paranjpye, *High Dams on the Narmada: A Holistic Analysis of the River Valley Projects*, New Delhi: INTACH, 1990. The government position is set forth in *Planning for Posterity: Sardar Sarovar Development Plan*, Gandhinagar: Sardar Sarovar Narmada Nigam Ltd., 1989, and *Sardar Sarovar Project: A Promise for Plenty*, ed. Mahesh T. Pathak, Gandhinagar: Narmada Planning Group, SSNNL, 1991. Balanced accounts may be found in Jean Dreze, Meera Samson and Satyajit Singh (eds.), *The Dam and the Nation: Displacement and Resettlement in the Narmada Valley*, Delhi: Oxford University Press, 1997, and William F. Fisher (ed.), *Toward Sustainable Development: Struggling Over India's Narmada River*, Jaipur and New Delhi: Rawat, 1997.
3. *Sardar Sarovar: Report of the Independent Review*, Chairman: Bradford Morse, Ottawa: Resource Futures International Inc., 1992.
4. See, my 'India's Narmada River Dams: Sardar Sarovar Under Siege', *Asian Survey* 33: 10 (October 1993), pp. 68–84.
5. Upendra Baxi, *Courage, Craft and Contention: The Indian Supreme Court in the Eighties*, Bombay: Tripathi, 1985, pp. 16-20.
6. For a critique, see, P.D. Mathew, *Public Interest Litigation*, New Delhi: Indian Social Institute, 1998.

7. In February 1999, the Supreme Court allowed the height of the dam to be raised from 80.3 to 85 m. See, 'SC nod for raising Narmada dam height', *Times of India (Ahmedabad)*, 19 February 1999.
8. See, Sharachchandram M. Lele, 'Sustainable Development: A Critical Review', *World Development*, 19: 6 (1991), pp. 607–21.
9. The others included Sanjeev Ahluwahlia of the Tata Energy Research Institute, an invited participant and Kalpana Sharma of *The Hindu*, an invited media representative. See, IUCN—The World Conservation Union and the World Bank Group, *Large Dams: Learning from the Past, Looking at the Future. Workshop Proceedings*. IUCN, Gland Switzerland and Cambridge, UK and the World Bank Group, Washington, DC, July 1997.
10. World Commission on Dams CD-ROM, *Dams and Development: A New Framework for Decision-Making: The Report of the World Commission on Dams*, London: Earthscan Publications. See http://www.earthscan. co.uk for further information.
11. L.C. Jain, a prominent public servant and academic, had been a member of the Five Member Group that reviewed the Sardar Sarovar project during 1996–7. He has published his views on Narmada and the Supreme Court decision of October 2000, in *Dam* v. *Drinking Water: Exploring the Narmada Judgement*, Pune: Parisar, 2001.
12. R. Rangachari, Nirmal Sengupta, Ramaswamy R. Iyer, Pranab Banerji and Shekhar Singh, 'Large Dams: India's Experience: A Report for the World Commission on Dams', New Delhi, 15 June 2000, typescript. This report is incorporated in the WCD Report CD-Rom, cited above.
13. See, for example, 'Luddite Sisters', *India Today*, 22 June 1998.
14. 'My argument not anti-Gujarat: Roy', *The Indian Express*, 31 July 1999.
15. 'Mapping the Mandate', *India Today*, 18 October 1999.
16. 'Will SSP ever be given national project status?' *Times of India* (Ahmedabad), 4 April 1998.
17. 'State reviews stand on Narmada oustees', *Times of India* (Ahmedabad), 17 March 1998.
18. 'Response of GRA, Gujarat to NCA's Questionnaire', typescript, n.d. (handed to me at GRA in August 2000), p. 4. See also *Narmada Ghati Vikas Patrika* (An Inhouse Magazine of the Narmada Control Authority), 8:4 (January–March 2001), p. 5.
19. See, 'The Relief Monitor', *The Indian Express*, 26 October 2000.
20. Narmada Bachao Andolan, Memo by Sripad Dharmadikary, 'Update and Action Alert on Maheshwar Project', 11 April 1998. According to one source, the list of companies that withdrew support from the Maheshwar Dam project included PacGen, Ogden and Harza International from the USA, Bayernwerk, VEW Energie and Siemens from Germany as well as Alstrom from France. See, Maggie Black, 'A Temple Too Far', *New Internationalist*, no. 336 (July 2001), p. 17.

21. The Court quoted an estimate that 'by the year 2050 the country needs to create storage of at least 600 billion cubic metre against the existing storage of 174 billion cubic metre' (Judgement, p. 46).
22. The majority judgement rejected the Independent Review's findings out of hand: '[W]e do not propose while considering the petitioners' contentions, to place any reliance on the report of Morse Committee. . . . There is no reason whatsoever as to why independent experts should be required to examine the quality, accuracy, recommendations and implementation of the studies carried out . . . the report of Morse Committee does not require our attention, the same not having been accepted either by the World Bank or the Government of India' (Judgement, pp. 78–9 and 91). The Independent Review is never mentioned in the minority judgement.
23. 'SC gives Gujarat "taller SSP" as bonus: Light at the end of the Narmada tunnel', *Times of India (Ahmedabad)*, 19 October 2000.
24. 'Fairytale ending eludes state shindig: Work on dam inaugurated', *Times of India* (Ahmedabad), 1 November 2000.
25. Narmada Bachao Andolan, *People* v. *Verdict* (self-published), November 2000, p. 74.
26. Ramaswamy R. Iyer, 'A Judgement of Grave Import', Commentary, *Economic and Political Weekly*, 4–10 November 2000.
27. L.C. Jain, op. cit., p. 3.
28. Ibid., p. 43.
29. Ibid., p. 126.
30. It is remarkable that authors like Iyer and Jain do not mention the GRAs, either to recognize or cast doubt on their achievement.

PART III

Judiciary and Secularism

11

Secular State in a Hyper-Religious Society: The Role of the Judiciary

C.P. BHAMBHRI

The greatest challenge for the secular state of India comes from the absolute majority of its own citizens who are fanatically devoted to their religion, gods, beliefs, rituals and priest-led, and priest-determined, norms of social and family conduct. In a series, *The People of India* of the Anthropological Survey of India, Kumar Suresh Singh informs us that India is inhabited by 4,694 communities (Biradris), and all these ethnic and linguistic groups are practitioners of multiple and diverse religious practices ranging from the most ritualized superstitions to worship of 'sacred' animals and animistic rituals. As inter-community conflicts are likely to arise, India requires a powerful adjudicator whose 'neutrality' is acceptable to the large majority of citizens. Not only this. A secular democratic State of India, unlike the Western democratic secular States, has a legal and constitutional obligation to legislate against many social practices which are against the norms of democratic and modern ways of life. Social transformative role of the Indian State is obstructed and vehmentally opposed by the majority of social groups, who view the social reformatory law as an interference in their religious way of life by the State. Indians follow religiously-sanctioned and priest-approved social traditions and whenever the State wishes to legislate against any 'religious-cum-social tradition' it meets with a China Wall of popular opposition. In his comparative study of secular States, Jacobson describes the United States as a case of 'Assimilative Secularism', Israel as a case of 'Visionary Secularism', and

India as a case of 'Ameliorative Aspiration' because its secularism has to be reconciled with the principle of 'The Good of the People'.[1]

INDIA AS A SECULAR STATE

Many doubts have been raised about the actual meaning, content, and even about the nomenclature of a secular State. This controversy should be buried once for all; instead, the focus should be on the actual practice of the secular State during the last half a century of post-Independence India and the institutional mechanisms which have 'adjudicated' disputes that have arisen between the law-makers and law-enforcers of secular State and the affected social groups which have felt that such laws have restricted and interfered in their religion and sacred practices.

There is no ambiguity about the secular character of the Indian State. According to Durga Das, a well-known constitutional expert, the 'unity and fraternity of the people of India, professing numerous faiths, has been sought to be achieved by enshrining the ideal of a "secular State", which means that the State protects all religions equally and does not itself uphold any religion as the State religion'.[2]

INDIAN JUDICIARY AND FREEDOM OF RELIGION

The Constitution of India guarantees to all individuals 'freedom of conscience and the right to freely profess, practise, and propagate religion' (Art. 25). Freedom of religion, to be meaningful, is to be guaranteed not only to individuals but to religious institutions as well. Religious freedom has both an individual as well as a corporate side; the latter is guaranteed by the Constitution which provides to every religious denomination or section the right '(a) to establish and maintain institutions for religious and charitable purposes; (b) to manage its own affairs in matters of religion; (c) to own and acquire movable and immovable property; and (d) to administer such property in accordance with law'. As these rights cannot be absolute, they are subject to statutory limitations in the interest of public order, morality and health and to the other provisions of Part III of the Constitution.

The Indian Constitution guarantees freedom of religion [Arts. 25, 26, 28, 30(1)], forbids religious discrimination on the part of the State [Arts. 15, 16, 29 (2), 30 (2), 325], and prohibits taxation for the support of religious institutions (Art. 27).[3] The Constitution lays down the foundations of a secular State which, according to Alexandrowicz, 'remains adamant in the exclusion of an establishment of religion, in the observance of strict non-discrimination between various churches and religious bodies and in the absention from any interference in their internal affairs'.[4] As a secular State, India has no official religion and officially-recognized and patronized church. The State is neutral in religious matters, though not hostile towards it.[5]

If any doubts had to be laid to rest, the Constitution (42nd Amendment) Act, 1976, inserted the word 'secular' in the Preamble itself. The 'the importance and utility of the Preamble', acknowledges D.D. Basu, has come to be recognized in several decisions of the Supreme Court. 'Though, by itself, it is not enforceable in a Court of law, the Preamble to a written Constitution states the objects which the constitution seeks to establish and promote and also aids the legal interpretation of the constitution where the language is found to be ambiguous.'[6]

The Supreme Court in its numerous judgements has described 'secularism as the basic structure' of the Indian Constitution; its implication is that secularism is a fundamental and foundational principle of the Indian Democratic State. Notwithstanding some critics, there is no ambiguity about the secular character of the Indian State, particularly after the 42nd amendment of the Constitution and following the numerous decisions of the highest judicial court of India which is the ultimate interpreter of laws and actions of every constitutional functionary of the Indian State.

SECULARISM—A DIFFICULT JOURNEY

It cannot be any one's case that the theory and actual praxis of democratic secular State in India can be smooth and free from controversies. The actual intentions of the law-makers and enforcers of law have generated, and would continue to generate, disputes and controversies by multiple religious and socio-cultural groups about the real intentions and religious biases of the functionaries of the State. Admitted that a formal and legal document like the Constitution can be bent to discriminate against, or show preferences to a religious group. State actions in democracy create dissent and the final word has to come from an impartial and independent judiciary which is the ultimate custodian of the philosophy and practice of constitutionalism. The shifting parliamentary majorities cannot be trusted to always act as 'impartial' players in governance. As such, citizens have to look towards an independent judiciary for the protection of their constitutionally guaranteed fundamental rights, if they feel that such rights have been infringed by arbitrary parliamentary majority governments. A very salient feature of religiously plural society like India is that the colonial rulers very effectively played the card of constructing homogeneous and monolithic religious identities with a view to playing one against the other, as they did with the Hindu-Muslim divide that led to the partition of India. The trauma of Partition was felt by every community; hence, the proclamation of the establishment of secular State in India provided a great healing touch to mutually-hostile religious communities. The Indian secular State is based on a social contract and the existence of plurality of religions will always act as a guide for actions of the State. Despite this, subjective feelings can come into the minds of the citizens that the State in a Hindu majority country is not always responsive to the sensibilities of the Muslims and other minority groups. Not only this. Some Hindu majoritarian groups have maintained that the post-independence secular State of India has been pro-minority and unfair to the Hindu majority community. And so have some intellectuals maintained that position. Writing on *Nehru and Secularism*, Bhiku Parekh observed: 'Protective provisions for the minorities aroused resentment among some groups of Hindus, who argued that they favoured minorities, stood in the way of their full integration into the national community, and discouraged the much-needed reform of their social practices. To counter this resentment, Nehru needed to reassure the majority that the protective provisions were in the long term interest of the country, appeal to its spirit of tolerance, mobilize its goodwill, and show patience towards its occasional impatience. He did not do this. Instead he dismissed their resentment as mean-spirited and petty, and lambasted them for being communal.'[7] If Nehru, the great renaissance man of the twentieth century India, and Gandhi, the Father of Nation, could be perceived as being anti-Hindu and pro-minority, and if their unwavering and firm belief in secularism could be doubted, it clearly substantiates the argument that the journey of the Indian secular State has indeed been a difficult one.

AREA OF CONFLICT

Disputes have arisen in many areas:

i. State regulation of places of worship.
ii. Right to conversion from one religion to the other.
iii. Management of Minority Educational Institutions.

iv. The issues concerning the sanctity of 'religious practices including rituals'.
v. Politically corrupt practices arising out of the provisions of the Representation of the People Act, 1951, 1952, etc., by using religious appeals during the elections.
vi. Management of places of religious worship, et al.

The above areas of conflict reveal that Parliament, the State Legislatures, the High Courts and the Supreme Court are continuously involved in dealing with one or the other issue having to with the religious belief and practice of one group or the other.

In a very important book edited by S.K. Verma and Kusum on *Fifty Years of the Supreme Court of India: Its Grasp and Reach,* three comprehensive chapters (out of 22)—K.C. Sunny, 'Election Laws'; Kusum, 'Matrimonial Adjudication Under Hindu Law'; and Danial Latifi, Muslim Law'[8]—are devoted to the examination of issues relating to the judicial interpretations of disputes regarding State and religion and citizens' approaching the courts for redressal of grievances based on either violations of secularism by the State or complaints against political groups and parties for bringing 'religion into politics', for electoral gains. Incidentally, the secular State of India is committed to the doctrine of Uniform Personal Law. It has also maintained a status quo in the case of respective 'religiously sanctioned', Personal Laws of every religious community. It is, however, unfortunate that almost every law of Parliament and State Legislatures dealing with any aspect of 'reform' of any Community's Personal Laws has been challenged before the courts. While K.C. Sunny's discussion on 'Election Laws' concerns us here only with regard to the judicial cases concerning the misuse of 'religion' in politics, Kusum's chapter on 'Matrimonial Adjudication under Hindu Law 'clearly shows that the judges are very busy in deciding cases on 'Marriage, Matrimonial House, Stridhana, Matrimonial Cruelty, Restitution of Conjugal Rights, Divorce by Mutual Consent, Irretrievable Breakdown of Marriage as ground for Divorce, Motivated Conversions and Bigamous Marriages, Permanent Alimony, Void Marriage and Maintenance under section 125, Award of Damages, Foreign Divorce Decrees, Guardianship of Minor Children and finally a Uniform Civil Code'. Under every 'item' mentioned by Kusum, the Indian State has legislated to reform the Hindu Law but disputants have invariably gone to the courts for interpretation and relief. The story is repeated in Danial Latifi's contribution on Muslim Law. He examines judicial cases concerning Muslim Personal Law beginning with 1953 to the most controversial case, popularly known as the *Shah Bano* case; in the process, the Holy Koran and other recognized sources of Muslim jurisprudence have received detailed attention of the judges. A former Chief Justice of the Supreme Court of India, A.S. Anand, refers to this issue and observes:

> In view of the enormous diversity of our population in terms of race, language, religion, community, caste and culture the Supreme Court has had the onerous task of protecting the ideal of secularism and respecting the sensitivities of all groups of people, and all this without compromising the need to impart real justice in the circumstances of the case. The *Shah Bano* case is an example of this.[9]

In an over-legislated country like India, judges are overloaded with cases and disputes linked with religious beliefs and practices.

COURTS IN THIS JOURNEY

In a country where religion plays an all-pervasive and dominant role in the life of the individual citizens, the State has to face many difficulties in practising 'non-interference' in religious matters. Hindus and Muslims have their personal laws which regulate their system of marriage, divorce, adoption, succession and inheritance. Many social traditions and norms of conduct, and many important social institutions have the sanction of religion e.g., the caste system.[10] Many a time, the State has to legislate with regard to various aspects of social life and organized religious institutions in the interest of social justice, social good, public order, health and morality. Many such laws passed by legislatures have been challenged in the courts of law on the ground of infringement of religious freedom by the State. Indian Courts had to decide many such cases requiring the interpretation of the 'religious freedom' as guaranteed in the Constitution to individuals as well as to corporate organized religious institutions like temples, *maths*, mosques and *gurdwaras*. The Supreme Court in India has permitted the State to exercise extensive control over a Hindu *math (The Commissioner, Hindu Religious Endowments, Madras*, v. *L.T. Swamiar*, A.I.R. 1954 S.C. 282), a Jain temple *(Ratilal* v. *State of Bombay*, A.I.R. 1954 S.C. 388), Sikh gurdwaras *(Sardar Sarup Singh* v. *State of Punjab*, A.I.R. 1959 S.C. 60) and a Muslims shrine *(Durgah Committee, Ajmer* v. *Syed Hussain Ali*, A.I.R. 1961, S.C. 1402). At the same time the Supreme Court has invalidated many of the clauses of various Temple-Regulation Laws which seemed to interfere in the freedom of religious practices, as also many governmental measures framed along religious lines e.g., *State of Rajasthan* v. *Pratap Singh,* A.I.R. 1960, S.C. 1208; *Nain Sukh Das* v. *State of U.P.,* A.I.R. 1953. S.C. 384; *State of Jammu and Kashmir* v. *Jagan Hath,* A.I.R. 1958, J&K (14). In 1962 the Supreme Court invalidated the Bombay Prevention of Ex-communication Act, 1949, in the appeal case of *Sardar Sydna Taher Saifuddin Saheb* v. *The State of Bombay;* here, the Court maintained that the Act was an interference in religious matters and was not a measure of 'social welfare and reform' as referred to in Article 25(2)(b) because this Article did not 'enable the legislature to reform a religion out of existence or identity'.[11]

While interpreting the various clauses of the Constitution relating to different aspects of religious freedom, one of the knotty questions before the judiciary has been the definition and meaning of the term 'religion'. The Constitution does not define religion; consequently, it is the judiciary, which is left to define and interpret it. In 1889 Justice Field undertook, for the American Supreme Court, a definition of the word 'religion'. He said: 'The term "religion" has reference to one's views of his relations to his Creator, and to the obligations they impose, of reverence for His Being and . . . of obedience to His will.'[12] But the Indian Supreme Court in *The Commissioner, Hindu Religious Endowments, Madras* v. *Lakshmindra Thirtha Swamiar of Sri Shirur Math,* considered this definition as inadequate and noted that '(t)here are well-known religions in India like Buddhism and Jainism which do not believe in God or in any Intelligible First Cause'.[13]

In the United States, it has been left to the individual to determine what is 'religion' for him. In *United States* v. *Bollard* (1944), the US Supreme Court observed: 'Men may believe what they cannot prove. (And) they may not be put to the proof of their religious doctrines or beliefs.'[14] The Court further said: 'The miracles of the New Testament, the Divinity of Christ, life after death and the power of prayer are deep in the religious convictions of many. If one could be sent to jail because a jury in a hostile environment found those teachings false, little indeed would be left of religious freedom.'[15] In that country, the freedom of 'belief' is defended, but not 'religious practices'. The Supreme Court has developed a 'belief-practice' dichotomy. In India also the Constitution wanted to defend religious 'beliefs' but not the 'religious practices', and subjected the latter to the 'control' of the State in the interest of social welfare, morality and public order.

Many people think that the freedom of religious 'belief' without the freedom of religious 'practices' and rituals is a contradiction in terms. Rituals, ceremonies, and other practices are considered to be the essence of religion. Any interference or regulation of religious practices by the State is viewed by many people as an infringement of the 'freedom of religion'. Moreover, if the State is given unlimited right to control and regulate 'religious practices' for social good, public welfare, health, order and morality, the result may be the massacre of the religious freedom of individuals. As Groves observes: 'Could not the State forbid religious parades under public order, plural marriages under morality, piercing the body or fire-walking under health. . . ?'[16]

RELIGIOUS PRACTICES: SEPARATING THE 'ESSENTIAL' FROM THE 'NON-ESSENTIAL'

In the light of the various cases decided by the Indian Supreme Court, the situation as it stands at present is as follows: the Indian Supreme Court recognizes that the religious practices which are 'essential' in a religion are to be given at least relative (not absolute) freedom and that such 'essential' practices are to be decided with reference to the doctrines of the religion itself.

In the case, *The Commissioner, Hindu Religious Endowments, Madras* v. *Lakshmindra Thirtha Swamiar of Sri Shirur Math,* the Indian Supreme Court opined that the religious denomination has the freedom to decide about essential rituals, though the Mutt's expenses and property could be controlled by the secular authority. In this case, the Supreme Court laid down a very important doctrine in relation to religious freedom i.e., religious practices have great importance and, many a time, they form an integral part of religion. Commenting on the scope of Article 25 in this case, Justice Mukerjea said, 'We now come to Article 25 which, as its language indicates, secures to every person, subject to public order, health and morality, a freedom not only to entertain such religious belief as may be approved of by his judgement and conscience, but also to exhibit his belief in such outward acts as he thinks proper and to propagate or disseminate his ideas for the edification of others.'[17]

The Court further observed:

> What constitutes the essential part of a religion is primarily to be ascertained with reference to the doctrines of that religion itself. If the tenets of any religious sect of the Hindus prescribe that offerings of food should be given to the idol at

particular hours of the day, those periodical ceremonies should be performed . . ., all these would be regarded as parts of religion and the mere fact that they involve expenditure of money, or employment of priests and servants or the use of marketable commodities would not make them secular activities partaking of a commercial or economic character; all of them are religious practices and should be regarded as matters of religion within the meaning of Article 26 (b).[18]

In the *Bombay Trust* case (based on an appeal from the Bombay High Court), the Supreme Court said: 'Article 25 guarantees to every person . . . freedom of conscience. . . . Thus . . . every person has a fundamental right under our Constitution not merely to entertain such religious belief as may be approved of by his judgement or conscience but to exhibit his belief and ideas in such overt acts as are enjoined or sanctioned by his religion.'[19]

Judicial decisions have made a distinction between 'essential' and 'non-essential' religious practices. While interpreting the 'right to religious freedom', the judiciary takes into consideration the essential religious practices and not the non-essential ones. In two important cases, the Supreme Court made a distinction between 'essential' and 'non-essential' religious practices. In *M.H. Qureshi* v. *State of Bihar*, the Supreme Court considered the constitutionality of Bihar, Uttar Pradesh, and C.P. and Berar (Madhya Pradesh) legislation banning cow-slaughter. It was argued that 'banning cow slaughter' was an infringement of religious freedom of the Muslim community as guaranteed under Article 25 of the Constitution of India. After consulting the Koran and *Hidyat*,[20] the Court observed that the slaughter of cow was not an obligatory act on Bakr-id day. The Islamic scriptures refer to 'a goat for one person, or a cow or camel for seven persons'; hence, the sacrifice of a cow on Bakr-id day is an option and not an obligatory act, and there is nothing wrong in State legislation prohibiting cow-slaughter. The Supreme Court observed: 'We have, however, no material on the record before us which will enable us to say that the sacrifice of a cow on that day is an obligatory overt act for a Mussalman to exhibit his religious belief and idea. It is not possible for us to uphold this claim of the petitioners.'[21] The same distinction between essential and non-essential religious practices was reiterated in *Masud Alam* v. *Commissioner of Police*. The neighbours of a mosque protested against the use of the loudspeaker for the calling of *Azan* as a consequence of which the permission to use the loudspeaker was withdrawn. Justice Sinha of the Calcutta High Court did not agree with the contention of the calling of *Azan*, by loudspeaker as an essential religious act of the Muslims and held: 'What is distasteful and abhorrent in the house of man is singularly inappropriate and even irrelevant when used in the House of God. Prayer is intended to be a silent communion with the Creator. It does not call for a tumultuous prelude or a noisy accompaniment.'[22]

The interpretation of 'religious freedom' by the judges has passed through several stages. The stand of the Bombay High Court was that the State protects religious beliefs and not practices. The High Court of Bombay in the case of *State of Bombay* v. *Narasu Appa M. Ali* observed: 'A sharp distinction must be drawn between religious faith and beliefs.' If religious practices 'run counter to public order, morality or health or a policy of social welfare upon which the State has embarked, then the religious practices must give way before the good of the people of the State as a whole.'[23] But in the *Shirur Math* case, the Supreme Court went beyond the Bombay High Court stand and accepted the importance of religious practices as an integral part of religious beliefs. In the case of *Ratilal* v. *State of Bombay,* the Supreme Court observed that the Constitution not only gives the right of religious belief but also of 'such overt acts as are enjoined or sanctioned by (one's) religion'. By including 'religious practices' in the freedom of religion, the courts had to make a distinction between 'essential' and 'non-essential' religious practices, and this distinction had to be resorted to, in upholding legislation with regard to monogamy for Hindus. In many cases, the Hindus have contended before the courts that prohibition of bigamy by the State is an infringement of 'religious freedom'. It has been argued that salvation for a Hindu lies in having a son. It is a religious obligation, and so bigamy should be allowed in order that a man may beget a son. The courts' response has been that it is not 'essential' for Hindus to marry another woman to beget a son as Hindu Law gives the 'option' of adopting a son. As such, prohibition of bigamy is not an interference in the religious freedom of the Hindus. While upholding the Bombay Prevention of Hindu Bigamous Marriages Act of 1946, the Chief Justice of the Bombay High Court said: '. . . it is rather difficult to accept the proposition that polygamy is an integral part of Hindu religion. It is perfectly true that Hindu religion recognizes the necessity of a son for religious efficacy and spiritual salvation. That same religion also recognizes the institution of adoption. Therefore, the Hindu religion provides for the continuation of the lines of a Hindu male within the framework of monogamy.' The enforcement of monogamy among Hindus is a measure of social reform which the

State is empowered to legislate by Article 25 (2) (b), 'notwithstanding the fact that it may interfere with the right of a citizen freely to profess, practise and propagate religion'.[24] In 1961, the Supreme Court re-affirmed its previous stand while deciding the case of *Durgah Committee, Ajmer* v. *Hussain Ali* by stating '. . . in order that the practices in question should be treated as a part of religion they must be regarded by the said religion as its essential and integral part; . . . in other words, the protection must be confined to such religious practices as are an essential and an integral part of it and no other'.[25]

In an important case, *Sardar Syedna Taker Saifuddin Saheb* v. *The State of Bombay*, the Supreme Court over-ruled the Bombay High Court and decided on 9 January 1962, that the Bombay Prevention of Ex-communication Act 1949 was invalid as it violated Article 26(b) of the Constitution in so far as it destroyed the right of *Dai-ul-Mutlaq* of excommunicating any member of the Dawoodi Bohra Community on religious grounds.

As seen above, the judiciary had to maintain a difficult balance between the Constitution, the legislative activities of the State to reform social life, and the concerns of citizens to defend religious freedom. Indian judiciary has been performing this difficult and delicate job by upholding the freedom of 'belief', and by laying down that while 'essential' religious practices cannot be regulated by State legislation, 'non-essential' religious practices can.

SECULARISM UNDER SIEGE—1990s AND THE SUPREME COURT

The last decade of the twentieth century witnessed the rise of militant and aggressive anti-minority Hindutva. Every institution meant for the governance of democratic secular State of India was confronted with fanatic anti-secular forces which seemed determined to convert a secular State into a theocratic Hindu State. The hands of judiciary have been full in dealing with litigations arising out of the activities of Hindutva and the defenders of the secular State, who felt that India had to be saved from the fanatic Hindutva forces. Not only this. Every earlier pronouncement of the High Courts or Supreme Court, while dealing with disputes arising out of inter-community disputes regarding religion, has been re-opened by the protagonists of militant Hinduism. The Supreme Court had passed an order in 1993 on the salary of Imams and Muajjins, where governments had been instructed to pay Rs. 1,600 to Imams and Rs. 1,400 to Muajjins. A complaint was filed against the Digvijay Singh government of Madhya Pradesh that the Supreme Court's 1993 salary order had not been implemented. The alibi provided by the (pro-Hindutva), BJP state government was that the court order was subject to the availability of Waqf Board properties. With this excuse offered by the state government, the helpless Imams and Muajjins were denied what the Supreme Court had wished in 1993.

The Indian judiciary had always adopted a balancing approach while dealing with emotive inter-community religious disputes. From Hanif Quereshi (1958) (Bihar) to Ashutosh Lahiri (1995) (West Bengal), the courts have acted as 'honest brokers' by balancing the Hindu sentiment for the 'cow' with the fundamental right of citizens to 'carry on any occupation trade or business'. Since state governments and legislatures are involved in quasi-religious matters concerning religious beliefs, the buck stops with the courts in adjudicating all such disputes. But given the nature of Indian communal cleavages, actions by one community, tend to invite opposite reactions from another community. The state government of Jammu & Kashmir took over from the Dharmarth Trust and made the Hindu state Governor, Jagmohan, Chairman of Shri Mata Vaishno Devi Shrine Board in 1986. If Jagmohan could implement his Hindutva agenda of reforming the management of a Hindu Temple, why would a Muslim Chief Minister stay behind? On 8 September 2003, the state government of Chief Minister Mufti Mohammad Sayeed, issued an Ordinance to take over the management of 89 shrines and 39 properties to be looked after by a body under the Muslim Auquaf Act. The opposition party in J&K, the National Conference, decided to challenge this action of the Mufti government in the High Court on 26 September 2003, but the decision is still pending. The story does not end here. In another case, the Kerala High Court appointed a Commissioner (an IAS officer), as administrator of the Guruvayur Temple (on 7 February 1993), who discovered 'irregularities in the management of the temple'. The Supreme Court on 18 August 2003, asked the Kerala state government to temper its action 'to ensure that the sentiments of the devotees are respected'.[26]

DEMOLITION OF THE BABRI MASJID

Everything mentioned above paled into insignificance, when a mob led by Hindu fanatic leaders destroyed the historic Babri Mosque at Ayodhya on 6 December 1992. By this action, it was implied that the Muslims of India were not equal citizens but a 'second class minority community' in India. After the destruction of the mosque, Kalyan Singh, the then BJP Chief Minister of Uttar Pradesh, resigned. This was followed by the Congress at the centre dismissing other BJP state governments in Himachal Pradesh, Madhya Pradesh, and Rajasthan under Article 356 of the Constitution for their responsibility in undertaking such a reprehensible activity of hurting the religious sentiments of the Muslim minority community of India. A flurry of activity was witnessed in the Supreme Court because every aggrieved party to the dispute knocked at its door for justice. The importance of the Supreme Court's judgements in this matter can be understood by reading the volume of commentaries written on the Hindutva judgement by legal luminaries, public commentators and the attention which the judgements have continued to invite even up to the end of 2003.[27] The Supreme Court upheld the dismissal of the BJP governments for offending the tenets of secularism, a part of the 'basic structure' of the constitution, and observed: '. . . the manifesto of a political party should be consistent with . . . the fundamental and basic features of the constitution—secularism, socio-economic and political justice, fraternity, unity, and national integrity.'[28] And in the *Bommai* case (1994), the Court affirmed that the basic structure of the Constitution was beyond the power to amend under Article 368 of the Constitution: 'There are certain basic features of the Constitution of India, which can not be altered in exercise of the power to amend it, under Article 368. . . . If therefore, a Constitution Amendment Act seeks to alter the basic structure or framework of the Constitution, the Court would be entitled to annul it on the ground of ultra vires, because the word "amend" in Article 368, means only changes other than altering the very structure of the Constitution, which would be tantamount to making a new Constitution.'[29]

GUJARAT: THE BEST BAKERY CASE

The Indian Supreme Court had to intervene once again, in the state of Gujarat, where the victims of communal holocaust of March–May 2002 were not getting justice because the BJP was in control of the state government. The Citizens of Justice and Peace demanded that the Nanavati Commission, set up to inquire into the post-Godhra communal carnage in Gujarat in 2002, be 'moved outside the state', because the relatives of the dead in riots, the media reported, were under 'pressure' from the BJP and Vishwa Hindu Parishad (VHP) to 'keep (their) mouth shut'.[30]

It was not an unfounded or ill-founded mistrust of the victims. In the *Best Bakery* case, the Session Judge had released all the 'guilty' people who were suspected to have burnt the victims of the riot. The National Human Rights Commission, headed by a former Chief Justice of the Supreme Court, J.S. Varma, filed a 'Public Interest Litigation' case before the Supreme Court of India advising that justice had not been done in the infamous and ghastly burning case of Best Bakery. While dealing with this PIL appeal, Chief Justice V.N. Khare observed on 12 September 2003: 'I have no faith left in the prosecution of the Gujarat Government'. The Chief Justice seemed so annoyed with the case that he asked the Gujarat government 'to quit' if it could not 'prosecute the guilty'. The Gujarat government, after great public protest, had filed an appeal before the Gujarat High Court against the verdict of the Special Judge, but Chief Justice Khare was unconvinced about the sincerity of the government's appeal. It was, the Chief Justice said, a 'sham'; 'an eyewash'. The Supreme Court, the Chief Justice continued, could not 'remain a silent spectator to government inaction'.[31]

Chief Justice Khare was certainly right in his assessment. The apex court asked the Chief Secretary and Director General of Police (DGP) of Gujarat to personally appear before the Court to explain the state government's conduct in dealing with those accused of participating in the riots and committing murders. On 19 September 2003, while cross examining the Gujarat DGP and the Deputy Superintendent of Police (DSP), Chief Justice Khare asked:

CJI: In may many witnesses in the case turned hostile. What steps did you take for their re-examination?

DGP: I came to know the fact much later.

CJI: Later, even more witnesses turned hostile. What did you do?

DSP: The Police Commissioner told me that they were won over.

CJI: Then why did you not take steps for re-examination of the hostile witnesses?

DGP: Yes, I did not take any step.[32]

Chief Justice Khare was stunned over the statement of the DSP to the effect that the Police Commissioner 'told me that the witnesses appear to have been either coerced or won over'.[33]

The Supreme Court had no alternative but to itself 'monitor' the ongoing case of Best Bakery in the Gujarat High Court. It asked Soli

Sorabjee, the Attorney General of the Government of India, to help the apex court in the process. 'We want a fair trial', said the Court on 18 October 2003, and advised the Attorney General to scrutinize the Gujarat Public Prosecutors who were alleged to be the members of the VHP, BJP, and the Rashtriya Swayamsevak Sangh (RSS). For sure, the rebuke of the Supreme Court had its effect; the Vadodra Police 're-registered the case against the so-called acquitted accused, the BJP legislator Madhu Srivastava, his brother Chandrakant, and two others for "threatening to kill" the Best Bakery case witnesses'.[34] The Court assured the witnesses of full protection and transferred the case from Gujarat to Mumbai for trial.

From 1989 to 2003, the Sangh Parivar has been actively involved in the Ayodhya politics and every institution of the state has been dragged into the religion-based politics of the Hindu organizations. Now that the BJP has lost its perch at the centre, there may be some relief to the courts from the hitherto overwhelming agenda of the Hindutava forces. In the cleavaged society of India however, the judiciary will continue to be the guardian of secularism.[35]

CONCLUSION

The Indian Judiciary has been active in dealing with all kinds of cases arising out of religion-linked beliefs of the protagonists of different religions. The list of such cases is quite long because the priestly class(es) is very active in making people believe that their religion and religious practices are in 'danger' of being 'interfered with' by the political executive and legislatures. Election of candidates is challenged, because it is maintained by the contestants that a candidate or a party has asked for 'votes' by appealing to religious sentiments, which is prohibited under the Representation of People Act of India. The Hindu fundamentalists are always raising the issue of 'ban cow slaughter' because the cow is a sacred animal; they also fault the Christian Missionaries who are alleged to be coercing people to convert to their religion by using the Fundamental Right's provision 'to practise and propagate religion'. Marriage and divorce cases also bring the issue of religion before the courts. The Constitution gives the 'minorities' the right to manage their own educational institutions, and every day, in some state or the other, disputes come before the courts on the legitimate meaning of this right. Following the Hindu agenda, the BJP-led state government of Gujarat passed a stringent anti-Conversion Law, 2003. The 2003 Act prohibits any conversion under any 'allurement' and every individual who wants to convert to another religion has 'to apply with name and address to the District Administration', which is expected to satisfy itself before giving permission for conversion. How can the district bureaucracy, one may legitimately ask, inspire confidence with the BJP government at the helm of affairs in Gujarat? The only saviour in India is the institution of last resort: the judiciary.

The above narration clearly substantiates the argument that the Indian Judiciary, while dealing with disputes arising out of the alleged 'violations' of the secular spirit of the Constitution, has faced many dilemmas and difficulties. It can not be any one's case that the Supreme Court which began its journey on 28 January 1950, and has witnessed the role of more than 142 judges, can remain consistent in its judicial pronouncements and interpretations on litigations. This 'reality' of the Supreme Court is very well documented by B.N. Kirpal et al. in *Supreme Court not Infallible: Essays in Honour of the Supreme Court*, in which twenty-four eminent contributors have focused attention on the inside story of the actual functioning of the Court. Govind Das, one of the contributors to the volume, clearly points out that changing social context determines the Court's judgements. He observes: 'The current political mood of the country, the prevailing economic situation, the dominant ideas prevalent in the society at a particular time have governed the activities of the Court.'[36] The telling example of the context determining the judgements and attitudes of the judges is provided by India of the 1990s, when society was violently polarized on the basis of religion-based politics, and aggrieved religious groups were knocking at the doors of courts to protect their constitutional right of freedom of religion which was threatened by the forces that did not believe in secularism as being a part of the basic structure of the Constitution. In a highly emotive and surcharged political and social atmosphere in the 1990s, many interpretations of the judges on the meaning of Hindutva were challenged by one section of society or the other. In this context, the difficult tightrope walking done by the judges on issues concerning 'secularism' makes us disagree with the conclusion of a comprehensive analysis of the Supreme Court on 'minority rights', when Rajeev Dhavan and Fali S. Nariman state: 'However, as we transit into the next millennium, the Supreme Court has a lot to reflect upon, and not least how to protect the minorities and their ilk from the onslaught of majoritarianism.'[37] By our account, the Indian judiciary, on the basis of its continuous involvement in dealing with contentious issues concerning 'religion', 'religious practices' and threats to 'religious practices' and threats to 'religious freedoms', has done a commendable job in a very difficult social situation.

NOTES

1. Garry Jeffrey Jacobson, *The Wheel of Law*, New Delhi: Oxford University Press, 2003.
2. Durga Das Basu, *Introduction to the Constitution of India*, New Delhi: Prentice-Hall, 1997 (18th edn.), p. 27.
3. The Supreme Court held that 'Article 25 of the Constitution guarantees to every person . . . the freedom of conscience and the right freely to profess, practise, and propagate religion.' This is 'subject, in every case, to public order, health and moraiity. . . . Subject to the restrictions which this article imposes, every person has a fundamental right under our Constitution . . . to entertain such religious beliefs as may be approved by his judgement or conscience . . . *Ratilal Panachand Gandhi* v. *The State of Bombay* (1951), S.C.R. 1055, p. 1062.; also refer to *Sardar Syedna Taher Saifuddin Sahch* v. *The State of Bombay*, A.I.R. 1962 S.C. H33, p. 863; *The State* v. *Narsu Appa M. Ali* (1951), I.L.R. Bombay, 775 at p. 778.
4. C.H. Alexandrowicz, 'The State in India and in the United States', *Journal of the Indian Law Institute*, New Delhi, 1959–60, vol. 2, p. 282.
5. Refer to Donald Eugene Smith, *India as a Secular State*, New Delhi: Oxford University Press 1963, pp. 3–12.
6. D.D. Basu: op. cit., p. 21. Also see, Granville Austin, *Working a Democratic Constitution: The Indian Experience*, New Delhi: Oxford University Press, 1999, especially the chapter on 'The Forty-Second Amendment: Sacrificing Democracy to Power', pp. 370–90.
7. Bhiku Parekh, 'Nehru and Secularism' in *Nehru Revisited*, Mumbai: Nehru Centre 2003, pp.165–6.
8. See, S.K. Verma and Kusum (eds.), *Fifty Years of the Supreme Court of India: Its Grasp and Reach* [Indian Law Institute], New Delhi: Oxford University Press, 2000, Chapters 5–7, pp. 210–87.
9. A.S. Anand, Foreword in Verma and Kusum (eds.), ibid., p. vi.
10. Dr. B.R. Ambedkar pointed out this fact in the Constituent Assemby when he said: 'The religious conceptions in this country are so vast that they cover every aspect of life from birth to death. There is nothing which is not religion and if personal law is to be saved I am sure about it that in social matters we will come to a standstill. . . . I personally do not understand why religion should be given this vast expansive jursidiction so as to cover the whole of life and to prevent the legislature from enchroaching upon that field.' *Constitutent Assembly Debates*, vol. VII, p. 781.

11. A.I.R. 1962 S.C. 853, p. 875.
12. *Davis* v. *Beason*, 133 US 333, p. 342 (1889).
13. A.I.R. 1954 S.C. 282, p. 290.
14. 322 US 78, 88 L.ED. 1148, p. 86.
15. Ibid., p. 87.
16. Harry E. Groves, 'Religious Freedom', *Journal of the Indian Law Institute*, New Delhi 1962, vol. 4, p. 198.
17. A.I.R. 1954 S.C. 282, p. 289. Rich sources of judgements and commentaries are available with the Indian Law Institute, New Delhi, and with the Supreme Copurt Library, New Delhi.
18. A.I.R. 1954 S.C. 282, p. 290.
19. *Ratilal* v. *State of Bombay*, A.I.R. 1954 S.C. 388, p. 391.
20. In Arabic, it is Hidyat and Sunnat (in English, 't' is not written); these refer to practices sanctioned by Prophet Muhammad.
21. A.I.R. 1958 S.C. 731, p. 740.
22. *Masud Mon* v. *Commissioner of Police*, A.I.R. 1956, Cal. 9, p. 10.
23. A.I.R. 1951 Bombay 775; also refer to *Syedna Taher Saifuddin* v. *Tyebbhai Moosaji Koicha*, A.I.R. (1953) Bombay 183. In this case also, religion was interpreted in terms of faith and belief.
24. *State of Bombay* v. *Narasu Appa*, A.I.R. 1951, Bombay, p. 184. Also see, Kusum 'Matrimonial Adjudication under Hindu Law', in S.K. Verma and Kusum (eds.), *Fifty Years of the Supreme Court of India: Its Grasp and Reach*, Oxford: New Delhi 2000, pp. 231–68.
25. A.I.R. 1961 S.C. 1404 at 1415.
26. *The Hindu*, New Delhi, 19 August 2003, p. 101.
27. Tahir Mahmood (ed.), *Religion and Law Review*, vol. V, 1996. *Hindutva Judgements of the Indian Supreme Court 1995-96* (Institute of Objective Studies, New Delhi: 1996, p. 315. Also see, Greg Jeffrey Jacobson, *The Wheel of Law: India's Secularism in Comparative Constitutional Context*, Oxford: New Delhi 2003.
28. Cited by Jacobson, p. 144.
29. Ibid., p. 139.
30. *The Statesman*, New Delhi, 5–6 October 2003; *The Hindustan Times*, New Delhi, 6 October 2003.
31. *The Hindustan Times*, New Delhi, 13 September 2003. Also see, C.P. Bhambhri, 'Are we ready for judge dread?', *The Pioneer*, New Delhi, 27 September 2003, p. 6.
32. *The Hindustan Times*, New Delhi, 20 September 2003, p. 1.
33. *The Indian Express*, New Delhi, 2 September 2003, p. 2.
34. The Hindustan Times, New Delhi, 7 October 2003. For the continuing saga of this case, *Frontline*, 14 January 2005, pp. 17-19.
35. For anti-Muslim and anti-Christian ideology of the Sangh Parivar, C.P. Bhambhri, *The Bharatiya Janata Party: From Periphery to Centre*, New

Delhi: Shipra Publication, 2003; also, *Hindutva: A Challenge to Multi-Cultural Democracy*, Shipra Publication, New Delhi, 2003.

36. Govind Das, 'The Supreme Court: An Overview', in B.N. Kirpal et al. (eds.), *Supreme But Not Infallible*: *Essays in Honour of the Supreme Court of India*, New Delhi: Oxford University Press, 2000, p. 17.
37. Rajeev Dhavan and Fali S. Nariman, 'The Supreme Court and Group Life: Religious Freedom, Minority Groups, and Disadvantaged Communities', in B.N. Kirpal et al. (eds.), ibid., p. 278.

12

Secularism and Justice: A Review of Indian Supreme Court Judgements

SANGHAMITRA PADHY

In the absence of a definition of secularism in the Indian Constitution, the Supreme Court's reading of it is noteworthy. Judicial interpretations, for the most part, have declared secularism as the fundamental law of the land and sought to delineate the boundaries of the sacred and the secular. This paper attempts to study judicial verdicts on secular issues in recent times. It argues that while the Supreme Court has increasingly taken upon itself the task of setting the policy, especially in its activist role, it needs to promote a vision of secularism that is consistent with a plural multicultural setting. While in some cases, the court has come out strongly on the issue, declaring secularism as an unamendable feature of the Indian Constitution, in some others the court's functional definition of secularism is susceptible to the interests of the majority impinging on the rights of minority communities, and in some others, it privileges minorities. This results in 'a weak' secularism that is susceptible to the interests of the majority as the secular agenda toes a path of uniformity and oneness.

Like in all common law systems, the Supreme Court is responsible for interpreting the Constitution. M.C. Setalvad, quoting Oliver Wendell Holmes, had said that the Constitution is an organic living character; he advised that the court's foremost task was to interpret the Constitution as a means of ordering the life of a 'progressive people'.[1] This fact has made the Supreme Court's position in the political process

*Reprinted with author's permission from the *Economic and Political Weekly*, 20 November 2004.

special—it functions as an adjudicating body and also in some ways as a policy maker; it has given the court considerable autonomy with respect to interpretation of the Constitution, notwithstanding legislative checks. In recent years the Court has augmented, in a strategic and purposive manner, substantive and due procedural rights, equal protection rights and other claims; it has handed down a series of rulings that increased its prominence as a legal and political institution. Many crucial issues concerning secularism were adjudicated during this time. The judiciary has been approached to settle disputes like the misuse of religion in politics of the *Bommai* case, or it has provoked a discourse in the larger public domain, such as on the issue of personal laws.

DELIBERATIONS ON SECULARISM

Unlike in the US, where secularism endorses the 'non-establishment' clause, its usage has been conditioned by the social milieu in India. The polemic is characterized by its appropriateness to Indian conditions. Critics of Indian secularism maintain that given the pervasive role of religion in the lives of people,[2] secularism—as the separation of religion from state—is an alien modernist imposition. Its proponents argue that this is a misreading of the constitutional vision, which enjoins the state to be equally tolerant of all religions. P.K. Tripathi[3] pointed out that the Constitution contemplated secularism as the product of India's social experience and genius. This does not envision a wall of separation between religion and politics, but neutrality of the State towards all religions.

Equivocalness on the definition of secularism is also reflected in the constitutional spirit. Shefali Jha[4] suggests that there were three different sets of views on secularism in the Constituent Assembly:

a. No-concern theory of secularism, which separated religion and the State.
b. No links theory between the State and religion, to prevent the demeaning of religion; and
c. The equal-respect theory of 'secularism' that respected all religions alike and granted religious liberty to all.

On the one hand, religious and cultural diversities made secularism indispensable for democracy and national integration. On the other, was the impending task of modernizing our traditional society and bringing in social reform that required state intervention in religious affairs. Unlike as in the West, in India, as Ambedkar[5] has pointed out, the two major religions in India do not confine themselves to spiritual and other worldly matters, but rather cover within their fold, social behavior as a whole. For example, in Hinduism, under the provision of the ancient *smritis*, all human actions from birth to death, and most human actions from day to day are regarded as religious in character. Roover[6] affirms that to make any separation of religion from the public realm possible, we should be able to recognize religion, that is, we should know the structure of 'the religious' (as in religious beliefs, religious institutions or religious conflicts), and understand what distinguishes it from the non-religious or the secular.

Given the polemic over the inclusion of the term, it was not adopted in the Constitution of 1950; in spirit, the Constitution did seek to promote a secular and plural society based on State neutrality towards all religions. State intervention in religious affairs was allowed to bring in social reform while guaranteeing religious freedom to all.

It was the 42nd Amendment of 1976 that declared secularism to be the fundamental basic feature of our polity, though the amendment did not define secularism.

Much has been left to the judiciary in determining the essence of secularism; the Constitution has only articulated it as a goal and is silent on its connotation. Interestingly, judicial use of the term predates its inclusion in the Constitution. Judges have freely used the term both judicially and extra judicially prior to 1976, while explaining the character and nature of the Indian Constitution. The Supreme Court's first recognition of secularism was in 1962, in the *Sardar Taheruddin Syedna Saheb* v. *State of Bombay*[7] case, where Justice Ayengar explained that Articles 25 and 26 of the Constitution, 'embody the principle of religious toleration . . . besides, they serve to emphasize the secular nature of Indian democracy which the founding fathers considered to be the very basis of the Constitution.'[8] Again, in the *Keshavananda Bharati* v. *State of Kerala*[9] case, 1972, the 13-judge constitutional bench declared secularism to be the fundamental law of the land in no uncertain terms. Chief Justice Sikri, 'enumerated secular character of the Constitution' as one of the basic features of the Constitution. This judgement declared secularism to be an unamendable feature of the Constitution, though it was silent on the meaning of secularism in the Indian context.

Yet in 1974, in *Ahmedabad St Xavier's College* v. *State of Gujarat*[10] case, the Supreme Court indicated that it was uncertain in its views. Justices Mathew and Chandrachud pointed that:

> The Constitution has not erected a strict wall of separation between the church and the state. We have grave doubts whether the expression 'secular state' as it denotes a definite pattern of relationship can with propriety be applied to India. It can only in a qualified sense that India can be said to be [a] secular state. There are provisions in our Constitution, which make one hesitate to characterize our state as secular. . . . Secularism in the context of our Constitution means only an attitude of live and let live developing into the attitude of live and help live.[11]

Whereas, in *Ziyauddin Burhanuddin Bukhari* v. *Brijmohan Ram Das Mehra*[12] case 1975, Justice Beg said our Constitution makers certainly intended to set up a secular democracy, the building spirit of which is summed up by the objectives set forth in it. The court set the role of the State as neutral or impartial in extending its benefits to citizens of all castes and creeds, and made it the State's duty to ensure through its laws that disabilities are not imposed based on persons practising or professing any particular religion. In the *Indra Sawhney*[13] case, Judge Kuldip Singh indicated that secularism envisages a cohesive, unified and casteless society and seems to have defined secularism to extend beyond religion. In these cases, the court indeed stepped in to declare secularism as a fundamental law of the land, and its stance on secularism was that of neutrality and tolerance rather than a separation of the temporal from the spiritual. It remains to be seen that while there is a consensus on secularism based on neutrality and tolerance, there are differences on the question of the separation of religion and politics.

In the landmark judgement of *S.R. Bommai* v. *Union of India*[14] 1994, a 9-judge bench again reiterated that secularism is a part of the basic structure of the polity. More importantly, here the court strongly held the opinion that secularism undeniably sought to separate the religious from the political. Justice B.P. Jeevan Reddy[15] in *S.R Bommai* v. *Union of India* argued that in matters of the State, religion was irrelevant. This case was the high point of the Supreme Court's protection of secular ideals. The court here justified the dismissal of the Bharatiya Janata Party (BJP)-led state governments of Uttar Pradesh, Rajasthan, Madhya Pradesh, and Himachal Pradesh in the aftermath of the Babri Masjid demolition. It was further added that the use of religion and caste to mobilize votes in the elections by any recognized political party would amount to corrupt practice, and was unconstitutional.

BJP's party manifesto, the close link of some of its members to the Rashtriya Swayamsevak Sangh (RSS)—a banned political outfit at that time, and support to 'Kar Sevaks' show how religion is used for the purpose of politics. This verdict gave practical shape to the principles enunciated in an earlier 13-judge bench judgement in the *Keshavananda*, case. It declared that any State government that pursues an unsecular course, contrary to the constitutional mandate, renders itself amenable to action under Article 356 of the Constitution that subjects them to dismissal. This judgement also stated that secularism in India is based on tolerance. It is not the opposite of religious devoutness. Justice Ahmadi stated that secularism is based on 'the principles of accommodation and tolerance'.[16] The court ruled that religion is a matter of one's personal belief and mode of worship; secularism operates at the temporal plane. Freedom and tolerance of religion is only to the extent of permitting the pursuit of spiritual life that is different from the secular life. The latter falls into the domain of the affairs of the State. Thus, while it supports equal respect for all religions, it also propagates a certain degree of separation of State and religion. In the same judgement, Justices Jeevan Reddy, Agrawal, and Ramaswamy,[17] also expressed the view that secularism in India is in broad agreement with the US Constitution's first amendment. They also stated that the State has the power to legislate on religion, including personal laws and secular affairs of temples and mosques, and other places of worship. It established, like the other judgements, the State's power to decide on what constituted religion for all practical purposes.

The reasoning of the *Bommai* case was absent in later judgements. In *Ismail Faruqui* v. *Union of India*,[18] the *Ram Janmabhoomi* case, the court seems to have endorsed a concept of secularism that had its rationale in Hindu scriptures. Justice Verma[19] (speaking for C.J. Venkatachaliah and J. Ray) justified a vision of secularism—'sarwa dharma sambhava', i.e. tolerance of all religions—that had its roots in the *Yajur Veda, Atharva Veda* and *Rig Veda* and Akbar's *Din I'lahi*. The court here seems to have also accepted the claim that secularism in India exists because of the tolerance of the Hindus who are the majority religion.[20] Such a perception of secularism is inconsistent with minority interests. The court's analysis, derived from the scriptures of religion alone, subverts secularism. It gives the impression of secularism as tolerance that is steadfast with Hindu interests, which subsumes other faiths within its philosophy. This leaves no space for plural values as it favours one set of values over the others.

Further, in a recent judgement on the *NCERT Textbook* case,[21] the Supreme Court decreed that all faiths are equal. The majority view was that the essence of every religion is common; only the practice differs. This is against the faith of tolerance because it is assimilative in its intent and does not give individual the autonomy of self. There are many different belief systems, cultures, viewpoints and groups and these differences need to be respected, so that they do not lose their identity. The problem with such notions is that they seek to create uniformity based on oneness, rather than allowing a space for diversity. This will favour majority interests and not protect minority rights.

COURT, STATE AND RELIGION

The Hindutva judgements add further details to the contradictions. In the *Ziyanuddin Bukhari* v. *Mehra* case of 1975, where the Supreme Court upheld the decision of the high court—to set aside the election of Bukhari to the Maharashtra state assembly on the grounds that he had asked Muslim voters to vote for him because he was a Muslim—which had decreed that religion could not be used for political ends. Following the precedent in *Ramesh Yashwant Prabhu* v. *Prabhakar K Kuntes*,[22] the court declared that an appeal to promote a candidate on the basis of his being a Hindu amounted to corrupt practice and was against the secular spirit of our Constitution. The substance of speech and the manner in which the audience understands it, notwithstanding a direct appeal, determines its nature. The Supreme Court 3-judge bench held that Bal Thackeray's speech in the election campaign in 1990 asking Hindu voters to vote for Ramesh Prabhu, a Hindu, and making derogatory remarks against Muslims amounted to corrupt practice.

Suryakant Mahadhik's statement on the necessity to vote for the Shiv Sena for the protection of 'Hindutva' was also a corrupt practice because it was an appeal by a Hindu to a congregation of Hindu devotees in a Hindu temple during a Hindu religious festival, with the emphasis on Hindu religion for giving votes to Hindu candidates.[23] However, the Supreme Court believed that Hindutva was understood as a way of life or a state of mind and was not to be equated with or seen as religious Hindu fundamentalism as in *Prabhu* v. *Kuntes* mentioned earlier. It held the 'words, "Hinduism" or "Hindutva" are not necessarily to be understood and construed narrowly, confined only to the strict Hindu religious practices, unrelated to the culture and ethos of the people of India, depicting the way of life of the Indian people'. Hindutva was a synonym for Indianization or the development of a uniform culture by the obliteration of the differences between all cultures co-existing in the country.

While the court has taken a broad meaning of Hindutva, it signifies a celebration of oneness rather than pluralism and diversity; this is suicidal for minority rights. T.B. Hansen[24] argues, that the ideology of Hindutva amounts to a principle of rule by Hindu majoritarianism; it is a peculiar co-articulation of brahmanical ideologies of purity, characteristic of RSS and its affiliated organizations. To consider Hindutva as the development of a uniform culture through the obliteration of differences between co-existing cultures negates the constitutional principle of giving each culture its own dignity. Austin[25] argues that to make 'Hinduness' a requirement for 'Indianness' is the worst kind of ugliness. First, it represents 'Hinduism' as having a monolithic structure, whereas there are multiple local faiths devoted to shared deities. Also, it is a denial of history and of India's rich and varied culture; in short, it is nationalism gone mad.

In the *Manohar Joshi*[26] case, the Supreme Court ruled that the promise to establish the first Hindu state in Maharashtra did not amount to appealing for votes in the name of religion. In the court's opinion, a mere statement that the first Hindu state will be established, is by itself not an appeal for votes on the ground of religion, but is the expression, at best, of such a hope. This, however, is against the secular parameters of neutrality. It is ultra-vires of the Constitution as no Hindu state can claim to be neutral. The court also failed to see the impact of the statement, especially since it was made during an election campaign. In the *Ram Kapse* v. *H.R. Singh*[27] judgement, the judiciary dithered again. Here, the three-judge bench dismissed the high court's contention that the BJP Member of Parliament was liable to lose his seat, because he was present at a meeting where Sadhvi Rithambara made an inflammatory speech on his behalf. The Supreme Court reinstated Kapse on the ground that he was opposed to the rhetorical appeal made in the public meeting and was not a part of it.

This leaves a huge gap between theory and practice. Contradictions in the judgements fail to bring out any clear judicial policy on religious and secular issues. The State has, rather, appropriated religious symbols. While the *Bommai* case strongly called for separating the two spheres, in the Hindutva judgements the Supreme Court has let manifest appeals to religion standby, redefining those appeals as appeals to culture or history, oblivious to the context that fosters those appeals. The court thus seems to have appropriated the symbols of Hindu India as Indian culture and history.

RELIGION AND THE SUPREME COURT

Interestingly it is the judiciary in India that tells us what constitutes religion. The Supreme Court is of the view that the problem with secularism in India is the demarcation between 'what are matters of religion and what are not. . . . Religion is not defined in the Constitution and it is a term that is hardly susceptible of any rigid definition'.[28] The Supreme Court[29] has not restricted the definition of religion to the relationship of an individual to the creator, and the obligation imposed for the reverence of 'his being'. For not all religions—like Buddhism and Jainism—believe in any Supreme Being. In *S.P. Mittal* v. *Union of India*,[30] the Court stated that religion is a matter of faith; belief in god is not essential to constitute religion. Religion includes not only a code of ethical rules for its followers to accept, it might prescribe rituals and observances, ceremonies and modes of worship, which are regarded as its integral parts. Further in *A.S. Narayan Deekshitulu* v. *State of Andhra Pradesh*,[31] it was held that religion in the Constitution was a personal matter for those who have faith and belief in it. Religion, therefore, had its basis in a system of beliefs and doctrines regarded by the practioners of the religion to be conducive to their spiritual well-being.

While in principle, the court seeks to protect the religious beliefs of all, they are subject to limitations imposed by the state on grounds of social welfare, public order, morality, health and any other provision of the fundamental rights of individuals. The judiciary evolved the doctrine of essentiality of religious practices to be the basis of protection of the freedom of conscience and free profession, practice and propagation of religion to manage religious affairs. Religion, as interpreted, was restricted to that which was essential to it, and non-essential features were not protected; courts determined the rationale. For example, the practice of untouchability is banned in India. Ambedkar[32] had held debates in the Constituent Assembly that we ought to strive to limit the definition of religion to beliefs and such rituals that may be connected with ceremonies that are essentially religious. The court has toed a similar line of practice.

While in the early cases, *Sirur Math Jagannath Temple*[33] and the

Bombay Trust cases of Justice B.K. Mukherjea, the Court assured all religions protection of their belief, practices and management of their religious institutions. In the later years, like in the *Nathdwara Temple* cases, the court propounded that only the essential practices of a faith would be protected.[34] Judges thereby became the custodians of faith. Justices Hansaria and Ramaswamy's judgements further extended the tentacles of State control over religion as the management of religious institutions was secularized in *Sri Lakshamana Yatendrulu* v. *State of Andhra Pradesh*.[35] Further, in *A.S. Narayana Deekshitulu* v. *State of Andhra Pradesh*,[36] it was established that the law's attempt to separate essential religious practice from non-essential was not unlawful but visionary. The essential practice of a religion is a question or fact to be considered in the context in which the question has a risen. It argued that the state could make laws in some areas, and hence justified the state taking over the secular affairs, here, the appointment of the *archak* or priest. Matters of religion that fell outside the precincts of essentiality could be secularized. It was held that the appointment of a priest is not an essential part of religion or of religious practice. This also reverberated in the special leave petition of the *Vaishnodevi Shrine* case.[37] Here the court made a distinction between religious service and the person who performs the service. The performance of religious service was considered an integral part of the religion's faith and belief, and could not be regulated by the state, but the service of the priest was considered a secular activity.

The Court also decides what constitutes a religious denomination. In *S.P. Mittal* v. *Union of India*,[38] the court denied the status of religion to the followers of Aurobindo, whose teachings were recognized as his philosophy and not a religion. In *Brahamachari Sidheswar Shai* v. *State of WB*,[39] the Court held that the followers of Ramakrishna, who are a collection of individuals and who adhere to a system of beliefs as conducive to their spiritual well-being, who have organized themselves collectively and who have an organization of a definite name – Ramakrishna Math, can be regarded as a religious denomination within the Hindu religion. While in another case, *Anand Margis*,[40] the Anand Margis' were recognized as a religious denomination. But the performance of *tandava* dance by its practitioners (in procession or at public places by Ananda Margis carrying lethal weapons and human skulls), was believed by the court to be a non-essential feature. On appeal, it did recognize the *tandava* dance to be essential to the religious beliefs of Anand Margis, but restricted it for the maintenance of public order.

In this phase, the court not only decided what constituted, religion but also what practice would be allowed.

In *Ismail Faruqui* v. *Union of India*, the Supreme Court's majority opinion was that the court could, in the exercise of sovereign power, acquire places of worship like mosques, churches, temples, etc., for the maintenance of law and order. It argued that while offering of prayer or worship, is an essential religious practice, its offering at every location where such prayers can be offered, is not an essential religious practice. The ban on cow slaughter further extends the debate on essentiality and non-essentiality of religion. Operating under a reified concept of Islam, the Supreme Court decreed in the *State of West Bengal* v. *Ashutosh Lahiri*[41] and earlier, in *M.H. Qureshi* v. *State of Bihar*,[42] that Muslims of India could not be given the freedom to kill cows by way of *qurbani* as part of Id-ul Adha. The court contended that the killing of cows could not be regarded as an essential practice of Muslims. After a scriptural search for a statement making cow sacrifice obligatory, the court found that it was optional for Muslims to sacrifice a cow or camel for every seven persons, and a goat for one person. Apparently, the Muslims had an option. Under the shelter of Article 48 of the Constitution, which sought to promote animal husbandry, the court banned cow slaughter—an unacknowledged recognition of Hindu belief in the sanctity of the cow.

Bijoe Emanuel v. *State of Kerala*[43] case added a new dimension, following similar dicta by the US Supreme Court. Here the court allowed the believers of the Jehovah faith, the right not to sing the national anthem on grounds of genuine conscientious religious objection. Justice Chinappa Reddy observed that there was no provision of the law that obliged anyone to sing the national anthem, and it was not disrespectful to the national anthem, if a person stood up respectfully when it was sung but did not join the singing.

'Imam' wages issue is another case in point. In the *All-India Imam Organisation* v. *Union of India*,[44] imams approached the court by way of a writ petition under Article 32, for the enforcement of their fundamental rights against exploitation by the Wakf board. It was contended that under Islamic religious practice, imams were not entititled to any emoluments as Islamic law ordains them to offer voluntary service. The court however decreed that under the Wakf Act of 1954, it was the duty of the Wakf Board to pay remuneration to imams. This speaks of state interference in matters of religion and in the management of religious affairs. Political overtones cloud the legal issues, where the issue of protecting vested interests, here that of imams have overridden all other considerations.

The judgements of the Supreme Court thus reiterate that in matters of religion, only essential practices, as determined by the court, can have absolute protection. This has allowed continual interference by the State in matters of religion. By their authority to decide what is religious, and what is not, the courts acquire the authority to regulate the meaning of religion. State control seems to be much more restrictive now than under the British, even though the Constitution guarantees religious freedom and the freedom to manage one's religious affairs.[45] Rajeev Dhavan[46] says these acts are a kind of juristic activism that entails judicial legislation of ideas. This has resulted in the transformation of the laws regarding religious freedom into an over-assimilationist mould, thus paving the way for an extensive control of religion and religious affairs by the State. Partha Chatterjee[47] has pointed out that in the name of national culture and a homogenized notion of citizenship, the State has overridden the toleration of religious, ethnic and cultural differences. In fact, even the decision of what is religion and what is not, lies no longer with the religious group/individual; the court determines it. Also, the legitimacy of a secular state to control religious institutions, even if the denominations agree, is questionable, so, what should be the extent of intervention. While it is argued that the secular State should be kept out of interfering with religious denominations, and the maximum interference that can be allowed is supervision alone,[48] social reforms necessitate state intervention. The difficulty of restricting the State, separating religion from the secular, and the inconsistency of the judiciary has undermined secularism. While this section focused on certain conceptual aspects, the next section discusses the issue of personal laws and its implications for a secular State. It maps the judiciary's response to demands of protection of personal laws, vis-à-vis demands of social justice and national integration. In effect, how does the judiciary adjudicate on conflicting goals set in the Constitution?

PERSONAL LAW AND THE COURT

The subject of personal law brings out yet another feature of secularism, i.e. the protection of minorities in a plural setting. Secularism sans protection to minority religious and cultural groups creates majoritarianism. To protect minority interests, special protection measures need to be undertaken to cover the need for different identities and cultures and this is at odds with strict secular principles. The Constitution is ambiguous on the issue of personal laws, as arguments in favour and against, are both based on provisions laid in the Constitution. Opposition to reform of personal laws is based on the freedom of religion and conscience, whereas the guarantee to citizens of equal protection from the law, and before the law, supports a uniform civil code. This issue also raises questions concerning the hierarchy of rights—can the right to be governed by personal laws (a component part of the right to freedom of conscience) have precedence over the right to equality—and legal pluralism in a diverse society.

In the constituent assembly debates, there were wide differences amongst the members on the issue of personal laws. On the one hand, there were demands to protect religious freedom, especially minority interests and, on the other, to have a uniform civil code for all, based on a notion of homogenized citizenship. Unable to arrive at an agreement, a uniform civil code was seen as a goal to be implemented, and was included in the directive principles. Personal laws of minorities were maintained and thus, the whole gamut of family, property, marriage, divorce and adoption rights were left within the fold of religious legislation.

Judicial pronouncements are important in determining the essence of the implications in our Constitution. As early as 1954, in the *State of Bombay* v. *Narasu Appa Mali*,[49] it was held that personal laws do not fall within the ambit of laws in force and, therefore, are not void even if they conflict with fundamental rights. Religious denominations had autonomy, while personal laws were recognized as extra-constitutional laws. The judicial perception was that personal laws did not fall within its purview; scriptures and religious texts were not subject to judicial review.

However, the *Shah Bano*[50] judgement of 1985 overturned this view and the Supreme Court took up the role of bringing in reform. The *Shah Bano* case concerns an old Muslim woman who went to court, against the way her husband had divorced her. In 1978, 65-year old Shah Bano filed a petition demanding alimony from her husband, who had abandoned her for another woman, after over 40 years of marriage. According to Muslim law, Shah Bano was entitled to three months maintenance. The Supreme Court heard the matter years later and upheld her right to maintenance. It ruled that Section 125 of the Criminal Procedure Code overrides Muslim Personal Law (Shariat) in matters of divorce. While doing so, the court also referred to the need to enact a uniform civil code to promote social justice. It held that no community is likely to bell the cat by making concessions on this issue; it is the state that is charged with the duty to do so. The political aftermath of this judgement—protest by patriarchal sections of the Muslim community—inverted the efforts of the court. The Rajiv Gandhi government, giving in to pressure, adopted legislation that abrogated the right of the Muslim woman divorcee to maintenance under Section 125 of the Criminal Procedure Code by passing the Muslim Women's Protection Bill.

In *Sarla Mudgal, President, Kalyani and Others* v. *Union of India*,[51] the Court again reiterated the need for a uniform civil code. Justice Kuldip Singh stated that the uniform civil code was required for national integration. It was stated that minorities should give up their commitment to the two-nation theory and accept reforms in a manner similar to the Hindus, and thus promote national unity. In the recent judgement of July 2003, *John Vallamattom and Anr.* v. *Union of India*,[52] Chief Justice V.N. Khare observed that it was a matter of great regret that Article 44 of the Constitution has not been given effect. It was argued that the common civil code would help national integration by removing contradictions based on ideologies. The semantics of the discourse conversely questions the intentions of the court. In the *Shah Bano* case the objective was social reform and the Court took upon itself this task, while in *Sarla Mudgal* and *John Vallamattom* cases, the objective was national integration. Secularism in such terms would mean uni-culturalism rather than multiculturalism, which has strong underpinnings for majoritarianism. Legal pluralism is not inconsistent with national integration, and hence to argue for uniformity on such grounds is indeed against the spirit of pluralism. S.P. Sathe[53] argues that an attempt to have a common law could be counter-productive. Religious groups with distinct identities are not against national integration and their personal laws cannot be obliterated for uniformity. More importantly, it is also to be seen whether the judiciary, the counter-majoritarian wing of polity, has the authority to introduce reforms in personal laws.

While the judiciary on the one hand propagated a uniform civil code on grounds of social justice and national integration, on the other hand, it has delayed taking up cases questioning the Muslim Women's Protection Bill, and has kept statutory enactments of personal laws out of the purview of Article 13, as in the Ahmedabad Women's and Allied

Cases verdict. This mirrors the inherent contradictions. The issue of religious personal laws reflects yet another aspect of secularism, limited secularism. In principle, it is articulated that secularism means equal respect and freedom of all religions, non-discrimination, and the separation of the sacred and secular but without special protection to minorities, it does become a form of majoritarianism.

CONCLUSION

The court's jurisdiction to interpret the Constitution has given it considerable authority. In the absence of any rigid positivist demarcation of the spheres of the secured and secular, the court has remarkable autonomy. Religion and secularism in India are given categories. The court decides, and more so in its activist phase, what is secular and what is not, what is religious and what is not, thereby regulating their meaning and thus the personal realm.

The judgements defy the logic of the positivist determination of outcomes. Judicial deliberations on issues of secularism, rather reveal that context takes centre-stage in decision-making. Judicial pronouncements on secular issues have thus been marked by contradictions. While in some of cases it has promoted majority interests, eroding the rights of minority groups, in others, it has privileged minority groups. On the one hand, minority interests were protected (by supporting personal laws in Ahmedabad Women's and Allied Cases, in the Imams' wage issue, and the protection to adherents of the Jehovah faith), on the other, their interests were subdued by majoritarianism as evident in the case of the ban on cow slaughter, its legitimizing of Hindutva, and its emphasis on a uniform civil code for national integration.

The spirit of the *S.R. Bommai* judgement that declared secularism to be a basic feature of the polity and defined it in terms of tolerance, accommodation, and separated the religious realm from the political, is not reflected in other verdicts. In principle, though the judiciary speaks of freedom of religion, tolerance, pluralism and non-discrimination, there is not much space for difference. The case of the *NCERT textbooks*, the *Hindutva judgements*, and the *Sarla Mudgal* and *John Vallamattom* cases reflect the court's intolerance towards difference. This standpoint subverts secularism. All in all, the vision of secularism endorsed by the judiciary favours the majority, as the emphasis is on uniformity based on oneness rather than respect for difference.

NOTES

1. Granville Austin (1999), *Working a Democratic Constitution: The Indian Experience*, New Delhi: Oxford University Press, 1999, p. 123.
2. Ashis Nandy, 'The Politics of Secularism and the Recovery of Religious Tolerance', *Alternatives*, 1988, p 192. He argues that Secularism is a part of the modern western package of scientific growth, nation building, national security and development. It is a legitimizing ideology for the national elites. To accept the ideology of secularism is to accept the ideologies of progress and modernity as the new justifications of domination, and the use of violence to achieve and sustain the ideologies as the new opiates of the masses. T.N. Madan, 'Secularism in its Place', *Journal of Asian Studies*, Nov. 1987. He is critical of secularism. Argues that the denial of religion in public life has led to the rise of fundamentalism.
3. P.K. Tripathi, *Secularism: Constitutional Provisions and Judicial Review in Secularism: Its implications for Law and Life in India*, ed. G.S. Sharma, N.M. Tripathi Pvt. Limited, 1966.
4. Shefali Jha, 'Secularism in the Constituent Assembly Debates, 1946–1950', *Economic and Political Weekly*, 27 July 2002.
5. D.E. Smith, *India as a Secular State*, Princeton: Princeton University Press, 1965, p. 105.
6. D.E. Jakob Roover, 'Secularism and Absence of theory', *Economic and Political Weekly*, 21 December 2002.
7. *Sardar Taheruddin Syedna Saheb* v. *State of Bombay*, AIR 1962 SC 853, 871.
8. Ibid.
9. *Keshavananda Bharati* v. *State of Kerala*, 1973 (4) SCC 225.
10. *Ahmedabad, St. Xaviers College* v. *State of Gujarat*, AIR, 1974, SC 1389.
11. *Ahmedabad, St. Xaviers College* v. *State of Gujarat*, AIR, 1974, SC 1434.
12. *Ziyauddin Burhanuddin Bukhari* v. *Brijmohan Ram Das Mehra*, 1975, 2 SCC 17.
13. *Indra Sawhney* v. *Union of India*, (1992) Supp (3) SCC 217.
14. *S.R. Bommai* v. *Union of India*, AIR, SC, December 1994.
15. Ibid., 232.
16. Ibid., 29.
17. Ibid., 304.
18. *Ismail Faruqui* v, *Union of India*, 1994 6 SCC 360.
19. *Ismail Faruqui* v. *Union of India*, 1994 6 SCC 399–400.
20. Ibid.
21. Pratap Bhanu Mehta 'Living with Difference', *Hindu*, 14 September 2002.
22. *Dr Ramesh Yashwant Prabhu* v. *Prabhakar K. Kuntes*, 1996 1 SCC 130.
23. *Suryakant Venkatrao Mahadik* v. *Smt. Saroj Sandesh Naik*, 1996 SCC(1) 384.

24. T.B. Hansen 'Globalization and Nationalist Imaginations: Hindutva's promise of Equality Through difference', *Economic and Political Weekly*, 9 March 1996, p. 608.
25. Granville Austin 'Comparative Frames', *Seminar*, 521.
26. *Manohar Joshi* v. *Nitin Rao Bhau Pate*, 1996 1 SCC169.
27. *Ram Kapse* v. *HR Singh*, AIR, S.C, December 1995.
28. *Commissioner Hindu Religious Endowments. Madra* v. *Dirur Math*. 26 SC J 1954, p. 348.
29. *S.P. Mittal* v. *Union Of India*, AIR, 1983, SC 1.
30. Ibid.
31. *A.S. Narayana Deekshitulu* v. *State of Andhra Pradesh*, AIR, 1996, SC 1765.
32. B.R. Ambedkar, Constitution Assembly Debates, vol. 7, p. 781.
33. Supra n. 28.
34. Rajeev Dhavan, 'The Temple at Vaishnodevi', *The Hindu*, 18 January 1997.
35. *Sri Lakshamana Yatendrulu* v. *State of Andhra Pradesh*, AIR, July 1996.
36. Supra n. 31.
37. Rajeev Dhavan,' The Temple at Vaishnodevi', The *Hindu*, 18 January 1997.
38. Supra n. 30.
39. *Brahamachari Sidheswar Shai* v. *State of W.B.*, 1995 4 SCC 646.
40. *Jagdishwaranand* v. *Police Commissioner*, AIR, 1984, SC 51.
41. *State of West Bengal* v. *Ashutosh Lahiri* AIR, 1995, SC 464.
42. *M.H. Querseshi* v. *State of Bihar*, AIR, 1958 SC 731.
43. *Bijoe Emanuel* v. *State of Kerala*, AIR, 1986, SC 615.
44. *All India Imam Organization* v. *Union of India*, 1993 SOL case no. 098.
45. Badar Ahmed, 'Religious Freedom under Article 25 of Constitution of India: A Critical Study', *Civil and Military Law Journal*, April–June 1991.
46. Rajeev Dhavan, 'The Apex Court and Personal Law', *the Hindu*, 14 March 1997.
47. Partha Chatterjee, 'Secularism and Toleration', *Economic and Political Weekly*, 9 July 1994.
48. V. Francis, 'Concept of Secular State and Adminstartion of Religious Institutions', *The Academy Law Review*, Center for Advanced Legal Studies, June–December 1978.
49. *State of Bombay* v. *Narasu Appa Mali*, AIR, 1952, Bombay, 1954.
50. *Mohd. Ahmed Khan* v. *Shah Bano Begum*, 1985, SOL case no. 085. http://www. supremecourtonline.com
51. *Sarla Mudgal, Smt., President, Kalyani and others* v. *Union of India*, 1995, 3 SCC 635.
52. *John Vallamattom and Anr.* v. *Union of India*, 2003 SOL case no. 388, http://www.supremecourtonline.com
53. S.P. Sathe, 'Uniform Civil Code', *Economic and Political Weekly*, 2 September 1995.

PART IV

Judiciary and Parliamentary Local Institutions

13

Parliamentary Privileges and Immunities in India: An Argument for Codification

M.P. SINGH

In the Spring of 2005 the Assembly elections in the state of Jharkhand yielded an uncertain verdict. The Bharatiya Janata Party-led National Democratic Alliance (NDA) emerged as the largest single coalition and appeared poised to form a coalition government, by somehow making up the shortage of half a dozen seats by roping in some smaller allies. However, Governor Syed Sibte Razi hurriedly invited a regional party leader, Shibu Soren (Jharkhand Mukti Morcha), who was aligned with the Congress Party, and appointed him as Chief Minister, and gave him several weeks to prove his majority on the floor of the legislature. President A.P.J. Abdul Kalam was anguished over the partisan role played by the constitutional head of the Jharkhand state and summoned him to New Delhi to explain his conduct. Meanwhile, the NDA moved the Supreme Court which ordered the Speaker of the Jharkhand Assembly to convene a meeting of the newly-elected Assembly for a composite floor test ahead of the time given by the Governor to the newly-appointed Chief Minister Shibu Soren.[1] When the Chief Minister failed to comply with the due date, he was advised by the Congress-led government (United Progressive Alliance) to resign and clear the way for the restoration of the due constitutional process. Eventually an NDA government headed by Arjun Munda was sworn in office by the discredited Governor. The Lok Sabha Speaker, Somnath Chatterjee, convened two meetings in the wake of the event: an all-party meeting of parliamentarians and a meeting of presiding officers of State legislatures in the country to protest the Court's interference in legislative proceedings, in solidarity with the Jharkand Legislature. Among other things, Chatterjee remarked:[2]

With all respect to Honourable Supreme Court, and without at all going into the political merits of the issue, to my mind, the order of the Honourable Supreme Court has created a disturbing situation. Separation of powers of different Constitutional Organs is a basic feature of the Constitution, giving sustenance to parliamentary democracy. Articles 122 and 212 of the constitution are the most important provisions, which symbolize the supremacy of the Legislatures within their own spheres. The Articles provide that no officer or member of Parliament, who is vested with the power of regulating procedure or conduct of the business in the House shall be subject to the jurisdiction of any court in respect of the exercise by him of those powers.

This episode is by no means the first of its ilk nor will it be the last. There are grey areas in some aspects of Indian constitutionalism. The purpose of this paper is to analyse one of them, namely, legislative privileges and immunities.

II

The law relating to privileges and immunities of Parliament and State legislatures in India, continues to rely on ill-defined conventions, and is largely lacking in positive constitutional law emanating from the Constitution, legislation, or case law. In a section of the Constitution entitled 'Powers, Privileges and Immunities of Parliament and its Members', Article 105 guarantees (a) 'freedom of speech in Parliament', 'subject to the provisions of this Constitution' and to the rules and standing orders regulating the procedure of Parliament; (b) immunity from legal proceedings arising from any parliamentary speech or vote or publications; and (c) all powers/privileges/immunities enjoyed by members (and non-members who have the right to partake in the parliamentary proceedings) 'by virtue of this Constitution'. In other respects, the powers, privileges, and immunities of the Houses are declared to be what they were 'immediately before coming into force of Section 15 of the Constitution (44th Amendment) Act 1978'. It is this point (c) in the above constitutional provision that has proved to be a nest of confusion and ambiguity. The reference to the 44th Amendment above replaced the original reference in the Constitution to the British House of Commons, to which the quest must now regress until the Indian Parliament chooses to define its rights and immunities 'by law' (Article 105, clause 3).

Article 194 of the Constitution repeats the same provisions (of Article 105) in relation to the State legislatures as with regard to the Parliament above. This compounds the confusion and contestation in the matter.

So far, neither has the Parliament nor any State legislature taken steps to define these powers, privileges, and immunities, either severally or singly. There have, of course, been numerous instances of flat assertions, sometimes bizarre from the perspective of constitutionalism and the rule of law. On each of these occasions, the courts were sucked into the legal or constitutional (or confrontational) crises thereby created. The ruling, rather advisory opinion, of courts or the Supreme Court has settled only limited issues in some cases and only provisionally defused the problem of the moment.

There is therefore neither a consensually agreed paradigm baring a vague reference to the British House of Commons as of 1950, precedents of the pre-Independence Indian legislatures, and a constitutional amendment by Parliament in 1978. There is no settled constitutional law or theory regarding parliamentary privileges in India and its federating states.[3]

III

Representative and responsible government in modern India was slow in its growth. The first statutory recognition of privileges of legislators was made in the Government of India Act 1919 enacted by the British Parliament:[4] 'Subject to the rules and standing orders affecting the council, there shall be freedom of speech in the Governor's legislative council. No person shall be liable to any proceedings in any court by reason of his speech or vote in any such council, or by reason of anything contained in any official report of the proceedings of any such council.'

Privileges of legislators were further reinforced by amendments to the civil procedure code in 1924, exempting them from arrest or detention under civil process in the course of meeting of the legislature or any of its committees. A similar amendment to the Civil Procedure Code exempted members from serving as jurors or assessors.

The Government of India Act 1935, also enacted by the British Parliament, renewed the above privileges and exemptions, but stopped short of granting to Indian legislatures the contempt power to punish alleged violators of their privileges.[5] It was left for the Constituent Assembly of independent India to equate the privileges of legislative institutions, to those of the British House of Commons.

In England, parliamentary privileges may be seen as the milestones of the growth of representative democracy in the struggle towards free and responsible institutions from the fetters of feudal royal absolutism. Instead of creating another chasm between the rulers and the ruled in Britain, parliamentary privileges were meant to enable people's representatives to perform their duty without fear or favour, pressures or intimidations. The history of the growth of these privileges in the Mother of Parliaments suggests that the privileges were fought for and won by the House of Commons from the Crown, the House of Lords, and the courts. The privileges were consolidated by constitutional conventions rather than in constitutional legislation. The privileges of the House of Commons, in the words of Thomas Erskine May, are 'the sum of [such powers of] the House and its individual members as against the prerogatives of the crown, the authority of the ordinary courts, and special rights of the House of Lords'. The privileges subsequently expanded into 'peculiar rights enjoyed by each House individually without which they could not discharge their functions, and which exceed those possessed by other bodies of individuals'.[6]

Major parliamentary privileges in the United Kingdom, include freedom from civil arrest, freedom of speech and debate, internal autonomy and the privilege of disciplinary power over members, ordering attendance of witness and punishment of non-members for disobedience, the right to open or close door debate, general warrant for contempt of the House, privilege to summon persons and to demand the assistance of civil and military authorities, and the right of access to the Queen.[7]

It is puzzling why the Constituent Assembly of India uncritically equated the privileges of Indian parliamentary institutions with those enjoyed by the House of Commons at the time of the commencement of the Constitution. After all, the founding fathers of the Indian republic were exceptionally gifted in law and discretion, and in most other cases went to the extent of creating elaborate provisions, producing in the process, probably the lengthiest written constitution in the world.[8]

In the Constituent Assembly Debates, the question of parliamentary privileges was discussed on two separate occasions.[9] Two objections to the drafting committee's version of Article 85, that finally became article 105 in the text of the Constitution, were articulated: (a) the 'nationalist' argument objecting to any reference to an alien imperial Parliament; and (b) the practical difficulty in definitively codifying the British privileges, when no one seemed to know what they really were. Alladi Krishnaswami Ayyar (Madras: General seat), who intervened in the debate and whose arguments were considered so sufficiently persuasive that the drafting committee chairman B.R. Ambedkar opted out from an official reply to the debate, dealt with the two major objections in the following way:[10]

(a) If the privileges are confined to the existing privileges of legislatures in India as at present constituted, the result will be that a person cannot be punished for contempt of the House. The actual question arose in Calcutta as to whether a person can be punished for contempt of the provincial legislature or other legislatures in this country. It has been held that there is no power to punish for contempt, any person who is guilty of contempt of the provincial or even the Central Legislature, whereas the Parliament in England has the inherent right to punish for contempt. The question arose in the Dominions and in the Colonies and it has been held that by reason of the wide wording in the Australian Commonwealth Act as well as in the Canadian Act, the Parliament in both the places have power similar to the power possessed by the Parliament in England and therefore have the right to punish for contempt. Are you going to deny to yourself that power? That is the question.

(b) If you have the time and if you have the leisure to formulate all the privileges in a compendious form, it will be well and good. I believe a committee constituted by the Speaker on the legislative side found it very difficult to formulate all the privileges, unless they went in detail into the whole working of parliamentary institution in England, and the time was not sufficient before the [central] legislature for that purpose, and accordingly the committee was not able to give any effective advice to the Speaker in regard to this matter. . . .The other point is that there is nothing to prevent the Parliament from setting up the proper machinery for formulating privileges. . . . It does not in any way fetter your discretion.

IV

Makers of the Constitution went straightaway to British parliamentary practice, and a subsequent amendment to the Constitution sought to rely on the law and conventions developed in India up to the time of the 44th Amendment in 1978.[11] Neither solution is satisfactory. In the former case, there is no law automatically and uncritically applicable to India. In the latter case, there are horrendous precedents, no conventions, and no positive law originating in parliamentary enactments/amendments or in case law.[12] There is no more than a sensible advisory opinion of the Supreme Court offered in a presidential reference case in 1960. Additionally, there are only limited Supreme Court rulings made on some specific points rather than in a comprehensive way. For example, in *Keshavram Reddy* v. *Nafisul Hasan and the State of UP,* popularly known as the *Blitz* case (after a Bombay weekly), the Supreme Court ordered the release of the editor of the weekly who had been arrested for breach of privilege of the UP Assembly (on the order of the Speaker), and lodged in a hotel in Lucknow without being produced before a magistrate as per Article 22(2).[13]

A landmark case *M.S.M. Sharma* v. *Sri Krishna Sinha and Others* involved the Patna English daily, *The Searchlight* (now the *Hindustan Times*). It published a vituperative portion of the speech by an MLA on the floor of the Assembly against Chief Minister S.K. Sinha, which the Speaker had ordered to be expunged. On a 'show cause' notice from the Assembly the editor moved the Supreme Court under Article 32 of the Constitution on the plea that the privileges of the legislature did not control his individual freedom of speech and expression under Article 19(1a). The Court by a majority of 4 to 1 noted that Parliament and/or State legislatures had not made any law relating to the privileges and on the basis of the then existing constitutional provisions, privileges were not subject to Article 19 (1a), excepting in the case of Article 21 on life and liberty.[14]

Another landmark case arose out of a conflict between the UP Legislative Assembly and the Allahabad High Court in 1964. The Assembly found one Keshav Singh, guilty of committing a breach of privilege for publishing a pamphlet against an MLA. On being produced before the House to be reprimanded by the Speaker, Keshav Singh defiantly misbehaved. He was ordered to be imprisoned for a week. Singh's Advocate, one Solomon, moved a petition at the Lucknow bench of the Allahabad High Court, under Article 226 of the Constitution and obtained an interim bail until the final disposal of the case. The Assembly proceeded in contempt for its breach of privilege and ordered the arrest of the two judges, who had granted the bail, along with Keshav Singh and Solomon. The two judges moved the High Court, under Article 226 contending that the resolution of the Assembly was unconstitutional. A full bench of 28 judges of the Allahabad High Court ordered a stay of the implementation of the order of the Assembly. The Nehru government asked the President to refer the case to the Supreme Court to defuse this constitutional crisis.[15]

The Supreme Court's 'advisory opinion' (6 to 1, chaired by Chief Justice Gajendragadkar) in the case was as follows:[16]

1. The Lucknow bench of the Allahabad High Court was competent to order the release of Keshav Singh on bail pending the disposal of the case.
2. The accused Keshav Singh, his advocate, and the two judges of the High Court 'did not commit contempt of the Legislative Assembly of Uttar Pradesh'.
3. On the facts and circumstances of the case, the Legislative Assembly of Uttar Pradesh was not competent to direct the production of the judges and the Advocate 'before it in custody or to call for explanation of its contempt'.
4. 'On the facts and circumstances of the case, the Full Bench of the High Court of Uttar Pradesh was competent to entertain and deal with the petitions of the victims of the Assembly.
5. 'In rendering our answer to' the President's questions 'which [are] very broadly worded, we ought to preface our answer with the observation that the answer is confined to cases in relation to contempt alleged to have been committed. . . .'

In a dissenting note, Justice A.K. Sarkar opined:[17]

> In a modern state it is often necessary for the good of the country that parallel powers should exist in different authorities. It is not inevitable that such powers will clash. It would be defeatism to take the view that in our country men would not be available to work these powers smoothly, and in the best interests of the people and without producing friction. I sincerely hope that what has happened will never happen again, and our Constitution will be worked by the different organs of the state amicably, wisely, courageously and in the spirit in which the makers of the constitution expected them to act.

H.M. Seervai is highly critical of the Supreme Court's majority view in the Presidential reference case regarding the privilege of the UP Assembly. He finds fault with the majority opinion both on the grounds of the intention of Constituent Assembly of India and on jurisprudence. His argument based on legal philosophy, opposes the

Court's majority opinion that the Assembly's power to commit for contempt by a non-speaking warrant is not a privilege. Instead, it is a flat assertion as 'courts have not scrutinized such general warrants on the grounds of comity, presumption, or agreement'. Seervai goes on to submit that:

> Sarkar J., in his dissenting opinion has dealt with these issues with satisfying finality. . . . If the privilege of committing by a general warrant is a right enforceable by law, it cannot be based on comity between courts, because comity confers no right but is merely a self-imposed restraint. Again, for comity between courts, there must be two courts and the House of Commons is not a court, and for its proper functioning, a court 'needs no civility or consideration' from the House. As regards the theory that a warrant of the House is presumed to be correct, the presumption is either a rule of law or it is not. If it is, then it is a part of *lex Parliamenti*; if it is not, it would depend upon the indulgence of courts and indulgence confers no rights. . . . I may add that reference to 'comity' or 'agreement' seems an odd way of describing the relation between two bodies each of which . . . denies the right claimed by the other. To my knowledge no decision or authoritative text-book has based the privilege of committing for contempt by a general warrant on comity, presumption or agreement. *Stockdale* v. *Hansard*, held that courts would take cognizance of *lex Parliamenti* and enforce it like laws.[18]

An extremely delightful exposition of the intentions of the framers of the Indian Constitution and of British constitutional law in this context! However, to my mind, the framers' provisional escape from codification for expedient reasons and the British convention and law cannot, on scrutiny, be validated for Indian constitutionalism, for India significantly departs from the United Kingdom, by virtue of its republican democracy, with a written constitution incorporating federalism, secularism, fundamental rights, and directive principles of State policy.

In 1984 the Andhra Pradesh Legislative Council raised a privilege issue and found the editor of *Eenadu*, a Telugu newspaper, guilty of contempt for publishing a news item 'elder's commotion'. It ordered him to present himself for a reprimand. On his refusal, the presiding offer of the House ordered his arrest. The editor moved the Supreme Court for the protection of his fundamental freedom of speech and expression. The Court stayed the Council's arrest order. The House invoked legislative supremacy and ordered the state police to carry out its order nevertheless. The Chief Minister of the state intervened at this point and advised the elders to drop the matter and requested the

President of India to refer the matter to the Supreme Court for its advisory opinion.[19] Commenting on this issue, A.G. Noorani has quoted from B.R. Ambedkar's observation in the Constituent Assembly on 14 October 1949: 'No constitutional government can work in any country unless institutions remember that their authority is limited by Constitution and that if there is any body created by Constitution which has to decide between that particular authority and any other authority, then the decision of that authority shall be binding upon any other organ.' Noorani adds that in Ambedkar's view, that final authority was clearly the judiciary.[20]

A number of years ago, the Maharashtra Assembly invoked its breach of privilege against Justice Lentin of the Bombay High Court and when N.A. Palkhivala wrote an article in defence of the judge he too was summoned. The Assembly retreated only after strong protest by bar associations en bloc.[21]

In *P.V. Narashimha Rao* v. *State (CBI/SPE)* (1998) the Supreme Court by a 3:2 judgement came to a rather contradictory conclusion that Members of Parliament and state legislatures are 'public servants' coming under the purview of the Prevention of Corruption Act 1968; however, they cannot be prosecuted for offences under Sections 7, 10 and 13 thereof for want of an authority competent to grant sanction for their prosecution under the Act, which was originally designed for civil servants alone. In addition, any charge of corruption/bribery in a Court proceeding having nexus with vote cast or speech made in Parliament, is protected by Article 105(3) dealing with powers, privileges, and immunities of a Member of Parliament (that are under the existing provisions of the Constitution ultimately equated with those of the British House of Commons at the time of the commencement of the Indian Constitution). The Court entertained the hope that Parliament would address itself to the task of removing the lacuna and the contradiction in the framework of the Constitution and the law of the land 'with due expedition'.[22]

The implication of the Court's verdict is clear. For one thing, the MPs/MLAs are 'public servants' for all intents and purposes of the Prevention of Corruption Act 1968. For another, parliamentary privileges of the classical British parliamentary vintage are alien to the Indian Constitutional design with its inbuilt additional features of federalism, judicial review, and fundamental freedoms of citizens, minority rights, and the press/media. But the Parliament has been tactfully avoiding any definitive attempt at codification by legislation under Article 105 of the Constitution.[23] For only the Parliament stands to bask in the continuing ambiguity about its privileges. There has not been a chance for the judiciary to settle the matter in a clinching judgement in an appropriate test case.

A more recent privilege case, as much bizarre as inconclusive, arose out of the resolution of the Tamil Nadu Assembly under the AIADMK government headed by J. Jayalalitha towards the end of the year 2003 ordering arrest and two-week imprisonment of, *The Hindu*, editor, N. Ram and his senior colleagues and the editor of the Tamil news magazine, *Murasoli* for the alleged breach of the privilege of the legislature by publishing some news about the government and editorially criticizing the Chief Minister, Speaker, and a committee. The journalists moved the Supreme Court which stayed the arrests and referred the matter to a 5-judge Constitution bench, as in the opinion of the Court, the case involved some important issues in constitutional law.[24] The case was subsequently withdrawn without a conclusive settlement of the matter.

The bases of the British constitution, as magisterially interpreted by Albert V. Dicey, are the twin principles of parliamentary sovereignty and rule of law. Notwithstanding the United Nations Charter and the European Union, this continues to be the case in theory and largely in practice as well. For any supranational obligations on British laws, are contingent on the will of the Westminster Parliament.

Indian constitutionalism, on the contrary, would appear to have widely diverged from British constitutional theory and the practice of parliamentary sovereignty. For, even though the transfer of power from the British Parliament to the Constituent Assembly of India under the Independence of India Act 1947 was *legal*, India emerged as a 'sovereign, democratic, republic' at the culmination of a long freedom struggle in which extra-legal methods of nonviolent agitation were freely used. Besides, the preamble to the Constitution of India invokes the principle of popular sovereignty in its opening lines 'We, the people of India. . . .'[25] In addition, the Constitution of India entrenched charters of fundamental rights of citizens and civil society institutions, and recognized federal rights of states. These features of the Indian Constitution are radically different from those of the Constitution of the United Kingdom. Further, the 'law peers' in the House of Lords are the highest Court of appeal in the United Kingdom, and the Parliament there is a 'court of record'. In India only the Supreme Court and High Courts have such a constitutional status under Articles 129 and 215 respectively.

V

The question of parliamentary privileges in India must be examined in the contemporary democratic context in India rather than in the archaic historical perspective of British constitutional history. Even in Britain the rethinking reflects the felt need for democratic reforms,[26] though, as in other constitutional matters, the British have a penchant for developing new conventions rather than by favouring direct intervention by constitutional legislation or 'positive' law. The Indian experience with constitutional reforms has been exactly the opposite.

So far in India the most frequent cases concerning parliamentary privileges have pitted the legislatures against fundamental freedoms of individuals and the press. With paradigm shifts in politics and the economy with the accent on economy, and with the revival of the civil society, recurrence of class and mass movements (including 'new' ones relating more to issues of quality of life than production and distribution), and privatization and globalization, the chances are that more complex conflicts between 'privileges' and 'rights' may surface with greater frequency.

Moreover, it would be too simplistic to assume that in a dispute between, say, the Parliament and the press, one side is automatically right and the other, wrong. Parliamentary institutions in India have undoubtedly gone down in functionality and public esteem. But the print and electronic media are also not entirely paragons of public virtue and reason. They often exhibit a crass commercialism, consumerism, and sensational entertainment, and public interest and information does not necessarily get a high rating with them. In a panel discussion on, *The Hindu* case referred to earlier, Rajni Kothari aptly observed: 'We have seen a series of distortions in respect of the growth of the privileges coming down all the way from the monarchy to a whole series of old and new vested interests. Therefore, whether it is the rights of the mass of the people or human rights, we have to be very careful about not locating it again in another institutional bind, namely, the media in the case that we are discussing.'[27]

The point has already been made that importing parliamentary privileges in the British mould and continuing this state of affairs *ad infinitum* is inconsistent with Indian constitutionalism properly interpreted. For even though the transfer of power from the British Parliament to the Indian Constituent Assembly may be construed to be made in terms of parliamentary sovereignty, the alternate heritage of the Gandhian freedom struggle prompted the Constituent Assembly to invoke the notion of popular sovereignty in the Preamble which proclaims 'We, the people of India', as the source of all political authority. Parliamentary immunities are essential for ensuring the autonomy of parliamentary proceedings from any external political, economic, and ecclesiastical pressures or intimations. However, fundamental civil, political, and economic rights of individuals and groups and media cannot be automatically subordinated to any general notion of parliamentary privileges.[28] I have postulated 'an informal theory of separation of powers, in which the institutions of government, organs of the state, and institutions of civil society check and balance each other in an extended theory of separation [and division] of powers'.[29]

To sum up, the powers and rights of Parliament and state legislatures in India must be reconciled with distinctively Indian features of evolving constitutionalism in this country, as explicated above. The contours of the unfolding case law is also consistent with this line of interpretation, even though a full crystallization of this constitutional principle must ultimately come from a parliamentary law and constitutional amendment or a clinching test case settled by the Supreme Court of India. Judicial review has already become a part of the 'basic structure' of the Constitution beyond the amending power of the Parliament. Any conclusion other than what is argued in this paper would appear to be questionable. For the Keshav Singh case clearly underlines the horrors of conflicts among the three organs of the state under their presumed powers, prerogatives, and contempt. Moreover, there are 29 legislatures in India, not one. The prospect of inter-legislative privilege fights may not be far behind, if Seervai's literal reading of privilege articles in the Constitution (that were adopted as a provisional compromise reached on considerations of convenience), is not critically interrogated. In my well-considered opinion the only defensible solution would be codification of parliamentary privileges by a law/constitutional amendment subject to judicial review.

NOTES

1. Shibu Soren was installed as Chief Minister on 2 March and was asked by the Governor to prove his majority on the floor of the House by 15 March 2005. The Supreme Court ordered that the Soren government prove its majority on 11 March instead of 15 March, over-ruling the Governor's

decision, and that a pro tem Speaker conduct the Assembly proceedings with just one agenda: the confidence vote. The apex court also ordered that the entire proceedings be video-recorded and reported. *Frontline*, 8 April 2005.

2. *Asian News Digest*, vol. VI, no. 14, 27 March–2 April 2005.
3. 'Lists of Parliamentary Privileges', writes Subhash C. Kashyap, 'can be drawn and have in fact been drawn. No such list, however, can be exhaustive'. He then proceeds to enumerate fourteen 'privileges and immunities' and five 'consequential powers necessary for the protection' of the same culled from the Constitution, Code of the civil procedure, rules of business of the House, report of the committee on privileges of the Lok Sabha, etc. See, his *Parliamentary Procedure: Law, Privileges, Practices and Precedents*, vol. 2, Delhi, 2000, pp. 1556–7.
4. *Government of India Act*, 1919, Calcutta: 1924, Section 72-D, subsection 7..
5. *Government of India Act*, 1935, as amended up to 15 August 1943, Delhi: 1943, Chapter 2, section 71.
6. Thomas Erskine May, *The Law, Privileges, Proceedings and Usages of Parliament*, London, 1964, 17th edn., p. 42.
7. Ibid., pp. 42–189.
8. In Chapter 1 of B. Shiva Rao, (ed.), *The Framing of Indian Constitution: Select Documents*, New Delhi, 1968, p.109, there is one comment and suggestion on article 85 in the draft constitution, which ultimately became article 105 in the final constitutional text, by one Atul Chandra Gupta, an Advocate of Calcutta High Court, who took exception to a reference to the privileges of the House of Commons of the United Kingdom and instead suggested a reference to the law and order of the old Indian Central Legislature. The editorial comment on this reads: 'It is not clear why Gupta prefers a subordinate legislature to a sovereign legislature'.
9. A longer discussion on 19 May 1949, and a briefer one on 16 October 1949. See, *Constituent Assembly Debates: Official Report*, Books 3 and 5, New Delhi: Lok Sabha Secretariat, 1999, 3rd rpt., pp. 143–56 and 373–75 respectively.
10. Quotes from Book 3; ibid., pp. 148–9.
11. For the text of the 44th Amendment, see M.V. Pylee, *Constitutional Amendments in India*, New Delhi, 2003, pp. 208–22. Section 15 is the point in reference and relevance here.
12. See, M.P. Jain, *Indian Constitutional Law*, New Delhi, 2003, pp. 370–80. During the last fifty years, there have been many cases leading to confrontation between the courts and the State Legislatures. In *S. Balasubramanian* v. *State of Tamil Nadu*, the Madras High Court full bench was quite upset: 'The all powerful postures or claims of sky-high powers or suzerain claim of sovereignty or over-lordism are to be brushed aside, as nothing but fossil of the tyrannical and anarchical past and not in tune with the basic and

fundamental principle of rule of law, the bedrock of the Constitution or the democratic ideals which are the avowed object of the Republic ushered in by the Constitution of India. The contentions [of the Speaker] to the contrary have no basis or recognition of law and do not have the merit of acceptance by the courts in this country.' Jain, p. 378.

13. *Keshavram Reddy* v. *Nafisul Hasan and the State of U.P.*, All India Reporter [AIR], 1954, Supreme Court Section, p. 636. Also, Jain, op. cit., p. 118.
14. *M.S.M. Sharma* v. *Sri Krishna Sinha*, AIR, 1959, Supreme Court Section, p. 396. The petitioner also argued that the proceedings before the Committee on Privileges violated his Fundamental Right under Article 21 as well. But the Court ruled that the 'rules of procedures' made by the legislature fulfilled the requirement of 'procedure established by law' as in Article 21 (unless someone was deprived of his personal liberty not in accordance with law but for capricious or *mala fide* reasons). Jain, op. cit., pp. 118–19.
15. Special Petition No. 1 of 1964 by the President of India to the Supreme Court. The judgement accessed from Supreme Court's website: www.supremecourtofindia.nic.in.
16. Ibid., p. 101.
17. Ibid., p. 241.
18. H.M. Seervai, *Constitutional Law of India: A Political Commentary*, vol. 2, 4th edn. (Bombay: 1993), pp. 2188–9. M.P. Jain lists two healthy aspects of the Supreme Court's advisory opinion: (a) 'First and foremost it seeks to maintain judicial integrity and independence, for if a House were to claim a right to question the conduct of a judge, then judicial independence would be seriously compromised. . . .; (b) 'In the second place, the Court seeks to concede to the House quite a large power to commit for its contempt or breach of its privileges for, even though the judiciary can scrutinize legislative committal for its contempt, in actual practice, this would not amount to much as the courts could interfere with the legislative order only in very extreme situation.' Incidentally, the Allahabad High Court in this case had rejected the argument that the facts found by the Assembly against the petitioner did not amount to contempt of the Assembly. The petitioner's argument that his committal by the Assembly was *mala fide* and violated Article 21 was also rejected. Jain, op. cit., pp. 125–7.
19. J.N. Pandey, *Constitutional Law of India,* 40th edn., Allahabad, 2003, p. 544. Incidentally, the controversy was ultimately defused when the Governor prorogued the Council on the advice of the Chief Minister on 30 March 1984.
20. A.G. Noorani, *Constitutional Questions in India: The President, Parliament and the States,* New Delhi, 2000, p. 161. Incidentally, there is a slight discrepancy in the narratives of the *Eenadu* case in Pandey and in Noorani. The latter says that Chief Minister N.T. Rama Rao recommended to the Governor to adjourn the session of the errant Council whereas the former

says he advised Presidential reference of the matter to the Supreme Court of India.

21. *Economic and Political Weekly*, vol. XXXIX, no. 13, 27 March–2 April 2004, p. 1381.
22. *P.V. Narashimha Rao* v. *State/CBI*, AIR 1998, Supreme Court, p. 2120. Photocopy courtesy Indian Institute of Public Administration, New Delhi, circulated on the occasion of a national seminar on 'MPs and MLAs as Public Servants: Privileges and Obligations' on 20 June 1998. The jurisprudence of the Supreme Court of India is puzzling in this case, especially in view of the absence of protection of parliamentary immunities in bribery cases in case laws in Canada and Australia, the two Commonwealth Parliaments directly comparable with India in view of their common constitutional legacies of parliamentary federalism. The Supreme Court takes note of the positions in these countries, as also in the American Congress where case law is no different but, in a literal legalistic vein, bases its judgement on the archaic British custom that cannot be rationally justified in liberal democratic theory or law. See, ibid., pp. 64–71.
23. 'Questions regarding the permissible limits of legislative privileges, the role of the courts in this area, the relation between legislative privileges and fundamental rights have been arising from time to time creating unnecessary tensions between the courts and the legislatures. The problem needs to be solved so that the court-legislature tensions which result in ugly incidents from time to time may be avoided.' M.P. Jain, op. cit., p. 370. If an exhaustive codification is too complex a matter, an amendment to Article 105 and 194, Jain argues, is called for to make legislative privileges subordinate to Fundamental Rights and judicial review.
24. *Asian News Digest*, New Delhi, vol. IV, 2003, pp. 3252–317. Also see, T.S. Subramanian, 'The Issue of Privilege', *Frontline*, 23 May 2003, pp. 34–6.
25. The spirit of 'We, the people' came alive in the 44th Constitutional Amendment (1979) which proposed in its Statement of Objectives and Reasons: 'Certain changes in the Constitution which would have the effect of impairing its secular and democratic character, abridging or taking away fundamental rights, prejudicing or impeding free and fair elections on the basis of adult suffrage, and compromising the independence of judiciary, can be made only if they are approved by the people of India by a majority of votes of a referendum in which at least fifty-one per cent of the electorate participate.' Though the device of 'referendum' was dropped in the final Amendment Act, it does speak for the thrust of popular sovereignty in our constitutionalism. See, M.V. Pylee, op. cit., p. 206 for background.
26. The Royal Commission on Standards of Conduct of Public Life [chair: Lord Salmon] observed that 'neither the statutory nor the common law applies to the bribery or attempted bribery of a Member of Parliament in respect of his parliamentary activities but corrupt transactions involving a

Member of Parliament of matters that had nothing to do with his parliamentary activities would be caught by the ordinary criminal law' [p. 98, paras 307 and 308]. The Commission recommended the bringing of such malpractices under common criminal law as Parliament's own powers of investigation and punishment were not equal to the task in view of the more well-developed common criminal law system of the state. See the judgement of the Supreme Court of India in *P.V. Narashimha Rao* v. *State [CBI/SPE]*, 1998, p. 64. Photocopy courtesy IIPA circulated on the occasion of the national seminar in New Delhi on 20 June 1998.

27. Dolly Arora (ed.), *Democracy and competing Claims: Should Privileges be Privileged over Rights?* [Proceedings of the Roundtable held on 19 November 2003], New Delhi: 2004. Kuldeep Nayyar in the panel subsequently made a point which may be of relevance in this context: '*The Hindu* has been run differently. It belongs to a family [Tamil Brahmans with left leanings] but the family members who run it are really professionals. . . . It runs in their blood. I would say they are the outstanding journalists of this country. . . . Very few papers like that are left now. But such papers do not make shopping profits like, *The Times of India* [which was also once a truly outstanding daily in its professionalism and journalistic standards], pp. 27–8.
28. Ibid., pp. 20–3. This issue becomes all the more relevant in the context of how the privileges have been used and abused. 'It needs to be appreciated,' writes M.P. Jain, 'that a legislature exercises its privileges against the same people who have elected it . . . legislatures use their privileges not for protection against the executive but to stifle criticism by the people. To a great extent, the claim of privilege by a democratically elected legislature borders on being undemocratic and anti-people. At times, the majority party in a House uses the issue of privileges as a political weapon to beat the minority.' M.P. Jain, op. cit., p. 380.
29. Dolly Arora, op. cit., p. 22.

14

Indian Judiciary and Local Governments

GEORGE MATHEW

INTRODUCTION

The Indian Independence movement had villages and their self-governing system at the top of its development agenda. But when the Constitution of independent India was written, the panchayats (village councils), and the municipalities did not get a place in its main body; instead, it got only a reference in the Directive Principles of State Policy (Article 40).[1] As the directive principles of state policy are not justiciable, the state governments did not take the rural (panchayats) and the urban (municipalities) bodies seriously. Thus the Indian State was functioning as a federation only at two levels—union and states. Over the years it was felt that without taking the local communities seriously and devolving powers to them, neither their governance nor their development could reach the desirable levels. Thus, when the Parliament passed the 73rd and 74th Amendments to the Constitution in 1992, giving powers of far-reaching significance to the panchayats and municipalities, it was to enable them to function as institutions of self-government. These amendments ushered in a new era, wherein the local government institutions of governance were recognized as instruments of economic and social development (Article 243G). These two amendments also took care of their composition, powers, functions, tenure, elections, finances and so on and ensured structural uniformity for local government institutions all over the country.

Within a year of the historic 73rd and 74th Amendments becoming part of the Constitution of India (Parts IX and IX A), all the states passed their own acts in conformity with the amended constitutional provisions. More than ten years have passed since the union government and the states committed to strengthen the local government institutions, but what is the ground reality today? The sad story is that the neither the provisions of the Constitution nor the panchayat acts legislated by the states, have been implemented in letter and spirit. Several state governments have been hesitant in giving the panchayats and the municipalities the due share of powers assigned to them in the Constitution. Without subscribing to a conspiracy theory, it appears that many vested interests (the contractors, the bureaucrats and politicians), feel threatened and humbled with the new local governments. As a consequence, a lot of frustration has grown among the people in general as well as among the citizens concerned and civil society organizations.

In this context, what is the last resort for setting things rights? Certainly, it has been the judiciary. Although the judiciary has been perceived as the saviour of these institutions and people have looked up to it to uphold the constitutional rights and powers guaranteed to local governments, what has been the experience in the last few years? Has the role played by the judiciary created the required norms (or prohibitions), so that could we say today with some degree of certainty, that such violations as have taken place in the functioning of these democratic institutions in the past, would not take place in the future? This paper examines these questions, focusing on the critical role of the judiciary in interpreting the provisions of the Constitution with regard to the panchayats and the municipalities. In view of the large scope of the subject matter, the paper limits itself to reviewing only a few sample cases of judicial intervention for an assessment, if these interventions have been able to defeat the nefarious designs of the adversaries of local government. The paper also examines cases where the judiciary has seemingly failed to rise to the expectations of the Constitution-makers and the ordinary people in the villages and towns of India.

JUDICIAL INTERVENTIONS BEFORE THE 73RD AND 74TH AMENDMENT ACTS

Even before the passing of the 73rd and 74th Constitution Amendment Acts, the Indian judiciary had on many occasions upheld the vital role of the local government institutions in the democratic governance of the country.

In the now famous judgement of *Anugrah Narain Singh* v. *State of UP*,[2] which was delivered in 1992, the Allahabad High Court underlined the crtitical role of local government institutions. The Court held that 'local self government was a basic feature of the Indian Constitution and that citizens are entitled as of right, to have elected representatives only, to administer them and any existence of or exercise of arbitrary power by the government was unconstitutional'. In this case, two main issues were brought before the Court:

a. Is it not unconstitutional for the state government to supersede local bodies having elected representatives and replace them with officials as functionaries? and
b. Does the Constitution of India leave local self governments at the mercy of the states which may switch them off whenever they wish?

The Court's response was positive for the local bodies when it held: 'Local self government was meant to go on progressively with greater participation of the people whether in rural or in urban areas.'[3] The Constitution, the Court emphasized, referred to the existence of local government and identified what local government was. 'The existence of local government has been part of the skeleton on which democracy is to be based under the Constitution. The Constitution goes further by explaining that local government would in fact be *local self government*. The entry 5 of the 7th Schedule of the Constitution enumerating the subjects for the state jurisdiction is self-explanatory. The interpretation of this entry is that there shall be a local government, but it will be constituted as local self-government. This means that there will be government of the people, by the people and for the people, but not a corporate entity run by those who are not the people.'[4] Reiterating the importance of local governments, the Court further noted: 'Local self-government is the arches upon which the parliamentary democracy in this nation rests and upon it a dome with state legislatures and federal Parliament. The structure will collapse without the arches. *Even the legislature ought not to and cannot legislate to kill local self-government*; that it may is another matter.'[5] The Court also said that local self-government through the elected bodies was the correct breeding ground for political experience and that local self-governments must function in continuity and should not be interrupted by replacing them with civil servants.

In deciding the legality of the legislative action by which civic elections to the local bodies remain suspended year by year, the High

Court held that the power to negate local-self government was not available to any state legislature, or for that matter even to the federal government. Entry 5 of state list of the Constitution of India did not lend itself to an interpretation that the law could retard local government. The Court also noted that the history of local self-government did not support the action of the state superseding local bodies and making them function through the agency of civil servants. The consequences of substituting elected representatives by bureaucrats would be, the Court warned, that vested interests would tend to dominate the domain of local self government.

The Allahabad High Court judgement was a benchmark verdict. It was referred to in an important judgement of the Karnataka High Court in *R. Venkategowda* v. *State of Karnataka.*[6] In this case, the petitioners challenged the state government of Karnataka for not holding elections to the Zilla Parishads and, instead, appointing Administrators in place of democratically-elected representatives. The Karnataka High Court referred to the Allahabad High Court judgement mentioned earlier[7] and observed that the process which degrades local self government is hostile to the text of the Constitution, and is arbitrary to the core; it undermines parliamentary government which cannot exist except for its roots in local self-government. The Court highlighted the fact that the Karnataka Zilla Parishads, Taluk Panchayat Samitis, Mandal Panchayats and Nyaya Panchayats Act 1983 was a comprehensive Act; that it assigned enormous powers and functions to the democratically-structured Zilla Parishads; and that it ensured genuine devolution of powers to local bodies for the purpose of securing the real Panchayati Raj System of Mahatma Gandhi's dream. The Court also referred to Article 40 of the Constitution to emphasize the point that the people had to have local self-government in the real sense of the term through their elected representatives.

The Court noted the significance of Section 272 of the Karnataka Act which laid down that: (a) the administration of every Zilla Parishad, constituted under the said Act, shall always be vested in the representatives of the people duly elected in accordance with the provisions of the Act; (b) except in a case where the general elections to any Zilla Parishad is stayed by an order of the Court, or in a case where all or more than two-thirds members have resigned, the administration of a Zilla Parishad could be placed in the hands of a civil servant; (c) the elections to Zilla Parishads must be held before the expiry of the term of office of the elected members, and, if for some reasons the elections could not be held, that the term of existing members could be extended by six months, but elections must be held within that time; and (d) the Act has ensured the citizens a local self-government of the people, by the people, and for the people, and not a local government run by a civil servant (as Administrator) appointed by the government. The Court ordered the state government to take all the necessary steps to hold and complete elections on or before 31 December 1992, so that elected representatives could take charge from the Administrators on or before that date.

The Allahabad and Karnataka High Court judgements before the 73rd and 74th Constitution Amendments should have prompted a regime of regular elections to the local bodies but this did not happen.

JUDICIAL INTERVENTIONS—LOCAL GOVERNMENT ELECTIONS

By April 1994, all state governments had passed conformity acts and therefore were obliged to hold elections immediately in those states where elected panchayats and municipalities did not exist. But under one pretext or the other, not holding elections or postponing them became the order of the day. In some states, stay orders from the courts were obtained against holding elections by vested interests. They could do so by challenging one clause or the other in the state panchayat acts or even questioning certain provisions of Article 243 of the Constitution. But it must be said to the credit of the Indian Judiciary that whenever the citizens concerned or civil society organizations, took such issues to the courts, the courts were generally firm in their judicial interpretation of Article 243E which specified, among other things, the tenure and election procedures and processes of panchayats.[8] The view that constitutional provisions with regard to the holding of local government elections were unambiguous and mandatory in nature were vindicated by several pronouncements of the High Courts and the Supreme Court. Some of the most significant judgements delivered in this regard deserve our attention.

Karnataka

To begin with, it may be noted that in spite of the powerful judgement of the Karnataka High Court cited earlier, holding elections on time had not become a norm in Karnataka. Under one pretext or the other, panchayat elections were postponed in the state.

The Karnataka High Court in a judgement delivered in 1999 in response to two writ petitions[9] held that Article 243G of the Constitution was mandatory and not directory. In this case, the petitioners had prayed to the High Court to issue a writ to the Karnataka State Election Commission to hold elections to the gram panchayats in the state so that newly-elected body in each panchayat was constituted well within the time frame as mandated under Article 243E of the Constitution irrespective of the Karnataka Panchayat Raj Amendment Ordinance No.1 of 1999 (which amended the Karnataka Panchayat Raj Act 1993). The Court, in delivering the judgement in this case, laid down some very important principles:

1. By the 73rd Amendment the state legislatures were deprived of their powers in respect of matters for which the provisions have been made in Part IX of the Constitution. Thus the state government has to follow Part IX of the Constitution without compromises.
2. Article 243 E limits duration of the panchayats to five years. Dissolution is therefore permissible but not an extension of the term.
3. Elections to fresh panchayats have to be completed before the expiry of the duration of the outgoing panchayat and in case of dissolution before the expiry of six months from the date of its dissolution.
4. The state governments should follow the Supreme Court verdict of August 1997 in which it has held: 'The concerned states cannot be permitted to withhold elections of panchayats except in cases of genuine supervening difficulties to hold such elections in the state like flood, earthquake, etc. Thus elections to panchayats have to be held before the expiry of tenure of five years in terms of Article 243E of the Constitution.'
5. When the Election Commission has taken all preparatory steps and the process of election has already been put in motion, the election cannot be postponed.
6. If an enactment of a state legislature results in defeating the constitutional mandate (as for example Article 243E which stipulates maximum period given to elected panchayats), the same is liable to be brushed aside and struck down.
7. Though the state legislature has competence to amend the provisions of the Panchayati Raj Act, but if the exercise of such competence results in nullifying the mandate of the Constitution, specially when the process of election has begun, it is not an appropriate exercise of competence or powers. If there is a conflict between

the mandatory provisions of the Constitution and the right of state legislature to enact laws which come under its legislative competence, the provisions of the Constitution would take precedence.

The High Court in this case held that the Karnataka State Election Commission should continue with the process of elections and hold the gram panchayat elections forthwith, notwithstanding the Karnataka Panchayat Raj Amendment Ordinance 1999 (which aimed at restricting the territorial jurisdiction of the Panchayats and which would have resulted in delaying the panchayat elections).

This was not the last case regarding the postponement of panchayat elections in Karnataka. Today the state government and the state election commission are embroiled in a case in the High Court, regarding the postponement of elections to Taluk Samitis and Zilla Panchayats. The petitioners in this case have contested the legality of the Karnataka Panchayat Raj (Reservation of Seats in Taluka and Zilla Panchayats by rotation), Rules 1998 which, the petitioners contend, defeat the very purpose and object of rotation. The petitioners have also challenged government notifications relating to the allotment of reserved category seats to different constituencies and the delimitation of areas for Taluk and Zilla Panchayats.[10]

Andhra Pradesh

The story of postponing panchayat elections in Andhra Pradesh is no different than the one in Karnataka. The Andhra government kept postponing the elections to the two tiers of panchayats at the Zilla and Mandal levels, and placed them under Administrators through an Ordinance. The reason for doing this was that the Andhra Pradesh Assembly had requested the centre to amend Article 243(C),[11] and until then the state would not hold elections. Even though the Ordinance had lapsed (and the 87th Constitution Amendment introduced in Parliament to amend Article 243(C) was not even taken up for discussion), the elections were nowhere in sight.

Several writ petitions were filed against the government in this matter. The Andhra Pradesh High Court[12] disposing the writ petitions directed that elections must be completed by 1 May 2000. The state government, however, did not comply with the order and went in appeal against the order to the Supreme Court. The Supreme Court upheld the order of the High Court and directed that the elections to Zilla and Mandal Parishads must be held by 31 March 2001.[13]

What could the Andhra Pradesh government do when the Supreme Court wanted the elections to be completed in a few months' time? The state went on appeal on 17 February 2001, pleading its inability to hold elections and praying for postponement. The state tried to convince the Court that an extension of time for conducting the elections was required in the light of limited time frame stipulated by the High Court within which it was difficult to identify backward class voters, according to Article 243(d) of the Constitution.[14] In the counter arguments, the Court was told that the state government was postponing the elections due in March 2000, on one pretext or the other and that Administrators (District Collectors) were discharging the functions of Zilla Parishads. The Court held that the attempt to defeat the electoral process and allow officials appointed by the political party in power to carry on the administration, was unacceptable. The Supreme Court finally ordered that elections be completed by 31 July 2001.

Bihar

Bihar was yet another state where no elections were held for Gram Panchayats, Block/Panchayat Samitis and Zilla Parishads since 1978. Several Public Interest Litigations (PIL) were filed in the High Court in Patna seeking the Court's intervention.[15] When the case came to the Supreme Court, the apex Court observed that 73rd Amendment of the Constitution was made with the stated object of continuity of panchayat bodies regulating their tenure. Article 243H of the Constitution envisages that the tenure of the panchayat shall be five years from the date appointed for its first meeting and shall continue no longer than that. It further noted that Article 243B provides that the election of the panchayat shall be held before the expiry of the said tenure of five years or within six months of its dissolution as the case may be. In order to ensure holding of elections, Article 243E also provides that laws relating to panchayats in the state inconsistent with the 73rd Amendment, shall continue in force only for a year from the commencement of the amendment.

The Supreme Court in this case held:

> It is necessary to emphasize that various clauses of Article 243 are to be followed in letter and spirit. The concerned state cannot be permitted to withhold elections of panchayats except in case of genuine supervening difficulties, e.g. unforeseen natural calamities in the state like flood, earthquake, etc., or extremely urgent situations prevailing in the state for which elections of the panchayats cannot be held within the time frame. It will be unfortunate if the concerned states remain

insensitive to the Constitutional mandate of holding election of panchayats in time and by unjustified inaction allow old bodies to continue in office of the panchayats. . . .[16]

Karnataka, Andhra Pradesh, and Bihar are not the only states that have defaulted in holding panchayat elections on time. It may be recalled here that panchayat elections were held only after judicial interventions in Orissa and Uttar Pradesh as well.[17] It is indeed a sad comment on the working our political system, that the Judiciary has to intervene to check the negligence of state governments in performing their constitutional responsibility of holding elections to local bodies.

JUDICIAL INTERVENTIONS – LOCAL GOVERNMENT JURISDICTION AND FUNCTIONS

In the last ten years or so, public interest litigations have been filed in the High Courts and Supreme Court of India by civil society organizations and citizens concerned, in respect to many areas relating to the jurisdiction and functioning of local governments. They include the duration of office, qualifications and disqualifications of members, term of office of chairperson, financial domain of panchayats, reservation for Other Backward Castes (OBC), personnel and service matters of employees, etc. According to a study, there are about 700 Court judgements regarding panchayats delivered by various High Courts and the Supreme Court from 1993 to 2004.[18]

A major concern has been the lack of understanding on the part of officials about the meaning and implications of Part IX of the Constitution. The courts had to come to the rescue of local governments and its elected members against the onslaught of senior civil servants. The following cases have a lot to tell about how officialdom looks at the panchayats and municipalities and the role played by the judiciary to protect the constitutional mandate given to these institutions of local self-government.

Punjab

Gurcharan Singh applied for transfer of a plot of land situated in village Ghai under Ferozepur tahsil, on the ground that he was in continuous possession of the land since *kharif* 1989. The Tahsildar (Sales), Ferozepur, recommended the case and was given appoval by the Ferozepur Sales Commissioner on 29 March 1994. The Panchayat Samiti of

Ferozepur filed an appeal in the court of the Sales Commissioner against the transaction. The appeal was turned down. The matter then moved to the Chief Sales Commissioner, Ferozepur. The appellate authority found that Singh had taken the land on lease from the Panchayat Samiti for Rs. 30,000 in 1989–90. Thereafter, he filed an application for allotment of the land, treating it to be in the ownership of the state as a 'package deal property' (land transferred by the central government to the state government on payment of a price). He also found that the land belonged to the District Board and when the District Board was abolished, it was transferred to the Panchayat Samiti. The appellate authority held that the land did not belong to the state of Punjab and that the transfer made in favour of Singh was fraudulent as well as bad in law. Singh appealed before the Ferozepur Commissioner against the decision of the appellate authority and was successful in getting his plea accepted. The Panchayat Samiti filed a writ petition before the Punjab and Haryana High Court. The High Court held that the land was not a package deal property and belonged to the Panchayat Samiti. Accordingly, the order of the Commissioner was set aside. However, the High Court order was challenged in the Supreme Court.

The Supreme Court reaffirmed the findings of the High Court regarding the ownership of the disputed land. Striking down the transfer of land by the government and restoring the ownership to the Panchayat Samiti, the Court ordered the state government to refund the amount deposited by the appellant as part of the sales price within a period of three months.[19]

Tamil Nadu

In 1997, the District Collector assigned two hectares of land in the jurisdiction of the Vengaivasal village panchayat to 71 employees of the Raj Bhavan without consulting or getting permission of the panchayat. The panchayat failed to convince the Collector that what he had done was against the Constitution and the state act. The Collector went ahead and directed the panchayat 'to pass a resolution in accordance with his request to transfer the land to the designated allottees'. When the Collector proceeded to enforce his order, the panchayat filed a writ petition in the Madras High Court. The government and the Collector did not even file a counter affidavit. Despite this, the single judge ruled in favour of the Collector's action. The judge held that the Collector was required only to hold consultations with the panchayats, and was not obliged to obtain the consent of the panchayat.

The ruling was challenged by the panchayat. A division bench reversed the order of the single judge. The judgement stated:

> In the post-independence period, realizing the fact that social, political and economic development of rural areas depends on the successful and effective working of local self-government, Gandhiji had aptly remarked that the democracy cannot be worked by 20 men sitting at the Centre. It has to be worked from below by the people of every village. . . . In our considered opinion, the panchayat cannot be lightly sidelined by the government by passing the appropriation order without the consent of the panchayat.

It was reported that the counsel for the government was not even able to point out to any provision of law under which the Collector's order was issued.[20]

Uttar Pradesh

Panchayats are also instruments to create a level playing field for all regardless of caste, religion, or social and economic hierarchy. The courts play a vital role when it doesn't work that way. The experience of a dalit woman sarpanch in her village in UP state is revealing. She had to face retribution by the defeated candidates belonging to the upper caste. She lodged a first information report (FIR) with the police station stating that the miscreants looted her house and used abusive language for her. The case was filed in the court. The high Court refused to quash the FIR and observed:

> The caste system in India, based on the feudal occupational division of labour in the past, is today totally outmoded and is a great hindrance to the nation's progress . . . no doubt, the word 'Chamar' is a word denoting a certain caste, but the word is also used in a derogatory sense for persons who are regarded as inferior by the so-called upper caste, and, therefore it should not be used by the members of the so-called upper castes or OBCs.[21]

NEED TO REVIEW SOME COURT JUDGEMENTS

While the silver lining on the otherwise dark horizon has been the positive intervention by the judiciary upholding the constitutional status of the panchayats and municipalities and protecting the jurisdiction of local institutions from the onslaughts of 'babudom', there have been a few setbacks from judicial action. One such case which has attracted nationwide attention recently is the Supreme Court judgement upholding the validity of the 'two child norm' for contesting elections to the panchayats imposed by some states. The 'two child norm' means that those having more than two children cannot contest the elections, and that if a third child is born to an incumbent member, the member must resign from office. In *Javed and Others* v. *State of Haryana* (2003),[22] the Supreme Court ruled that even if a member had given away his third or fourth child for adoption, the said member could not claim the benefit of being not covered under the law. Needless to say, this norm is undemocratic, and could result in curtailing the democratic right to contest elections for a large number of people. Moreover, there is no such stipulation for contesting elections to the Parliament and state legislatures.

Another case is that of *Perumatty Panchayat* v. *Coca Cola Factory* in Plachimada, Kerala. The Perumatty Panchayat filed a case in the Kerala High Court against the Hindustan Coca Cola Beverages (P) Ltd., for drawing scarce underground water excessively resulting in the groundwater level going down in the area. The Coca Cola Factory has caused enormous water shortage and pollution, thus causing misery to the local people by its sludge disposal and commercial use of the water. When the panchayat filed a case against the company, the single Judge of the High Court, in a judgement delivered on 16 December 2003, held that the company's extraction for ground water was illegal. The Judge also directed the company to stop over-exploiting the ground water resources of the village. 'Ground water', the Judge said, 'is a public property held in trust by the government' which had no right to allow a private party to over-exploit the resources to the detriment of the people. Although the company could not be permitted to draw ground water like any other landowner, 'it has no right to claim a huge share of it'. The single bench ruled that the company could be allowed to use only the quantity of ground water equal to the amount 'normally used for irrigating crops in a 34 acre plot.'[23]

But on 7 April 2005, the Division Bench of the Kerala High Court rejected the above judgement. The Division Bench said:

> We do no find justification for upholding the finding of the learned judge that extraction of ground water is illegal. It is definitely not something like digging out a treasure-trove. We cannot endorse the finding that the company has no legal right to extract this 'wealth'. If such restriction is to apply to a legal person, it may have to apply to a natural person as well. Abstract principles cannot be the basis for the Court to deny basic rights, unless they are curbed by valid legislation.[24]

The Court also said that even reference to the mandatory function of a panchayat, i.e. the maintenance of traditional drinking water resources, as envisaged in the Panchayati Raj Act, could not prevent the owner of a well from extracting water as he wished. 'The Panchayat has no ownership,' said the Court order, 'about such private water sources, in effect denying the proprietary rights of the occupier'.

The implications of the judgement were serious. First, it meant that a person owning just a square foot of land (just sufficient to sink a bore well) could extract, as owner of what is underneath the land, any amount of water irrespective of the concerns of the community. Second, the Court's declaration that as a 'legal person' the multinational corporation has all the rights of a 'natural person' was frightening.[25] The judgement also raised the basic question about the right of the local government to issue, suspend or cancel licences for factories and commercial establishments working within its jurisdiction.

Another judgement of the Kerala High Court on 1 June 2005, directed the Perumatty Panchayat to renew the factory's licence within one week. It said that if a formal licence was not issued by the panchayat within the time prescribed, it should be deemed that the company possessed the renewed licence and that the company would have the right to carry on its functions for a period of two years with effect from 10 June 2005. Further, the Court rejected the panchayat's plea to keep this order in abeyance so as to enable it to file an appeal before the Supreme Court. It also flayed the panchayat for not taking action on Coca Cola's application for the renewal of licence pending before it for more than a year for 'extraneous' reasons. The panchayat complied with the orders of the High Court but, as R. Krishna Kumar reports, issued Coca Cola a licence valid for three months, pending company's compliance of 13 conditions, including production of a fresh certificate under the Hazardous Wastes (Management and Handling) Rules, a licence under the panchayat laws for drawing, using, and supplying water (to the affected people) according to an earlier directive of the Supreme Court Monitoring Committee on Hazardous Wastes, and the submission of a detailed plan for the social security measures it was required to implement for the benefit of the affected villagers. The company rejected the three-month conditional licence describing it as 'arbitrary and in violation of High Court orders', claiming that the 13 conditions put forth by the panchayat were well outside its legal powers.[26]

Justice V.R. Krishna Iyer, former Supreme Court Judge and a legal luminary, reacted to the High Court judgement by issuing a public statement. He said:

> May be I am wrong or may be the concerned judges are in error. When the licence has been refused for Coa Cola by the local authority, which is necessary under the Municipal Law, the Court cannot hold that, in certain circumstances, the licence may be deemed to have been granted, thus nullifying the statute. The procedure of invoking the jurisdiction of the Court for getting an earlier decision modified smacks of 'bench shopping' by a powerful litigant. The circumstances of the case when fully disclosed may suggest a 'riddle wrapped in a mystery inside an enigma'.

Reasserting his great respect for the judiciary, Justice Iyer continued:

> But [non] criticism of judicial pronouncements when one considers them as aberrational, is a failure of a jurist's duty to the Constitution and the non-exercise of the fundamental right of freedom of expression. We are governed by the Constitution but it has been said that the Constitution, is what the judges say it is. This does not mean that the 'robed brethren' can go haywire, reduce the law to mere judicial *ipse dixits.* I suspect the wisdom and the constitutionality of the *Coca Cola* judgement pronounced by the Division Bench of the Kerala High Court.[27]

According to Justice Iyer, the jurisprudence as laid down by the Kerala Court requires a second look. The Perumatty village panchayat has appealed to the Supreme Court for revocation of the 7 April, High Court order. The panchayat in its appeal said that 'the rights of a gram panchayat to drinking water and for agricultural purposes in contrast to the right of a multinational company to extract water' has been made the main bone of contention.[28] The apex Court has issued notices to the Hindustan Coca Cola Company, the Kerala government, and the Kerala State Pollution Control Board for a hearing of the case. The panchayat has also filed a review petition in the Kerala High Court saying that apparently there are various errors of law in the order 'which need to be immediately reviewed and corrected'. It has further submitted that the Court had 'failed to notice that in the absence of licence, mandatorily required to be possessed by the company considering the health hazard, permitting the company to function would pose a serious threat to the residents of the area'.[29] The Supreme Court judgement in this case will have far-reaching implications all over the country in the working of the panchayats as well as their authority and powers to protect the interests of local residents and natural resources.

SIGNIFICANCE OF JUDICIAL INTERVENTIONS

It is clear that the judiciary has been playing a significant pro-active and progressive role in interpreting the provisions of the Constitution relating to local governments, notwithstanding the Coca Cola aberration. The citizens concerned and civil society groups have found the judiciary, the last pillar of hope for obtaining the constitutional entitlements and legal rights. Indeed, the judiciary can be seen as the saviour of the people in the villages and towns of India who perceive it as a bright ray of hope for achieving their democratic rights through the local government institutions. It is specially true when there is a great resistance, even after more than ten years of the passage of the historic 73rd and 74th Constitutional Amendment Acts, to granting constitutionally mandated powers and functions to local government by vested interests who perceive the strength of local institutions as a threat to their power and prestige. These vested interests are doing whatever they can to maintain the pre-1992 status quo.

The judicial interpretations of the constitutional provisions for Panchayati Raj Institutions have aided in the emergence of local government jurisprudence defining the rights of these institutions. And as judicial decisions of the higher judiciary are binding, and can be cited as precedence in latter cases based on similar facts, one can expect increasing standardization in the interpretation of constitutional provisions and state acts relating to local bodies. Judicial orders are also mandatory, and have to be followed by governments or other persons against whom the judgements have been passed (their violation can invite contempt proceedings), with the consequence that one can expect greater respect given to the jurisdictional boundaries of local bodies.

It is, however, unfortunate that local institutions, which are regarded as the alpha and omega of democracy, should be overrun by vested interests, at times in collaboration with state government bureaucrats and politicians. Despite court cases and judicial verdicts, the state of Jharkhand and the union territory of Pondicherry have yet to hold panchayat elections. How long, one may ask, will it take for the states to accept panchayat elections on par with the elections to State Assemblies and the Parliament? The Panchayati Raj Institutions are the third tier of the Indian federal system and deserve to be recognized as such.

While the judiciary has been helpful and generally positive in the interpretation of the constitutional provisions relating to Panchayati Raj institutions, there has been a genuine concern that the judicial process has become more and more time consuming and delays in deciding cases are common even for matters which require expeditious disposal. A writ petition filed in the Chhattisgarh High Court, in the nature of public interest litigation against the Chhattisgarh government, for passing an amendment in the Panchayati Raj Act making literacy a pre-requisite for contesting elections, has not yet been taken up for hearing even after the lapse of one year.[30] The petitioners had contended that the move of the state government was undemocratic and unconstitutional—the state has a large tribal population which is illiterate and the state's move would result in depriving them of their democratic right to contest elections. There are several other cases pending before the High Courts and the Supreme Court as well. An important case among them that deserves mention, is that of Members of Parliament Local Area Development Scheme which has a direct negative impact on the working of the local governments. According to one study, more than half a dozen petitions have been pending before the Supreme Court for years now.[31]

CONCLUSION

Although the 73rd and 74th Amendment Acts were revolutionary in giving wide powers of governance to the panchayats and municipalities and, for all practical purposes, envisaging them as the third stratum of governance in the country, these provisions remain by and large on paper, and have not resulted in any substantial devolution of powers to the panchayats. Even where some functions were devolved to these local institutions, the state governments did not give adequate funds and functionaries to implement them, making them virtually ineffective. Generally speaking, the state governments were found to be unsympathetic to the cause of local governments and, at times, tried to throttle them by withholding elections or postponing them indefinitely. In place of the elected representatives, government officials were appointed to carry on the business of local governments with the tacit support of the bureaucrats, the big landowners, the upper castes, the politicians, and other vested interests. The failure of the state governments to live up to the constitutional provisions relating to local governments and to implement even their own conformity legislations in full measure, invited multiple judicial interventions which, in most cases, kept alive the basic principles of the new generation of local institutions. As the guardian of the Constitution, the judiciary has time and again underlined the fundamental importance of these institutions in the grassroots governance of the country, and it will continue to oversee the sustained progress of these institutions in the interest of true democracy until such time that the state governments pull themselves up to recognize and acknowledge the real value and virtues of local governments.

It is needless to emphasize that Panchayati Raj Institutions are closer to the people; they alone can understand local problems and advocate for people's interests. Concerned citizens and civil society groups have been playing a crucial role in accessing justice for them by taking recourse to judicial interventions. While the courts have done their job to the best of their understanding of the local problems (notwithstanding the disappointing judgement in the *Coca Cola* case), the process of the justice delivery system has been extraordinary slow, much to the sorrow of the local people. There are many subject areas in local governance that would require judicial interpretation in the years to come, though there is an urgent need for the Supreme Court to clarify grey areas in Articles 243 and 243G (the meaning of 'Institutions of local self government'), for the proper implementation of the two constitutional amendments. The sooner the Court acts and crystallizes ambiguities associated with these two amendments, the better the prospects for the growth and development of Panchayati Raj Institutions.

NOTES

1. Article 40 of the Constitution states: 'The state should take steps to organize village panchayats and endow them with such power and authority as may be necessary to enable them to function as units of self government.'
2. AIR 1992 Allahabad 1962.
3. Ibid.
4. Ibid.
5. Ibid.
6. ILR 1992 Karnataka 1447.
7. AIR 1992 Allahabad 1962.
8. Article 243E states: (1) Every panchayat, unless sooner dissolved under any law for the time being in force, shall continue for five years from the date appointed for its first meeting and no longer. (2) No amendment of any law for the time being in force, shall have the effect of causing dissolution of a

panchayat at any level, which is functioning immediately before such amendment, till the expiration of its duration specified in clause (1). (3) An election to constitute a Panchayat shall be completed (a) before the expiry of its duration specified in clause (1); (b) before the expiration of a period of six months from the date of its dissolution. Provided that where the remainder of the period for which the dissolved Panchayat could have continued is less than six months, it shall not be necessary to hold any election under this clause for constituting the panchayat for such a period. (4) A panchayat constituted upon the dissolution of a panchayat before the expiration of its duration shall continue only for the remainder of the period for which the dissolved panchayat would have continued under clause (1) had it not been so dissolved.

9. AIR 1999 Karnataka 461.
10. Writ petitions, Karnataka High Court 2005.
11. Article 243C refers to the composition of panchayats.
    (1) Subject to the provision of this Part, the Legislature of a State may, by law, make provisions with respect to the composition of panchayats: Provided that the rates between the population of a territorial area of a panchayat at any level and the number of seats in such panchayat to be filled by election shall, so far as practicable, be the same throughout the state.
    (2) All the seats in a panchayat shall be fiiled by persons chosen by direct election from territorial constituencies in the panchayat area and, for this purpose, each panchayat area shall be divided into territorial constituencies in such manner that the ratio between the population of each constituency and the number of seats allotted to it shall, so far as practicable, be the same throughout the panchayat area.
    (3) The Legislature of a State may, by law, provide for the representation of (a) the Chairpersons of the panchayats at the village level, in the Panchayats and the intermediate level, or in the case of a state not having panchayats at the intermediate level, in panchayats at the district level; (b) the Chairpersons of the panchayats at the intermediate level, in the panchayats at the district level; (c) the members of the House of the People and the members of the Legislative Assembly of the State representing constituencies which comprise wholly or partly a Panchayat area at a level other than the villege level, in such panchayat; (d) the members of the Council of States and members of the Legislative Council of the State, where they are registered as electors with (i) a Panchayat area at the intermediate level, in panchayat at the intermediate level; (ii) a Panchayat area at the district level in Panchayat at the district level.
    (4) The Chairperson of a panchayat and other members of a panchayat whether or not chosen by direct election from territorial constituencies

in the panchayat area shall have the right to vote in the meeting of the panchayats.

(5) The Chairperson of (a) a panchayat at the village level shall be elected in such manner as the Legislature of a State may, by law, provide; and (b) a panchayat at the intermediate level or district level shall be elected by, and from amongst, the elected members thereof.

12. George Mathew, 'Panchayats Powerless in A.P.', *The Hindu*, New Delhi, 17 April 2001.
13. Ibid.
14. Article 234(d) of the Constitution gives powers to state legislatures for making reservation for Backward Class persons for the posts and seats of the panchayat bodies.
15. *RLEK* v. *Government of UP and others* (Writ Petition No. 719 of 1995).
16. Ibid.
17. Consultation paper on the Working of the Constitutional Provisions (Part IX), for Decentralization—Panchayats: 2001, Institute of Social Sciences, New Delhi.
18. *Judgements on Panchayati Raj*, Rural Litigation and Entitlement Kendra, Dehradun.
19. AIR 2004 Supreme Court 2438, reported in *Panchayati Raj Update*, May 2005.
20. L.C. Jain, 'Panchayats make collectors obey the law', *Asian Age*, 20 June 2005.
21. *Panchayat Raj Update*, March 2001.
22. *Panchayat Raj Update* [2003 (8) SCC], August 2003.
23. For details of this case and related issues, see, *Hindustan Coca Cola Beverages (P) Ltd.* v. *Perumatty Grama Panchayat* judgement dated 7 April 2005; P.N. Venugopal and M. Suchitra, 'Rain or no rain, Water for Coke', 10 May 2005; Mukundan C. Menon, 'Tale of Two Verdicts on Water', *Indian Currents*, 12 June 2005; K. Ravi Raman, 'Corporate Violence, Legal Nuances and Political Ecology', *Economic and Political Weekly*, 18–24 June 2005, p. 2481.
24. High Court of Kerala judgement dated 7 April 2005.
25. P.N. Venugopal & M. Suchitra, 'Rain or no rain, Water for Coke', Plachimada Solidarity Committee, Trivandrum, 10 May 2005.
26. See, R. Krishnakumar, 'Coa-Cola's battle', *Frontline*, 15 July 2005, p. 133.
27. 'Krishna Iyer criticizes ruling on Coke Plant', *The Hindu*, New Delhi, 4 June 2005, p. 13.
28. P.N. Venugopal & M. Suchitra, op. cit.
29. 'Panchayat files review plea on coke plant', Press Trust of India, 14 June 2005.
30. *Institute of Social Sciences* v. *State of Chhattisgarh* writ petition 2004.
31. Era Sezhiyan, 'MPLADS: Concept, Confusion, Contradictions', Institute of Social Sciences, New Delhi, 2005, p. 107.

PART V

Judiciary and Central Executive

15

Indian Superior Judiciary: The Selection and Impeachment of Judges

K.G. KANNABIRAN

How should we appoint our judges and how should they be removed from office? It is widely believed that the answer to these twin questions is crucial for assessing the character of the superior judiciary in the country. People in general know less about courts, the judges who are appointed to this hierarchical structure called the justice system, the way the system operates or the method or content of judges' functions, than they know about the working of the Legislative Assemblies, or the Parliament and the members elected to those bodies.

After the recognition of the right to vote as a fundamental right we have come to know more about our representatives and also about the aspirants. This transparency has enlarged the content of our democracy. Where the judiciary is concerned, at the lower level, up to the level of district judges, there is some understanding of their uses to the people and generally about their jurisdiction to try offenders. As we go up the hierarchy of courts, mystery shrouds appointments, the powers of the appointees and their activity. Yet, it is the high court and the Supreme Court that are always debated about during periods of crisis—internal or external—and when the executive puts the fundamental freedoms in jeopardy. During such periods we are told that the justice system, as delineated in our Constitution, is the index of democratic governance.

*Published with some editorial changes from the *Economic and Political Weekly*, 4 December 2004, with the permission of the author.

After we attained independence we were left with an administration trained to administer colonial interests and a judiciary trained to protect colonial rule against popular struggles with special laws to contain popular protests and revolts. The structure of the high courts and the Supreme Court are testimony to this legacy. In fact, as late as 1964 the Supreme Court opined that nothing changed in terms of structures after the Constitution came into force on 26 January 1950. No new structures were created to herald the change, though we did make some changes with reference to the judiciary. Although we did not adopt the theory of separation of powers fully, the view was that we should have an independent judiciary to prevent arbitrary law-making by the legislature and arbitrary exercise of power in governance. The superior judiciary was designed to be the 'sentinel on the qui vive' and protect the rights of the citizens guaranteed in Part III of the Constitution. In practice, however, the superior judiciary was partial to the protection of property rights and biased against parliament's imposition of restraints on the personal liberty of the people. Be that as it may, it was during the periods when the executive introduced laws to abridge property rights on the one hand and imposed restraints on liberty on the other that a major debate took place on the independence of judiciary.[1]

What was achieved was the independence of the judiciary sans the vision required, leading to an erosion of purpose and philosophy in the judiciary. The problem is not one of executive interference in the appointment process but the choice of persons who have intellectual capabilities to understand the constitutional scheme and its goals, and an enthusiasm to mould the law, and interpret it in a manner that would secure the objectives set out in the Preamble to the Constitution, evolving in the process a jurisprudence that would be able to resolve our own constitutional dilemmas. Courts were never committed to maintain the status quo. And Indira Gandhi was not the first leader of a government to introduce the concept of committed judiciary.

LACK OF VISION

Judges in an institution devoid of vision are committed to maintaining the status quo. A state of affairs has more or less come to stay, whereby the court staffing pattern ensures that it shall play no role in the country's affairs in terms of the Constitution. It is this commitment to one's own career that has been continuously eroding the value system in our society. The aberration of the Best Bakery trial,[2] and the use of the administration of justice as a doormat as the Tamil Nadu Chief Minister has done, are all manifestations of this erosion. Every retiring Chief Justice cries about the enveloping corruption in the judiciary. And yet while in tenure, not only does he not do anything, he does not even suggest steps to cleanse the Augean stables. The profession with its value neutral stance, and the consequent tunnel vision, enables its members to enjoy the independence it is assured without the attendant responsibilities of practicing the profession diligently. Not being saddled with institutional responsibilities or a professional vision committed to constitutional morality, the profession continues to be the only institution which has the licence to be amoral in practising its calling. In such situations, the aggrandizement by professional leaders and corruption in the decision-making process, appear to be inevitable. Personal corruption interferes with the decision-making processs; thus the much talked-about independence gets eroded much faster than it is realized. And that is why the method and manner of staffing the judiciary at every level assumes importance.

JUDICIAL APPOINTMENTS

Article 124(2) of the Constitution deals with the appointment of judges of the Supreme Court, and Article 217(1) deals with the appointment of judges to the High Courts. And all that is said is that the President shall appoint these judges. The judges of the Supreme Court are to be appointed after consultation with such of the judges of the Supreme Court and the judges of the High Courts as the President may deem necessary. For an appointment of a judge other than the Chief Justice, the Chief Justice of India must be consulted. A judge to the High Court shall be appointed after consultation with the Chief Justice of India, the Governor of the state and, in case of the appointment of a judge other than the Chief Justice, the Chief Justice of the state High Court. Nowhere is the required intellectual calibre or the intellectual standing necessary for appointment stipulated for making the recommendation. The Constituent Assembly debates also do not mention anywhere the qualities and capabilities required for an advocate to be appointed as a judge. A judge either to the High Court or the Supreme Court, undoubtedly a constitutional appointment, has enormous powers that can be uncritically exercised, while the interpretive authority entrusted to them has destructive potentialities. E. Cahn points out that the best and worst propositions of social ethnics, politics and law will not preserve us if men who apply them are themselves philistines and mediocrities, even affable mediocrities. Nothing earthly can preserve us without sharply improved human qualities of leadership and citizenship.[3] Ralf Dahrendorf is yet another who stressed the importance of the personal qualities of the incumbents in enhancing the prestige of institutions. It is very often said that a few stray sheep cannot unmake an institution. But it is not realized that it is the silent sheep that unmake an institution.

JUDICIAL NORMS AND VALUES

After so many years of almost inaudible criticism about the conduct of judges, in 1992 a resolution was passed at the Chief Justices Conference held in New Delhi on 18 and 19 September, where it was resolved to restate the pre-existing and universally accepted norms, guidelines and conventions, reflecting the high values of judicial life to be followed. A committee was appointed by the CJI, to submit a draft of the restatement of values that should guide their conduct whether in office or in their personal lives. The draft came up for consideration and was approved by the full court of the Supreme Court, and a resolution was passed, adopting the Restatement as binding on the judges.

The Restatement empowers the CJI, to take action against errant judges for violating its provisions. It reads:

1. The judges of the High Court should make a declaration to the Chief Justice of their High Court, regarding assets standing in their names, standing in the names of their spouses and other dependents. The Chief Justice shall file a similar declaration for purposes of records. The declarations so made are treated as confidential.
2. No judge shall contest for any position in a club or any other association. He can, however, stand for an elective post in any association or society connected with law.
3. [No judge shall have] close association with members of the Bar, particularly those who practise in the same court. No member of his family whether a spouse, son(s), sons-in-law, or other close relative–being in the profession should appear before him or in the court presided over by him or be associated with a case to be dealt with him. No judge should deal with a case in which his family or a close relation is interested or concerned.
4. A judge shall not enter into a public debate or express his views in public on political matters or on matters pending or likely to arise for judicial determination.

5. A judge should allow his judgements to speak for themselves, and he shall not campaign for their correctness in the media, electronic or otherwise. He shall avoid media interviews.
6. A judge shall not accept hospitality or gifts excepting from his family, close relations and friends.
7. [A judge] shall not hear and decide cases of a company in which he holds shares, unless he discloses his interest and if no objection is raised he can proceed to decide the matter.
8. A judge shall not speculate in shares and stocks. A judge shall not engage in any trade or business either by himself or with any other person. A judge shall not indulge in any activity of fund-raising for any purpose and this will include his accepting contributions.
9. A judge shall not seek any financial benefit in the form of a perquisite or privilege attached to his office unless it is clearly available. In case of doubt, the CJ has to clarify.
10. A judge should be conscious that he is constantly working under the public gaze and he shall not commit any acts of omission or commission unbecoming of the high office he is holding, and the public esteem in which it is held. That was why he is advised to practice a degree of aloofness consistent with the dignity of office.[4]

These have remained mere moral aphorisms to which few pay lip-service. A soliloquy of the Chief Justice of India! A CJ of the High Court is not superior to the puisne judge. He is only a first among equals. The ostensible subservience one witnesses is a way of getting on in life. The High Court is not administratively subordinate to the Supreme Court. The ostensible subordination one witnesses, is for reasons of expediency. Such relationships were brought into existence in the belief that, holding such high constitutional appointments, the incumbents will acquit themselves with responsibility. The Restatement of Judicial Values is itself a recognition of deteriorating standards.

Thomas Jefferson complained about the Federalists in a letter: 'by a fraudulent use of the Constitution, which has made the judges irremovable, they multiplied useless judges merely to strengthen their phalanx'.[5] Jefferson was carrying on a debate with his adversaries. We are in much the same position, though adversarial politics has nothing to do with the deterioration. It is about the staffing pattern by the superior judiciary in the High Courts and the Supreme Court. It is about independence of the judiciary in the real sense and not in the formal sense. Independence of the judiciary has been reduced to a fetish, and guarding this independence in the outer ramparts is the contempt power of the Court, often quite arbitrarily exercised. The *Second judges* case,[6] where nine judges sat and liberated the Court from the trammels of the executive has no mechanism to appoint persons to judgeships, from those persons who have an understanding of the constitutional vision and philosophy. That, I believe, is the minimum requirement.

A NEW STRUGGLE FOR INDEPENDENCE

The earlier struggle for independence of the judiciary was avowedly for protecting property and business interests. There is a necessity to start a struggle for independence of the judiciary to protect the right to life, of the poor, the socially and economically deprived, and the underprivileged, and when this happens the institution can be said to be democratic. As it is structured, it is the inheritor of the colonial tradition, super-imposed by upper caste dominant culture. That the personal element of the persons chosen has not been discussed and considered in the famous *Second judges* case which appropriated all the powers interpretatively cannot be disputed. In this case they say that the executive in one form or the other is the single largest litigant before the courts, and in this view of the matter, the judiciary is the principal mediating factor between the people and the executive. The dispute in this case is on account of a crisis in the relationship between the executive and the judiciary. There was no imminent erosion or attempted erosion of the independence of the judiciary. It was by way of abundant caution that the decision was rendered. They say that the CJI is the *pater familias* of the Indian judiciary. In another case the Supreme Court was likened to the Vatican and the CJI to the Pope. And he is the person who guards the integrity and independence of the institution. And in that capacity he evaluates the merit of the candidates with regard to his and her (occasionally appointed), legal ability, etc., and offers his opinion. There is no necessity to question his opinion or have his recommendation vetted by any other person or authority, for such a procedure interferes with the independence of the judiciary. This reasoning proceeds on the basis that the Chief Justice of the High Court and the CJI have the wherewithal to know and assess the worth of the candidates and their suitability to hold the position of judges in the High Courts, as also the Supreme Court. All this exercise is meant to do is to eliminate political influence, which may sully the independence of the judiciary at the very threshold.

In this approach, they assume they alone are competent to talk about independence of the judiciary and how to bring about such independence and prevent its erosion. They, therefore, presume that they alone know how to pick up the qualified among the lawyers to be appointed as judges. They were for a long time under the mistaken impression that the executive alone was interested in destroying the independence of the judiciary. They have not yet recognized the erosion of independence wrought by litigants by playing upon caste and religious sentiments. Downright corruption, making dispensation of justice a marketable commodity, is also a threat to the independence of these institutions. These reasons have made Rule of Law a fugitive which, with the kind intervention the Supreme Court has had to make, had to take shelter in neighbouring state courts.[7]

The system, as it existed, was of elevating persons to the High Court, on the basis of impressions of the High Court judges about lawyers practising in their courts and/or on the basis of the ruling party's selection of lawyers for elevation, very often this practice resembled some barter-like transaction between the executive and the judiciary. The ruling party's nominee was also elevated along with the judges' choice for elevation. This exercise in consensus worked until Indira Gandhi wanted a loaded judiciary. The smooth working of the mechanism was ruptured because of the executive insisting on its candidate, or a stubborn judge, refusing to yield to the machinations of the executive. This is because from the beginning there was no transparency in selecting persons for elevation, and the manner in which judges were elevated was never democratic. The method of appointing judges was quite arbitrary and was entrusted to a small oligarchy. The President consulted the CJI and the Chief Justice of the High Court for appointment to the High Court and elevation to the Supreme Court—and that was the culmination of constitutional requirement.

The Constituent Assembly (CA) did not provide guidelines for appointing as judges, persons equipped to discharge constitutional obligations. Being a lawyer is not a sufficient qualification to be a judge. Being a lawyer with a large clientele may also not fit the bill. It also calls for a philosophical understanding of what the Constitution is all about. A commitment to bring about transformation of the society in terms of the Constitution by using adjudicating and interpretative skills is called for. Ralph Dahrendorf deals with the personal requirements of the person who should staff these institutions.[8] According to him, and rightly so, institution-building requires primary attention in democracies. While democratization may lead to extensive participation, this itself creates its veto group, and to make this democratization meaningful, there is a necessity for restructuring the institutions of democracy. Where institutions are staffed by the elective process they can be reformed by the process of election or by subsequent legislation. The restructuring of judicial processes and functioning are very cumbersome, and tradition-bound. The opaqueness of the British method of appointment was because they had no obligation to share with the subjects, the process of staffing these institutions, in fact any institution. But that process ill fits a democracy consisting of several crores of citizens with fundamental rights, including the fundamental right to vote. That is why Dahrendorf says that institution-building should begin with first principles: 'Democracy is about seeking progress in a world of uncertainty. Its Constitution must make change possible, [and] move it away from the arbitrary acts of the few. This means it must create conditions for initiative but also for control and both must be related to the rights and interests of the citizens.'

After liberating them from the regulation of authoritarian interference and control, the real issue remains as to how one encourages initiatives and retains control in the functioning of these institutions. Lack of norms at the time of entry, admits people who have never even paid lip-service to norms that have been stipulated or implied. These are people admitted to these institutions who feel that their idea of what is good for the people, without reference to constitutional values and laws passed in furtherance of those values, may not yield to the collective wisdom reflected in the Constitution. Thus one will find the enervation of the Constitution, which occurs while interpreting laws pertaining to violence on women, the laws pertaining to dalits, or the interpretation of liberty in the succeeding decades after Gopalan, the *Best Bakery* case in the High Court, and later in the Supreme Court, the corruption charges against Jayalalitha. Part of this impotence is manifested in the failure to innovate reliefs to assure people that rule of law and democracy will stay, and that chief ministers will be the fugitives and not the rule of law.

And what shall we do with the errant judges? This question remains unanswered. The institution is avoiding facing the issue on a very misleading premise that debating these issues might bring down the prestige this institution enjoys, and disable it from a proper discharge of its constitutional obligations. An elected appointee is only removable from office by impeachment as provided in Article 124(4) of the Constitution. A judge who is charged with misbehaviour has to be arraigned in each house of parliament by an address in each house, and the voting for removal is cumbersome ensuring failure of voting recess. While parliament acts as the high court against these high constitutional appointees, its decision is partisan, the party whip controlling the result.

IMPEACHMENT AND SELECTION OF JUDGES

This spectacle has been witnessed in the course of the impeachment of the Tamil Nadu judge, Ramaswamy. There is, in the case of a whip, only a collective decision without either a collective or individual application of mind to the issue of misbehaviour of the judge in the dock. This arraignment before parliament has to be preceded by an investigation in accordance with the provisions set out in the Judges (Inquiry) Act 1968. The proposal should have the support of the majority of the house with two-thirds majority in each house of the parliament present and voting. As a judge can be tried for misbehaviour, his tenure can only be a tenure on good behaviour. It can not be anything else. Unfortunately, the cumbersome disciplinary proceeding can only be on proven misbehaviour. This is too comprehensive an expression and when undefined, it gives licence to regular misbehaviour of various grades leading to an erosion of norms rendering the institution useless for constitutional purposes. Tenure to last till the persons reach the age of superannuation, is subject to good behaviour. The misbehaviour results in termination of the office. The judges are not even aware that their term is not so completely protected as they imagine. They should realize that it is not the cumbersome procedure for their impeachment that protects their tenure. Their tenure is conditional upon good behaviour, irrespective of the age of their superannuation. The first time the attempt at impeachment failed because Parliament did not function as the High Court of Parliament. Issuing a whip to control the voting in impeachment is an injudicious and arbitrary exercise of power by a body, which claims to run a democracy. The second time such an approach to judicial proceedings of the Parliament may not succeed because there is, I believe, a mood to restructure institutions. How can one control, short of impeachment, the ever-increasing judicial misbehaviour?

The only way out found by the Supreme Court was to transfer undesirable judges from one High Court to another, taking care to inform the public that there was no stigma attached to these transfers. Even campaigning for impeachment to secure the 100 signatures of the representatives of the people can be viewed as contempt. The strategy is to overawe the public at large, by increasing the power of judges to proceed on the basis of contempt of Court. This is not going to help matters and it will lead to a more and more brazen response by the incumbents. This will leave the institution festering. People are paying a very heavy price for maintaining the independence of the judiciary, where it has been made into a fetish, preventing any attempt to cleanse the institution.

Impeachment for misbehaviour is in fact a process, which is impossible to achieve under the procedures now prescribed. It appears to be the most inefficacious remedy one can think of. The US experience is no different. Raoul Berger in his treatise on impeachment quotes the opinion of Senator McAdoo after the conviction of Judge Halstead Richter:

> the nature of the process is such that, as evidenced in the recent proceedings, it seriously interrupts for long periods the necessary transaction of important legislative business, places an intolerable burden of hearing and weighing testimony upon senators already heavily charged with the responsibilities, and for this alone is always resorted to with extreme reluctance even in cases of flagrant misconduct.[9]

He goes on to say that this gives an assurance that the errant judges will never be visited with impeachment, which is then, a standing invitation for judges to abuse their authority with impunity and without fear of removal. Woodrow Wilson described impeachment as an 'an empty menace'. The Congress was, said some, willing to suffer a misbehaving judge.

In the earlier period of constitutional history, both in the US and UK, a judge's term was pleasure tenure, and removal presented no problems. It was felt that when power was granted to be held during good behaviour, to carry the law into execution, the English law provided for a proceeding to forfeit the office by a writ *scire facias*. This practice was used to appeal a patent in case of forfeiture. This remedy was used to protect offices held during good behaviour by persons under Royal patent (appointment) to protect them from arbitrary removal. Since then in the UK, the writ *scire facias* was available for the removal of judges for bad behaviour. The termination of office on bad behaviour may be an instrument of checks and balances in a parliamentary and presidential system, but the citizen too, has a fundamental right to clean governance in institutions and the remedy to repair these institutions is necessary as an innovative alternative relief, which does not invite executive invasion, and thus also preserves the independence of the judiciary.

It is time that some thought was given to re-defining the 'independence of judiciary'. There should be a legislative mechanism to set the limits of good behaviour by defining misbehaviour. The definition would inform every judge what constitutes the removable cause. Given that the removal of judges is, as Raoul Berger suggests, likely to be controversial, it may be useful to tighten and clarify the definition, and entrust it to a special court comprising a committee of judges. The National Commission to Review the Working of the Constitution (NCRWC) in its report of 31 March 2002 (Chapter 7), deals with the removal of judges. It recommends the establishment of a National Judicial Commission. At the preliminary stage, a committee comprising the CJ1 and the two senior-most judges, is to inquire into the complaint of deviant behaviour of all kinds, including complaints of mishebaviour and incapacity against judges of the Supreme Court and the High Courts. If the committee finds that the matter is serious enough, it may call for a full investigation by a committee constituted under the Judges' Inquiry Act 1968. This committee shall submit its report to the CJI who, in turn, shall place its report before a bench of the seven senior-most judges of the Supreme Court. Impeachment is reserved for misbehaviour of a serious nature affecting national interests. The investigation should be completely divorced from the function of hearing and judging. The fact that the judges alone will try the erring judge should be a safeguard for the independence of judiciary.[10] Persisting with a judge found to be guilty of deviant behaviour by transferring him to another High Court, is unethnical and highly objectionable. How can a judge found guilty of misdemeanour be foisted on the litigant public of another state? No option but to resign, should be given to those found guilty of misbehaviour.

How should one select our judges? There is extensive campaigning for the setting up of a National Judicial Commission, under the Constitution (Ninety-eight) Amendment Bill 2003, consisting of (a) the CJI of India; (b) two other judges of the Supreme Court, next to the CJI in seniority; (c) the Union Minister in-charge of Law and Justice; and (d) one eminent citizen nominated by the President of India in consultation with the Prime Minister. The last is a homage to democracy.

Another kind of composition is recommended by the judicial accountability committee, comprising prominent lawyers and constitutional experts located currently at New Delhi. The National Judicial Commission recommended by them should consist of: (a) the Chairman to be appointed by a collegium consisting of all the judges of the Supreme Court; (b) one member to be appointed by a collegium comprising all Chief Justices of the High Courts; (c) one to be nominated by the union cabinet; (d) one member to be appointed by the leader of the Opposition in parliament in consultation with other opposition parties in both the houses; and (c) one member recommended by the collegium comprising all the members of the Bar Council of India.

The NCRWC, of course, did not bother about the representative status of the body it recommended. There is a large population of lawyers who provide the staff for the judiciary, from the magistrate at the lower level to the judges of the districts, High Courts and the Supreme Court, apart from the tribunals for various purposes at various levels; it is odd therefore, that this large community of 10 lakh plus is not even given consultative status in the composition of the National Judicial Commission. They are members of Bar Associations, which are working as professional bodies in every nook and corner of the country wherever there is legal work to do. It may not be difficult to work out a consultative status for this community in the matter of appointment to the higher judiciary. At the lower levels, there are methods to test competency while it is at the higher levels, that there is no such test. As I often say, we get good and competent persons by culpable oversight. Entrusting responsibility will discipline the profession and will give meaning and vision to their independence. The effort should be to announce the names of the contenders to the office. Wider consultation will give transparency to the appointment process which need not be shrouded in opacity.

NOTES

1. Golaknath AIR 1967 SC 1642; Keshavananda Bharati AIR 1973 SC 1461.
2. See, *Frontline*, 7 May 2004, pp. 34–5. 'The court expressed its shock over the manner in which the State government came to the aid of the perpetrators of violence against the minority community during the roits.'
3. E. Cahn (1967) 'Confronting Injustice', in Lord Loyd of Hampstead, *Introduction to Jurisprudence*, 4th edn., ed. MDA Freeman, Steven and Sons, London, 1979.

4. V.R. Krishna Iyer (2001), *Off the Bench.*
5. Wallace Mendelson (1987), *Supreme Court Statecraft: The Rule of Law and Men,* New Delhi: Asian Books, p. 219.
6. Second Advocates on Record Association, AIR 1994 SC 268.
7. For example, the transfer of the Best Bakery case from Gujarat to Mumbai.
8. Ralph Dahrendorf (1985), *Law and Order* (The Hamlyn Lectures), London: Steven and Sons.
9. Raoul Berger (1974), *Impeachment: The Constitution Problems,* Harvard University Press, Cambridge, MA., p. 167.
10. Ibid., pp. 173–7. Also, see, *Report of the National Commission to Review the Working of the Constitution,* Delhi: Universal Law Publishing Co. Ltd., 2002 (vol. 1, Ch. 7, p. 139).

16

India: A Study in Executive–Judicial Relations Revisited

B.D. DUA

INTRODUCTION

When Justice Imam of the Supreme Court was unwell in 1964, Jawaharlal Nehru, writes that Chief Justice P.B. Gajendragadkar, 'met him half a dozen times to come to the conclusion' that it 'would not be fair to Imam himself, and to the Court, to ask him to be the Chief Justice after Sinha's retirement'.[1] Thus, instead of the ailing Justice Imam, Justice Gajendragadkar, the senior most on the Bench, became the Chief Justice of India without there being any protest. Gajendragadkar CJ recommended the transfer of two High Court judges and requested Lal Bahadur Shastri to accept his recommendation for good reasons, otherwise, he wrote, 'the position of the Chief Justice of India would be extremely anomalous and, I am sure, you will not drive me to an embarrassing position'. Shastri responded: 'No, Chief Justice, that situation will never arise'.[2] After due consultations, the transfers took place without any fuss. By all accounts, both Nehru and Shastri were very respectful of the judiciary. No doubt, Nehru was critical of some of the earlier judgements of the Supreme Court relating to property rights, but he relied on constitutional ways and means to override them (9th Schedule of the Constitution). During his tenure, judgements were criticized, not the men in the black robes who rendered them. This is, however, the history of the time long past in executive-judicial relations.

The universe of executive-judicial relations changed dramatically during the prime ministership of Mrs. Indira Gandhi. Not only the judgements, but also the judges came under attack. In this process of confrontation, which escalated during the period of the Emergency (1975–7). The Supreme Court caved in, although most of the High Courts stood their ground (the *Habeas Corpus* case). The Janata interregnum (1977–9), repaired some Emergency-caused damage to the Constitution and restored to judges a certain degree of confidence in themselves, but the return of Mrs. Gandhi to power in 1980 spread new fears in the judicial circles. If Mohan Kumaramangalam's doctrine of 'committed' judiciary was the anathema of the higher judiciary during Mrs. Gandhi's first regime (1966–77), it was Shiv Shankar's contentious 'transfer of High Court judges' policy that Chief Justice Y.V. Chandrachud had to wrestle with, during her second regime (1980–4). Once again, the Supreme Court submitted to the regime in the 1981 *Judges transfer* case (or committed 'collective suicide', as Ram Jethmalani said[3]). Not much changed in the afflicted executive-judicial relations during the Prime Ministership of Rajiv Gandhi (1984–9).

The decline of the one-party dominance of the political system that followed the 1989 parliamentary elections had, it appears, a catalytic effect on the Supreme Court. In the 1993 *Second judges* case, it wrested from the Executive the power in respect to the selection and appointment of judges of the Supreme Court and the High Courts, as also the transfer of the High Court judges, virtually claiming to be the exclusive master of its own home. The decision was certainly uncomfortable for the executive, but the minority (coalition) governments that followed the 1989 parliamentary elections could not do much about it, though they wished they could. The short-lived Inder Kumar Gujral government attempted (82nd Constitutional Amendment drafted by Union Law Minister Ramakant D. Khalap), to limit the power of the Chief Justice of India (CJI) in matters of judicial appointments, but had to give it up for want of support from the Bharatiya Janata Party (BJP). Interestingly, the statement of objectives for the Amendment read: 'It is felt that the majority view of the Supreme Court does not seem to be in consonance with the letter and spirit of the language and scheme of the Constitution'.[4] The statement certainly did not augur well for the Supreme Court.

Few will deny that the Supreme Court in particular has come a long way to earn public applause for its innovative and creative jurisprudence. In the process however, it has exercised, some constitutional pundits argue, extravagant jurisdiction, transgressing the executive and legislative domains, contrary to the original 'checks and balances' design of the Constitution.[5] This judicial transformation of the original scheme of the Constitution, it is further argued, has been facilitated because of the dysfunctionality of the other two branches of the government both at the centre and in the states, and on account of the widespread criminalization of politics. In the process of correcting this dysfunctionality, the Court has, so it is argued, over-reached its adjudicating role to become the governing institution of the country. Besides its frequent forays into the legislative and executive domains, the Court has limited the constitutional space for the other two branches of the government—its doctrine of 'basic structure' of the Constitution has constrained parliamentary sovereignty; its reading of the 'procedure established by law' as 'due process of law', has given it almost an all-pervasive power to scrutinize legislative and executive action (or inaction), on the touchstone of 'reasonableness'; and its public interest litigation (PIL) pronouncements have, at times, been too brave for the administration to live with. These constitutional anomalies, coupled with the judicial activism of the courts at all levels in dealing with the increasing number of political fugitives of justice, have raised the stakes of the executive in judicial selections and appointments.

Uncomfortable as the *Second judges* decision (subsequently elucidated in 1998), was for the executive, tensions did erupt at odd times on both sides of the fence, in making judicial appointments. For example, when Law Minister Thambi Durai in the Atul Behari Vajpayee government suggested to Chief Justice Madan Mohan Punchhi in 1998, that his recommendation for appointments and transfer of judges was 'short on consultation', CJ Punchhi was not exactly pleased. *India Today*, records the angry exchange of letters that followed between the two constitutional functionaries, with the Chief Justice dispatching the 'entire heap of appointment-transfer files—contained in four trunks according to a ministry source—back to [the] *Shastri Bhavan*'.[6]

In 2000, the Vajpayee government set up a National Commission to Review the Working of the Constitution (NCRWC), to settle multiple consti-tutional issues. In respect to the higher judiciary, the Commission examined, *inter-alia*, the appointment, transfer, and removal of judges and remedies for deviant judicial behaviour. In its report submitted in 2002, the Commission recommended, to a mixed reaction, the constitution of a National Judicial Commission responsible for recommending Supreme Court appointments, and streamlined disciplinary procedures short of removal of judges by impeachment.

With this introduction, this paper proceeds in the following sequence. Part I discusses executive-judicial relations for the period 1966 to 1989. This period spans the two regimes of Mrs. Indira Gandhi (1966-77; 1980–4), the Janata interregnum of Morarji Desai (1977–9), and the Congress(I) rule of Prime Minister Rajiv Gandhi (1984–9). Although few anticipate that the history of Congress(I) parliamentary majorities that allowed Mrs. Gandhi to domesticate and Rajiv Gandhi to reform (pack?), the higher judiciary will repeat itself, the discussion here serves as a historical background to subsequent developments in executive-judicial relations focused in particular on the appointment, transfer, and disciplinary issues in the higher judiciary. Part II of the paper summarizes the two Supreme Court judgements—the *Second judges* case 1993; the *Presidential reference* case 1998—and discusses executive-judicial relations in the context of minority (coalition) governments at the center from 1990 to 2004. Part III discusses the recommendation of the NCRWC for a National Judicial Commission and concludes with some observations.

PART I: EXECUTIVE-JUDICIAL RELATIONS—1966–1989

The First Gandhi Regime: 1966–1977

With the enactment of a series of constitutional amendments (24th, 25th, 26th, 29th), in 1971–2 to overcome the decisions of the Supreme Court in the *Golak Nath* (1967), *Bank Nationalization* (1970), and *Privy Purses* (1970) cases,[7] one might have thought that the issue of parliamentary sovereignty versus judicial review was settled, and that the Court would not challenge the constituent power of Parliament in the future. However, this did not happen. In *Keshavananda* v. *State of Kerala* (1973), the Court decided that whereas the Parliament had the power to amend the Constitution, it had no power to emasculate or destroy its 'basic structures'. It further held that the Parliament could not abrogate fundamental rights, though reasonable abridgment of such rights could be effected in the public interest.[8]

The judgement was disturbing enough for the champions of parliamentary sovereignty, but some of the extra-judicial comments made by Justices Hegde and Mukherjea—that the government could not 'speak on behalf of the entire people of this country' and that, given the vagaries of the electoral system, it did not 'represent even the majority of the people in the country'[9]—were simply too harsh for a government that had received a heavy mandate in the 1971 elections. As Upendra Baxi noted: 'It was one thing to deny Parliament the last word in the matter of constitutional change; and quite another—and devastating—to deny the legitimacy of the constitutionally prescribed procedures in fulfilment of which the then government was deemed to be the majority government.'[10]

The *Keshavananda* decision was delivered on 24 April 1973. Mrs. Gandhi struck back the next day. The government announced the appointment of Justice A.N. Ray as the Chief Justice of India, in preference to three senior judges who had dared to interpret *Keshavananda* boldly and in the face of open threats from the regime. As N.A. Palkhivala records:

> During the hearing . . . the Attorney-General appearing for the Union of India and the counsel for some States expressly referred in open Court, both orally and in writing, to the alternative of 'political action' if the Supreme Court's rulings did not find favour with the government. This background is not without significance in considering the cases of supersession.[11]

The supersession of judges provoked volumes of protest from all across the country, but the government refused to admit that it had compromised the independence of the judiciary by its unprecedented action.[12] On the contrary, Steel Minister Mohan Kumaramangalam formulated a 'committed judiciary' theory and insisted that it was incumbent on the part of the government to consider not merely 'judicial integrity' but also the 'philosophy and outlook' of judges.[13] The controversy continued, almost unabated, for several years, but the judges received the message in unmistakable terms: behave or else.

During the Emergency (1975–7), the Supreme Court survived because it did not confront Mrs. Gandhi head-on. The Court did not formally give up its power of judicial review, but some judges began interpreting the Constitution in the light of the new political climate. Justice Krishna Iyer, for example, not only granted a quasi-absolute stay to Mrs. Gandhi against the operation of the Allahabad High Court judgement, but also went out of his way to suggest that the Prime Minister had committed no 'graver electoral vices' under the 'draconian' Section 123 of the Representation of People Act. 'Draconian laws', the Justice added, 'do not cease to be law [*sic*] in courts but must alert a wakeful and quick-acting legislature'.[14] If this was a message to the Prime Minister on how to proceed, she received it well. The besieged Parliament quickly passed the 39th Amendment (Article 329A) to the

Constitution, which not only validated the Prime Minister's election but also placed certain electoral laws beyond the pale of judicial review. The Supreme Court upheld Mrs. Gandhi's election on 7 November 1975, under the retroactively changed electoral laws. However, it struck down Article 329A(4) as *ultra vires* on the ground that it offended the rule of law—a part of the basic structure of the Constitution (vide *Keshavananda*). Thus, the Court accomplished a very difficult task: it provided relief to Mrs. Gandhi and, at the same time, preserved its own legitimate role by asserting the power of judicial review. There were, of course, arguments over the meaning of 'basic structure', but it was astonishing to note Justice Chandrachud's comment that the 39th amendment Act did not 'destroy the democratic framework of our Government'.[15]

Three days after the above judgement was delivered, the government requested the Court to reconsider *Keshavananda*. The Chief Justice assembled a full bench but dissolved it in indecent haste after two days of awkward exchange of arguments between 'brother' justices and the Attorney-General of India. The outcome of the episode was unfortunate for Chief Justice Ray, for he was accused of playing to the tune of the regime which, as the Attorney-General pointed out unintentionally, was seeking review of the case in order to amend 'the very structure of the Government'.[16]

Though the theory of 'basic structure' survived, the emergence of Sanjay Gandhi on the political stage coupled with the deliberations of the Swaran Singh Committee to reform the Constitution,[17] generated new fears in the corridors of the Court in early 1976. To begin with, Chief Justice Ray agreed, voluntarily or otherwise, with the President of India to the mass transfer of High Court judges who were allegedly out of line with the regime; this unprecedented move and the controversy surrounding it seriously undermined the prestige of the Chief Justice.[18] Following this, came the *Habeas Corpus* (1976) case in which the Court (with the exception of Justice H.R. Khanna) not only refused to grant relief to the victims of the preventive detention orders but also came close to endorsing the Emergency regime itself.[19] The conclusion of the Court in this case, that the emergency provisions (MISA) lifted the rule of law in the country was tragic both for the victims and for the doctrine of 'basic structure' of the Constitution, but the observations of some of the judges were highly inappropriate. For example, Justice Chandrachud, who turned a perfect somersault during the Janata regime and admitted having lacked the courage to resign after this judgement,[20] said at the time: 'Counsel after counsel expressed the fear that during the Emergency the executive may whip and strip and starve the detenu and, if this be our judgement, even shoot him. Such misdeeds have not tarnished the image of free India and I have diamond-bright, diamond-hard hope that such things will never come to pass'.[21]

Justice M.H. Beg went a step further. He not only appreciated the regime for taking good care of the detenus, but also complimented the government for having averted the 'dangers of tomorrow' by taking the necessary security steps. And, in the *Union of India* v. *Bhanudas* (1977) case, the Court seemed so nervous that it almost, as Baxi suggests, abdicated its judicial function by declining to intervene in the conditions, much less in the legality, of detention. Once again, Beg's comments shocked civil libertarians: 'Speaking for myself, I am inclined to suspect that a number of allegations made on behalf of detenus have the oblique motive of partisan vilification or political propaganda for which Courts are not proper places.'[22]

Despite the pro-regime decisions of the Supreme Court, the Parliament enacted the 42nd Amendment (18 December 1976), which not only abrogated *Keshavananda*, but also subordinated fundamental rights to the directive principles of state policy and restricted the writ jurisdiction of State High Courts. And even though Mrs. Gandhi announced elections to the Lok Sabha on 18 January 1977, she did not hesitate to strike yet another blow at the Supreme Court ten days later, when she announced the appointment of Justice Beg as the Chief Justice of India, in preference to Justice Khanna, who had refused to toe the government line in the *Habeas Corpus* case.

Like other institutions in society, the judiciary suffered enormously during the Emergency period; it yielded in substance to the strong rule of Mrs. Gandhi and in the process, lost its institutional prestige and cohesiveness. The identification of judges and lawyers either as pro-regime or anti-regime created schisms in the membership of the Bench and the Bar, and the courtrooms across the country became sites for partisan clashes and conflicts.

The Janata Interegnum: 1977–1979

The victory of the Janata party in March 1977 brought new hopes for the restoration of democratic government in the country. Prime Minister Morarji Desai, in his very first broadcast to the nation on 4 April, said: 'I yield to none in my zealous regard for the independence of judiciary. . . . I recognize that the right to liberty is the natural right of all the citizens of the country. We are resolved fully to restore those rights as embodied in the Constitution as it was before the eclipse in the last two years or so.'[23]

Three days later, Shanti Bhushan, Union Law Minister, began restoring the lost constitutional balance. He introduced the 43rd Amendment Bill in the Lok Sabha (finally enacted in April 1978), to wipe out those provisions of the 42nd Amendment Act that had given sweeping powers to the Parliament, to make laws dealing with 'anti-national' activities, and had required extraordinary majorities of the Supreme Court and High Court judges to declare on the constitutionality of central and state laws, respectively.[24] In May 1978, the government introduced the 45th Amendment Bill (renumbered as the 44th Amendment Bill), not only to eliminate the remaining repressive features of the 43nd Amendment Act but also to establish a liberal democratic regime in the country. Unfortunately, the bill had a rough journey through the Congress-dominated upper house (Rajya Sabha), which passed it, only after five of its crucial clauses—dealing *inter alia* with (a) the primacy of fundamental rights over the directive principles of state policy; and (b) the compulsory use of a *referendum* to amend the basic structures of the Constitution—were dropped by the government. The bill, as enacted in May 1979, thus failed in some of its significant provisions, though it placed considerable restrictions on the emergency powers of the executive, in order to prevent manipulation of the rules of the game in the future.[25]

Though the government could not restructure the Constitution the way it had promised, it made major efforts to restore confidence in the community of judges. For one thing, the 44th Amendment Bill and the debate that followed it did convey a welcome message to the judiciary that the government, unlike the Emergency regime, was willing to recognize the correctness of *Keshavananda*, and to limit the constituent powers of the Parliament. For another, the government, through its proposed device of a referendum to amend the basic structures of the Constitution, indicated to the judiciary that it had a coordinate status with the Parliament and that the sovereign will of the people alone could change this structural balance. In addition, the government reaffirmed the 'seniority principle' in judicial appointments, and appointed, despite some loud protests, Justice Chandrachud as the Chief Justice of India in February 1978. It also cancelled Mrs. Gandhi's mass transfer of High Court judges to emphasize that the Constitution did not contemplate punitive transfers (i.e. transfers without the 'effective' consultation of the CJI) of judges.[26]

In view of the reassuring political climate, the Supreme Court began demonstrating a renewed sense of confidence and vitality. In most of the decisions made between 1977 and 1979, the Court exhibited a new social awareness of its role in the political system—*Pathak* (1977); *Haskot* (1978); *Hussainara* (1979). But, the sound and fury that accompanied the ruling in *Maneka* (1978) left no doubt that the Court was burying its emergency past and emerging as the final guardian of fundamental rights. 'Governments come and go,' said Justice Iyer, 'but the fundamental rights of the people cannot be subject to wishful value-sets of the political regimes of the passing day.'[27] If the restriction imposed on personal freedom indicated any abuse of power, added Justice Bhagwati, 'the arms of the Court (were) long enough to reach it and to strike it down'.[28]

Though the Court would have preferred to stay out of the vortex of national politics, it was drawn into it in the *Dissolution* (1977), and in the *Special Courts Reference* (1978) cases. In the *Dissolution* case, the Court upheld the Janata's move to dismiss nine Congress State governments (a decision under which Mrs. Gandhi removed an equal number of Janata state governments when she returned to power in 1980), and suffered some justified criticism for the elaborate defensive policy statements that it made in support of its decision.[29] In the *Special Court Reference* case, the Court almost got co-opted in the Janata's task of bringing the sinners of the Emergency to quick trial, when it not only affirmed the legislative competence of the Parliament to enact the Special Courts bill, but also suggested such modifications in the bill that would make it constitutionally valid.[30] Though it was argued that the bill, which selected offenders with special reference to the emergency period, created a separate class of offenders, the Court over-ruled the objection on pragmatic grounds and in the interest of speedy trials. The Court was accused (and perhaps rightly so) of legitimizing the move of the new political masters to make the trial of their adversaries look unusual, if not unfair.

While the Court was skilful in dealing with political issues, it must be admitted that it failed to operate as a cohesive institution. Chief Justice Beg (Mrs. Gandhi's appointee who retired in February 1978), came in for heavy criticism from the press (particularly for his *Habeas Corpus* decision), and from his own 'brother' justices for hobnobbing with the Acting President of India during the *Dissolution* case. Justice Goswami put it on record, much to the embarrassment of the Chief Justice:

I part with the records with a cold shudder. The Chief Justice was good enough to tell us that the acting President saw him during the time we were considering judgement after having announced the order, and that there was mention of this pending matter during the conversation. I have given this matter most anxious thought, and even the strongest judicial restraint which a judge would prefer to exercise, leaves me no option but to place this on record hoping that the majesty of the High Office of the President, who should be beyond the high watermark of any controversy, suffers not in the future.[31]

As the retirement of Chief Justice Beg drew closer, a Bombay Memorandum (prepared by fifty-two public men and advocates), called into question the integrity of both Justice Chandrachud (next-in-line of seniority) and Justice Bhagwati for their decision in the *Habeas Corpus* case, and appealed to the government not to appoint either of them as the next CJI. The Memorandum said: 'The people of the country can hardly be expected to allow the Supreme Judicial Power in the State to pass into the hands of judges whose record can do no credit to any freedom loving people or to the Supreme Court.'[32]

Criticism notwithstanding, the Janata government embraced the 'seniority principle' and appointed Justice Chandrachud as the next CJI though attacks on his personal integrity continued long thereafter. Arun Shourie wrote:

Thus, we have our 'leaders' and our 'laws'. We have our judges too. Judges represented at the top by a judge who one day upholds the fascist decision of a clique to deny six hundred and fifty million the right to *habeas corpus*, who the next day wishes he had the courage to resign rather than pronounce that judgement, who the day after addresses one of the principal culprits of the Emergency [Sanjay Gandhi] again and again as 'a very responsible member of society'.[33]

Thus, public criticism put both the Chief Justices (Beg and his successor, Chandrachud) on the defensive; they were made to feel guilty for their decisions during the Emergency, and this robbed both of them of their capacity to give a corporate identity to the Court. Chief Justice Beg did not receive much respect from his colleagues while Chief Justice Chandrachud sought to build his credibility in the judicial circles, until he ran into difficulties when the Congress(I) party returned to power in January 1980.

The Second Gandhi Regime: 1980–1984

Mrs. Gandhi's return to power in January 1980 revived memories of the old Emergency regime. Even before Mrs. Gandhi had the time to settle into office, Justice P. N. Bhagwati of the Supreme Court dispatched the following letter to her:

> May I offer you my heartiest congratulations on your resounding victory in the elections and your triumphant return as the Prime Minister of India. . . . I am sure that with your iron will and firm determination, uncanny insight and dynamic vision, great administrative capacity and vast experience, overwhelming love and affection of the people and above all, a heart which is identified with the misery of the poor and the weak, you will be able to steer the ship of the nation safely to its cherished goal.[34]

The letter was written in confidence. The Press, however, received a copy of it, allegedly through the prime minister's office. Within days, Justice V.D. Tulzapurkar referred to it in a bitter attack: 'If judges start sending bouquets or congratulatory letters to a political leader on his political victory, eulogizing him on assumption of a high office in adulatory terms, the people's confidence in the judiciary will be shaken.'[35] The wide debate that followed the episode not only put Bhagwati on the defensive, but also exposed the shifting loyalties of the members of the Bench and the Bar.

Mrs. Gandhi, who had often viewed the courts as unfriendly, watched the widening cracks in the judicial edifice. And then, on 18 March 1981, she called into question the judicial integrity of the Janata-appointed judges: 'The former Janata regime had made a lot of appointments in the judiciary on political basis . . . a dilemma faced by us was whether these persons appointed on political basis in the judicial services should be allowed to continue; and if they were continued, how can we expect justice from them? What is their credibility?'[36] It was an intimidating statement for the 110 Janata-appointed judges. A showdown with the judiciary had begun.

Even before Mrs. Gandhi spoke, her Law Minister was already on the move. On 14 January 1980, Shiv Shankar promised (a) that the system of appointment of judges would be reviewed in order to make the judiciary more committed to the ideals of the Constitution; and (b) that the 'obnoxious' Act relating to special courts would be repealed.[37] As if to escape the wrath of new masters, all courts dealing with cases against Mrs. Gandhi and others began moving with the winds of political change. A day after the Law Minister Shiv Shankar made his statement, Justice Jain invoked 'improper procedure' in the creation of his special court and hastily closed its doors after summarily dismissing all cases against Mrs. Gandhi and others. The judge said that 'the creation and establishment of this court and the declaration and designations to try the said cases were not made in accordance with the provisions of the Constitution and are, therefore, of no effect and confer no jurisdiction on this court'.[38] A month later, Justice Joshi declared the establishment of his special court unconstitutional, and dismissed the 'jeep scandal' case against Mrs. Gandhi.[39] In the last week of March, Justice Aggarwal discharged Sanjay Gandhi and his co-accused Singh, in the polymix case, observing that 'accusations against them lacked reasonable ground to expect a conviction and as such could be regarded as groundless'.[40]

The Supreme Court, it appears, carefully distinguished constitutional matters from issues involving a 'cocktail of law and politics'. While the Court held its own in constitutional matters and refused to play the politics of the establishment until mid-1981, it awarded politically expedient justice on 'cocktail' issues. In April 1980, a three member Bench set aside the conviction of both Sanjay Gandhi and V.C. Shukla in the notorious *Kissa Kursi Kaa* case, leaving without cover, both Justice O.N. Vohra (who had convicted them and who, later on, paid the price for doing so when he was refused a permanent position on the Delhi Bench), and Chief Justice Chandrachud (who, as a member of the Supreme Court Bench, had cancelled Sanjay Gandhi's bail on 5 May 1978, and sent him to jail for one month for 'tampering with witnesses' in this case[41]). The Supreme Court, as A.G. Noorani wrote, did not take note of the fact that Sanjay Gandhi had been charged for 'attempting to suborn the prosecution witnesses' and that 'the innocent ought not to and, indeed, do not tend to tamper with witnesses'.[42]

In May 1980, another Supreme Court Bench, consisting of Justices Reddy and Iyer, gave a politically expedient decision when it dismissed two appeals, one challenging the withdrawal of the *Baroda Dynamite* case by the erstwhile Janata government, and another arising out of the withdrawal of cases against Bansi Lal by the Mrs. Gandhi government.[43] Describing the submission in the case as a 'cocktail of law and politics', Justice Reddy, who wrote the judgement, warned that 'criminal justice is not a plaything and a court is not a playground for politicking. . . . If political fortunes are to be reflected in the process of the court, very soon the credibility of law will be lost.' And yet, the judgement concluded: 'To persist with prosecutions, where emotive issues are involved, in the name of vindicating the law may even be utter foolishness bordering on insanity.'[44] The Court's ruling that politically motivated prosecutions were different, and could be treated differently was, of course, good politics but bad jurisprudence. Relying on this judgement, the Delhi Metropolitan Magistrate, V.B. Gupta, allowed the prosecution to withdraw, in the so-called public interest, a criminal case against Sanjay Gandhi and others who were involved in violent clashes with the Delhi police while protesting against the setting up of Special Courts in May 1979.[45] In fact, once the Supreme Court had given the lead, all 35 criminal cases against Sanjay Gandhi were gradually withdrawn or settled in his favour.

While decisions in 'cocktail' cases brought no special honour to the courts, a few constitutional decisions of the Supreme Court were highly irksome for the ruling party. In May 1980, a five-member Bench of the Supreme Court, presided over by Chief Justice Chandrachud, struck down two of the most crucial clauses of the controversial 42nd Amendment Act in the *Minerva Mills* case and reaffirmed *Keshavananda*. The Court ruled that Section 55 of the Amendment Act 'is beyond the amending power of the Parliament and is void, since it removes all limitations on the power of Parliament to amend the Constitution, and confers power upon it to amend the Constitution so as to damage or destroy its basic or essential features or its basic structure'.[46] This reassertion of the power of judicial review by the Supreme Court upset many ruling politicians, who saw in it a new challenge to the progressive policies of their government. The General Secretary of the Congress(I) party warned that the judgement would have 'serious political and constitutional implications', and the Law Minister suggested that the government would 'appeal to the Supreme Court to constitute a larger bench to reconsider the order'.[47]

The controversy relating to the *Minerva Mills* case never abated. At the same time, however, the Supreme Court became the target of yet another Congress(I) attack when it held in the *LIC Bonus* case (1980), that the old bonus settlements to lower employees of the Corporation were valid and must be paid. The government brought in new legislation to nullify this judgement, but the Court passed an interlocutory order refusing to stay payments pending the validity of the new legislation.[48] And when the Supreme Court began admitting writ petitions in early 1981 challenging the validity of the preventive detention law (i.e. the National Security Ordinance and the National Security Act 1980 which replaced it), and of the Special Bearer Bonds Act 1981 (which was designed to recover black-market money in the country), the Mrs. Gandhi government renewed its attempt to cut the Court to size. Besides blaming the judiciary for many of the ills afflicting society, the ruling circles began debating the virtues of a presidential form of government in which the judiciary, stripped of its constitutional power to review legislation, would be made accountable to some kind of a politically appointed Superior Council. Such debates became so irksome that Justice Iyer of the Supreme Court, in one of his public lectures, remarked that a 'presidential system had the potential to subvert democracy' and that the Parliament would be well-advised to consider if such a change would not 'violate the basic structure of the Constitution'.[49]

Though the entire judicial system was under pressure to conform, the ruling party zeroed in its attack on the *pater familias.* Unlike Justice Bhagwati, who was labelled as a Congress(I) man for his laudatory letter to Mrs. Gandhi, Chief Justice Chandrachud had a very low rating with the ruling household. Appointed Chief Justice of the Supreme Court by the Janata government—a disqualification in itself under the new regime—Chandrachud had not exactly endeared himself to the Gandhis for sending Sanjay to jail in 1978, or for turning *volte face* during the Janata period. By mid-1981, the estrangement between Chandrachud and the ruling party was so great that Ashoke Sen, a Congress(I) MP and President of the Supreme Court Bar Association, even hinted at his impeachment by Parliament.[50] Undaunted, the Chief Justice continued to defend the judiciary against executive interference, and called upon the Bench and the Bar to be united as this was 'the only way we could fight the provocation and attack on the judges'.[51] On 12 July 1981, Chandrachud made his stand clear: 'As the head of the judiciary does not interfere with the functioning of the Cabinet or ministry, so the head of the executive should not interfere with the functioning of the judiciary.'[52]

The issue that had forced Chief Justice Chandrachud to give a clarion call for unity was the government's insistence in having a free hand in the appointment, confirmation, and transfer of High Court judges—a constitutionally questionable power but used by the government during the Emergency period.[53] Throughout 1980, the Chief Justice had refused to submit to pressures, and made the government appoint eight Chief Justices to High Courts (and five judges to the Supreme Court) according to well-established constitutional practices. Thus, when the Law Minister announced his 'appointment and transfer policy'—that each High Court should have one-third of its judges and its chief justices from outside the State, and such a task should be accomplished by transferring judges from one High Court to another—Chief Justice Chandrachud was quick to react:

> I do not think it will be either feasible or proper to transfer each and every sitting Chief Justice of the High Court to another High Court or to appoint an outside Judge as Chief Justice. . . . [The question is] so replete with practical difficulties and involves question of such high principles that a very careful thought shall have to be given to it before a final decision is taken.[54]

Chandrachud's stand was in line with the decision of the Supreme Court in *Sheth* v. *Union of India* (1977), which held that 'transfers on a wholesale basis' that left no scope for careful deliberations of the 'facts in each particular case' were outside the 'contemplation of our Constitution'. The Court had concluded that even individual transfers could not be effected by the government without the 'effective' and 'real' consultation of the CJI as provided in Article 222(1) of the Constitution. Thus, the CJI was willing to consider individual cases, and, in fact, did recommend the transfer of Madras High Court Chief Justice Ismail to Kerala, and of Patna High Court Chief Justice Singh to Madras in January 1981, but he was adamant in not endorsing the government policy of wholesale transfers.[55] Despite the fact that these were cases of individual transfers duly recommended by Chandrachud, both the Chief Justice and the government did suffer some embarrassment, when Ismail resigned[56] in protest and Singh appealed the decision to the Supreme Court.

While the transfer policy was still being debated in early 1981, the government began reviewing Janata-appointed temporary or additional judges. Initially appointed for a period of two years, it was a well-established convention before the Emergency interregnum, either to extend their term if the business of the courts so warranted or to confirm them against permanent vacancies in various High Courts. By mid-1981, the government had confirmed a few of the additional judges but kept most of them on tenterhooks either by giving them last-minute short-term extensions[57] or by dropping them unceremoniously on the expiry of their term. Justice Tulzapurkar of the Supreme Court was, in fact, constrained to remark that the government was treating judges 'worse than clerks'.[58]

The government had also asked the additional judges (vide Ministry of Law circular of 18 March 1981), to give an undertaking that they would have no objection to being transferred outside their States on appointment to permanent positions. This brought angry response from Chandrachud:

What is involved in the issue is not the motive or intentions of someone but the principles. When Article 222 of the Constitution clearly says that a judge can be transferred [or appointed under Article 224], after consultation with the Chief Justice of India . . . how can the executive then assume that it alone has the right to transfer a judge or grant an extension to an additional judge. Since the executive is controlled by political leaders . . . it may, it is feared, transfer a judge to a far-off place like Sikkim, the Andaman Islands or Assam, or refuse to grant him further extension if he does not toe the line.[59]

In June 1981, the government refused extensions to O.N. Vohra (who had convicted Sanjay Gandhi in the *Kissa Kursi Kaa* case), and S.N. Kumar (who was labelled a Janata candidate, but was recommended for appointment by Chief Justice Chandrachud against the wishes of the Delhi Chief Justice[60]), of the Delhi High Court. While Vohra did not challenge the decision, some legal luminaries took Kumar's case to the Supreme Court.

Thus, when a seven-member Constitution Bench of the Supreme Court, presided over by Justice Bhagwati, met on 20 July 1981, it was asked to decide on three thorny questions. The first was whether Singh had been properly transferred from Patna to Madras; the second was whether the circular of 18 March 1981, seeking advance consent of additional judges for transfer, was within the brief of the Minister of Law; and the third was whether the government had acted correctly in dispensing with the services of Kumar.

Before the Constitution Bench reached its decision (*S.P. Gupta* v. *Union of India*), on these crucial issues, it was obvious that the Court was badly disunited. Besides the usual ideological divisions—left, centre, right—that had overtaken the Court, the extent of backbiting among the judges had gained a certain measure of notoriety in legal circles. Justice Tulzapurkar had attacked Justice Bhagwati for eulogizing the Prime Minister; Justice Desai had stalked off to his chamber in anger when one of his colleagues reminded him that the oath of office was more important than social sympathies; Justice Bhagwati had found Chief Justice Chandrachud 'guilty' of not fulfilling the judicial requirements of circulating his own judgement among 'brother' judges in the *Minerva Mills* case; and Justice Iyer had responded from the public platform to Justice Tulzapurkar, when the latter had attacked him for his 'irrelevant perorations and sermons'.[61] Given the tendency among judges to fight out their political and personal battles in public, the Court seemed wanting both in will[62] and in cohesiveness to fight the government in the present case.

Thus, when the Constitution Bench, by a majority of four-to-three, announced its judgement on 30 December 1981, it was hailed as the most precious New Year's gift to the ruling party. The gloomiest aspect of the judgement was the devastating *obiter dicta* against the supreme figure of the judiciary, Chief Justice Chandrachud. Chandrachud stood humiliated, ironically by his own 'brothers', and the government rejoiced at the fissure running through the Court. 'The judiciary', commented the *Statesman*, 'shall never be the same again'.[63]

The essence of the majority decision was that (a) Singh's transfer from Patna to Madras was in order;[64] (b) the Law Ministry's circular was valid since it applied to judges who had yet to be confirmed; and (c) the government was correct in dispensing with the services of Kumar, even though Chief Justice Chandrachud was opposed to it. The implications of the decision were obvious—*consultation* with the Chief Justice of India, as provided in the Constitution, did not mean *concurrence* of the Chief Justice, and the government was free to hire (including the Supreme Court judges), fire, and transfer all of the additional judges, provided it had gone through certain formal constitutional procedures. The more ominous rider in the judgement was that the last word in these matters rested with the President of India alone.[65] In contravention of well-established conventions, the President could even initiate proposals[66] for the appointment of judges to High Courts and to the Supreme Court. As one Supreme Court advocate put it: 'The President means the Congress(I), under the present circumstances. This is a scandal. From now on, the ragamuffins of the ruling party will have the right to decide who will be a High Court judge, or even its Chief Justice.'[67]

While the government celebrated the judgement, the Court lost most of its aura of respectability by exposing its internal divisions. Justice Bhagwati was unsparing in nailing down Chandrachud—'figuratively described as *pater familias*', *w*ho could claim no 'primacy over other constitutional functionaries' and who had taken a 'constitutionally impermissible' position in the *Kumar* case[68]—and the attack became more vicious as the arguments proceeded in the case. Though Chandrachud's move to recommend Singh's transfer from Patna to Madras was upheld (and this was the only saving grace for Chandrachud), there was a sinister move to destroy his personal credibility even on this issue. Chandrachud had filed an affidavit before the Constitution Bench stating that he had consulted the President of India in regard to Singh's transfer. However, when the issue came up before the Bench, President Sanjiva

Reddy sent a special message to the Court denying that he had been consulted *in person* by Chandrachud.[69] This gave yet another opportunity to Bhagwati to criticize the Chief Justice. 'It is an affidavit which is made by the Chief Justice [and yet] the statement made . . . is delightfully vague.'[70] And when Justice Desai insisted that he must know the constitutional connotation of the term 'President', K. Parasaran, Solicitor General for India, asked: 'Why did we have a Supreme Court if we could not take as truth the sworn statement of the Chief Justice of India?'[71] The affidavit, of course, was accepted but Chandrachud's credibility was definitely put on the line.

A rather unusual feature of the judgement that caused great jubilation among the ruling politicians was the peroration by the majority of the Constitution Bench on the 'value-packing' of judges in order to get rid of the 'cancer-ridden' judicial system. The chorus on value-packing was loud and clear. 'The judiciary', said Bhagwati, 'has a socio-economic destination' because the Constitution is 'not a non-aligned parchment'.[72] Justice Desai went a little further: 'The three organs of the government created by the Constitution must march in step. All must be imbued with the same values. Judges must be value-packed.'[73] And Justice Venkataramiah talked of the desirability of having 'people's judges' who alone could 'fit into the scheme of popular democracy'.[74] Even Mrs. Gandhi could not have said it better!

The perception that the Supreme Court had committed political *hara-kiri* was further strengthened by a Catch-22 questionnaire (with suggestive answers), of the Law Commission which appeared to be seeking alternatives to this august body. As R.K. Makhija, President of the Delhi Court Bar Association, put it:

> Mathew [head of the Commission and a retired Supreme Court judge], wants to complete his unfinished task of reducing the Supreme Court to the status of a serf. He wants to block the writs in the name of reducing the work load. He wants to cut back on hearing so that the points that do not suit the executive cannot be clarified. . . . Finally, he wants to do away with the very Supreme Court which cradled him for six long years and wants to play the Frankenstein to it.[75]

Makhija's fears turned out to be unfounded though his statement did reflect the climate of the day.

But when Chief Justice Chandrachud advised in early 1983, that we should give a 'decent burial'[76] to the constitutional consultation process and instead establish a nine-member collegium for the selection and appointment of Supreme Court and High Court judges, it was difficult to speculate (the government had announced four appointments to the Supreme Court), if he were speaking out of personal despair with the consultation process or otherwise.[77] On retirement, two years later in 1985, Chandrachud re-emphasized: 'The appointment of judges is too much of a clandestine affair. There should be wider consultation and freer discussion on the question of judicial appointments.'[78]

If the issue of judicial appointments was a 'clandestine affair', it became all the more so with the government's policy (1981) to have one-third of the judges and the Chief Justice in each High Court from outside the state.[79] The guidelines for transfer were set by the government in November 1983,[80] but these were often breached by the government itself. The poor implementation of the policy, whatever its merits, provoked resentment and resistance—the community of judges, particularly those appointed by the previous regime, resented it for fear of being tossed around in turbulent waters (transferred to Sikkim?); the non-Congress(I) state governments resisted it for political and partisan reasons.[81] A non-Tamil speaking Chief Justice, argued Chief Minister M.G. Ramachandran of Tamil Nadu, would have a difficult time understanding the court proceedings when K.B.N. Singh of Patna High Court was transferred to Madras in 1983.[82] The Karnataka Chief Minister, Ramakrishna Hegde, was more forthright: 'We will not be a party to any attempt of the Central Government which either destroys the independence of the judiciary or aims to politicize it.'[83]

The experiment of shuffling chief justices of High Courts across states not only undermined the confidence of the judiciary, but also damaged the credibility of the government. It was by no means easy for the government, for example, to refute the charge that it was dangling carrots before acting Chief Justices (a necessary consequence of the transfer policy), to seek partisan and unmeritorious nominations,[84] or that it was elevating junior judges as Chief Justices, through its careful manipulation of the transfer policy. Nor did it do any good to the government when a Chief Justice resigned in protest, or when the lawyers went on strike, as in Ahmedabad, to protest against the arrival of an out-of-state Chief Justice',[85] or when the transfer of a Chief Justice, as in the case of *Satish Chandra* (transferred from Allahabad to Calcutta), became the subject of a writ petition in the Supreme Court of India.[86] The transfer guidelines had promised respect for 'seniority' for the purposes of elevation as Chief Justice, but the government could not live up to its promise. As *India Today* reported in 1983: 'An analysis of the recent appointments and transfers reveals that in a majority of the cases the Law Ministry has violated its own norms. Of the 343 permanent judges of various High Courts, over 20 were superseded while selecting new Chief Justices for Jammu & Kashmir, Rajasthan and Gujarat.'[87] While the courts were being buried under the weight of pending cases, the deadlocks in the triangular consultation process for appointments and transfers, left many High Courts understaffed and over-worked.[88]

The Rajiv Gandhi Regime: 1984–1989

The situation did not improve during the tenure of Rajiv Gandhi either. Rather, it got worse in some ways. In 1985, a three-member Bench of the Supreme Court, hearing *Satish Chandra's* case,[89] questioned the government's 'arbitrariness' in making transfers of High Court Chief Justices in violation of its own guidelines. The Court also took note of the fact that a large number of appointments of High Court judges were made on the recommendation of acting Chief Justices on considerations other than merit and that junior judges were being elevated as chief justices. This disturbed Justice Tulzapurkar: 'If the sycophant element amongst the chief justices is not eschewed from consideration, the entire judiciary is doomed.'[90] And Justice Sen remarked: 'The policy of appointing chief justices from outside of their own courts seems to be a pernicious principle.'[91] Undaunted by criticism, transfers and appointments continued to be made in disregard of the policy guidelines.

The politics of judicial patronage flourished and the criticism of the policy—that unworthies were being nominated for appointments; that juniors were over-riding seniors in the appointment of Chief Justices; that Chief Ministers were pushing their own candidates over the heads of their Chief Justices; that party affiliations and caste considerations were weighing heavy in the selection process; that the non-Congress(I) state governments in particular were not agreeable to transferred Chief Justices; and that some nominees were caught in the turnover of Chief Ministers and Chief Justices, causing undue delay in appointments[92]—became louder over time. Even President Zail Singh expressed concern about the policy guidelines and the selection process (he questioned the rejection of one duly recommended candidate for appointment to the Punjab and Haryana High Court and Rajiv, it was reported, 'backed down'.[93]) and asked the government to re-state its policy more clearly.

Chief Justice P.N. Bhagwati (a brilliant jurist who succeeded Chandrachud CJ in 1985) of the Supreme Court held the judicial fort, but not quite (the 'primacy' of the Chief Justice's advice in judicial appointments was lost in the *Judges transfer* case). During his eighteen-month tenure as Chief Justice, 'several of the 40-odd High Court judges he assented to because of executive pressures', commented *India Today*, had 'little to recommend them except proximity to ruling party bigwigs'.[94] Chief Justice R.S. Pathak (who succeeded Bhagwati CJ), sailed through the rough political waters, but, at times, it was no smooth sailing for him.[95]

In an opinion poll conducted by the Operations Research Group in 1987, two-thirds of the 310 practising lawyers of the Supreme Court and the Delhi High Court believed that the judiciary was no longer independent, and an almost equal number felt that it was not attracting the best talent from the bar.[96] However, it appears that the government was so set to reform (pack) the judiciary that it recommended a dozen high court appointments even after the parliamentary elections were called in 1989, which President R. Venkataraman, of course, deemed inappropriate to make.[97]

PART II: EXECUTIVE–JUDICIAL RELATIONS—1990–2004

Preoccupied with the politics of Mandal, the V.P. Singh coalition government (1989–90), did not stay in power long enough to re-structure executive-judicial relations. However, even during its short tenure, Union Law Minister Dinesh Goswami gave the assurance that 'he would not appoint any Supreme Court judge who had not been recommended by the chief justice and that no judge would be transferred without the recommendation of the chief justice.'[98] He even proposed the 67th Amendment Bill to constitute a National Judicial Commission (which Chief Justice Sabyasachi Mukharji opposed), but the curtain fell on the government, not long thereafter in November 1990. Prime Minister Chandrashekhar succeeded in forming a minority government but he too was soon out-manoeuvred and lost his perch in March 1991. After the 1991 parliamentary elections, the Congress(I) formed a minority government under the leadership of P.V. Narashima Rao.

The Narasimha Rao Regime: 1991–1996

While there was a crisis of governance at the centre, the judiciary suffered its own crisis of credibility when a corruption scandal erupted in the Bombay High Court in 1990 at the same time that Justice V. Ramaswami of the Supreme Court came under investigation for embezzlement of funds, when he was the Chief Justice of the Punjab and Haryana High Court.[99] Supreme Court Chief Justice Mukharji recommended the transfer of two High Court judges (allegedly involved in corruption) out of Bombay, but the solution failed to work.[100] He forced his brother Justice Ramaswami to proceed on leave pending inquiry (by a three-judge committee), into corruption charges against him, but whether a Chief Justice (as one among the equals as per the *Judges transfer* case), could withdraw work from a colleague, became the subject of constitutional debate.[101] When Ramaswami was called back to work after five months of leave by the next Chief Justice, Ranganath Mishra, the Supreme Court Bar Association (SCBA) resolved to boycott his Court.[102] The credibility of the judiciary suffered a severe blow as controversies surrounding these scandals contaminated public narratives and demonstrated how widespread the malaise of corruption was in the higher judiciary—it was reported that the former Chief Justice, E.S. Venkataramiah (Mukharji's predecessor), had recommended a large number of transfer of High Court judges for their questionable ethics.[103] Commenting on the situation, P.N. Bhagwati regretted: 'The credibility of the judiciary has gone down. People's faith and confidence have been shaken.'[104] If the degeneration 'within' the judiciary was to be checked, so argued some legal circles, then the role of the constitutional functionaries, particularly that of the *pater familias,* in judicial appointments and transfers had to be re-examined.

In *Subhash Sharma* v. *Union of India* (1991), a three Judge Bench of the Supreme Court acknowledged this need, when it observed that the role of the institution of the Chief Justice of India should be 'recognized as of crucial importance in the matter of appointments to Supreme Court', and that the word 'consultation' as in Article 124(2) of the Constitution 'required to be expounded in the context of separation of powers and judicial independence'.[105] The Bench also decried the practice of state governments sending their list of nominees for High Court appointments to the centre over the heads of their Chief Justices.[106] These questions and others, the Bench advised, should be considered by a larger Bench. In other words, the Bench wished a review of the *Judges transfer* case.

'If you sow the wind, you reap the whirlwind.' This is what exactly happened when the Supreme Court wrested control of appointments and transfers to the higher judiciary from the Executive in the *Second judges* case in 1993. In the *Supreme Court Advocates-on-Record Association*

(SCAORA) v. *Union of India*, a nine-Judge Constitution Bench of the Supreme Court (with a majority of seven), over-ruled the decision in the *Judges transfer* case and recognized the 'primacy' of the CJI in appointments to the Supreme Court, so long as his opinion was a 'collective opinion' formed after consulting with two of his senior-most colleagues. Further, the Bench laid down that: (a) the Chief Justice *alone* could initiate the appointment proposal; (b) the President, for stated and cogent reasons disclosed to the Chief Justice, may decline to make the appointment; however, if the stated reasons were not accepted by the Chief Justice and other judges who were consulted in the matter, on reiteration of the recommendation of the Chief Justice, the appointment should be made as a healthy convention; and (c) no appointment of any judge to the Supreme Court could be made by the President, unless it was in conformity with the final 'collectively-formed' opinion of the CJI.

For the High Courts, the Bench laid down that (a) the recommendation for appointment shall be made by the Chief Justice of the High Court concerned in consultation with his two senior-most colleagues; and (b) the 'collectively-formed' opinion of the Chief Justice of India will have 'primacy' in the matter and shall prevail (if inconsistent) over that of the Governor of the state or even that of the High Court. In forming his opinion, the CJI, the Bench said, is expected 'to take into account the views of his colleagues in the Supreme Court who are likely to be conversant with the affairs of the concerned High Court. The Chief Justice of India may also ascertain the view of one or more senior Judges of that High Court.'[107] In respect to the transfer of High Court judges, the Bench laid down that (a) the Chief Justice of India *alone* shall have the power to initiative transfer proposal; and (b) his opinion in the matter shall not only be 'primate' but '*determinative*' in nature. In forming his opinion however, the Chief Justice shall consult (i) any Supreme Court judge whose opinion may be significant for the purpose; (ii) the Chief Justice of the High Court from where the judge is to be transferred; (ii) at least one other senior High Court Chief Justice, or any other person whose views he considers relevant for transfer. The transfers could not be 'punitive' in character; the power of transfer could be used only in 'public interest'.

Thus, the Court established the pre-eminent position of the Chief Justice of India and institutionalized a 'participatory consultative process' (with a nominal role for the Executive), in appointments and transfers in the higher judiciary, much to the lament of the shaky Congress(I) minority government of Prime Minister P.V. Narasimha Rao.[108] The government could have challenged the Court for over-reaching itself, but it had neither the political strength (surviving in office as it was through legitimate and not so legitimate coalitions), nor the moral courage [mired as it was in corruption, stonewalling the probe into 'Bofors' and other scams[109]), to tangle with the Court which was getting increasingly popular as the 'Court of First Resort' for its 'victim abuse' jurisprudence. While the political system was undergoing dis-rythemic changes (fragmentation of the party system; economic reforms; defection politics and disorderly scenes in state legislatures), while the criminalization of politics was on the increase (the Vohra Committee Report 1995 highlighted the 'nexus' among politicians-bureaucrats, and businessman[110]), the moral bankruptcy of the government was exposed in the *Ramaswami impeachment* case in 1993. Appointed to the Supreme Court bench by the Rajiv Gandhi government without the consent of the Chief Justice of India in 1989,[111] the ruling Congress(I) party bailed Ramaswami out despite the fact that he was found guilty of financial irregularities by the Lok Sabha Speaker's three-member judicial committee, of which Supreme Court Justice P.S. Sawant was a member. Justice Sawant's verdict said that Ramaswami was:

> guilty of wilful and gross misuse of office, purposeful and persistent negligence in the discharge of duties, intentional and habitual extravagance at the cost of the public exchequer, moral turpitude by using public funds for private purposes in diverse ways and reckless disregard of statutory rules, and brings disrepute to the high judicial office and dishonor to the institution of the judiciary and undermines the faith and confidence which the public reposes in the administration of justice.

And Sawant J concluded: 'The acts are of such a nature that his continuance in office will be prejudicial to the administration of justice and to public interest.'[112]

After SCAORA, the Rao government did not dabble in appointments and transfers, letting the chips fall where they may most of the time, but it watched with concern, the expanding reach of the higher judiciary that particularly touched the conventional authority of other political institutions: the President, Parliament, Governors, Speakers of State Assemblies and others.[113] The government also noted the judicial unfolding of the universe of basic structures of the Constitution,[114] the dynamic interplay between fundamental rights and the directive principles of state policy,[115] and, to its discomfort, the judicial assertiveness in PIL cases (the number increased because of relaxed *locus standi* rule[116]). As some judicial decisions, particularly in the social, labour, health, and environment areas (bridged with the expanded jurisprudence of fundamental rights and the directive principles of state policy), had wide-ranging consequences, the Court had often to remind the executive authorities of Article 144 of the Constitution: 'All authorities, civil and judicial, in the territory of India shall act in aid of the Supreme Court.'[117] The leadership of the apex Court in these areas had an emboldening effect on the High Courts (and even on the lower courts) too. In fact, the dwindling legitimacy of the executives and the legislatures at both the levels of federal system compelled wide judicial intervention, creating a somewhat healthy fear of the rule of law (though heads of as many as 15 ministers in Rao's cabinet rolled, on corruption charges; the Congress, the worst hit by the courts, wished a special session of the Parliament to discuss the limits of judicial intervention).[118] That the chips were up for the judiciary came out clearly in the high-sounding (or heavy-sounding!) expression of the Chief Justice of India, J.C. Verma, in 1996: 'As far as I am concerned, we are only making the executive work. We are not usurping its role. And while the courts are making the executive work, what is needed is very deft handling. It is like a sharp-edged tool which has to be used as a scalpel in the hands of a skilful surgeon to cure the malady. Not as a Rampuri knife which can kill.'[119] The analogy of the surgeon-patient was interesting and spoke volumes for the state of changed judicial-executive relations. Not surprisingly, V.N. Gadgil, a Congress(I) Member of the Parliament, introduced a private member's bill (1996) to take the appointment of judges outside the exclusive domain of the judiciary.[120]

With power, however, comes responsibility, and the *pater familias* had a lot of it after the SCAORA decision. Although the Chief Justices' Conference in September 1992, had endorsed the government's policy, that one-third of the judges in each High Court should be from other States, and that such a policy should be implemented (through 'initial' appointments and 'lateral' transfer in equal numbers), on the recommendation of a 'peer committee',[121] it was no smooth sailing for Supreme Court Chief Justice M.N. Venkatachaliah, when the President of India, on the recommendation of the Chief Justice, and in accordance with the SCAORA procedures, ordered the transfer of as many as 50 High Court judges in April 1994 under Article 222 of the Constitution. As the goals of the transfer policy were ambiguous (was it national integration?), the transfer orders provoked concern, even resentment, among a section of lawyers in certain parts of the country.[122] But if one of the unarticulated objectives of the transfer policy was to eliminate corruption in High Courts (widespread as the disease of 'son-stroke' and 'uncle judge' was, Venkatachaliah CJ having checked out for this malady in preparing his transfer list[123]), the policy simply did not work. However, despite the fact that judges were, more or less, beyond the reach of law,[124] the watchful media and the active Bar associations began to expose the hidden skeletons in the cupboards of some of the High Courts. In 1995, Chief Justice A.M. Bhattacharjee (Bombay) was forced to resign following a lawyers' agitation and allegations of corruption.[125] A year later, the Supreme Court banned public demonstrations against judges accused of corruption or misbehaviour.[126] Short of removal by impeachment (a nearly impossible constitutional process), there were no effective complaint remedial mechanisms in place to deal with errant judges. In the *Bhattacharjee* case, a two-judge bench of the Supreme Court had placed the responsibility of dealing with allegations of misconduct against a member of the higher judiciary, on the CJI, but no action strategy was streamlined to resolve such matters. Although transferring a tainted judge to another location could help (though it created its own problems), such an action offered no long-term solution to cleansing the higher judiciary. With a view to dealing with disciplinary matters therefore, the brotherhood of chief justices turned their attention to revamping the 'in-house procedures' for their effectiveness, and adopted a revised Code of Conduct—Restatement of Values of Judicial Life—in 1996.[127]

Rao's leadership came to a disgraceful end after a prolonged uneasy tenure—a tenure marked by corruption in high places eroding the credibility of the democratic system—after the Congress(I) suffered its most unprecedented defeat in the 1996 parliamentary elections, which returned a very fractured verdict. The BJP, which was returned with the largest number of parliamentary seats, formed a minority government under the leadership of Atal Behari Vajpayee on 28 May 1996, but resigned thirteen days later. Thereafter, H.D. Deve Gowda formed a 13-parties United Front government in June 1996 which, besieged from within by disparate regional leaders and from without by the Congress(I) and the Marxists, muddled through for ten months. Unable to meet the ever-expanding Congress(I) charter of demands, Congress President Sitaram Kesri pulled the plug on the Gowda ministry in April 1997 but, on second thought, agreed to support the United Front government under the new leadership of I.K. Gujral, which lasted until November

1997 (caretaking until March 1998). The 1998 parliamentary elections returned a fractured verdict once again. Atal Behari Vajpayee (BJP) formed a rainbow coalition government (a combination of 17 parties and Independents) in March 1998, but the government lost on a confidence vote, and resigned in April 1999. The BJP did not improve its score of seats in the 1999 parliamentary polls but formed, once again, a coalition government in alliance with 24 parties (the National Democratic Alliance) under the leadership of Atal Behari Vajpyee which continued in office until the next elections in 2004.

The United Front Interegnum: 1996–1998

Both Deve Gowda and Inder Kumar Gujral (1996–8) were Prime Ministers by default. Both were tossed around by regional leaders and both were rudderless in the midst of all-pervasive political normlessness. But the worst aspect of their tenure was that both were the prisoners of the Congress(I) party which expected them to sabotage the 'law taking its own course' in the several scam-related prosecutions of many of the 'jail to bail' top Congress leaders.[128] Likewise, some regional leaders—allies of the United Front—who were caught in the cobweb of judicial trials (the Election Commission noted in August 1997, that 40 sitting Members of the Parliament and 700 Members of State Assemblies had criminal records[129]), wished to be protected too. Suspected of pulling some strings to help out Narasimha Rao (who was under judicial trial for corruption), the media cried foul when Deve Gowda rushed to bail out the Bihar Chief Minister, Laloo Prasad Yadav, in the multi-crore fodder scam. The *Statesman Weekly's* editorial observed, 'The humble farmer may have a great deal to be humble about but he has nothing to learn as regards the misuse of power to protect the guilty.'[130]

After Congress(I) dumped Deve Gowda, I.K. Gujral went overboard to appease Congress President Sitaram Kesri, who (like many other tall leaders involved in the Jain Hawala[131] and other cases) was under investigation by the Central Bureau of Investigation (CBI), for foreign financial contributions to his party. Warning that 'there will be no witch-hunting',[132] Gujral shot himself in the foot when he removed the overzealous CBI Director Joginder Singh and suffered a reprimand from the Supreme Court. 'If someone in the probe team is changed', said Chief Justice J.S. Verma, 'the government must come to us for permission . . . his [Joginder Singh's] removal should have come earlier'.[133] Gujral's alleged intervention in the *Jain Hawala* case did not add to his reputation either. In the *Kesri* case, Gujral 'got his government to say' that there was no case for Sitaram Kesri to answer in the matter where four nondescript foreign firms sent the party almost Rs. 4 crore out of the goodness of their corporate heart'. The Delhi High Court was upset and sharply reminded all concerned that the government's satisfaction was 'not enough and [that] the Court must be satisfied'.[134] 'The Emperor has no clothes', headlined the *Statesman Weekly,* and 'Go—even if you leave in chaos!',[135] 'That Mr. Gujral is not personally corrupt is accepted', commented the *Statesman Weekly,* editorial of 2 August 1997, 'that he is well out of his depth in dealing with corruption is no longer in doubt, that he is quite at ease tolerating it and misusing his office to protect family and friends both political and personal is, on the evidence, all too painfully apparent. The Prime Minister is not aware of the damage he is inflicting on the body politic. . . .'[136]

The United Front government, weak-kneed as it was, could not meddle in judicial appointments and transfers, but its agenda to circle the higher judiciary (which was closing on the tainted supporters of the regime) was obvious. In 1997, Union Law Minister Ramakant D. Khalap attempted (and drafted 82nd Amendment Bill) to limit the powers of the Chief Justice of India with regard to appointments ('The policy for judges' appointments,' he said, 'doesn't reflect the spirit of the Constitution.'[137]) and to legislate eligibility parameters for the admission of PILs. 'The present-day situation is', a cabinet note fulminating against judges said, 'that the judiciary is cooperating, encouraging and promoting PIL. The judiciary has digressed from its traditional duties and functions and has entered into a field in which it has no competence or safe standards for judicial action.'[138] While the judges stood their ground on the usefulness of PIL, and blamed the investigating agencies for their failure to successfully prosecute the accused in corruption cases, the government decried 'the judiciary's penchant for admitting the most flippant of public-interest litigation [increasingly instrumental in nailing down corrupt politicians], to pass administrative directives (like such and such officer cannot be shifted), over the heads of the executive, to show scant regard for the practicality of their orders, and to use the court-room as a forum for arraignment of the political class'.[139] The lament of the government was not without reason. On 12 August 1997, the judicial over-activism of the Patna High Court was reflected in its flippant remark that Bihar was fit for President's rule (a centre's privilege on report from the Governor, or otherwise) in view of the dysfunctional state administration.[140] And one month before Chief Justice J.S. Verma retired in January 1998, a three-judge Jain Hawala Bench headed by him wrote a comprehensive handbook of rules for the central investigating agencies—the CBI was no longer to report to the Prime Minister but instead to the Central Vigilance Commission (CVC); and neither the CBI nor the Enforcement Directorate (ED) were required to seek the top level permission to investigate public servants.[141] The Court had indeed pushed itself over the edge.

The Vajpayee Regime(s): 1998–2004

If the United Front was the prisoner of Congress(I), Vajpayee's NDA government (1998–9) was the prisoner of the AIADMK supremo, J. Jayalalitha (with a loyal brigade of 18 MPs), who wished to seek cover in corruption cases which were being hotly pursued by the CBI and the Tamil Nadu DMK government of M. Karunanidhi. In addition, she was being investigated by the income tax authorities. Although the Vajpayee government did not give into her multiple wish list, it did accommodate many of her unbecoming demands. She successfully claimed critical ministerial berths (including the law portfolio), for her nominees in the Union cabinet, sought a veto over high-level appointments, and drew on the resources of the Centre in her relentless fight in the courts to stop her prosecution. In April 1998, she was reported to have handpicked 33 AIADMK advocates and got them appointed as senior central government counsels in the Madras High Court, through her nominated Union Minister of Law.[142] The credibility of the centre was seriously undermined when it herded out M.K. Bezbaruah from the Enforcement Directorate of the CBI. 'The (transfer) order must be revoked with immediate effect', reprimanded the Supreme Court, 'and he should be reinstated as Enforcement Director'.[143] New Delhi stumbled once again when it transferred Jayalalitha's corruption cases from special courts to ordinary courts after the Madras High Court had rejected her petition against special courts.[144] In respect to the Bofors case, the Supreme Court expressed concern about the non-prosecution of any one by the CBI 'years after the event and wished to be informed, why this forbearance'.[145] In a somewhat overdrawn comparison, the *Statesman Weekly*, editorial commented in November 1998: Prime Minister Vajpayee 'has shown disturbing similarities with his predecessor; the same indecision; the same tolerance for corruption, even the same propensity to interfere with investigations into criminal offences allegedly committed by political allies like Jayalalitha and rescuing friends and relatives in trouble with law, as Gujral was wont to do.'[146]

The NDA government, perhaps, had no intention to confront the judiciary (because of its own precarious existence even after the 1999 parliamentary elections), though it would have liked to revert to the pre-1993 situation in respect to judicial appointments and transfers. Thus, when the Union Law Minister, M. Thambi Durai, and the Chief Justice of India, Madan Mohan Punchhi (who had succeeded J.S. Verma in January 1998 in the midst of controversy[147]), deadlocked in the matter of certain appointments and transfers[148] (Punchhi had returned all files to the Law Mantralya, and there was a lurking suspicion that he did not subscribe to the 1993 SCAORA decision in which he had dissented along with Ahmadi), the government preferred to seek the advisory opinion of the Supreme Court under Article 143 of the Constitution.[149] In the opinion rendered on the *Presidential reference* (1998), the 9-judge Bench of the Supreme Court, without any dissent, reaffirmed SCAORA with some improvements. In making recommendation for appointment to the Supreme Court, the Chief Justice of India must consult four (not two as in SCAORA), senior-most judges of the Supreme Court. Exceptions to the seniority principle for appointments from among the High Court judges could be made to accommodate outstanding merit and regional balance on the Supreme Court. For appointment to High Courts, the 'primacy' of the Chief Justice of India must reflect the elements of plurality of opinions, as formed in consultation with his two senior-most judges. 'They would in making their decision take into account the opinion of the Chief Justice of the High Court, which "would be entitled to greatest weight", the views of other high court judges who may have been consulted and the views of the Supreme Court judges who are conversant with the affairs of the concerned high court.'[150] For High Court transfers, the Chief Justice of India must consult (a) the Chief Justice of the High Court from which the judge is to be transferred; (b) the Chief Justice of the High Court to which the transfer is to be effected; and (c) any other judge of the Supreme Court whose opinion may be relevant and significant in the case. Following such a consultation, a collegium consisting of the CJI and four other senior-most judges of the Supreme Court would consider the matter of transfer with due consideration given to the response of the judge to be transferred. Thus, the Court elucidated SCAORA, and embedded, more deeply than before, a wider 'participatory consultative process' in judicial appointments and High Court transfers.

However, if one thought that the Executive had accepted judicial supremacy in appointments and transfers after the *Presidential reference,* the President of India, K.R. Narayanan, did not think so. In November 1998, the President questioned the procedure followed in the appointment of four Chief Justices and several judges of various High Courts despite the fact that the union cabinet had concurred with the recommendations (which included seven appointments to the Supreme Court and about 150 appointments to High Courts) of the Chief Justice of India, Dr. A.S. Anand.[151] While President Narayanan finally gave his belated assent, he wrote a potentially explosive suggestion on the file: 'I would like to record my views that while recommending the appointment of Supreme Court judges, it would be consonant with constitutional principles and the nation's social objectives if persons belonging to the weaker sections of society like Schedule Castes and Scheduled Tribes, who comprise 25 per cent of the population, and women, are given due consideration.' And he further added: 'Eligible persons from these categories are available and their under-representation or non-representation would not be justifiable.'[152] Chief Justice Anand's response was simple: 'Our Constitution envisages that merit alone is the criterion for all appointments to the Supreme Court and High Courts. And we are scrupulously adhering to these provisions.'[153] It was certainly a correct but not an exhaustive response, to the President's concern which boiled down to '*how and who* gets selected under the new regime of judicial supremacy'? This concern was to become the major focus of the media and the Bar associations, particularly whenever the integrity of a judge or a community of judges was called into question. Over the years, the often-heard criticism against the Supreme Court was that it was not transparent about its internal consultation process in judicial appointments and that such a non-transparent system was turning the judiciary into an 'enclosed community', with the rules of entry entirely dictated by its own members.[154]

'If wars cannot be left to generals alone', Justice V.R. Krishna Iyer had commented after the *Second judges* decision, 'judicial administration cannot be left to the "robed brethren" alone.'[155] At a national convention on judicial corruption and judicial accountability in August 2003, Justice P.B. Sawant, former judge of the Supreme Court, deplored the fact that persons known for their integrity-deficit had been appointed to the High Courts, and that there was a 'give and take' between the members of the judicial collegium which had selected judges since 1993. 'Caste, religion and political considerations have played a role;

the device is to keep a seat in the Supreme Court vacant as a carrot hanging before the Chief Justice of the High Court, to secure the appointment of one's nominees on the High Court.'[156] While Chief Justice S.P. Bharucha of the Supreme Court admitted in early 2003, that the integrity of about 20 per cent of judges in the higher judiciary was in serious doubt, the Union Law Minister Jana Krishnamurthy lamented: 'Earlier such deviant behavior,' referring to charges of misconduct against some High Court judges, 'was confined to the lower judiciary. Now it has reached the high courts. Unfortunately, we have no mechanism at present to deal with the situation.'[157] Although the 'in-house procedures' evolved since 1997 to deal with allegations of judicial misconduct had worked reasonably well in settling cases of misconduct in the Punjab, Rajasthan, Karnataka, and Delhi High Courts,[158] questions were raised about the non-transparency nature of investigations conducted by the Chief Justice of India. In August 2003, the Bar Council of India requested the centre and the CJI to transfer as many as 131 High Court judges whose relatives were practising in the same High Courts.[159]

Prime Minister Vajpayee was anguished over the deteriorating state of law and order in the country—'there is an all-pervasive perception that the law has become a shield of the unscrupulous'[160]—and with the increasing number of pending cases before the courts, but his government (1999–2004) lived with the *Presidential reference* decision, even though irksome, and relied on the CJI to handle matters of judicial indiscipline. That the government wished to give no offence to the higher judiciary became obvious when the Union Law Minister, Ram Jethmalani, was asked to resign, for engaging himself in a 'turf war' with Chief Justice A.S. Anand in mid-2000.[161] However, as the government was concerned with multiple constitutional issues, including the issue of judicial selections and appointments, it set up a Judicial Commission to Review the Working of the Constitution in 2000.

During the second tenure of the Vajpayee government, no dramatic changes took place in executive-judicial relations. While the government continued to live with the criticism that it was soft-pedalling investigations (Tehelka expose[162]), that it was covering the Sangh Parivar excesses (the *Babri Masjid demolition* case, the Godhra violence in Gujarat, etc.[163]), that some of its disinvestments policies were misguided,[164] and that it was encouraging a 'wheeler-dealer' political culture to stay in power, the higher judiciary, particularly the Supreme Court, continued to be praised for many of its landmark judgements (*Fatima Beevi* case 2001; striking down Section 33B of the Representation of

People Act Amendment, 2003; and others[165]), though it also continued to be blamed for transgressing its boundaries in its crusade against executive-legislative mismanagement and the abuse of power.[166] Referring to the Supreme Court's deadline for using CNG buses in Delhi, a former retired High Court judge said: 'While the executive has collapsed and no excuses can be made for them, the Supreme Court is not justified in issuing what is almost a *firman*.'[167] And Delhi Chief Minister Sheila Dikshit complained: 'The courts have not been listening to the elected governments.'[168]

Over the years, the Supreme Court in particular has come under attack for its lack of judicial restraint. Praful Bidwai of the *Frontline* said it all:

> The Supreme Court has, regrettably, blurred the separation of powers demarcations. This [the Jharkhand episode 2005], is one more step toward the expansion of the court's remit and the erosion of the domains of the legislature and the executive. This is part of the process which has been in motion since the *Second judges case*. This created a higher judiciary, that is virtually self-appointing and not fully answerable to anyone in its exercise of a number of self-defined powers. The courts have entered into areas—for instance, micro-management of urban transport and the right fuel to be used, or banishing lakhs of people from cities in the name of 'environmenal protection'—which should be considered out of bounds for the judiciary. At the same time, they have tended to ignore or dismiss well-thought out petitions that seek to restrain or punish corporate malfeasance (for instance, Bhopal or Enron's Dabhol project), or prevent enormous human rights violations, as in the Narmada displacement case.[169]

Commenting on the order of the Supreme Court in respect to the Jharkand legislature—when and how long the Assembly should meet; what should the Speaker do; and that the session be videotaped,[170] Fali Nariman said: 'It is as if it [the Supreme Court], was dealing with some *administrative body*, and as if it were part of administrative law. . . . If it can happen here, it can happen anywhere else and the High Court has the same power.'[171] However, when Lok Sabha Speaker Somnath Chatterjee protested against the Court's 'encroachment on well-demarcated areas of powers of the legislatures',[172] interestingly there were few who were willing to pursue this controversy.[173] The Manmohan Singh coalition government (United Progressive Alliance) rather took the view that the Speaker's statement was 'an unwarranted exercise against the judiciary'.[174] In the politics of existentialism where the distinction between the lawmakers and lawbreakers has become unclear, the Court perhaps had no choice but to do what it did. 'We now have politics', regretted Era Sezhiyan, 'that is deinstitutionalised, demoralized, devalued and dehumanized'.[175] This, to a large extent, explains the expanding universe of the higher judiciary. Juristocracy (particularly when the courts have a high reputation for rectitude and political impartiality), triumphs when public's elected representatives cannot be trusted for good governance. The unprecedented judicialization of politics, functionalists will argue, is an organic response to pressures within the political system itself.[176]

PART III: NATIONAL JUDICIAL COMMISSION

The National Commission to Review the Working of the Constitution (NCRWC), or the Venkatachaliah Commission, appointed by the Vajpayee government in February 2000, reported its recommendations in 2002. The Commission's recommendations in respect to the higher judiciary were brief. It did not discuss the underlying tensions between the executive-legislative and judicial powers and privileges,[177] nor did it raise other controversial concerns such as the expanding scope of judicial review in the context of the theory of 'the basic structure' of the Constitution.[178] It did, however, acknowledge the need for judicial restraint: 'Judicial activism', the Commission said, 'has not gone too well with groups of democratic theorists, who object to the kind of judicial activism which has tended to turn social and political processes to legal processes and obliterate the line of demarcation between interpretation and adjudication, exhibiting an ever eager tendency to intervene in the governing process. Constitutional adjudications do have an inevitable legislative element. Judges need great wisdom and restraint in wielding these great judicial powers, lest they should build their own predilections into principles.'[179] Undoubtedly, the NCRWC's comments were well loaded.

With regard to judicial appointments, the NCRWC recognized that there was 'a movement throughout the world to move this function away from the exclusive fiat of the executive, and involve some institutional framework, where under consultation with the judiciary at some level [was] provided for, before making such appointments'. However, it would be worthwhile, the NCRWC added, 'to have a participatory mode with the participation of both the executive and the judiciary in making such recommendations'.[180]

In this spirit, it recommended, for the purpose of appointments to the Supreme Court *alone*, the constitution of a National Judicial Commission (NJC) composed of (i) The Chief Justice of India as Chairman; (ii) Two senior-most judges of the Supreme Court; (iii) The Union Minister of Law and Justice; and (iv) One eminent person nominated by the President of India after consulting with the CJI.

The NCRWC did not recommend any role for the National Judicial Commission in High Court appointments and transfers, and in the removal of judges for deviant behaviour. Perhaps, it wished to exclude the executive representatives in such matters. Instead, it suggested that (a) the President would transfer a judge from one High Court to another after consultation with a committee comprising the CJI and the two senior-most judges of the Supreme Court; and (b) a committee consisting of the CJI and two senior-most judges of the Supreme Court would be *exclusively* empowered to examine complaints of deviant behaviour of all kinds and complaints of misbehaviour and incapacity against the Supreme Court and High Court judges. The NCRWC laid down a 3-step procedure for investigating judicial misbehaviour and suggested remedies based on the gravity of misbehaviour (administering a warning to the errant judge; change in the allotment of work; transfer; and removal through impeachment). However, any proposed action for misbehaviour required of the CJI to place the proposal before a committee of seven senior-most judges of the Supreme Court.[181] In addition, the NCRWC recommended the appointment of Judicial Councils at the apex, and at the high court level, under a parliamentary statute for the preparation of plans and annual budgets for judicial administration and development, and for consideration by the Finance Commission, the Planning Commission, and by the two orders of government.

The Vajpayee government, it appears, was not satisfied with the NCRWC recommendations. It did not wish to be excluded in the appointment and transfer of High Court judges, nor from examining complaints of judicial misconduct. Thus, when Law Minister Arun Jaitley introduced the Constitution (98th Amendment), Bill during the budget session of the Parliament in 2003, the National Judicial Commission (now with one significant change—the President of India was to appoint one eminent person on advice from the Prime Minister for a period of three years), was put in charge of appointing the Supreme Court judges, as also appointing and transferring High Court judges (in association with the High Court Chief Justice concerned and the state Chief Minister). Besides, the NJC was authorized to draw a code of conduct for judges, inquire into cases of misconduct or deviant behaviour of a judge, and advise the Chief Justice of India or the Chief Justice of the concerned High Court as appropriate. The NJC's recommendations with respect to appointments and transfers were made binding on the President of India.

The main purpose of the Amendment Bill, Arun Jaitley explained, was 'to provide transparency in the appointment of judges'. The rationale given for the Bill was 'the general dissatisfaction with the present system of appointment and transfer of judges of the higher judiciary and the in-house procedure evolved by the Supreme Court to inquire into cases of misconduct or deviant behaviour of judges'.[182]

The reaction to the Bill was swift. 'Despite the avowed objective to ensure transparency in the selection process', wrote Venkatesan, 'there is nothing in the Bill that makes transparency mandatory. It empowers the NJC to regulate its own procedure. With three judicial members and two executive appointees, the Commission is under no obligation to make its selection process public or declare the rationale behind its decisions.'[183] Further, Venkatesan added, 'With two political appointees on the NJC sharing the responsibility to draw a code of ethics for judges and to inquire into charges of misconduct against judges, will judicial independence not be compromised, observers wonder.'[184] The Committee on Judicial Accountability (CJA), an association of eminent legal experts which has consistently demanded the establishment of a National Judicial Commission, faulted the composition of the proposed NJC. Instead of including any member of the executive or the judiciary, the 'National Judicial Commission', said Prashant Bhushan of the CJA, 'should consist of former judges, eminent advocates, and legal experts. Only then can it ensure objectivity and transparency in the process of selection of judges and disciplining judges accused of misconduct.'[185] Bhushan's suggestion may not be practical, but it does reflect the current deficit of trust in the executive and the judiciary to handle matters of judicial appointments and discipline.

While every country designs its own political institutions and processes, no political system in the world provides for a self-appointing judiciary as is the case in India. Neither in Canada nor in the United States is there a requirement that the Chief Justice of the country has to be consulted while making high judicial appointments. While the United States provides for confirmation hearings of Supreme Court appointments by the Senate,[186] a parliamentary committee was set up to review the latest appointments to the Supreme Court of Canada though, constitutionally, judicial appointments continue to be the preserve of the Governor-General of Canada. For other federal appointments to superior and appellate courts, each Canadian province has an independent expert committee that advises the federal justice minister on whether candidates are highly qualified, qualified, or not qualified, leaving the final selection to the federal government. While it is a given in the United States that partisan (not necessarily non-meritorious[187]) appointments are made, the emphasis in Canada has been to purge judicial patronage by constituting non-partisan vetting committees in each province, with the recent move to let a parliamentary committee review appointments to the top court.[188] In other words, the general thrust in Canada as also in many other democratic countries has been to democratize and make more transparent, the process of high judicial appointments by including more stakeholders in the selection process. The proposed Bill for the constitution of a National Judicial Commission, therefore, is a right move except that its composition should be enlarged to include other stakeholders. A representative of the Bar Association of India [and of the State Bar Association(s) in the case of High Court appointments] and a spokesperson of the Lok Sabha (preferably the Speaker) will certainly go a long way in making the judicial appointment process more open, if not more transparent. [Incidentally, despite a great deal of political patronage, Rajeev Dhavan writes, 'the most crucial appointments to the higher judiciary have not been arbitrarily made by politicians. . . . Once appointed, those selected have ensured that judicial processes are fair . . .'[189]]. Disciplinary matters and inter-state transfer of High Court judges should be the preserve of the higher judiciary, so that it is held accountable for smooth and clean judicial administration.

The matter of judicial appointments, however, is a part of the larger issue having to do with the expanding ambit of judicial powers at the cost of the other two branches of government. Even though it be argued that the higher judiciary has acted in the public interest, that it has expanded and created new fundamental rights in line with the international 'rights jurisprudence', that it has opened its doors to the marginalized sectors of society through the public interest litigation process, that it has enlarged the contours of secular democracy, checkmated political corruption (notwithstanding the low conviction rate[190]), and entrenched the rule of law more firmly than ever before, and that it has, to some extent, provided relief even to the other two branches of government by dealing with divisive political and social issues,[191] there is no denying the fact that its activist role has distorted the original scheme of power distribution as provided in the Constitution. The political response of the minority and coalition governments—weak and fractious—has been not to challenge judicial aggrandizement (but to focus on judicial selections as a means to restoring the constitutional balance of powers), but the dangers of an all-powerful judiciary cannot be overlooked. As former Additional Solicitor General Santosh Hegde pointed out: 'Things are so bad today that any and every approach adopted by the courts is applauded. But the damage suffered by the checks and balances of our Constitution makes me apprehensive about tomorrow.'[192]

There is another downside to judicial activism. The judiciary does not have the resources or the capacity to monitor and micro-manage the administrative Leviathan. And as the judiciary cannot quick fix all problems, the public is likely to be disappointed sooner than later. 'Justices and intelligent citizens understand that judicial activism', writes Upendra Baxi, 'cannot provide an element of permanent revolution against the ways of the Indian State. It can (and does), of course, hold a constitutional mirror to wielders of state power reflecting the ugly face of anti-people politics and inhumane practices of power. But the task of making that image more friendly to the plight of India's worst affected or situated citizens may not be wholly performed by any transformation of courts into activist jurisprudential boutiques.'[193] And Justice S.P. Bharucha of the Supreme Court has warned: 'The Court must refrain from passing orders that cannot be enforced, whatever the fundamental right may be, and however good the cause. It serves no purpose to issue some high profile mandamus or declaration that can only remain on paper. It is counter-productive to have people say, 'The Supreme Court has not been able to do anything or worse. It is of cardinal importance to the confidence that people have in the Court that its orders are implicitly and promptly obeyed and it is, therefore, of cardinal importance that orders that are incapable of obedience and enforcement are not made.'[194] Obviously, the stakes are too high for the higher judiciary if it does not restrain itself. At the same time however, the issue of judicial transgressions (which makes the question of judicial selections super significant for the executive), and boundary maintenance will have to be addressed for better executive-legislative-judicial relations. Constitutional systems, needless to emphasize, work best when the sub-systems are in proper equilibrium.

NOTES

1. P.B. Gajendragadkar, *To the Best of my Memory*, Bombay, 1983.
2. Ibid., p. 169.
3. For other comments, see, B.P. Jeevan Reddy, 'Judiciary and its Accountability', in *Indian Judicial System: Need and Direction for Reforms*, New Delhi, 2004, p. 388. V.R. Krishna Iyer, *Constitutional Miscellany*, New Delhi, 2003, Chapter XIV.
4. *India Today*, 28 July 1997.
5. For excellent analysis, see, Arun Shourie, *Courts and their Judgements*, New Delhi, 2001; S.P. Sathe, *Judicial Activism in India: Transgressing Borders and Enforcing Limits*, New Delhi, 2002.
6. *India Today*, 10 August 1998.
7. The confrontation between the Parliament and the Judiciary began with the decision of the Supreme Court in the *Golak Nath* case. The Court not only upheld the contention of the petitioners that certain Land Reforms Acts were *ultra vires* of the Constitution because they infringed fundamental rights, but also declared that 'the Parliament will have no power from the date of this decision to amend any of the provisions of Part III of the Constitution'. In the *Bank Nationalization* case, the Court declared as invalid the Banking Companies Act 1969, under which fourteen banks were nationalized; the Court's view was that the Act violated fundamental rights. In the *Privy Purses* case, the Presidential order de-recognizing the former rulers of princely states, was struck down on the ground that it was outside the competence of the President to issue such an order. The Court's judgements in the two last-mentioned cases created serious uneasiness in political circles. See, S.N. Ray, *Judicial Review and Fundamental Rights* (Calcutta, 1974); S.M.N. Raina, *Law, Judges, and Justices*, Indore, 1979.
8. The four of the nine judges who did not sign this judgement were A.N. Ray, K.K. Mathew, M.H. Beg and S.N. Dwivedi. See, D.C. Gupta, *Indian Government and Politics*, New Delhi, 1979.
9. Upendra Baxi, *The Indian Supreme Court and Politics*, Lucknow, 1980, pp. 21–3.
10. Ibid., p. 25.
11. N.A. Palkhivala, *Our Constitution Defaced and Defiled*, Delhi, 1974, pp. 93–4.
12. See, Mohan Kumaramangalam, *Judicial Appointments: Analysis of the Recent Controversy over the Appointment of the Chief Justice of India*, New Delhi, 1973; Kuldip Nayar (ed.), *The Supersession of Judges*, New Delhi, 1973; G.G. Mirchandani, *Subverting the Constitution in India*, New Delhi, 1978; N.A. Palkhivala (ed.), *A Judiciary Made to Measure*, Bombay, 1973; K.S. Hedge, *Crisis in Indian Judiciary*, New Delhi, 1973.
13. For Kumaramangalam's view on the subject of a committed judiciary,

see, his *Judicial Appointments.* Also see, Kuldip Nayar, *India After Nehru*, New Delhi, 1975, pp. 215–16.

14. Baxi, *Indian Supreme Court*, p.51. The Allahabad judgement was delivered on 12 June 1975. It was the verdict on the petition filed by Raj Narain for quashing Mrs. Gandhi's election to the Lok Sabha on the plea that she had employed corrupt methods to win her election. The verdict went against her. For a detailed reaction to this verdict, see, J.S. Bright, *Allahabad High Court to Shaw Commission*, New Delhi, 1979.
15. Justice Chandrachud's observations, writes Baxi, were 'astonishing at the level of statesmanship and disconcerting at the level of juristic technique'. Baxi, *Indian Supreme Court*, p. 59.
16. The dialogue between a few judges and the Attorney-General is reported in Anil Divan, 'The Supreme Court: Legitimacy and Accountability', *The Radical Humanist*, August 1981.
17. The Swaran Singh Committee, set up by the Congress High Command on 26 February 1975, recommended those drastic changes in the Constitution that became part of the notorious 42nd amendment Act. For a brief purview of the Committee's report, see, *Keesing's Contemporary Archives*, 18 June 1977.
18. The government had long followed the principle not to transfer a High Court judge without his consent and without effectively consulting the Chief Justice of India. See, *Lok Sabha Debates*, XVIII, 25 April–7 May 1963. The experience of sixteen transfers during the Emergency violated this principle. See, A.G. Noorani, 'Transfer of High Court Judges', *Economic and Political Weekly*, 20 September 1980.
19. A number of persons were detained after the promulgation of Presidential Order dated 27 June 1975, which suspended the right to move the courts for the enforcement of right to life and personal liberty. However, some of the detainees challenged their detention by *habeas corpus* petitions under Article 226 of the Constitution. For details, see, S.M.N. Raina, *Law, Judges, and Justice*, pp. 122–7.
20. Speaking at the Bar Association meeting in Bangalore, See, *India Today*, 1–15 July 1981, p. 80.
21. Baxi, *Indian Supreme Court*, p. 113.
22. Baxi, *Indian Supreme Court*, p. 119. Baxi headlines this case as 'the last nail in the coffin of personal liberty'.
23. G.G. Mirchandani, *Subverting the Constitution*, p. 191.
24. The 42nd amendment laid down (a) that no High Court could hear cases involving the constitutional validity of Central laws; (b) that only two-thirds of a minimum five-judge High Court Bench could decide the constitutional validity of any State law; and (c) that only two-thirds of a minimum of a seven-judge Supreme Court Bench could determine the constitutional validity of Central laws. See, Sunder Raman, *Fundamental Rights and the 42nd Constitutional Amendment* (Calcutta, 1977).

25. For two excellent articles on the subject, see, A.G. Noorani, 'Cleaning up the Constitution', *Seminar*, January 1979, and Lloyd I. Rudolph and Susanne Hoeber Rudolph, 'Judicial Review versus Parliamentary Sovereignty: The struggle over Stateness in India', *Journal of Commonwealth and Comparative Politics*, XIX: 3, November 1981.
26. Article 222(1) of the Constitution reads: 'The President may, after consultation with the Chief Justice of India, transfer a judge from one High Court to any other High Court.' However, Law Minister Sen had stated in the *Lok Sabha* in 1963, that the government 'had accepted it as a principle that so far as High Court Judges were concerned, they should not be transferred excepting by consent. This convention has worked without fail during the last twelve years, and all transfers have been made not only with the consent of the transferees, but also in consultation with the Chief Justice of India.' In the *Union of India* v. *S. II. Sheth* (1977), the Supreme Court ruled that (a) the Constitution contemplated only individual transfers, and (b) transfers by the President only after an 'effective and meaningful' consultation with the Chief Justice of India. See, *Lok Sabha Debates; Union of India* v. *S. II. Sheth*, in N.R. Madhava Menon, 'Judicial Appointments and Transfers', *Journal of the Bar Council of India*, VIII(1), 1981; *Gujarat Law Reporter*, No. 17, 1976, pp. 1017–1140. For a reflection on Chandrachud's appointment, see, Henry J. Abraham, 'Merit or Seniority. . . ', *Journal of Commonwealth and Comparative Politics*, XVI: 3, November 1978.
27. Baxi, *Indian Supreme Court*, p. 155. The case arose when the government impounded Mrs. Maneka Gandhi's passport under Section 10 of the Passport Act. The Court ruled that Section 10 was arbitrary and offended fundamental rights, establishing the principle that the procedure contemplated by Article 21 must be 'right, just and fair' and must pass the test of 'reasonableness'. In the words of Justice Bhagwati, '. . . though the right to go abroad is not a Fundamental Right, the denial of the right to go abroad may, in truth and in effect, restrict freedom of speech and expression or freedom to carry on a profession . . . '. See, M.P. Jain, *Indian Constitutional Law* (Nagpur, 2003), pp. 1169–70. In *Pathak*, the Court ruled that the State could not abrogate the bonus settlement with the LIC workers; in *Madhav Haskot*, it ruled that free legal service to the poor was an integral component of 'reasonable, fair, and just' procedure; in *Hussainara Khatoon*, speedy trial was ruled as part of the right to life and liberty.
28. Baxi, *Indian Supreme Court*, p. 163.
29. See, *Times of India*, 7 May 1977; Baxi, *Indian Supreme Court*, pp. 127–36; Bhagwan D. Dua, 'India: A Study in the Pathology of a Federal System'. *Journal of Commonwealth and Comparative Politics*, XIX:3, November 1981; Alice Jacob and Rajeev Dhavan, 'The Dissolution Case: Politics at the Bar of the Supreme Court', *Journal of Indian Law Institute*, 19:4, October–December 1977.

30. See, S.S. Sahay, 'Significance of Special Courts', *Statesman Weekly*, 23 December 1978.
31. Alice Jacob and Rajeev Dhavan, 'The Dissolution Case . . .', p. 390.
32. See, Rajeev Dhavan, *Justice on Trial: The Supreme Court Today*, Allahabad, 1980, pp. 73–4.
33. Arun Shourie, *Symptoms of Fascism*, New Delhi, 1978, p. 308.
34. The full text of the letter dated January 15, is published in the *Overseas Hindustan Times*, 3 April 1980. Justice Bhagwati who made sterling contribution to social justice during his tenure on the Supreme Court was next in line of seniority to Chandrachud CJ. Also see, Arun Shourie, *Indian Express*, 25 January 1982, for 'startling inconsistencies' in his judgements during and after the Emergency.
35. *Overseas Hindustan Times*, 3, 17 and 24 April 1980.
36. *India Today* 31 January 1982, p. 62.
37. *Statesman Weekly*, 19 January 1980.
38. The cases pending before the special court were in relation to the arrest of Bhimsen Sachar during the Emergency, and the alleged harassment of four officials detained to collect information regarding the Maruti car project of Sanjay Gandhi. See, *Overseas Hindustan Times*, 28 February 1980; A.G. Noorani, 'Judgement in Special Court No. 2', *Economic and Political Weekly*, 23 February 1980.
39. In this case, Mrs. Gandhi and others were accused of procuring jeeps without payment from some industrialists and companies for use in the Lok Sabha election campaign in 1977 at Rae Bareilli and Amethi. See, *Overseas Hindustan Times*, 28 February 1980.
40. *Overseas Hindustan Times*, 3 April 1980.
41. Before Justice Vohra convicted Sanjay Gandhi and V.C. Shukla for entering into a conspiracy during the Emergency to destroy the film 'Kissa Kursi Kaa' produced by Amrit Nahata, the Supreme Court Bench, consisting of Chief Justice Chandrachud, Justices Ali and Shinghall, had cancelled Sanjay Gandhi's bail for 'abusing his liberty by attempting to suborn the prosecution witnesses'.
42. A.G. Noorani, 'Kissa Kursi Kaa Case', *Economic and Political Weekly*, 14–21 June 1980.
43. The Baroda Dynamite case involved George Fernandes and others who were charged with blowing up bridges and derailing passenger trains in various parts of Bombay and Karnataka during the Emergency. The Janata government withdrew the case from the Delhi High Court in March 1977. However, R.K. Jain challenged the withdrawal in the Supreme Court. See, *Overseas Hindustan Times*, 24 April 1980.
44. *Overseas Hindustan Times*, 15 May 1980.
45. Ibid., 22 May 1980.
46. But for Justice Bhagwati, a five-member Bench of the Court ruled that the 'Parliament could not have unlimited power to amend the Constitution

and it could not write into the Constitution that an amendment made by it shall not be called into question in any court on any ground'. In other words, 'the Parliament could not debar the courts from their right of judicial review simply by declaring that such amendments were not to be touched by the courts'. *Overseas Hindustan Times*, 22 May 1980.

47. Ibid., Also see, S. Sahay, 'A Close Look: No Place for Firmans', *Statesman Weekly*, 24 May 1980.
48. See, Anil Divan, 'Supreme Court', *Times of India*, 29 December 1981.
49. *Overseas Hindustan Times*, 22 May 1980. Also see, A. Prasad, *Presidential Government or Parliamentary Democracy* (New Delhi, 1981); S. Sahay, 'Not Wiser Than Before', *Statesman Weekly*, 6 December 1980.
50. See, *India Today*, 1–15 July 1981; *Himmat*, 1 July 1981; *Onlooker*, 16–31 July 1981; *Link*, 21 June 1981; *Illustrated Weekly*, 12–18 July 1981.
51. *India Today*, 1–15 July 1981.
52. *Illustrated Weekly*, 12–18 July 1981.
53. Besides the transfer of sixteen High Court judges, two additional judges of the Delhi High Court, Aggarwal and Lalit, were neither confirmed nor given a further extension when their two-year term expired during the Emergency. See, *Illustrated Weekly*, 12–18 July 1981.
54. Chandrachud's correspondence with the Minister of Law dated 31 July 1980, appears in the *Overseas Hindustan Times*, 31 December 1981. Also see, A.G. Noorani, 'Transfer of High Court Judges', *Overseas Hindustan Times*, 5, 12 and 19 November 1981. Law Minister Shiv Shankar believed his policy will overhaul the increasingly 'communal and partisan' justice system and promote national integration.
55. By the end of the year 1980, seven High Courts had remained without permanent chief justices for over six months because Chandrachud wanted individual cases considered on merit. See, *India Today*, 1--15 February 1981. Chandrachud experienced difficulties in reconciling seniority with merit, in recommending the transfer of Chief Justices of High Courts to the Union Law Minister on 7 December 1980. See, *Hindustan Times*, 19 November 1981
56. See, M.M. Ismail, 'The Decision was Mine', *India Today*, 1–15 August 1981; *Statesman Weekly*, 18 and 25 July 1981.
57. 'Two High Court judges in the Punjab and Haryana High Court, who were to end their temporary tenure in the afternoon on 19 February 1981, got their extension only that morning—and the extension was only for four months. In Madhya Pradesh the swearing-in of judges who had been confirmed belatedly, had to be held at midnight because they could not have continued in office beyond that.' Kuldip Nayar in, *The Daily*, Ahmedabad, 30 July 1981. Also see, *Overseas Hndustan Times*, 31 December 1981.
58. *Illustrated Weekly*, 12–18 July 1981.
59. Ibid. The Law Minister defended his circular on the basis of the recom-

mendations made by the Law Commission of India and suggested that the transfer policy would bring about greater 'national integration.' See, *Eightieth Report, Law Commission of India* (New Delhi, 1979), p. 24; *Tribune*, 16 July 1981 for the text of the circular; *Statesman Weekly* of, 2 May 1981, for criticism.

60. Article 217(1) of the Constitution states that every judge of a High Court shall be appointed by the President after consultation with the CJI, the Governor of the state, and the Chief Justice of the High Court concerned. Prakash Narain, Chief Justice of the Delhi High Court, had charged Kumar with corrupt practices in his letter to the Minister of Law dated 7 May 1981; however, he had requested the Minister not to show the letter to the CJI. Since Kumar's wife had switched her party loyalty during the Janata regime, the whole episode was labelled as a grand conspiracy to get Kumar. The Supreme Court, in its final judgement on 30 December 1981, passed strictures against Narain for going over and above the head of the judiciary. See, *Overseas Hindustan Times*, 25 June, 5 and 12 November 1981; *Statesman Weekly*, 25 July 1981; *Onlooker*, 1–15 July 1981, p. 10; *Tribune*, 31 December 1981.
61. Salman Khursheed and Sudershan Kumar Misra, 'Supreme Court: A Bench Divided', *India Today*, 1–15 February 1981. For widening ideological differences (*Tulzapurkar* v. *Bhagwati*), see, Chaitanya Kalbag, 'A Battle Supreme', *India Today*, 15 December 1982, pp. 32–5.
62. See, Supreme Court's somewhat apologetic judgements in relation to the Special Bearer Bonds, and National Security Act. *Overseas Hindustan Times*, 5 November 1981; *Times of India*, 29, 30 December 1981.
63. *Statesman Weekly*, 9 January 1982.
64. Justice Bhagwati disagreed. For him, the transfer was bad because (a) it was not in public interest; and (b) the consultation between the CJI and the Central government was not 'full and effective'. M.P. Jain, *Indian Constitutional Law*, New Delhi, 2003, p. 443.
65. Justice Bhagwati observed: 'It would therefore be open to the Central Government to override the opinion given by constitutional functionaries required to be consulted and to arrive at its own decision in regard to the appointment of a Judge in the High Court or the Supreme Court . . . *Even if the opinion given by all the Constitutional functionaries consulted by it is identical, the Central Government is not bound to* act *in accordance with such opinion.*' Ibid., p. 473 (emphasis added).
66. The proposals were generally initiated by the High Court Chief Justice in the case of appointment of a High Court judge and by the Supreme Court Chief Justice in the case of a Supreme Court judge. It was only in overriding circumstances that the President rejected such proposals. See, *Eightieth Report, Law Commission of India*. M. Hidayatulla, *My Own Boswell*, New Delhi, 1980, p. 178.

67. *India Today*, 21 November 1981.
68. Since 1980, Bhagwati had never concurred with Chandrachud on any judgement. See, ibid., *Tribune*, 31 December 1981.
69. *Statesman Weekly*, 21 November 1981. Justice Tulzapurkar was critical of the President's action: 'I fail to appreciate the desirability or necessity of the statement made on behalf of the President disowning the personal discussion with the Chief Justice of India. . .'. *Tribune*, 31 December 1981.
70. *India Today*, 31 January 1982.
71. *Statesman Weekly*, 21 November 1981.
72. Ibid., 16 January 1982.
73. S. Sahay, 'A Close Look: You Said Value-Packing, Milord?', *Statesman Weekly*, 23 January 1982. Sahay's comments are very appropriate: 'The grave danger of the Judiciary playing to the gallery is that sooner than we imagine, it may be politically packed, and not merely "value-packed". The majority judgement has created conditions for such a development.'
74. Ibid., *Tribune*, 31 December 1981. V.S. Deshpande regrets that the Supreme Court's approach in the *Judges transfer* case was that of 'mechanical jurisprudence. It was not the approach to the spirit of the Constitution'. 'High Court Judges: Appointment and Transfer', in *The Journal of the Law Institute*, vol. 27, April–June 1985, p. 189.
75. Sumit Mitra, 'Judiciary: Sinister Implications', *India Today*, 28 February 1982. Also see, *Statesman Weekly*, 6 February 1982; *Overseas Hindustan Times*, 11, 18 February and 15 April 1982. For a cursory understanding of the government's point of view on judiciary, see, 'Law Minister likes Soviet Legal Set-up', in *Overseas Hindustan Times*, 16 August 1981; 'Question of Commitment', *Statesman Weekly*, 11 October 1980. Also, 'Judges at Loggerheads', in *Times of India*, 1 January 1982. Considering the rising number of cases in the Court, Jagannath Kaushal, Union Law Minister, announced in late 1982 that he planned to introduce administrative tribunals and limit the work of the Supreme Court and High Courts to constitutional matters. Prabhu Chawla, 'A Losing Battle', *India Today*, 15 September 1982, pp. 64–5.
76. Quoted in Krishan Mahajan, 'A Negotiated Judiciary', *Hindustan Times*, 15 December 1986.
77. One week after he spoke at the all-India law seminar in Patna, the government announced four appointments to the Supreme Court and declared that the Chief Justice had consented to these appointments. See, Sumit Mitra, 'Uneasy on the Bench', *India Today*, 31 March 1983, p. 44.
78. Shekhar Gupta's interview with Chandrachud, *India Today*, 31 July 1985, pp. 42–4. Also, see, Rajeev Dhavan, *Justice on Trial: The Supreme Court Today*, Allahabad, 1980, p. 81.
79. In an interview with the author in August 1981, the Hon'ble Shiv Shankar, then Union Law Minister, insisted that the transfer policy will get rid of

'inbreeding' in judicial nominations, eliminate judicial parochialism, and promote (as the 14th Law Commission Report had suggested), national integration at the same time.

80. Union Law Minister Jagannath Kaushal laid down the guidelines in Parliament on 15 November 1983: (i) A Chief Justice who has only one year or less to retire may not be transferred to any other high court; (ii) A judge in a high court who has one year or less to retire should be considered for appointment as Chief Justice of his own High Court, subject to his seniority in the profession; and (iii) for the purposes of elevation as Chief Justices, the all-India seniority of judges will be taken into account for appointment as chief justices in high courts of other states. *India Today*, 15 December 1983, p. 54.
81. See, Bhagwan Dua, 'The Judicial Landscape', *Seminar* 357, May 1989.
82. 'We are not in favour of a non-Tamil speaking judge to be appointed as chief justice of our court.' MGR quoted in *India Today*, 31 May 1983, p. 61, although MGR was at odds with the incumbent Chief Justice Chandurkar. See, *India Post*, 6 November 1987.
83. Ibid.; The conflict between the Karnataka Chief Minister and the Union Minister for Law and Justice was open and engaging. See, Ramakrishna Hegde's address to the Bar Association of India, 27 June 1986.
84. At times, sharp differences between the Chief Justice and the Chief Minister paralysed nominations with the consequence that vacancies would not be filled up until some more convenient time.
85. The lawyers went on strike when P. Subramaniam Poti was transferred from Kerala to Ahmedabad in 1983. It had not much to do with Poti. The lawyers were supporting the acting Chief Justice, P.D. Desai, senior-most judge in the Court, who should have normally become the Chief Justice of the Court. *India Today*, 15 November 1983, p. 29. Poti's transfer out of Kerala removed Chief Minister Karunakaran's headache as well. See, *India Today*, 30 June 1984.
86. By 1983, the government had moved twelve Chief Justices; and four High Courts had acting Chief Justices.
87. Ibid.
88. Deadlocks were common; Chief Ministers would often sit on the list of nominees submitted by Chief Justices in case of sharp differences. One of the senior judges in the Punjab and Haryana High Court said: 'The chief ministers will not even acknowledge a letter from the highest judicial authority [the Janata-appointed Chief Justice Sandhawalia] for weeks'. *India Today*, 15 October 1982, p. 53. Sandhawalia was later transferred to the Calcutta High Court. Ten vacancies in Madhya Pradesh in 1983 were stalled because of the differences between Chief Justice Guru Prasanna Singh and the state government. *India Today*, 15 December 1983, p. 55.

89. Virendra Singh's writ petition to the effect that Satish Chandra (Allahabad) was transferred to benefit some high caste judges who were accommodated by the acting Chief Justice, M.N. Shukla, following Chandra's departure to Calcutta in 1983. *India Today*, 15 June 1985, pp. 78–9.
90. Ibid.
91. Ibid.
92. Prabhu Chawla, 'Judiciary: Controversial Appointments', *India Today*, 30 November 1986; 15 November 1987. For the dilemma of Brij Mohan Lal who was caught between two chief ministers—Moti Lal Vohra and Arjun Singh, *India Today*, 30 June 1989, pp. 52–3. The issue of caste representation on the court was raised in Tamil Nadu. see, Prabhu Chawla, 'On a Collision Course', *India Today*, 31 May 1983, pp. 60–1. Incidentally, the practice of chief ministers pushing their own candidates was not uncommon even in the Nehru era. M. Hidayatullah, then Chief Justice of Madhya Pradesh High Court, has reported: 'Chief Minister Shukla (MP) had his own candidate for each vacancy for whom he would canvass the Chief Justice.' *My own Boswell: Memoirs*, New Delhi, 1980, p. 178.
93. *India Today*, 28 February 1987, p. 20
94. *India Today*, 15 January 1987.
95. Pathak CJ was listened to with respect, but his advice was ignored at times. He could not do much when J.S. Verma superseded acting Chief Justice Lodha of the Rajasthan High Court, or when Justice B.N. Jha was made the Chief Justice of Allahabad High Court barely 24 hours before he was to retire. *India Today*, 15 November 1987.
96. *Indian Express*, 16 December 1987.
97. R. Venkataraman, *My Presidential Years*, New Delhi, 1994, p. 315. 'It was represented to me', writes the President, 'that the present government was in office commanding a majority in the Lok Sabha and not just a caretaker government and therefore these appointments which had been approved by the CJI and the States, might be accepted. I explained that though legally the contention was right, propriety and democratic conventions called for restraint in such matters after the election process had started.'
98. *India Today*, 13, 31 July 1990. For comments on the proposed National Judicial Commission, see, *Economic and Political Weekly*, 16–23 June 1990, p. 1307.
99. *India Today*, 15 July 1990.
100. Mukharji's recommendation to transfer Justice Desai to Kerala and Justice Kenia to Allahabad did not work. Desai resigned, and Kenia's order was deferred for medical reasons. Besides, 'punitive' transfers were not permissible. Ibid.
101. Mukharji (CJ) himself admitted, that legally he was on slippery ground

though he had the moral right of authority. *India Today*, 28 March 1991, p. 41. Ramaswami survived the impeachment motion—the first of its kind—in the Lok Sabha because the Congress(I), which had formed the government after 1991, decided not to support his impeachment, and the motion simply lapsed.

102. *India Today*, 28 February 1991, p. 41. On the basis of the findings of the three-judge committee, which was also endorsed by the full Court, Chief Justice Mishra reinstated Justice Ramaswami. *India Today*, 31 March 1991. In October 1991, a constitution bench expressed the hope that Justice Ramaswami would abstain sitting the bench in the interest of judicial propriety, though it ruled that he can 'legally continue his judicial functions'. *India Today*, 30 November 1991.
103. *India Today*, 15 July 1990, p. 22. It was pointed out that many of the judges' relatives practised in the same high courts ('son stroke'; 'uncle judge'?), and that a large number of them were 'winning and dining', either at a lawyer's house or at a foreign embassy.
104. *India Today*, 15 July 1990.
105. M.P. Jain, *Indian Constitutional Law*, New Delhi, 2003, p. 227.
106. 'This is a distortion', the Bench said, 'of the constitutional scheme which is wholly impermissible'. Ibid., p. 437.
107. M.P. Jain, *Indian Constitutional Law*, New Delhi, 2003, pp. 229, 439. Unless there were cogent and explainable reasons, the Court ruled that the order of seniority (*inter se* combined with seniority on all-India basis), among the high court judges should be given due weight if a high court judge was to be elevated to the Supreme Court.
108. Lord Cooke of Thorndon, 'Where Angels Fear to Tread', in B.N. Kirpal et al. (eds.), *Supreme But Not Infallible*, New Delhi, 2000, for a critique of the judgement.
109. Narasimha Rao government was perhaps the most corrupt government; virtually one-half of Rao's cabinet was involved in one or the other scam—securities, telecom, housing allotment, petrol pump allocations, Jain Hawala, *St. Kitts forgery* case, *JMM bribery* case, etc., *India Today*, 31 October 1996, pp. 20–3.
110. It required the Supreme Court's intervention to release the Vohra Committee report. For an overview of the report, *Hindu International Weekly*, 5, 12 and 19 August 1995.
111. *India Today*, 15 June 1993, p. 65.
112. *Indian Today*, 31 May 1993, p. 15. Ramaswami's father-in-law, K. Veeraswami, Chief Justice of the Madras High Court, was also charged with corruption in 1976. His objection that the Prevention of Corruption Act did not apply to judges was over-ruled by the Supreme Court in 1991. *India Today*, 31 August 1991, p. 44.
113. It was in *S.R. Bommai* v. *Union of India* (1994), that the Supreme Court

ruled that the President's satisfaction under Article 356 was justifiable. Also see, Suryaprasad, 'Judicial Review of Presidential Proclamation . . .', Ravi P. Bhatia, 'Federalism in India and the Supreme Court Rulings', in B.D. Dua and M.P. Singh (eds.), *Indian Federalism in the New Millennium*, New Delhi, 2003; *India Today*, 30 April 1993, pp. 42–3. Prime Minister Rao said: There was no question of reinstating the Patwa government (BJP) after the Jabalpur Bench of the MP High Court set aside President's rule. *Statesman Weekly*, 10 April 1993; *Hindu International Weekly*, 17 April 1993, p. 12. For conflict between Manipur Speaker H. Borobabu (who said that it was an affront to the institution of the Speaker and to the democratic system itself, to be summoned by the Supreme Court), and the Supreme Court, *Statesman Weekly*, 10 October 1992; *Hindu International Weekly*, 13 February 1993. For conflict between the Tamil Nadu State Assembly and the Madras High Court, *The Hindu International Weekly*, 30 July 1994. A.G. Noorani called for codifying the legislative privileges in *Statesman Weekly*, 11 July 1992. R.D. Sharma for a historical account of the privileges of the legislature in *Statesman Weekly*, 23 May 1992.

114. For background, *Waman Rao* v. *Union of India* (1981). The Supreme Court in this case applied the doctrine of basic structure when it held that (a) any amendment of the Constitution after 24 April 1973 (including laws in the Ninth Schedule) would have to be tested by reference to the basic structure doctrine; and (b) the First and Fourth Amendments, which were passed to effectuate the purpose of Directive Principles contained in Article 39(b) and (c), strengthened the basic structure of the Constitution. For perils of the doctrine, see, Raju Ramachandran, 'The Supreme Court and the Basic Structure Doctrine', in B.N. Kirpal et al. (eds.), *Supreme But Not Infallible*, New Delhi, 2000.

115. The Supreme Court read Article 41 (the right to education, a directive principle) into the right to life guaranteed under Article 21. See, *Mohini Jain* v. *State of Karnataka*; *Unni Krishnan J.P.* v. *State of Andhra Pradesh, and Other* cases. In *M.H. Hoskote* v. *State of Maharashtra*, the Court described Article 39A as an 'interpretative tool' for Article 21.

116. See, Gobind Das, 'The Supreme Court: An Overview'; Ashok H. Desai and S. Muralidhar, 'Public Interest Litigation: Potential and Problems', in B.N. Kirpal et al. (eds.), *Supreme But Not Infallible*, New Delhi, 2000; S.P. Sathe, *Judicial Activism in India*, New Delhi, 2002; Upendra Baxi, 'The Avatars of Indian Judicial Activism: Explorations in the Geographies of Justice', in S.K. Verma and Kusum (eds.), *Fifty Years of the Supreme Court of India*, New Delhi, 2000, *India Today*, 31 October 1996.

117. Arun Shourie writes: '. . . when the neglect of their duties by other institutions compels courts to "take the law in their own hands," so to say, they should at the least look to the practicality of their decrees; monitor the

implementation of what they have decreed, [and] assess the meta-consequences of their decrees.' *Court and their Judgements*, New Delhi, 2001), p. 61.

118. *India Today*, 31 October 1996, p. 20.
119. Ibid., 15 March 1996, p. 99.
120. Ibid., 21 July 1997. Gadgil argued that even though the US appointment process was purely political, no one questioned the independence of US Supreme Court. In no other democracy, he said, does the judiciary enjoy primacy in the selection of judges.
121. *The Hindu International Weekly*, 23 April 1994.
122. Ibid. Lawyers associations in Tamil Nadu, Pondicherry, Bombay and Allahabad planned to go on strike.
123. *India Today*, 15 July 1990; 31 October 1993.
124. Section 154 of the Criminal Procedure Code prohibited the registration of a criminal case against a judge of the higher judiciary (K. Veeraswami case). The Contempt of Courts Act 1971 shielded judges against personal attacks on the plea that such attacks scandalized the court. The shield of contempt was once used by Justice Ajit Sengupta of the Calcutta High Court, to ward off an inquiry into the source of funds for his daughter's education abroad. He was arrested the day after his retirement. See, Sumit Mitra, 'The Judiciary—Losing Face', in *India Today*, 20 January 2003, pp. 15–17.
125. See, *India Today*, 31 December 1996; *Frontline*, 6 December 2002 for V. Venkatesan, 'A Transition in the Supreme Court', pp. 29–30. Also, *Hindu International Weekly*, 4, 11, 18 March 1995. Chief Justice Bhattacharjee (Bombay) was charged with accepting $80,000 as royalty from an unknown publisher in the UK for his book.
126. *India Today*, 31 December 1996, pp. 52–4.
127. In 1992, a resolution was passed in the Chief Justices Conference to restate high values of judicial life; a committee, appointed by the Chief Justice of India, drafted the statement, which was duly endorsed by the Supreme Court . . . re-adopted in 1996. See, K.G. Kannabiran's paper in this book.
128. For details, see, *India Today*, 30 April 1997; *Statesman Weekly*, 26 April 1997, p. 8.
129. *The Hindu International Weekly*, 22 March 2003.
130. *The Statesman Weekly*, editorial, 4 January 1997; *The Hindu International Weekly*, editorial, 21 January 1997. Deve Gowda toyed with the idea of superseding Justice Verma for appointment as the CJI but was dissuaded. See, *Sunday*, 22–8 December 1996, p. 19.
131. *India Today*, 31 October 1996. *Jain Hawala* case involved 15 tall Congress MPs. By the time Rao's government was voted out, almost every member of his cabinet had been charged with abuse of power, if not downright criminality.

132. *India Today*, 7 July 1997, p. 30. Chief Minister Mahanta of Assam, partner in the UF, was also in trouble in the Letter of Credit scam. For details, *Statesman Weekly*, 18 October and, 22 November 1997.
133. The three-judge bench of the Supreme Court was hearing a petition of *amicus curiae* in respect to the removal of Joginder Singh in July 1997, when Chief Justice Verma disclosed that someone was trying to contact him to influence the Jain Hawala bench. Joginder Singh, it was alleged, was replaced under Kesri's pressure. *Statesman Weekly*, 5 and 19 July 1977; *India Today*, 14 and 28 July 1977, pp. 22–7.
134. *Statesman Weekly*, editorial, 6 December 1997.
135. Ibid., 28 june and 12 July 1977.
136. Ibid., editorial, 2 August 1977. Gujral resigned in November 1997 after the UF refused to cave in because of the Congress(I) demand that the UF should disassociate itself from the DMK and its leader, Chief Minister K. Karunanidhi, who, the Jain Commission Report mentioned, had had links with the LTTE, the killer of Rajiv Gandhi in May 1991.
137. *India Today*, 28 July 1997, p. 23.
138. Ibid., pp. 22–7. A PIL led to the closure of 39,000 industries in Delhi (1996). PILs were responsible for exposing many scams–the Satish Sharma petrol pump allotments scandal (1996); the Sheila Kaul housing allotments scandal (1996); the Narasimha Rao JMM bribery scandal (1997); Kesri's foreign contribution scandal (1997), etc. There were 300 PILs before the Supreme Court and another 2,000 in the high courts.
139. Ibid., pp. 23–4.Chief Justice A.S. Anand warned in 1999: 'It is necessary and essential that *PIL* should develop on a consistent and firm path. Care has to be taken to see that *PIL* essentially remains Public Interest Litigation and does not become either *Political* Interest Litigation or *Personal* Interest Litigation or used for *Persecution.*' A.S. Anand, 'Indian Judiciary and Challenges of 21st Century', in S.P. Verma and Kusum (ed.), *Indian Judicial System*, New Delhi, 2004.
140. *India Today*, 25 August 1997, p. 5.
141. Ibid., 29 December 1997. The Court also laid down that the CBI and the ED directors would have a fixed tenure of two years regardless of their due retirement dates, to provide for their continuity in combating corruption without fear or favour. For background, *India Today*, 31 October 1996, pp. 24–6.
142. *Statesman Weekly*, 11, 25 April and 2 May 1998. *India Today*, 4 January 1999. In July, some key Income Tax officials dealing with the cases received marching orders. *Statesman Weekly*, 18 July 1998, p. 4.
143. To the urging of *amicus curiae*, Anil Divan, their Lordship characterized the transfer at this time as an 'extremely distressing factor' and said that they were 'very, very bothered by this'. *Statesman Weekly*, 25 July, 24 August and 12 September 1998. Dr. U.N. Biswas investigating the fodder scam was shuffled around as well.

144. The Madras High Court had ruled that special courts were neither 'malafide nor arbitrary'. *Statesman Weekly*, 7 November 1998. The Supreme Court of India cleared Jayalalitha's trial by special courts on November 26: 'Let it be understood that the interim stay is refused.' *Statesman Weekly*, 5 December 1998, p. 3. In Chennai, three special judges dismissed with contempt Centre's notification of transfer of cases. *India Today*, 22 February 1999. Chief Minister Karunanidhi characterized the central action as 'abuse of power'. *Hindu International Weekly*, 20 February 1999. Tamil Nadu Advocate General challenged the notification in the Supreme Court on 5 February 1999. *Hindu International Weekly*, 20 March 1999, p. 2. *India Today*, 12 April 1999, p. 12 for a list of cases Jayalalitha was involved in. It was also alleged that she was responsible for the transfer of the Madras High Court Chief Justice, Manmohan Singh Liberhan who dealt with most of her cases. *Statesman Weekly*, 2 May 1998; *India Today*, 4 January 1999, p. 9; *Hindu International Weekly*, 12 December 1998, p. 2.
145. *Statesman Weekly*, 27 February 1999, p. 1. It should however be noted that the CBI had become more active than before under pressure from the Supreme Court. Bihar was paralysed by the state-sponsored *bandh* to protest against the CBI raid on the residence of Chief Minister Rabri Devi. *Statesman Weekly*, editorial, 29 August 1998.
146. *Statesman Weekly*, 14 November 1998.
147. A committee of three judges, set up by Chief Justice Verma, cleared the Judicial Accountability Committee's charge of impropriety against Punchhi J. Interestingly, the complainants waited to bring the charge against him on the eve of his appointment as the next Chief Justice. *India Today*, 24 November 1997.
148. For Punchhi's recommendations, see, *India Today*, 6 May 1998, p. 22. Ram Jethmalani, Minister of Urban Affairs, openly expressed reservations on Punchhi's recommendations. Kapil Sibal, a supporter of Punchhi, questioned Jethmalani in the Rajya Sabha. *India Today*, 10 August 1998.
149. When asked by the Court as to where did the Union government stand with respect to SCAORA decision, the Attorney-General of India, Soli Sorabjee, assured the Court that the government was not seeking a review or reconsideration of the SCAORA decision, and that the government would treat as binding the answers of the Court to the nine questions referred to it.
150. M.P. Jain, *Indian Constitutional Law*, New Delhi, 2003, p. 439. Also see, Prem Kumar and Raj Bhatia, 'Independence of Judiciary and the Appointment of Judges', in *Indian Judicial System: Need for Reforms*, New Delhi, 2004.
151. Prabhu Chawla, 'Courting Controvery', *India Today*, 25 January 1999. In the matter of transfers, the President was right on a technicality.
152. Ibid. The Presidents have become sensitive to procedural correctness in

appointments and transfers. Recently, President A.P.J. Abdul Kalam returned the recommendation for the transfer of Chief Justice B.K. Roy of the Punjab and Haryana High Court to the Guwahati High Court because Roy was not consulted. *The Hindu*, 9 January 2005.

153. *India Today*, 25 January 1999. 'Merit' and 'representativeness' are not necessarily opposing principles—this was the basic argument of the President of India. In Canada, regional representation on the Supreme Court bench is an accepted principle. Of the nine judges, three must come from Quebec, three from Ontario, one from the Atlantic provinces, and two from the Prairies. There is also gender consideration. Recently, there is a feeling that the Supreme Court should also have an aboriginal judge on the bench. *Globe and Mail*, 5 October 2005, editorial.

154. *India Today*, 6 October 1997.

155. V.R. Krishna Iyer, *Constitutional Miscellany*, Delhi, 2003, p. 278.

156. *Frontline*, 29 August 2003.

157. Sumit Mitra, 'The Judiciary—Losing Face', *India Today*, 20 January 2003.

158. The 'cash for jobs' scandal in the Punjab and Haryana High Court involved three judges. One of the judges was exonerated; another one proceeded on leave until retirement, and the third was issued a warning. *Frontline*, 17 January 2003. Justice Arun Madan of the Rajasthan High Court resigned after the inquiry committee indicted him for 'sex exchange' and corruption charges. *Frontline*, 17 January 2003. The three Karnataka judges allegedly involved in 'sex, sleaze and power' were exonerated; the Karnataka high court had issued notice of contempt to as many as 56 persons from 14 newspaper to stop 'scandalizing the court' through rumour-mongering. *Frontline*, 3 January and 28 February 2003. The DDA scandal inquiry made Shamit Mukherjee to resign from the Delhi high court, though President Kalam advised that he should be prosecuted. *Frontline*, 23 May 2003; *Statesman Weekly*, 5 and 12 April 2003. Any time the suggestion that one or the other judge should be transferred, was met with opposition from the 'receiving' court.

159. *Hindu International Weekly*, 9 August 2003, p. 12. Also, *Frontline*, 29 August 2003, pp. 40–1. Currently, there is a moratorium on transfer policy; only judges appointed as Chief Justices are transferred. The Committee on Judicial Accountability demanded that Chief Justice A.H. Ahmadi and his daughter Tasneem, who had a roaring practice in the Delhi High Court, should not live in the same house. *India Today*, 20 January 2003, pp. 15–17.

160. Vajpayee speaking at the Golden Jubilee of the Supreme Court on 26 November 1999. See, *India Today*, 20 December 1999.

161. It all began when Ram Jethmalani asserted that he did not have to consult Chief Justice Anand in the appointment of retiring Chief Justice B.M. Lal (Patna) as Chairman of the MRTP. The battle turned ugly when Jethmalani began investigating Anand's age and some property deal that

involved Anand's wife. See, Ram Jethmalani, *Big Egos, Small Men,* New Delhi, 2000.

162. BJP's bigwigs were video-taped accepting bribes in defence procurement deals. George Fernandes, Defence Minister, was exonerated by the Justice Phukan Commission which attributed procedural failures to bureaucracy in the Ministry of Defence. The Manmohan Singh government did not accept the Commission's report. The revelation that Fernandes as Defence Minister had allowed Justice Phukan to use Indian Air Force aircraft to visit holiday and pilgrimage destinations, strengthened the government's position. *Frontline,* 3 June 2005, p. 26.
163. In the *Best Bakery* case (Godhra violence in Gujarat), Chief Justice V.N. Khare was quite upset with the way the Gujarat BJP government drafted the appeal in response to the Human Rights Commission's special leave petition. 'I have no faith left,' Khare (CJ) told the Additional Solicitor General, 'in the prosecution and the Gujarat government. I am not saying Article 356. You have to protect people and punish the guilty.' V. Venkatesan, 'A Judicial Crackdown', *Frontline,* 10 October 2003, pp. 37–8.
164. The Supreme Court virtually stopped the privatization of the HPCL-BPCL when it ruled, in a public interest litigation petition, that the government's move to sell these companies was in contravention of existing statutes unless suitably amended by the parliament (knowing that the minority government could not get a majority support in the Parliament for its proposal). See, *Frontline,* 10 October 2003.
165. Governor Fatima Beevi erred and lost her tenure when she installed J. Jayalalitha (convicted of corruption), as the Chief Minister of Tamil Nadu on 14 May 2001, despite the fact that she was banned from contesting elections. She stepped down on 21 September 2001, in the wake of Supreme Court judgement. *India Today,* 7, 19 and 28 May; 6 and 23 July, and 17 December 2001. Also see, *Frontline,* 3, 17 and 31 August; 14 and 28 September and 12 October (SC verdict) 2001. There is a long history to this amendment. The Delhi High Court's ruling that it was the right of the voter (Article 19.1: freedom of speech and expression), to be properly informed about the criminal antecedents, wealth, and education qualifications, etc., of the candidates for elections was set at naught by the Vajpayee government through an ordinance on 24 August 2002. The ordinance was challenged; in its place, an amendment to the Representation of People Act was brought into force retrospectively. On 13 March 2003, the SC set aside the Amendment and restored the earlier judgement. *The Hindu International Weekly,* 22 March 2001; *Statesman Weekly,* 22 March 2003.
166. The Supreme Court had used commissioners to investigate facts as also appointed lawyers as *amicus curiae* to draft regular petitions. Under guide of interpretation of Article 142 'doing complete justice', the SC has

assumed plenary powers to pass any decree or order for doing what it thinks is 'complete justice'. Practically, nothing remained out of the jurisdiction of SC.

167. H.L. Anand quoted in *India Today*, 16 April 2001.
168. *India Today*, 16 April 2001. It has invariably been the case that the executive tends to sit on the Court's directives. The courts have been forgiving most of the time and the deadlines for the implementation of their directives have been postponed (and, at times, neglected) resulting in long delays. *The Nav Bharat Times* of 21 February 2005, headlined: 'The Supreme Court Directives: Subject of Ridicule'. The courts have hauled up top civil servants (IAS) for disobeying their orders. For Karnataka, Madras, Kerala cases, *Hindu International Weekly*, 23 September 1995, p. 5.
169. Praful Bidwai, *Frontline*, 8 April 2005. He could have also added to micromanagement, the Supreme Court's prescription of 'environmental courses' for University education. Of course, the Court has recently been sensitive to the issue of judicial restraint in the matter of PILs. It, in *Lakshmikant R. Bhojawanti* v. *Paratapsing Mohansingh Pardesh* case (1995), observed: 'The High Court under Article 227 cannot assume unlimited prerogative to correct all species of hardship or wrong decisions. It must be restricted to cases of grave dereliction of duty and flagrant abuse of fundamental principles of law or justice, where grave injustice would be done unless the High Court interferes.'
170. See, Venkitesh Ramakrishnan, 'Beyond Jharkhand'; Purnima S. Tripathi, 'Games without Rules'; V. Venkatesan, 'A defective law'; *Frontline*, 8 April 2005. For background, *Statesman Weekly*, 5 March 2005.
171. *Frontline*, 8 April 2005, p. 17.
172. Ibid., p. 8
173. Speaker Somnath Chatterjee called two meetings of the Assembly Speakers–20 May, 21 July 2005 to discussed judiciary's alleged transgression into legislative space. B.P. Saha considers Chatterjee's moves as 'deplorable attempts to demoralize the Judiciary.' *The Statesman Weekly*, 1 October 2005, pp. 10–11.
174. Ibid., p. 8. Though the pent-up feelings exploded when the Parliament criticized the Supreme Court for its judgement that barred the Centre and the state governments from enforcing admission quotas in private colleges. Chief Justice R.C. Lahoti reaction to criticism was strong: 'Shut us down if you are so intolerant', *Overseas Statesman Weekly*, 27 August 2005.
175. Former member of the Parliament Era Sezhiyan, 'A Democracy in Disarray', *Frontline*, 8 April 2005, pp. 20–1.
176. For an excellent analysis on judicial empowerment, see, Ran Hirschl, *Towards Juristocracy: The Origins and Consequences of the New Constitutionalism*, Harvard, 2004.

177. NCRWC seemed more concerned to re-state that the power of court to punish for contempt of itself was a sovereign power and could be exercised only by the Supreme Court and the High Courts, Parliament and the State Legislatures, and by no other court, tribunal or authority. Further, it recommended that 'in matters of contempt, it shall be open to the Court on satisfaction of the bona fides of the plea and the requirements of public interest to permit a defence of justification by truth.' *Report of the National Commission to Review the Working of the Constitution* (Delhi, 2002), pp. 140–1. The government introduced the Contempt of Courts (Amendment) Bill to accommodate NCRWC recommendation in the Contempt of Courts Act 1971. NCRWC had recommended that this be done through a constitutional amendment because the power of the Supreme Court and High Courts to punish for contempt was provided in the Constitution.
178. NCRWC clarified that judicial review could only be used by the Supreme Court and the High Courts. 'The decisions of courts to the effect that an authority constituted under a statute . . . can adjudicate on the unconstitutionality and lack of legislative competence of other legislative enactments may be inconsistent with basic postulates of the constitution.' Ibid., p. 141.
179. Ibid., p. 136.
180. Ibid., pp. 137–8.
181. Ibid., pp. 138–9.
182. V. Venkatesan, 'A Flawed Mechanism', *Frontline*, 6 June 2003, pp. 40–1. The Bill lapsed with the dissolution of the 13 Lok Sabha in January 2004.
183. Ibid., p. 40.
184. Ibid., p. 41
185. Ibid.
186. Many people consider the US process as too political and damaging of the reputation of the nominees. Since 1789, 156 people has been nominated to join the US Supreme Court. Of those, 35 have been either rejected, withdrawn, or dropped from consideration. President George W. Bush's recent nominee, Ms. Harriet Miers, withdrew her nomination in October 2005 in the face of opposition from the Christian right. *Globe and Mail*, 28 October 2005, p. A13.
187. The vast majority of presidential nominees are approved by the Senate, usually without much rancour or partisanship. The ratification procedure hasn't stopped quality candidates from allowing their names to go forward. . . . Its virtue lies not in preventing good people getting onto the court, but preventing under-qualified or highly controversial ones from making it. Lyndon Johnson tried to appoint an old political crony, Abe Fortas, to the Supreme Court and that nomination failed. Richard Nixon proposed two clearly unqualified candidates, and those nominations failed.

Robert Bork, a strict constructionist, failed to make it because his views were too far removed from the mainstream; and Clarence Thomas was rejected because the nation's legal community considered him underqualified. See, Jeffrey Simpson, 'Filling a Supreme vacancy the see-through way', *Globe and Mail*, 22 July 2005.

188. See, *Globe and Mail*, editorial, 19 May 2005. The nominated judges did not appear before the parliamentary committee, instead, the Minister of Justice did. Also, *Globe and Mail*, 24 May 2005. Former Chief Justice Patrick LeSage (Ontario) suggested that candidates could be vetted and ranked by a committee composed of Commons members, senators and experienced lawyers appointed by legal organizations. He argued that politicians being involved in the culling process is valuable, because 'politicians have a sense and understanding of what is required'. Also, *Globe and Mail*. 26 February, 5, 6 and 28 April 2005; *The Ottawa Citizen*, 13 June 2005, p. A12.

189. Rajeev Dhavan, 'Judges and Indian Democracy: the lesser evil?', in Francine R. Frankel et al. (eds.), *Transforming India: Social and Political Dynamics of Democracy*, New Delhi, 2000.

190. Large-scale acquittal of stained politicians has been the concern of the courts as well public. Recently, the Bofors case fell flat in the Delhi High Court after a decade of investigations by the CBI at the cost Rs. 250 crores in public expenses. *India Today*, 20 June 2003, p. 14. Recently, when the Manmohan Singh government decided to close the *Mayawati* case (the Congress was keen to woo her in UP), and the CBI was asked to comply, the Supreme Court did not buy the argument. However, this does reflect on how the government(s) uses the scales of justice for partisan purposes in 'cocktail' cases, resulting in low prosecutions. See *India Today*, 23 May 2005, p. 16.

191. S.P. Sathe writes: 'The political establishment has used the Court to legitimize its own decisions. the controversial decision to reserve twenty-seven per cent of public service jobs for the backward classes . . . was accepted without protest after the Supreme Court endorsed it by a majority in *Indra Sawney* v. *Union of India*.' Sathe, *Judicial Activism in India*, New Delhi, 2002, p. 21. However, at times, the Court goes overboard in deciding social issues and attracts criticism of its judgements. Recently, its seven-judge Bench decision that in unaided private institutions, including engineering and medical colleges, the state could neither impose a reservation policy nor carve out its quota from the total number of seats, has upset many state governments which have asked the centre to override this decision through a national policy on this issue. The Court's decision, some political parties have argued, is 'against the constitutional principle of social justice.' *Overseas Statesman Weekly*, 20 August 2005; also, *Frontline*, 9 September 2005, pp. 28–37. The Chief Justice, R.C. Lahoti, reacted strongly to 'unwanted criticism' of the

judgement in the Parliament. He told the Attorney General: 'Tell us, we will wind up the courts and then do whatever you want.' *Overseas Statesman Weekly*, 27 August 2005.

192. Quoted in, *India Today*, 31 October 1996, p. 54
193. Upendra Baxi, 'The *Avatars* of Indian Judicial Activism: Explorations in the Geographies of [In]Justice', in S.K. Verma and Kusum (eds.), *Fifty Years of the Supreme Court of India*, New Delhi, 2000.
194. Quoted in B.N. Kirpal et al. (eds.), *Supreme But Not Infallible*, New Delhi, 2000, p. 182.

17

Supranational Intergovernmental Relations and the Role of Judiciary

REKHA SAXENA

> The GATT Treaties and the WTO affect the sovereignty of the nation and trench upon the federal character of the polity. I am convinced that the Supreme Court has to examine these treaties. . . . (V. R. Krishna Iyer)[1]

India—and the world at large—is passing through rapidly changing times. Within India, the years since the 1990s have witnessed tremendous transformation which may be encapsulated in two rather vague terms, i.e. federalization of the polity and the neo-liberal reforms in the economy. In the world at large, the forces of globalization and regional integration have gathered unprecedented momentum, paving the way for a new world order—an order mediated by the sole superpower, the United States, and other regional powers defined in military as well as in economic terms. Whatever hopes and fears may mark the dawning of this new order, India has joined the forces of globalization, liberalization, and privatization.

In his powerful indictment of the 'ultra-modern mantras' of the new economic order, Justice Krishna Iyer has warned that developing nations are deluding themselves if they think that they can 'trade themselves out of poverty' by being a part of the World Trade Organization (WTO) or, for that matter, by signing international commercial agreements which are corrosive of their sovereign powers.[2] 'The legal methodology of treaties legitimizes the process of economic exploitation', argues

*First published in *Economic and Political Weekly*, 6–12 January 2007. Reprinted with permission from the author with some modifications.

Justice Iyer, 'and international treaty jurisprudence is today a "Might is Right" manoeuver to subjugate, without arms, nations which are forced to jettison their national sovereignty and abandon their commitment to their people, by the diplomacy of signatures. The *pen* has done without blood what needed a *gun* before; what once required wars of conquest, is accomplished by words of treaties'.[3] India, Justice Iyer regrets, 'without consulting Parliament or people, signed on the dotted line, signing away the safeguards for crucial sectors such as agriculture on which nearly 70 per cent of the Indian population still depends for a living'.[4] There is a need, argues Justice Iyer, to check the treaty-making power of the central executive. 'Assuming vast powers in the Executive (Article 73), it is outrageous to use it to make treaties and stultify the essentials of the very Constitution sans which no power subsists. It follows that the potential terrorism of treaty power desiderates sharp checks on its adventurist use.'[5]

This paper argues that the union government should develop mechanisms of consultation with state governments before signing international treaties—commercial or non-commercial—and conventions which affect state jurisdictions under the Constitution of India. The Indian polity, needless to emphasize, is more federated today than it was during the dominance of the one-party system. Not only have some of the state governments protested against the Union Executive unilateralism in signing some international treaties and conventions (aside from entertaining foreign investors in their competitive bids to attract foreign investment and multinational corporations), but also approached the Supreme Court of India to adjudicate in such matters. Before the docket of the Supreme Court gets flooded with such petitions, the politics of current federalism (and there is little hope that it is going to change in favour of a centralized federalism of the earlier years), demands that the interests of the state governments be accommodated within a broad centre-state consultation framework. It was in this context that the National Commission to Review the Working of the Constitution (2002) recommended: 'The Commission recommends that for reducing tension or friction between States and the Union and for expeditious decision-making on important issues involving States, the desirability of prior consultation by the Union Government with the inter-State Council may be considered before signing any treaty vitally affecting the interests of the States regarding matters in the State List.'[6]

It is well known that in the wake of Independence and partition in

1947, India drafted and adopted a federal constitution with a strong parliamentary centre. Taking the lessons of history and contemporary times, the Constituent Assembly of India settled for a Constitution which, as B.R. Ambedkar put it, would work as a federal one but would be amenable to transformation into a unitary one in constitutionally contemplated emergencies. Without going into the details of controversial centralization of a potentially federal constitution and the displacement of the cabinet system by a Prime Ministerial system in the 1970s, it is evident that the system has been in for a remarkable degree of federalization since the 1990s. The economic reforms have reversed the process of state-led strategy of growth and given a greater leeway to the market forces both in national and multinational terms. Federalization and marketization have conjointly augmented the autonomy of both the State governments and the private sector. In this new ambience, the channels of communication between the state governments or the sub-national governments (SNG), and foreign governments and between the Indian corporate companies and the foreign companies, are expanding at a remarkable pace. This symbolizes the growing trends of federalization in the country as much as it represents the 'state-building' activities of the SNGs, in collaboration with multi-lateral financial institutions like the International Monetary Fund, World Bank, and other foreign investors. Several of the state governments have entered into, or are in the process of negotiating contracts with foreign governments and multi-lateral international agencies for development of the infrastructure and vital sectors of the economy. During his previous visit to India, the World Bank President spent more time in some state capitals than in New Delhi. And the state chief ministers, as the Rudolphs noted, have become 'the marquee players in India's federal market economy'.[7] This changed context requires a fresh look at our constitutional and legal frameworks with a view to bringing about positive reforms in policy coordination between the centre and the states.

A reading of the Constituent Assembly debates as well as the text of the Constitution indicates that the framers of the Constitution were essentially motivated by the theory that external affairs and treaty-making powers should be an exclusively union jurisdiction, and primarily an executive affair. Presumably, the colonial practice and nationalist sentiment had made them oblivious of the fact that the matter at some stage would become federally sensitive and that states and regions would develop a desire for being effectively consulted and represented in the process of treaty making. This argument appears to be validated by observations made by K.M. Munshi (Bombay: General), who made a rather detailed comment on the nature of the union executive in the draft constitution, strongly advocating the British model against the American model, but completely glossing over the difference between the two models with regard to the treaty-making power. As is well known, the treaty-making power in the US is shared between the executive and the federal second chamber whereas the British follow a unitary executive model of treaty-making. Munshi argued that the model of the British executive 'is the best form suited to Indian conditions'. He went on to say:

> We must not forget a very important fact that during the last 100 years, the Indian public life has largely drawn upon the traditions of the British constitutional law. Most of us, and during the last several generations before us, public men in India, have looked up to the British model as the best. For the last thirty or forty years, some kind of responsibility has been introduced in the governance of the country. Our constitutional traditions have become parliamentary, and we have now all our provinces functioning more or less on the British model. As a matter of fact, today the Dominion Government of India is functioning as a full-fledged Parliamentary Government. After this experience why should we go back upon the tradition that has been built for over 100 years, and try a novel experiment which was, as I said, formed 150 years ago and which has been found wanting even in America.[8]

Nevertheless, Article 51 of the Part IV of the Constitution on the Directive Principles of State Policy, dealing with promotion of international peace and security, uses the term 'the state' rather than the union. This Article provides that 'the State shall endeavour to (a) promote international peace and security; (b) maintain just and honourable relations between nations; (c) foster respect for international law and treaty obligations in the dealing of organized people with one another; and (d) encourage settlement of international disputes by arbitration'.[9] It may be argued academically as also by the judiciary with greater authoritativeness that this article leaves enough scope for greater participation of SNGs, in the exercise of the treaty-making power of the union—after all, the concept of the 'state' has to be inclusive of the federal units.

In terms of the original constitutional design, the treaty-making power appears to be an essentially executive power. This is for two reasons. First, prior parliamentary sanction is not required for the executive signing a treaty. Second, parliamentary legislation is required pro facto for implementing a treaty. Thus, the executive can very well present the Parliament with a fait accompli and constrain its options by the argument that treaty is already signed and the federal state cannot go back on the commitments already made to a foreign government. On the face of it, it appears to be a historical hangover of the imperialist British tradition which is a mixture of royal executive prerogative as well as undemocratic colonial heritage. This state of affairs however can be questioned and an alternative point of view may even assert itself on an unwilling executive whose survival is dependent on coalitional majority support with parties supporting the government from outside. For instance, in 2005–6, the Indo-US nuclear deal was formalised in a series of steps whereby prime minister Manmohan Singh and president George W Bush signed an agreement in the first instance in July 2005 which was followed up by subsequent deliberations and signing of documents by the two governments. Interestingly, around the same time, when this treaty was going through process of ratification by the American congress, especially the senate, the Indian parliamentary scene was also replete with heated debates in which the left parties supporting the Congress-led minority coalition government insisted and were assured that the government would proceed in the matter on the basis of the sense of the houses of Parliament as revealed in the long drawn out debates. A similar demand was made by the Bharatiya Janata Party. Recently (Winter of 2006), Jayalalitha, the former Chief Minister of Tamil Nadu suggested that the Constitution should be amended to the effect of making the treaty making power of the union executive subject to approval by the Rajya Sabha.

Some scholars have argued that the treaties made by the union executive should be subject to ratification by the Parliament and that the Supreme Court should watch them if they are in conformity with the 'basic structure' of the Constitution.[10] 'Under the scheme of the Constitution', writes Rajeev Dhavan, 'it is Parliament that needs to legis-late on the manner and extent to which the union may participate in international conferences, associations and other bodies, enter into treaties and agreements and implement whatever decisions are made at these meeting through these instruments. . . . There is nothing to prevent Parliament from passing legislation which will place treaty negotiations within a framework of democratic accountability of India.'[11] In the same vein, Justice Krishna Iyer wrote: 'So it is fair to implant parliamentary ratification as a condition precedent to validation of a treaty negotiated, even signed by a Minister or Head of the State.'[12]

Similarly, the NCRWC's consultation paper observed: 'The power of treaty-making is so important and has such far-reaching consequences to the people and to our polity that the element of accountability should be introduced into the process.'[13] It is my argument that this democratic accountability needs to be expanded into federal accountability in the sense that the Centre should consult SNGs before concluding international treaties and agreements which affect the interests of the SNGs (state governments).

Under the Constitution, SNGs are not authorized to contact foreign authorities directly. Under the Union list, Article 246 read with the Seventh Schedule of the Constitution specified by Entries numbers 10 (foreign affairs), 11 (diplomatic representation), 12 (United Nations Organization), 13 (International conferences), 14 (War and Peace), and 41 (International Trade), give exclusive authority in this regard to the Union Parliament.[14]

According to Article 73(b), the extent of executive power of the Union extend 'to the exercise of such rights, authority and jurisdiction as are exercisable by the Government of India by virtue of any treaty or agreement'.[15] Treaty-making power is thus an executive act performed by the Government of India on behalf of the Parliament. The executive power of the Union (particularly when it commands solid partisan majority in the Parliament), is further enhanced by Article 253 which confers overriding power to Parliament for giving effect to international agreements. According to Article 253, 'Parliament has the power to make any law for the whole or any part of the territory of India for implementing any treaty, agreement or convention with any other country or countries or any decision made at any international conference, association or other body'. Thus, the treaty-making power of the centre overrides the normal federal-state jurisdictional lines.[16]

The constitutional provision in India with regard to the power of the central executive to conclude treaties is consistent with the practice in the British Empire, though the parliamentary power to override the normal federal state jurisdictional lines is not consistent with the framework of a federal system. In a 1937 case, *Attorney General of Canada* v. *Attorney General of Ontario*, the Privy Council observed: 'Within the British Empire there is a well-established rule that the making of a treaty is an executive act, while performance of its obligations, if they entail alteration of the existing law, requires legislative action. Unlike some other countries, the stipulations of a treaty duly ratified do not, within the empire, by virtue of the treaty alone, have the force of law.'[17] At the same time, however, the Privy Council noted that this practice is simple enough in case of unitary countries but somewhat complex in the Canadian case by virtue of it being a federal system. 'There being no such thing as treaty legislation', the judgement said, 'but only a distribution of legislative powers between the Dominion and the Provinces, the distribution being based on classes of subjects and it being one of the essential conditions in the inter-provincial compact to which BNA Act gives effect, the Dominion Parliament *could not be said to have power to legislate for obligation arising out of treaty and make the same binding on the Provinces in [the] face of Section 91 and 92 of the Act.*'[18]

The Supreme Court of India, in the few cases having to do with international treaties and agreements, has affirmed the constitutional position to the effect that (a) the executive power of the centre extends to the exercise of such rights, authority, and jurisdiction as are exercisable by the Government of India by virtue of any treaty or agreement (Article 73); and (b) the Parliament has full authority to enact legislation to implement any international treaty, agreement or convention even if the subject matter falls within the provincial jurisdiction (entries 13, 14, and Article 253). This means that the Union Executive's treaty-making power is unfettered so long as it does not require any implementing parliamentary legislation (Supreme Court's ruling in the Rann of Kutch boundary dispute settlement, 1969).[19] The powers of the union executive and Parliament, however, are subject to the provisions of the Constitution, i.e. limited by the fundamental rights of the citizens as guaranteed in the Constitution, and by the judicially-invented doctrine of 'basic structure' of the Constitution.

In *Maganbhai Ishwarbahi* v. *Union of India* (1969), the Supreme Court, speaking through Justice J.C. Shah, held:

> The effect of Article 253 is that if a treaty, agreement or convention with a foreign State deals with a subject within the competence of the State Legislature, the Parliament alone has, notwithstanding Article 246(3), the power to make laws to implement the treaty, agreement or convention or any decision made at the international conference, association, or other body . . . thereby power is conferred upon the Parliament which it may not otherwise possess. But it does not seek to circumscribe *the extent of power conferred [on the central executive] by Article 73.* If, in consequence of the exercise of executive power, *rights of the citizens or others are restricted or infringed,* or laws are modified, the exercise of power must be supported by legislation; *where there is no restriction, infringement of the right or modification of the laws, the executive is competent to exercise the power.*[20]

This judgement of the Supreme Court was endorsed in the *P.B. Samant* v. *Union of India* case (1994). A petition was filed in the Bombay High Court invoking its power to issue a writ of Mandamus under Article 226 to restrain the Union of India to enter into the final treaty relating to Dunkel proposals without the prior consent of the Parliament and state legislatures. It was contended that the intended treaty would affect agricultural products, irrigation facilities, and raw cotton, which fall within the jurisdiction of state legislatures. The Court overruled these contentions and endorsed the earlier decision of the Supreme Court in the *Maganbhai Patel* case. 'It is undoubtedly true', surmised the Court, 'that the executive power of the Central Government flows from the provisions of Article 73 of the Constitution of India. It is equally true that the proviso set out that the executive power shall not, save as expressly provided in this Constitution or in any State, extend to matters with regard to which the Legislature of the State has the power to make laws.'[21] In other words, the central executive has the power to conclude treaties, but it has no power to *legislate* for the purpose of implementing these treaties—a power that rests with the state legislatures or the Parliament (Article 253).

Notwithstanding the above judgements, the Supreme Court, in *Vishaka* v. *State of Rajasthan* (1997),[22] ruled that international conventions signed by the Government of India that are consistent with the spirit of the fundamental rights, even though not exactly in terms of letters of the Constitution, can be read into fundamental rights, although the union and state legislatures may not have passed an implementing legislation to that effect. It, therefore, follows by implication that such judicial expansions of fundamental rights by the courts are equally binding on the Government of India and the state governments. Thus, by entering into such international conventions, the Government of India binds itself as well as the state governments.

In the constitutional scheme, the treaty-making power was treated as a special aspect of executive power. Article 131 of the Constitution dealing with original jurisdiction of the Supreme Court over union, state and inter-state disputes adds a clarification to the effect that the Supreme Court's jurisdiction 'shall not extend to a dispute arising out of any treaty, agreement, covenant, engagement, sanad or other similar instruments which, having been entered into or executed before the commencement of this Constitution, continue in operation after such commencement, or which provide that the said jurisdiction shall not extend to such a dispute'.[23] However, for an activist Court like the

Supreme Court of India, the inhibition in this Article may not stand the litmus test of the doctrine of 'basic structure', of the Constitution of which federalism has been declared to be an essential part of the Constitution. Further, Article 131 does not prevent the aggrieved parties to approach the Court for a decision on questions of law, or of fact on which 'the existence or the extent of legal right claimed depends'.[24]

In the absence of an institutionalized consultation process between the centre and the states prior to making treaties, the exclusive monopoly of the central executive in this area is likely to run into conflict. In respect to participation at international conferences, the centre alone is entitled to send delegations which the state governments may join as a matter of courtesy. This speaks to the ad hoc nature of the consultation process which is certainly a fertile ground for tensions between the union and the state governments. For example, at least three petitions, one each by governments of Tamil Nadu, Rajasthan, and Orissa were filed in the Supreme Court under Article 131 of the Constitution. The cases have been withdrawn, but the pressure from the SNGs, for participation in the treaty-making power is not likely to disappear in the growing context of federalization within and globalization without.

There are other unanticipated problems that the treaty-making power of the union may give rise to in the context of India's growing integration with global and supranational regional economies. For example, there is a widely-shared apprehension that relatively low prices of medicines in India may increase phenomenally as a result of the TRIPS clauses of the WTO treaty. To quote Dhavan:

> The Indian Constitution guarantees life and liberty to each person in India. This has been interpreted to include the right to health. Read with the Directive Principles, there is a positive obligation on the state to ensure the health of persons. If the patent regime is changed or EMR protection is given for drugs and medicine, there would be good public interest reasons for asserting, that by virtue of the executive action of agreeing to these patent law changes and committing the legislature to change its laws, the direct and inevitable effect of these changes would be that India would not be able to fulfil its constitutional obligations to its own people. . . . It is these considerations (amongst others) which persuaded the Sates of Tamil Nadu, Rajasthan and Orissa to raise federal disputes with the Union on the signing and implementing of the GATT treaty.[25]

The economies of the SNGs are affected by trade treaties made in pursuit of globalization and liberalization. While some states may be winners in the competition to attract foreign investment, others may be losers in this competition. Market solutions may also generate inequalities within each state as well, endangering its political stability. In other words, the state governments have great stake in the commercial or trade treaties that are concluded by the centre for, in most cases, they have to live with the consequences of such treaties. The Rudolphs see in the dawn of liberalization, the gradual emergence of what they call 'a federal market economy' which places an extra-ordinary burden of responsibility on the state governments:

> Our use of the term 'federal market economy' is meant to draw attention to the fact that the new imagined economy evokes not only the decentralization of the market, but also new patterns of shared sovereignty between the states and the centre for economic and financial decision-making. This increased sharing shifts India's federal system well beyond the economic provisions of its formal constitution. Over the last decade it has become clear that if economic liberalization is to prevail, it is the state governments and their chief ministers that can and must break the bottlenecks holding back economic growth. Can they and their governments negotiate a path that avoids surrender to populist pressures and yet effectively respond to the inequalities generated by market solutions?[26]

Obviously, the more the state governments become partners in economic and financial decision-making both in the domestic and external arenas (particularly in trade or commercial treaties), the more effective is likely to be their response to the challenge(s) referred to by the Rudolphs.

In the larger context of new trends in comparative federalism, John Kincaid has conceptualized what he calls 'constituent diplomacy' to refer to relations between sub-national political units (states/provinces/cantons/lander) and organizations beyond the boundaries of the nation state or the federal state.[27] Rob Jenkins has tried to explore developments in this direction in the recent trends in Indian federalism. Both Kincaid and Jenkins are of the opinion that India is not yet a clear cut case of constituent diplomacy in the sense defined above. For the Indian states are considerably less autonomous in the area of foreign economic policy than paradigmatic cases of constituent diplomacy. For example, the state governments exercised marginal influence over India's multilateral talks on agricultural trade at the WTO and other forums. Yet some new trends are noticeable. To quote Jenkins: 'During the 1990s (and into the new millennium), several of India's state governments conducted negotiations and concluded agreements with international economic institutions such as the Asian Development Bank and the International Labour Organization. Some bilateral aid agencies, like the United Kingdom's Department for International Development, have begun to focus much of their efforts directly on state governments as well.'[28]

Notwithstanding Kincaid and Jenkin's argument, the fact of the matter is that India cannot speak in different voices to world organizations and international audiences, without undermining its credibility. The centre may have the predominant constitutional power in concluding international treaties and agreements, but neither the centre nor the states can fully honour treaty obligations unless there is a broad consensus between the two levels of government to do so. The centre, unlike in the old days of one-party dominant system, can no longer coerce state governments into submission to discharge treaty obligations, leaving aside the question, whether a particularly treaty or agreement affects the resources or legislative powers of the states. The situation in Canada is somewhat similar to that of India; the federal government has the power to conclude international agreements, but the Canadian system has come to institutionalize the Premiers' conference(s) as a means to evolving consensus among the provinces prior to the federal government's agreement on critical international commitments. It is by no means a perfect system—the Kyoto Accord to control environmental pollution was signed by Prime Minister Jean Chretien much to the protest of some provinces, and Quebec always insists on participation with the federal delegation, when it comes to signing international agreements particularly in respect to cultural and educational matters. Quebec also maintains its own trade missions abroad though other provincial premiers do trot the globe for more business opportunities for their provinces. Minor difficulties notwithstanding, the Canadian system works through consultation and negotiations between the federal and the provincial governments.

In view of the growing trend of federalization in India wherein 'province' or 'state-building' has captured the psychology of provincial leaders and coalition-building at the centre has become a governing mode of administration, it is fortunate that foreign relations particularly having to do with trade treaties, agreements and conventions with foreign countries, even though enumerated exclusively under the centre's jurisdiction, should be conducted on a broad-based consensus between the centre and the states through a well-institutionalized process of mutual consultation and negotiations. In the absence of such a mechanism, it is likely that the centre will face more and more challenges to its treaty-making powers from the state governments. So far, the Supreme Court has recognized that the treaty-making power of the centre overrides the normal federal-state jurisdictional lines, according to the constitution, in the limited number of cases it has dealt with (except in the *Berubari* case[29] where the Court called for a constitutional amendment for the cession of Indian territory to another country), but the centre's power is not absolute. International treaties and other agreements can be challenged in the court of law if these are in violation of fundamental rights of the people but more so if they are not in line with the 'basic structure' of the Constitution. First, enunciated in the *Keshavananda* v. *State of Kerala* (1973),[30] the doctrine of 'basic structure' as developed by the Supreme Court gives the Court the power to review the constitutionality of any legislative and executive action, if it is not in conformity with the basic structure of the Constitution. This doctrine is still in the making, but federalism has certainly been recognized as falling within the ambit of 'basic structure'. Before treaty-making and treaty-implementation conflicts become the burden of the Supreme Court of India to settle, it will augur well for centre-state relations if some cooperative mechanism is put in place whereby the state governments become partners with the centre in concluding international treaties, accords and agreements.

NOTES

1. V.R. Krishna Iyer, *Constitutional Miscellany*, Lucknow, 2003, p. 10.
2. Ibid., Chap. II.
3. Ibid., p. 11.
4. Ibid., p. 22.
5. Ibid., p. 14.
6. *Report of the National Commission to Review the Working of the Constitution*, vol. I, Delhi, 2002, p. 165.
7. Lloyd I. Rudolph and Susanne Hoeber Rudolph, 'Iconization of Chandrababu: Sharing Sovereignty in India's Federal Market Economy', *Economic and Political Weekly*, vol. XXXVI, #18, 5–11 May 2000, p. 1541.
8. K.M. Munshi's speech in Constituent Assembly, *CAD*, Book 2, vol. 7, 4 November 1948–8 January 1948, pp. 984–5.
9. *Constitution of India*, Article 51.
10. See, Justice Iyer, op. cit., p. 13.
11. Rajiv Dhavan, 'Treaties and People: Indian Reflections', PILSARC Working Paper no. 131, Old Series, 1996, p. 50.
12. V.R. Krishna Iyer, op. cit., p. 14.

13. Quoted in V.R. Krishna Iyer, op. cit., p. 17.
14. M.P. Jain, *Indian Constitutional Law*, New Delhi: 2003, pp. 564–5.
15. Ibid., p. 214.
16. Ibid., p. 565.
17. *All India Reporter*, 1937 Privy Council, p. 82.
18. Ibid., p. 83. Section 91 of the BNA Act 1867 (amended: Constitution Act 1982) lists the powers of the Parliament; Section 92 lists the exclusive powers of the provincial legislatures; and Section 93 lists Education, Old Age Pensions, Agricultural and Immigration as concurrent powers where both the Parliament and the Provincial legislatures can legislate.
19. A boundary dispute between India and Pakistan was referred to an arbitration tribunal. It was argued, based on the decision in the *Berubari case*, that the Government of India could not implement the award without a constitutional amendment. But the Supreme Court held that it was not a case of cession of Indian territory, and that the Central Government could amend the award, treating it as an operative treaty, without any law or constitutional amendment. See, M.P. Jain, *Indian Constitutional Law*, New Delhi, 2003, p. 565.
20. *Maganbhai* v. *Union of India*, Hidayatullah (CJ), AIR 1969, Supreme Court, p. 784.
21. *P.B. Samant* v. *Union of India*, AIR 1994, Bombay 324.
22. *Vishaka* v. *State of Rajasthan*, 1997, *6 Supreme Court Cases*, p. 241.
23. *Constitution of India*, Article 131. Also see, Article 363(1) which excludes the jurisdiction of the courts in disputes with respect to agreements (treated as treaties) concluded between the princely states and the Government of India before the inauguration of the new Constitution.
24. M.P. Jain, op. cit., p. 255. The Court can always make a 'declaration' on questions of law or of fact on which the existence of a legal right claimed depends; it may not be able to give relief though it has moved in this direction as well to meet the ends of justice. . . . *State of Rajasthan* v. *Union of India (1977); State of Karnataka* v. *State of Andhra Pradesh (1978).*
25. Rajeev Dhavan, 'Treaties and People: Indian Reflections', op. cit., p. 29.
26. Lloyd I Rudolph and Susanne Hoeber Rudolph, *supra* n. 1, p. 1542.
27. John Kincaid, 'Constituent Diplomacy in Federal Politics and the Nation State: Conflict and Cooperation', *Federalism and International Relations: The Role of Subnational Units* (ed.), Hans Michelmann and Panayotis Soldatoes (Oxford, 1990), pp. 55–76.
28. Rob Jenkins, 'India's State and the Making of Foreign Economic Policy: The Limits of the Constituent Diplomacy Paradigm', *Publius*, vol. 33, no. 4, Fall 2003, p. 71.
29. In Re Berubari, AIR 1960 SC 845: (1960)3 SCR 250.
30. *Keshavananda Bharati* v. *State of Kerala*, AIR, SC 1973.

PART VI

Judiciary and Reforms

18

Indian Judiciary and the New Economy

S.K. VERMA

The last decade of the twentieth century saw a lot of upheaval in the economic and political relations of the world. The setting of the World Trade Organization (WTO), was the hallmark which opened up the frontiers of the nation-states. Liberalization and globalization[1] became the buzzwords, which emphasize the market-oriented free economy, governed by market forces, with minimal intervention by the state. Every country, to be a part of globalization, is expected to put in place new economic policies, devised to accelerate economic development, in compliance with the WTO and other agreements under its umbrella, such as Trade-related Intellectual Property Rights (TRIPS), Trade-related Investment Measures (TRIMS) and General Agreement on Trade in Services (GATS) as well as plethora of regional and bilateral free trade agreements.

The new economy, as envisaged under globalization, is aimed at the removal of national barriers to trade and investment. It is associated with the contemporary phenomenon of privatization, de-regulation, the expanded provision of incentives for entrepreneurial behaviour, structural adjustment programmes[2] for the economy and opening-up of markets by developing countries for international financial institutions and developed countries.

Under pressure from the international financial institutions and the new dispensation of the WTO, privatization and structural adjustment policies, imposed or adopted by many developing countries have minimized the role of the state in framing its policies or setting its development goals. State sovereignty is no more absolute when it comes to economic policies, which are dictated by international financial institutions or donor countries. These developments have resulted in the international mercenization of domestic economies wherein the movement of capital, goods and services are made dependent on exterior factors, as national barriers to trade and investments have been removed. In order to integrate into the global economy, after four decades of mixed economy and planned development, India embarked on a new economic policy (NEP) in 1991 by providing market-oriented free economy as the model. The new economy, with its thrust on global trade and greater interdependence among nations, has thrown new challenges in practically every walk of life, social structure and governance of the country. In this dispensation, the judiciary has a very crucial role. The fast track dispute resolution and proper judicial behaviour are the important determinants in giving effect to the NEP, and integrating the Indian markets with global economy. The judiciary has not only to play its role more effectively to ensure that the new dispensation works in the national interest towards the goal of development, but it has also to ensure security, predictability and transparency in the working of the legal regime with a well-entrenched legal mechanism for quick disposal of cases under which the foreign entrepreneurs, the multinational corporations (MNCs) and investors, should be able to work towards the national goals enshrined in the Constitution as socialism, justice and equality.

How to fulfil these goals in the context of new liberal and market-oriented mandates a close look on the existing state of the judiciary and the future challenges before it.

ROLE OF THE STATE AND JUDICIARY IN THE NEW ECONOMY

The 'judges do not make the law, but only interpret the law', is a well-known quote but in the process of interpretation, judges also give new directions to law, bordering thereby on law making. The laws made by the State, when interpreted, should further the goals of new economy. In the new economy, based on market economy model, the state's role, *inter alia*, would be as under:

(a) In the new economy, the *legal regulation* of economic activity and the *managerial behaviour* of the state will be reduced. In the market economy model, while there would be legal determination of the market behaviour of entrepreneurs, it should also have enough scope for healthy competition. The law should not allow business to monopolize the market. There should be a legal mechanism to protect the interests of the marginal and small-scale entrepreneurs as well as of consumers, ensured through appropriate legislative and administrative measures. Thus, the operation of the law of the market and consequently the maintenance of competitive conditions are to be regulated by an appropriate mechanism in which the judiciary will have an active role.

(b) There are certain areas which will be outside the purview of normal economic activity and hence under the control of the state, where state will be required to regulate it through law. The areas so identified are:

- Those compelled by public interest, viz., public health, environment standards, labour policy and standards, free legal aid, etc. Proper laws are to be framed to look after these spheres (presently they are covered by the Directive Principles of State Policy), and the judiciary has to work as a watchdog to ensure their realization.
- Effective upholding and supervision of *legal* requirements in the sphere of economic venture. This type of legal control is conducted by the court system, even though the role of public administrative organs cannot be ignored.
- In the new economy, the legal settlement of foreign economic activities, including foreign trade activities is part of the legal regulation of the economy. The main aim of regulation of this field is the protection of national economic interests and the realization of foreign trade objectives. The role of the judiciary in this sphere is very crucial and significant. It is not only the early settlement of disputes that is paramount, but an easy access to the judicial system, while predictability and transparency of the outcome is equally important to create a faith in the system, which will allow foreign trade and investment to flow and help in development.

A proper judicial system is a *sine quo non* for this.

JUDICIAL SYSTEM—PRESENT SCENARIO

India is a democratic republic with a federal system of government. The preamble of the Constitution declares it as a 'sovereign, socialist, secular, democratic republic'. The Constitution provides for the separation of powers between the legislative, executive and judiciary.

There is a fine-tuning of the centre-state relations. The mode of establishment and jurisdiction of courts and the appointment of judges are also defined therein. The Constitution guarantees specific fundamental rights, enforceable through the Supreme Court and high courts.[3]

India's court system is a coordinated, pyramid structure of judicial authority. At the head is the Supreme Court with a high court for each state or group of states. Under the high courts, subordinate courts, including district and sessions courts, function, while at the grass-roots level, in some states, Nyaya Panchayats decide petty civil and criminal matters.[4] The subordinate judiciary is divided into civil and criminal courts, presided over by a district (civil matters) and/or sessions (criminal matters) court judge. Below district and sessions courts are courts of civil jurisdiction, known as *munsifs* or civil judges, and magistrates courts that exercise criminal jurisdiction. Small causes courts have been established in some districts. Courts apply central and state law. Besides, there are Family Courts, Consumer Forums, Administrative Tribunals and others from which appeal may lie to High Court or Supreme Court.

Though the country has a vibrant legal system with progressive laws, well established institutions, independent judiciary and private activists organizations (NGOs), the system still faces a few insurmountable challenges, viz., a huge backlog of court cases and delay in dispensing justice, lack of accountability and transparency, high cost of litigation and large scale acquittals in the criminal cases.[5] Among these, the greatest challenge is the failure of the judiciary to deliver justice expeditiously. There is a near consensus among all the stakeholders in the broad spectrum that backlog and delay in justice administration system is the most serious problem. There has been an estimated backlog of over 2.85 crore cases as towards the year of 2004, which include over 20,0000 under-trials.[6] This has brought about a sense of frustration among the litigants.

The problem of delay on account of arrears has been a topic of discussion for decades. Criminal and civil cases quite often take years to be resolved. The average time taken by the Indian courts for deciding a case varies between 5–15 years.[7] This has given a feeling of the justice system failing to provide effective and timely dispute resolution processes for a democratic, culturally diverse, and market-oriented society. Despite constitutional guarantees, judicial decisions,[8] and the reports by various high-powered committees, the concept of speedy justice has remained an elusive goal. Backlog and delay erodes public trust and confidence in the legal and judicial system, undermines social justice and the realization of human rights, and slows down socio-economic development. It may also have potent effects on the economic development of the country in the emerging scenario and could keep the foreign investors and business out of the reach of the country, which would otherwise flourish upon the quick disposal of cases. The lack of a speedy dispute resolution system has a direct impact on law and order in a society, which provides a conducive atmosphere to foreign investors. A peaceful society is a necessary pre-requisite for any kind of development.

Reasons for backlog and delay are linked to a plethora of problems, viz., poor infrastructure; minimal access to new technology, such as computerization in every segment of the justice delivery system, including courts; inadequate resources; procedural complexity; outdated laws or provisions in certain laws, particularly in the Indian Evidence Act, Code of Civil Procedure, 1973, Code of Criminal Procedure, Indian Penal Code, etc., inadequate, inequitable and arbitrary implementation of laws and judicial decisions; lack of training in the law enforcement agencies, inadequate remuneration, with no accountability mechanism for judicial Acts. Added to this, is the fact that the central and state governments are the single largest litigant, abetted by the government-owned corporations, semi-government bodies and other statutory organizations. Lack of responsiveness and transparency in administration, increase in access to information and institution of cases, rise in population, radical changes in the pattern of litigation, multifarious litigation, etc., are the other reasons for this dismal state.

ALTERNATIVE DISPUTE RESOLUTION (ADR) MECHANISM

Because of the manifold problems afflicting the court system in India, the ADR movement was initiated in the 1970s to make the judicial system accessible to everybody. The aim of the ADRs is to make the system predictable, less expensive and one in which the parties will have more control over the outcome, such as arbitration, conciliation and mediation. ADR is the speedier justice delivery system and its procedure helps in the reduction of the workload of the courts. Today the following prototypes of ADRs exist in the country for dispute resolution at the national level: tribunals, commissions and boards under different laws, which border more than 90 in number at present; Lok Adalats (under the Legal Services Authorities Act, 1987); Nyaya

Panchayats; arbitration and conciliation bodies (under the Arbitration and Conciliation Act, 1996) and Ombudsman(s). To make the justice delivery system accessible to poor people, the provisions for legal aid have also been introduced.[9] But they have not proved to be too effective as they are afflicted with many weaknesses.

For example, there are no uniform standards and practices in respect to the establishment of the tribunals. There are large variations in the composition, qualifications of members, powers, procedures and provisions for appealing against the decisions or orders of the tribunals. Also there are no statutory guidelines regarding the principles applicable to the tribunals or their nomenclature. The party faced with an unfavourable decision tries to avoid its implementation, by filing appeals in the appropriate court since there is no finality attached to the decisions of these tribunals. In fact, except for Lok Adalats, decisions rendered under any ADR mechanism are appealable. The decisions of the Nyaya Panchayats, are not even the decree of the court. The new Arbitration and Conciliation Act similarly does not rule out the intervention of the court at different stages of the arbitration. This makes the ADR system ineffective, and despite inordinate delays in the court system, litigants prefer the regular courts for their own reasons, leading to cramming of the court-dockets. Furthermore, not all types of disputes can be resolved through ADRs. For example, ADR fora cannot resolve disputes arising out of illegal contracts or illegal transactions. Criminal offences, which are non-compoundable, cannot be referred to any ADR mechanism, except to a regular court of law. Also, important matters related to constitutional rights can not be touched by these foras.[10]

On the recommendation of the Eleventh Finance Commission, a novel experiment aimed at clearing the massive backlog of Court cases was started in 2001 by setting up 'fast track' courts in different states. A total of 1,734 such courts are expected to be set-up by the Government of India under a wholly centrally-funded scheme.[11] The laudable objective of the five-year experimental scheme is to take up on priority basis sessions case pending for more than two years and other cases involving under-trials. The scheme envisages the appointment of *ad hoc* judges from amongst the retired sessions or additional judges, judges promoted on *ad hoc* basis and posted in these courts or from the members of the Bar. The states, which are lagging behind their targets, are being persuaded by the centre to speed up the work.[12] The fast track court system has come under a lot of criticism for its high rate of acquittals (90 to 95 per cent). The Supreme Court in its order of 8 November

2001, under a Public Interest Litigation challenging the scheme, noted that though the scheme is aimed at reducing the backlog of cases in criminal matters, it is not an absolute solution and called for deriving maximum benefit from it.[13]

EFFORTS TO IMPROVE THE COURT SYSTEM

In its 114th Report on Gram Nyayalaya (1986), the Law Commission of India observed that the judicial system suffers from inordinate delays, excessive costs, legal technicalities and even uncertainty of judicial decision. The Commission added that the task of solving the problems of backlog of pending cases in law courts is stupendous.[14] Beside the Law Commission, other commissions also made recommendations for improvement in judicial system. For example, the 11th Finance Commission gave directions to the government to take specific measures to tackle the backlog of cases.[15]

The report of the Arrears Committee (1989–90),[16] highlighted and identified some of the causes for delay and backlog of cases. Though this report was not based on any scientific study, it opined that unfilled vacancies in the high courts largely accounted for the accumulation of cases, as loss of man-days was directly proportionate to the accumulation of cases. The observations made in the report of the Arrears Committee,[17] however, reflect the general mindset regarding the court system in India:

> . . . Settlement of cases by mutual compromise is a much better method than seeking adjudication in the adversary system. Fighting litigation to its bitter and final end apart from generating tension and leaving a trail of bitterness, burdens the parties with heavy financial expenditure. Besides, the successful party has to wait for years before enjoying the fruits of litigation. Results in consonance with justice, equity and good conscience can sometimes be achieved by having a mutual settlement of the dispute, than by inviting the court to decide a case one way or the other. . . .

Inadequate judge strength throughout the country is similarly one of the biggest factors for the huge backlog of cases. Added to this, is sluggishness shown by the high courts and various state governments in filling up the vacancies of judges on time, which further aggravates the problem of speedy disposal of cases.[18] The ratio of judges per million population in India is the lowest in the world. In 1987, India had only 10.5 (presently, it is 11)[19], judges per million, as against 41.6 in Australia,

75.2 in Canada, 50.9 in England and 107 in USA.[20] However, it is not merely the raising of strength of the judges in the subordinate courts and the high courts which is needed, it is equally crucial that the right appointments are made, based on merit, suitability, ability and integrity. The job of judgeship needs to be made attractive to have the best brains and persons with integrity on the Bench. It is a known fact that the leading members of the Bar are always reluctant to adore the mantle of judgeship.

There is, nevertheless, a real need to assess the judge-strength, more particularly in the subordinate judiciary and its impact on the disposal rate of cases. A proper study is also required to work out the requirement of infrastructure and the number of judges in the country on the basis of the pendency, rate of inflow of legal matters into the courts and the estimated growth of litigation in the future. Such a scientific study will help in chalking out the future course of action and to meet the problem of backlog head-on.

To examine court work, methods, and work environment, and to suggest improvements thereof, the National Judicial Pay Commission[21] engaged the services of the Indian Institute of Management, Bangalore (IIMB). The IIMB, after an in-depth study, concluded that most people having stakes in judicial work, are of the opinion that the justice delivery system is unsatisfactory and poor. The main reason given by them is the delay in disposal of cases. IIMB went through the order sheets of several cases and after carefully analysing them noted as follows:

1. The time taken to serve summons and emergency notices to defendants varied from three months to three years.
2. The time taken to file written statements ranged from six months to twenty-four months.
3. Interlocutory applications caused delays ranging from four months to four years.
4. Framing of issues consumed as much as three years and six months in one case.[22]
5. Other stages that delayed the cases were absence of advocates and, of course, innumerable adjournments given for a variety of reasons.
6. The major causes of delays were 'summons not being served on time' and 'witnesses not being present in court'. For criminal cases, the most widely-felt source of delay was 'inadequate number of concerned personnel'. For civil cases, it was 'filing of unwarranted Interlocutory Applications'.

7. The delay in most of the cases is due to multiplicity of interlocutory applications, which are not promptly dealt with by the courts.[23]

The above findings concur with the views of several commissions and reinforces the felt need to introduce long over-due reforms.

The National Judicial Pay Commission, in its first report submitted in 1999, examined the work methods and environment in courts and noted the following difficulties faced in court system that affect the interests of litigant public:

1. The courts are over-burdened with work. The experience is that even at the stage of framing of issues, there is no assistance from advocates in most of the courts. Interrogatories are seldom resorted to and very often documents are filed after the commencement of trial with an application seeking permission.
2. Advocates produce hindrance in observing the procedure and a very insistent officer is likely to be harassed in many ways. Rules are not observed because of non-cooperation of various agencies responsible for producing witnesses.
3. Considerable time is being wasted in securing the presence of the parties for the purpose of admission and denial and seeking reply to the interrogatories.
4. The language of the courts is an additional problem. In almost all states, the judicial proceedings in lower courts are recorded in the local language of the state concerned. Proceedings, including evidence, are recorded by the *Peshkar* (Reader) in vernacular, while the presiding officer records the proceedings in English. On account of implementation of transfer policy of judges of the High Courts, generally judges in a High Court are from outside the state concerned. The transferee judges, who are not familiar with local language of the state, face considerable difficulty in dealing with cases when the records are only in the local language. The translation of all the records into English is an enormous task besides the cost factor and even if it were to be done, it would cause delay in the disposal of cases. Therefore, language also becomes a hindrance to attain speedy disposal of cases.[24]

Thus appointment of more judges is merely *tinkering at the fringes.* It is also necessary that the procedure for disposal of cases be made more exact and time bound. Cumbersome features of the procedural law contribute in no small measure to the delay in the disposal of cases.

Too many appeals and revisions against even interim orders help vested interests to prolong litigation. These need to be curtailed. The Code of Civil Procedure, 1908, was first amended in 1976, to address some of these aspects to curtail delays in court procedure, but the experience has been that cases were still adjourned for the asking either for filing written statements or documents and even for settlement of issues. There are technical flaws on many accounts in the procedural law, beside an unlimited right to appeal to the higher courts, which need to be addressed. Attempts have been made to amend the Code of Civil Procedure in order to speed up the tardy justice delivery system by settling cases within a time frame, with minimum adjournment on stated grounds and a limited rights to appeal. The Act amending the Code of Civil Procedure was passed by Parliament in 1999, and came into force in October 2002. The amendments to the Code are devised with the purpose of speeding up the tardy justice delivery system.[25] The amendments to the Code faced stiff opposition from the advocates. While the government felt that the amendments would benefit poor litigants, the lawyers held the view that the amended law would cause hardship to poor litigants. The amended Act has also provided the mechanism of recording evidence through video-conferencing.

The scenario on the criminal side is equally disappointing. Often, investigating (police) and prosecuting agencies are not well-equipped with modern means and scientific training to deal with the volume and types of crimes occurring, which leads to rising crime and acquittal rates. The average conviction rate is 39.02 per cent, according to the information from the National Crime Records Bureau.[26] The reasons for the poor conviction rate are attributed to the nature of the procedural laws and practices followed by criminal courts, and also to a great extent because of improper and deficient investigations. Speedy trials hold the key to the sentencing policy. In this regard, the Indian Penal Code 1862, Indian Evidence Act 1872 and Code of Criminal Procedure 1973,[27] are in many respects antiquated laws. Delay, procedural complexity and unlimited appeal mechanisms also make litigation costly. The heavy backlog of cases, increasing rate of acquittal, lack of trained police staff[28] lead to overcrowding of jails as well.[29] There are an estimated 2 lakh under-trials in different jails of the country, on whom the states spend more than 461 crores annually.[30] Sentencing procedures are strict with limited alternatives to incarceration. Corruption within the police and among lower-level court administrators is said to be quite widespread.

A Code of Criminal Procedure (Amendment Bill), 1994, proposed an overhaul of criminal procedure law and practice. Various government committees and the Law Commission of India[31] have over the past forty years produced comprehensive reports and recommendations for the reform of India's criminal law and procedure. Different stakeholders[32] in the criminal administrative system, including the Supreme Court, High Courts and Sessions Courts, prison authorities and legal services authorities (constituted under the Legal Services Authorities Act, 1987), have implemented a variety of *ad hoc* measures within their jurisdictions to reduce delay and increase efficiency. However, a coordinated and comprehensive plan to reform criminal law and procedure has not been initiated by the Government of India. In November 2000, the Government constituted another committee under the chairmanship of Justice Malimath to look into different aspects of the criminal justice system. The Committee with 158 recommendations submitted its report on 21 May 2003. The recommendations have since become very controversial and are stated to be in violation of basic human rights of the accused.

The delay in the disposal of cases, to some extent, is also 'judge-made'. Lack of punctuality, laxity and lack of control over the case file and court proceedings, contribute in no small measure to the delay in the disposal of cases. Habitually coming late to court, or rising early, or failing to deliver judgements for long periods of time, are part of the malaise afflicting the judiciary, which in no small measure compound the problem of the justice delivery system and compromise the image of the judiciary. The grant of unnecessary adjournments on the mere asking or on account of any flimsy ground or 'strike call' by lawyers, further adds to the problem. Whereas it is pertinent that judges at all levels must respect the court time and remain punctual, any aberration thereto should be taken seriously, calling for appropriate action. Delay in the pronouncement of judgements is another serious problem deserving appropriate attention. It is another manifestation of the denial of justice. Slow motion justice is no justice, particularly when significant rights of the parties are involved in litigation.

In its structure and organization, the administration of justice in India at present is in analogue mode and bears the stamp of 'Made in UK'. It is adversial in character, which renders the position of a judge to a passive listener, denying him an active participation in unravelling the truth. The court battle is conducted according to medieval rules of evidence. There is no system of case management in the courts, worth the name, and the concept of pre-trial meeting of the parties is totally non-existent, after the lawsuit is being filed. This may help in identifying the key legal issues of the case and avoid unnecessary litigation.

Integrity of the judiciary is an important aspect in order to create trust, transparency and predictability in the judicial system. Corruption in the judiciary will be a fatal blow to its reputation and will shake the faith of people. In order to maintain the health of the judiciary, it is imperative to deal with the malaise of corruption with a firm hand. Whereas the problem in the subordinate judiciary can be addressed with the help of Vigilance Cells in the High Courts and judges found to be guilty may be terminated from service, the procedure prescribed for higher judiciary is cumbersome. A judge of the Supreme Court or High Court can be removed from service only through impeachment by the Parliament (Arts. 124(4) and 217(1)(b) respectively). The mechanism should be devised through law to deal with less serious cases, not deserving impeachment, by an independent judicial body. There is a move to constitute a National Judicial Commission to address this issue beside the appointment and transfer of judges in the higher judiciary.

MAIN CHALLENGES FOR REFORM

In order to reap the benefits of the new economy, and to play its role in the new dispensation effectively, it is imperative that the prevalent legal and judicial situation in India should be changed. The business thrives on quick disposal of cases and a foreign investor would like to see transparency and predictability in judicial matters and an early resolution of disputes would help in building his confidence in the legal system of the country. He would also like to have a certain measure of control over the system, which may be possible under an ADR mechanism.

There are multifarious reasons for the present dismal state of the judiciary, which need to be addressed. The legal and judicial reforms must be initiated and adopted to improve the efficiency of the justice delivery system and to reduce backlog and delay through initiatives to reform procedural laws and increase in the number of judges along with much-desired infra-structural changes in the context of information technology. As mentioned above, many studies and proposals have been made in the past to deal with the single most important problem inflicting the judiciary, i.e. how to deal with arrears and delay in dispensation of justice on account of arrears. As outlined above, the problem has many facets requiring amending/implementing the procedural law; appointing more judges; training judges, law enforcement agencies—prosecutors, police, investigating agencies, etc., strengthening the machinery of legal aid/services; devising an effective ADR mechanism, Lok Adalats, Nyaya Panchayats and updating the archaic laws.

(a) *Arrears and Delay*

Studies have revealed the need to improve the infrastructure—qualitatively and quantitatively, at each level of justice delivery system. There is an urgent need to improve the infra-structural facilities in the courts. Computerization of courts would bring much desired transparency in the court system and help in case management in the courts.

Studies have also highlighted the need to appoint more judges, particularly in the subordinate judiciary. The edifice of the administration of justice rests on the shoulders of the district judiciary, as the majority of the litigants go only up to district level.[33] In this context, it is necessary that the judiciary must be granted financial and administrative autonomy. Presently, the power to make appointments in the lower judiciary rests with the state, with the consent of the Chief Justice of the state High Court, who does not have the power to fill up the vacancies at will, though the High Court has the power of superintendence over the subordinate judiciary. The High Court does not enjoy any power to create any new post in the judiciary. Transferring this power to the High Court will not only ensure speedy trial, but will also ensure the independence of the judiciary, one of the cardinal principles of democracy.

(b) *Reform in Criminal and Civil Procedure and Processes*

In order to help in overcoming the problem of delay in dispensation of justice, all the stakeholders in the justice delivery system—lawyers, judges, legal experts, litigants and court administrators—are of the unanimous view to reform the criminal and civil law procedure. The 1999 amending Act of the Code of Civil Procedure 1908, has become effective from 1 October 2002, and its full impact has yet to be realized. Similarly, the reforms in the Code of Criminal Procedure, 1973 and the Indian Penal Code should be brought in, reducing the delay and making the procedure simple. These reforms should also be aimed at cutting the cost of litigation and avoiding technicalities, thereby making the law simple and within the reach of the common man.

(c) *Judicial Training*

In order to reform legal and judicial practices, training of the judiciary in procedural laws, case management and court administration is an important aspect. In certain states, there are judicial training institutions, controlled and managed by state high courts, viz., Andhra Pradesh, Delhi, Tamil Nadu, Uttar Pradesh, Karnataka. The High Courts and District Courts in several other states are taking steps to improve their professional capacity through participation in joint training programmes with other stakeholders. Increased and improved training for subordinate judiciary, including magistrates, remains a key area. The Supreme Court, very recently (March 2002), has highlighted the need for judicial training and establishing state judicial academies for that purpose.[34] For the higher judiciary, the National Judicial Academy at Bhopal has been established.

(d) *Law Enforcement Agencies*

It is high time that necessary training and reforms should be introduced in the law enforcement agencies to conduct scientific investigation, with proper coordination among them, so that the guilty are prosecuted and punished. This will help in solving the problem of large-scale acquittals and cutting down the arrears. In fact, a large number of acquittals results out of faulty, non-scientific and disoriented investigation. The Police Act, 1861 needs to be re-written in consonance with the needs of the twenty-first century.

(e) *ADRs*

In the new economy, the ADRs will have the central role in the quick disposal of cases and will enhance the trust of the foreign parties in the legal areas of concern to them. To meet the demands of the new economy, a well-crafted ADR mechanism needs to be devised. The government, in 1996, enacted Arbitration and Conciliation Act, replacing thereby the earlier laws on arbitration—the Arbitration Act, 1940, the Arbitration (Protocol and Convention) Act, 1937, and the Foreign Awards (Recognition and Enforcement) Act, 1961. The new Act is based on the UNCITRAL's Model Law on International Commercial Arbitration, 1985, and is meant to repose the confidence of the foreign entrepreneurs in the legal system. ADRs give the party a certain degree of control over the procedure, law, venue and speed in the disposal of a commercial dispute. To make the ADR system to work effectively, there should be minimal intervention from the court.

In order to lessen the burden of the courts, it is also imperative to enhance the powers and jurisdiction of different tribunals, constituted for various purposes such as tax, administrative matters, debt relief, consumer, labour, etc., with a very restricted right to appeal to the Supreme Court. It is also necessary to increase the number of these tribunals as well as to create more benches of the existing tribunals. This will help in providing less expensive, easy and quick justice within a stipulated time frame. Their procedure needs to be less technical and cumbersome.

(f) *Lok Adalats, Nyaya Panchayats*

The Legal Services Authority Act 1987, has constituted the National Legal Services Authority (NALSA) and state legal services authorities, which provide legal aid to poor and hold Lok Adalats for quick disposal of cases. These authorities function under the Supreme Court and the respective High Courts. Through their legal aid programmes, they help in spreading the legal literacy among the masses about their rights. The cases disposed of by Lok Adalats are final, with no right to appeal. At present, these Lok Adalats are limited mainly to road accident and matrimonial cases, primarily to marginalized groups. It is necessary that they should be expanded to new substantive areas and regions.

Similarly, Nyaya Panchayats, constituted under the 73rd Amendment of the Constitution in 1992, be assigned an accelerated role in dispute settlement, whose judgement should have the sanctity of a court verdict and the right to appeal against such settlements be restricted.

CONCLUSION

In the new economy, the judiciary is in a very pivotal position to make India an effective player in the global trade. Its efficiency, transparency, predictability of its judgements will create an atmosphere of trust in the judicial system for the foreign entrepreneurs and investors. It is high time that the necessary reforms, as suggested above, be introduced in the judiciary to enable it to play its role effectively. In this respect, the role of the Government is very important in initiating these reforms, and also in granting financial and administrative independence to the judiciary.

NOTES

1. Globalization is understood to be a western model of market economy, see, Asghar Ali Engineer, 'Globalization, Democracy and threat to Diversity', *Mainstream* 10 (1 November 1997). In economic terms, globalization is the opening up of the markets, which will operate under market forces, where State will have very little role to play. Liberalization is an offshoot of globalization.
2. The term 'structural adjustment programme', describes policies advocated by international institutions such as the International Monetary Fund (IMF), and by individual governments in order to enable beneficiary states to achieve an improved balance of payments. In the case of IMF, such states must agree to implement those policies in order to qualify for future assistance. The policies generally involve a move towards greater market ordering and one or the other measure of fiscal austerity through heavy taxation and reduction of governmental subsidies and in welfare funding, see, Steiner and Alston (eds.), *International Human Rights in Context* 1139 (1996), citing Sigrun Skogly, 'Structural Adjustment and Development: Human Rights—An Agenda for Change', 15 *H Rs Q* 751 (1993).
3. See, Articles 32 and 226 of the Constitution.
4. The Constitution (Seventy-third Amendment) Act, 1992, effective from 24 April 1993, made provision for Panchayats which will exercise such powers at the village level as the legislature of a state may, by law, provide. The states are responsible to set up Nyaya Panchayats at the district level, block level, etc., in the villages. Many state governments, by law, have authorized these *Panchayats* to decide petty matters. For example, Madhya Pradesh government in 1996 set up 'Village Courts' to decide civil matters pertaining to disputes involving a sum below Rs. 1,000, besides criminal cases involving theft, quarrels and threats. Each Village Court is established for a cluster of 10 or more Village Panchayats. However, there are no official statistics available indicating the number of cases handled by the Nyaya Panchayats, set up all over the country. Their decisions are mostly informal and no data is kept about them. The disputes decided by the Nyaya Panchayats, have no finality and the courts can be approached for the same disputes.
5. The conviction percentage in criminal cases is falling over the years. It was 64.8 per cent in 1961, which fell to 42.9 per cent in 1994. The All India average conviction rate in the year 1997 was as low as 38.2 per cent and 39.02 per cent in 1999. The disposal rate is equally dismal. In 1997, it stood at as low as 20.8 per cent. See, Government of India, *Crimes in India,* 1998. Also see, PIB Release, *Low Conviction Rate in Criminal Cases,* 22 August 2001. It is reported that the average disposal of cases in the apex court was 42,200 against 40,400 cases filed every year; in the High Courts, it was 12,41,000 against 11,23,500 cases and in subordinate

courts, it was 142,43,500 against the 132,29,000 cases filed. See, *The Hindu*, 27 November 2004, p. 12.
Also see, http://pib.nic.in/archive/Ireleng/1yr2001/raug2001/22082001/r220820012.html.

6. Out of 2.85 crore cases, 29,315 cases are lying with the Supreme Court; 32,24,144 with different high courts and over 2,53,50,370 with the subordinate courts. See, http://164.100.24.219/rsq/quest.asp?gref=37489.
7. It is stated that some civil cases take as long as 25 to 30 years and even in criminal cases, it sometimes takes more than 8 years. See, the statement of the Law Minister, in a written reply, to the Lok Sabha on 4 August 2000.
8. See, *Hussainara* v. *State of Bihar*, AIR 1979 SC 1360.
9. Article 39-A of the Constitution provides: 'The State shall secure that the operation of the legal system promotes justice, on a basis of equal opportunity, and shall, in particular, provide free legal aid, by suitable legislation or schemes or in any other way, to ensure that opportunities for securing justice are not denied to any citizen by reason of economic or other disabilities.' In 1987, the Legal Services Authorities Act was enacted to give a statutory base to the legal aid programme throughout the country on a uniform basis. The Act finally became effective from 9 November 1995. A National Legal Services Authority (NALSA) has been created under the Act to lay down policies and principles for making legal services available under the Act. Despite a press release by the NALSA to create awareness about its activities, there still exists a tremendous knowledge gap in this respect. The income ceiling of Rs. 50,000 per annum for legal aid before the Supreme Court and Rs. 25,000 per annum for legal aid to High Court has been set.
10. For more details on the ADR system in India, see, *Dispute Resolution Process in India*, study conducted by S.K. Verma, S.C Srivastava and Geeta Obrai for Institute of Developing Economies (IDE-JETRO), 2002.
11. The Finance Commnission committed Rupees 502.9 crores to set up fast track courts in the country.
12. See, http://pib.nic.in/welcome.html.
13. 'Supreme Court on Efficacy of Ast Track Court System', *Times of India*, 9 November 2001, p. 7.
14. For Law Commision's report, see, ttp://www.nic.in/lawmin/legalcon.html#LAW%20COMMISSION.
15. See, http://cbi.nic.in/case.html.
16. The Committee was constituted byu the Government of India in 1989 on the recommendation of the Chief Justices' Conference; report published by the Supreme Court of India in 1990.
17. Ibid., p. 109.
18. As on December 2001, there were 15.24 per cent vacancies in the Subordinate Courts, High Courts, and the Supreme Court of India out of a total strength of 13140 judges. See, Government of India, Ministry of Law,

Justice & Company Affairs; Rajya Sabha unstarred question #2223, answered on, 10 December 2001.

19. According to the records, presently there exist more than 1,500 unfilled vacancies in the subordinate judiciary against the sanctioned strength of 12,205 and 155 vacancies exist in the high courts out of 647 sanctioned posts as on 8 June 2002. See, *The Hindu*, 8 June 2002, p. 8.
20. Krishan Mahajan, 'Judges the right number', *Indian Express*, 18 May 2000, p. 8.
21. Constituted by the Government of India in 1996 on the direction of the Supreme Court given in *All India Judges' Association* v. *Union of India*, AIR 1992 SC 165.
22. Sometime it takes longer than this.
23. Chapter 21, Report of First National Judicial Pay Commission (1999); see, http://www.kar.nic.in/fnjpc/cwcm&adr.html
24. Ibid.
25. Act 46 of 1999, Bill #50 of 1999, which received the assent of the President of India on, 30 December 1999.
26. See, PIB Release, Government of India, 22 August 2001.
27. The Code of Criminal Procedure, 1973 repealed the earlier Code of 1898. It has since been amended in 1974, 1978, 1980, 1983, 1988, 1990, and 1993 for specific purposes. See, Institute of Developing Economies (IDE-JETRO) study by S.K. Verma, S.C. Srivastava, Sadiq Jilani Syed, and Geeta Obrai, *India Judicial System and Reforms in Asian Countries: The Case of India*, p. 130 *et. seq.* (March 2001, Japan).
28. The Police Act 1861 is also an antiquated law. It does not stress scientific training of the police force.
29. In Tihar Jail, Delhi, as against the sanctioned capacity of 3,300, there are 9,000–10,000 inmates, out of which 90 per cent are undertrials. This is against the Supreme Court decision on speedy trial in *Hussainara Katoon* v. *States of Bihar*, (1980) 1 SCC 81.
30. See, *The Hindu*, 15 June 2002, p. 8. Also see, PIB Press Release, 8 November 2001.
31. See, 113th Report of the Law Commission of India (1985); 154th Report on the Code of Criminal Procedure, in two volumes (1996).
32. The Act was amended in 1994 (by Act #59 of 1994), which has provided the statutory base to Lok Adalats by conferring wide powers on Lok Adalat judges in the matter of summoning and examining witnesses on oath, discovery and production of documents, reception of evidence of affidavits, requisitioning of public records or documents. See, Section 22.
33. It is estimated that about 20 per cent cases go in appeal.
34. See, *All India Judges' Association* v. *Union of India*, 2002 (3) Scale 291.

19

Judicial Reforms and Market Institutions: The Emerging Scenario

DOLLY ARORA

In the changing global scenario, the question of judicial reforms has acquired a new sense of urgency in most Third World countries. Three significant developments characterize the emerging discourse on judicial reforms: one, weakening of perceived boundaries between legal and judicial reforms; two, emergence of economic development as the primary objective and the driving force of legal-judicial reforms; and three, increasing interest in downloading the responsibilities of a formal judicial system in favour of mechanisms of alternative dispute resolution. Significantly enough, this discourse has been shaped in a context characterized by the growing role of multilateral and bilateral aid agencies in financing of legal-judicial reforms. In order to delineate the true nature and implications of reforms which are taking shape, it is imperative to comprehend the forces which define and dominate their context. This article seeks to do so in the context of Third World countries which have introduced significant changes in their legal-judicial systems in recent years.

REFORM ADVOCACY: CONDITIONALITY AS CONTEXT

Legal and judicial reforms have been vigorously advocated by multilateral and bilateral aid providers in many countries of Latin America and

*Published with the permission of the author from *Indian Judicial System: Need and Directions of Reforms*, New Delhi, 2004.

Asia. Since 1994, the World Bank, the International Development Bank and the Asian Development Bank have either approved or initiated more than $500 million in loans for judicial reform projects in 26 countries. The US Agency for International Development has spent close to $200 million on similar projects in the past decade. Many other groups and private organizations are also funding programmes to modernize the judiciary in many countries.[1]

It is noteworthy that Articles of Agreement of World Bank prohibit if from interfering in the 'political affairs of any member country', unless it is established that they have direct and obvious economic effects relevant to its work, which is 'to promote the economic development of member countries by providing loans and guarantees for the financing of specific projects of technical assistance', and to assist a member country 'to stabilize or revive its economy and thus enhance or facilitate investment for productive purposes inits territory'.[2]

The implication of this clause, however, has been far from prohibitive. The World Bank (WB) in effect tends to justify nearly all kinds of its interference in political, administrative and judicial matters of its member countries in the interest of its own economic objectives. Economic goals of the Bank are not considered distinct from political issues in absolute terms. Rather, in case of a conflict, the former are invariably assigned priority over questions of political rights of the countries which borrow from it. This implies that even though political interference is not regarded as the objective of the Bank, economic logic can always be asserted to justify it. The Bank does not even proclaim that it has an obligation to stay out of political matters when its economic interests are at stake either directly or indirectly. Its recent interest in promotion of 'good governance' as well as 'judicial reforms' is also justified in terms of this logic.[3]

The Bank's approach, it underlines, allows legal reforms to proceed in harmony with economic reforms, rather than lag behind or go off on tangents which my not be germane to the critical needs of the countries' economies as a whole.[4] It has used a wide range of instruments for the purpose. Its major lending instruments include adjustment loans, legal components of investment loans, and free-standing technical assistance and institution capacity building loans. Besides, studies and pilot projects on judicial reforms are also financed by a grant from the recently established Fund for Institutional Development.

COMPONENT OF ADJUSTMENT LOAN

Judicial reforms have often been advocated as a component of the measures to be implemented under a structural or sectoral adjustment loan. The Second Structural Adjustment Credit provided to Benin, for example, had a conditionality attached to itself, which required specific measures to enhance recovery of Bank loans—these measures included reform of judicial procedures, land titles and commercial laws. Likewise, in Bolivia, the structural adjustment credit included conditionality concerning the enactment of new banking laws and regulations for their enforcement.[5]

The sectoral adjustment credits to Bangladesh and Cote d'lvoire, are other cases indicative of judicial reforms being thrust upon as a part of loan conditionality. Bangladesh was provided assistance for agreeing to enact a Financial Loan Courts Act in 1990, whereby special commercial courts were established in major economic centers of the country. These courts enabled the financial institutions to bring actions against defaulting borrowers and the loans could be adjudicated. In Cote d'Ivoire, under the Economic Management Project of 1993, support was provided to the Ministry of Justice to strengthen the legal framework and judicial system in commercial areas, including updating of economic legislation; establishment of arbitration court for commercial disputes and provision of logistical support to this court; computerization of selected courts' registrars' offices; design and implementation of training programmes in commercial and financial legislation for the legal community; assistance for publication of legal and judicial data and acquisition of law books and periodicals for courts and tribunals; and institutional strengthening of the Supreme Court through training of staff and acquisition of computers and equipment.[6]

FREE STANDING AND PROJECT LOANS

The most significant of the instrumentalities used by the Bank for executing judicial reforms, however, has been the provision of free-standing loan for judicial reform as a self-contained project. The Judiciary Infrastructure Project of 1993 involving a $30 million loan to Venezuela was the first World Bank-supported operation with the exclusive purpose of judicial reform. Its objective was to upgrade institutional infrastructure of the judiciary, improve judicial training, modernize court management and finance further studies on judicial reform. The project consisted of four components. The first component included a programme for institutional strengthening of the constitutional body in charge of the administration of the judiciary; the second component involved a programme to modernize the system of courtroom administration; the third component involved training programmes for judges and other judiciary personnel as well as technical assistance to strengthen institutional capabilities of the judicial school; and the last component involved construction, rehabilitation and upgrading of court buildings.[7]

Project loans of a broader scope, normally of an institutional development character, which include judicial reforms as a component of the project are also provided. Financial and Upgrading Project of Tanzania, for instance, provided credit to, among other things, finance activities designed to strengthen the judiciary in the area of commercial law developments and to streamline procedures to ensure the speedy disposal of cases. These activities included the training of High Court judges, resident and district magistrates, registry assistants and registrars of the Court of Appeal and High Courts, and provisions for typewriters and computers for use by magistrates and High Court registries. Likewise, the Capacity Building, Public Sector and Legal Institutions Development Project in Mozambique provided, among other things, for the training of judges and court staff, provision of financing to improve institutional facilities, including legal information systems, acquisition of books for law libraries as well as support for a new centre of judicial studies. World Bank's first direct financial assistance for judicial reform effort was also a component of a 1988 public sector management loan which was provided to Argentina to, among other things, improve the information systems in courts.[8] Judicial sectors have been assisted as a part of its institution-building projects in East European countries and the republics of the former Soviet Union also.

Inasmuch as the problems pertaining to the judicial sector are traced by the bank to the existing legal framework in specific countries in general, and sectors in particular, reforms in the legal framework are considered crucial to bring about positive effects at the level of judicial system too. Law reform and reform of regulatory framework of the economy has accordingly been assigned considerable significance in deciding assistance, and countries willing to undertake reforms in desired directions are readily offered assistance to execute these. Thus, for instance, under a Financial Sector Deepening and Intermediation Project Loan, Pakistan has been offered an assistance of $213 million by the IBRD, to help prepare a legal and judicial reform programme to improve the environment of debt recovery. Provision of legal consultants' services has been made to partially reorganize the corporate law authority and to assist in revising the insurance law. *India* was provided under the Technical Assistance Private Power Development Project a loan of $3 million to review the contractual arrangements for private power projects. Peru was offered a $30 million Privatization Technical Assistance Project loan in connection with the preparation and implementation of the privatization programme and related sectoral policy, legal and regulatory reforms, primarily in the mining, hydrocarbons, telecommunications, power, fisheries, air and urban transport, industry, water and banking sectors.[9]

CO-OPERATION WITH OTHER AGENCIES

Besides providing direct assistance, the World Bank also cooperates with other bilateral and multilateral donor agencies, such as the USAID, the German GTZ and non-governmental organizations like the Central and East European Law Institute of the American Bar Association. It has actively been coordinating legal technical assistance from other sources in its member countries. Many other donors either appoint it as the executive agency for their programmes or join forces with the bank in a variety of co-financing arrangements. Many of bank's projects have been co-financed by agencies like African Development Bank, European Investment Bank, Asian Development Bank, etc. The Japanese government has also been co-financing many of its projects.

In Cape Verde, for instance, it executed and coordinated the Public Sector Reform and Capacity Building Project which was financed by IDA and co-financed by UNDP, Switzerland, France and EC. The project had a strong judicial reform component involving advisory services and training for the judiciary, registrars and key ministries' legal departments; business law training for magistrates and lawyers; strengthening of drafting skills in the Ministry of Justice; development of arbitration facilities and procedures for economic matters; and provision of equipment, materials and publications to the Ministry of Justice and its agencies. In Albania, the World Bank and GTZ co-operate in funding a resident legal advisor who assists a legal reform group within the Ministry of Finance in drafting legislation for privatization and financial sector restructuring.[10]

In the case of Bolivia, under the IDA financed Judicial Reform Project 1993, support was provided for preparation of the judicial reform programme which should include development of policies in the area of case management and judicial adjudication, legislative reform, alternative dispute resolution and legal education. Another project involving $95 million worth of IDA credit aimed at development of judicial procedures, guidelines and training of judges in implementation thereof, a study on the judiciary's organization and development of alternative organization structures, judicial legal training, institution strengthening of the judiciary and the Ministry of Justice, support for establishment of mediation and conciliation centres, and a study on legal education.[11]

Under the Financial Resources Development Japanese Grant Agreement of 1993, Japanese grant of Y39 million was provided to Pakistan to prepare for legal and regulatory reforms relating to divestiture, restructuring of state financial institutions and revision of anti-trust legislation. Another Japanese grant of Y86.1 million was provided to it under the Financial Sector Deepening and Income Generation Agreement to design a legal and regulatory reform programme to support private sector development. Separate agreements were entered into to meet the legal requisites for privatization of telecommunications and power sector development too. These projects, as mentioned before, are also executed through the World Bank itself.[12]

MAJOR THRUST AREAS

The major thrust areas for judicial reforms have been perceived by most aid providers as having to with, apart from legal reforms, questions of autonomy, speed, accessibility and professionalism. These are expected to be resolved primarily through provision of resources, training, procedural reforms and creation of alternative institutions of justice. Efforts have been made to push several of these countries in the direction of these reforms. In many cases, research studies either preceded or accompanied their adoption. Despite variations in specific details, it is not difficult to delineate some common thrusts which characterize these interventions. The most significant of these is the predominance of economic development as the objective of judicial reforms; the second feature pertains to the merging boundaries between legal and judicial reforms; and the third feature relates to the extension of reforms to sites for alternative justice.

ON REASONS, MEANINGS AND ALTERNATIVES

A series of questions arise at this point. Why is so much interest being evinced by powerful multilateral and bilateral donor agencies in promoting judicial and legal reforms in Third World countries? What motivates them to pursue these ends? Do these motives have any implications for the strategy or content of reforms? Are the effects likely to be conditioned by these motives and strategies? Does this pattern of interventions for reform have any adverse policy implications for the recipient countries? Do reforms need to be reconsidered? And finally, are there any possibilities of more meaningful alternatives which may be closely related to the specific contexts of societies? It may be desirable to address these questions systematically before any meaningful conclusions can be derived about the kind of efforts required in a country like India. The following section attempts to raise some issues which need to be further examined in the light of specific experiences of reforms introduced in various contexts.

PREDOMINANCE OF ECONOMIC MOTIVE

First, the question of motives of those who have been keen to Fund reforms should the considered. One of the primary concerns of donors, emphatically, has been to create institutional conditions for their own economic expansion into the Third World countries which offer immense economic opportunities to them. As a World Bank study by Buscaglia and Dakolias underlines while discussing the experience of Argentina and Equador: 'An accessible and efficient judicial sector is necessary to handle more complex transactions, i.e. takeovers and mergers, which have arisen as a result of market reforms. The judiciary can impact market transactions by ensuring predictable dispute resolution costs and effective enforcement of property and contractual rules. In this context, the judiciary has a major role to play in assuring the growth of markets. Governments are therefore, forced to address this crisis in the judicial system in order to create a reliable environment for foreign investment and for enforcement of individual rights.'[13]

The major concern of the World Bank and other providers of assistance is improvement of conditions for the operation of foreign investors. The statement of Ibrahim F.I. Shihata, Vice-President of the Bank, is quite revealing in respect of motives. 'Successful implementation of fundamental policy changes in business environment and in the financial sector,' he stated, 'normally requires equally fundamental changes in the overall legal and institutional framework. More broadly, civil service reform, legal reform, and judicial reform are often prerequisites for the facilitation of investment.'[14] In his study of the judicial sector in Latin America and the Caribbean, undertaken for the World Bank, Maria Dakolias similarly emphasizes, that:

> economic integration between countries and regions demands a judiciary that meets international standards. . . . Economic integration requires greater harmonization of laws which in turn requires that they be consistently applied by the member countries. Member countries must have the assurance that the law will be interpreted in accordance with these international or regional standards. In this way, the countries around the world must modernize their judiciaries in order to accommodate these demands and provide a level-playing field in the international arena.[15]

There is an eagerness to transform the judicial systems in Third World countries to serve the needs of capital in exploiting their newly emerging markets.

SELECTIVE LOCAL PARTICIPATION

One of the primary objectives of donors has always been to ensure maximum compliance from the countries being assisted. Efforts are made to ensure this from the very beginning of the process of decision-making about it. The World Bank usually interacts with the executive branches in the borrowing countries. In the case of legal reforms, however, it has to deal with other branches too. In order to ensure that conflicting pressures are easily set aside, in many countries, governments have been asked to establish separate legal reforms units (Lures) within the executive branch. These are meant to ensure that legal reforms are guided by a coherent strategy and frequent dialogue and coöperation with the agencies managing legal reforms.[16]

A recent overall review of its legal and judicial reforms support by the bank in order to identify issues of concern and draw lessons for future underlines that legal reforms must 'take root' in the local legal community as well as the population at large in order to be successful and to have long-term effects. For this purpose, however, it does not underline the need for it to be at the listening end. Rather, it suggests that training and education programmes for government officials, judges, local lawyers and administrators as well as members of the legal profession are an indispensable part of legal assistance.[17] The bank has over time supported various training activities as a part of projects it financed. It has also financed participation of local lawyers in training seminars abroad. The Bank's commitment to local participation in the process of reforms appears superficial rather than real, when seen in the light of its actual conduct. Despite admitting that unless a country is committed to reforming its legal regime, and either requests assistance for its reform process or agrees with assistance providers, legal technical assistance may be a waste of resources. Despite this, it has not refrained from evoking conditionalities for execution of certain reforms while providing general economic assistance.

The World Bank's legal department advises that any reform programme must essentially be owned by the country and problems have to be identified by the authorities in the country through consultation with the people involved.[18] The remarks of Shihata, the Vice-President of the World Bank, regarding who should be involved in legal reforms at a World Bank Conference to discuss judicial reforms, however, are worth noting in this connection. Even as he admitted that 'the reforms should not be a closed operation between a ministry and the Bank', and that, these are important to others in the country, such as 'judiciary, the bar associations, law professors, groups likely to be affected by certain legislation, and so on', it was emphasized that 'it is generally useful to be able to deal with a legal judicial focus unit in charge of the country's reforms' for 'we have found that when too many people speak for reform, it is difficult to get things done efficiently'.[19] Some countries have addressed this issue by establishing a unit in the cabinet, the ministry of justice, or sometimes even the ministry of finance to act as interlocutor between foreign donors and local authorities. Governments are easily pressurized in this manner than would be possible if there were to be greater interaction.

TOP DOWN APPROACH

One of the major failures of the reforms programme in the Third World countries has been its top-down nature. A major problem with such an approach is that even sincere efforts often end up in an advocacy of remedies which are standardized solutions, wherein local contexts are objectified and expected to comply. Neither their genuine concerns, nor their real priorities find themselves reflected in such solutions which are offered to them by way of these exogenous, or top down exercises.

The local context, where reforms are to be introduced, does not get the opportunity to voice its problems; it is not allowed to speak for itself. Rather, the diagnosis as well as solutions reflect the interests and priorities of those who provide the assistance to executive reforms.[20]

The limits of a top-down approach to reforms and the constraints experienced at the level of countries which are expected/assisted to carry out the suggested package have been admitted by the evaluation studies of various projects also. In a study of judicial reform projects in 15 Latin American countries, Martinez Neira found that there had been too much emphasis on increasing the number of judges, courts, buildings and computers at the expense of more fundamental changes in the legal system.[21] The US General Accounting Office concluded on the basis of an analysis of USAID programmes in Central America and Colombia, that providing computers, training and other technical assistance to the judiciary in countries where a strong commitment to reform was lacking had not been productive.[22] Yet another study which undertook an evaluation of six judicial reform projects of USAID in Argentina, Colombia, Honduras, Philippines, Sri Lanka and Uruguay found that training judges, improving management systems and supplying computers and other resources to the judiciary had little impact in countries where a consensus for judicial reforms was lacking.[23]

ROLES REDEFINED

While these reviews have emphasized the problems which come in the way of any reform efforts unless these are able to ensure local involvement, these are not open to the idea of reforms agenda and its objectives themselves being locally determined. The interest is confined to mobilization of local opinion in favour of reforms as conceived by the World Bank and its co-financers. There is a predefined framework within which all participation must fit. This is the framework which facilitates market transactions and private sector development. A powerful or socially committed state is not considered desirable any more. Instead the state is expected to be prepared to give space to the formal as well as informal mechanisms of justice. It is expected to be active to the point of creating a favourable institutional context for enforcement of contracts between private and public parties, and thereby provide a conducive legal environment for business. But it is not required to assert itself over and above the power of the capital.

The power of judiciary is sought to be both asserted and contained in this framework of reform. For the judiciary is not supposed to be an instrument of State power; its autonomy from political rulers must be established. Yet is must not be the only site of justice. Informal and alternative mechanisms for dispute resolution are considered essential to provide respite to an overburdened judiciary, thus giving it an opportunity to recover its prestige. At the same time, these are also considered a source of challenge to the final power of judiciary, which can thereby be bypassed in dealing with many economic disputes, particularly affecting foreign investors. In Latin American countries, for instance, the World Bank has been keen that disputes with foreign investors should be settled through independent arbitration, preferably outside the host country, rather than in accordance with Calvo doctrine which requires that disputes between a government and foreign investor be settled by national courts according to national law.

The problem area is not that informal justice is being supported or being formalized as a preferred institution over the formal state judicial structure. The problem is, that this is being suggested to safeguard the interests of business or to protect those with resources rather than in the interest of welfare or social justice. The socially beneficial effects of such innovative and locally sensitive institutions of justice as Lok Adalats or Public Interest Litigation in India are significant instances of how formal and informal sites of justice can relate in a meaningful way. However, the manner in which alternative institutions are being advocated raises more questions about the objectives as well as strategies than it answers. It is, therefore, desirable to do some rethinking on the nature of reforms which are required without bypassing the very people who would experience the effects of these reforms. Active political participation in the debate on reforms is more and not less desirable in the present context where centralization of policy processes raises question marks on the very genuineness of policy processes and necessitates the search for new ways of democratization of the policy regime.

SOCIAL CONTENT

Legal and judicial reforms are no doubt a major necessity in most Third World countries. And it is no doubt possible to approach the question of judicial reforms via legal reforms. Yet, it is not possible to achieve much from these unless these are related to the objectives of the wider society. The context of objectives which a particular society seeks to accomplish through these reforms is what defines their meaning. To conceptualize either legal or judicial reforms in terms of the objectives of establishing or supporting market institutions, is at the cost of a debate on the very meaning of these institutions. When assistance flows in to support such reforms regardless of their social content, society is not likely to fully integrate with the process or ends of reforms. Dualities and contradictions are likely to emerge, or persist if these already exist, in consequence of reforms. Unless the recipients already possess egalitarian frameworks of power, difficulties are unlikely to be lessened except for some who benefit from the reforms.

Pressure or support to introduce a certain pattern of reforms in a fragmented manner need not necessarily imply that a process has started, and other sectors or levels would soon be engulfed in the process. Instead, a reduced pressure for change from the resource rich on account of selective reforms in arenas which affect them most may increase the vulnerability of those who lack a powerful voice. The possibilities for more comprehensive and socially sensitive reforms may shrink rather than expand as a consequence of these selective reforms. There is in any case little justification for prioritizing reforms to cater to the needs of capital and committing huge amount of borrowed public money to these. Since a large part of assistance which is offered is in the form of credit which has to be paid back, it is important that priorities for reform are determined not on the basis of availability of money for their execution, but on the basis of needs of society to ensure justice for all.

CONCLUSION

The purpose of the foregoing discussion is not imply to suggest that judicial reforms, which are funded from outside, are not without a political or ideological agenda and that societies which take such assistance must understand the limits of choice such support imposes. It is also to underline that specific societies must remain sensitive to their social and economic contexts as well as the possibilities of justice which need to be created amidst or through the constraints and opportunities thrown up by such contexts. To conceive of reforms, which shall enhance the possibilities of justice, requires not only cultural sensitivity, an encounter with history, but also active commitment and participation from the citizenry. It also requires an active political context where conflicting pressures can be exposed and resolved in a creative and committed manner. To append judicial reforms to the agenda for institutional reforms embedded in market ideology may not, therefore, take the societies striving for justice for the common people very far. The search for justice must necessarily take these people alongwith it.

NOTES

1. Richard E. Messick, 'Judicial Reforms and Economic Development: A Survey of the Issues', *The World Bank Research Observer*, vol. XIV, no. 1, p. 117.
2. World Bank, *Governance and Development*, Washington DC, 1992.
3. See, Abrahim F.L. Shihata, 'Judicial Reform in Developing Countries and the Role of World Bank', in Malcolm Rowat, Waleed H. Malik and Maria Dakolias (eds.), *Judicial Reforms in Latin America and the Caribbean*, WB, Washington DC, 1995. Also see, Noble Laureate Joseph L. Stiglitz, *Globalization and Its Discontent*, London, 2002.
4. The World Bank Legal Department, *The World Bank and Legal Technical Assistance, Initial Lessons,* Policy Research Working Papar 1414, Washington DC, 1995.
5. Ibid.
6. The World Bank Legal Department, op. cit.
7. Ibid.
8. Ibid.
9. Ibid.
10. Ibid.
11. Ibid.
12. Ibid.
13. Edgard Buscaglia and Maria Dakolias, *Judicial Reform in Latin American Courts: The Experience in Argentina and Equador*',World Bank Technical Paper no. 350, Washington DC, World Bank, 1996.
14. Ibrahim F.I. Shihata, '*Legal Framework for Development: The World Bank's Role in Legal and Judicial Reform*', *in* Rowat, Malik and Dakolias (eds.), op. cit., p. 14.
15. Maria Dakolias, *The Judicial Sector in Latin America and the Caribbean,* World Bank Technical Paper no. 319, Washington DC, World Bank, 1996, pp. 304.
16. The World Bank Legal Department, op. cit., p. 20.
17. Ibid.
18. The World Bank Legal Department, op. cit., p. 20. For a comparison of

World Bank vs. International Monetary Fund approaches, see, Joseph Stiglitz, op. cit., Chapter 2.

19. The World Bank Legal Department, op. cit.
20. See, Patrick McAuslan, 'Laws, Governance and the Development of the Market: Practical Problems and Possible Solutions', in Julio Faundez (ed.), *Good Governance and Law: Legal and Institutional Reforms in Developing Countries*, London, 1997.
21. Cited in Messick, op. cit.
22. Ibid.
23. Ibid.

20

Reforms in the Criminal Justice System

V.K. OHRI

The problem of the growing incidence of corruption and criminality in politics cannot be adequately understood in a vacuum. Although the problem must be seen in a wider socio-economic and political perspective, my attempt here is to take a close look at the legal dimension of this problem with special reference to the criminal justice system. Given my background, I will restrict myself to the proposed frame of legal reference, leaving the electoral and political dimensions to be studied in greater detail by other scholars. I would begin by referring to the Vohra Committee Report constituted by the Government of India in July 1993, which was a five member committee at the administrative level headed by the then Home Secretary, N.N. Vohra. This committee has made a very perceptive comment that our criminal law was originally devised with the individual criminal within its frame of reference, but now it must deal with criminal activities by syndicates of mafia.

The Vohra Committee was appointed 'to take stock of all available information about the activities of crime-syndicate/mafia organizations which had developed links with and were being protected by government functionaries and political personalities'.[1]

The Vohra Committee report was tabled in both the Houses of the Parliament in October 1993. It made the following sinister submission: 'Organized crime syndication/mafia have overtime acquired currency amounting to crores of rupees invariably packed in suit cases and gunny bags' which are used to develop an extensive network of contacts with bureaucrats/government functionaries at the local level, and politicians, media persons and strategically located individuals in the non-state sector, who are pressured not to take action against the offenders or go slow in the cases against them. These processes go unchecked owing to 'the utter inadequacy of the criminal justice system; cases are not heard timely; functioning of the Government lawyers is grossly inadequate'. They have also indulged in narcotics trade (or narco-terrorism) which have close links with terrorists from within and without 'smuggling arms, ammunition, explosives, etc., into the country'. The CBI reported that all over India such crime syndicate 'have become law unto themselves', with 'considerable political clout, seriously jeopardizing the smooth functioning of the administration and the safety of life and property of the common man', to an extent that 'the network of mafia is virtually running a parallel government pushing the state apparatus into irrelevance'. 'Even the members of the judicial system have not escaped the embrace of the mafia. The cost of contesting an election has thrown the politicians into the lap of these elements'. It further remarked,

> the mafias too big to be tackled have graduated to big business and their muscle power is sustained by their enormous financial power. This in turn is protected by the such elements committing economic offences with impunity. These 'mafia giants', 'economic lobbies', 'the big smuggling syndicates', 'having internal linkages, have spread into and infected the various economic and financial activities, including havala transactions, circulation of black money and operations of a vicious parallel economy causing serious damage to the economic fibre of the country.

The Vohra Committee Report observed that there are various agencies to deal with such corrupt activities, but they have resulted in ineffectiveness and irrelevance due to corruption and kickbacks, as 'the financial stakes are astronomically high and the pressures are brought to bear through shiftings and postings from sensitive assignments or sharing the huge funds. Besides, there is no proper co-ordination, sharing of information and any operational use of information relating to the activities of crime syndicates.'[2]

WHY REFORMS?

For more than two decades, there has been a growing demand for amending the criminal justice system. Several amendments have been made since independence in this regard. To this effect, the entire

Criminal Procedure Code (CrPC) was amended in 1973. Still the inadequacy of the system has been posing not only grave challenge to legitimacy of the entire system, rather also eating into the body politic in the form of growing criminalization of electoral politics. All the parts of the criminal justice system are in the dire need of an overhaul. The former President R. Venkataraman held that the three adjuncts of criminal justice system were: prosecution, trial and sentence or punishment. The bane of criminal justice system were tardy investigation, absence of witnesses, delay, cumbersome procedures, lengthy judgements, paucity of criminal courts and large number of vacancies of judges.[3]

The social, economic and cultural environment around the system has also undergone a sea change. Distance has narrowed down. Technology is available in a way never before known or heard of. Communication is easy and quick. Population and poverty have visibly increased. All these factors have helped the emergence of more crime and new kinds of crime. The perpetrators are very quick to take advantage of the advance in communication and technology and to literally get away with it much before the long arm of the law catches up with them. Such is the speed and ingenuity of their escape that society is a mute witness to the pathetic helplessness of those who have to look after the prevention of crime and to bring to book the criminals and ensure quick justice.

Political influence on members of all the agencies involved (namely, the police, the public prosecutors, the courts and their staff) seems to make them vulnerable. Money and power are behind many of the unresolved cases, which have got inordinately delayed, thereby denying justice. Often, the upholders of law commit crimes to hide the crimes of 'important' people. Many people are reported to be vanished from prison; many people die an unnatural death, which is often made to appear natural.

All the parties involved in the matter of criminal justice—be it the police, the courts, the lawyers, the prisons—seem to be reeling under heavy pressure of work and years of arrears. The police have many duties now that they had much less of earlier. It is said that the time and care needed to be devoted to the skilled and professional work of interrogation is hardly treated with the seriousness that it deserves. So little training for so onerous and responsible a task is imparted that it is something of a farce and cases are more prone to failure on this account alone. An average investigating officer has to handle 122 cases a year—an enormous burden—and hence inefficient.[4] As for arrears of cases in courts, there is an enormous backlog of cases (around 3.4 crores) that must be disposed of in each court. The situation in the subordinate judiciary is more serious where 2 crore 78 lakh cases are pending. It is a sorry state of affairs in the Lower Courts that none is bothered about the merit of the case. Nor the complainant neither the accused understand what is happening, some time even the lawyers don't understand the proceedings. Of late new duties have been taken on by the courts, where the Executive has abdicated its functions. Besides, there is also what in recent years has come to be termed as 'public litigation', where the court can *suo motu* take up cases on the basis of a petition from a member of the public. Besides, more people are going to court for anything and everything despite the cost, the mystery of procedures, the adjournments sought by lawyers on excuses which in many cases may not be truly what they are made out for, and such other hassles.

Undertrial prisoners form 64 per cent of the inmates of prisons in most of the states and union territories. This means that in addition to overwork for the prison staff, the high occupancy may lead to more crime. The highest number of undertrial prisoners over five years and above is 423 in Bihar. Perhaps if convicted, some of them may have to undergo a lesser punishment than being put in jail as an undertrial waiting for justice. The National Human Rights Commission says that 60 per cent of arrests are unnecessary and unjustifiable. Former Chief Justice Anand also cited the case of an accused in West Bengal police custody for 37 years, awaiting trial.

Then there is the case of the number of convictions being very few considering the number of cases booked. The conviction rate in IPC crime has declined from 64.81 in 1961 to 38.2 per cent in 1997.[5] It seems self evident that a mechanism be evolved to secure coordination between the police and the prosecutors.

The police are functioning under a very old Police Act of 1861 and there are umpteen proposals for comprehensive reforms, including the Police Commission Report of the 1970s. Power and control dominate police thinking rather than initiative, humaneness, integrity and commitment. There is a serious alienation of our police with the public. The politician wants illegal things done by them; they are helpless in the matter of arresting corruption and illegality in society; overpopulation and poverty are causes for the increase in the incidence of crime; the media sometimes blows the wrong thing out of all proportion; and the attitude of courts is also not very helpful to them.

The legal system is also old and outdated. It is facing these severe problems for which lawyers, investigating agencies, judges and politicians have all to account for: (1) prolonging cases; (2) not increasing the number of judges; (3) the inadequate education of lawyers and their dilatory procedures, adopted in self interest; and (4) lack of awareness amongst members of the public about legal systems and procedures. Adjournments are rampant, and prosecutors are not selected on the basis of merit. Our system is more concerned with the accused than with the victim—the victim has to prove the guilt of the accused.

As legal processes are too time consuming, only rich people can buy time and people and get justice in their favour. This has shaken the confidence of the people in the capacity of the courts to redress grievances and give timely relief and justice. 'Since problems are not confined to one agency or point in the process, the entire apparatus from the point of making a complaint to the delivery of justice needs to be reviewed, and re-engineered'.[6]

AGENDA FOR REFORMS

In November 2000, the Ministry of Home Affairs (MHA), Government of India set up the Committee on Reforms of the Criminal Justice System under the Chairmanship of Justice V.S. Malimath to do a comprehensive review of all the functionaries of the criminal justice system, fundamental principles and relevant laws and to suggest reforms in the system. Before this, the NDA government came out with a 'National Policy on Management of Crime and Delivery of Effective Criminal Justice', the objectives of which were as following:

(a) to consolidate and reiterate sectoral policies many of which are already enunciated;
(b) to set clear targets towards achieving the goal;
(c) to plan increased spending where it is most needed;
(d) to assess future needs and requirements in a realistic frame; and
(e) to give a direction for co-ordinated criminal justice reform on a continuing basis.

The Committee gave 158 recommendations under 23 heads attracting bricks and bouquets from the scholars as well as practitioners. Stressing the need for reforms, the Committee observed:

It is the duty of the State to protect fundamental rights of the citizens as well as the right to property. The State has constituted the criminal justice system to protect the rights of the innocent and punish the guilty. The system devised more than a century back, has become ineffective; a large number of guilty go unpunished in a large number of cases; the system takes years to bring the innocent to justice; and has ceased to deter criminals. Crime is increasing rapidly everyday and types of crimes are proliferating. The citizens live in constant fear.[7]

The Committee gave its serious consideration to the question as to whether this system had been satisfactory or whether we should consider recommending any other system. The Committee examined in particular the inquisitorial system followed in France, Germany and other Continental countries. The inquisitorial system is certainly efficient in the sense that the investigation is supervised by the Judicial Magistrate which results in a high rate of conviction. The Committee on balance felt that, a fair trial and in particular, fairness to the accused, are better protected in the adversarial system. However, the Committee felt that some of the good features of the Inquisitorial System could be adopted to strengthen the Adversarial System and to make it more effective. This includes the duty of the Court to search for truth, to assign a proactive role to the judges, to give directions to the investigating officers and prosecution agencies in the matter of investigation and leading evidence with the object of seeking the truth and focusing on justice to victims.

The recommendations made by the Malimath Committee did not serve the purpose for which it was constituted. While the report contains some useful suggestions, the overall thrust of the report is dangerous for the health of the criminal justice system. Rather than engaging in a serious critical diagnosis of what ails the system, the report's central premise seems to be that arming the state with more discretionary and punitive measures, weakening the constitutionally guaranteed rights of the accused, relaxing the presumption of innocent until proven guilty, is the surest way of creating a better criminal justice system. 'It is in the end, more a reflection of the frustration with the ills of the current system than a sober diagnosis of what can reform it. But it is in line with the clamour for punitive measures that is becoming acceptable increasingly in wide sections of Indian society.' The report states that 'more specifically, the aim is to reduce the level of criminality in society by ensuring the maximum detection of reported crimes, conviction of the accused persons without delay, awarding appropriate punishments to the convicted to meet the ends of justice and prevent recidivism'.[8]

The report assumes, first, that crime rates are simply a function of the ability of the state to detect them. There is no evidence for this proposition whatsoever. Even countries with more punitive legal systems and efficient detection mechanisms as the United States of America have also had high crime rates compared to their European counterparts.

The major flaw lies also in the fact that it is against the interest of common people as it tends to give lot of powers to the police authorities who are likely to misuse it against the public at large, as seen in the past. The Committee observed that there are two major problems inherent in the Criminal Justice System relating to huge pendency of criminal cases on the one hand, and a very low rate of convictions in cases involving serious crimes, on the other. But the Committee has not taken into consideration the fact that a large number of false cases are being registered everyday therefore at the time of evidence either the matter is settled among the parties or the party becomes hostile.

Further, Committee also observed that justice suffers not only when an innocent person is punished or a guilty person is exonerated but also when there is enormous delay in deciding the criminal case. However, the Committee overlooked the issue that reform in Criminal Justice System should be brought about on the point that an innocent should not be punished for the act for which he is not guilty. Furthermore, the Committee recommends that the standard of 'proof beyond reasonable doubt' which is presently followed in criminal cases shall be done away with, without realizing that it will bring innocent persons into conviction even though the prosecution is not able to establish his/her guilt.

The Committee falls woefully short of offering either a comprehensive examination or reforms. The approach of the Committee, its basic assumptions are not only faulty but also appear exclusionary and biased in nature. It also seems that the direction and content of the reforms recommended and the silences in the report suggest that the Committee is actually attempting to undermine the entire normative framework of the criminal justice system rather than addressing the real systemic problems facing the criminal justice system today.

The Committee has failed to take into account international human rights standards, which establish a framework for human rights protection within the criminal justice system throughout the world. It also disregards those human rights treaties to which India is a party and is therefore bound to uphold. The Committee appears to ignore important judgements indicting the police for human rights violation and misuse of the criminal justice system, including members of the judiciary, who routinely fail to implement safeguards in law designed to protect the human rights of both victims and the accused. Instead the Committee has given tremendous power into the hands of the police authorities. This may lead to misuse of such powers and create chaos in the society. It will lead to the excessive inconvenience to the public at large.

As Ujjwal Singh has also argued, the Malimath Committee appeared to be determined to use the paranoia created by terrorism to import highly punitive and liberty-restricting measures into ordinary law. For example, in its discussion of the need to intercept communication, the Committee recommended that the Prevention of Terrorism Act be followed: 'a suitable provision should be made on the lines of Sections 36 to 48 of POTA, 2002 for the interception of wired, electric or oral communication'.[9]

There is a need to amend and simplify criminal laws; compensate victims; introduce plea-bargaining; introduce an inquisitorial system; punish perjury; increase manpower in the police and judiciary; maintain coordination between the police and prosecution; bring the criminal justice system under plan budget for better assessment and allocation of financial resources, and to encourage people's participation in the administration of criminal justice.[10]

There is urgent necessity for a meaningful and healthy dialogue between the people and criminal justice functionaries, especially the police. Formation of voluntary schemes can help bring the people closer to the police.

Several recommendations have been made by the Law Commission from time to time. Considering all the recommendations given by various committees and Law Commissions, the Congress-led United Progressive Alliance (UPA) government finally prepared a Criminal Law Amendment Bill 2005 which was passed by both the houses and notified but due to nation wide agitation by the legal community, the Amendment was kept in abeyance. The reason is obvious. All the committees, which were dealing with Criminal Justice System, had no knowledge about the ground realities of the functioning of Criminal Justice System. They acquired the knowledge through books or by reading news reports about the failure of Criminal Justice System. None of the committee member knew in reality about the failure of the system and went only by what was portrayed by the media.

Like the Malimath Report, the Bill also has certain flaws. The Bill intends to retain certain provisions, which already existed in the code but were not followed by the judicial system. Some provisions regarding bail are anti-people. The recommendations qua anticipatory bail will make common man suffer who are being falsely involved in the case by the police and interested parties. It is curtailing their right to seek bail from higher courts in case their request is rejected at the lower court.

Even making Section 324 of the code not compoundable will make things worse, the matter will be settled between the parties and they will be left with no option except to turn hostile in the court and give a setback to the judicial system. In fact, there should be more compoundable offences and punishment for such offences should be made easier. The recommendations of Justice Malimath Committee and the government have not taken into consideration the real problems and have made recommendations without consulting the legal fraternity who practice the criminal justice system. The Committee sent a questionnaire to over 3,000 individuals, and received 264 responses. There had been no categorization of responses into the different sectors of society they came from. There was also little input from criminal lawyers dealing with cases on the ground. Nobody seems to have realized that the Criminal Justice System is the most misused justice system in this country. The citizens, police, politicians and all others misuse the system. The main reason for misuse is that there is no accountability of any person who has set the law in motion wrongly and achieved the desired result. The system is misused by the person who has the money and influence with the local police. The entire system is centred around one person, namely, the Station House Officer (SHO). No case is registered without his concurrence, howsoever serious offence is committed in his area. In most cases, it is found that whenever any person has gone to lodge a report about theft or other offences, mostly persons are turned back as police do not want to show the rise in crimes in their area. Most of the theft cases and other offences go unreported for police misadventure to keep crime rate low in their respective areas. This issue was raised by the duty officers under training of Delhi Police recently with their superiors during training that even they are not allowed to register the crime without the concurrence of SHO although cognizable offences are to be reported to them. The misuse at the level of lodging of First Information Report (FIR) is rampant in this country. But no mechanism is suggested to prevent the misuse of the law by the Police. So, law should be amended recommending that whenever a person comes to Police Station with a complaint, the same should be reproduced in writing by the duty officer or by the person if he is literate in his own words so the clear FIR is registered if it discloses a cognizable offence. And in case no offence is made out, the complaint should be numbered and kept on record for a minimum period of three years. If this provision is not complied with, there should be a mandatory punishment for such an officer for non-compliance to the above section. This amendment will prevent the misuse of the power by the police qua registration of cases as well as the addition and alteration made by the police in order to make false cases against the persons for *malafide* motives.

Most of the time, the crime reported do not make a cognizable offence, but by little changes by the police for obvious reasons, cognizable offence is made, the persons are arrested and detained. People misuse the law by use of money and influence to get the desired result under the threat of arrest and detention. Those who misuse the law takes advantage and the victim of such nexus suffers as there is no method to redress his grievance against the mighty police and the influential persons. In my view, Section 358 of Chapter 27 of the CrPC which gives power to award compensation on groundless arrest should be suitably amended which was Rs. 100 but raised to Rs. 1,000 vide Code of Criminal Procedure (Amendment) Act, 2005, which is still too meagre to act as a deterrent. Further, it should be made mandatory for the Magistrate to pass orders awarding compensation at the culmination of the trial whenever the Court is convinced that the person was involved in a false case, arrested without any ground, and the compensation should be as per the status of the affected person. This will prevent the multiplicity of litigation and if the person is not satisfied with the claim awarded, he/she will have remedy to claim further sum through civil proceedings for the losses caused to him/her and the Court should also pass order as to who shall be liable to pay such compensation to the affected party. Stiffening of this provision will prevent registration of false cases and frivolous litigation which is rampant.

Another area which has been overlooked by the agencies recommending amendment in criminal law is relating to case property involved in criminal cases. Most of the times, the properties involved in criminal cases lose their value in terms of money and use as the same cannot be transferred being involved in criminal case. Any movable property including cash, if stolen and recovered, are subject matter of Chapter 34 of CrPC. The properties are not released to the owners unconditionally. The condition is that the property is released on *supardari*. The property released on *supardari* cannot be put to its proper use, especially in case of cash and automobiles. It is a known fact that automobile loses its value fast and nobody wants to buy a property which is involved in criminal case. There are large number of accident cases involving criminal law in which a vehicle is released on *supardari* and cases run for years and the vehicle owner is unable to transfer the vehicle at the time of need. Eventually losses are invaluable at the time of transfer of the automobile. In case of cash, it cannot be put to utility because one is required to produce the same notes so released on *supardari*. A suitable amendment is required in Chapter 34 of CrPC in which property is released to the rightful owner in shortest possible time say within three months of such seizure and the same should be released on furnishing an indemnity bond securing the investigation agencies and the government against other claimants. Chapter 7-A has been added which deals with the properties derived from or in use in commission of offence but on the request of foreign States (contracting States) but no such clear provision exist for identification of such properties qua properties involved in crime in India. Similar provisions are required to be made to identify such properties and their disposal to the person found entitled. Further, Chapter 34 should be amended to give better justice to innocent and cheated purchaser.

With regard to blind cases where the accused is declared a proclaimed offender, the Investigation Officer should report the matter to the Chief Judicial Magistrate (CJM) or any other Magistrate authorized and seek orders for further investigation. In reality, in the cases where the accused is known and charge sheet is filed, and he/she is declared proclaimed offender and warrants are issued, there is no further action by the courts or investigating agencies. Influential people take advantage of this situation as in the case of a MP and a former Union Minister from the State of Jharkhand, Shibu Soren who escaped murder trial for twenty years. There were arrest warrants against him and he was declared a proclaimed offender but still he remained a public figure and was in the union cabinet. He was not arrested or taken to court to face the charges till a public interest litigation (PIL) was filed in the Supreme Court by the author.[11] It was then that he resigned from the cabinet and surrendered though he was later released on bail. He still enjoyed the silence of the system as by the time, he reappeared in the court and trial started, most of the witnesses had died. Soren took the advantage, delayed the trial and reaped its benefit and he may be acquitted for want of evidence. There are many such cases involving important members of Parliament and State Legislatures including ministers, therefore in my view, in case a person is declared a proclaimed offender, the court should seek report about such person's arrest from time to time and provision 82–3 of the CrPC should be suitably amended. Further all such orders authorizing further investigation should be 'speaking' (self explanatory) orders. This amendment will ensure that criminal case registered with police go unattended and all matters will receive judicial attention.

The frequently misused Sections of CrPC are Sections 161 and 162, which empower the police to record the statement of the persons who have the knowledge and information of the crime under investigation. The said statement is not required to be signed by the person making it. The collapse of entire Criminal Justice System as reported is based on this section alone. The statement recorded under Section 161 of CrPC is not been relied upon by the Court except in the case of any contradiction. The statement recorded by the police under this section is not considered by the Courts during trial. Most of the people who come to the Court for deposing in the Criminal Court have a common complaint that they never made the statement as recorded by the police and the moment the person changes from the statement produced by the police, the accused gets the benefit. The person who changes his statement as given by him to the police cannot be punished for perjury as the statement given under Section 161 has no evidentiary value. The person who makes the statement is not given the copy of his statement and he can always deny having made such statement to police. In most of the cases where people are acquitted of serious offences, the witnesses come and say they never gave such statements as produced by the police in the charge-sheet and with one line statement, the Court becomes helpless. It is also commonly noticed that the police misuse Section 161 of CrPC, they record statement of their own to suit to their case and to falsely implicate other persons for hidden motives who are not connected with the crime committed. This Section requires to be amended so that nobody is able to retract from the statement and the Section is not misused by the investigation agencies.

It can also be argued that Section 162 should require that statements of all persons examined by the police who are acquainted with the facts of the case should be recorded in the language known to the person in writing and the signature of the person making such statements should be obtained. A copy of such statements must be given to the party against a receipt. In case the person is illiterate the said proceeding should be conducted in presence of an independent person, who could act as an interpreter and the signature of the interpreter should be obtained.

Further, Section 167 of the CrPC also needs to be amended which gives power to investigate the offence beyond twenty-four hours. This Section gives limitation for the summons cases but no limitation has been provided for the Warrant trial and the Sessions trial cases. Even the provisions of limitation given in Section 468 of the CrPC are not adequate to control the period of investigation by the court as such people with influence get their investigation delayed with the connivance of the police. Due to lapse of time and change of circumstances, witnesses disappear and persons accused of serious offences go free. It is therefore recommended that the limit of investigation for the offences such as Warrant trial and Session trial should also be set up. In cases of Warrant trial and Session trial whether the accused is arrested or not, if the investigation is not concluded within one year, the Magistrate should make an order stopping further investigation into the offence, unless the officer making the investigation satisfies the Magistrate that for special reasons and in the interest of justice the continuation of the investigation beyond the period of six months is necessary.

Besides, the other area which requires immediate attention of the law amending agencies relates to the provisions of the bail, i.e. Chapter 33 of CrPC. It is often seen that poor people remain in jail for longer period for the small crimes committed by them and the rich and influential get the benefit of Bail even for heinous offences committed by them. The provisions of bail should be made more rational. The person arrested for the first time should be mandatorily released on bail for the offences punishable up to seven years and for the second and subsequent offences there should be no provision for grant of bail unless the accused is able to establish that he/she is innocent and falsely implicated. In the event of multiple crime detected, law should be amended for the persons involved in more than one crime if it is in one series. There should be further amendment in the law for the persons who are released on bail once and they commit the similar crime while being on bail. These changes in law related to bails will deter criminals from getting involved in further crimes and will solve the purpose of law.

Another Section which has caused legal hassles for people involved in Criminal Judicial System is Section 251 of the CrPC. Most of the cases are covered under Chapter 20 of CrPC, being summon trial cases. Section 251 reads as follows: 'Substance of accusation to be stated—When in a summons-case the accused appears or is brought before the Magistrate, the particulars of the offence of which he is accused shall be stated to him, and he shall be asked whether he pleads guilty or has any defense to make, but it shall not be necessary to frame a formal charge'.

There is no provision for a person to seek release even if he is wrongly summoned or involved in the summon trial case. Most of the summon trial cases are instituted upon complaint. People are summoned on false complaints or due to wrong facts and laws. The person has no remedy except to face trial or file revision petition before Hon'ble High Court which involves huge expenses and time. Hon'ble Supreme Court has given some relief to such persons in the K.N. Mathew Judgement,[12] wherein a person can approach and seek dismissal. But this judgement was overruled by the Hon'ble Supreme Court in the *Adalat Prasad* case.[13] This section requires a complete overhaul and there should be a provision as in Chapter 19 of CrPC, i.e. Section 245 CrPC Similar provision should also be inserted in Section 251 so that a person wrongly summoned can seek redressal from the same court. If the court can recall the order of summoning or pass order of discharge in a warrant trial case, what prevents the same court from discharging or recalling order in a summon case?

The above said facts and legal positions and practice have not been considered by the law amending agencies., such aspects should be looked into and law should be amended in the light of above recommendations. Further, legal reforms alone would not take us far in dealing with such a complex situation. A concerted effort has to be made both by the state and the civil society on economic, cultural, social, and political planes as well.

NOTES

1. Vohra Committee Report, Government of India, Ministry of Home Affairs, 1993, 1.1.
2. Ibid., 1993.
3. http://pib.nic.in/archieve/lreleng/lyr2002/rapr2002/27042002/r270420021.html

4. Padma Ramchandran, 'Revamping the Criminal Justice System', *Hindu*, 28 January 2003.
5. Ibid.
6. Ibid.
7. 'The Malimath Committee', *Combat Law*, vol. 2 issue 2, June–July 2003, p. 46. Also see Report of Malimath Committee on Reforms of Criminal Justice System, Government of India, Ministry of Home Affairs (Chairman Dr. Justice V.S. Malimath).
8. Pratap Bhanu Mehta, 'Presumed Guilty', *Telegraph*, 20 November 2003.
9. Pratap Bhanu Mehta, 'Presumed Guilty', *The Telegraph*, 20 November 2003.
10. See Dalbir Bharti, *The Constitution and Criminal Justice Administration*, New Delhi: APH Publishing Corporation, 2006.
11. *V.K. Ohri* vs. *Union of India* (pending in the Court).
12. *K.N. Mathew* vs. *State of Kerala & Ors*, 1992(1) SCC 217 AIR 1992 SC 2206, 1992 GILJ 3779, 1991 (3) Crimes 820(SC).
13. *Adalat Prasad* vs. *Rooplal Jindal & Ors.*, 2004(7) scale 137 2004(4) CTC 608, 113(2004) DLT 356 (SC)(2005) IGLR 546 JT 2004(7) SC 243, 2004(4) MHLJ 274 (2004)7 SCC 338, 2004(2) UJI 342(SC).

Index